Contemporary Moral Issues

Contemporary Moral Issues

DIVERSITY AND CONSENSUS

SECOND EDITION

Lawrence M. Hinman
UNIVERSITY OF SAN DIEGO

Prentice Hall, Upper Saddle River, New Jersey 07458

Library of Congress Cataloging-in-Publication Data

Hinman, Lawrence M.
Contemporary moral issues: diversity and consensus / Lawrence M. Hinman.—2nd ed.
p. cm.
Includes bibliographical references.
ISBN-0-13-086219-3
1. Ethics. I. Title.
BJ1012.H56 2000 99-044843
170—dc21

Editor-in-Chief: *Charlyce Jones-Owen*
Acquisitions Editor: *Karita France*
Editorial Assistant: *Jennifer Ackerman*
Managing Editor: *Jan Stephan*
Production Liaison: *Fran Russello*
Project Manager: *Publications Development Company of Texas*
Prepress and Manufacturing Buyer: *Tricia Kenny*
Marketing Manager: *Ilse Wolfe*
Art Director: *Jayne Conte*
Cover Designer: *Bruce Kenselaar*
Cover Image: *Roxana Villa/Stock Illustration Source, Inc.*

Acknowledgments for essay contributions appear on the base of opening pages, which constitute a continuation of the copyright page.

This book was set in 9.5 point Times Roman by Publications Development Company of Texas and was printed and bound by RR Donnelley & Sons Company. The cover was printed by Phoenix Color Corp.

Printed in the United States of America

10 9 8 7 6 5 4 3 2 1

ISBN 0-13-086219-3

Prentice-Hall International (UK) Limited, *London*
Prentice-Hall of Australia Pty. Limited, *Sydney*
Prentice-Hall Canada Inc., *Toronto*
Prentice-Hall Hispanoamericana, S.A., *Mexico*
Prentice-Hall of India Private Limited, *New Delhi*
Prentice-Hall of Japan, Inc., *Tokyo*
Pearson Education Asia Pte. Ltd., *Singapore*
Editora Prentice-Hall do Brasil, Ltda., *Rio de Janeiro*

To Laura,
my daughter

Contents

* indicates new readings in this edition

Preface

The second edition of *Contemporary Moral Issues* contains over twenty new articles and, for instructors, is accompanied with a free set of ABC videos, with a total of eleven new segments. A new chapter on reproductive technologies and cloning has been added to Part One. An introductory section on academic integrity precedes the main sections of the book. The bibliographical essays have been updated throughout the book.

Even with these changes, the book retains the strengths that characterized the first edition. First, each chapter contains narratives that position the issues within the context of lived experiences. The issues discussed in this book—from abortion and euthanasia to questions of famine relief and animal experimentation—are questions of social policy as well as issues within individual lives. Indeed, contemporary social ethics exists at the intersection of large-scale policy decisions and personal narratives. Throughout this anthology, I have tried to give voice to the stories of individual lives that are woven—sometimes skillfully, sometimes crudely—into the tapestry of social policy decisions. It is crucial that we understand the way in which these social policies impact individual lives. Thus, each chapter contains at least one narrative account that places these larger issues within the context of an individual life. Often truth is to be found in the detail of our personal lives—what philosophers call "thick descriptions"—not just in general principles. It is my hope that these narrative selections will help to provide some of that detail.

Issues of diversity play an important role in questions of social policy and in the stories of individual lives. Throughout this book, I have tried to provide the opportunity for as many voices of diversity as possible to be heard. In addition to this, one-third of this book—Part Two: Issues of Diversity and Equality—is explicitly devoted to a number of specific issues about diversity and equality in regard to race, gender, sexual orientation, and economic status.

This book is "user-friendly" for students. *Critical introductions* to each chapter provide a conceptual map of the moral terrain to be covered, while a short, *general introduction to moral theory* helps to specify some of the common issues that arise in each chapter. Each selection is introduced with *prereading questions* to focus the students' attention. *Discussion questions* at the end of each selection are designed to help students develop their own positions on the issues raised, while journal questions—in italics—explore more personal issues raised by the readings. A *bibliographical essay* at the end of each chapter highlights key works and points the way to valuable resources for students. A guide about critical reading in philosophy and writing philosophical papers on moral issues is now available on Ethics Updates. It includes tips on choosing and refining a topic, developing a bibliography, refining arguments, and using counterexamples.

I have retained the *Moral Problems Self-Quiz* at the beginning of this book that surveys your position on a number of issues discussed throughout the book. At the end of each chapter, there is a retest of the relevant questions. Take the initial test before you read any of the individual chapters, and then retake it at the end of each chapter. Check your responses against your initial answers, and see in what ways—if any—you've changed.

Finally, the integration with the World Wide Web, which was begun with the first edition, is even more extensive in this new edition. Two sites now provide support for this book. Prentice-Hall has developed an excellent site (http://www.prenhall.com/hinman) and my own site, *Ethics Updates* (http://ethics.acusd.edu), continues to provide extensive resources on all the topics covered in this book. These resources are increasingly multimedia and interactive and contain several types of sources. First, continually updated versions of the bibliographical essays in this book will be available online, with references to the latest work in each area. Second, hypertext links to numerous Web sites will provide additional resources for the book. For example, the section on abortion contains links to the Web pages of both pro-choice and pro-life groups, and also contains links to the full texts of major court decisions about abortion. Third, there will be brief descriptions of current news articles and popular books that relate to issues raised in this book. Fourth, an opportunity will be provided for you—both students and instructors—to forward interesting articles, references, and so on for posting on this site. Finally, discussion groups are available on each of the main topics in this book. Please come, visit, and contribute.

This book, like Caesar's Gaul, is divided into three parts. *Part One* centers around issues of life and death, including abortion, *in vitro* fertilization, euthanasia, and the death penalty. Central to this section is the question of the right to life and the sanctity of human life. *Part Two* deals explicitly with questions of diversity and equality, including issues of race, ethnicity, gender, sexual orientation, and economic status. Here one of the central issues is how we balance the recognition of diversity with the demands for community. *Part Three* turns to a consideration the boundaries of the moral domain. Morality may begin at home, but how far from home does it extend? Do our moral obligations extend to the poor and starving of other countries? To animals? To the environment? These three questions provide the basis for the final three chapters of this book.

For instructors who are interested in using it, a videotape is available with segments dealing with the topics in each of these chapters. The segments are short (about 12 minutes), and intended to stimulate discussion of the issues. They are drawn from ABC News sources, primarily *Nightline.*

I wish to thank, first of all, the authors who kindly allowed their work to be reprinted in this book, for their contributions, which form the heart of this work. Moreover, I would like to thank the anonymous reviewers at Prentice-Hall for their comments and suggestions for making this a better book; any shortcomings are my own. At Prentice-Hall, I am especially grateful to Karita France, for her patience and support in a project that took longer than either of us anticipated. At the University of San Diego, many contributed to the success of this project: Pat Drinan, dean of the College of Arts and Sciences, for his support for computer resources that saved me countless hours on this project; Leeanna Cummings, our departmental secretary, for invaluable assistance in managing permissions requests; and many of my colleagues, including Mike Soroka, George Bryjak, Joe Colombo, Rodney Peffer, and Mark Woods, and my students in my Social Ethics course.

Most of all, I would like to thank my wife, Virginia, for her continued love as well as her support. Without her, this book would not have been written.

Finally, I would greatly appreciate comments from readers, both students and professors. Please feel free to write to me either via e-mail (hinman@acusd.edu) or the old fashioned way to Lawrence M. Hinman, Department of Philosophy, University of San Diego, 5998 Alcalá Park, San Diego, CA 92110-2492. Your comments and suggestions are most welcome.

Lawrence M. Hinman

Contemporary Moral Issues

INTRODUCTION

A Pluralistic Approach to Contemporary Moral Issues

Moral Disagreement

As we move through the chapters of this book, we will see one area of moral disagreement after another. Abortion, surrogacy, euthanasia, the death penalty, racism, sexism, homosexuality, welfare, world hunger, animal rights, and environmental issues—all are areas characterized by fundamental disagreements, often intense, sometimes bitter and acrimonious.

This situation is made even more perplexing by the fact that in all of these debates, each side has good arguments in support of its position. In other words, these are not debates in which one side is so obviously wrong that only moral blindness or ill will could account for its position. Thus, we cannot easily dismiss such disagreements by just saying that one side is wrong in some irrational or malevolent way. Ultimately, these are disagreements among intelligent people of good will. *It is precisely this fact that makes them so disturbing.* Certainly part of moral disagreement can be attributed to ignorance or ill will, but the troubling part is the moral disagreement among informed and benevolent people.

What kind of sense can we make of such disagreement? Three possible responses deserve particular attention.

Moral Absolutism

The first, and perhaps most common, response to such disagreements is to claim that there is a single, ultimate answer to the questions being posed. This is the answer of the *moral absolutists,* those who believe there is a single Truth with a capital "T." Usually, absolutists claim to know what that truth is—and it usually corresponds, not surprisingly, to their own position.

Moral absolutists are not confined to a single position. Indeed, absolutism is best understood as much as a way of *holding* certain beliefs as it is an item of such belief. Religious fundamentalists—whether Christian, Muslim, or some other denomination—are usually absolutists. Some absolutists believe in communism, others believe just as absolutely in free-market economics. Some moral philosophers are absolutists, believing that their moral viewpoint is the only legitimate one. But what characterizes all absolutists is the conviction that their truth is *the* truth.

Moral absolutists may be right, but there are good reasons to be skeptical about their claims. If they are right, how do they explain the persistence of moral disagreement? Certainly there are disagreements and disputes in other areas (including the natural sciences), but in ethics there seems to be persistence to these disputes that we usually do not find in other areas. It is hard to explain this from an absolutist standpoint without saying such disagreement is due to ignorance or ill will. Certainly this is part of the story, but can it account for all moral disagreement? Absolutists are unable to make sense out of the fact that sometimes we have genuine moral disagreements among well-informed and good-intentioned people who are honestly and openly seeking the truth.

Moral Relativism

The other common response to such disagreement effectively denies that there is a truth in this area, even with a lower case "t." Moral *relativists maintain* that moral disagreements stem from the fact that what is right for one is not necessarily right for another. Morality is like beauty, they claim, purely relative to the beholder. There is no ultimate standard in terms of which perspectives can be judged. No one is wrong; everyone is right within his or her own sphere.

Notice that these relativists do more than simply acknowledge the existence of moral disagreement. Just to admit that moral disagreement exists is called *descriptive relativism,* and this is a comparatively uncontroversial claim. There is plenty of disagreement in the moral realm, just as there is in most other areas of life. However, *normative relativists* go further. They not only maintain that such disagreement exists; they also say that each is right relative to his or her own culture. Incidentally, it is also worth noting that relativists disagree about precisely what morality is relative *to.* At the one end of the spectrum are those (*cultural moral relativists*) who say that morality is relative to culture; at the other end of the spectrum are those (*moral subjectivists*) who argue that morality is relative to each individual. When we refer to moral relativists here, we will be talking about normative relativists, including both cultural moral relativists and moral subjectivists.

Although moral relativism often appears appealing at first glance, it proves to be singularly unhelpful in the long run. It provides an explanation of moral disagreement, but it fails to provide a convincing account of how moral *agreement* could be forged. In the fact of disagreement, what practical advice can relativists offer us? All they can say, it would seem, is that we ought to follow the customs of our society, our culture, our age, or our individual experience. Thus cultural moral relativists tell us, in effect, "When in Rome, do as the Romans do." Moral subjectivists tell us that we should be true, not to our culture, but to our individual selves. But relativists fail to offer us help in how to resolve disputes when they arise. To say that each is right unto itself is of no help, for the issue is what happens when they come together.

While this might be helpful advice in an age of moral isolationism when each society (or individual) was an island unto itself, it is of little help today. In our contemporary world, the pressing moral question is how we can live together, not how we can live apart. Economies are mutually interdependent; corporations are often multinational; products such as cars are seldom made in a single country. Communications increasingly cut across national borders. Satellite-based telecommunication systems allow international television (MTV is worldwide and news networks are sure to follow) and international telephone communications. Millions of individuals around the world dial into the Internet, establishing a virtual community. In such a world, relativism fails to provide guidance for resolving disagreements. All it can tell us is that everyone is right in his or her own world. But the question for the future is how to determine what is right when worlds overlap.

Moral Pluralism

Let's return to our problem: in some moral disputes, there seem to be well-informed and good-intentioned people on opposing sides. Absolutism fails to offer a convincing account of how opposing people could be both well informed and good intentioned. It says there is only one answer, and those who do not see it are either ignorant or ill willed. Relativism fails to offer a convincing account of how people can agree. It says no one is wrong, that each culture (or individual) is right unto itself. However, it offers no help about how to resolve these moral disputes.

There is a third possible response here, which I will call *moral pluralism.* Moral pluralists maintain that there are moral truths, but they do not form a body of coherent and consistent truths in the way that one finds in the science or mathematics. Moral truths are real, but partial. Moreover, they are inescapably *plural.* There are many moral truths, not just one—and they may conflict with one another.

Let me borrow an analogy from government. Moral absolutists are analogous to old-fashioned monarchists: there is one leader, and he or she has the absolute truth. Moral relativists are closer to anarchists: each person or group has its own truth. The U.S. government is an interesting example of a tripartite pluralist government. We don't think that the president, the Congress, or the judiciary alone has an exclusive claim to truth. Each has a partial claim, and each provides a check on the other two. We don't—at least not always—view conflict among the three branches as a bad thing. Indeed, such a system of overlapping and at times conflicting responsibilities is a way of hedging our bets. If we put all of our hope in only one of the branches of government, we would be putting ourselves at greater risk. If that one branch is wrong, then everything is wrong. However, if there are three (at least partially conflicting) branches of government, then the effect of one branch's being wrong are far less catastrophic. Moreover, the chance that mistakes will be uncovered earlier is certainly increased when each branch is being scrutinized by the others.

We have an analogous situation in the moral domain. As we shall see, there are conflicting theories about goodness and rightness. Such conflict is a good thing. Each theory contains important truths about the moral life, and none of them contains the whole truth. Each keeps the others honest, as it were, curbing the excesses of any particular moral absolutism. Yet each claims to have the truth, and refuses the relativist's injunction to avoid making judgments about others. Judgment—both making judgments and being judged—is crucial to the moral life, just as it is to the political life. We have differing moral perspectives, but we must often inhabit a common world.

It is precisely this tension between individual viewpoints and living in a common world that lies at the heart of this book. The diversity of viewpoints is not intended to create a written version of those television news shows where people constantly shout at one another. Rather, these selections indicate the range of important and legitimate insights with which we approach the issue in question. The challenge, then, is for us—as individuals, and as a society—to forge a common ground which acknowledges the legitimacy of the conflicting insights but also establishes a minimal area of agreement so that we can live together with our differences. The model this book strives to emulate is not the one-sided monarch who claims to have the absolute truth, nor is it the anarchistic society that contains no basis for consensus. Rather, it is the model of a healthy government in which diversity, disagreement, compromise, and consensus are signs of vitality.

A Pluralistic Approach to Moral Theories

Just as in the political realm there are political parties and movements that delineate the main contours of the political debate, so also in philosophy there are moral theories that provide characteristic ways of understanding and resolving particular moral issues. In the readings throughout this book, we will see a number of examples of these theories in action. It is helpful, to look at some of the main characteristics of each of these theories. Just as Republicans and Democrats, liberals and conservatives, libertarians and socialists all have important, and often conflicting, insights about the political life, so too does each of these theories have valuable insights into the moral life. Yet none of them has the whole story. Let's look briefly at each of these approaches.

Morality As Consequences

What makes an action morally good? For many of us, what counts are *consequences.* The right action is the one that produces good consequences. If I give money to Oxfam to help starving people, and if Oxfam saves the lives of starving people and helps them develop a self-sustaining economy, then I have done something good. It is good because it produced good consequences. For this reason, it is the right thing to do. Those who subscribe to this position are called *consequentialists.* All consequentialists share a common belief that it is consequences that make an action good, but they differ among themselves about precisely which consequences.

Ethical Egoism

Some consequentialists, called *ethical egoists,* maintain that each of us should look only at the consequences that affect us. In their eyes, each person ought to perform those actions that contribute most to his or her own self-interest. Each person is the best judge of his or her own self-interest, and each person is responsible for maximizing his or her own self-interest. The political expression of ethical egoism occurs most clearly in *libertarianism,* and the best-known advocate of this position was probably Ayn Rand.

Ethical egoism has been criticized on a number of counts, most notably that it simply draws the circle of morality much too closely around the isolated individual. Critics maintain that self-interest is precisely what morality has to overcome, not what it should espouse. Egoism preaches selfishness, but morality should encourage altruism, compassion, love, and a sense of community—all, according to critics, beyond the reach of the egoist.

Utilitarianism

Once we begin to enlarge the circle of those affected by the consequences of our actions, we move toward a utilitarian position. At its core, *utilitarianism* believes that we ought to do what produces the greatest overall good consequences for *everyone,* not just for me. We determine this by examining the various courses of action open to us, calculating the consequences associated with each, and then deciding on the one that produces the greatest overall good consequences for everyone. It is consequentialist and computational. It holds out the promise that moral disputes can be resolved objectively by computing consequences. Part of the attraction of utilitarianism is precisely this claim to objectivity based on a moral calculus.

This is a very demanding moral doctrine for two reasons. First, it asks people to set aside their own individual interests for the good of the whole. Often this can result in great individual sacrifice if taken seriously. For example, the presence of hunger and starvation in our society (as well as outside of it) places great demands on the utilitarian, for often more good would be accomplished by giving food to the hungry than eating it oneself. Second, utilitarianism asks us to do whatever produces the *most* good. Far from being a doctrine of the moral minimum, utilitarianism always asks us to do the maximum.

Utilitarians disagree among themselves about what the proper standard is for judging consequences. What are "good" consequences? Are they the ones that produce the most *pleasure*? The most *happiness*? The most truth, beauty, and the like? Or simply the consequences that satisfy the most people? Each of these standards of utility has its strengths and weaknesses. *Pleasure* is comparatively easy to measure, but in many people's eyes it seems to be a rather base standard. Can't we increase pleasure just by putting electrodes in the proper location in a person's brain? Presumably we want something more, and better, than that. *Happiness* seems a more plausible candidate, but the difficulty with happiness is that it is both elusive to define and extremely difficult to measure. This is particularly a problem for utilitarianism, for since its initial appeal rests in part on its claim to objectivity. *Ideals* such as truth and beauty are even more difficult to measure. *Preference satisfaction* is more measurable, but it provides no foundation for distinguishing between morally acceptable preferences and morally objectionable preferences such as racism.

The other principal disagreement that has plagued utilitarianism centers on the question of whether we look at the consequences of each individual act—this is called *act utilitarianism*—or the consequences that would result from everyone following a particular rule—this is called *rule utilitarianism.* The danger of act utilitarianism is that it may justify some particular acts that most of us would want to condemn particularly those that sacrifice individual life and liberty for the sake of the whole. The classic problem occurs in regard to punishment. We could imagine a situation in which punishing an innocent person—while concealing his innocence, of course—would have the greatest overall good consequences. If doing so would result in the greatest overall amount of pleasure or happiness, then it would not only be permitted by act utilitarianism, it would be morally required. Similar difficulties arise in regard to an issue such as euthanasia. It is conceivable that overall utility might justify active euthanasia of the elderly and infirm, even involuntary euthanasia, especially of those who leave no one behind to mourn their passing. Yet are there things we cannot do to people, even if utility seems to require it? Many of us would answer such a question affirmatively.

In response to such difficulties, utilitarian theorists pointed out that, while consequences may justify a particular act of punishing the innocent, they could never justify living by a *rule* that said it was permissible to punish the innocent when doing so would produce the greatest utility. Rule utilitarians agree that we should look only at consequences, but maintain that we should look at the consequences of adopting a particular rule for everyone, not the consequences of each individual action. This type of utilitarianism is less likely to generate the injustices associated with act utilitarianism, but many feel that it turns into rule-worship. Why, critics ask, should we follow the rule in those instances where it does not produce the greatest utility?

Feminist Consequentialism

During the past twenty years, much interesting and valuable work has been done in the area of feminist ethics. It would be misleading to think of feminist approaches to ethics as falling into a single camp, but certainly some feminist moral philosophers have sketched out consequentialist accounts of the moral life in at least two different ways.

First, some feminists have argued that morality is a matter of consequences, but that consequences are not best understood or evaluated in the traditional computational model offered by utilitarianism. Instead, they focus primarily on the ways in which particular actions have consequences for relationships and feelings. Negative consequences are those that destroy relationships and that hurt others, especially those that hurt others emotionally. Within this tradition, the morally good course of action is that one that preserves the greatest degree of connectedness among all those affected by it. Carol Gilligan has described this moral voice in her book *In a Different Voice.*

Second, other feminists have accepted a roughly utilitarian account of consequences, but have paid particular attention to—and often given special weight to—the consequences that affect women. Such consequences, they argue, have often been overlooked by traditional utilitarian calculators, supposedly impartial but often insensitive to harming women. Unlike the work of Gilligan and others mentioned in the previous paragraph, feminists in this tradition do not question the dominant utilitarian paradigm, but rather question whether it has in fact been applied impartially.

Conclusion

Despite these disagreements about the precise formulation of utilitarianism, most people would admit that utilitarianism contains important insights into the moral life. Part of the justification for morality, and one of the reasons people accept the burdens of morality, is that it promises to produce a better world than we would have without it. This is undoubtedly part of the picture. But is it the whole picture?

Morality As Act and Intention

Critics of utilitarianism point out that, for utilitarianism, no actions are good or bad in themselves. All actions in themselves are morally neutral, and for pure consequentialists no action is intrinsically evil. Yet this seems to contradict the moral intuition of many people, people who believe that some actions are just morally wrong, even if they have good results. Killing innocent human beings, torturing people, raping them—these are but a few of the actions that many would want to condemn as wrong in themselves, even if in unusual circumstances they may produce good consequences.

How can we tell if some actions are morally good or bad in themselves? Clearly, we must have some standard against which they can be judged. Various standards have been proposed, and most of these again capture important truths about the moral life.

Conformity to God's Commands

In a number of fundamentalist religious traditions, including some branches of Judaism, Christianity, and Islam, what makes an act right is that it is commanded by God and what makes an act wrong is that it is forbidden by God. In these traditions, certain kinds of acts are wrong just because God forbids them. Usually such prohibitions are contained in sacred texts such as the Bible or the Koran.

There are two principal difficulties with this approach, one external, one internal. The external problem is that, while this may provide a good reason for believers to act in particular ways, it hardly gives a persuasive case to nonbelievers. The internal difficulty is that it is often difficult, even with the best of intentions, to discern what God's commands actually are. Sacred texts, for example, contain numerous injunctions, but it is rare that any religious tradition takes *all* of them seriously. (The Bible tells believers to pick up venomous vipers, but only a handful of Christians engage in this practice.) How do we decide which injunctions to take seriously and which to ignore or interpret metaphorically?

Natural Law

There is a long tradition, beginning with Aristotle and gaining great popularity in the Middle Ages, that maintains that acts which are "unnatural" are always evil. The underlying premise of this view is that the natural is good, and therefore what contradicts it is bad. Often, especially in the

Middle Ages, this was part of a larger Christian worldview that saw nature as created by God, who then was the ultimate source of its goodness. Yet it has certainly survived in twentieth-century moral and legal philosophy quite apart from its theological underpinnings. This appeal to natural law occurs at a number of junctures in our readings, but especially in the discussions of reproductive technologies and those of homosexuality. Natural law arguments lead quite easily into considerations of human nature, again with the implicit claim that human nature is good.

Natural law arguments tend to be slippery for two, closely interrelated reasons. First, for natural law arguments to work, one has to provide convincing support for the claim that the "natural" is (the only) good—or at least for its contrapositive, the claim that the "unnatural" is bad. Second, such arguments presuppose that we can clearly differentiate between the natural and the unnatural. Are floods and earthquakes natural? Is disease natural? Either the natural is not always good, or else we have to adopt a very selective notion of natural.

Proper Intention

A second way in which acts can be said to be good or bad is that they are done for the proper motivation, with the correct intention. Indeed, intentions are often built into our vocabulary for describing actions. The difference between stabbing a person and performing surgery on that person may well reside primarily in the intention of the agent.

Acting for the sake of duty. Again, there is no shortage of candidates for morally acceptable intentions. A sense of duty, universalizability, a respect for other persons, sincerity or authenticity, care and compassion—these are but a few of the acceptable moral motivations. Consider, first of all, the motive of duty. Immanuel Kant argued that what gives an action moral worth is that it is done for the sake of duty. In his eyes, the morally admirable person is the one who, despite inclinations to the contrary, does the right thing solely because it is the right thing to do. The person who contributes to charities out of a sense of duty is morally far superior to the person who does the same thing in order to look good in the eyes of others, despite the fact that the consequences may be the same.

Universalizability. How do we know what our duty is? Kant avoided saying duty was simply a matter of "following orders." Instead, he saw duty as emanating from the nature of reason itself. And because reason is universal, duty is also universal. Kant suggested an important test of whether our understanding of duty was rational in any particular instance. We always act, he maintained, with a subjective rule or maxim that guides our decision. Is this maxim one that we can will that everyone accept, or is it one that fails this test of universalizability?

Consider cheating. If you cheat on an exam, it's like lying: you are saying something is your work when it is not. Imagine you cheat on all the exams in a course and finish with an average of 98 percent. The professor then gives you a grade of "D." You storm into the professor's office, demanding an explanation. The professor calmly says, "Oh, I lied on the grade sheet." Your reply would be, "But you can't lie about my grade!" Kant's point is that, by cheating, you've denied the validity of your own claim. You've implicitly said that it is morally all right for people to lie. But of course you don't believe it's permissible for your professor to lie—only for you yourself to do so. This, Kant says, fails the test of universalizability.

Notice that Kant's argument isn't a consequentialist one. He's not asking what would happen to society if everyone lied. Rather, he's saying that certain maxims are *inconsistent* and thus irrational. You cannot approve of your own lying without approving of everyone else's, and yet the advantage you get depends precisely on other people's honesty. It is the irrationality of making an exception of my own lying in this way that Kant feels violates the moral law. We have probably all had the experience of acting in a morally sleazy way, of making an exception for ourselves that (at least in retrospect) we know isn't justified.

Kant's argument captured something valuable about the moral life: the insight that what's fair for one is fair for all. Yet critics were quick to point out that this can hardly be the entire story. Consequences count, and intentions are notoriously slippery. A given act can be described with many different intentions—to cheat on a test, to try to excel, to try to meet your parents' expectations, to be the first in the class—and not all of them necessarily fail the test of universalizability.

Respect for other persons. Kant offered another formulation of his basic moral insight, one that touches a responsive chord in many of us. We should never treat people merely as things, Kant argued. Rather, we should always respect them as autonomous (i.e., self-directing) moral agents. Both capitalism and technology pressure us to treat people merely as things, and many have found Kant's refusal to do this to be of crucial moral importance.

It is easy to find examples at both ends of this spectrum. We use people merely as things when we do not let them make their own decisions and when we harm them for our own benefit without respect for their rights. Consider the now infamous Tuskegee experiment, in which medical researchers tracked the development of syphilis in a group of African-American men for over thirty years, never telling them the precise nature of their malady and never treating them—something which would have been both inexpensive and effective. Instead, the researchers let the disease proceed through its ultimately fatal course in order to observe more closely the details of its progress. These men were used merely as means to the researchers' ends.

Similarly, we have all, hopefully, experienced being treated as ends in ourselves. If I am ill, and my physician gives me the details of my medical condition, outlines the available options for treatment (including nontreatment), and is supportive of whatever choice I finally make in this matter, then I feel as though I have been treated with respect. Timothy Quill's selection in the chapter on euthanasia offers a good, real-life example of such respect in the doctor-patient relationship.

The difficulty with this criterion is that there is a large middle ground where it is unclear if acting in a particular way is really using other people merely as things. Indeed, insofar as our economic system is based on commodification, we can be assured that this will be a common phenomenon in our society. To what extent is respect for persons attainable in a capitalist and technological society?

Compassion and caring. Some philosophers, particularly but not exclusively feminists, have urged the moral importance of acting out of motives of care and compassion. Many of these philosophers have argued that caring about other persons is the heart of the moral life, and that a morality of care leads to a refreshingly new picture of morality as centering on relationships, feelings, and connectedness rather than impartiality, justice, and fairness. The justice-oriented person in a moral dispute will ask what the fair thing to do is, and then proceed to follow that course of action, no matter what effect that has on others. The care-oriented individual, on the other hand, will try to find the course of action that best preserves the interests of all involved and that does the least amount of damage to the relationships involved.

Many in this tradition have seen the justice orientation as characteristically male, while the care orientation as typically female. (Notice that this is not the same as claiming that these orientations are exclusively male or female.) Critics have argued that such correlations are simplistic and misleading. Both orientations may be present to some degree in almost everyone, and particular types of situations may be responsible for bringing one or the other to the fore.

Respect for Rights

Kant, as we have just seen, told us that we ought to respect other persons. Yet what specific aspects of other persons ought we to respect? One answer, which has played a major political as well as philosophical role during the past two centuries, has been framed in terms of human rights. The Bill of Rights was the first set of amendments to the U.S. Constitution. At approximately the same time, the French were drafting the *Declaration of the Rights of Man and Citizen.* Concern for human rights has continued well into the twentieth century, and the past forty years in the United States have been marked by an intense concern with rights—the civil rights movement for racial equality, the equal rights movement for women, the animal rights movement, the gay rights movement, and equal rights for Americans with disabilities. Throughout the selections in this book, we will see continual appeals to rights, debates about the extent and even the existence of rights, and attempts to adjudicate conflicts of rights.

Rights provide the final criterion to be considered here for evaluating acts. Those acts which violate basic human rights are morally wrong, this tradition suggests. Torture, imprisoning, and executing the innocent; denial of the right to vote; denial of due process—these are all instances of actions that violate human rights. (The fact that an act does not violate basic human rights does not mean that it is morally unobjectionable; there may be other criteria for evaluating it as well as rights.) Human rights, defenders of this tradition maintain, are not subject to nationality, race, religion, class, or any other such limitation. They cannot be set aside for reasons of utility, convenience, or political or financial gain. We possess them simply by virtue of being human beings, and they thus exhibit a universality that provides the foundation for a global human community.

Criticisms of the rights tradition abound. First, how do we determine *which* rights we have? Rights theorists often respond that we have a right to those things—such as life, freedom, and property—which are necessary to human existence itself. Yet many claim that such necessities are contextual, not universal. Moreover, they maintain that there is something logically suspicious about proceeding from the claim that "I need something" to the claim that "I have a right to it." Needs, these critics argue, do not entail rights. Second, critics have asked whether these rights are *negative rights* (i.e., freedoms from certain kinds of interference) or *positive rights* (i.e., entitlements). This is one of the issues at the core of the welfare debate currently raging in the United States. Do the poor have any positive rights to welfare, or do they only have rights not to be discriminated against in various ways? Finally, some critics have argued that the current focus on rights has obscured other, morally relevant aspects of our lives. Rights establish a moral minimum for the ways in which we interact with others, especially strangers we do not care about. But when we are dealing with those we know and care about, more may be demanded of us morally than just respecting their rights.

Morality As Character

It is rare that a philosophy anthology reaches the bestseller lists, and it is even more unusual when that book is a relatively traditional work about character. William Bennett's *The Book of Virtues,* however, has done just that. Staying on the bestseller list for week after week, Bennett's book indicates a resurgence of interest in a long-neglected tradition of ethic: Aristotelian virtue theory.

The Contrast between Act-Oriented Ethics and Character-Oriented Ethics

This Aristotelian approach to ethic, sometimes called *character ethics* or *virtue ethics,* is distinctive. In contrast to the preceding act-oriented approaches, it does not focus on what makes *acts* right or wrong. Rather, it focuses on *people* and their moral character. Instead of asking, "What should I do?" those in this tradition ask, "What kind of person should I strive to be?" This gives a very different focus to the moral life.

An analogy with public life may again be helpful. Consider the American judiciary system. We develop an elaborate set of rules through legislation, and these rules are often articulated in excruciating detail. However, when someone is brought to trial, we do not depend solely on the rules to guarantee justice. Ultimately, we place the fate of accused criminals in the hands of people—a judge and jury. As a country, we bet on both rules and people.

A similar situation exists in ethics. We need good rules—and the preceding sections have described some attempts to articulate those rules—but we also need good people to have the wisdom and good will to interpret and apply those rules. Far from being in conflict with each other, act-oriented and character-oriented approaches to ethics complement one another.

Human Flourishing

The principal question that character-oriented approaches to ethics asks is the following: What strengths of character (i.e., virtues) promote human flourishing? Correlatively, what weaknesses of character (i.e., vices) impede human flourishing? *Virtues* are thus those strengths of character that contribute to human flourishing, while *vices* are those weaknesses that get in the way of flourishing.

To develop an answer to these questions, the first thing that those in this tradition must do is to articulate a clear notion of human flourishing. Here they depend as much on moral psychology as moral philosophy. Aristotle had a vision of human flourishing, but it was one that was clearly limited to his time—one that excluded women and slaves. In contemporary psychology, we have seen much interesting work describing flourishing in psychological terms—Carl Rogers and Abraham Maslow are two of the better-known psychologists who attempt to describe human flourishing. The articulation of a well-founded and convincing vision of human flourishing remains one of the principal challenges of virtue ethics today.

The Virtue of Courage

We can better understand this approach to ethics if we look at a sample virtue and its corresponding vices. Consider courage. Aristotle analyzed it primarily in military terms, but we now see that it is a virtue necessary to a wide range of human activities—and those who lack courage will rarely flourish. Courage is the strength of character to face and overcome that which we fear. Fears differ from one person to the next, but we all have them. Some may fear physical danger; some may fear intimacy and the psychological vulnerability that comes with it; some may fear commitment; some may fear taking risks to gain what they desire. We all have things we fear, and for most of us, we must overcome those fears if we are to achieve our goals, to attain what we value in life.

Imagine people who lack the courage to take chances in their careers. They desire a more challenging position, but they are unwilling to give up the old position to make the move. Imagine those who fear the vulnerability that comes with genuinely intimate relationships. They long for intimacy, but are unable or unwilling to take the risk necessary to attain it. Those who lack courage will be unable to take the necessary risks, and this is the sense in which cowardice is a vice: it prevents us from flourishing.

Yet Aristotle also suggests that virtues are usually a mean between two extremes. One of the extremes here is clear: cowardice. But what would it mean to have too much courage? It is easy to imagine examples. First, one could be willing to risk too quickly. Rashness is one way of having too much courage. Or one could risk much for too little. To run into a burning building to save a trapped child is courage; to run into the same building to save an old pair of shoes is foolhardy. Of course, the phrase "too much courage" here can be misleading. Too much courage in the end isn't really courage; it's something else.

Compassion

Aristotle talked a lot about virtues such as proper pride, courage, fortitude, and the like. Compassion was not among them. Yet many today would argue that compassion is a virtue—and this becomes a pivotal issue in a number of our readings in this book. What would an Aristotelian analysis of compassion look like?

First, let's define compassion and bracket it between its two extremes, the vices that correspond to a deficiency or an excess of compassion. *Compassion* itself is a feeling for our fellow moral beings (human beings and perhaps animals). It is literally a "feeling with . . ." an ability to identify with the feelings of another being, especially feelings of suffering. Moreover, it is usually oriented toward action. The compassionate person is moved to help those who are suffering, and we would doubt the genuineness of the compassion if it never led to action. Those with too little compassion are cold-hearted, indifferent to the suffering of others. Unfortunately, there is no shortage of examples here. Yet what is "too much" compassion? Presumably, it is being overly concerned with the suffering of others. There are several ways in which this could occur. First, we might be so concerned with the suffering of others that we neglect ourselves and those to whom we have direct duties. Second, we might be so concerned with the suffering of others that we neglect the nonsuffering parts of their personality, turning them into pure victims when they are not. Third, we may be appropriately concerned with the suffering of others, but we may manifest this in inappropriate ways. If compassion for a child crying in pain during a medical procedure leads us to kidnap the child to save it from suffering, we have expressed our compassion in an inappropriate way.

Compassion has an emotional element to it, but it is not just a blind feeling. Rather, it is also a way of perceiving the world—the world looks different through the eyes of the compassionate person than through the eyes of the sociopath. Moreover, it is also a way of thinking about the world, a way of understanding it. Compassion has to make judgments about the nature and causes of suffering, and also about the possible remedies for suffering. Compassion, finally, is also a way of acting, a way of responding to the suffering of the world. Compassion can be both deeply passionate and smart at the same time. As we shall see in our discussion of issues about poverty and starvation, it is not enough to feel compassion. We also have to know how to respond to suffering in effective ways that not only relieve the immediate suffering but also help the sufferers to free themselves from future suffering. Compassion needs to be wise, not just strongly felt.

Virtue Ethics as the Foundation of Other Approaches to Ethics

We can conclude this section by reflecting once again on the relationship between virtue ethics and act-oriented approaches to ethics. One of the principal problems faced by moral philosophers has been how to understand the continuing disagreement among the various ethical traditions described above. It seems implausible to say that one is right and all the rest are wrong, but it also seems impossible to say that they are all right, for they seem to contradict each other. If we adopt a pluralistic approach, we may say that each contains partial truths about the moral life, but none contains the whole truth. But then the question is: How do we know which position should be given precedence in a particular instance?

There is no *theoretical* answer to this question, no meta-theory that integrates all these differing and at times conflicting theories. However, there is a *practical* answer to this question: We ultimately have to put our trust in the wise person to know when to give priority to one type of moral consideration over another. Indeed, it is precisely this that constitutes moral wisdom.

Analyzing Moral Problems

As we turn to consider the various moral problems discussed in this book, each of these theories will help us to understand aspects of the problem that we might not originally have noticed, to see connections among apparently unconnected factors, and to formulate responses that we might not previously have envisioned. Ultimately, our search is a personal one, a search for wisdom.

But it is also a social approach, one that seeks to discern how to live a good life with other people, how to live well together in the community. As we consider the series of moral issues that follows in this book, we will be attempting to fulfill both the individual and the communal goals. We will be seeking to find the course of action that is morally right for us as individuals, and we will be developing our own account of how society as a whole ought to respond to these moral challenges.

An Initial Self-Quiz

Drawing on your current moral beliefs, answer the following questions as honestly as possible. You may feel that these check boxes do not allow you to state your beliefs accurately enough. Please feel free to add notes, qualifications, and so on, in the margins. You will be asked to return to reassess your answers to these questions throughout the semester.

To participate in an on-line version of this self-quiz, and to see how others have responded, visit the Ethics Surveys section of *Ethics Updates* (http://ethics.acusd.edu)

	Strongly Agree	*Agree*	*Undecided*	*Disagree*	*Strongly Disagree*	*Chapter 1: Abortion*
1.	❑	❑	❑	❑	❑	The principal moral consideration about abortion is the question of whether the fetus is a person or not.
2.	❑	❑	❑	❑	❑	The principal moral consideration about abortion is the question of the rights of the pregnant woman.
3.	❑	❑	❑	❑	❑	The only one who should have a voice in making the decision about an abortion is the pregnant woman.
4.	❑	❑	❑	❑	❑	Abortion should be legal but morally discouraged.
5.	❑	❑	❑	❑	❑	Abortion protesters are justified in breaking the law in order to prevent abortions

	Strongly Agree	*Agree*	*Undecided*	*Disagree*	*Strongly Disagree*	*Chapter 2: Cloning and Reproductive Technologies*
6.	❑	❑	❑	❑	❑	*In vitro* fertilization is morally wrong.
7.	❑	❑	❑	❑	❑	Any procedure that helps infertile couples to have children is good.
8.	❑	❑	❑	❑	❑	Surrogate mothers should never have to give up their babies if they don't want to do so.
9.	❑	❑	❑	❑	❑	Surrogate motherhood should be illegal.
10.	❑	❑	❑	❑	❑	Genetic manipulation of embryos should be forbidden.

	Strongly Agree	*Agree*	*Undecided*	*Disagree*	*Strongly Disagree*	*Chapter 3: Euthanasia*
11.	❑	❑	❑	❑	❑	Euthanasia is always morally wrong.
12.	❑	❑	❑	❑	❑	Euthanasia should be illegal at least under almost all circumstances.
13.	❑	❑	❑	❑	❑	The principal moral consideration about euthanasia is the question of whether the person freely chooses to die or not.
14.	❑	❑	❑	❑	❑	Actively killing someone is always morally worse than just letting them die.
15.	❑	❑	❑	❑	❑	Sometimes we have a duty to die.

	Strongly Agree	*Agree*	*Undecided*	*Disagree*	*Strongly Disagree*	*Chapter 4: Punishment and the Dealth Penalty*
16.	❑	❑	❑	❑	❑	The purpose of punishment is primarily to pay back the offender.
17.	❑	❑	❑	❑	❑	The purpose of punishment is primarily to deter the offender and others from committing future crimes.
18.	❑	❑	❑	❑	❑	Capital punishment is always morally wrong.
19.	❑	❑	❑	❑	❑	The principal moral consideration about capital punishment is the question of whether it is administered arbitrarily or not.
20.	❑	❑	❑	❑	❑	The principal moral consideration about capital punishment is that it doesn't really deter criminals.

	Strongly Agree	*Agree*	*Undecided*	*Disagree*	*Strongly Disagree*	*Chapter 5: Race and Ethnicity*
21.	❑	❑	❑	❑	❑	African Americans are still often discriminated against in employment.
22.	❑	❑	❑	❑	❑	Affirmative action helps African Americans and other minorities.
23.	❑	❑	❑	❑	❑	Racial separatism is wrong.
24.	❑	❑	❑	❑	❑	Hate speech should be banned.
25.	❑	❑	❑	❑	❑	We should encourage the development of racial and ethnic identity.

Chapter 6: Gender

	Strongly Agree	*Agree*	*Undecided*	*Disagree*	*Strongly Disagree*	
26.	❑	❑	❑	❑	❑	Women's moral voices are different from men's.
27.	❑	❑	❑	❑	❑	Women are still discriminated against in the workplace.
28.	❑	❑	❑	❑	❑	Sexual harassment should be illegal.
29.	❑	❑	❑	❑	❑	Affirmative action helps women.
30.	❑	❑	❑	❑	❑	Genuine equality for women demands a restructuring of the traditional family.

Chapter 7: Sexual Orientation

	Strongly Agree	*Agree*	*Undecided*	*Disagree*	*Strongly Disagree*	
31.	❑	❑	❑	❑	❑	Gays and lesbians should be allowed to serve openly in the military.
32.	❑	❑	❑	❑	❑	Gays and lesbians should not be discriminated against in hiring or housing.
33.	❑	❑	❑	❑	❑	Homosexuality is unnatural.
34.	❑	❑	❑	❑	❑	Same-sex marriages should be legal.
35.	❑	❑	❑	❑	❑	Homosexuality is a matter of personal choice.

Chapter 8: Poverty and Welfare

	Strongly Agree	*Agree*	*Undecided*	*Disagree*	*Strongly Disagree*	
36.	❑	❑	❑	❑	❑	People are poor mainly because they do not have the proper ability, training, motivation, or interest in working hard.
37.	❑	❑	❑	❑	❑	Everyone has a right to a minimum income, whether they work or not.
38.	❑	❑	❑	❑	❑	Everyone has a right to a minimum income, if they want to work but cannot find a job.
39.	❑	❑	❑	❑	❑	Society ought to continue welfare support for women with illegitimate children.
40.	❑	❑	❑	❑	❑	Society ought to provide welfare support to elderly people who are no longer able to work.

	Strongly Agree	Agree	Undecided	Disagree	Strongly Disagree	*Chapter 9: World Hunger and Poverty*
41.	❑	❑	❑	❑	❑	Only the morally heartless would refuse to help the starving.
42.	❑	❑	❑	❑	❑	We should help starving nations until we are as poor as they are.
43.	❑	❑	❑	❑	❑	In the long run, relief aid to starving nations does not help them.
44.	❑	❑	❑	❑	❑	Overpopulation is the main cause of world hunger and poverty.
45.	❑	❑	❑	❑	❑	The world is gradually becoming a better place.

	Strongly Agree	Agree	Undecided	Disagree	Strongly Disagree	*Chapter 10: Living Together with Animals*
46.	❑	❑	❑	❑	❑	There's nothing morally wrong with eating veal.
47.	❑	❑	❑	❑	❑	It's morally permissible to cause animals pain in order to do medical research that benefits human beings.
48.	❑	❑	❑	❑	❑	All animals have the same moral standing.
49.	❑	❑	❑	❑	❑	Zoos are a morally good thing.
50.	❑	❑	❑	❑	❑	There is nothing morally wrong with hunting.

	Strongly Agree	Agree	Undecided	Disagree	Strongly Disagree	*Chapter 11: Environmental Ethics*
51.	❑	❑	❑	❑	❑	Nature is just a source of resources for us.
52.	❑	❑	❑	❑	❑	The government should strictly regulate toxic waste.
53.	❑	❑	❑	❑	❑	We should make every effort possible to avoid infringing on the natural environment any more than we already have.
54.	❑	❑	❑	❑	❑	We owe future generations a clean and safe environment.
55.	❑	❑	❑	❑	❑	We should not impose our environmental concerns on developing nations.

Center for Academic Integrity Philosophical Foundations of the "Fundamental Principles of Academic Integrity"

This document was written by a group of faculty, administrators, and students at the Center for Academic Integrity and revised, in a collaborative process, with various groups around the country.

This document provides a comprehensive view of the foundations of academic integrity for students, professors, administrators and educational institutions. Further information is available on the Center's website at http://www.academicintegrity.org

As You Read, Consider This:

1. What are the five fundamental values of academic integrity?
2. Why isn't it sufficient simply to equate academic integrity with academic honesty?

Academic integrity provides the foundation upon which a flourishing academic life rests. Building on discussions with faculty, students, and administrators throughout the land, the Fundamental Principles of Academic Integrity Project seeks to develop a definition of "academic integrity." Like the word "integrity" itself, academic integrity is a complex concept, difficult to define. Yet it is so axiomatic to the work of higher education that for many institutions, the meaning and definition of academic integrity literally go without saying: they simply state that "academic integrity is essential to the educational mission of the university" and go on to other policy and procedural matters. Those that do attempt a definition generally declare that academic integrity means "academic honesty," or define it by example, listing prohibited cheating behaviors and/or required honest and fair behaviors.

We define academic integrity in terms of a commitment to five fundamental values and to the principles that flow from those values. Just as personal integrity involves standing up for one's fundamental commitments, even in difficult circumstances, so too academic integrity involves standing up for what is fundamental as well. In the case of academic integrity, it is standing up for the values that are fundamental to the academic process, even when it is difficult to do so. In the Committee's discussions with faculty, students, and administrators, five values emerged as fundamental to the academic process: *honesty, trust, fairness, respect, and responsibility.* Academic integrity, in our view, is the commitment to stand up for these five values, even in the face of adversity.

An academic community cannot flourish without these values. Without honesty, the free exchange of ideas is distorted. Without trust, the willingness to engage collaboratively in the learning process is stunted. Without fairness, the foundation of the critical dimension of educational inquiry is eroded. Without respect, the civility necessary to public discourse is drowned out. Without responsibility, we will not acknowledge ourselves as accountable for supporting and enforcing these fundamental values. Supporting and affirming these five values, as expressed in the following principles, is essential to promoting and maintaining a high level of academic integrity. The five values provide reasons and motives for actions; the corresponding principles provide specific ways in which those five values can be translated into action. While these values and principles necessarily overlap one another to some extent, each expresses a key and separate aspect of academic integrity.

Academic integrity, thus defined, is both intrinsically valuable and also instrumentally valuable. The educational mission of colleges and universities entails a belief that academic integrity is a value in and of itself. A commitment to academic integrity also yields certain tangible benefits in, for example, maintaining the reputation and credibility of an institution's students and faculty, as well as the meaning, value and validity of the degrees it awards.

We seek, through this document, to affirm the importance of these five values and the principles that flow from them for all those who participate in the academic life. In so doing, we seek to encourage a culture of integrity within which the academic life can more fully flourish. The cultivation of integrity within institutions of higher learning is especially pressing now for two reasons. First, there is strong evidence to suggest that academic dishonesty is on the rise. Initial studies of cheating and plagiarism in high schools suggest alarming trends. Our colleges and universities will be increasingly challenged by problems relating to academic integrity. Second, as Professor Stephen Carter and others have pointed out, we face a "crisis of integrity" in society as a whole. Educational institutions have a special responsibility in such a crisis, for they are often society's last good chance at defusing that crisis. If habits of integrity are not strongly instilled before students leave school for the workforce, there is little hope that they will be developed after that point.

I. Honesty

An academic community should advance the quest for truth and knowledge by requiring intellectual and personal honesty in learning, teaching, and research.

Honesty is crucial to the academic mission, especially to the tasks of learning, teaching, and research. Although sometimes difficult to achieve and fraught with obstacles, honesty is a necessary condition for the flourishing of the academic life. Uniformly, campus honor codes and/or standards of conduct deplore cheating, lying, misrepresentation, deception, fraud, forgery, theft, and dishonesty in all its forms, whether in class, in the laboratory, in writing and research, or in our dealings with one another as students, teachers, colleagues.

Honesty with oneself as well as others is essential to learning. In order to grow in both knowledge and insight, students must be honest to themselves as well as to others about what they know and what they do not know. Only when they build on such a foundation of honesty can students develop an accurate sense of their own academic progress and receive accurate assessment from their professors. Professors have a particular responsibility to articulate for students the specific standards of academic honesty, especially in less traditional areas such as collaborative learning.

Honesty is equally important in teaching and research, where the professor often provides a role model for the students' developing sense of academic honesty. To be effective teachers, professors should model and practice honesty in their own quest for knowledge, as well as in interactions with students and colleagues. Professors, in both their teaching and their research, provide the model of academic honesty that is most visible to students.

Dishonesty undermines the process of education. Those who cheat do not learn, do not develop the skills, knowledge, and expertise necessary for the exercise of their profession, and make a mockery and a fraud of any degrees they may be awarded. They may be dangerous as well, because they profess to know what they do not, jeopardizing the rights and welfare of other individuals and their community for the false goal of grades at any cost.

Although each of these five values is essential to academic integrity, honesty holds a special place. Honesty is necessary for the other values. Trust, fairness, respect, and responsibility presuppose a foundation of honesty. Without honesty, we can only realize diminished versions of these other values. Yet in recognizing the special place of honesty in the academic life, we do not intend to reduce academic integrity simply to honesty. Honesty is the foundation of academic integrity, not its fullness.

The cultivation of such honesty plays a crucial role in moral development. Virtue, Aristotle tells us, is a habit. In stressing the importance of academic integrity to our students, we seek to encourage the development of a lifelong habit of honesty. Nor can honesty be cultivated without other virtues. To act with academic integrity requires courage, insight, and self-awareness: the courage to face hard choices honestly, and to choose to do what is right, as well as to accept responsibility for one's actions and their consequences, even at personal cost.

II. Trust

An academic community should foster a climate of mutual trust to encourage the free exchange of ideas and enable all to reach their highest potential.

Honesty breeds trust, just as surely as dishonesty breeds mistrust and suspicion. Trust is the natural response to consistent honesty. We seek not only to encourage trust in the academic community, but even more importantly to encourage those actions and policies that encourage and justify an attitude of trust from others.

For example, when faculty set clear guidelines for assignments and for the evaluation of student work, they act in a way that encourages students to trust them. Similarly, when students reply to assignments by faculty with honesty and thoughtfulness, they encourage faculty to listen more closely to students and to participate more openly in the academic dialogue, even when it leads in unexpected directions. So, too, when administrators interact with faculty and students in respectful and responsible ways, they encourage a response of trust.

Without trust, the academic life is impoverished. Without trust, the reliance on the communal dimension of knowledge is lost. Without trust, each member of the academic community must begin the quest for knowledge over again from the beginning, alone. Only when we trust can we take for granted the work of others and begin where they have left off. On both the individual level and on the level of disciplines as a whole, trust is necessary to the advancement of knowledge. Without trust, collaborative research is discouraged or even corrupted, and many of our greatest intellectual achievements would not have been possible. The absence of trust means individuals decline to share ideas and information for fear that work or credit will be stolen, careers stunted, reputations diminished. Such a climate is antithetical to creativity and the search for knowledge.

Many institutions have sought to promote a climate of trust through honor systems, which are virtually unique to educational communities. Honor systems are a respected and long-standing tradition among colleges and universities, and there is empirical evidence of their positive effect on the behavior and attitudes of their students and faculty. Honor systems may not be an option at all institutions, however, and they are not requisite either to academic integrity or to trust. There are many paths to academic integrity.

All institutions, whether they have honor codes or not, should act in ways which encourage and justify trust. Here the importance and interconnectedness of the other four values comprising academic integrity emerge most clearly: acting with honesty, fairness, respect, and responsibility fosters an attitude of trust.

Just as we seek to encourage trust within the academic community, we also seek to encourage trust between the academic community and communities outside of it. Society must have confidence in our scholarship and degrees in order for our work and awards to have social value and meaning. Whether it be through clear and consistent academic standards or honest and impartial research, we strive to act in ways that encourage and justify the trust of those outside the academic community.

III. Fairness

An academic community should seek to ensure fairness in institutional standards, practices, and procedures for academic integrity as well as fairness in interactions with each other.

Evaluation plays an important role in the educational process: faculty and students alike are constantly evaluating ideas, data, and even one another. Justice requires that fairness be fundamental to the evaluative process; without it, evaluation is false, misleading and unjust to the persons and positions being evaluated.

Students and faculty alike want their work to be evaluated fairly and accurately, using relevant forms of assessment. For students, predictability, clear expectations, and explicit standards are important components of fairness, as is a consistent and just response to cheating behaviors.

Students also want faculty and administration to confront and address dishonest and unfair conduct which jeopardizes their grades, the quality of learning in the classroom, and the reputation and value of their degrees. Fairness demands that honest students not be put at a disadvantage for their honesty. To maintain fairness, one should fully acknowledge any collaboration or use of sources. Otherwise, the work of students who struggle to produce papers in their own words may be downgraded when compared with the work of students who have copied without acknowledgment or detection whole paragraphs verbatim from the Internet.

Similarly, faculty are right to expect fairness not only from their students, but also from their colleagues and from their administration. This aspect of academic integrity enjoins faculty to evaluate one another fairly and administration to treat faculty and students with fairness.

Finally, while all have roles to play in ensuring fairness, this mutuality should not imply that a lapse by one would excuse misconduct by another. Rationalizations such as "everyone does it" or "the curve was too low" (and therefore allegedly unfair) are unacceptable and cannot justify dishonesty.

IV. Respect

An academic community should promote respect among students, staff, and faculty: respect for self, for others, for scholarship and research, for the educational process, and for our intellectual heritage.

To be most potent and rewarding for all concerned, teaching and learning demand active engagement and mutual respect. Respecting people means acknowledging their worth and treating them as ends in themselves, not just as a means to our own purposes. It is a fundamental virtue of community; without respect, people are often treated as mere objects. Effective teaching, because it recognizes the communal and participatory nature of the learning process, requires mutual respect. So, too, do collegiality and collaborative work, which have always been a valued part of the academic enterprise.

Respect for oneself implies participating actively in the learning, research, and teaching processes, trying one's wings, testing one's skills, building on successes, and learning from mistakes. For students, showing respect for others includes attending classes, being on time, paying attention, listening rather than simply arguing one's own point of view, being prepared and contributing to discussion, completing homework and papers in a timely fashion, and doing one's best. It also means not engaging in *ad hominem* attacks, profanity, intimidation, inappropriate demands for re-grading of work, and other disruptive, demeaning, or degrading behavior during class, office hours, or in other faculty-student interactions.

These requirements of respect and civility are of course mutual, and bind faculty, staff, and administration as well as students. For faculty, showing respect for students involves taking their ideas seriously, valuing their aspirations and goals, and recognizing them as individuals.

Respect for the work of others means appropriate acknowledgment of that work—words, ideas, discoveries, facts, charts or other graphics, or research, whether incorporated through collaboration, copying, or paraphrase. Both students and faculty are held to this standard. It means acknowledging any intellectual indebtedness to others, and giving credit where credit is due. Proper acknowledgment of academic debts requires citation of exact sources, and if verbatim language is used, it must be set off by quotation marks or indentation. Credit should be given whether the source is written or oral, published or unpublished, from the Internet, a database, a video or audio recording, a faculty lecture, course text, or class handout, an encyclopedia or other reference work, or the work of another student.

Once again, we see the interdependence of the values that constitute academic integrity. Part of respecting other people involves treating them fairly and dealing with them honestly, and all of this supports an environment of trust.

V. Responsibility

An academic community should uphold high standards of conduct in learning, teaching, and research by requiring shared responsibility for promoting academic integrity among all members of the community.

Responsibility for academic integrity lies with every member of the community; each should hold him/herself and others accountable. There is a responsibility not only to act with integrity in our own learning, teaching, and research, but also to take action in the face of wrongdoing. To tolerate dishonesty and unfairness is to perpetuate its existence.

Accordingly, each individual student, faculty member, and administrator is responsible for upholding the integrity and quality of scholarship and learning, and for ensuring fairness of the academic endeavor. Shared responsibility distributes the power to effect change, helps overcome apathy, and helps each individual to understand and feel that he/she is an integral part of the academic community.

One of the most difficult issues in regard to our shared responsibility for maintaining standard of academic integrity is how we deal with the dishonesty of others. Not only must we refrain from dishonesty, but we also must not permit it in others. The requirement of taking action often comes into direct conflict with peer pressure, with fear, with loyalty, and with misguided compassion. There is peer pressure not to "snitch" on one's peers. There is fear of ruining another's education, reputation, or life. There is concern that one might be mistaken and might unjustly accuse an innocent party. There is the specter of retaliation or blame, of harm to one's own standing if known to be a "snitch."

Some institutions do not explicitly require action, others permit anonymous reports. Anonymous reporting, however, is not without controversy; for some, it is an abdication of responsibility, and sends a mixed message by implying that the accuser does not have the strength of his/her convictions. It may also undermine due process by denying the accused an opportunity to confront and question the witness.

At a minimum, an academic integrity system should require that individuals take responsibility for their own honesty, and seek to discourage and prevent misconduct by others. This may be as simple as covering one's own answers during a test. The ultimate responsibility is to report any misconduct of others which one witnesses or discovers, and to self-report any transgressions in which one is an intentional or unintentional participant. Only in so doing are we willing to take full responsibility for our participation in the academic community.

Conclusion

This call for academic integrity places a heavy responsibility upon everyone in the academic community. Throughout this process of academic integrity, it is imperative that we balance a strong sense of our standards with compassion and a deep concern for healing. Academic institutions are dedicated to learning, and we must seek to insure that, when violations of academic integrity occur, everyone learns from them. Moreover, even in those instances in which breaches of academic integrity must be met with expulsion, we should strive to bring as much healing to all concerned through a process that is sensitive, fair, respectful, and responsible.

As members of academic communities, we can play a unique role in responding to the "crisis of integrity" in which our society finds itself embroiled. Institutions and individuals can initiate and sustain an ongoing dialogue about these issues and act in ways which support the values and principles outlined above.

Acknowledgments

A document on academic integrity would hardly be complete or consistent without acknowledging its sources. We do so, not only out of honesty, but also out of a deep sense of gratitude to the many who have given of their time, effort, and insight to advance this project. It is a far better document because of their participation.

The following individuals participated in the planning and preparation of early drafts of this document: Sally Cole, The Center for Academic Integrity; Mary Olson, Oakton Community College; Patrick Drinan, University of San Diego; Julian Harris, Duke University; James Lancaster, University of North Carolina, Greensboro; Donald L. McCabe, Rutgers University; James Larimore, Stanford University; John Margolis, Northwestern University; and Elizabeth Kiss, Duke University.

Written comments on the October 1997 draft were submitted by: Bill Taylor, Oakton Community College; Mark A. Hyatt, U.S. Air Force Academy; Sally Kuhlenschmidt, Western Kentucky University; Beverly Foster, University of North Carolina, Chapel Hill; Bruce Johnston, Lyon College; R. Michael Haines, Keene State College; and Patricia Bass, Rice University.

Jeanne M. Wilson, University of California, Davis, prepared the February 1998 draft. Comments on the February 1998 came in written form from Lawrence M. Hinman, University of San Diego, and in discussion from San Diego participants in a two-day workshop on academic integrity.

Lawrence M. Hinman, University of San Diego, prepared the May 1998 draft.

In addition to insights of the individuals mentioned above, the present document rests on the shoulders of the work done by countless college and university boards on academic integrity and on the statements of academic integrity that emerged from those groups. It continues to be a work in progress.

PART ONE

Matters of Life and Death

In the following four chapters, we will be concerned primarily with matters of life and death. In abortion, cloning, euthanasia, and the death penalty, we are faced time after time with decisions in which lives hang in the balance. It is helpful, before looking at any of these specific issues, to look at the general background issue in all these chapters, the question of the value of life.

The Value of Life

Immanuel Kant, one of the most influential moral philosophers of modern times, said that human life was priceless. His insight was a tremendously important one. He argued that human beings are fundamentally different from mere objects. Objects or things have a price. It is entirely appropriate to buy and sell things. I might purchase a new book, sell an old car, and all of that is entirely morally appropriate. I cannot, however, buy or sell human beings, because human beings—if Kant is right—are not the kind of entities that can properly have a price or be bought and sold. Human beings are ends in themselves, not mere means to be used to an end.

Although Kant thought human life was priceless, he was not a pacifist. Some, however, go even further than Kant and maintain that all human life is sacred and, as a result, no one is ever justified in taking a human life. There are strains of this in Christianity, Buddhism, and other religions as well. What these positions have in common is a belief that human life is sacred and inviolable, a gift given by God and not to be taken away by human beings. In the Catholic tradition, this position translates into an opposition to abortion, active euthanasia, war, the death penalty, and other forms of killing human beings. Respect for life becomes a "seamless garment."

These perspectives contrast starkly with utilitarian accounts of the value of human life. Utilitarianism is about weighing things, comparing the suffering and happiness that various alternatives might produce. As such, it has to put a price tag on human life.

At first glance, the utilitarian approach may seem morally noxious and we may be inclined to dismiss it out of hand. However, we often place a value on human lives, even innocent human lives. Consider such a simple matter as speed limits. If we lower the speed limit, there will be fewer traffic-related fatalities. Yet there is a trade-off here. When the speed limit is lowered, it takes longer to get from one place to another. The price of shipped goods goes up. Commuting takes longer, perhaps with more pollution as a by-product. We are able to save a number of lives by reducing the speed limit to 55 mph. What about reducing it to 45 mph? Perhaps 35 mph? In each case, we would (presumably) save additional innocent lives, but we may be unwilling to make the trade-off. Whether we like it or not, we often think in utilitarian terms, even about matters of life and death.

As you work through the following four chapters, you will continually be asked to weigh the value of human life against other values, including safety, medical progress, suffering, and justice. As you develop your position on this issue, look for issues of consistency and inconsistency in your thinking about the value of life across a range of different issues.

CHAPTER 1

Abortion

Videotape:

Topic: Survivor of Abortion Clinic Bombing Speaks

ABCNEWS *Source:* ABC *Nightline* (January 28, 1999)

Anchor: Ted Koppel

Experiential Accounts

Linda Bird Francke
"There Just Wasn't Room in Our Lives Now for Another Baby"

Linda Bird Francke is a journalist whose articles have appeared in The New York Times, Harper's Bazaar, The Washington Post, Esquire, Ms., *and* McCalls. *Her books include* The Ambiguity of Abortion *and* Growing Up Divorced. *She has three children and lives in Sagaponack, New York.*

The present selection originally appeared anonymously in the Letters to the Editor section of The New York Times. *The article itself brought forth a number of letters in reply. Eventually her concern with the issue of abortion led to her book on* The Ambivalence of Abortion, *which presents first-hand accounts of the decision about abortion from women in numerous positions in life.*

We were sitting in a bar on Lexington Avenue when I told my husband I was pregnant. It is not a memory I like to dwell on. Instead of the champagne and hope that had heralded the impending births of the first, second and third child, the news of this one was greeted with shocked silence and Scotch. "Jesus," my husband kept saying to himself, stirring the ice cubes around and around. "Oh, Jesus."

Oh, how we tried to rationalize it that night as the starting time for the movie came and went. My husband talked about his plans for a career change in the next year, to stem the staleness that fourteen years with the same investment-banking firm had brought him. A new baby would preclude that option.

The timing wasn't right for me either. Having juggled pregnancies and child care with what freelance jobs I could fit in between feedings, I had just taken on a full-time job. A new baby would put me right back in the nursery just when our youngest child was finally school age. It was time for us, we tried to rationalize. There just wasn't room in our lives now for another baby. We both agreed. And agreed. And agreed.

How very considerate they are at the Women's Services, known formally as the Center for Reproductive and Sexual Health. Yes, indeed, I could have an abortion that very Saturday morning and be out in time to drive to the country that afternoon. Bring a first morning urine specimen, a sanitary belt and napkins, a money order for $125 cash—and a friend.

My friend turned out to be my husband, standing awkwardly and ill at ease as men always do in places that are exclusively for women, as I checked in at 9 A.M. Other men hovered around just as anxiously, knowing they had to be there, wishing they weren't. No one spoke to each other. When I would be cycled out of there four hours later, the same men would be slumped in their same seats, locked downcast in their cells of embarrassment.

The Saturday morning women's group was more dispirited than the men in the waiting room. There were around fifteen of us, a mixture of races, ages and backgrounds. Three didn't speak English at all and a fourth, a pregnant Puerto Rican girl around eighteen, translated for them.

There were six black women and a hodgepodge of whites, among them a T-shirted teenager who kept leaving the room to throw up and a puzzled middle-aged woman from Queens with three grown children.

"What form of birth control were you using?" the volunteer asked each one of us. The answer was inevitably "none." She then went on to describe the various forms of birth control available at the clinic, and offered them to each of us.

The youngest Puerto Rican girl was asked through the interpreter which she'd like to use: the loop, diaphragm, or pill. She shook her head "no" three times. "You don't want to come back here again, do you?" the volunteer pressed. The girl's head was so low her chin rested on her breastbone. "Si," she whispered.

We had been there two hours by that time, filling out endless forms, giving blood and urine, receiving lectures. But unlike any other group of women I've been in, we didn't talk. Our common denominator, the one which usually floods across language and economic barriers into familiarity, today was one of shame. We were losing life that day, not giving it.

The group kept getting cut back to smaller, more workable units, and finally I was put in a small waiting room with just two other women. We changed into paper bathrobes and paper slippers, and we rustled whenever we moved. One of the women in my room was shivering and an aide brought her a blanket.

"What's the matter?" the aide asked her. "I'm scared," the woman said. "How much will it hurt?" The aide smiled. "Oh, nothing worse than a couple of bad cramps," she said. "This afternoon you'll be dancing a jig."

I began to panic. Suddenly the rhetoric, the abortion marches I'd walked in, the telegrams sent to Albany to counteract the Friends of the Fetus, the Zero Population Growth buttons I'd worn, peeled away, and I was all alone with my microscopic baby. There were just the two of us there, and soon, because it was more convenient for me and my husband, there would be one again.

How could it be that I, who am so neurotic about life that I step over bugs rather than on them, who spend hours planting flowers and vegetables in the spring even though we rent out the house and never see them, who make sure the children are vaccinated and inoculated and filled with vitamin C, could so arbitrarily decide that this life shouldn't be?

"It's not a life," my husband had argued, more to convince himself than me. "It's a bunch of cells smaller than my fingernail."

But any woman who has had children knows that certain feeling in her taut, swollen breasts, and the slight but constant ache in her uterus that signals the arrival of a life. Though I would march myself into blisters for a woman's right to exercise the option of motherhood, I discovered there in the waiting room that I was not the modern woman I thought I was.

When my name was called, my body felt so heavy the nurse had to help me into the examining room. I waited for my husband to burst through the door and yell "stop," but of course he didn't. I concentrated on three black spots in the acoustic ceiling until they grew in size to the shape of saucers, while the doctor swabbed my insides with antiseptic.

"You're going to feel a burning sensation now," he said, injecting Novocaine into the neck of the womb. The pain was swift and severe, and I twisted to get away from him. He was hurting my baby, I reasoned, and the black saucers quivered in the air. "Stop," I cried. "Please stop." He shook his head, busy with his equipment. "It's too late to stop now," he said. "It'll just take a few more seconds."

What good sports we women are. And how obedient. Physically the pain passed even before the hum of the machine signaled that the vacuuming of my uterus was completed, my baby sucked up like ashes after a cocktail party. Ten minutes start to finish. And I was back on the arm of the nurse.

There were twelve beds in the recovery room. Each one had a gaily flowered draw sheet and a soft green or blue thermal blanket. It was all very feminine. Lying on these beds for an hour or more were the shocked victims of their sex, their full wombs now stripped clean, their futures less encumbered.

It was very quiet in that room. The only voice was that of the nurse, locating the new women who had just come in so she could monitor their blood pressure, and checking out the recovered women who were free to leave.

Juice was being passed about, and I found myself sipping a Dixie cup of Hawaiian Punch. An older woman with tightly curled bleached hair was just getting up from the next bed, "That was no goddamn snap," she said, resting before putting on her miniskirt and high white boots. Other women came and went, some walking out as dazed as they had entered, others with a bounce that signaled they were going right back to Bloomingdale's.

Finally then, it was time for me to leave. I checked out, making an appointment to return in two weeks for an IUD insertion. My husband was slumped in the waiting room, clutching a single yellow rose wrapped in a wet paper towel and stuffed into a baggie.

We didn't talk the whole way home, but just held hands very tightly. At home there were more yellow roses and a tray in bed for me and the children's curiosity to divert.

It had certainly been a successful operation. I didn't bleed at all for two days just as they had predicted, and then I bled only moderately for another four days. Within a week my breasts had subsided and the tenderness vanished, and my body felt mine again instead of the eggshell it becomes when it's protecting someone else.

My husband and I are back to planning our summer vacation and his career switch.

And it certainly does make more sense not to be having a baby right now—we say that to each other all the time. But I have this ghost now. A very little ghost that only appears when I'm seeing something beautiful, like the full moon on the ocean last weekend. And the baby waves at me. And I wave at the baby. "Of course, we have room," I cry to the ghost. "Of course, we do."

Journal/Discussion Questions

✍ *Write about your reactions to the case described above. What, if anything,* touched *you the most in Francke's essays? What would be the questions that would run through your mind in this situation? What would you do if you were in this situation?*

1. Was there anything about the Francke selection that surprised you? If so, what was it? Explain.

2. Francke says that she does not regret having an abortion. Does that claim seem

consistent with the rest of what she says? Explain.

3. Francke says that she is still as strongly "pro-choice" as she ever was. Yet she depicts abortion as a morally profoundly ambiguous experience? Is this consistent? Explain.

4. Do you think that Francke and her husband made the right decision? What do you mean by "the right decision"? Explain.

Naomi Wolf
"A Call for Truth"

Naomi Wolf, a feminist writer, is the author of The Beauty Myth, Fire with Fire: The New Female Power and How It Will Change the 21st Century, *and most recently* Promiscuities: The Secret Struggle for Womanhood. *This article is adapted from a longer version in* The New Republic *magazine.*

Pro-choice advocates should defend abortion honestly, says this prominent feminist author. "The death of a fetus is a real death." By failing to recognize that this is a real death, feminism has given up the moral high ground in the discussion of abortion.

As You Read, Consider This:

1. What, according to Wolf, should the principal imperative of feminism be?
2. What dangers does Wolf see in the position of contemporary feminism in regard to abortion?

I had an abortion when I was a single mother and my daughter was 2 years old. I would do it again. But you know how in the Greek myths, when you kill a relative you are pursued by furies? For months, it was as if baby furies were pursuing me.

These are not the words of a benighted, superstition-ridden teenager lost in America's cultural backwaters. They are the words of a Cornell-educated, urban-dwelling, Democratic-voting 40-year-old cardiologist—I'll call her Clare.

Clare is exactly the kind of person for whom being pro-choice is an unshakable conviction. If there were a core constituent of the movement to secure abortion rights, Clare would be it. And yet, her words are exactly the words to which the pro-choice movement is not listening.

At its best, feminism defends its moral high ground by being simply faithful to the truth—to women's real-life experiences. But to its own ethical and political detriment, the pro-choice movement has relinquished the moral frame around the issue of abortion. It has ceded the language of right and wrong to abortion foes.

Such a position causes us to lose political ground. By refusing to look at abortion within a moral framework, we lose the millions of Americans who want to support abortion as a legal right but still need to condemn it as a moral iniquity. Their ethical allegiances are then addressed by the pro-life movement, which is willing to speak about good and evil.

But we are also in danger of losing something more important than votes; we stand in jeopardy of losing what can only be called our souls. Clinging to a rhetoric about abortion in which there is no life and no death, we entangle our beliefs in a series of self-delusions, fibs, and evasions. And we risk becoming precisely what our critics charge us with being: callous, selfish, and casually destructive men and women who share a cheapened view of human life.

I argue for a radical shift in the pro-choice movement's rhetoric and consciousness about abortion. We need to contextualize the fight to defend abortion rights within a moral framework that admits that the death of a fetus is a real death; that there are degrees of culpability, judgment, and responsibility involved in the decision to abort a pregnancy; that the best understanding of feminism involves holding women as well as men to the responsibilities that are inseparable from their rights; and that we need to be strong enough to acknowledge that this country's high rate of abortion—which ends more than a quarter of all pregnancies—can only be rightly understood as what Dr. Henry Foster was brave enough to call it: "a failure."

Any doubt that our current pro-choice rhetoric leads to disaster should be dispelled by the famous recent defection of the woman who had been Jane Roe. What happened to Norma McCorvey? To judge by her characterization in the elite media and by some prominent pro-choice feminists, nothing very important. Her change of heart about abortion was relentlessly explained away as having everything to do with the girlish motivations of insecurity, fickleness, and the need for attention, and little to do with any actual moral agency.

To me, the first commandment of real feminism is: When in doubt, listen to women. What if we were to truly, respectfully listen to this woman? We would have to hear this: Perhaps McCorvey actually had a revelation that she could no longer live as the symbol of a belief system she increasingly repudiated.

McCorvey is more astute than her critics; she seems to understand better than the pro-choice activists she worked with just what the woman-in-the-middle believes. "I believe in the woman's right to choose. I'm like a lot of people. I'm in the mushy middle," she said. McCorvey still supports abortion rights through the first trimester—but is horrified by the brutality of abortion as it manifests more obviously further into a pregnancy.

What McCorvey and other Americans want and deserve is an abortion-rights movement publicly willing to mourn the evil—necessary evil though it may be—that is abortion.

The abortion debate has tended to focus on the question of "personhood" of the fetus. Many pro-choice advocates developed a language to assert that the fetus isn't a person, and this, over the years, has developed into a lexicon of dehumanization.

In one woman's account of her chemical abortion, in the January/February 1994 issue of *Mother Jones,* the doctor said, "By Sunday you won't see on the monitor what we call the heartbeat" [my italics]. The author of the article, D. Redman, explained that one of the drugs the doctor administered would "end the growth of the fetal tissue." And we all remember Dr. Joycelyn Elders' remark, hailed by some as refreshingly frank and pro-woman, but which I found remarkably brutal, that, "We really need to get over this love affair with the fetus."

How did we arrive at this point? In the early 1970s, second-wave feminism adopted this rhetoric in response to the reigning ideology in which motherhood was invoked as an excuse to deny women legal and social equality.

Yet this has left us with a bitter legacy. For when we defend abortion rights by emptying the act of moral gravity, we find ourselves cultivating a hardness of heart.

Too often our rhetoric leads us to tell untruths. What McCorvey wants, it seems, is for abortion-rights advocates to face, really face, what we are doing. "Have you ever seen a second-trimester abortion?" she asks. "It's a baby. It's got a face and a body, and they put him in a freezer and a little container." Well, so it does; and so they do.

The "Good Mother" Myth

Other lies are not lies to others, but to ourselves. An abortion-clinic doctor, Elizabeth Karlin, who wrote a recent "Hers" column in *The New York Times,* declared that "There is only one reason I've ever heard for having an abortion: The desire to be a good mother."

Though that may well be true for many poor and working-class women—and indeed research shows that poor women are three times more likely to have abortions than are better-off women—the elite, who are the most vociferous in their morally unambiguous pro-choice language, should know perfectly well how untrue that statement often is in their lives.

Many women, including middle-class women, have abortions because, as one woman put it, "They have a notion of what a good mother is and don't feel they can be that kind of mother at this phase of their lives." In many cases, that is still a morally defensible place on the spectrum; but it is not the place of absolute absolution that Karlin claims it to be. It is, rather, a place of moral struggle, of self-interest mixed with selflessness, of wished-for good intermingled with necessary evil.

Other abortions occupy places on the spectrum that are far more culpable. Of the abortions I know of, these were some of the reasons: to end a "test" pregnancy to find out whether the woman could get pregnant; to force a boy or man to take a relationship more seriously; and, again and again, to enact a right of passage for affluent teenage girls. In my high school, the abortion drama was used to test a boyfriend's character. Seeing whether he would accompany the girl to the operation or, better yet, come up with the money for the abortion almost could have been the 1970s San Francisco Bay area equivalent of the 1950s' fraternity pin.

Not to judge other men and women without judging myself, once I made the choice to take a morning-after pill. The heavily pregnant doctor looked at me, as she dispensed it, as if I were the scum of the Earth.

If what was going on in my mind had been mostly about the well-being of the possible baby, that pill would never have been swallowed. For that potential baby, brought to term, would have had two sets of loving middle-income grandparents, an adult mother with an education and even, as I discovered later, the beginning of diaper money for its first two years of life (the graduate fellowship I was on forbade marriage but, frozen in a time before women were its beneficiaries, said nothing about unwed motherhood). Because of the baby's skin color, even if I chose not to rear the child, a roster of eager adoptive parents awaited him or her. If I had been thinking only or even primarily about the baby's life, I would have had to decide to bring the pregnancy, had there been one, to term.

No: There were two columns in my mind—"Me" and "Baby"—and the first won out. And what was in it looked something like this: unwelcome intensity in the relationship with the father; desire to continue to "develop as a person" before "real" parenthood; wish to encounter my eventual life partner without the off-putting encumbrance of a child; resistance to curtailing the nature of the time remaining to me in Europe. Essentially, this column came down to: "I am not done being responsive only to myself yet."

In that moment, feminism came to one of its logical if less-than-inspiring moments of fruition: I chose to sidestep biology; I acted—and was free to act—as if I were in control of my destiny, the way men more often than women have let themselves act. I chose myself on my own terms over a possible someone else, for self-absorbed reasons. But "to be a better mother"? Nonsense.

True Freedom to Choose

Freedom means that women must be free to choose self or to choose selfishly. Certainly for a woman with fewer economic and social choices than I had—for instance, a woman struggling to finish her higher education, without which she would have little hope of a life worthy of her talents—there can indeed be an obligation to choose self. There is no easy way to deny the powerful argument that a woman's equality in society must give her some irreducible rights unique to her biology, including the right to take the life within her life.

But we don't have to lie to ourselves about what we are doing at such a moment. Let us at least look with clarity at what that means and not whitewash self-interest with the language of self-sacrifice.

That decision was not my finest moment. The least I can do, in honor of the being that might have been, is simply to know that.

Using amoral rhetoric, we weaken ourselves politically because we lose the center.

In a time of retrenchment, how can I be so sure that a more honest and moral rhetoric about abortion will consolidate rather than scuttle abortion rights? Look at what Americans themselves say.

When a recent *Newsweek* poll asked about support for abortion using the rare phrasing, "It's a matter between a woman, her doctor, her family, her conscience and her God," a remarkable 72 percent of the respondents called that formulation "about right." When participants in the Gallup poll were asked whether they supported abortion "under any circumstances" only 32 percent agreed; only 9 percent more supported it under "most" circumstances. Clearly, abortion rights are safest when we are willing to submit them to a morality beyond just our bodies and ourselves.

How could one live with a conscious view that abortion is an evil and still be pro-choice? Through acts of redemption, or what the Jewish mystical tradition calls *tikkun;* or "mending." Laurence Tribe, in *Abortion: The Clash of Absolutes,* notes that "Memorial services for the souls of aborted fetuses are fairly common in contemporary Japan," where abortions are both legal and readily available. Shinto doctrine holds that women should make offerings to the fetus to help it rest in peace; Buddhists once erected statues of the spirit guardian of children to honor aborted fetuses.

If one believes that abortion is killing and yet is still pro-choice, one could try to use contraception for every single sex act; if one had to undergo an abortion, one could then work to provide contraception, or jobs, or other choices to young girls; one could give money to programs that provide prenatal care to poor women; if one is a mother or father, one can remember the aborted child every time one is tempted to be less than loving—and give renewed love to the living child. And so on.

As the world changes and women, however incrementally, become more free and more powerful, the language in which we phrase the goals of feminism must change as well.

Try to imagine real gender equality. Actually, try to imagine an America that is female-dominated, since a true working democracy in this country would reflect our 54–46 voting advantage.

Now imagine such a democracy, in which women would be valued so very highly, as a world that is accepting and responsible about human sexuality; in which there is no coerced sex without serious jail time; in which there are affordable, safe contraceptives available for the taking in every public health building; in which there is economic parity for women—and basic economic subsistence for every baby born; and in which every young American woman knows about and understands her natural desire as a treasure to cherish, and when the time is right, on her own terms, to share responsibly.

In such a world, in which the idea of gender as a barrier has become a dusty artifact, we probably would use a very different language about what would be—then—the rare and doubtless traumatic event of abortion. That language probably would call upon respect and responsibility, grief and mourning. In that world we might well describe the unborn and the never-to-be-born with the honest words of life.

And in that world, passionate feminists might well hold candlelight vigils at abortion clinics, standing shoulder to shoulder with the doctors who work there, commemorating and saying goodbye to the dead.

Journal/Discussion Questions

1. Why, according to Wolf, has American feminism given up seeing abortion as a moral issue? Do you agree with her assessment?
2. Who was Norma McCorvey? What point is Wolf making by mentioning her?
3. What does Wolf mean by the "good mother" myth? Do you agree with her analysis of this issue? Discuss.
4. Wolf asks, "How could one live with a conscious view that abortion is an evil and still be pro-choice?" How does she answer this question? Evaluate her answer.
5. What does Wolf mean by true gender equality? What role does this notion play in the development of her position on abortion?

An Introduction to the Moral Issues

Abortion: The Two Principal Moral Concerns

The ongoing discussion of abortion in American society is often framed as a debate between two sides, usually called *pro-life* and *pro-choice.* The labels themselves are instructive. Whereas one label points our attention toward the fetus, the other emphasizes the pregnant woman. Each position highlights a different aspect of the situation as the principal focus of moral concern. Pro-life supporters emphasize the issue of the rights of the unborn, while pro-choice advocates stress the importance of the rights of the pregnant woman.

Notice that these two moral concerns are not immediately mutually exclusive in the same way that, for example, the pro- and anti-capital-punishment positions are. (They may, of course, be secondarily exclusive insofar as the consequences of one exclude the other.) This results in a certain murkiness in debates about abortion, since the opposing sides are often talking primarily about quite different things, either the moral status of the fetus or the rights of the pregnant woman. Let's examine each of these issues.

The Moral Status of the Fetus

Initially, much of the debate about abortion centered around the question of the moral status of the fetus—in particular, if and when the fetus is a person. Most participants in the discussion took for granted that if the fetus can be shown to be a person, then abortion is morally wrong. Thus the discussion focused primarily on whether the fetus could be shown to be a person or not. To answer this question, it was necessary to specify what we meant by *a person.*

Criteria of Personhood

What characteristics does a being have to have in order to be a person?

In attempting to define personhood, philosophers have looked for the criteria by means of which we determine whether a being is a person or not. This is a search for *sufficient conditions,* that is, conditions which if present would guarantee personhood. The argument moves in the following way: Some criterion is seen as conferring personhood, and personhood is seen as conferring certain rights, including the right to life. Thus the overall structure of the argument looks like this:

Criterion ⇨ Personhood ⇨ Right to life

We can see the two critical junctures in the argument just by looking at this diagram. The first is in the transition from the criterion to personhood. What justification is there for claiming that this criterion (or group of criteria) justifies the claim that a being is a person? The second transition has sometimes been seen as less problematic, but it may have more difficulties than are initially apparent. The issue in this transition is whether personhood always justifies the right to life.

A number of criteria have been advanced for personhood. Some of these result in conferring personhood quite early in fetal development, sometimes from the moment of conception.

The *conceived-by-humans* criterion is, at least on the surface, the most straightforward: "if you are conceived by human parents, you are human." (Noonan, in Feinberg, p. 9) But this straightforwardness turns out to be misleading. We obviously acknowledge the personhood of anyone *born of human parents.* This is the indisputably true sense of "conceived-by-humans." However, we do not obviously and necessarily acknowledge the personhood of everything "conceived-by-humans" in the strict sense. This either equivocates or begs the question.

The *genetic structure* argument maintains that a human genetic code is a sufficient condition for personhood. All the genetic information for the fully-formed human being is present in the fetus at the time of conception; therefore, it has the rights of a person. Nothing more needs to be added, and if nothing interferes with the development of the fetus, it will emerge as a full-fledged human baby.

The *physical resemblance* criterion claims that something that looks human is human. Advocates of this criterion then claim that the fetus is a person because of its physical resemblance to a full-term baby. Movies such as *The Silent Scream* (which graphically depicts the contortions of a fetus during an abortion) depend strongly on such a criterion. This criterion seems rhetorically more powerful than the appeal to DNA (since DNA lacks the same visual and emotive impact), but less rigorous, since resemblance can be more strongly in the eye of the beholder than DNA structures.

The *presence-of-a-soul* criterion is often evoked by religious thinkers. The criterion is then used in an argument maintaining that God gives an immortal soul to the fetus at a particular moment, at which time the fetus becomes a person. Although contemporary versions of this argument usually maintain that the implantation of a soul takes place at the time of conception, St. Thomas Aquinas—one of the most influential of modern theologians—claimed that implantation usually occurs at quickening, around the third month. (Aquinas also thought that this event occurred later for females than it did for males.) The principal difficulty with this argument is that it attempts to clarify the opaque by an appeal to the utterly obscure: God's will, at least in matters such as the implantation of a soul, is even more difficult to discern than the personhood of the fetus.

The *viability* criterion sees personhood as inextricably tied to the ability to exist independently of the mother's womb. A fetus is thus seen as a person and having a right to life when it could survive (even with artificial means) outside the body of the mother. This criterion is clearly dependent on developments in medical technology that make it possible to keep increasingly young premature babies alive. If artificial wombs are eventually developed, then viability might be pushed back to a much earlier stage in fetal development.

Finally, the *future-like-ours* criterion maintains that fetuses have a future, just as adult human beings have a future. Just as killing of adults is wrong because it deprives them of everything that comprises their future, so too the killing of a fetus deprives it of its future. Don Marquis develops this argument in his selection, "Why Abortion Is Immoral."

Some philosophers have argued that there are other criteria that are *necessary* conditions of personhood, and that fetuses usually lack these characteristics. These are criteria that we usually associate with adult human beings: *reasoning,* a *concept of self, use of language,* and so on. (These criteria are often particularly relevant in discussions of the end of life: at what point, if any, does a breathing human being cease to be a person?) There are several dangers with appeals to such criteria. Most notably, such criteria may set the standard of personhood too high and justify not only abortion, but also infanticide, the killing of brain-damaged adults, and involuntary euthanasia.

There are a number of possible responses to this lack of consensus in regard to the conditions of personhood. Two arguments have been advanced which see this lack of consensus as supporting a conservative position on the morality of abortion. The *Let's Play It Safe* argument states that we cannot be absolutely sure when the fetus becomes a person, so let's be careful to err on the safe side. This is often coupled with the *Let's Not Be Arbitrary* argument, which states that, since we do not know precisely the moment at which a fetus assumes personhood, we should assume that it becomes a person at the moment of conception and act accordingly. The moment of conception provides, according to this argument, the only nonarbitrary point of demarcation.

Other philosophers have taken a quite different tack in the face of this disagreement about the conditions of personhood. They have argued that it is impossible to define the concept of a person with the necessary precision. Instead, we should turn to other moral considerations to determine whether and when abortion is morally justified.

Relevance of Personhood

There was a widespread assumption that if the fetus is a person, then abortion is morally wrong. The first major article to challenge this assumption was Judith Jarvis Thomson's "A Defense of Abortion," (1971), which presented an intriguing example. Imagine that, without your prior knowledge or consent, you are sedated in your sleep and surgically connected to a famous violinist, who must share the use of your kidneys for nine months until he is able to survive on his own. Even granting that the violinist is obviously a full-fledged person, Thomson argues that you are morally justified in disconnecting yourself from the violinist, even if it results in his death. Going back to our diagram of the two main stages of the abortion argument, we can see that Thomson's strategy is to question the transition from "personhood" to "right to life." Even granting that the dependent entity is a full person (whether fetus or violinist), we may still be morally justified in cutting off support and thereby killing that person. Thus, Thomson argues, the morality of abortion does not depend on our answer to the question of whether the fetus is a person or not. A more developed version of Thomson's example is to be found in Jane English's selection, "Abortion and the Concept of a Person."

Thomson's article has been criticized on many fronts, but despite these criticisms, the major impact of her piece has been to open the door to the possibility that the answer to the question of abortion does not depend solely on the moral status of the fetus. This opened the door to a more extensive consideration of the other principal moral consideration in this situation, the rights of the pregnant woman.

The Rights of the Pregnant Woman

The second principal focus of moral concern is on the rights of the pregnant woman. Yet what precisely are these rights? At least three main candidates have been advanced: the right to privacy, the right to ownership and control over one's own body, the right to equal treatment, and the right to self-determination.

The Right to Privacy

Does the right to privacy guarantee the right to an abortion?

In *Roe v. Wade* (1973), the Supreme Court based its support for a woman's right to abortion in part on the claim that the woman has a right to privacy. In constitutional law, the right to privacy seems to have two distinct senses. First, certain behaviors—such as sexual intercourse—are usually thought to be private; the government may not infringe upon these behaviors unless there is some particularly compelling reason (such as preventing the sexual abuse of children) for doing so. Second, some decisions in an individual's life—such as the choice of a mate or a career—are seen as matters of individual autonomy or self-determination; these are private in the sense that the government has no right to tell an individual what to do in such areas. This second sense of privacy will be discussed below in the section on the right to self-determination. In this section, we will confine our attention to the first sense of privacy.

This appeal to the right of privacy as the basis for a woman's right to choice has proved to be a peculiar justification for two reasons. First, privacy claims are difficult to justify constitutionally, since in fact there is no explicit mention of a right to privacy in the Constitution or Bill of Rights. Second, the abortion *procedure* is certainly not usually private in the way in which, for example, sexual intercourse is private. It takes place outside of the home (at a clinic or hospital) and involves a second party (a physician and staff). To be sure, the *decision* may be made in private, but what is at issue is the procedure for implementing that decision. Interestingly, this will change significantly if and when the French-developed abortion pill, RU-486, is more widely used. Under new protocols being developed for the drug, the pregnant woman may only have to make a single visit to a physician to obtain the prescription.

The Right to Ownership of One's Own Body

Some have argued that the right to abortion is based on a woman's right to control her own body, and in some instances this is seen as a property right. This approach also seems wide of the mark. To be sure, no one else owns our bodies, and, in this sense, there seems to be a right to control our own bodies. However, it is doubtful whether the relationship we have with our own bodies is best understood in terms of ownership, nor is the presence of the fetus most perceptively grasped as the intrusion onto private property.

The Right to Equal Treatment

Some jurists, most notably Ruth Bader Ginsburg, have suggested that a woman's right to abortion may be best justified constitutionally through an appeal to the right to equal protection under the law. Pregnancy results from the combined actions of two people, yet the woman typically bears a disproportionate amount of the responsibility and burden. This line of reasoning certainly seems highly relevant to striking down laws and regulations that discriminate against women because of pregnancy, but it is unclear whether it alone is sufficient to support a right to abortion. In fact, it would seem that there must be some other, more fundamental right which is at stake here.

The Right to Self-Determination

When we consider the actual conflict that many women experience in making the decision about abortion, it would seem that it centers primarily around the effects that an unwanted pregnancy and child would have on their lives. The most fundamental right at issue for the pregnant woman in this context would seem to be the right to determine the course of her own life. In this context, it is relevant to ask *how much* the pregnancy would interfere with the woman's life. As John Martin Fisher has pointed out, one of the misleading aspects of Thomson's violinist example is that it suggests that pregnancy would virtually eliminate one's choices for nine months. In actuality, the violinist case would be comparable only to the most difficult of pregnancies, those which require months of strict bed rest. Yet in most cases, pregnancy does not involve such an extreme restriction on the woman's everyday life; the restrictions on self-determination are much less.

In what ways do pregnancy and childbirth potentially conflict with self-determination? Consider, first of all, the extremes on the spectrum. On the one hand, imagine a most grave threat to self-determination: a rape that results in an extremely difficult pregnancy that required constant bed rest, childbirth that contained a high risk of the mother's death, and the likelihood that the child would require years of constant medical attention. Conception, pregnancy, delivery, and the child would all severely limit (if not destroy) the mother's choices in life. These carry enormous moral weight. On the other hand, an easy pregnancy and birth of a perfectly healthy baby are potentially much less restrictive to a woman's power of self-determination. Raising a child, of course, is potentially quite restrictive to self-determination, but in those cases where adoption is a reasonable option, raising the child is not necessary.

There is a further perplexity about self-determination. It is reasonable, as Fisher and others have done, to distinguish between what is central to one's self-determination and what is peripheral to it. We intuitively recognize this when we hear, for example, of a pianist whose hands have been crushed. Although such an accident would be terrible for anyone, it is especially terrible for a person whose life is devoted to making music with his or her hands. If the pianist were to become color-blind, this would be much less serious since it would not strike as centrally at the pianist's sense of self. (We would have a quite different assessment of color-blindness in a painter, however.) Yet the perplexity centers around those cases in which people make something central to their sense of identity that we, as outsiders, would consider peripheral at best. For example, the couple who want an abortion because bearing a child would force them to postpone a vacation for two months seems to be giving undue weight to the timing of their vacation. What if, to take an even more extreme case, a woman bank robber decided on an abortion because pregnancy would interfere with robbing banks? Are there any limits to what can legitimately be taken as central to self-determination?

Other Moral Considerations

Feminist Concerns about Abortion

For many thinkers, especially feminists, the issue of abortion must be understood within the context of the oppression of women. Indeed, this gives a special importance to the right of self-determination as one which must be defended all the more vigilantly in a context of oppression. Rape provides the most extreme example of this oppression within the realm of sexuality, but the oppression of women is not confined to this sphere. For some women, rape has become a metaphor for understanding many of the sexual relations between men and women. Whether we choose to use the word "rape" or not, most of us can agree that there are many areas outside of paradigmatic rape cases (forcible intercourse by a stranger) in which sexual intercourse is less than fully consensual. There is a growing recognition that rape often occurs between acquaintances, friends, and even spouses. Moreover, it is increasingly clear that there are many situations in which women are pressured (although the threat of physical force is not present) into sexual intercourse without their full consent. In addition to this, we live in a society in which men value highly the feeling that they are the ones in control of sexuality. Given all of this, feminists argue that it is imperative that women have the right to determine whether to bring a pregnancy to term or not.

Abortion and Racism

Among some African Americans and other minority groups in the United States, there is a concern that the emphasis on abortion rights has racist overtones. In particular, their concern is that abortion—and forced sterilization—might be used as a means of controlling minority populations. This concern is not limited to the United States; in many countries, members of oppressed minority populations fear that the majority government may be using abortion (and enforced sterilization) as means of reducing the minority population. The history of the relationship between the medical establishment in the United States and African Americans makes such fears understandable. The Tuskegee syphilis experiment, in which African American men were allowed to die from syphilis without treatment until the early seventies in order to further research in this area, typifies the cases to which African Americans point in order to make their concerns more understandable to those who have not suffered such discrimination. Similarly, as pressure grows to reduce or eliminate support for Aid to Families with Dependent Children, some see a growing pressure on women, and perhaps especially on minority women, to choose abortion. Ironically, this has resulted in some very conservative, anti-abortion Christian groups being on the same side as outspoken opponents of white racism who are at the other end of the political spectrum.

The Rights of the Father

During the past twenty-five years, there has been an increasing interest in our understanding of fatherhood. This raises important issues in regard to the proper role of the father in making decisions regarding abortion. What rights, if any, does a biological father have when he disagrees with the woman's choice either to have an abortion or not to have an abortion? Are there any circumstances in which the man's choice should take precedence over the woman's preferences? Two types of cases are imaginable. On the one hand, the man may wish to have the fetus brought to term but the woman may want to abort it; on the other hand, these roles may be reversed. Under what conditions, if any, do the father's preferences count? Do those conditions have to do with the initial circumstances of conception? With the present state of their relationship? With the assumption of future responsibilities for the child?

What rights, if any, do fathers have in deciding whether their partner should have an abortion?

Some feminist concerns seem to conflict directly with concerns about the rights of the father in the decision-making process. The issue, of course, is that women's oppression has been primarily at the hands of men—and any attempts at recognizing the rights of the father may seem at the same time to be an act of returning power to the oppressors. Moreover, it seems to ignore the asymmetry between men and women in regard to child-bearing. Although the act of conception requires both a male and female contribution, it is the woman who carries the fetus to term and undergoes childbirth. A man can be a father and never know it, but the same is not true for a woman. A woman bears the direct weight of pregnancy and childbirth is a way that men do not and cannot. The strongest argument against giving the father a decisive voice in this decision is precisely the fact that the woman bears the responsibilities of pregnancy and childbirth so much more directly, strongly, and unavoidably than the man.

Given these reservations, two additional points need to be made about the rights of fathers. First, rights entail responsibilities. To the extent that a father has a voice in the decision, he presumably also has correlative responsibilities toward the baby (and indirectly toward the mother). Second, this situation is perhaps not best understood in terms of rights; rather, especially within the context of long-term committed relationships, the appeal to rights may usually occur only when the situation has disintegrated.

The Principle of Double Effect

Centuries of Christian theology and philosophy have finely honed what is known as the *Principle of the Double Effect,* which allows us to perform certain actions that would otherwise be immoral. Typically, four conditions have to be met for an action to be morally permissible: (1) the action itself must be either morally good or at least morally neutral; (2) the bad consequences must not be intended; (3) the good consequences cannot be the direct causal result of the bad consequences; and (4) the good consequences must be proportionate to the bad consequences. For example, the principle of the double effect allows a physician to remove a cancerous uterus from a pregnant woman, even if the fetus is thereby killed. Removal of the uterus is in itself morally neutral; it is not done in order to abort the fetus; the elimination of the cancer does not result from the killing of the fetus; and the saving of the woman's life is proportionate to the termination of the pregnancy.

A Consequentialist Concern

Some philosophers have expressed concern about the possible consequences of widespread abortion if it is used for sex selection. The argument is a simple enough one, even if it is not easy to judge the factual claims on which it is based. If abortion is widely used as a means of choosing to bring primarily male babies to term, it may well create a gender imbalance in society with undesirable long-term consequences. This concern does not center on abortion per se, and would be equally applicable to preconception sex-selection methods, if such methods became available.

Abortion and Compromise: Seeking a Common Ground

Initially, it might seem that there is no room for compromise in matters of abortion. If it is the intentional killing of an innocent human being, then it cannot be countenanced. If it does not involve killing a human being, then it should not be prohibited. It is either wrong or right, and there seems to be little middle ground. Yet as we begin to reflect on the issue, we see that there are indeed areas of potential cooperation. Let's briefly consider several such areas.

Is there any common ground that pro-choice and pro-life supporters can accept?

Reducing Unwanted Pregnancies

One of the striking aspects of the abortion issue is its potential avoidability. Abortions occur when there are unwanted pregnancies. To the extent that we can reduce unwanted pregnancies, we can reduce abortions. Certainly there are cases of unwanted pregnancy due to rape or incest, and there are certainly other cases due to the failure of contraceptive devices. Unfortunately, despite our best efforts, none of these types of cases will probably be completely eliminated in the future. Yet they comprise only a small percentage of the cases of unwanted pregnancies; moreover, there is already agreement that these should be further reduced.

The single most common cause of unwanted pregnancies is sexual intercourse without contraception. To the extent that this can be reduced, the number of abortions can be reduced. Conservatives, liberals, and strong feminists can agree on this goal, although they may emphasize quite different ways of achieving it. Conservatives will stress the virtue of chastity and the value of abstinence. Liberals will stress the importance of contraceptives and family planning. Strong feminists will urge social and political changes that will ensure that women have at least an equal voice in decisions about sexual intercourse. Some will respond to the conservative call, others to the liberal program, still others to the feminist concerns. Yet the common result may be the reduction of unwanted pregnancies and, with that, the reduction of abortions. In addition to this, an increase in responsibility in the area of sexuality may help to reduce the spread of AIDS and other sexually communicated diseases.

Ensuring Genuinely Free and Informed Choice

There is widespread agreement among almost all parties that a choice made freely is better than one made under pressure or duress. There are several ways of increasing the likelihood of a genuinely free and informed choice. First, *the earlier the choice, the better.* Many people maintain that the more the fetus is developed, the more morally serious is the abortion decision. Although conservatives would maintain that all abortions are equally wrong, encouraging an early decision would not contradict their beliefs. Second, *women should have the opportunity to make the choice without undue outside pressure.* There are a number of ways in which undue outside pressure can be reduced, most notably through providing genuinely impartial counseling in an atmosphere devoid of coercion (demonstrations, etc.). Third, *alternatives to abortion should be available.* These include adoption (for those who wish to give their baby up for adoption), aid to dependent children (for those who wish to raise their own babies), day care (for those who work full-time and raise children), and adequate maternity leave.

Abortion and Sorrow

Naomi Wolf refers to a Japanese practice that honors the memory of departed fetuses. This is called *Mizuko Kuyo.* I have gathered together a number of resources relating to this practice on the

Web page on abortion at *http://ethics.acusd.edu/abortion.html.* Philosophically, one of the most interesting aspects of this practice is that it unites two elements that are rarely brought together in the American philosophical discussion of abortion. In the practice of *Mizuko Kuyo,* couples who have had an abortion dedicate a doll at a temple to the memory of the departed fetus. To some extent, this is analogous to the practice of lighting a votive candle in Christian churches. What is noteworthy is that Japanese society both permits abortion and at the same time recognizes that it is a sorrowful occasion. In most instances, American philosophical literature chooses one or the other of these elements, but not both simultaneously.

Living Together with Moral Differences

Abortion is a particularly interesting and important moral issue in contemporary America, for it poses most clearly to us as a society the question of how we can live together with deep moral differences. People on all sides of the abortion controversy are intelligent people of good will, genuinely trying to do what they believe is right. The challenge for all of us in such situations is to view one another in this light and seek to create a community that embraces and respects our differences while at the same time preserving our moral integrity. It is in this spirit that you are urged to approach the articles contained in this section. None provides the final answer to all our questions about the morality of abortion, but each helps to shed light on the moral complexity of the situation and the differing moral insights with which we as a society approach this difficult issue. Even if none of these articles provides the complete answer to the problem of abortion, each does help us to better understand ourselves and others.

The Arguments

Jane English
"Abortion and the Concept of a Person"

Jane English (1947–1978) received her doctorate from Harvard University. She authored several articles in the field of ethics before her untimely death in a mountain climbing accident on the Matterhorn at the age of thirty-one.

English challenges a common belief often shared by both advocates and critics of abortion. Both sides often claim that the permissibility of abortion turns on the question of whether the fetus is a person or not. English argues (1) that the notion of personhood is not precise enough to offer a decisive criterion for judging whether the fetus is a person; and (2) that there are a number of cases in which we can reasonably conclude that (a) abortion is permissible even if the fetus is a person, and (b) abortion is not permissible even if the fetus is not a person. The issue of abortion, in other words, does not turn on the issue of the personhood of the fetus.

As You Read, Consider This:

1. What reasons does English offer for claiming that the notion of personhood is not precise enough to serve as a foundation for deciding the abortion issue? Do you agree with her reasons?
2. Why, according to English, do we need "an additional premise" to move from the claim that the fetus is a person to the conclusion that abortion is always morally wrong?

The abortion debate rages on. Yet the two most popular positions seem to be clearly mistaken. Conservatives maintain that a human life begins at conception and that therefore abortion must be wrong because it is murder. But not all killings of humans are murders. Most notably, self-defense may justify even the killing of an innocent person.

Liberals, on the other hand, are just as mistaken in their argument that since a fetus does not become a person until birth, a woman may do whatever she pleases in and to her own body. First, you cannot do as you please with your own body if it affects other people adversely.[1] Second, if a fetus is not a person, that does not imply that you can do to it anything you wish. Animals, for example, are not persons, yet to kill or torture them for no reason at all is wrong.

At the center of the storm has been the issue of just when it is between ovulation and adulthood that a person appears on the scene. Conservatives draw the line at conception, liberals at birth. In this paper I first examine our concept of a person and conclude that no single criterion can capture the concept of a person and no sharp line can be drawn. Next I argue that if a fetus is a person, abortion is still justifiable in many cases; and if a fetus is not a person, killing it is still wrong in many cases. To a large extent, these two solutions are in agreement. I conclude that our concept of a person cannot and need not bear the weight that the abortion controversy has thrust upon it.

I

The several factions in the abortion argument have drawn battle lines around various proposed criteria for determining what is and what is not a person. For example, Mary Anne Warren[2] lists five features (capacities for reasoning, self-awareness, complex communication, etc.) as her criteria for personhood and argues for the permissibility of abortion because a fetus falls outside this concept. Baruch Brody[3] uses brain waves. Michael Tooley[4] picks having-a-concept-of-self as his criterion and concludes that infanticide and abortion are justifiable, while the killing of adult animals is not. On the other side, Paul Ramsey[5] claims a certain gene structure is the defining characteristic. John Noonan[6] prefers conceived-of-humans and presents counterexamples to various other candidate criteria. For instance, he argues against viability as the criterion because the newborn and infirm would then be non-persons, since they cannot live without the aid of others. He rejects any criterion that calls upon the sorts of sentiments a being can evoke in adults on the grounds that this would allow us to exclude other races as non-persons if we could just view them sufficiently unsentimentally.

These approaches are typical: foes of abortion propose sufficient conditions for personhood which fetuses satisfy, while friends of abortion counter with necessary conditions for personhood which fetuses lack. But these both presuppose that the concept of a person can be captured in a straightjacket of necessary and/or sufficient conditions.[7] Rather, "person" is a cluster of features, of which rationality, having a self-concept and being conceived of humans are only part.

What is typical of persons? Within our concept of a person we include, first, certain biological factors: descended from humans, having a certain genetic make-up, having a head, hands, arms, eyes, capable of locomotion, breathing, eating, sleeping. There are psychological factors: sentience, perception, having a concept of self and of one's own interests and desires, the ability to use tools, the ability to use language or symbol systems, the ability to joke, to be angry, to doubt. There are rationality factors: the ability to reason and draw conclusions, the ability to generalize and to learn from past experience, the ability to sacrifice present interests for greater gains in the future. There are social factors: the ability to work in groups and respond to peer pressures, the ability to recognize and consider as valuable the interests of others, seeing oneself as one among "other minds," the ability to sympathize, encourage, love, the ability to evoke from others the responses of sympathy, encouragement, love, the ability to work with others for mutual advantage. Then there are legal factors: being subject to the law and protected by it, having the ability to sue and enter contracts, being counted in the census, having a name and citizenship, the ability to own property, inherit, and so forth.

Now the point is not that this list is incomplete, or that you can find counterinstances to each of its points. People typically exhibit rationality, for instance, but someone who was irrational would not thereby fail to qualify as a person. On the other hand, something could exhibit the majority of these features and still fail to be a person, as an advanced robot might. There is no single core of necessary and sufficient features which we can draw upon with the assurance that they constitute what really makes a person; there are only features that are more or less typical.

This is not to say that no necessary or sufficient conditions can be given. Being alive is a necessary condition for being a person, and being a U.S. Senator is sufficient. But rather than falling inside a sufficient condition or outside a necessary one, a fetus lies in the penumbra region where our concept of a person is not so simple. For this reason I think a conclusive answer to the question whether a fetus is a person is unattainable. Here we might note a family of simple fallacies that proceed by stating a necessary condition for personhood and showing that a fetus has that characteristic. This is a form of the fallacy of affirming the consequent. For example, some have mistakenly reasoned from the premise that a fetus is human (after all, it is a human fetus rather than, say, a canine fetus), to the conclusion that it is a human. Adding an equivocation of "being," we get the fallacious argument that since a fetus is something both living and human, it is a human being.

Nonetheless, it does seem clear that a fetus has very few of the above family of characteristics, whereas a newborn baby exhibits a much larger proportion of them—and a two-year old has even more. Note that one traditional anti-abortion argument has centered on pointing out the many ways in which a fetus resembles a baby. They emphasize its development ("It already has ten fingers . . .") without mentioning its dissimilarities to adults (it still has gills and a tail). They also try to evoke the sort of sympathy on our part that we only feel toward other persons ("Never to laugh . . . or feel the sunshine?"). This all seems to be a relevant way to argue, since its purpose is to persuade us that a fetus satisfies so many of the important features on the list that it ought to be treated as a person. Also note that a fetus near the time of birth satisfies many more of these factors than a fetus in the early months of development. This could provide reason for making distinctions among the different stages of pregnancy, as the U.S. Supreme Court has done.[8]

Historically, the time at which a person has been said to come into existence has varied widely. Muslims date personhood from fourteen days after conception. Some medievals followed Aristotle in placing ensoulment at forty days after conception for a male fetus and eighty days for a female fetus.[9] In European common law since the seventeenth century, abortion was considered the killing of a person only after quickening, the time when a pregnant woman first feels the fetus move on its own. Nor is this variety of opinions surprising. Biologically, a human being develops gradually. We shouldn't expect there to be any specific time or sharp dividing point when a person appears on the scene.

For these reasons I believe our concept of a person is not sharp or decisive enough to bear the weight of a solution to the abortion controversy. To use it to solve that problem is to clarify *obscurum per obscurius.*

II

Next let us consider what follows if a fetus is a person after all. Judith Jarvis Thomson's landmark article, "A Defense of Abortion,"[10] correctly points out that some additional argumentation is needed at this point in the conservative argument to bridge the gap between the premise that the fetus in an innocent person and the conclusion that killing it is always wrong. To arrive at this conclusion, we would need the additional premise that killing an innocent person is always wrong. But killing an innocent person is sometimes permissible, most notably in self-defense. Some examples may help draw out our intuitions or ordinary judgments about self-defense.

Suppose a mad scientist, for instance, hypnotized innocent people to jump under the bushes and attack innocent passers-by with knives. If you are so attacked, we agree you have a right to kill the attacker in self-defense, if killing him is the only way to protect your life or to save yourself from serious injury. It does not seem to matter here that the attacker is not malicious but himself an innocent pawn, for your killing of him is not done in a spirit of retribution but only in self-defense.

How severe an injury may you inflict in self-defense? In part this depends upon the severity of the injury to be avoided: you may not shoot someone merely to avoid having your clothes torn. This might lead one to the mistaken conclusion that the defense may only equal the threatened injury in severity; that to avoid death you may kill, but to avoid a black eye you may only inflict a black eye or the equivalent. Rather, our laws and customs seem to say that you may create an injury somewhat, but not enormously, greater than the injury to be avoided. To fend off an attack whose outcome would be as serious as rape, a severe beating or the loss of a finger, you may shoot; to avoid having your clothes torn, you may blacken an eye.

Aside from this, the injury you may inflict should only be the minimum necessary to deter or incapacitate the attacker. Even if you know he intends to kill you, you are not justified in shooting him if you could equally well save yourself by the simple expedient of running away. Self-defense is for the purpose of avoiding harms rather than equalizing harms.

Some cases of pregnancy present a parallel situation. Though the fetus is itself innocent, it may pose a threat to the pregnant woman's well-being, life prospects or health, mental or physical. If the pregnancy presents a slight threat to her interests, it seems self-defense cannot justify abortion. But if the threat is on a par with a serious beating or the loss of a finger, she may kill the fetus that poses such a threat, even if it is an innocent person. If a lesser harm to the fetus could have the same defensive effect, killing it would not be justified. It is unfortunate that the only way to free the woman from the pregnancy entails the death of the fetus (except in very late stages of pregnancy). Thus a self-defense model supports Thomson's point that the woman has a right only to be freed from the fetus, not a right to demand its death.[11]

The self-defense model is most helpful when we take the pregnant woman's point of view. In the pre-Thomson literature, abortion is often framed as a question for a third party: do you, a doctor, have a right to choose between the life of the woman and that of the fetus? Some have claimed that if you were a passer-by who witnessed a struggle between the innocent hypnotized attacker and his equally innocent victim, you would have no reason to kill either in defense of the other. They have concluded that the self defense model implies that a woman may attempt to abort herself, but that a doctor should not assist her. I think the position of the third party is somewhat more complex. We do feel some inclination to intervene on behalf of the victim rather than the attacker, other things equal. But if both parties are innocent, other factors come into consideration. You would rush to the aid of your husband whether he was attacker or attackee. If a hypnotized famous violinist were attacking a skid row bum, we would try to save the individual who is of more value to society. These considerations would tend to support abortion in some cases.

But suppose you are a frail senior citizen who wishes to avoid being knifed by one of these innocent hypnotics, so you have hired a body-guard to accompany you. If you are attacked, it is clear we believe that the bodyguard, acting as your agent, has a right to kill the attacker to save you from a serious beating. Your rights of self-defense are transferred to your agent. I suggest that we should similarly view the doctor as the pregnant woman's agent in carrying out a defense she is physically incapable of accomplishing herself.

Thanks to modern technology, the cases are rare in which a pregnancy poses as clear a threat to a woman's bodily health as an attacker brandishing a switchblade. How does self-defense fare when more subtle, complex and long-range harms are involved?

To consider a somewhat fanciful example, suppose you are a highly trained surgeon when you are kidnapped by the hypnotic attacker. He says he does not intend to harm you but to take you back to the mad scientist who, it turns out, plans to hypnotize you to have a permanent mental block against all your knowledge of medicine. This would automatically destroy your career which would in turn have a serious adverse impact on your family, your personal relationships and your happiness. It seems to me that if the only way you can avoid this outcome is to shoot the innocent attacker, you are justified in so doing. You are defending yourself from a drastic injury to your life prospects. I think it is no exaggeration to claim that unwanted pregnancies (most obviously among teenagers) often have such adverse life-long consequences as the surgeon's loss of livelihood.

Several parallels arise between various views on abortion and the self-defense model. Let's suppose further that these hypnotized attackers only operate at night, so that it is well known that they can be avoided completely by the considerable inconvenience of never leaving your house after dark. One view is that since you could stay home at night, therefore if you go out and are selected by one of these hypnotized people, you have no right to defend yourself. This parallels the view that abstinence is the only acceptable way to avoid pregnancy. Others might hold that you ought to take along some defense such as Mace which will deter the hypnotized person without killing him, but that if this defense fails, you are obliged to submit to the resulting injury, no matter how severe it is. This parallels the view that contraception is all right but abortion is always wrong, even in cases of contraceptive failure.

A third view is that you may kill the hypnotized person only if he will actually kill you, but not if he will only injure you. This is like the position that abortion is permissible only if it is required to save a woman's life. Finally we have the view that it is all right to kill the attacker, even if only to avoid a very slight inconvenience to yourself and even if you knowingly walked down the very street where all these incidents have been taking place without taking along any Mace or protective escort. If we assume that a fetus is a person, this is the analogue of the view that abortion is always justifiable, "on demand."

The self-defense model allows us to see an important difference that exists between abortion and infanticide, even if a fetus is a person from conception. Many have argued that the only way to justify abortion without justifying infanticide would be to find some characteristic of personhood that is acquired at birth. Michael Tooley, for one, claims infanticide is justifiable because the really significant characteristics of a person are acquired some time after birth. But all such approaches look to characteristics of the developing human and ignore the relation between the fetus and the woman. What if, after birth, the presence of an infant or the need to support it posed a grave threat to the woman's sanity or life prospects? She could escape this threat by the simple expedient of running away. So a solution that does not entail the death of the infant is available. Before birth, such solutions are not available because of the biological dependence of the fetus on the woman. Birth is the crucial point not because of any characteristics the fetus gains, but because after birth the woman can defend herself by a means less drastic than killing the infant. Hence self-defense can be used to justify abortion without necessarily thereby justifying infanticide.

III

On the other hand, supposing a fetus is not after all a person, would abortion always be morally permissible? Some opponents of abortion seem worried that if a fetus is not a full-fledged person, then we are justified in treating it in any way at all. However, this does not follow. Non-persons do get some consideration in our moral code, though of course they do not have the same rights as persons have (and in general they do not have moral responsibilities), and though their interests may be overridden by the interests of persons. Still, we cannot just treat them in any way at all.

Treatment of animals is a case in point. It is wrong to torture dogs for fun or to kill wild birds for no reason at all. It is wrong Period, even though dogs and birds do not have the same rights persons do. However, few people think it is wrong to use dogs as experimental animals, causing them considerable suffering in some cases, provided that the resulting research will probably bring discoveries of great benefit to people. And most of us think it all right to kill birds for food or to protect our crops. People's rights are different from the consideration we give to animals, then, for it is wrong to experiment on people, even if others might later benefit a great deal as a result of their suffering. You might volunteer to be a subject, but this would be supererogatory; you certainly have a right to refuse to be a medical guinea pig.

But how do we decide what you may or may not do to non-persons? This is a difficult problem, one for which I believe no adequate account exists. You do not want to say, for instance, that torturing dogs is all right whenever the sum of its effects on people is good—when it doesn't warp the sensibilities of the torturer so much that he mistreats people. If that were the case, it would be all right to torture dogs if you did it in private, or if the torturer lived on a desert island or died soon afterward, so that his actions had no effect on people. This is an inadequate account, because whatever moral consideration animals get, it has to be indefeasible, too. It will have to be a general proscription of certain actions, not merely a weighing of the impact on people on a case-by-case basis.

Rather, we need to distinguish two levels on which consequences of actions can be taken into account in moral reasoning. The traditional objections to Utilitarianism focus on the fact that it operates solely on the first level, taking all the consequences into account in particular cases only. Thus Utilitarianism is open to "desert island" and "lifeboat" counterexamples because these cases are rigged to make the consequences of actions severely limited.

Rawls's theory could be described as a teleological sort of theory, but with teleology operating on a higher level.[12] In choosing the principles to regulate society from the original position, his hypothetical choosers make their decision on the basis of the total consequences of various systems. Furthermore, they are constrained to choose a general set of rules which people can readily learn and apply. An ethical theory must operate by generating a set of sympathies and attitudes toward others which reinforces the functioning of that set of moral principles. Our prohibition against killing people operates by means of certain moral sentiments including sympathy, compassion and guilt. But if these attitudes are to form a coherent set, they carry us further: we tend to perform supererogatory actions, and we tend to feel similar compassion toward person-like non-persons.

It is crucial that psychological facts play a role here. Our psychological constitution makes it the case that for our ethical theory to work, it must prohibit certain treatment of non-persons which are significantly person-like. If our moral rules allowed people to treat person-like non-persons in ways we do not want people to be treated, this would undermine the system of sympathies and attitudes that makes the ethical system work. For this reason, we would choose in the original position to make mistreatment of some sorts of animals wrong in general (not just wrong in the cases with public impact), even though animals are not themselves parties in the original position. Thus it makes sense that it is those animals whose appearance and behavior are most like those of people that get the most consideration in our moral scheme.

It is because of "coherence of attitudes," I think, that the similarity of a fetus to a baby is very significant. A fetus one week before birth is so much like a newborn baby in our psychological space that we cannot allow any cavalier treatment of the former while expecting full sympathy and nutritive support for the latter. Thus, I think that anti-abortion forces are indeed giving their strongest arguments when they point to the similarities between a fetus and a baby, and when they try to evoke our emotional attachment to and sympathy for the fetus. An early horror story from New York about nurses who were expected to alternate between caring for six-week premature infants and disposing of viable 24-week aborted fetuses is just that—a horror story. These beings are so much alike that no one can be asked to draw a distinction and treat them so very differently.

Remember, however, that in the early weeks after conception a fetus is very much unlike a person. It is hard to develop these feelings for a set of genes which doesn't yet have a head, hands, beating heart, response to touch or the ability to move by itself. Thus it seems to me that the alleged "slippery slope" between conception and birth is not so very slippery. In the early stages of pregnancy, abortion can hardly be compared to murder for psychological reasons, but in the latest stages it is psychologically akin to murder.

Another source of similarity is the bodily continuity between fetus and adult. Bodies play a surprisingly central role in our attitudes toward persons. One has only to think of the philosophical literature on how far physical identity suffices for personal identity or Wittgenstein's remark that the best picture of the human soul is the human body. Even after death when all agree the body is no longer a person, we still observe elaborate customs of respect for the human body; like people who torture dogs, necrophilics are not to be trusted with people.[13] So it is appropriate that we show respect to a fetus as the body continuous with the body of a person. This is a degree of resemblance to persons that animals cannot rival.

Michael Tooley also utilizes a parallel with animals. He claims that it is always permissible to drown newborn kittens and draws conclusions about infanticide.[14] But it is only permissible to drown kittens when their survival would cause some hardship. Perhaps it would be a burden to feed and house six more cats or to find other homes for them. The alternative of letting them starve produces even more suffering than the drowning. Since the kittens get their rights secondhand, so to speak, via the need for coherence in our attitudes, their interests are often overridden by the interests of full-fledged persons. But if their survival would be no inconvenience to people at all, then it is wrong to drown them, contra Tooley.

Tooley's conclusions about abortion are wrong for the same reason. Even if a fetus is not a person, abortion is not always permissible, because of the resemblance of a fetus to a person. I agree with Thomson that it would be wrong for a woman who is seven months pregnant to have an abortion just to avoid having to postpone a trip to Europe. In the early months of pregnancy when the fetus hardly resembles a baby at all, then, abortion is permissible whenever it is in the interests of the pregnant woman or her family. The reasons would only need to outweigh the pain and inconvenience of the abortion itself. In the middle months, when the fetus comes to resemble a person, abortion would be justifiable only when the continuation of the pregnancy or the birth of the child would cause harms—physical, psychological, economic or social—to the woman. In the last months of pregnancy, even on our current assumption that a fetus is not a person, abortion seems to be wrong except to save a woman from significant injury or death.

The Supreme Court has recognized similar gradations in the alleged slippery slope stretching between conception and birth. To this point, the present paper has been a discussion of the moral status of abortion only, not its legal status. In view of the great physical, financial and sometimes psychological costs of abortion, perhaps the legal arrangement most compatible with the proposed moral solution would be the absence of restrictions, that is, so-called abortion "on demand."

So I conclude, first, that application of our concept of a person will not suffice to settle the abortion issue. After all, the biological development of a human being is gradual. Second, whether a fetus is a person or not, abortion is justifiable early in a pregnancy to avoid modest harms and seldom justifiable late in pregnancy except to avoid significant injury or death.

Endnotes

1. We also have paternalistic laws which keep us from harming our own bodies even when no one else is affected. Ironically, anti-abortion laws were originally designed to protect pregnant women from a dangerous but tempting procedure.
2. Mary Anne Warren, "On the Moral and Legal Status of Abortion," *Monist* 5 (1973), p. 55.
3. Baruch Brody, "Fetal Humanity and the Theory of Essentialism" in Robert Baker and Frederick Elliston (eds.) *Philosophy and Sex* (Buffalo, NY, 1975).
4. Michael Tooley, "Abortion and Infanticide." *Philosophy and Public Affairs* I (1971).
5. Paul Ramsey, "The Morality of Abortion," in James Rachels (ed.), *Moral Problems* (New York, 1971).
6. John Noonan, "Abortion and the Catholic Church: A Summary History," *Natural Law Forum* 12 (1967), pp. 125–131.
7. Wittgenstein has argued against the possibility of so capturing the concept of a game, *Philosophical Investigations* (New York, 1958), § 66–71.
8. Not because the fetus is partly a person and so has some of the rights of persons but rather because of the rights of person-like non-persons. This I discuss in part III.
9. Aristotle himself was concerned, however, with the different question of when the soul takes form. For historical data, see Jimmye Kimmey "How the Abortion Laws Happened," *Ms.* I (April, 1973), p. 48 ff. and John Noonan, *loc. cit.*
10. J.J. Thomson, "A Defense of Abortion," *Philosophy and Public Affairs* I (1971).
11. *Ibid.*, p. 52.
12. John Rawls, *A Theory of Justice* (Cambridge, MA, 1971), §§ 3–4.
13. On the other hand, if they can be trusted with people, then our moral customs are mistaken. It all depends on the facts of psychology.
14. *Op. cit.*, pp. 40, 60–61.

Journal/Discussion Questions

✍ *In your own experience, do you think of the fetus as a person? In what sense(s)? In what ways did English's remarks shed light on your moral feelings toward the unborn?*

1. English indicates that it is not always morally wrong to kill an innocent person. What support does she give for this claim? Do you agree with her?
2. What does English mean by "coherence of attitudes"? What role does this term play in the development of her argument?
3. Under what circumstances would English hold that abortion is morally wrong? What are her reasons? Do you agree with her? Why or why not?

Edward Langerak
"Abortion: Listening to the Middle"*

Edward Langerak is a professor of philosophy at St. Olaf College in Minnesota.

Langerak notes that most philosophers writing about abortion tend to see the issue in terms of extremes, either that abortion is always wrong or that it is never wrong. The American public, however, has a much more nuanced position, seeing some abortions as permissible and others as much more problematic. Langerak offers a philosophical justification for that middle position.

As You Read, Consider This:

1. What are the apparently incompatible beliefs of liberals and conservatives about abortion? How does Langerak attempt to find a middle ground?
2. What does Langerak mean by the potentiality principle? What role does it play in his argument?
3. On what basis does Langerak claim that later abortions are morally more serious than earlier abortions?

Says one critic of the philosophical debate on abortion: "Philosophers are not listened to because they do not listen." Though I believe the charge is too strong, my own review of the literature makes it uncomfortably understandable. If there is any public consensus on abortion, as reflected in legal systems as well as in public opinion surveys, it is the middle-of-the-road view that some abortions are not permissible but that others are, and that some of the permissible abortions are more difficult to justify than others. But many of the most widely cited philosophical writings on abortion argue that the only coherent positions tend toward the extremes: all or most abortions are put into the same moral boat with either murder or, more frequently, elective surgery. In fact, proponents of the

* *Hastings Center Report,* October, 1979, pp. 24–28.

extremes tend to respect one another as at least being self-consistent, while joining in swift rebuttal of those who want it both ways and ignominiously try to be moderates on either murder or mandatory motherhood.

This reaction against the middle derives from some basic beliefs of those on the extremes. On the liberal side are those who believe that fetuses, and perhaps even very young infants, lack some necessary condition (say, self-consciousness) of personhood. This view is often combined with the further assertion that the social consequences of society's conferring on the fetus a claim to life are such that the conferral should not be made until birth or shortly thereafter. On the conservative side there are those who believe that from conception (or very shortly thereafter) the fetus has as strong (or almost as strong) a claim to life as does any person. This claim resides either in some property thought sufficient for personhood (say, genetic endowment) that the fetus has in itself, or in the immediate conferral of personhood on the fetus *by* God or society.

Of course, as Schopenhauer said, arguments are not like taxicabs that you can dismiss when they become inconvenient; and the two extremes are quick to point out the problematic implications of each other's positions. The liberals are accused of courting infanticide and the conservatives of trivializing the moral category of murder. Such implications would be more damaging to the extremes were it not that most moderate positions have an equally problematic flaw—that of arbitrary line-drawing. My reading of the abortion literature suggests that there are two widely shared beliefs that moderate positions seek to incorporate in their approaches to the abortion issue. The first belief is that something about the fetus itself, not merely the social consequences of abortion, makes abortions (or at least many abortions) morally problematic. The second belief is that late abortions are significantly more morally problematic than early abortions. Not only are these beliefs widely shared by moderates, but I find that liberals and conservatives, whose positions implicitly reject one or both of these beliefs, often feel uncomfortable in rejecting them.

In accounting for these two beliefs, most middle positions maintain variations of what I call the "stage" approach and what its critics call the "magic moment" approach. The assertion is that at some point in the development of the fetus, say at the point of acquiring some vital sign, of sentience, of quickening, or of viability, the fetus suddenly moves from having no claim to life to having as strong (or almost as strong) a claim as an adult human. While the "stage" approach is consistent with the two beliefs underlying the moderate position, its difficulty has always been to explain the tremendous moral weight put on some specific point in what really amounts to a continuum in development. Critics on both extremes argue that, no matter what stage is picked as the "magic moment," the whole approach is prima facie arbitrary.

The implications of the liberal and conservative positions, including their denial of one or both of the moderate beliefs, and the prima facie arbitrariness of the stage positions, motivate consideration of an alternative that both is coherent and listens to the middle by accounting for the two beliefs.

Without examining all the alternatives. I will argue that the potentiality principle is plausible and accounts for the first belief—that something about the fetus itself makes abortion morally problematic—but that, by itself, it cannot account for the second belief—that late abortions are significantly more problematic than early abortions. I will then argue that a conferred claims approach is plausible, consistent with the potentiality principle, and accounts for the second belief though it cannot account for the first. I will suggest that combining the potentiality principle with a conferred claims approach provides moderates with a coherent framework for thinking through the central questions of the abortion debate: (1) When does an individual human being attain either an inherent claim to life or such properties that society ought to confer on it a claim to life? (2) When do a person's or a group of persons' claims to life, physical or mental health, freedom, privacy, and self-actualization override another human being's claim to life? (3) When should answers to the first two questions be incorporated into the law of a pluralistic society?

The Potentiality Principle

I formulate the potentiality principle as follows: "If in the normal course of its development, a being will acquire a person's claim to life, then by virtue of that fact it already has some claim to life." To understand this principle, one must distinguish among "actual person," "a capacity for personhood," "potential person," and "possible person." An *actual person* is a being that meets a sufficient condition (whatever that may be) for personhood and thereby has as strong a claim to life as normal adult human beings. Roughly, a *capacity for personhood* is possessed by any being not currently exhibiting that capacity, but who has proceeded in the course of its development to the point where it could currently exhibit it (for example, a temporarily unconscious person). A *potential person* is a being, not yet a person, that will become an actual person in the normal course of its development (for example, a human fetus). A *possible person* is a being that could, under certain causally possible conditions, become an actual person (for example, a human sperm or egg).

This technical set of distinctions is important because the potentiality principle asserts that potential persons, but not possible persons, have a claim to life. Some attacks on the principle confuse these categories. Also, the principle is consistent with granting full personhood to those with a capacity for personhood, a fact ignored by those who collapse "capacity" and "potentiality" and argue, for example, that the category of "potential person" endangers sleeping persons. Moreover, the distinctions can help us avoid sloppy language, such as that of the Supreme Court in *Roe v. Wade* when it asserted that at viability the state begins to have a compelling interest in "potential life." Clearly a fetus is actually alive and is even an actual human being, genetically defined; its unique status is that, given most criteria of personhood, it is neither an actual person nor a merely possible person—it is a potential person.

Potentiality and Temporality

The potentiality principle asserts that a potential person has a claim to life, albeit one that may be weaker than the claim of an actual person. Many people find this assertion intuitively plausible, but are unable to persuade those who challenge it. Here is my attempt to persuade. It is clear that the unique status of the potential person has to do with its inherent "thrust" or predetermined tendency. A potential person is not simply a set of blueprints, it is an organism that itself will become the actual person toward which it is already developing. Controversial issues of personal identity arise here, but two points seem obvious. First, we cannot simply assume that its predetermined tendency already grants it the claims it will have in the future. To paraphrase H. Tristram Engelhardt, Jr., we must not lose the ability to distinguish between the claims of the future and those of the present; or as S.I. Benn succinctly puts it, a potential president is not already commander-in-chief.

Second, those attracted to the potentiality principle do see some derivative relationship between the claims that a being will have in the normal course of its development and those that it has in the present.

I believe that the plausibility of the last point rests in perceiving humans as basically temporal beings. For actual persons this is true, first of all, from an internal point of view (a fact Heidegger uses for his entire ontology). Our self-consciousness so orients us to our past and our future that, in an important sense, we *are* our history and our projections as well as our present. A premedical student, for example, sees himself or herself as a future physician, not just as a science student. This temporal perception is also true from an external point of view, a point of view that extends to humans that are not yet persons. When we see a very young child, we see something of the adult it will, in the normal course of its development, become, as well as something of the baby that it once was. In this temporal perception lies, I believe, the respect we feel is due former persons (for example, respectful treatment of corpses) and, for that matter, former presidents. The respect we give former persons and presidents is not as great as that which we give actual ones, but that does not undermine the fact that some respect is due the former and that it is derivative from, indeed proportional to, the respect due to the latter.

Similarly, perceiving humans in a temporal context accounts for the respect many feel is due to humans by virtue of their potential. As an analogy, consider a potential president. Following my distinctions, such a person is not merely a possible president (something civics teachers used to say about every American child); he or she has already won the election but has not yet been inaugurated (on a somewhat arbitrarily selected date). The person is not yet commander-in-chief but, in the normal course, *will* (not *could*) be. Already that person receives some of the perquisites of the future office. The fact that the news media and others give the potential president more attention than the actual president, of course, may be the result of prudence, if not exploitation (the same derivation for much of the respect given actual presidents). But, at least pre-Watergate times, some of the respect given actual presidents, and most of that given former presidents, derives from the high office that the person has or had, even when the person is not particularly deserving. Those who perceive a person in a temporal context and who, like myself, still respect an actual or former president by virtue of the office (apart from achievements in it), will derivatively have some respect toward a potential president by virtue of the office he or she will have.

Even those who deny that presidents ought to be respected simply by virtue of their office, should agree that some of the respect given persons derives from their "office" of personhood, apart from their achievements. In fact, traditionally the respect involving a claim to life derives from what persons are, rather than what they achieve or fail to achieve. If so, then perceiving humans in a temporal context should elicit some respect for former and potential persons, respect that is derivative from and proportional, though not identical, to the respect elicited by the actual persons they were or will become.

Temporality and Probability

Some may grant the strength of this argument as it applies to former persons, sensing that it accounts, for example, for our aversion to artificially keeping former persons "alive" in order to harvest their organs at a convenient time. However, whatever else we may say about former persons, they were certainly, at one time, actual persons. But the personhood of potential persons is still "outstanding" and there is no guarantee that it will be realized. The contingency of the "not yet" makes it asymmetrical with the "has been" even when we perceive humans in a temporal context.

This objection forces us to ask just what is the moral significance of the predetermined tendency of a potential person. Though the tendency does not guarantee personhood, it does distinguish the organism from possible persons by guaranteeing a dramatic shift in probabilities. This difference in probabilities is similar to that which distinguishes a potential president from a possible president. The potentiality principle asks us to respect a potential person by virtue not of what it *could* be, but of what it *will* be in the normal course of its development. Even those of us who refuse to mythologize the predetermined tendency in potential persons must agree that this tendency makes it highly likely that, without outside interference, they will become persons. Is this shift in probabilities of moral significance?

Consider the other end of the life span. Those who believe that it is sometimes permissible to cease striving officiously to keep humans in an irreversible coma artificially alive, must agree that the irreversibility of the coma is seldom, if ever, absolutely guaranteed. But we believe it is morally irresponsible to allow the rare "miraculous recovery" to prevent acting on the best medical prognosis, when it indicates no reasonable hope of recovery. To shut off a respirator when there is a 50 percent chance of recovery (or even a 5 percent chance, given our laudable bias toward erring in favor of personal life), is morally wrong, but not when the probability of recovery approaches (without reaching) zero. In an uncertain world, judgments of high probabilities are often the only kind we have. This makes dramatic shifts in probabilities morally significant.

So I believe that the high probability of future personhood, inherent in a potential person, is of moral significance to those who perceive humans in a temporal context, and that this makes plausible the assertion of the potentiality principle. I hope I have at least shifted the burden of proof on to those who deny that the high probability of a fetus's becoming a person with a strong claim to life already grants it some (proportional) claim to life and respect.

Conferred Claims

Although the potentiality principle, as defended, accounts for the first belief—that something about the fetus itself makes abortion morally problematic—it leaves open the question of just how strong a claim to life should be attributed to the fetus. There are extreme liberals on the abortion issue who may grant the fetus some claim to life but simply argue that the claims of an actual person—claims to freedom and mental health—always override the claim to life of a fetus. Among those who use the potentiality principle, there will be intramural debates on how strong a claim to life it implies. I cannot argue the case here, but I believe that the most plausible use of it is one that allows the use of RIDs and "morning after" pills (both of which probably act as abortifacients), as well as abortions during the first trimester for such reasons as the woman's being too young for motherhood. But then the claim to life attributed to the very early fetus cannot be very strong. The incidence of early spontaneous abortion is "estimated" variously from 15 percent to over 50 percent, and second-trimester fetuses have a somewhat higher natural death rate than postviable fetuses. In other words, the probability of an older fetus becoming an actual person is perhaps double the probability of a zygote becoming a person. While this shift in probability is noteworthy, and marks implantation as a point of some moral significance, it is not nearly as significant as the difference in moral seriousness moderates see between a very early abortion and a late one. Consequently, if the inherent claim to life of a potential person is derived from and proportional to the probability of its becoming an actual person, one cannot in good faith allow the claim to life of a zygote to be easily overridden and then assert that the inherent claim to life of an older fetus is so vastly stronger that it all but cannot be overridden. Therefore, although the potentiality principle can account for the belief that something about the fetus itself makes abortion morally problematic, it cannot by itself account for the belief that late abortions are significantly more morally problematic than very early abortions.

However, the conferred claims approach can account for the second belief, although it cannot account for the first. Assume that, whatever moral claim to life an older fetus may have by virtue of its potentiality, the claim may not be strong enough to override the claim of a pregnant woman for an abortion. At what point should society confer a stronger claim to life on the fetus? At what point should society treat it as if it were a person?

The conferral approach to the status of the fetus is not an unusual one, though it is sometimes thought incompatible with an approach that asserts an inherent claim in the fetus itself. But an approach that *confers* claims rubs an approach that *recognizes* inherent claims only if the inherent claim to life is thought to be as serious as an actual person's claim to life. In this case it would be futile (rather than contradictory) to ask what claims society ought to confer on it. However, when the recognized inherent claim is weaker than a normal adult's claim to life, as can be the case with the potentiality principle, one can coherently ask whether society ought, in addition, to confer on the fetus a stronger claim to life.

The argument in favor of such a conferral basically appeals to the social consequences of abortions and infanticide. For example, infants are so similar to persons that allowing them to be killed would generate a moral climate that would endanger the claim to life of even young persons. And older fetuses are so similar to infants that allowing them to be killed without due moral or legal process would endanger infants. Of course there must be a cutoff for this sort of argument. For example, most would agree that preventing the implantation of zygotes would have no discernible effect on our sympathetic capacities toward persons. At what point would abortions begin to have such effects, especially on medical personnel, that it is in society's interest to endow becoming a person. While this shift in probability is noteworthy, and marks implantation as a point of some moral significance, it is not nearly as significant as the difference in moral seriousness moderates see between a very early abortion and a late one. Consequently, if the inherent claim to life of a potential person is derived from and proportional to the probability of its becoming an actual person, one cannot in good faith allow the claim to life of a zygote to be easily overridden and then assert that the inherent claim to life of an older fetus is so vastly stronger that it all but cannot be overridden. Therefore, although the potentiality principle can account for the belief that something about the fetus itself makes abortion morally problematic, it cannot by itself account for the belief that late abortions are significantly more morally problematic than very early abortions.

However, the conferred claims approach can account for the second belief, although it cannot account for the first. Assume that, whatever moral claim to life an older fetus may have by virtue of its potentiality, the claim may not be strong enough to override the claim of a pregnant woman for an abortion. At what point should society confer a stronger claim to life on the fetus? At what point should society treat it as if it were a person?

The conferral approach to the status of the fetus is not an unusual one, though it is sometimes thought incompatible with an approach that asserts an inherent claim in the fetus itself. But an approach that *confers* claims rubs an approach that *recognizes* inherent claims only if the inherent claim to life is thought to be as serious as an actual person's claim to life. In this case it would be futile (rather than contradictory) to ask what claims society ought to confer on it. However, when the recognized inherent claim is weaker than a normal adult's claim to life, as can be the case with the potentiality principle, one can coherently ask whether society ought, in addition, to confer on the fetus a stronger claim to life.

Implantation, Quickening, Viability, and Birth

My combined approach escapes the problematic implications of the extremes but does it escape the flaw of arbitrary line-drawing that I attributed to those moderate positions that appeal to the stage or "magic moment" approach? Two related considerations show that it does. First, notice that the word "arbitrary" should not be used loosely. For example, there is a certain arbitrariness in making eighteen the age of majority rather than seventeen or nineteen. But the relevant criteria nonarbitrarily imply that, if a legally precise line must be drawn within the continuum of growth, the debate must focus on that time span rather than, say, the span between seven and nine.

Second, I submit that the two criteria I use—important shifts in probabilities and dangerous social consequences—nonarbitrarily suggest four spans (beyond that of conception) for moral and legal line-drawing in a potential person's continuum of growth. Although these criteria imply distinct spans for definite increments in the strength of the claim to life, at no stage does a potential person move from having no claim to having one as strong as an adult.

The first span, as we saw, is that of implantation, when the shift in probabilities of actual personhood signifies a somewhat stronger inherent claim to life, at least from the moral point of view. The recognition of this change is due apart from any consequentialist considerations about the difference between more or less unknowingly preventing implantation and knowingly detaching an implanted embryo. However, the remaining spans are suggested by consequentialist considerations about the psychological and social impact of abortions, considerations in favor of conferring an even stronger claim to life on the fetus.

The second span involves the traditional indicator of "quickening." When the fetus begins making perceptible spontaneous movements (around the beginning of the second trimester), its shape, its behavior, and even its beginning relationship with the mother and the rest of society (every father recalls when he first felt the fetus's movements) all suggest that abortions after this point will have personal and social consequences specifiably more serious than those of earlier abortions.

The third is that of viability, when a fetus is capable of living with simple medical care, outside the womb (around the end of the second trimester). Recall the "infanticide" trials of physicians who, claiming they were inducing abortions, were charged with participating in premature births and murders. This controversy is only one indication that killing potential persons after viability has social consequences (apart from legal ones) even more serious than abortions soon after quickening.

Finally, consider that allowing infanticide is generally regarded as a *reductio* of those positions that allow it. The aversion to infanticide is shared even by most of those whose criteria for personhood imply that a newborn is still only a potential person and not an actual one. This suggests that most people agree that at birth the potential person attains properties and relationships so close to those of actual persons that the consequences of killing at this point are practically the same as killing young persons.

If these observations are true, they justify conferring on new newborns a claim to life as strong as that of adult persons. They also suggest partial wisdom in the Supreme Court's decision allowing states to grant a rather strong claim to life to postviable fetuses, a claim overridden only by the claim to life or health (I would specify "physical health") of the mother. But the court decision, in effect, mandates the allowing of abortion on demand for all previable fetuses. If my observations about quickening are correct, we should also draw an earlier line, conferring a claim to life on the fetus at the beginning of the second trimester, a claim less strong than that conferred at viability, but one overridden only by such serious claims as that of the mother to mental or physical health. Probably the moral line drawn at implantation should remain outside the legal realm.

I admit the difficulties in legally implementing such an approach, but I doubt that they are insurmountable or as deep as the moral and legal difficulties of alternative approaches. Therefore I believe I have presented a plausible approach to the abortion issue that is coherent, is not arbitrary, and listens well to the considered intuitions of those in the middle.*

Journal/Discussion Questions

✍ *Consider Langerak's attempt to mark out a middle ground in the abortion debate. How does this compare with your own position?*

1. In what way is Langerak's position sensitive to the moral concerns of liberals? Of conservatives?
2. What do you think is the strongest objection that Langerak's position still faces?

Don Marquis
"Why Abortion Is Immoral"†

Don Marquis is a professor of philosophy at the University of Kansas who specializes in medical ethics. He originally became interested in the issue of abortion while teaching medical ethics. He was also motivated by his belief that American involvement in the Vietnam War was profoundly immoral and he wanted to understand why that was so in a philosophically respectable way.

In order to demonstrate precisely what is wrong with abortion, Marquis first develops a theory of what is wrong with killing in general. The principal moral objection to killing is that it deprives beings of their futures—hopes, projects, dreams. If this is what is objectionable about killing, it is easy to see that abortion is morally wrong, for it deprives a living being of its future.

* Patricia Fauser, James Gussafson, Gary Iseminger, Daniel Lee, and Frederick Stousland gave me very helpful comments on an earlier draft of this essay.

As You Read, Consider This:

1. Marquis considers several possible answers to the question of why killing is wrong. Which of these is closest to your own?
2. On what basis does Marquis support his claim that the fetus is an innocent human being?

The view that abortion is, with rare exceptions, seriously immoral has received little support in the recent philosophical literature. No doubt most philosophers affiliated with secular institutions of higher education believe that the anti-abortion position is either a symptom of irrational religious dogma or a conclusion generated by seriously confused philosophical argument. The purpose of this essay is to undermine this general belief. This essay sets out an argument that purports to show, as well as any argument in ethics can show, that abortion is, except possibly in rare cases, seriously immoral, that it is in the same moral category as killing an innocent adult human being.

The argument is based on a major assumption. Many of the most insightful and careful writers on the ethics of abortion—such as Joel Feinberg, Michael Tooley, Mary Ann Warren, H. Tristram Engelhardt, Jr., L.W. Sumner, John T. Noonan, Jr., and Philip Devine[1]—believe that whether or not abortion is morally permissible stands or falls on whether or not a fetus is the sort of being whose life it is seriously wrong to end. The argument of this essay will assume, but not argue, that they are correct.

Also, this essay will neglect issues of great importance to a complete ethics of abortion. Some anti-abortionists will allow that certain abortions, such as abortion before implantation or abortion when the life of a woman is threatened by a pregnancy or abortion after rape, may be morally permissible. This essay will not explore the casuistry of these hard cases. The purpose of this essay is to develop a general argument for the claim that the overwhelming majority of deliberate abortions are seriously immoral.

I

A sketch of standard anti-abortion and pro-choice arguments exhibits how those arguments possess certain symmetries that explain why partisans of those positions are so convinced of the correctness of their own positions, why they are not successful in convincing their opponents, and why, to others, this issue seems to be unresolvable. An analysis of the nature of this standoff suggests a strategy for surmounting it.

Consider the way a typical anti-abortionist argues. She will argue or assert that life is present from the moment of conception or that fetuses look like babies or that fetuses possess a characteristic such as a genetic code that is both necessary and sufficient for being human. Anti-abortionists seem to believe that (1) the truth of all of these claims is quite obvious, and (2) establishing any of these claims is sufficient to show that abortion is morally akin to murder.

A standard pro-choice strategy exhibits similarities. The pro-choicer will argue or assert that fetuses are not persons or that fetuses are not rational agents or that fetuses are not social beings. Pro-choicers seem to believe that (1) the truth of any of these claims is quite obvious, and (2) establishing any of these claims is sufficient to show that an abortion is not a wrongful killing.

In fact, both the pro-choice and the anti-abortion claims do seem to be true, although the "it looks like a baby" claim is more difficult to establish the earlier the pregnancy. We seem to have a standoff. How can it be resolved?

As everyone who has taken a bit of logic knows, if any of these arguments concerning abortion is a good argument, it requires not only some claim characterizing fetuses, but also some general moral principle that ties a characteristic of fetuses to having or not having the right to life or to some other moral characteristic that will generate the obligation or the lack of obligation not to end the life of a fetus. Accordingly, the arguments of the anti-abortionist and the pro-choicer need a bit of filling in to be regarded as adequate.

Note what each partisan will say. The anti-abortionist will claim that her position is supported by such generally accepted moral principles as "It is always prima facie seriously wrong to take a human life" or "It is always prima facie seriously wrong to end the life of a baby." Since these are generally accepted moral principles, her position is certainly not obviously wrong. The pro-choicer will claim that her position is supported by such plausible moral principles as "Being a person is what gives an individual intrinsic moral worth" or "It is only seriously prima facie wrong to take the life of a member of the human community." Since these are generally accepted moral principles, the pro-choice position is certainly not obviously wrong. Unfortunately, we have again arrived at a standoff.

Now, how might one deal with this standoff? The standard approach is to try to show how the moral principles of one's opponent lose their plausibility under analysis. It is easy to see how this is possible. On the one hand, the anti-abortionist will defend a moral principle concerning the wrongness of killing which tends to be broad in scope in order that even fetuses at an early stage of pregnancy will fall under it. The problem with broad principles is that they often embrace too much. In this particular instance, the principle "It is always prima facie wrong to take a human life" seems to entail that it is wrong to end the existence of a living human cancer-cell culture, on the grounds that the culture is both living and human. Therefore, it seems that the anti-abortionist's favored principle is too broad.

On the other hand, the pro-choicer wants to find a moral principle concerning the wrongness of killing which tends to be narrow in scope in order that fetuses will *not* fall under it. The problem with narrow principles is that they often do not embrace enough. Hence, the needed principles such as "It is prima facie seriously wrong to kill only persons" or "It is prima facie wrong to kill only rational agents" do not explain why it is wrong to kill infants or young children or the severely retarded or even perhaps the severely mentally ill. Therefore, we seem again to have a standoff. The anti-abortionist charges, not unreasonably, that pro-choice principles concerning killing are too narrow to be acceptable; the pro-choicer charges, not unreasonably, that anti-abortionist principles concerning killing are too broad to be acceptable.

Attempts by both sides to patch up the difficulties in their positions run into further difficulties. The anti-abortionist will try to remove the problem in her position by reformulating her principle concerning killing in terms of human beings. Now we end up with: "It is always prima facie seriously wrong to end the life of a human being." This principle has the advantage of avoiding the problem of the human cancer-cell culture counterexample. But this advantage is purchased at a high price. For although it is clear that a fetus is both human and alive, it is not at all clear that a fetus is a human *being*. There is at least something to be said for the view that something becomes a human being only after a process of development, and that therefore first trimester fetuses and perhaps all fetuses are not yet human beings. Hence, the anti-abortionist, by this move, has merely exchanged one problem for another.[2]

The pro-choicer fares no better. She may attempt to find reasons why killing infants, young children, and the severely retarded is wrong which are independent of her major principle that is supposed to explain the wrongness of taking human life, but which will not also make abortion immoral. This is no easy task. Appeals to social utility will seem satisfactory only to those who resolve not to think of the enormous difficulties with a utilitarian account of the wrongness of killing and the significant social costs of preserving the lives of the unproductive.[3] A pro-choice strategy that extends the definition of "person" to infants or even to young children seems just as arbitrary as an anti-abortion strategy that extends the definition of "human being" to fetuses. Again, we find symmetries in the two positions and we arrive at a standoff.

There are even further problems that reflect symmetries in the two positions. In addition to counterexample problems, or the arbitrary application problems that can be exchanged for them, the standard anti-abortionist principle "It is prima facie seriously wrong to kill a human being," or one of its variants, can be objected to on the grounds of ambiguity. If "human being" is taken to be a *biological* category, then the anti-abortionist is left with the problem of explaining why a merely biological category should make a moral difference. Why, it is asked, is it any more reasonable to base a moral conclusion on the number of chromosomes in one's cells than on the color of one's skin?[4] If "human being," on the other hand, is taken to be a *moral* category, then the claim that a fetus is a human being cannot be taken to be a premise in the anti-abortion argument, for it is precisely what needs to be established. Hence, either the anti-abortionist's main category is a morally irrelevant, merely biological category, or it is of no use to the anti-abortionist in establishing (non-circularly, of course) that abortion is wrong.

Although this problem with the anti-abortionist position is often noticed, it is less often noticed that the pro-choice position suffers from an analogous problem. The principle "Only persons have the right to life" also suffers from an ambiguity. The term "person" is typically defined in terms of psychological characteristics, although there will certainly be disagreement concerning which characteristics are most important. Supposing that this matter can be settled, the pro-choicer is left with the problem of explaining why *psychological* characteristics should make a *moral* difference. If the pro-choicer should attempt to deal with this problem by claiming that an explanation is not necessary, that in fact we do treat such a cluster of psychological properties as having moral significance, the sharp-witted anti-abortionist should have a ready response. We do treat being both living and human as having moral significance. If it is legitimate for the pro-choicer to demand that the anti-abortionist provide an explanation of the connection between the biological character of being a human being and the wrongness of being killed (even though people accept this connection), then it is legitimate for the anti-abortionist to demand that the pro-choicer provide an explanation of the connection between psychological criteria for being a person and the wrongness of being killed (even though that connection is accepted).[5]

Feinberg has attempted to meet this objection (he calls psychological personhood "commonsense personhood"):

> The characteristics that confer commonsense personhood are not arbitrary bases for rights and duties, such as race, sex or species membership; rather they are traits that make sense out of rights and duties and without which those moral attributes would have no point or function. It is because people are conscious; have a sense of their personal identities; have plans, goals, and projects; experience emotions; are liable to pains, anxieties, and frustrations; can reason and bargain, and so on—it is because of these attributes that people have values and interests, desires and expectations of their own, including

> a stake in their own futures, and a personal well-being of a sort we cannot ascribe to unconscious or nonrational beings. Because of their developed capacities they can assume duties and responsibilities and can have and make claims on one another. Only because of their sense of self, their life plans, their value hierarchies, and their stakes in their own futures can they be ascribed fundamental rights. There is nothing arbitrary about these linkages. (*op. cit.*, p. 270)

The plausible aspects of this attempt should not be taken to obscure its implausible features. There is a great deal to be said for the view that being a psychological person under some description is a necessary condition for having duties. One cannot have a duty unless one is capable of behaving morally, and a being's capability of behaving morally will require having a certain psychology. It is far from obvious, however, that having rights entails consciousness or rationality, as Feinberg suggests. We speak of the rights of the severely retarded or the severely mentally ill, yet some of these persons are not rational. We speak of the rights of the temporarily unconscious. The New Jersey Supreme Court based their decision in the Quinlan case on Karen Ann Quinlan's right to privacy, and she was known to be permanently unconscious at that time. Hence, Feinberg's claim that having rights entails being conscious is, on its face, obviously false.

Of course, it might not make sense to attribute rights to a being that would never in its natural history have certain psychological traits. This modest connection between psychological personhood and moral personhood will create a place for Karen Ann Quinlan and the temporarily unconscious. But then it makes a place for fetuses also. Hence, it does not serve Feinberg's pro-choice purposes. Accordingly, it seems that the pro-choicer will have as much difficulty bridging the gap between psychological personhood and personhood in the moral sense as the anti-abortionist has bridging the gap between being a biological human being and being a human being in the moral sense.

Furthermore, the pro-choicer cannot any more escape her problem by making person a purely moral category than the anti-abortionist could escape by the analogous move. For if person is a moral category, then the pro-choicer is left without the resources for establishing (noncircularly, of course) the claim that a fetus is not a person, which is an essential premise in her argument. Again, we have both a symmetry and a standoff between pro-choice and antiabortion views.

Passions in the abortion debate run high. There are both plausibilities and difficulties with the standard positions. Accordingly, it is hardly surprising that partisans of either side embrace with fervor the moral generalizations that support the conclusions they preanalytically favor, and reject with disdain the moral generalizations of their opponents as being subject to inescapable difficulties. It is easy to believe that the counterexamples to one's own moral principles are merely temporary difficulties that will dissolve in the wake of further philosophical research, and that the counterexamples to the principles of one's opponents are as straightforward as the contradiction between A and O propositions in traditional logic. This might suggest to an impartial observer (if there are any) that the abortion issue is unresolvable.

There is a way out of this apparent dialectical quandary. The moral generalizations of both sides are not quite correct. The generalizations hold for the most part, for the usual cases. This suggests that they are all *accidental* generalizations, that the moral claims made by those on both sides of the dispute do not touch on the *essence* of the matter.

This use of the distinction between essence and accident is not meant to invoke obscure metaphysical categories. Rather, it is intended to reflect the rather atheoretical nature of the abortion discussion. If the generalization a partisan in the abortion dispute adopts were derived from the reason why ending the life of a human being is wrong, then there could not be exceptions to that generalization unless some special case obtains in which there are even more powerful countervailing reasons. Such generalizations would not be merely accidental generalizations; they would point to, or be based upon, the essence of the wrongness of killing, what it is that makes killing wrong. All this suggests that a necessary condition of resolving the abortion controversy is a more theoretical account of the wrongness of killing. After all, if we merely believe, but do not understand, why killing adult human beings such as ourselves is wrong, how could we conceivably show that abortion is either immoral or permissible?

II

In order to develop such an account, we can start from the following unproblematic assumption concerning our own case: it is wrong to kill us. Why is it wrong? Some answers can be easily eliminated. It might be said that what makes killing us wrong is that a killing brutalizes the one who kills. But the brutalization consists of being inured to the performance of an act that is hideously immoral; hence, the brutalization does not explain the immorality. It might be said that what makes killing us wrong is the great loss others would experience due to our absence. Although such hubris is understandable, such an explanation does not account for the wrongness of killing hermits, or those whose lives are relatively independent and whose friends find it easy to make new friends.

A more obvious answer is better. What primarily makes killing wrong is neither its effect on the murderer nor its effect on the victim's friends and relatives, but its effect on the victim. The loss of one's life is one of the greatest losses one can suffer. The loss of one's life deprives one of all the experiences, activities, projects, and enjoyments that would otherwise have constituted one's future. Therefore, killing someone is wrong, primarily because the killing inflicts (one of) the greatest possible losses on the victim. To describe this as the loss of life can be misleading, however. The change in my biological state does not by itself make killing me wrong. The effect of the loss of my biological life is the loss to me of all those activities, projects, experiences, and enjoyments which would otherwise have constituted my future personal life. These activities, projects, experiences, and enjoyments are either valuable for their own sakes or are means to something else that is valuable for its own sake. Some parts of my future are not valued by me now, but will come to be valued by me as I grow older and as my values and capacities change. When I am killed, I am deprived both of what I now value which would have been part of my future personal life, but also what I would come to value. Therefore, when I die, I am deprived of all of the value of my future. Inflicting this loss on me is ultimately what makes killing me wrong. This being the case, it would seem that what makes killing *any* adult human being prima facie seriously wrong is the loss of his other future.[6]

How should this rudimentary theory of the wrongness of killing be evaluated? It cannot be faulted for deriving an "ought" from an "is," for it does not. The analysis assumes that killing me (or you, reader) is prima facie seriously wrong. The point of the analysis is to establish which natural property ultimately explains the wrongness of the killing, given that it is wrong. A natural property will ultimately explain the wrongness of killing, only if (1) the explanation fits with our intuitions about the matter and (2) there is no other natural property that provides the basis for a better explanation of the wrongness of killing. This analysis rests on the intuition that what makes killing a particular human or animal wrong is what it does to that particular human or animal. What makes killing wrong is some natural effect or other of the killing. Some would deny this. For instance, a divine command theorist in ethics would deny it. Surely this denial is, however, one of those features of divine-command theory which renders it so implausible.

The claim that what makes killing wrong is the loss of the victim's future is directly supported by two considerations. In the first place, this theory explains why we regard killing as one of the worst of crimes. Killing is especially wrong, because it deprives the victim of more than perhaps any other crime. In the second place, people with AIDS or cancer who know they are dying believe, of course, that dying is a very bad thing for them. They believe that the loss of a future to them that they would otherwise have experienced is what makes their premature death a very bad thing for them. A better theory of the wrongness of killing would require a different natural property associated with killing which better fits with the attitudes of the dying. What could it be?

The view that what makes killing wrong is the loss to the victim of the value of the victim's future gains additional support when some of its implications are examined. In the first place, it is incompatible with the view that it is wrong to kill only beings who are biologically human. It is possible that there exists a different species from another planet whose members have a future like ours. Since having a future like that is what makes killing someone wrong, this theory entails that it would be wrong to kill members of such a species. Hence, this theory is opposed to the claim that only life that is biologically human has great moral worth, a claim which many anti-abortionists have seemed to adopt. This opposition, which this theory has in common with personhood theories, seems to be a merit of the theory.

In the second place, the claim that the loss of one's future is the wrong-making feature of one's being killed entails the possibility that the futures of some actual nonhuman mammals on our own planet are sufficiently like ours that it is seriously wrong to kill them also. Whether some animals do have the same right to life as human beings depends on adding to the account of the wrongness of killing some additional account of just what it is about my future or the futures of other adult human beings which makes it wrong to kill us. No such additional account will be offered in this essay. Undoubtedly, the provision of such an account would be a very difficult matter. Undoubtedly, any such account would be quite controversial. Hence, it surely should not reflect badly on this sketch of an elementary theory of the wrongness of killing that it is indeterminate with respect to some very difficult issues regarding animal rights.

In the third place, the claim that the loss of one's future is the wrong-making feature of one's being killed does not entail, as sanctity of human life theories do, that active euthanasia is wrong. Persons who are severely and incurably ill, who face a future of pain and despair, and who wish to die will not have suffered a loss if they are killed. It is, strictly speaking, the value of a human's future which makes killing wrong in this theory. This being so, killing does not necessarily wrong some persons who are sick and dying. Of course, there may be other reasons for a prohibition of active euthanasia, but that is another matter. Sanctity-of-human-life theories seem to hold that active euthanasia is seriously wrong even in an individual case where there seems to be good reason for it independently of public policy considerations. This consequence is most implausible, and it is a plus for the claim that the loss of a future of value is what makes killing wrong that it does not share this consequence.

In the fourth place, the account of the wrongness of killing defended in this essay does straightforwardly entail that it is prima facie seriously wrong to kill children and infants, for we do presume that they have futures of value. Since we do believe that it is wrong to kill defenseless little babies, it is important that a theory of the wrongness of killing easily account for this. Personhood theories of the wrongness of killing, on the other hand, cannot straightforwardly account for the wrongness of killing infants and young children.[7] Hence, such theories must add special ad hoc accounts of the wrongness of killing the young. The plausibility of such ad hoc theories seems to be a function of how desperately one wants such theories to work. The claim that the primary wrong-making feature of a killing is the loss to the victim of the value of its future accounts for the wrongness of killing young children and infants directly; it makes the wrongness of such acts as obvious as we actually think it is. This is a further merit of this theory. Accordingly, it seems that this value of a future-like-ours theory of the wrongness of killing shares strengths of both sanctity-of-life and personhood accounts while avoiding weaknesses of both. In addition, it meshes with a central intuition concerning what makes killing wrong.

The claim that the primary wrong-making feature of a killing is the loss to the victim of the value of its future has obvious consequences for the ethics of abortion. The future of a standard fetus includes a set of experiences, projects, activities, and such which are identical with the futures of adult human beings and are identical with the futures of young children. Since the reason that is sufficient to explain why it is wrong to kill human beings after the time of birth is a reason that also applies to fetuses, it follows that abortion is prima facie seriously morally wrong.

This argument does not rely on the invalid inference that, since it is wrong to kill persons, it is wrong to kill potential persons also. The category that is morally central to this analysis is the category of having a valuable future like ours; it is not the category of personhood. The argument to the conclusion that abortion is prima facie seriously morally wrong proceeded independently of the notion of person or potential person or any equivalent. Someone may wish to start with this analysis in terms of the value of a human future, conclude that abortion is, except perhaps in rare circumstances, seriously morally wrong, infer that fetuses have the right to life, and then call fetuses "persons" as a result of their having the right to life. Clearly, in this case, the category of person is being used to state the *conclusion* of the analysis rather than to generate the *argument* of the analysis.

The structure of this anti-abortion argument can be both illuminated and defended by comparing it to what appears to be the best argument for the wrongness of the wanton infliction of pain on animals. This latter argument is based on the assumption that it is prima facie wrong to inflict pain on me (or you, reader). What is the natural property associated with the infliction of pain which makes such infliction wrong? The obvious answer seems to be that the infliction of pain causes suffering and that suffering is a misfortune. The suffering caused by the infliction of pain is what makes the wanton infliction of pain on me wrong. The wanton infliction of pain on other adult humans causes suffering. The wanton infliction of pain on animals causes suffering. Since causing suffering is what makes the wanton infliction of pain wrong and since the wanton infliction of pain on animals causes suffering, it follows that the wanton infliction of pain on animals is wrong.

This argument for the wrongness of the wanton infliction of pain on animals shares a number of structural features with the argument for the serious prima facie wrongness of abortion. Both arguments start with an obvious assumption concerning what it is wrong to do to me (or you, reader). Both then look for the characteristic or the consequence of the wrong action which makes the action wrong. Both recognize that the wrong-making feature of these immoral actions is a property of actions sometimes directed at individuals other than postnatal human beings. If the structure of the argument for the wrongness of the wanton infliction of pain on animals is sound, then the structure of the argument for the prima facie serious wrongness of abortion is also sound, for the structure of the two arguments is the same. The structure common to both is the key to the explanation of how the wrongness of abortion can be demonstrated without recourse to the category of person. In neither argument is that category crucial.

This defense of an argument for the wrongness of abortion in terms of a structurally similar argument for the wrongness of the wanton infliction of pain on animals succeeds only if the account regarding animals is the correct account. Is it? In the first place, it seems plausible. In the second place, its major competition is Kant's account. Kant believed that we do not have direct duties to animals at all, because they are not persons. Hence, Kant had to explain and justify the wrongness of inflicting pain on animals on the grounds that "he who is hard in his dealings with animals becomes hard also in his dealing with men."[8] The problem with Kant's account is that there seems to be no reason for accepting this latter claim unless Kant's account is rejected. If the alternative to Kant's account is accepted, then it is easy to understand why someone who is indifferent to inflicting pain on animals is also indifferent to inflicting pain on humans, for one is indifferent to what makes inflicting pain wrong in both cases. But, if Kant's account is accepted, there is no intelligible reason why one who is hard in his dealings with animals (or crabgrass or stones) should also be hard in his dealings with men. After all, men are persons: animals are no more persons than crabgrass or stones. Persons are Kant's crucial moral category. Why, in short, should a Kantian accept the basic claim in Kant's argument?

Hence, Kant's argument for the wrongness of inflicting pain on animals rests on a claim that, in a world of Kantian moral agents, is demonstrably false. Therefore, the alternative analysis, being more plausible anyway, should be accepted. Since this alternative analysis has the same structure as the anti-abortion argument being defended here, we have further support for the argument for the immorality of abortion being defended in this essay.

Of course, this value of a future-like-ours argument, if sound, shows only that abortion is prima facie wrong, not that it is wrong in any and all circumstances. Since the loss of the future to a standard fetus, if killed, is, however, at least as great a loss as the loss of the future to a standard adult human being who is killed, abortion, like ordinary killing, could be justified only by the most compelling reasons. The loss of one's life is almost the greatest misfortune that can happen to one. Presumably abortion could be justified in some circumstances, only if the loss consequent on failing to abort would be at least as great. Accordingly, morally permissible abortions will be rare indeed unless, perhaps, they occur so early in pregnancy that a fetus is not yet definitely an individual. Hence, this argument should be taken as showing that abortion is presumptively very seriously wrong, where the presumption is very strong—as strong as the presumption that killing another adult human being is wrong.

III

How complete an account of the wrongness of killing does the value of a future-like-ours account have to be in order that the wrongness of abortion is a consequence? This account does not have to be an account of the necessary conditions for the wrongness of killing. Some persons in nursing homes may lack valuable human futures, yet it may be wrong to kill them for other reasons. Furthermore, this account does not obviously have to be the sole reason killing is wrong where the victim did have a valuable future. This analysis claims only that, for any killing where the victim did have a valuable future like ours, having that future by itself is sufficient to create the strong presumption that the killing is seriously wrong.

One way to overturn the value of a future-like-ours argument would be to find some account of the wrongness of killing which is at least as intelligible and which has different implications for the ethics of abortion. Two rival accounts possess at least some degree of plausibility. One account is based on the obvious fact that people value the experience of living and wish for that valuable experience to continue. Therefore, it might be said, what makes killing wrong is the discontinuation of that experience for the victim. Let us call this the *discontinuation account.*[9] Another rival account is based upon the obvious fact that people strongly desire to continue to live. This suggests that what makes killing us so wrong is that it interferes with the fulfillment of a strong and fundamental desire, the fulfillment of which is necessary for the fulfillment of any other desires we might have. Let us call this the *desire account.*[10]

Consider first the desire account as a rival account of the ethics of killing which would provide the basis for rejecting the anti-abortion position. Such an account will have to be stronger than the value of a future-like-ours account of the wrongness of abortion if it is to do the job expected of it. To entail the wrongness of abortion, the value of a future-like-ours account has only to provide a sufficient, but not a necessary, condition for the wrongness of killing. The desire account, on the other hand, must provide us also with a necessary condition for the wrongness of killing in order to generate a pro-choice conclusion on abortion. The reason for this is that presumably the argument from the desire account moves from the claim that what makes killing wrong is interference with a very strong desire to the claim that abortion is not wrong because the fetus lacks a strong desire to live. Obviously, this inference fails if someone's having the desire to live is not a necessary condition of its being wrong to kill that individual.

One problem with the desire account is that we do regard it as seriously wrong to kill persons who have little desire to live or who have no desire to live or, indeed, have a desire not to live. We believe it is seriously wrong to kill the unconscious, the sleeping, those who are tired of life, and those who are suicidal. The value-of-a-human-future account renders standard morality intelligible in these cases; these cases appear to be incompatible with the desire account.

The desire account is subject to a deeper difficulty. We desire life, because we value the goods of this life. The goodness of life is not secondary to our desire for it. If this were not so, the pain of one's own premature death could be done away with merely by an appropriate alteration in the configuration of one's desires. This is absurd. Hence, it would seem that it is the loss of the goods of one's future, not the interference with the fulfillment of a strong desire to live, which accounts ultimately for the wrongness of killing.

It is worth noting that, if the desire account is modified so that it does not provide a necessary, but only a sufficient, condition for the wrongness of killing, the desire account is compatible with the value of a future-like-ours account. The combined accounts will yield an anti-abortion ethic. This suggests that one can retain what is intuitively plausible about the desire account without a challenge to the basic argument of this paper.

It is also worth noting that, if future desires have moral force in a modified desire account of the wrongness of killing, one can find support for an anti-abortion ethic even in the absence of a value of a future-like-ours account. If one decides that a morally relevant property, the possession of which is sufficient to make it wrong to kill some individual, is the desire at some future time to live—one might decide to justify one's refusal to kill suicidal teenagers on these grounds, for example—then, since typical fetuses will have the desire in the future to live, it is wrong to kill typical fetuses. Accordingly, it does not seem that a desire account of the wrongness of killing can provide a justification of a pro-choice ethic of abortion which is nearly as adequate as the value of a human-future justification of an anti-abortion ethic.

The discontinuation account looks more promising as an account of the wrongness of killing. It seems just as intelligible as the value of a future-like-ours account, but it does not justify an anti-abortion position. Obviously, if it is the continuation of one's activities, experiences, and projects, the loss of which makes killing wrong, then it is not wrong to kill fetuses for that reason, for fetuses do not have experiences, activities, and projects to be continued or discontinued. Accordingly, the discontinuation account does not have the antiabortion consequences that the value of a future-like-ours account has. Yet, it seems as intelligible as the value of a future-like-ours account, for when we think of what would be wrong with our being killed, it does seem as if it is the discontinuation of what makes our lives worthwhile which makes killing us wrong.

Is the discontinuation account just as good an account as the value of a future-like-ours account? The discontinuation account will not be adequate at all, if it does not refer to the *value* of the experience that may be discontinued. One does not want the discontinuation account to make it wrong to kill a patient who begs for death and who is in severe pain that cannot be relieved short of killing. (I leave open the question of whether it is wrong for other reasons.) Accordingly, the discontinuation account must be more than a bare discontinuation account. It must make some reference to the positive value of the patient's experiences. But, by the same token, the value of a future-like-ours account cannot be a bare future account either. Just having a future surely does not itself rule out killing the above patient. This account must make some reference to the value of the patient's future experiences and projects also. Hence, both accounts involve the value of experiences, projects, and activities. So far we still have symmetry between the accounts.

The symmetry fades, however, when we focus on the time period of the value of the experiences, etc., which has moral consequences. Although both accounts leave open the possibility that the patient in our example may be killed, this possibility is left open only in virtue of the utterly bleak future for the patient. It makes no difference whether the patient's immediate past contains intolerable pain, or consists in being in a coma (which we can imagine is a situation of indifference), or consists in a life of value. If the patient's future is a future of value, we want our account to make it wrong to kill the patient. If the patient's future is intolerable, whatever his or her immediate past, we want our account to allow killing the patient. Obviously, then, it is the value of that patient's future which is doing the work in rendering the morality of killing the patient intelligible.

This being the case, it seems clear that whether one has immediate past experiences or not does no work in the explanation of what makes killing wrong. The addition the discontinuation account makes to the value of a human future account is otiose. Its addition to the value-of-a-future account plays no role at all in rendering intelligible the wrongness of killing. Therefore, it can be discarded with the discontinuation account of which it is a part.

IV

The analysis of the previous section suggests that alternative general accounts of the wrongness of killing are either inadequate or unsuccessful in getting around the anti-abortion consequences of the value of a future-like-ours argument. A different strategy for avoiding these anti-abortion consequences involves limiting the scope of the value of a future argument. More precisely, the strategy involves arguing that fetuses lack a property that is essential for the value-of-a-future argument (or for any anti-abortion argument) to apply to them.

One move of this sort is based upon the claim that a necessary condition of one's future being valuable is that one values it. Value implies a valuer. Given this one might argue that, since fetuses cannot value their futures, their futures are not valuable to them. Hence, it does not seriously wrong them deliberately to end their lives.

This move fails, however, because of some ambiguities. Let us assume that something cannot be of value unless it is valued by someone. This does not entail that my life is of no value unless it is valued by me. I may think, in a period of despair, that my future is of no worth whatsoever, but I may be wrong because others rightly see value—even great value—in it. Furthermore, my future can be valuable to me even if I do not value it. This is the case when a young person attempts suicide, but is rescued and goes on to significant human achievements. Such young people's futures are ultimately valuable to them, even though such futures do not seem to be valuable to them at the moment of attempted suicide. A fetus's future can be valuable to it in the same way. Accordingly, this attempt to limit the anti-abortion argument fails.

Another similar attempt to reject the anti-abortion position is based on Tooley's claim that an entity cannot possess the right to life unless it has the capacity to desire its continued existence. It follows that, since fetuses lack the conceptual capacity to desire to continue to live, they lack the right to life. Accordingly, Tooley concludes that abortion cannot be seriously prima facie wrong (*op. cit.,* pp. 46–47).

What could be the evidence for Tooley's basic claim? Tooley once argued that individuals have a prima facie right to what they desire and that the lack of the capacity to desire something undercuts the basis of one's right to it (*op. cit.,* pp. 44–45). This argument plainly will not succeed in the context of the analysis of this essay, however, since the point here is to establish the fetus's right to life on other grounds. Tooley's argument assumes that the right to life cannot be established in general on some basis other than the desire for life. This position was considered and rejected in the preceding section of this paper.

One might attempt to defend Tooley's basic claim on the grounds that, because a fetus cannot apprehend continued life as a benefit, its continued life cannot be a benefit or cannot be something it has a right to or cannot be something that is in its interest. This might be defended in terms of the general proposition that, if an individual is literally incapable of caring about or taking an interest in some X, then one does not have a right to X or X is not a benefit or X is not something that is in one's interest.[11]

Each member of this family of claims seems to be open to objections. As John C. Stevens[12] has pointed out, one may have a right to be treated with a certain medical procedure (because of a health insurance policy one has purchased), even though one cannot conceive of the nature of the procedure. And, as Tooley himself has pointed out, persons who have been indoctrinated, or drugged, or rendered temporarily unconscious may be literally incapable of caring about or taking an interest in something that is in their interest or is something to which they have a right, or is something that benefits them. Hence, the Tooley claim that would restrict the scope of the value of a future-like-ours argument is undermined by counterexamples.[13]

Finally, Paul Bassen[14] has argued that, even though the prospects of an embryo might seem to be a basis for the wrongness of abortion, an embryo cannot be a victim and therefore cannot be wronged. An embryo cannot be a victim, he says, because it lacks sentience. His central argument for this seems to be that, even though plants and the permanently unconscious are alive, they clearly cannot be victims. What is the explanation of this? Bassen claims that the explanation is that their lives consist of mere metabolism and mere metabolism is not enough to ground victimizability. Mentation is required.

The problem with this attempt to establish the absence of victimizability is that both plants and the permanently unconscious clearly lack what Bassen calls "prospects" or what I have called "a future life like ours." Hence, it is surely open to one to argue that the real reason we believe plants and the permanently unconscious cannot be victims is that killing them cannot deprive them of a future life like ours; the real reason is not their absence of present mentation.

Bassen recognizes that his view is subject to this difficulty, and he recognizes that the case of children seems to support this difficulty, for "much of what we do for children is based on prospects." He argues, however, that, in the case of children and in other such cases "potentiality comes into play only where victimizability has been secured on other grounds" (ibid., p. 333).

Bassen's defense of his view is patently question-begging, since what is adequate to secure victimizability is exactly what is at issue. His examples do not support his own view against the thesis of this essay. Of course, embryos can be victims: when their lives are deliberately terminated, they are deprived of their futures of value, their prospects. This makes them victims, for it directly wrongs them.

The seeming plausibility of Bassen's view stems from the fact that paradigmatic cases of imagining someone as a victim involve empathy, and empathy requires mentation of the victim. The victims of flood, famine, rape, or child abuse are all persons with whom we can empathize. That empathy seems to be part of seeing them as victims.[15]

In spite of the strength of these examples, the attractive intuition that a situation in which there is victimization requires the possibility of empathy is subject to counterexamples. Consider a case that Bassen himself offers: "Posthumous obliteration of an author's work constitutes a misfortune for him only if he had wished his work to endure" (*op. cit.,* p. 318). The conditions Bassen wishes to impose upon the possibility of being victimized here seem far too strong. Perhaps this author, due to his unrealistic standards of excellence and his low self-esteem, regarded his work as unworthy of survival, even though it possessed genuine literary merit. Destruction of such work would surely victimize its author. In such a case, empathy with the victim concerning the loss is clearly impossible.

Of course, Bassen does not make the possibility of empathy a necessary condition of victimizability; he requires only mentation. Hence, on Bassen's actual view, this author, as I have described him, can be a victim. The problem is that the basic intuition that renders Bassen's view plausible is missing in the author's case. In order to attempt to avoid counterexamples, Bassen has made his thesis too weak to be supported by the intuitions that suggested it.

Even so, the mentation requirement on victimizability is still subject to counterexamples. Suppose a severe accident renders me totally unconscious for a month, after which I recover. Surely killing me while I am unconscious victimizes me, even though I am incapable of mentation during that time. It follows that Bassen's thesis fails. Apparently, attempts to restrict the value of a future-like-ours argument so that fetuses do not fall within its scope do not succeed.

V

In this essay, it has been argued that the correct ethic of the wrongness of killing can be extended to fetal life and used to show that there is a strong presumption that any abortion is morally impermissible. If the ethic of killing adopted here entails, however, that contraception is also seriously immoral, then there would appear to be a difficulty with the analysis of this essay.

But this analysis does not entail that contraception is wrong. Of course, contraception prevents the actualization of a possible future of value. Hence, it follows from the claim that futures of value should be maximized that contraception is prima facie immoral. This obligation to maximize does not exist, however; furthermore, nothing in the ethics of killing in this paper entails that it does. The ethics of killing in this essay would entail that contraception is wrong only if something were denied a human future of value by contraception. Nothing at all is denied such a future by contraception, however.

Candidates for a subject of harm by contraception fall into four categories: (1) some sperm or other, (2) some ovum or other, (3) a sperm and an ovum separately, and (4) a sperm and an ovum together. Assigning the harm to some sperm is utterly arbitrary, for no reason can be given for making a sperm the subject of harm rather than an ovum. Assigning the harm to some ovum is utterly arbitrary, for no reason can be given for making an ovum the subject of harm rather than a sperm. One might attempt to avoid these problems by insisting that contraception deprives both the sperm and the ovum separately of a valuable future like ours. On this alternative, too many futures are lost. Contraception was supposed to be wrong, because it deprived us of one future of value, not two. One might attempt to avoid this problem by holding that contraception deprives the combination of sperm and ovum of a valuable future like ours. But here the definite article misleads. At the time of contraception, there are hundreds of millions of sperm, one (released) ovum and millions of possible combinations of all of these. There is no actual combination at all. Is the subject of the loss to be a merely possible combination? Which one? This alternative does not yield an actual subject of harm either. Accordingly, the immorality of contraception is not entailed by the loss of a future-like-ours argument simply because there is no nonarbitrarily identifiable subject of the loss in the case of contraception.

VI

The purpose of this essay has been to set out an argument for the serious presumptive wrongness of abortion subject to the assumption that the moral permissibility of abortion stands or falls on the moral status of the fetus. Since a fetus possesses a property, the possession of which in adult human beings is sufficient to make killing an adult human being wrong, abortion is wrong. This way of dealing with the problem of abortion seems superior to other approaches to the ethics of abortion, because it rests on an ethics of killing which is close to self-evident, because the crucial morally relevant property clearly applies to fetuses, and because the argument avoids the usual equivocations on "human life," "human being," or "person." The argument rests neither on religious claims nor on Papal dogma. It is not subject to the objection of "speciesism." Its soundness is compatible with the moral permissibility of euthanasia and contraception. It deals with our intuitions concerning young children.

Finally, this analysis can be viewed as resolving a standard problem—indeed, *the* standard problem—concerning the ethics of abortion. Clearly, it is wrong to kill adult human beings. Clearly, it is not wrong to end the life of some arbitrarily chosen single human cell. Fetuses seem to be like arbitrarily chosen human cells in some respects and like adult humans in other respects. The problem of the ethics of abortion is the problem of determining the fetal property that settles this moral controversy. The thesis of this essay is that the problem of the ethics of abortion, so understood, is solvable.

Endnotes

1. Feinberg, "Abortion," in *Matters of Life and Death: New Introductory Essays in Moral Philosophy,* Tom Regan, ed. (New York: Random House, 1986), pp. 256–293; Tooley, "Abortion and Infanticide," *Philosophy and Public Affairs* 11, 1 (1972), 37–65, Tooley, *Abortion and Infanticide* (New York: Oxford, 1984); Warren, "On the Moral and Legal Status of Abortion," *The Monist* LVIX, 1 (1973), 4361; Engelhardt, "The Ontology of Abortion," *Ethics* LXXXIV, 3 (1974), 217–234; Sumner, *Abortion and Moral Theory* (Princeton: University Press, 1981); Noonan "An Almost Absolute Value in History," in *The Morality of Abortion: Legal and Historical Perspectives,* Noonan, ed. (Cambridge: Harvard, 1970); and Devine, *The Ethics of Homicide* (Ithaca: Cornell, 1978).
2. For interesting discussions of this issue, see Warren Quinn, "Abortion: Identity and Loss," *Philosophy and Public Affairs* XIII, 1 (1984), 24–54; and Lawrence C. Becker, "Human Being: The Boundaries of the Concept," *Philosophy and Public Affairs* IV, 4 (1975), 334–359.
3. For example, see my "Ethics and the Elderly: Some Problems," in Stuart Spicker, Kathleen Woodward, and David van Tassel, eds., *Aging and the Elderly: Humanistic Perspectives in Gerontology* (Atlantic Highlands, NJ: Humanities, 1978), pp. 341–355.
4. See Warren, *op. cit.,* and Tooley "Abortion and Infanticide."
5. This seems to be the fatal flaw in Warren's treatment of this issue.
6. I have been most influenced on this matter by Jonathan Glover, *Causing Death and Saving Lives* (New York: Penguin, 1977), ch. 3; and Robert Young, "What Is So Wrong with Killing People?" *Philosophy* LIV, 210 (1979), 515–528.
7. Feinberg, Tooley, Warren, and Engelhardt have all dealt with this problem.
8. "Duties to Animals and Spirits," in *Lectures on Ethics,* Louis Infeld, trans. (New York: Harper, 1963), p. 239.
9. I am indebted to Jack Bricke for raising this objection.
10. Presumably a preference utilitarian would press such an objection. Tooley once suggested that his account has such a theoretical underpinning. See his "Abortion and Infanticide," pp. 44–45.
11. Donald VanDeVeer seems to think this is self-evident. See his "Whither Baby Doe?" in *Matters of Life and Death,* p. 233.
12. "Must the Bearer of a Right Have the Concept of That to Which He Has a Right?" *Ethics* XCV, 1 (1984), 68–74.
13. See Tooley again in "Abortion and Infanticide," pp. 47–49.
14. "Present Sakes and Future Prospects: The Status of Early Abortion," *Philosophy and Public Affairs* XI, 4 (1982), 322–326.
15. Note carefully the reasons he gives on the bottom of p. 316.

Journal/Discussion Questions

✍ *Take some time to reflect on what makes killing wrong* for you. *Why do you think it is wrong? Is it because you believe people have a right to life? If so, what is the basis for that right? Is it because of the suffering that the person being killed experiences? What if the killing were sudden and painless? Would that make it less objectionable?*

1. Marquis maintains that what's wrong with killing someone is that the person who is killed suffers the loss of his or her life, and "the loss of one's life deprives one of all the experiences, activities, projects, and enjoyments that would otherwise have constituted one's future." Do you agree that this is what makes killing wrong?
2. At the beginning of his article, Marquis dismisses two proposed candidates for explaining the wrongness of killing—the effects on the perpetrator and the effects on the victim's family and friends—in favor of his own analysis. Why do you think that Marquis considers and rejects these two particular claims? Can there be more than one thing that is wrong with killing people or must wrongness always be reduced to a single factor?
3. Imagine that you are the First Officer of the U.S.S. Enterprise and head of a landing party being beamed down to a planet that you don't have any previous knowledge of. How would you decide which beings on the planet ought not to be killed? Marquis suggests that it would be morally wrong to kill any being that has a future like ours. Is this the criterion that you would use?
4. Marquis argues that "personhood theories of the wrongness of killing . . . cannot straightforwardly account for the wrongness of killing infants and young children." Recall the discussion of personhood theories presented in Jane English's article. Do you think that Marquis's criticism of such theories is justified? Why?
5. The future-like-ours argument, Marquis maintains, does not entail the claim that contraception is morally wrong. Do you think that Marquis is justified in this claim? Does it depend on the kind of contraception? At what point does an entity have a future like ours? At the moment of conception? Implantation? Or later?
6. Do you think that abortion involves killing an innocent human being? If it does, is it murder?

Concluding Discussion Questions

Where Do You Stand Now?

Instructions

You have already answered the following questions in your moral problems self-quiz at the beginning of this book. Now that you have studied the material in this section, take a moment to answer the same questions again.

	Strongly Agree	*Agree*	*Undecided*	*Disagree*	*Strongly Disagree*	*Chapter 1: Abortion*
1.	❑	❑	❑	❑	❑	The principal moral consideration about abortion is the question of whether the fetus is a person or not.
2.	❑	❑	❑	❑	❑	The principal moral consideration about abortion is the question of the rights of the pregnant woman.
3.	❑	❑	❑	❑	❑	The only one who should have a voice in making the decision about an abortion is the pregnant woman.
4.	❑	❑	❑	❑	❑	Abortion should be legal but morally discouraged.
5.	❑	❑	❑	❑	❑	Abortion protesters are justified in breaking the law in order to prevent abortions.

Now compare your answers to the present self-quiz with the answers to the initial self-quiz. How, if at all, have your answers changed? How have the *reasons* for your answers changed?

Journal/Discussion Questions

- ✍ *You have now read, thought, and discussed a number of aspects of the morality of the abortion decision. How have your views* changed *and developed? What idea had the greatest impact on your thinking about abortion?*
- ✍ *Imagine that a close friend at another college just called you to tell you that she was pregnant and that she didn't know what to do. Although she is not asking you to tell her what to do, she does ask you to tell her what* you *believe about abortion. Write her a letter in which you tell her what your own beliefs are. Talk, among other things, about what sorts of factors should be taken into consideration.*

✍ *If you were going to have a baby, to what extent would you want to select its characteristics in advance? Which characteristics, if any, would you not want to consciously select? Physical characteristics? Physical and mental capabilities? Personality traits? Sex? Sexual orientation?*

1. What, in the readings in this chapter, was the most thought-provoking idea you encountered? In what ways did it prompt you to reconsider some of your previous beliefs?
2. Has your overall position on the morality of abortion changed? If so, in what way(s)? If your position has not changed, have your reasons developed in any way? If so, in what way(s)? Has your understanding changed of the reasons supporting other positions that are different from your own? If so, in what way(s)?

For Further Reading

Web Resources

For an overview of Web-based resources relating to abortion, including relevant Supreme Court decisions, see the abortion page of *Ethics Updates (http://ethics.acusd.edu).* Among the resources listed there on abortion is an excellent article in the *Boston Review* on abortion by Judith Jarvis Thomson and Philip L. Quinn, Donald Regan, Douglas Laycock, Drucilla Cornell, Peter de Marneffe, and a rejoinder by Judith Jarvis Thomson. A link to George McKenna's "On Abortion: A Lincolnian Position," on the *Atlantic Monthly* site is also provided. Steven Schwartz's *The Moral Question of Abortion* is also available on-line. I have also gathered a set of on-line resources on *Mizuko Kuyo,* the memorial rites for the spirits of departed fetuses in Japan. There is also a link to a real audio interview of Don Marquis by Hugh LaFollette.

Journals

There are a number of excellent journals in ethics which contain articles on virtually all of the topics treated in this book. These include *Ethics,* the oldest and arguably the finest of the ethics journals; *Philosophy and Public Affairs,* which—as its name implies—places special emphasis on questions of public rather than private morality; *Journal of Social Philosophy,* which often contains articles on the cutting edge of social controversies; *Social Philosophy and Policy,* which is devoted to a particular topic each issue (such as Liberalism and the Economic Order; Altruism; Property Rights; and Crime, Culpability, and Remedy); and *Public Affairs Quarterly,* which contains a number of articles on the ethical dimensions of public policy issues. In addition to these, see the *Hastings Center Reports, BioEthics, Kennedy Institute of Ethics, Journal of Medicine and Philosophy, Biomedical Ethics Reviews,* and *Law, Medicine & Health Care* for discussion of issues relating specifically to biomedical ethics.

Review Articles and Reports

For a comprehensive bibliographical guide to *abortion,* see Diane E. Fitzpatrick, *A History of Abortion in the United States: A Working Bibliography of Journal Articles* (Monticello, IL: Vance Bibliographies, 1991). For excellent surveys of the philosophical issues, see Mary Anne Warren, "Abortion," in *A Companion to Ethics,* edited by Peter Singer (Oxford: Blackwell, 1991), pp. 303–314, and Nancy (Ann) Davis, "Abortion," *Encyclopedia of Ethics,* edited by Lawrence C. Becker and Charlotte B. Becker (New York: Garland, 1992), Vol. I, pp. 2–6. For demographic data, see Paul Sachdev, *International Handbook on Abortion* (New York: Greenwood Press, 1988).

Anthologies and Books

There are a number of excellent *anthologies* of selections dealing solely with the issue of abortion. *The Problem of Abortion*, 3rd ed., edited by Susan Dwyer and Joel Feinberg (Belmont, CA: Wadsworth, 1996) contains a number of important pieces covering a wide range of positions, as does *The Ethics of Abortion: Pro-Life vs. Pro-Choice,* rev. ed., edited by Robert M. Baird and Stuart E. Rosenbaum (Buffalo: Prometheus Books, 1993). Lewis M. Schwartz's *Arguing about Abortion* (Belmont, CA: Wadsworth, 1993) not only contains a number of important essays, but also (a) provides a well-done introduction to reconstructing and evaluating argumentative discourse and (b) offers an outline and analysis of six of the essays contained in the anthology. *Abortion: Moral and Legal Perspectives,* edited by Jay L. Garfield and Patricia Hennessey (Amherst: University of Massachusetts Press, 1984) contains several new essays as well as reprints of some previously published pieces. Also see Marshall Cohen, Thomas Nagel, and Thomas Scanlon, eds., *Rights and Wrongs of Abortion* (Princeton: Princeton University Press, 1974) and John T. Noonan, Jr., ed., *The Morality of Abortion: Legal and Historical Perspectives* (Cambridge: Harvard University Press, 1970). The anthology, *Abortion: Understanding Differences,* edited by Sidney Callahan and Daniel Callahan (New York: Plenum Press, 1984) contains a number of perceptive essays. For an excellent selection of both philosophical and popular articles, see *Abortion: Opposing Viewpoints,* edited by Tamara L. Roleff (San Diego, CA: Greenhaven Press, 1997).

Among the many excellent books on abortion, see L.W. Sumner, *Abortion and Moral Theory* (Princeton: Princeton University Press, 1981) for a carefully reasoned moderate view on the permissibility of abortion. Rosiland Hursthouse's *Beginning Lives* (Oxford: Basil Blackwell, 1987) includes a perceptive account of the issue of abortion. John T. Noonan, Jr., who represents a conservative Catholic view, has several books on this issue, including *How to Argue About Abortion* (New York, 1974) and *A Private Choice: Abortion in America in the Seventies* (New York: The Free Press, 1979); Germain G. Grisez's *Abortion: The Myths, the Realities, and the Arguments* (New York: Corpus Books, 1970) also argues for a strongly conservative view. Baruch Brody's *Abortion and the Sanctity of Human Life: A Philosophical View* (Cambridge, MA: The MIT Press, 1975) defends a fairly conservative view, arguing that the fetus becomes a person when brain activity begins. Michael Tooley's *Abortion and Infanticide* (Oxford: Clarendon Press, 1983) presents some controversial arguments in support of abortion and situates the issue within the larger context of infanticide and the killing of non-human animals. Bonnie Steinbock's *Life Before Birth: The Moral and Legal Status of Embryos and Fetuses* (New York: Oxford, 1992) concentrates primarily on the issue of the status of embryos and fetuses, while F.M. Kamm's *Creation and Abortion* (New York: Oxford, 1992) develops a broader theory of creating new people responsibility, and explores the issue of abortion within this context. Also see Stephen D. Schwarz, *The Moral Question of Abortion* (Chicago: Loyola University Press, 1990). For an excellent CD-ROM introduction to this issue, see *The Issue of Abortion in America,* by Robert Cavalier, Liz Style, Preston Covey, and Andrew Thompson (Routledge, 1998).

Key Essays

Among philosophers, there are several key essays that have set the stage for the philosophical discussion of abortion. The most reprinted essay in contemporary philosophy is probably Judith

Jarvis Thomson's "A Defense of Abortion," which originally appeared in the inaugural issue of *Philosophy and Public Affairs* Vol. 1, No. 1 (Fall 1971), pp. 47–66 and is reprinted in her *Rights, Restitution, & Risk: Essays in Moral Theory* (Cambridge: Harvard University Press, 1986)—which also contains her "Rights and Deaths," a reply to several critics of her initial essay—and in both the Feinberg and the Schwarz anthologies cited above. Thomson's article has elicited a number of replies; one of the more recent and insightful of these is John Martin Fisher, "Abortion and Self-Determination," *Journal of Social Philosophy* Vol. XXII, No. 2 (Fall 1991), pp. 5–13. On the issue of responsibility for pregnancy in Thomson's example, see David Boonin-Vail, "A Defense of 'A Defense of Abortion': On the Responsibility Objection to Thomson's Argument," *Ethics* 107, 2 (January 1997), 286–313. John T. Noonan, Jr.'s "An Almost Absolute Value in History," is also widely reprinted (including in Noonan's *The Morality of Abortion,* cited above) and is a strong, classic statement of the conservative view. Joel Feinberg's "Abortion," in *Matters of Life and Death,* edited by Tom Regan (New York: Random House, 1980), pp. 183–217 is a careful and nuanced discussion of the question of the moral status of the fetus. Roger Werthheimer's "Understanding the Abortion Argument," *Philosophy and Public Affairs* Vol. 1, No. 1 (Fall 1971), pp. 67–95 presents strong arguments for a fairly conservative view. Mary Anne Warren's "On the Moral and Legal Status of Abortion," *The Monist* Vol. 57 (1973) argues for a strongly liberal position, maintaining that the fetus is not a person.

For a good collection of essays on the *status of the fetus,* see *Biomedical Ethics Reviews: Bioethics and the Fetus: Medical, Moral, and Legal Issues,* edited by James M. Humber and Robert Almeder (Clifton, NJ: Humana Press, 1991) and Peter Singer et al., eds., *Embryo Experimentation* (New York: Cambridge University Press). For a critique of the philosophical viability of the notion of the "pre-embryo," see A.A. Howsepian, "Who or What Are We?" *Review of Metaphysics* Vol. 45, No. 3 (March 1992), pp. 483–502, which replied to Richard McCormick's "Who or What is the Pre-embryo?" in the *Kennedy Institute of Ethics Journal* Vol. 1 (1991), pp. 1–15; Alan Holland, "A Fortnight of My Life Is Missing: A Discussion of the Status of the Human 'Pre-Embryo,'" *Applied Philosophy,* edited by Brenda Almond and Donald Hill (London: Routledge, 1991), pp. 299–311.

For background on the *principle of double effect,* see Joseph T. Mangan, "An Historical Analysis of the Principle of Double Effect," *Theological Studies* Vol. 10 (1949), pp. 41–61. G. E. M. Anscombe's "Modern Moral Philosophy," *Philosophy* Vol. 33 (1958), pp. 26–42, raises important questions about the distinction between intended consequences and foreseen consequences. Phillipa Foot expresses doubts about the moral significance of this distinction in her article, "Abortion and the Doctrine of Double Effect," in her *Virtues and Vices and Other Essays* (Berkeley: University of California Press, 1978), pp. 19–32. For a short survey of the philosophical issues surrounding this principle, see William David Solomon, "Double Effect," *Encyclopedia of Ethics,* edited by Lawrence C. Becker and Charlotte B. Becker (New York: Garland, 1992), Vol. I, pp. 268–269.

Narratives

On *women's experiences with the abortion decision,* see Carol Gilligan, *In a Different Voice* (Cambridge: Harvard University Press, 1982), which contains in-depth interviews with young women who have faced the abortion decision. Linda Bird Francke's *The Ambiguity of Abortion* (New York: Random House, 1978) is an excellent source of interviews with women of all ages who have had abortions. Martha Bolton's "Responsible Women and Abortion Decisions," in

Having Children: Philosophical and Legal Reflections (New York: Oxford University Press, 1979), pp. 40–51 places the decision within the context of the narratives of individual women's lives. For collections of narratives about abortion, see *The Choices We Made: Twenty-five Women and Men Speak Out About Abortion,* edited by Angela Bonavoglia (New York: Random House, 1991). For a fascinating portrait of individuals involved on all sides of the abortion controversy, see Faye D. Ginsburg, *Contested Lives: The Abortion Debate in an American Community* (Berkeley: University of California Press, 1989). Also see Denise Winn, *Experiences of Abortion* (London: Macdonald, 1988) and Ellen Messer and Kathryn E. May, *Back Rooms: Voices from the Abortion Era* (New York: Simon & Schuster, 1988) and *The Voices of Women: Abortion, in Their Own Words* (Washington, DC: National Abortion Rights Action League, 1989).

Abortion and the Law

On *Roe v. Wade,* see especially David J. Garrow, *Liberty and Sexuality. The Right to Privacy and the Making of Roe v. Wade* (New York: Macmillan, 1994). For a broader history, see Mary Ann Glendon, *Abortion and Divorce in Western Law* (Cambridge: Harvard University Press, 1987).

On Finding a Common Ground

Several recent contributions to the search for common ground in the abortion discussion are Laurence H. Tribe, *Abortion: The Clash of Absolutes* (New York: Norton, 1992); Roger Rosenblatt, *Life Itself* (New York: Vintage Books, 1992); Ronald Dworkin, *Life's Dominion: An Argument about Abortion, Euthanasia, and Individual Freedom* (New York: Knopf, 1993); and Elizabeth Mensch and Alan Freeman, *The Politics of Virtue. Is Abortion Debatable?* (Durham: Duke University Press, 1993). For an excellent review of Tribe's book, see Nancy (Ann) Davis, "The Abortion Debate: The Search for Common Ground," *Ethics* Vol. 103, No. 3 (April 1993), pp. 516–539 and Vol. 103, No. 4 (July 1993), 731–778. For a discussion of abortion within the general context of a theory of compromise, see Martin Benjamin, *Splitting the Difference: Compromise and Integrity in Ethics and Politics* (Lawrence, KS: University of Kansas Press, 1990), esp. pp. 151–171.

CHAPTER 2

Cloning and Reproductive Technologies

NARRATIVE ACCOUNT

David Shenk
"Biocapitalism: What Price the Genetic Revolution?"

David Shenk is a writer who lives in Washington, D.C. His most recent books are The End of Patience *and* Data Smog: The Information Glut.

In this article, Shenk combines personal narrative with fundamental questions about the limits of the genetic revolution.

About a year ago, my wife phoned to say that something might be wrong with our unborn child. A blood test suggested the possibility of Down syndrome, and the doctor was recommending amniocentesis and genetic counseling. As it happened, I was almost finished writing a book about the paradoxical nature of information technology—the strange realization that more, faster, even better information can sometimes do more harm than good. When my wife's obstetrician reported the alarming news, it seemed as though the God of Technology was already looking to settle the score. The doctor, after all, was merely reading from a computer printout. Test results poured over us in a gush of formulas and statistics. My wife's blood contained such-and-such a ratio of three fetal hormones, which translated statistically into a such-and-such increased chance of our child having an extra chromosome, a forty-seventh, which can cause severely limited intellectual capacity, deformed organs and limbs, and heart dysfunction. The amniocentesis would settle the matter for certain, allowing a lab technician to count the fetus's actual chromosomes. But there was a dark statistical specter here, too, a chance that the procedure itself would lead to a spontaneous miscarriage whether the fetus was genetically abnormal or not. Testing a healthy fetus to death: many times in the days ahead, I wondered if I could come to terms with that ultracontemporary brand of senselessness. The computer thought it a risk worth taking: the chance of miscarriage was slightly lower than the chance of discovering Down syndrome.

My wife and I put our faith in the computer.

Few of these details will seem familiar to parents of children born before this decade; nor will any parents of children born after, say, 2010 face our specific predicament. The discoveries in the field have been generating one astonishing headline after another about genes related to Alzheimer's, breast cancer, epilepsy, osteoporosis, obesity, and even neurosis; the fetal-genetics revolution is now so accelerated that remarkable technologies become obsolete almost as quickly as they are invented. Although the "triple marker" blood test was invented in the late 1980s, it probably will be a historical footnote a decade or so from now. So will amniocentesis. Both will be replaced by a genetic sampling of fetal cells extracted from the mother's blood, a test that will be risk free for both mother and fetus. That's hundreds of healthy fetuses every year who will not be lost just for the sake of a genetic snapshot. We will know much more for much less.

But the odd question arises: Will we know too much? Fetal and embryonic genetic karyotypes may ultimately be as legible as a topographical map: Your son will be born healthy; he will be allergic to cashews; he will reach five foot ten and a half inches; math will not come easily to him; in his later years, he will be at high risk for the same type of arteriosclerosis that afflicted his great-grandfather. Here are secrets from the heretofore indecipherable text "The Book of Man," the wishful term used by researchers to refer to the complete translation of human genetic information that they one day hope to acquire. Such a discovery is what C.S. Lewis foresaw when he warned, in a prescient 1944 essay The Abolition of Man, "The final stage is come when Man by eugenics, by pre-natal conditioning . . . has obtained full control over himself."

I'm jumping ahead, far beyond present facts and into the future. "The Book of Man" will not be finished for some time, if ever. But with the U.S. government's staunch support of the Human Genome Project, the $3 billion mega-research sprint to map out and decode all of the estimated 100,000 human genes by the year 2005, genetic knowledge has suddenly become a national priority. It is this generation's race to the moon, but we're not quite sure what we'll do when we get there; what the dark side looks like most of us don't particularly want to imagine.

We're pursuing the human genome for good reasons, of course. With our new syllabus of genetic knowledge, we will become healthier and live longer. But even with the few facts that we now have, there is already cause to worry about the unintended consequences of acquiring such knowledge. If genes are the biological machine code the software—containing the instructions for each person's development and decay, unlocking that code portends the ability to fix the bugs and even to add new features. When people worry aloud that we may soon be "playing God," it's because no living creature has ever before been able to upgrade its own operating system.

Lewis suggests that such absolute biotechnological power is corruptive, that it robs humanity of its instinctive duty to posterity. "It is not that they are bad men," he writes of future genetic "Conditioners." "They are not men at all. Stepping outside the Tao"—that is, outside the moral order as dictated by Nature—"they have stepped into the void." Although not yet close to a moral void, we do, even at this primitive stage of biotechnology, effortlessly step outside the Tao. Consider, for example, that when my wife and I went in for amniocentesis, we did so with the tacit understanding that we would abort our child if we discovered that he or she was carrying the extra chromosome; otherwise, there would have been no point in risking miscarriage. The fact that we did not abort our child, that she was born healthy, with forty-six chromosomes and four chambers in her heart and two lungs and two long legs, is morally beside the point. We had made our if then choice to terminate. I suppose I'm glad I had the legal freedom to make that choice; I know, though, that I'm still haunted by the odd moral burden it imposed on me: Here is a preview of your daughter. If she's defective, will you keep her?

We all want a world without Down's and Alzheimer's and Huntington's. But when the vaccine against these disorders takes the form of genetic knowledge and when that knowledge comes with a sneak preview of the full catalogue of weaknesses in each of us, solutions start to look like potential problems. With the early peek comes a transfer of control from natural law to human law. Can the U.S. Congress (which seems intent on shrinking, not expanding, its dominion) manage this new enlarged sphere of influence? Can the churches or the media or the schools? To mention just one obvious policy implication of this biotechnological leap beyond the Tao: The abortion debate, historically an issue in two dimensions (whether or not Individuals should have the right to terminate a pregnancy), suddenly takes on a discomfiting third dimension. Should prospective parents who want a child be allowed to refuse a particular type of child?

From that perspective, I wonder if today's crude triple marker/amnio combination isn't just an early indication of the burdens likely to be placed on future generations of parents: the burden of knowing, the burden of choosing. I imagine my daughter, pregnant with her first child. The phone rings. The doctor has reviewed the karyotype and the computer analysis. He is sorry to report that her fetus is carrying a genetic marker for severe manic-depressive illness, similar in character to that of my great-uncle, who lived a turbulent and difficult life. Will she continue the pregnancy?

Or perhaps she is not yet pregnant. In keeping with the social mores of her day, she and her partner have fertilized a number of eggs in vitro, intending to implant the one with the best apparent chance for a successful gestation. The doctor calls with the karyotype results. It seems that embryos number 1 and 6 reveal a strong manic-depressive tendency. Will my daughter exclude them from possible implantation? The choice seems obvious, until the doctor tells her that embryos 1 and 6 are also quick-witted, whereas 2 and 3 are likely to be intellectually sluggish. The fourth and fifth embryos, by the way, are marked for ordinary intelligence, early-onset hearing impairment, and a high potential for aggressive pancreatic cancer. Which, if any, should be implanted?

Now add a plausible economic variable: Suppose that my daughter gets a registered letter the next day from her health maintenance organization, which also has seen the karyotype and the analysis (both of which they happily paid for). The HMO cannot presume to tell her which embryo to implant, but she should know that if she chooses to implant embryo number 1 or 6, the costs of her child's manic depression will not be reimbursed, ever. Now that the genetic marker is on the record, it is officially a "pre-existing condition"—in fact, the term has never been more appropriate.

Such are some of the specific scenarios now being bandied about by bioethicists, who, because of the Human Genome Project, are flush with thinking-cap money. Five percent of the project's funds (roughly $100 million over fifteen years) is being dedicated to social and ethical exploration, an allotment that prompted Arthur Caplan, director of the University of Pennsylvania's Center for Bioethics, to celebrate the HGP as the "full-employment act for bioethicists." The Department of Energy, the National Institutes of Health, and the international Human Genome Organisation all have committees to study the social and ethical implications of genetic research. Popping up frequently are essays and conferences with titles like "Human Gene Therapy: Why Draw a Line?" "Regulating Reproduction," and "Down the Slippery Slope." While genetic researchers plod along in their methodical dissection of chromosomes, bioethicists are leaping decades ahead, out of necessity. They're trying to foresee what kind of society we're going to be living in when and if the researchers are successful. In Sheraton and Marriott conference halls, they pose the toughest questions they can think of. If a single skin cell can reveal the emotional and physical characteristics of an individual, how are we going to keep such information private? At what level of risk should a patient be informed of the potential future onset of a disease? Will employers be free to hire and fire based on information obtained from their prospective employees' karyotypes? Should a criminal defendant be allowed to use genetic predisposition toward extreme aggressiveness as a legitimate defense, or at least as a mitigating factor in sentencing? Should privately administered genetic tests be regulated for accuracy by the government? (Currently, they are not.) Should private companies be able to patent the gene sequences they discover? Should children of sperm donors have the right to know the identity and genetic history of their biological fathers? The only limitation on the number of important questions seems to be the imagination of the inquirer.

Most fundamental of all, though, are questions regarding the propriety of futuristic gene-based medical techniques. Suppose for a moment that the power to select on the basis of, and possibly even alter, our genetic code does, as many expect, turn out to be extensive. What sort of boundaries should we set for ourselves? Should infertile couples be allowed to resort to a clone embryo rather than adopt a biological stranger? Should any couple have the right to choose the blond-haired embryo over the brown-haired embryo? Homosexuality over heterosexuality? Should we try to "fix" albinism in the womb or the test tube? Congenital deafness? Baldness? Crooked teeth? What about aortas that if left alone will likely give out after fifty-five years? Should doctors instead pursue a genetic procedure that would give the ill-fated embryo a heart primed for ninety-nine years?

To address these questions, bioethicists need to determine what competing interests are at stake. If a father wants a blue-eyed, stout-hearted son and is able to pay for the privilege, which will cause no harm to anyone else, what's the problem? Consider the prospect of a pop-genetics culture in which millions choose the same desirable genes. Thousands of years down the line, the diversity in the human gene pool could be diminished, which any potato farmer can tell you is no way to manage a species. While public policy generally arbitrates between individual rights and social responsibilities, genetics raises a new paradigm, a struggle between contemporary humanity and our distant descendants.

The considerable support for legislation that would suppress some of these technologies draws its strength from a sense of moral indignation as well as from the fear of an alien future. In a *New Republic* essay entitled "The Wisdom of Repugnance," University of Chicago philosopher Leon Kass argues for a permanent ban on human cloning, a ban grounded not in hysteria but in moral principle. "We are repelled by the prospect of cloning human beings not because of the strangeness or novelty of the undertaking," he writes, "but because we intuit and feel, immediately and without argument, the violation of things that we rightfully hold dear."

On the other end of the spectrum, some scientists argue against any boundaries, proposing that whatever we can do to better ourselves is not only ethically appropriate but also imperative. "The potential medical benefits of genetic engineering are too great for us to let nebulous fears of the future drive policy," argues Gregory Stock, director of the Center for the Study of Evolution and the Origin of Life at UCLA. Stock and others contend that we know better than Nature what we want out of life, and we owe it to ourselves and future generations to seek genetic improvement as a component of social progress. In his article "Genetic Modifications," for example, Anders Sandberg, a young Swedish scientist and self-described "Transhumanist," not only recommends the removal of genetic "defects" and such less harmful "undesirable traits" as drug abuse, aggression, and wisdom teeth but proposes a wide selection of enhancements to benefit the entire race. Systemic improvements would involve reprogramming cells to be more resistant to aging, toxins, and fat. "Cosmetic modifications" would be the plastic surgery for the next millennium—alteration of hair color/texture, eye color, skin color, muscular build, and so on. Sandberg even fancies deluxe new features such as built-in molecular support for frozen cryonic suspension. We can chuckle now at the improbability of these ideas, but when we do we might also try to imagine how people might have reacted 150 years ago (before electricity, before the telegraph) to someone suggesting that people in the late twentieth century would routinely converse with people on other continents using portable devices the same size and weight as an empty coin purse. "It basically means that there are no limits," Princeton biologist Lee Silver remarked after the announcement of Dolly, the cloned sheep. "It means all of science fiction is true. They said it could never be done and now here it is, done before the year 2000."

The attitude within the ranks of the Human Genome Project community is, not surprisingly, quite a bit more conservative than Sandberg's. Nowhere in the project summaries will an affiliated researcher be found yearning publicly for a world filled with fat-proof, freezable people (although no one seems to have misgivings about any conceivable genetic engineering of pigs, cows, or other nonhumans). More modestly, the stated hopes for the application of gene mapping include a greater understanding of DNA and all biological organisms; new techniques for battling genetic diseases; a new prevention-oriented type of medicine, and a windfall for agribusiness and other biotech industries.

The fact that researchers are careful to limit their publicly stated goals reflects not so much a deeply ingrained social ethic, says Arthur Caplan, as a canny political awareness. "If uncertainty about what to do with new knowledge in the realm of genetics is a cause for concern in some quarters," he writes in the book *Gene Mapping,* "then those who want to proceed quickly with mapping the genome might find it prudent to simply deny that any application of new knowledge in genetics is imminent or to promise to forbear from any controversial applications of this knowledge. . . . [This] is the simplest strategy if one's aim is not applying new knowledge but merely to be allowed to proceed to acquire it." Caplan thus exposes a built-in tension between researchers and ethicists. Ethicists are paid to arouse concern, but researchers lose funding if too many people get too worried.

Spotlighting the personal motivations of their researcher counterparts might seem a little beyond the purview of bioethicists, but in fact bioethicists are obliged, as part of the exploration of propriety, to not only hope for the ideal social circumstances of genetic engineering but also to consider the more probable landscape for it, an approach we might call Real Ethik. To simply declare certain procedures immoral and call for an immediate and permanent ban is to ignore brazenly the history of technology, one lesson of which might fairly be summarized as "If it can be done, it will be done." E.g., the atomic bomb. The genie found its way out of that bottle in short order, almost instantaneously revolutionizing the way we think about conflict. Real Ethik dictates that other genies will escape from their bottles no matter what we do to stop them. Glenn McGee, a Caplan protégé at the University of Pennsylvania and the architect of what he calls a "pragmatic approach" to genetics, argues that while we may be able to revolutionize our technology, there is no escape from human nature. We're wasting our time, says McGee, huffing and puffing about an international ban on human cloning. "Get over it. It's not going to happen. We are fundamentally in an unpoliceable realm." Human cloning will occur, probably in Chelsea Clinton's lifetime. And considering the current trajectory of genetic research, so will a host of other exotic and frightening developments.

If one accepts McGee's worldview, genethical considerations shift abruptly from policies of stark authorization/prohibition to a web of regulation and incentive, from ultimatums to real diplomacy, from grandstanding to nuance and compromise. Instead of regarding advanced genetic engineering as taboo, as a eugenic catastrophe waiting to happen, one plunges straight into the facts, and works to maximize the general social welfare and to minimize harm. From the pragmatic perspective, the warning about "playing God" is a distracting irrelevance, since we're already playing God in so many ways. In Escondido, California, for example, the Repository for Germinal Choice, a.k.a.

the "Nobel sperm bank," collects and distributes sperm from an exclusive group of extraordinary men—top athletes, scientists, executives, and so on. A number of clinics in the United States now enable prospective parents to sex-select their children in advance of fertilization, sorting "male" (Y chromosome) sperm from "female" (X chromosome) sperm according to their volume and electrical charge, with an estimated success rate of 90 percent.

What about the horrifying prospect that parents might react irresponsibly to the genetic sneak preview of their fetus or embryo? That genie has escaped already, too. In what has become a powerful cautionary tale in bioethicist circles, an American couple was advised recently that their fetus had a rare extra chromosome that would not cause a debilitating disease like Down syndrome but that potentially, possibly, was linked to tall stature, severe acne, and aggressive—even criminally aggressive—behavior. The couple responded to this information by aborting their child. Their decision was ice water in the face of bioethicists, who concluded that the couple should not have been informed of the unusual, vague condition. The hard truth, says McGee, is that "when given the opportunity, people can do things that are inappropriate and unwise."

This inescapable element of human nature is why industrialized societies that respect the basic freedoms of their citizens nonetheless impose so many niggling restrictions on them—speed limits, gun control, waste-disposal regulations, food-and-drug preparation guidelines, and so on. As technologies advance further, conferring even more power and choice on the individual—the abilities to travel at astonishing rates of speed, to access and even manipulate vital pieces of information, to blow up huge structures with little expertise—societies will have no option but to guard against new types of abuse. Real Ethik is, therefore, inevitably a prescription for aggressive and complex government oversight of society and its powerful new tools.

Scratch the surface of both the information and biotech revolutions, in fact, and what one discovers underneath is a "control revolution," suggests political theorist Andrew Shapiro, a massive transfer of power from bureaucracies to individuals and corporations. In an unregulated control revolution, free markets and consumer choice become even more dominant forces in society than they already are, and in virtually every arena social regulation gives way to economic incentive. Unrestrained consumerism augments the ubiquitousness of pop culture and the free-for-all competition for scarce resources. Ultimately, even such social intangibles as privacy become commodified.

The unpleasant extremes of this climate are not very difficult to imagine: an over-class buying itself genetic immunity from industrial waste, leaving the working class gasping in its wake; conglomerates encoding corporate signatures onto genetic products, rendering competing products ineffective and enforcing the ultimate brand loyalty; parents resorting to all available legal means to ensure their kids can compete effectively, including attempts to, in the parlance of the Repository for Germinal Choice, "get the best possible start in life." In the absence of legal restrictions, one envisions the development of a free-market eugenic meritocracy—or, to coin a term, biocapitalism. If left up to the marketplace, designer genes could even allow the wealthy to pass on not only vast fortunes but also superior bioengineered lineages, thereby exacerbating class divisions.

With that much freedom and independence, the paradoxical question one must finally ask is: Can freedom and independence, as we know them, survive? The genetic revolution may well deliver the apex of "life, liberty, and the pursuit of happiness," but it seems destined to conflict with another bedrock American principle. Two centuries after it was first proclaimed, we still abide by the conceit—the "self-evident" truth—that "all men are created equal." We know, of course (as did our founding fathers), that this is not literally true: people are born with more, less, and different varieties of strength, beauty, and intelligence. Although we frequently celebrate these differences culturally, from a political and legal standpoint we choose to overlook them. For the purposes of sustaining a peaceful, just, and functional society, we are all considered equal.

An unregulated, unrestricted genetic revolution, by highlighting our physical differences and by allowing us to incorporate them in our structures of enterprise, might well spell the end of this egalitarian harmony. In this pre-genetics era, we are all still external competitors, vying for good jobs, attractive mates, comfortable homes. After the revolution has begun in earnest, much of the competition will likely take place under the skin. We will compete for a better code. Such a eugenic culture, even one grounded in a democracy, will inevitably lead to the intensified recognition and exaggeration of certain differences. In a newly human-driven evolution, the differences could become so great that humans will be literally transformed into more than one species. But even if this doesn't happen, our thin metaphysical membrane of human solidarity might easily rupture under the strain. "The mass of mankind has not been born with saddles on their backs," Thomas Jefferson wrote two centuries ago, "nor a favored few booted and spurred, ready to ride them . . ." Who today can consider the momentum of genetic research and be confident that in another two centuries Jefferson's words will still hold true?

Journal/Discussion Questions

1. In what way, according to Shenk, is the biotech revolution a "control revolution?" Do you agree with Shenk's claim? Discuss.
2. In a number of the examples Shenk gives, the issues of privacy of information is central. Who has a right to genetic information about you? What protections should be available to individuals who do not wish to divulge genetic information about themselves?
3. Genetic information may contain unpleasant surprises for us. Do individuals have the right to refuse genetic information about themselves? What obligations do they have to others (e.g., spouses) to make this information available?

An Introduction to the Moral Issues

Many of the moral problems we face today—such as euthanasia, punishment, hunger, and discrimination—have been perennial issues for humanity. In the past few decades, however, we have been faced with a new range of moral problems, problems arising out of the advance of medical technology. Perhaps nowhere are these more pressing and more complex than in the areas of cloning and reproductive technology. The past two decades of scientific advances have now turned fiction into fact. Indeed, so-called "test-tube babies"—more precisely, babies conceived in a Petrie dish from human sperm and eggs and then implanted in a woman's uterus—used to be the stuff of science fiction. Now the question is more likely to be whether the cost of such procedures should be covered by health insurance.

In this chapter, we will be looking at a number of the moral issues raised by this and other advances in reproductive technology. Some of these relate directly to the moral status of what is variously called the embryo, the pre-embryo, or the conceptus. To a large extent, the issues here repeat those explored in our discussion of abortion. However, some completely new issues arise as well. For example, there have been several cases in which divorcing couples have gone to court to settle disagreements about the disposition of frozen embryos from their own eggs and sperm.

A quite different set of issues arises in those situations where a surrogate mother carries the embryo to term, and these issues center primarily on the relationship among three parties: (1) the couple—or, occasionally, the single individual—who wants to raise the child, (2) the surrogate mother who carries the baby to term, and (3) the baby that the surrogate mother bears.

A third set of issues arises through the intersection of reproductive technologies and genetic manipulation. We are only on the verge of confronting such issues, but they are sure to become more pressing as medical science becomes increasingly skilled at genetic manipulation and as the Human Genome Project maps out the genetic code with increasing precision. The questions are primarily hypothetical at present. What if we can decide whether a given embryo develops as a male or a female? What if we can select physical characteristics? Personality traits? Sexual orientation? The specter of "designer babies" looms, if not in the immediate future, at least in the not-too-distant future. How should such choices be made, if at all? The final step in this process is cloning.

Let's consider each of these three areas in more detail.

In Vitro Fertilization

Current estimates suggest that one in twelve American couples who want to have a child experience significant medical barriers to fertility. For such couples, once the nature of the medical problem(s) has been diagnosed, there are often initial therapeutic techniques, such as hormone therapy or surgery, that can enable the couple to have children without further medical assistance. However, this is not possible for all. For some couples, it is still impossible to conceive. In those cases, it is necessary to turn to more radical means. If conception cannot take place in the woman, then the next step is to try to bring about conception externally—in a glass laboratory dish, *in vitro.* The man's sperm and the woman's egg are combined in a glass dish (*in vitro* just means "in glass" in Latin) in a way that allows the sperm to fertilize the egg, producing the embryo. This creates a double separation. First, the act of creating a human life is separated from sexual intercourse. Second, and even more importantly, the embryo itself is separate (if only for a short period of time) from the mother. At this point, the embryo is implanted, either in the woman whose egg was fertilized or in another woman who will bear the baby.

The Vocabulary of the New Parenthood

How many parents can a child have?

We can begin to see the myriad of possibilities in this arrangement and how our traditional vocabulary fails us. To help describe the various possibilities, we can distinguish among the:

- Intentional mother: the woman who wants to have the child;
- Intentional father: the man who wants to have the child;
- Genetic mother: the woman who supplies the egg for the embryo;
- Genetic father: the man who supplies the sperm for the embryo;
- Gestational mother: the woman who carries the embryo to term and gives birth to it;
- Nurturing mother: the woman who raises and nurtures the child from infancy as her own;
- Nurturing father: the man who raises and nurtures the child from infancy as his own.

In the simplest case, both sperm and egg may come from the couple wanting to have the child, and then the embryo may be implanted back in the woman. In this case, we may say that the *intentional parents* are also the *genetic parents,* the *birth parents,* and the *nurturing parents.* However, it is not uncommon for either the sperm or the egg—sometimes, even both—to come from a donor. (The male's sperm count may be too low or too abnormal or unable to penetrate the egg, or the female may be unable to produce eggs that can be fertilized.) In those cases, the genetic mother or father is different from the birth mother and the nurturing parents. The simplest of these cases does not even require *in vitro* fertilization; it can simply be achieved through artificial insemination by a donor (AID). Compared with *in vitro* procedures, AID is comparatively cheap and effective. However, it is only helpful in cases of male infertility. The corresponding procedure for women, which involves donor eggs instead of donor sperm, is much more complicated and expensive and generally requires *in vitro* techniques.

In some cases, the embryo may be implanted in a surrogate, who then bears the child. She is then the birth mother, but she may not be the genetic mother. Nor, if things go according to the plan of the intentional parents, will she be the nurturing mother. The whole point of the process for them is for the surrogate to bear their child for them. As we shall see in our readings, the issue of surrogacy is a thorny one, especially in those cases where a surrogate changes her mind and wants to raise the baby herself.

We can easily see the complex possibilities. It is possible for a child to have three mothers: a genetic mother, a birth mother, and a nurturing mother. (Presumably the intentional mother and the nurturing mother are the same, although in unusual circumstances they could be two different women.) Similarly, a child can have at least two fathers: the genetic father and the nurturing father.

Who, then, are the *real* parents? Our initial answers often reveal a lot about our most fundamental beliefs about what counts as "real." Some see biology as constituting what is most real, and for them the "real" parents are either the genetic parents or, in some cases, the birth mother. Some see relationships and love as being the most "real," and for them the "real" parents are often the nurturing parents. But there is no simple and unchallenged answer to this question, and little is to be gained by pursuing it too far. Rather, the answer—as Ruth Macklin indicates in "Artificial Means of Reproduction and Our Understanding of the Family"—is to be found in making the various senses of "real" more precise and then specifying the ways in which a given person meets, or fails to meet, that more specific sense.

Who is the "real" mother—the intending, the genetic, the gestational, or the nurturing mother?

The Moral Status of the Pre-Embryo

We have already discussed many of the arguments about the moral status of the *fetus* in the introduction to the chapter on abortion. However, when we are dealing with *in vitro* fertilization, we are dealing with what is sometimes called a pre-embryo, which arguably has a different moral status than an embryo.

What is a pre-embryo? Some have argued that it is simply an embryo at its earliest stage of development, and that the attempt to call it a *pre-embryo* is simply an attempt to make anything relating to it appear morally unobjectionable. Yet giving something a new name does not change its moral status. We will follow common usage and employ the term *pre-embryo,* but note that this does not entail any judgment about its moral status.

Is the pre-embryo a human person?

At least two points are relevant here to the moral status of the pre-embryo. First, at this early stage, the pre-embryo is microscopic, smaller than the period at the end of this sentence. Usually, it is implanted or frozen when it has reached eight cells. There is nothing visually resembling a human being, although the pre-embryo certainly contains the coded genetic information for a full human being. Second, in contrast to its situation when it is *in utero,* the pre-embryo in a Petrie dish will not develop into a human being unless someone takes positive steps to implant it. This is very different from the situation of abortion, where someone has to intervene to prevent the pre-embryo from developing. Of course, the positive steps necessary when the pre-embryo is *ex utero* are only necessary because the woman's eggs have been artificially removed and fertilized.

One of the principal moral issues here is that it is standard procedure during *in vitro* fertilization to harvest a number of eggs, to fertilize them outside of the uterus, and then to implant the pre-embryo most likely to thrive. What happens to the remaining pre-embryos? In some instances, they may be frozen to be used later by the couple if this attempt is unsuccessful or if they want additional children. Otherwise they are usually destroyed. Some people are opposed to *in vitro* fertilization primarily because it produces pre-embryos that are then discarded.

Access to *in vitro* Fertilization

Unusual cases often find their way into the newspaper headlines, and unusual cases involving *in vitro* fertilization are no exception. In 1995 in Italy, a woman in her early sixties gave birth to a healthy baby boy, with the help of donor eggs and her husband's sperm. She decided to try IVF after the death of their 17-year-old son and after they were told that they were too old to adopt. Such a case inevitably raises questions. Should there be age limits on couples seeking IVF? Moreover, should there be any restrictions about motivation? In the Italian case, the woman gave her new baby the same name as her previously deceased son. In another case in 1995, a black woman in Italy with a husband of mixed race obtained *in vitro* fertilization using the eggs of a white woman. One of the reasons she gave was her belief that a light-skinned child would have an easier time in life than a dark-skinned one, given the existence of racism. Again, questions about motivation immediately arise.

Should in vitro *fertilization be available to everyone?*

What interest, if any, does the state have in regulating such IVF? While we might raise questions about the motives of the women mentioned in the preceding paragraph, we could certainly raise questions about the motives of many parents, and yet that is not sufficient grounds for state intervention. The situation changes significantly if public money is used to finance such procedures; but as long as they are done with private funds, it seems that the state has little basis for questioning the motivation of the couples involved.

Conflicting Claims: The Embryos of Divorcing Couples

One of the more perplexing issues arising out of the fact that embryos can—at least temporarily—exist outside the mother's womb is that couples, when in the process of divorcing, make competing claims for custody of the embryos. Usually such embryos are frozen, and this allows such battles to be protracted. Several issues are intertwined here.

The first of these issues is the moral status of the pre-embryo, which we have already considered above. If they have the moral status of persons, then they have a right to life. If one member of the couple wants the embryos destroyed, this would not be morally permissible if they have a right to life. If, on the other hand, they do not yet have this moral status, then destroying embryos would be morally permissible.

Who, if anyone, has the right to frozen embryos when a couple decides to divorce?

Second, what kind of rights and responsibilities do the genetic parents have toward the embryo as *parents?* Is it a relationship of ownership? Of parenthood? In the case of one divorcing couple, the woman wanted possession of the embryos in order to have them implanted in herself and to bring them to term. The divorcing husband did not want to be the (genetic) father, with its accompanying responsibilities, when he and his wife were getting a divorce. Does the wife have the right to go ahead and have the embryos implanted? Does the husband have the right to have the embryos destroyed, since he no longer wants to be their father? What role should the courts play in settling such disputes?

Conservative Objections to *in vitro* Fertilization

Some critics of the current rise in *in vitro* fertilization recognize that it may be effective in achieving its goal, but that it ought not to be used anyway. Several motives come into play in such criticisms.

Religiously based critiques of assisted reproduction. Many religious traditions are profoundly opposed to the development of reproductive technologies. At its deepest level, just as we have seen in our discussion of abortion, this view questions the technological society's presumption that we can control our destiny. Instead, it believes that our fates are ultimately in divine hands, and that intrusive technological procedures are *hubris.*

The second principal concern within religious traditions is that reproductive technologies almost always involve manipulating and destroying embryos. Embryos, many religious thinkers maintain, are persons and thus are not the proper objects of manipulation. Certainly, it is immoral to destroy them. Since *in vitro* fertilization almost inevitably involves such destruction of embryos, many religious thinkers believe it should be condemned.

Anti-technology critiques of assisted reproduction. Not all critics of assisted reproduction are motivated solely by religious concerns. Many are concerned with the way in which technology distorts the reproductive process, as our selection from Paul Lauritzen, "What Price Parenthood?" indicates. Ideally—and almost everyone would admit that the actual case often falls short of the ideal—conception is part of a larger process, one with both human and natural elements. Technological intervention breaks both the natural and the human cycle. Ideally, human intercourse is motivated by love and is open to the possibility that this love will result in children.

Surrogacy

From Donors to Surrogates

What is the moral standing of sperm donors, egg donors, and surrogates in pregnancies?

Many of these situations become more complicated with the introduction of a surrogate who is the birth mother. The role that the birth mother plays in this process is different from the role played by donors. In the case of sperm donors, their contributions may be made in a way that does not personally involve them in the process at all. Their sperm is frozen, and those in need of donor sperm consult lists of available donors which give information such as physical characteristics, interests, and so on. Moreover, donor sperm may be mixed with the husband's sperm in some cases, thus making its contribution less prominent and less certain. Donor eggs are a different matter, since they are much more difficult to harvest—currently, this requires laproscopic surgery—and often the harvesting must be coordinated with the cycle of the gestational mother. Whereas sperm is donated to a general sperm bank, eggs are usually donated with a specific recipient in mind. However, the interests of the sperm or egg donors do not come close to rivaling the interests of the hopeful couple, and there would be scant basis for such donors to claim the child as their own.

The case of surrogate mothers is much different from that of donors. Surrogate mothers have a nine-month relationship with the child they are carrying and which they eventually bear. This is an intimate and emotionally charged relationship, and it is understandable if unanticipated feelings of attachment develop during it. Moreover, there is often a relationship between the surrogate mother and the couple desiring the child. A surrogate carries the baby for a particular couple, with whom in some cases she has personal contact. The interests of the surrogate have a kind of standing that we would not accord to the interests of either sperm or even egg donors.

The Case of Baby M

The interests of the surrogate have even greater standing if the surrogate is also the genetic mother. This was the situation in the case of Baby M, where the surrogate mother—Mary Beth Whitehead—was also the genetic mother of the baby she was carrying for William and Elizabeth Stern; William Stern was the genetic father through artificial insemination. Mr. Stern contracted with Mrs. Whitehead for her to be the surrogate mother for the Stern's child; in return, they promised to pay her $10,000 and to pay her medical expenses. Several days after the birth, she asked the Sterns to allow her to take the baby back for a week, and the Sterns agreed. The next day, Mrs. Whitehead left the state to visit her mother. Shortly thereafter, Mrs. Whitehead told the Sterns that she wanted to keep the baby, and she eluded a subsequent court order requiring her to return the baby to the Sterns. She ran away with the baby for almost three months. After numerous press conferences, suits and countersuits, the court awarded custody of the baby to the Sterns but gave Mrs. Whitehead visitation rights. However, the court did not uphold the enforceability of the surrogacy contract itself; rather, it awarded custody on the basis of what it considered to be "the best interests of the child."

The public reaction to the case of Baby M was both deep and widespread. Many sympathized with Mrs. Whitehead and decried the action of the court as taking a child from her "real" mother. Others sympathized with the Sterns, who had placed their trust and hopes for a family with Mrs. Whitehead. They saw Mrs. Whitehead's promise to the Sterns as binding. Some sympathized with both sides, as well as with the baby, and denounced the situation itself; they often called for the banning of all surrogacy arrangements, precisely because they could lead to such Solomonic outcomes.

The case of Baby M was exceptional. Most surrogacy arrangements proceed without such difficulties. However, it focused attention on a number of moral issues about the practice of surrogacy that deserve attention. How should we deal with changes of heart on the part of surrogates? Is the relationship between the intending parents and the surrogate best understood in terms of family law or contract law? Does surrogacy involve buying and selling babies? Does surrogacy usually exploit women, especially poor women? Let's turn to some of these questions.

Models for Understanding the Relationship between the Surrogate and the Intending Parents

There are several ways in which we might attempt to understand the relationship between the surrogate mother and the intentional parents. Our choice of a model affects both our moral evaluation of the situation and the ways in which we respond when something goes wrong in the arrangement.

The contractual model. Since there is often a contract between the surrogate mother and the intending parents, we are often inclined to understand their relationship primarily in terms of a contract. This can lead to either of two results. On the one hand, those who see this contractual model as appropriate to surrogacy will maintain that surrogate mothers as well as intending parents should be held to the terms of their contract. The contract, in their eyes, is the only morally salient aspect of the situation. On the other hand, some see surrogacy as a matter of contracts, but maintain contracts for carrying babies are inappropriate. Among the reasons for seeing such contracts as objectionable is that they involve "selling babies" or that they are exploitative of women, especially poor women. From this, they conclude that surrogacy itself is wrong.

The drawback of the contractual model is that it overlooks much in the process of surrogacy that is morally relevant but which is not part of the contract. Among the neglected factors are the best interests of the child and the feelings of natural bonding that the surrogate mother may experience.

The adoption model. Some have suggested that we understand the relationship between the intending parents and the surrogate in terms of pre-natal adoption. One of the advantages of such a model is that the adoption model usually has a specified period of time (up to six months) during which the birth mother can change her mind about her decision to allow the baby to be adopted. Moreover, birth mothers receive no payment for their baby, although their living expenses (including medical costs and counseling) may be paid by the intending parents.

Such a model seems to avoid the two principal drawbacks of the contractual model, but there are important differences between surrogacy and adoption. First, in adoption, the birth mother is not getting pregnant *for* the intending parents, and thus there is no direct connection with the intending parents as there is in surrogacy. In recent years, this has changed somewhat, since birth mothers may well have selected—and be emotionally quite close to—the couple that hopes to adopt. Second, there is no genetic connection in adoption between the intending parents and the birth mother, whereas in most cases of surrogacy there is a genetic contribution from at least one of the intending parents. Often the embryo will have no genetic links to the surrogate mother, but it always does in adoption.

The cooperative model. If we ask ourselves what is taking place in the ideal relationship between intending parents and surrogate, we can get a fuller picture of the moral aspects of this relationship and a better idea of what we want to strive for in this area. Let's look at the two parties in the relationship, the intending parents and the surrogate.

First, the intending parents are presumably a couple that either is infertile (thus unable to have children on their own) or is at risk through pregnancy. These at-risk factors are presumably on the intending mother's side, and usually relate to the physical risks of pregnancy. For example, in the Baby M case, it was reported that the intending mother (Mrs. Stern) had a mild case of multiple sclerosis, which could have been greatly exacerbated by pregnancy. Presumably, we would look with much greater suspicion at intending parents who wanted to hire a surrogate for reasons of convenience, career, and the like.

Second, the surrogate mother usually has special characteristics as well. Although they often welcome the payment ($10,000 is currently the usual amount), their motives are usually much more than monetary. (There are often other, easier, and less intrusive ways of making money; and some surrogates, especially family members, do not accept money.) They are usually not desperately poor women, but rather middle-class women who use the money for things like college tuition for other children, a new car, or home improvements. They understand, often through the experiences of a close friend or family member, how painful it can be for a couple to want to have children but to be unable to. Moreover, they usually have children themselves, and they value parenthood highly. Interestingly, some even enjoy the experience of being pregnant, despite its obvious discomforts and the pain of childbirth. They often become surrogates in order to help a couple who otherwise would be unable to have children. And it is this which makes surrogacy unique. *Surrogates become pregnant, not in order to have children of their own, but in order to help others to have children of their own.* Indeed, often the babies they have are not genetically their own at all; rather, they are *carrying* a baby *for* someone else.

The issue, then, is how to structure the surrogacy arrangement so that it most often approximates this ideal. Here it seems that the first step is screening to insure, as much as possible, that both parties come as close as possible to this ideal. Intending parents should not be people who simply want to avoid the inconveniences of pregnancy or the career interruptions it can cause. Similarly, surrogates should not be women who have ambivalent feelings about carrying another couple's child for them or about giving up the child once it is born. The more thoroughly those who facilitate surrogacy arrangements can assure these issues, the more smoothly the process will proceed.

This does not mean that contracts have no place in surrogacy arrangements, but it does mean that the relationship is not primarily *about* contracts. Consider the difference between getting married and buying a car. Both may involve contracts of types, but marriage in not primarily about a contract. Buying a car, on the other hand, is mainly a matter of contract, and any personal relationship between buyer and seller is incidental. Marriage, on the other hand, is mainly about a certain kind of relationship between two people. What is morally salient here is, first and foremost, the relationship; only secondarily, the contract. Similarly, with surrogacy. The relationship is primarily *about* one woman bearing a child for another couple.

Remaining moral issues. Many issues obviously remain to be resolved in this area. Who does the screening? What standards are legitimate in such screening? What interest does the state have in regulating this process? Most difficult of all, what should happen in those cases where a surrogate changes her mind about turning over the child? Here it is important to distinguish three types of cases: (1) those in which the surrogate is also the genetic mother; (2) those in which the intending parents are also the genetic parents; and (3) those in which the genetic parents are neither the surrogate nor the intending parents. The interests of the surrogate seem strongest in the first case. The interests of the intending parents certainly seem strongest in the second case. In the third case, both the surrogate and the intending parents have strong, although quite different, interests. The surrogate may well have strong feelings of bonding which she had not, in all good faith, anticipated; the intending parents certainly have invested deeply, emotionally as well as financially, in this process. When neither side can claim genetic lineage to tip the scales, there seems to be no clear and easy basis for deciding whose interests are stronger.

Genetic Manipulation, Cloning, and Parenthood

Two areas of development have recently combined to open possibilities that were previously thought to be only in the realm of science fiction. First, in just the past few years, scientists have developed the ability to *manipulate* the genes of an embryo or fetus. Although such techniques are still in their infancy, as it were, there is little reason to doubt that they will develop further, probably fairly rapidly. Second, in the late 1980s, the U.S. government and others launched the Human Genome Project, which is intended eventually to provide a complete map of the human genome. A vast undertaking, this project is gradually uncovering the genetic markers for numerous diseases as well as for a number of human conditions that are not diseases. The combination of the technology to manipulate genes and the knowledge of the human genetic code is a powerful and awesome prospect.

Is it moral to use genetic screening of embryos? To change gene structure?

From Abortion to Genetic Manipulation

The moral terrain opened up by advances in genetic manipulation is still largely uncharted. One of the first things we notice is that, with the advent of genetic manipulation, abortion is no longer the only option when tests reveal an unwanted condition in the embryo or fetus. This makes the situation morally much more complex, because it is no longer a question—as it was in the case of abortion—of depriving the fetus of a future through terminating it. Instead, the issue is now one of giving it a *different* future, one that results from conscious human choice rather than genetics.

What is the moral difference between abortion and genetic manipulation?

Some alternative futures are clearly preferable to others, especially when we are dealing with disease. A child facing a future of Tay-Sachs disease or multiple sclerosis or other debilitating and eventually lethal ailments clearly has a bleaker future than a child who does not face that. There seems to be little moral problem here. However, other cases are much more difficult. What do we say about dwarfism? Genetically-based deafness? Obesity? Eye color? Skin color? Sex? Sexual orientation? If it is possible to do so, do parents have the right to choose whatever characteristics they desire for their child?

Consider the following example. It is already possible to test to determine whether a fetus has the gene for acondroplegia, a form of dwarfism. If the fetus has that gene from both parents—a double dominant—then it can be expected to live only a few days after birth. If it has the gene just from one side, then it will be a dwarf. If it does not have the gene from either side, its height will be normal. It is important to note that dwarfism is not a medical illness and that, although they encounter problems with back pain and the like, dwarfs are not at medical risk. At present, the only option available to parents is to have the child or to abort it. Should a couple be allowed to abort a fetus because it will be a dwarf? Should a couple, both of whom are dwarfs, be allowed to abort a fetus if it is *not* a dwarf? Should genetic counselors (and genetic testing laboratories) provide prospective parents with such information? Let's imagine, furthermore, that the choice did not involve abortion, but rather genetic manipulation. Should prospective parents be allowed to request genetic manipulation to insure that the child does not die shortly after birth? To insure that the child is not a dwarf? To insure that the child is not of normal height?

Individual Choices and Social Policy

Once we begin to raise questions about the limits of individual choice in these matters, we also have to distinguish between the moral issues surrounding the individual decision and those that arise if large numbers of people make the same decision. This is not a major issue in regard to acondroplegia, which is a relatively rare condition (it affects one in every 20,000 to 30,000 births) and does not directly impact social policy. Consider two other areas that are more perplexing.

First, if it becomes possible genetically to manipulate the sex of an embryo, this could have a far-reaching impact on society. If more couples have a preference for a male child than a female, and if an increasing number of couples have only one child, then such selection can seriously upset the balance of males and females in society. We do not know what consequences this may have, but a number of undesirable scenarios—especially undesirable for women—have been sketched out. Many of these involve women, because of their scarcity, being turned into breeding machines in a male-dominated society. If only a handful of parents were to engage in genetic sex selection for their developing embryos, then it may be unnecessary or unwise to legislate such practices. If, however, large numbers of parents do so, and if in doing so they affect the balance of males and females in our society, then there may be harmful effects of the practice as a whole and reasons for intervening.

What limits should be placed on genetic manipulation of embryos?

Second, imagine if it eventually becomes possible to determine sexual orientation. Some researchers feel that they are on the trail of a gene for "homosexuality." Whether this will actually occur remains an open question, and to many it seems improbable that such a complex thing can be reduced to a single genetic marker. Nonetheless, it is certainly possible. Moreover, it is possible that, if such a genetic marker is found, it may become possible to change it. Several factors might discourage couples from having homosexual children, if the choice were up to them. First, the vast majority of couples having children are not homosexual. Second, in our society there is a significant amount of anti-homosexual sentiment. Some parents may be against having homosexual children; others may simply feel that a child will have an easier time in our society if he or she is not homosexual. It is not unimaginable that, given genetic manipulation, the percentage of persons who are homosexual might decrease.

Common Ground

When we are hiking in a new area, we often are particularly aware of possible dangers. These dangers often serve as landmarks, hazardous and to be avoided. Similarly, as we explore the new moral terrain opened up by recent reproductive technologies, there are several dangers that can serve as initial reference points as we begin to formulate our positions.

Unforseeable Consequences

Genetic manipulation opens up previously undreamed-of possibilities. It is all too easy, at least for some of us, to focus on the possible benefits of such developments rather than the possible—and, at least in some cases, largely unforeseeable—negative effects. For example, reports in May 1999, now indicate that the cloned sheep Dolly is showing unanticipated signs of genetic aging. It is wise to tread carefully in such uncharted terrain.

Using Persons as Commodities

Many people, regardless of political and ideological commitments, would agree that one of the principal dangers of contemporary capitalist, technological society is that it turns people into commodities. Persons, Kant once reminded us, are priceless, but mere things can always be bought and sold. We honor this admonition with our firm conviction that people—or even parts of people, their body parts—cannot be bought or sold. The danger we face with the development of reproductive technologies is that this tendency to turn everything into a commodity will only increase. We are moving at least dangerously close—some would say we have already crossed the line—to buying and selling sperm, eggs, and even the use of wombs.

The Arguments

Paul Lauritzen
"What Price Parenthood? Social and Ethical Aspects of Reproductive Technology"

Paul Lauritzen, an assistant professor of religious ethics at John Carroll University in Cleveland, Ohio, is the author of Religious Belief and Emotional Transformation: A Light in the Heart *and* Pursuing Parenthood: Ethical Issues in Assisted Reproduction.

Drawing on personal experience in infertility therapy as well as recent scholarship in the ethical aspects of reproductive technology, Lauritzen argues that we "must combine careful attention to the experience of pursuing parenthood by technological means with principled reflection on the morality of this pursuit." Lauritzen relates feminist objections to IVF, AID, and surrogacy to his own experience, and concludes that such technologies must be approached with great caution and only—if at all—as a final resort.

As You Read, Consider This:

1. What, according to Lauritzen, is the reason for including personal experiences with infertility within a philosophical discussion of the ethical issues raised by reproductive technologies? In what ways does this add or detract from his argument?
2. How, according to Lauritzen, does the very existence of new reproductive technologies become coercive? In what ways do you agree with Lauritzen? Disagree with him?

The ceremony goes as usual.

> I lie on my back, fully clothed except for the healthy white cotton underdrawers. What I could see, if I were to open my eyes, would be the large white canopy of Serena Joy's outsized colonial-style four-poster bed, suspended like a sagging cloud above us . . .
>
> Above me, towards the head of the bed, Serena Joy is arranged, outspread. Her legs are apart, I lie between them, my head on her stomach, her pubic bone on the base of my skull, her thighs on either side of me. She too is fully clothed.
>
> My arms are raised; she holds my hands, each of mine in each of hers. This is supposed to signify that we are one flesh, one being. What it really means is that she is in control, of the process and thus of the product . . .
>
> My red skirt is hitched up to my waist, though no higher. Below it the Commander is fucking. What he is fucking is the lower pan of my body. I do not say making love, because this is not what he's doing. Copulating too would be inaccurate, because it would imply two people and only one is involved. (Margaret Atwood, *The Handmaid's Tale*).

This chilling depiction of the process of reproduction in the fictional Republic of Gilead provides a vision of what many feminists believe will soon be reality if the new reproductive technologies (NRTS) proceed unchecked. Children will be thought of exclusively as products. Women will be valuable merely as breeders. Reproductive prostitution will emerge as women are forced to sell wombs, ovaries, and eggs in reproductive brothels.[1] Men will be more fully in control than ever.

There was a time when I would have dismissed such claims as wildly alarmist. I still believe these worries to be overblown. Yet I have been haunted by this passage from *The Handmaid's Tale* as I have stood, month after month, holding my wife Lisa's hand as she, feet in stirrups, has received my sperm from the catheter that her doctor has maneuvered into her uterus. Indeed, once, when the nurse asked me to stand behind her to hold steady an uncooperative light, I wondered perversely whether I shouldn't, like Serena Joy, play my symbolic pall by moving rhythmically as the nurse emptied the syringe.[2] Having experienced the world of reproductive medicine firsthand, I believe we need to take a closer look at feminist objections to NRTS.

Here, then, I will review objections that some feminists have raised to such technologies as *in vitro* fertilization (IVF), artificial insemination with donor sperm (AID), and surrogate motherhood, and relate these objections to my own experience. I take up feminist objections because, although there is no one "feminist" response to reproductive technology, some of the most forceful objections to this technology have come from writers who are self-consciously feminist and understand their opposition to the NRTS to be rooted in their feminism.[3] Moreover, the international feminist organization FINRRAGE (Feminist International Network of Resistance to Reproductive and Genetic Engineering) is committed to opposing the spread of reproductive technology, and it is from this group that we have the most sustained and systematic attack on NRTS in the literature.[4] I relate these objections to my own experience because, in my view, all serious moral reflection must attend to the concrete experience of particular individuals and thus inevitably involves a dialectical movement between general principles and our reactions to particular cases. The need to balance appeals to abstract rules and principles with attention to the affective responses of particular individuals has not always been sufficiently appreciated in moral theory or in medical ethics.[5] Yet such a balance is necessary if we are to understand both how moral decisions are actually made and how to act compassionately when faced with troubling moral situations.

My experience leads me to believe that there are some real dangers in pursuing these technologies, that individuals should resort to them only after much soul searching, and that society should resist efforts to expand their use in ways that would make them available as something other than a reproductive process of last resort. In the case of my wife and me, this soul searching is upon us. It now appears that artificial insemination with my sperm will not be successful. We are thus confronted with the decision of whether to pursue *in vitro* fertilization, artificial insemination with donor sperm, or adoption. This paper is one moment in that process of soul searching.

Like many couples of our generation and background, my wife and I delayed having children until we completed advanced degrees and began our jobs. With careful deliberation, we planned the best time to have children given our two careers, and were diligent in avoiding pregnancy until that time. What we had not planned on was the possibility that pregnancy would not follow quickly once we stopped using birth control. This had not been the experience of our friends whose equally carefully laid plans had all been realized. For them, birth control ended and pregnancy followed shortly thereafter. For us, a year of careful effort, including charting temperatures and cycles, yielded only frustration.

Because we had indeed been careful and deliberate in trying to conceive, we suspected early on that there might be a problem and we thus sought professional help. A post-coital examination by my wife's gynecologist revealed few, and rather immobile sperm. I was referred to a specialist for examination and diagnosed as having two unrelated problems: a varicocele and retrograde ejaculation. A varicocele is a varicose vein in the testicle that is sometimes associated with a reduction in both the numbers and quality of sperm. Retrograde ejaculation is a condition in which a muscle at the neck of the bladder does not contract sufficiently during ejaculation to prevent semen from entering the bladder. As a result, during intercourse semen is ejaculated into the bladder rather than into the vagina. Both conditions are treatable, in many cases. Indeed, the doctor's diagnosis was followed almost immediately by a presentation of possible "therapies," given roughly in the order of the doctor's preferences, all presented as points on the same therapeutic continuum. A varicocele can be repaired surgically. Retrograde ejaculation can sometimes be eliminated through the use of drugs and, failing that, can be circumvented by recovering sperm from urine and using it for artificial insemination. Should both these treatments fail, *in vitro* fertilization might be successful. And, if all else fails, donor insemination is always a possibility.

Since surgery for a valicocele is not always successful and since surgery is more invasive than either of the treatments for retrograde ejaculation, I tried these latter treatments first. Unfortunately, neither drug therapy nor artificial insemination was of any avail. Possibly because of damage done to the sperm as the result of the varicocele, the numbers and quality of sperm recovered from urine for insemination were not such as to make conception likely. After trying artificial insemination (AIH) for six months, we decided to attempt to repair the varicocele. Following this surgery, there is generally a three to nine month period in which a patient can expect to see improvement in his sperm count. After nearly seven months, we have seen virtually no improvement. Although we have begun AIH once again, we do not have high hopes for success.

This is the bare chronicle of my infertility experience. A complete record would be too personal, too painful, and too long to present here. But something more should be said. For someone who loves children, who has always planned to have children, infertility is an agonizing experience. In a culture that defines virility so completely in phallocentric terms, infertility can also threaten male identity, for infertility is often confused with impotence. Infertility is damaging in other ways as well. The loss of intimacy as one's sex life is taken over by infertility specialists strains a relationship. More generally, the cycle of hope and then despair that repeats itself month after month in unsuccessful infertility treatment can become unbearable. Nor is the experience of infertility made easier by the unintended thoughtlessness or uncomfortable attempts at humor of others. It is hard to know which is worse: to endure a toast on Father's Day made with great fanfare by someone who knows full well your efforts to become a father or to suffer yet another comment about shooting blanks.

With this as background, I would like to consider four interrelated, but distinct objections that have been raised to NRTS. According to feminist opponents, the new reproductive technologies are inescapably coercive; lead to the dismemberment of motherhood; treat women and children as products; and open the door to widespread genetic engineering.

The Tyranny of Technology

Although opponents of reproductive technology do not generally distinguish types of coercion, there are typically two sorts of claims made about NRTS. The first is that the very existence (and availability) of these technologies constitutes a sort of coercive offer; the second, that the future of these technologies is likely to include coercive threats to women's reproductive choices.[6] The first claim is often a response to the standard reasons given for developing these technologies. Advocates of NRTS typically argue that these techniques are developed exclusively to help infertile couples, expanding the range of choices open to them.[7] Moreover, the medical community is portrayed as responding to the needs and interest of infertile patients to find technological means to produce pregnancy if the natural ones fail. IVF programs, for example, are almost always defended on the grounds that however experimental, painful, or dangerous they may be to women, women choose to participate in them. Thus, it is said, IVF increases choice.

Feminists who believe NRTS to be coercive claim that such a choice is illusory, because in a culture that so thoroughly defines a woman's identity in terms of motherhood, the fact that women agree to participate in IVF programs does not mean they are truly free not to participate. According to this view, we must not focus too quickly on the private decisions of individuals.[8] Individual choices are almost always embedded in social contexts, and the context in our culture is such that a childless woman is an unenviable social anomaly. To choose to be childless is still socially disapproved and to be childless in fact is to be stigmatized as selfish and uncaring. In such a situation, to offer the hope of becoming a mother to a childless woman is a coercive offer. Such a woman may well not wish to undergo the trauma of an *in vitro* procedure, but unwillingly do so.

Robyn Rowland has appreciated the significance of this social context for infertile women. "In an ideological context where child bearing is claimed to be necessary for women to fulfill themselves," she writes, "whether this is reinforced by patriarchal structures or by feminist values, discovering that you are infertile is a devastating experience."[9] The response may be a desperate search to find any means of overcoming this infertility, a search that may render the idea of choice in this context largely meaningless.

Moreover, feminists insist, developing these technologies is not about increasing choice. They are not, by and large, available to single women—infertile or not—or to lesbian women. Further, if doctors were truly concerned for the suffering of infertile women, we would expect much greater effort to publicize and to prevent various causes of infertility, including physician-induced sterility, as well as to inform women more fully about the physical and emotional trauma that various types of fertility treatments involve.[10] This neglect became dramatically apparent to me when I discovered Lisa at home weeping quietly but uncontrollably after a "routine" salpingogram for which she was utterly unprepared by her doctor's description of the procedure.[11] I will return to this theme below but I hope the claim of feminist opponents of the NRTS is clear. If doctors were in fact concerned about the well-being of their infertile patients, they would treat them less as objects to be manipulated by technologies and more as persons. The fact that this is often not the case should reveal something about the underlying motivations.[12]

The second claim about the possibility of coercive threats is really a concern about the future. While we may debate whether a desperately infertile woman really is free to choose not to try *in vitro* fertilization, still, no one is forcing her to participate in an IVF program. But what about the future? This question is meant to point to how thoroughly medicine has encroached on the birth process. The use of ultrasound, amniocentesis, genetic testing and counseling, electronic fetal monitoring, and cesarean sections have all increased the medical community's control over the process of birth. Why should the process of conception be any different? If anything, a pattern suggests itself. What was originally introduced as a specialized treatment for a subclass of women quickly expanded to cover a far wider range of cases. What was originally an optional technology may quickly become the norm.[13]

Such interventions can be coercive not only in the sense that, once established as the norm they are difficult to avoid, but in the stricter sense that women may literally be forced to submit to them, as with court-ordered cesarean sections. Will compulsory treatment be true of the new technologies as well? Will the technology that allows for embryo flushing and transfer in surrogate cases be required in the future as part of a process of medical evaluation of the fetus? The concern that the answer to these questions is too likely to be "yes" stands behind some claims that the NRTS are dangerously coercive. The potential for a loss of control over one's reproductive destiny is increased with the development of these technologies. And the coercion that could follow such a loss of control is worrisome.

Have I experienced a loss of control or coercion? The answer is a qualified yes. I certainly have not felt coerced in the second sense. I have not been physically forced to undergo infertility treatment nor has there been any threat, actual or implied, connected with the prospect of avoiding NRTS altogether. Still, I have experienced the existence of these technologies as coercive. And here the notion of a coercive offer is helpful. Although the inability to have children has not threatened my social identity in the same way it might were I a woman, nevertheless, the pressure is real. Having experienced this pressure, and having met others whose desperation to bear a child was almost palpable, I do not doubt that the offer of hope held out by available technologies, however slim and unrealistic in some cases, is indeed a form of coercion.

The problem here might reasonably be called the tyranny of available technologies. This "soft" form of coercion arises from the very existence of technologies of control. Increased control by the medical profession over the birth process, for example, has not resulted because of a conspiracy to gain control, but rather because, once the technology of control exists, it is nearly impossible not to make use of it. If, as I believe, this pressure to make use of existing technologies is a type of coercion, I have experienced this coercion powerfully during my infertility treatment. If surgery might repair the problem, even if the chances are not great, how can I not have surgery? If surgery and artificial insemination have not worked, but some new technique might, how can I not try the new technique?

The very existence of the technology inevitably changes the experience of infertility in ways that are not salutary. One of the peculiar aspects of infertility is that it is a condition that a couple suffers. Individuals can have retrograde ejaculation or blocked tubes, but only couples can be infertile. As Leon Kass has noted, infertility is as much a relationship as a condition.[14] Yet infertility treatment leads us to view infertility individually, with unfortunate consequences. The reason is that couples will often not be seen together in infertility treatment, and, even when they are, they will receive individual workups and be presented with individual treatment options. Now it might be said that providing individuals with options increases agency rather than diminishes it. Yet with this agency comes a responsibility that may not itself be chosen and that reduces the prospects for genuine choice. For once an individual is presented with a treatment option, not to pursue it is, in effect to choose childlessness and to accept responsibility for it. From a situation in which infertility is a relational problem for which no one is to blame, it becomes an individual problem for which a woman or man who refuses treatment is to blame.[15] Reproductive technology structures the alternatives such that a patient is "free" to pursue every available form of assisted reproduction or to choose to be childless.

This problem is compounded by the fact that infertility specialists simply assume that patients will pursue all available treatments and typically present the variety of treatment options as just different points on the same therapeutic spectrum, distinguished primarily by degree of invasiveness. In our case, taking relatively mild drugs in an effort to make an incontinent muscle more efficient lies at one end of the continuum, at the other end of which lies IVF. Surgery, I suppose, falls somewhere in the middle. At no time in my experience, however, has anyone suggested that treatments differ qualitatively. (The only exception to this was my urologist's opposition to an experimental treatment for malefactor infertility.) It has generally been assumed that if one therapy fails, we will simply move on to the next. And that is the problem. If the technology exists, the expectation is that it will be used. Again, if IVF might work, how can we not try it? The force of these questions covers us like a weight as we consider what to do next.

The Dismemberment of Motherhood

A second objection raised against the NRTS is that they question the very meaning of motherhood. The reality of oocyte donation, embryo flushing, and embryo transfer produces another possible reality: the creation of a child for whom there are three mothers: the genetic mother, the gestational mother, and the social mother.[16] In such a situation, who is the real mother? In the absence of a compelling answer, the claim of each of these three women to the child will be tenuous. Maternity will be as much in dispute as paternity ever was. And whatever criteria are used to settle this issue, the result for women is that the reproductive experience may become discontinuous in much the way it has traditionally been for men. Just as paternity has been uncertain because the natural, biological relation between the father and child could always be questioned, so too might maternity become a sort of abstract idea rather than a concrete reality. Just as paternity has been a fight rather than a natural relation, so too might maternity become.[17]

The significance of this can be seen if one takes seriously Mary O'Brien's claim that men's reproductive experience of discontinuity, that is, the inevitable uncertainty of genetic continuity, has contributed significantly to men's need to dominate. The problematic nature of paternity, O'Brien suggests, can account for the sense of isolation and separation so common in men, in part because for men the nature of paternity is such that the natural experiental relation of intimacy with another is missing.

Feminists' celebrations of motherhood have also made much of the biological continuity women have traditionally experienced with their children. Caroline Whitbeck and Nancy Hartsock, for example, have both discussed how the biological differences between men and women, especially as they are manifested in reproduction, account for some of the differences in how men and women experience the world.[18] Many women do not experience the sharp separation between self and others so common to male experience, Hartsock and Whitbeck note, a fact both explain by appeal to the way in which female physiology mediates female experience. In the case of women who are mothers, the experience of pregnancy, labor, childbirth, and nursing shape a way of responding to the world and to others. For a mother whose milk lets down at the sound of her child's cry, a sense of deep connection and continuity is established.[19]

On this view, the danger of the new technologies of birth is precisely that they alienate women from procreation and thus rob them of one of their most significant sources of power and identity. It is precisely this realization that leads Connie Ramos, a character in Marge Piercy's *Woman on the Edge of Time,* to react with such horror at the division of motherhood envisioned by Piercy. In a world where gestation takes place in artificial wombs, where men as well as women nurse the young, women have lost something of tremendous value and men have gained something they always wanted: control of reproduction. Connie's response to seeing a breast feeding male poignantly expresses this point:

> She felt angry. Yes, how dare any man share that pleasure. These women thought they had won, but they had abandoned to men the last refuge of women. What was special about being a woman here? They had given it all up, they had let men steal from them the last remnants of ancient power, those sealed in blood and in milk.[20]

One of the gravest concerns raised about the new technologies of birth, then, is that they represent the culmination of a patriarchal imperative: to gain for men what they have always lacked, namely, the power to reproduce. The fear is that this desire is close to realization. Gena Corea has put this point forcefully:

> Now men are far beyond the stage at which they expressed their envy of woman's procreative power through couvade, transvestism, or subincision. They are beyond merely giving spiritual birth in their baptismal-font wombs, beyond giving physical birth with their electronic fetal monitors, their forceps, their knives. Now they have laboratories.[21]

Since this objection essentially focuses on the impact on women of the NRTS, my experience cannot speak directly to this issue. Nevertheless, because part of what is at stake is the importance of the unity of genetic and social parenthood, as well as the unity of genetic and gestational parenthood, this is not a concern exclusively of women; it is a concern I have confronted in reflecting about donor insemination and adoption. One of the most striking aspects of my experience is how powerfully I have felt the pull of biological connection. Does this mean that genetic and social parenthood should never be separated or that parenthood should be defined strictly as a biological relation? I believe the answer to both questions is "no," but my experience leads me to believe also that a unity of genetic, gestational, and social parenthood is an ideal that we ought to strive to maintain.

The Commodification of Reproduction

The third objection found in some of the feminist literature on NRTS is that they tend to treat human beings as products. Not only can these technologies divide up motherhood, they can divide up persons into parts. Even when they are used to treat infertility, it is often not men or women who are being treated, but testicles, sperm, ovaries, eggs, wombs, etc. While this is true to some extent of all treatment in the specialized world of modern medicine, it is acute in reproductive medicine. Robyn Rowland has described the situation as one in which women especially are treated as "living laboratories" in which body parts and systems are manipulated in dramatic fashion without knowledge about the consequences of such manipulation.[22] Clearly, this has been the case in the development of *in vitro* fertilization, where women have not been adequately informed about the experimental nature of the procedure, possible side effects, or poor success rates.

In addition, the language of reproductive medicine can also be dehumanizing. Eggs are "harvested" as one might bring in a crop. Body parts are personified and thus attributed a sort of individuality and intentionality; cervical mucus is said to be hostile, the cervix itself is said to be incompetent, and the list could go on.

Yet as troubling as the language and practice surrounding this technology may be in treating persons like products, it is the application of this technology that treats persons as products that is completely objectionable. This has clearly happened with the development of a commercial surrogate industry and donor sperm banks, and it is the danger that attends the establishment of oocyte donor programs. Indeed, Corea's idea of a reproductive brothel seems inescapable. If there are not yet houses of ill repute where one can go to purchase embryos and women to gestate them, there are brochures available containing pictures and biographical information of women willing to sell their services. Nor can the development of commercial surrogacy arrangements be dismissed as the misguided and unintended application of reproductive techniques, an application of NRTS mistakenly and uncharacteristically driven by the profit motive. Treatment of infertility is big business, and the drive to develop reproductive technology is clearly fueled by financial incentives.[23]

Nothing perhaps illustrates this more clearly than the development of an embryo flushing technique by a team of physicians at Harbor-UCLA Medical Center. In April 1983, this team successfully flushed an embryo from one woman and transferred it to a second woman who carried the fetus to term. The project was funded by Fertility and Genetics Research, a for-profit company begun by two physicians who envisioned the establishment of a chain of embryo transfer clinics where infertile women could purchase embryos to gestate themselves. Indeed, to insure maximum profits for themselves, the Harbor-UCLA team sought to patent the equipment and the technique they developed.[24]

Not only do men and women get treated as products, so do children. The logic here is clear enough. If women are paying for embryos or being paid for eggs, the embryos and the eggs cannot but be understood as products. Because they are products, buyers will place demands on them. We will expect our products to meet certain standards and, if they fail, we will want to be compensated or to return the damaged goods. In a society that sells embryos and eggs for profit, children will inevitably be treated as property to be bought and sold, and just as inevitably it follows that different children will carry different price tags. As Barbara Katz Rothman puts it, "some will be rejects, not salable at any price: too damaged, or the wrong colour, or too old, too long on the shelf."[25]

My own experience leads me to believe that this tendency toward the commodification of reproduction is one of the most worrisome aspects of the NRTS.[26] In part, this tendency is troubling because it manifests itself not simply in commercial surrogacy transactions—transactions that many if not most people find morally problematic—but in applications of these technologies that almost no one questions. For example, few, I believe, would have qualms about the sort of artificial insemination that Lisa and I have undertaken and yet perhaps the most difficult part of AIH for us has been the struggle to maintain a degree of intimacy in the process of reproduction in the midst of a clinical environment designed to achieve results. As Katz Rothman has pointed out, the ideology of technology that fuels this commodification is not reducible to particular technological tools or to particular commercial transactions. Rather it is a way of thinking of ourselves and our world in "mechanical, industrial terms," terms that are incompatible with intimacy.[27] Interestingly, the Roman Catholic Church has rejected AIH precisely because it separates procreation from sexual intercourse and the expression of love manifest in the conjugal act.[28] While I reject the act-oriented natural law reasoning that stands behind this position, there is an insight here that should not be overlooked. Once procreation is separated from sexual intercourse, it is difficult not to treat the process of procreation as the production of an object to which one has a right as the producer. It is also difficult under these circumstances not to place the end above the means; effectiveness in accomplishing one's goal can easily become the sole criterion by which decisions are made.

This anyway, has been my experience. Although Lisa and I tried for a time to maintain a degree of intimacy during the process of AIH by remaining together during all phases of the procedure as well as after the insemination, we quickly abandoned this as a charade. The system neither encourages nor facilitates intimacy. It is concerned, as it probably should be, with results. And so we have become pragmatists too. We do not much enjoy the process of AIH, to say the least, but we also do not try to make it something it is not. A conception, if it takes place, will not be the result of an act of bodily lovemaking, but a result of technology. We have come to accept this. Yet, such acceptance comes at a price, for our experience of reproduction is discontinuous. A child conceived by this method is lovingly willed into existence, but it is not conceived through a loving, bodily act.

Having accepted the separation of sexual intercourse and procreation, however, it is difficult to resist any sort of technological manipulation of gametes that might result in conception. We have, so to speak, relinquished our gametes to the doctors and once this has been done, how can various technological manipulations be judged other than by criteria of likelihood of success? This is precisely the problem: once one has begun a process that inevitably treats procreation as the production of a product, the methods of production can only be evaluated by the end result.

Reproductive Technologies and Genetic Engineering

The fourth objection to NRTS is that their general acceptance and use is an inevitable route to widespread use of genetic engineering. It should be no mystery why this might be thought to be the case. Once the embryo, for example, is treated as a product to be bought and sold, there will be great pressure to produce the perfect product. The attraction of genetic engineering under such circumstances should be obvious. Genetic screening and therapy would be a sort of quality control mechanism by which to insure customer satisfaction.[29] Moreover, the greater access to embryos and to eggs provided by IVF and embryo flushing means that genetic manipulation of the eggs or the developing embryo is now more feasible than it once was. Even more importantly, however, this greater access to embryos and eggs, combined with the possibility of freezing and storing those not used to attempt a pregnancy, means that experimentation can go forward at a much faster rate. Scientists have experimented with the injection of genetic material into non-human eggs for some time, and a recent issue of *Cell* reported the introduction of foreign genetic material into mouse sperm.[30] It is not unreasonable to suppose that such manipulations will one day extend to human gametes. Indeed, one experimental technique being developed to treat forms of male infertility in which sperm is unable to penetrate the egg involves isolating a single sperm in order to introduce the sperm directly into the egg.[31] The obvious question is: How will this sperm be selected? The most likely answer will be: by a determination that it is not genetically abnormal.

Thus far, most genetic experimentation, manipulation, and screening has been defended by appeal to the goal of eliminating human suffering. If genetic abnormalities can be detected or even treated, much human suffering might either be avoided or alleviated. Yet, how does one distinguish between attempts to eliminate suffering and attempts at eugenics? The fact that it is so difficult to answer this question is one reason to be concerned about NRTS. Moreover, the equation of genetic abnormality or disability with suffering can be questioned. As Marsha Saxton has pointed out, we cannot simply assume that disabled people "suffer" from their physical conditions any more than any other group or category of individuals "suffer."[32] Indeed, decisions about bearing genetically damaged fetuses are generally made in relative ignorance of what sorts of lives potential offspring might actually have.[33] "Our exposure to disabled children," Saxton writes, "has been so limited by their isolation that most people have only stereotyped views which include telethons, and displays on drugstore counters depicting attractive crippled youngsters soliciting our pity and loose change" (306).

If reproductive technology is developed because every person has a right to bear a child, does it not follow that every person has a right to bear a perfect child? Advocates of NRTS would not admit this, and yet it seems to be the logical conclusion of the commitment to produce a child, no matter the cost. To see the difficulties here, we need only ask how we are to define the perfect child, and whether a commitment to eliminate genetic abnormalities means that women will lose the freedom not to test for or to treat abnormalities.[34]

In my view, the concern here is a real one for, once one has begun to think in terms of producing a product, it becomes exceedingly difficult to distinguish between technological interventions except on the basis of the resulting product. And since the product one desires in this instance is a healthy baby, a technological intervention that helps to achieve this, even one that involves genetic manipulation, is likely to be both initially attractive and ultimately irresistible. My own reaction to the new technique of overcoming male infertility by isolating a single sperm and injecting it into an egg it would otherwise be unable to penetrate is instructive. My initial response was that of tremendous excitement. Here was a treatment that could clearly overcome our problem. The fact that I did not produce great numbers of sperm or that the ones I produced were not likely to be capable of penetrating an egg did not matter. In theory, very few sperm are required and the work of penetration is done for them. The fact that such a technique involves placing an extraordinary amount of control in the hands of the doctor who selects the single sperm from among the many millions that even a man with a low sperm count is likely to produce did not even occur to me. In fact, it was my doctor, who had moral reservations about this technique, who first pointed this out to me. What is perhaps more troubling, however, is that when the issue of control was pointed out to me, I found no immediately compelling reason to object. I had, after all, been routinely providing sperm for a lab to manipulate in an effort to produce a collection that was capable of penetrating my wife's egg. Was selecting a single sperm that could accomplish the goal really so different?

In light of these various objections and my own experience, then, my basic response is one of concern. I do not believe that the predominantly male medical profession is acting in bad faith in developing reproductive technologies, as some critics suggest. Much of the feminist literature on NRTS is cynical and deeply contemptuous of what is seen as a patriarchal and conspiratorial medical establishment. My own experience, however, does not bear this out. Although there is much about my treatment for infertility that I have found frustrating, anxiety-producing, and distasteful, and although I have felt at turns coerced by the existence of the technologies themselves; angry at the loss of intimacy in my relationship with Lisa; and worried by my own near obsession with the goal of achieving a pregnancy, I have never had reason to doubt the sincerity of my doctor's care and concern. That my experience has been so negative despite treating with a doctor who is very much aware of the potentially dehumanizing aspects of infertility treatment is further evidence of how serious the problems with these technologies may be.

This is not to deny that infertility specialists are too concerned with technological fixes; in my view, they are. While there is no conspiracy to gain control of the process of reproduction, there is increased control. And if one theme joins the various objections to the new reproductive technologies, it is that they increase the medical profession's control over the process of reproduction and that such control has deleterious consequences. We have not, by and large, thought through the consequences of this sort of intervention and control. Neither infertile couples nor those who try to alleviate their suffering, nor indeed the community that is generally supportive of the desire to have children has really asked whether that desire should be met at all costs. Is the desire to have children a desire for a basic human good? Can it be met through adoption or only through biological offspring? Are there other, competing social goods that set limits on how far we, as a community, should go to meet this need? These are certainly questions that I had not addressed before my experience of infertility. Even now I am not certain how to answer all of them. I am certain, however, that my desire to have children is strong. I am also equally certain that we need to attend to these questions as a society. For anyone not blinded by self-deception will admit that wanting something does not always make it right.

Acknowledgments

A number of individuals both encouraged me to go forward with this essay, and provided me with very helpful suggestions for revisions. Thanks to Lisa Cahill, Lisa de Filippis, Howard Eilberg-Schwartz, Tom Kelly, Gilbert Meilaender, Louis Newman, John P. Reeder, Jr., David H. Smith, Claudia Spencer, John Spencer, and Brian Stiltner. I also received very helpful comments from the works-in-progress group at the Center for Bioethics at the Case Western Reserve University School of Medicine and the participants in a NEH-sponsored Humanities and Medicine Institute at Hiram College held in collaboration with the Northeastern Ohio Universities College of Medicine.

Endnotes

1. See Gena Corea, "The Reproductive Brothel" in *Man-made Woman,* Gena Corea *et al.,* eds. (Bloomington: Indiana University Press, 1987), 38–51.
2. The medical profession has gone to some lengths to insure that artificial insemination is defined as a medical procedure, and thus controlled by doctors. Most of my wife's inseminations have been administered by doctors, even when this has been inconvenient for us. The two exceptions have been when Lisa ovulated on the weekend and then, apparently, insemination did not need to be performed by a doctor.
3. Although for convenience I will refer in this paper to "feminist" objections, I cannot stress enough that there is not one feminist response to reproductive technology, but several. Indeed,

feminist responses range from enthusiastic support to moderate and cautious support to radical opposition. See Anne Donchin, "The Future of Mothering: Reproductive Technology and Feminist Theory," *Hypatia* (1986), 121–137.

4. Patricia Spallone and Deborah Lynn Steinberg, eds., *Made to Order* (Oxford: Pergamon Press, 1987).
5. But see Sidney Callahan, "The Role of Emotion in Ethical Decisionmaking," *Hastings Center Report* 18:3 (1988), 9–14.
6. On the difference between coercive offers and coercive threats, see Virginia Held, "Coercion and Coercive Offers," in *Coercion,* J. Roland Pennock and John Chapman, eds. (Chicago: Atherton, 1972), 49–62.
7. I use "couples" here intentionally. The justification for developing reproductive methods is almost always to help infertility within marriage. There is an irony in this: Although physicians tend to treat infertility as a problem for an individual, they insist that that individual be part of a heterosexual marriage. Thus it is not just infertility that is of concern, but infertility in certain types of situations.
8. For a discussion of the difficulty of providing an adequate account of free choice given the assumptions of modern liberalism, see Barbara Katz Rothman, *Recreating Motherhood* (New York: WW Norton, 1989), 62.
9. Robyn Rowland, "Of Woman Born, But for How Long?" in *Made to Order,* 70.
10. See Spallone and Steinberg, eds., *Made to Order,* 6–7.
11. The test involves injecting radiopaque dye into the uterine cavity after which X-rays are taken. The fallopian tubes are outlined wherever the dye has penetrated. Using this procedure, it is sometimes possible to determine whether a woman's tubes are blocked.
12. Here my experience and Lisa's differ dramatically. The infertility specialist I have seen could not be more sensitive or attentive to the human dimension of our difficulties. By contrast, Lisa's experience with the gynecologists involved with insemination has been almost entirely negative, in part because she has not been treated fully as a person by them.
13. Spallone and Steinberg, eds., *Made to Order,* 4–5.
14. Leon Kass, *Toward a More Natural Sex* (New York: The Free Press, 1985), 45.
15. I am, in effect, suggesting that more choice is not always better. This is not a popular view in our culture, but it can be persuasively defended. For such a defense, see Gerald Dworkin, "Is More Choice Better than Less?" *Midwest Studies in Philosophy* 7, Peter A. French, Theodore E. Uehling, Jr., and Howard K. Wettstein, eds. (Minneapolis: University of Minnesota Press, 1982), 47–61.
16. Gena Corea, *The Mother Machine* (New York: Harper and Row, 1985), 290.
17. Mary O'Brien, *The Politics of Reproduction* (Boston: Routledge and Kegan Paul, 1981), 55.
18. See Nancy Hansock, "The Feminist Standpoint: Developing the Ground for a Specifically Feminist Historical Materialism," in *Discovering Reality,* Sandra Harding and Merrill B. Hintikka, eds. (Dordrecht: D. Reidel, 1983), 283–310; and Caroline Whitbeck, "A Different Reality: Feminist Ontology," in *Beyond Domination,* Carol C. Gould, ed. (Totowa, NJ: Rowman and Allanheld, 1983), 64–88.

19. Emily Martin, *The Woman in the Body* (Boston: Beacon Press, 1987).
20. Marge Piercy, *Woman on the Edge of Time* (New York: Ballantine Books, 1976), 134.
21. Corea, *The Mother Machine,* 314.
22. Robyn Rowland, "Women as living Laboratories: The New Reproductive Technologies," in *The Trapped Woman,* Josefina Figueira-McDonough and Rosemary Sani, eds. (Newbury Park, CA: Sage Publications, 1987), 81–112.
23. According to the Office of Technology Assessment, $164 million is paid to close to 11,000 physicians every year for artificial inseminations alone. Add to this the variety of other infertility services provided every year to childless couples and the total cost is at least $1 billion (U.S. Congress, Office of Technology Assessment, Artificial Insemination Practice in the United States: Summary of a 1987 Survey, Washington: Government Printing Office, 1988).
24. Although there are currently no franchised clinics in the U.S., the ovum transfer procedure using uterine lavage is commonplace. See Leonard Fonnigli, Graziella Fonnigli, and Carlo Roccio, "Donation of Fertilized Uterine Ova to Infertile Women," *Fertility and Sterility* 47:1 (1987), 162–165.
25. Barbara Katz Rothman, "The Products of Conception: The Social Context of Reproductive Choices," *Journal of Medical Ethics* 11 (1985), 191.
26. The tendency to treat children as commodities is not solely the product of developing NRTS, of course, but the culmination of a process begun with the old reproductive technology of contraception. Once the inexorable connection between sexual intercourse and procreation was broken, it became possible to choose when to have children. From that point on, it made sense to treat children in some ways as products, the purchase of which, so to speak, could be planned as one planned the purchase of other expensive items.
27. Katz Rothman, *Recreating Motherhood,* 49.
28. Sacred Congregation for the Doctrine of the Faith, Instruction on Respect for Human Life in Its Origin and on the Dignity of Procreation, in *Origins* 16 (March 1987), 697–711.
29. Katz Rothman, "The Products of Conception," 188.
30. For a discussion of the transgenic animals that result from the genetic manipulation of eggs, see V.G. Pursel et al., "Genetic Engineering of Livestock," *Science* 244 (1989), 128–188. Also see M. Lavitrano et al., "Sperm Cells as Vectors for Introducting Foreign DNA into Eggs: Genetic Transformation of Mice," *Cell* 57:5 (1989), 717–724.
31. Actually, there are at least three different techniques being investigated. See Jon W. Gordon et al., "Fertilization of Human Oocytes by Sperm from Infertile Males After Zona Pellucida Drilling," *Fertility and Sterility* 50:1 (1988), 68–73.
32. Marsha Saxton, "Born and Unborn: The Implications of Reproductive Technologies for People with Disabilities," in *Test-Tube Women,* Rita Arditti, Renate Duelli Klein, and Shelley Minden, eds. (London: Pandora Press, 1984), 298–313.
33. Anne Finger, "Claiming All of Our Bodies: Reproductive Rights and Disabilities," in *Test-Tube Women,* 281–297.
34. See Ruth Hubbard, "Fetal Rights and the New Eugenics," *Science for the People* (March/April 1984), 7–9, 27–29.

Journal/Discussion Questions

✍ *Do you know anyone who has gone through any of the types of fertility programs that Lauritzen describes? In what ways was their experience similar to Lauritzen's? In what ways dissimilar?*

1. Why do feminists think that advances in reproductive technologies actually *reduce* women's choices? Do you agree with this reasoning? Why or why not?
2. Should reproductive technologies be made available to single women? To lesbian women? Why or why not?
3. Lauritzen states that, "A child conceived by this method [AID] is lovingly willed into existence, but it is not conceived through a loving, bodily act." What moral implications follow from this, according to Lauritzen. In what ways do you agree with him? Disagree?
4. Lauritzen asks, "How does one distinguish between attempts to eliminate suffering and attempts at eugenics?" How does he answer this question? In what ways do you agree with him? Disagree?

Leon Kass
"The Wisdom of Repugnance"

Leon Kass is the Addie Clark Harding Professor at the University of Chicago. He holds both an M.D. (University of Chicago) and a Ph.D. in biochemistry (Harvard), and regularly teaches courses on science and ethics. His books include Toward a Moral Natural Science, The Ethics of Cloning, *and* The Hungry Soul.

Kass, trained as a physician and biochemist, places cloning within the perspective of human lives and argues that we ought to feel a moral repugnance toward it. In this selection, he explores the philosophical justification for such a feeling.

As You Read, Consider This:

1. Why, according to Kass, is asexual reproduction such a profound departure from the traditional path to reproduction?
2. What does Kass mean by the "profundity of sex"?

. . . cloning shows itself to be a major alteration, indeed, a major violation, of our given nature as embodied, gendered and engendering beings—and of the social relations built on this natural ground. Once this perspective is recognized, the ethical judgment on cloning can no longer be reduced to a matter of motives and intentions, rights and freedoms, benefits and harms, or even means and ends. It must be regarded primarily as a matter of meaning: Is cloning a fulfillment of human begetting and belonging? Or is cloning rather, as I contend, their pollution and perversion? If pollution and perversion, the fitting response can only be horror and revulsion; and conversely, generalized horror and revulsion are prima facie evidence of foulness and violation. The burden of moral argument must fall entirely on those who want to declare the widespread repugnances of humankind to be mere timidity or superstition.

Yet repugnance need not stand naked before the bar of reason. The wisdom of our horror at human cloning can be partially articulated, even if this is finally one of those instances about which the heart has its reasons that reason cannot entirely know.

The Profundity of Sex

To see cloning in its proper context, we must begin not, as I did before, with laboratory technique, but with the anthropology—natural and social—of sexual reproduction. Sexual reproduction—by which I mean the generation of new life from (exactly) two complementary elements, one female, one male, (usually) through coitus—is established (if that is the right term) not by human decision, culture or tradition, but by nature; it is the natural way of all mammalian reproduction. By nature, each child has two complementary biological progenitors. Each child thus stems from and unites exactly two lineages. In natural generation, moreover, the precise genetic constitution of the resulting offspring is determined by a combination of nature and chance, not by human design; each human child shares the common natural human species genotype, each child is genetically (equally) kin to each (both) parent(s), yet each child is also genetically unique. These biological truths about our origins foretell deep truths about our identity and about our human condition altogether. Every one of us is at once equally human, equally enmeshed in a particular familial nexus of origin, and equally individuated in our trajectory from birth to death—and, if all goes well, equally capable (despite our mortality) of participating, with a complementary other, in the very same renewal of such human possibility through procreation. Though less momentous than our common humanity, our genetic individuality is humanly trivial. It shows itself forth in our distinctive appearance through which we are everywhere recognized, it is revealed in our signature marks of fingerprints and our self-recognizing immune system, it symbolizes and foreshadows exactly the unique, never-to-be-repeated character of each human life.

Human societies virtually everywhere have structured child-rearing responsibilities and systems of identity and relationship on the bases of these deep natural facts of begetting. The mysterious yet ubiquitous "love of one's own" is everywhere culturally exploited, to make sure that children are not just produced but well cared for, and to create for everyone clear ties of meaning, belonging, and obligation. But it is wrong to treat such naturally rooted social practices as mere cultural constructs (like left- or right-driving, or like burying or cremating the dead) that we can alter with little human cost. What would kinship be without its clear natural grounding? And what would identity be without kinship? We must resist those who have begun to refer to sexual reproduction as the "traditional method of reproduction," who would have us regard as merely traditional, and by implication arbitrary, what is in truth not only natural but most certainly profound.

Asexual reproduction, which produces "single-parent" offspring, is a radical departure from the natural human way, confounding all normal understandings of father, mother, sibling, grandparent, etc., and all moral relations tied thereto. It becomes even more of a radical departure when the resulting offspring is a clone derived not from an embryo, but from a mature adult to whom the clone would be an identical twin; and when the process occurs not by natural accident (as in natural twinning), but by deliberate human design and manipulation; and when the child's (or children's) genetic constitution is pre-selected by the parent(s) (or scientists). Accordingly, as we will see, cloning is vulnerable to three kinds of concerns and objections, related to these three points: cloning threatens confusion of identity and individuality, even in small-scale cloning; cloning represents a giant step (though not the first one) toward transforming procreation into manufacture, that is, toward the increasing depersonalization of the process of generation and, increasingly, toward the "production" of human children as artifacts, products of human will and design (what others have called the problem of "commodification" of new life); and cloning—like other forms of eugenic engineering of the next generation—represents a form of despotism of the cloners over the cloned, and thus (even in benevolent cases) represents a blatant violation of the inner meaning of parent-child relations, of what it means to have a child, of what it means to say "yes" to our own demise and "replacement." Before turning to these specific ethical objections, let me test my claim of the profundity of the natural way by taking up a challenge recently posed by a friend. What if the given natural human way of reproduction were asexual, and we now had to deal with a new technological innovation—artificially induced sexual dimorphism and the fusing of complementary gametes—whose inventors argued that sexual reproduction promised all sorts of advantages, including hybrid vigor and the creation of greatly increased individuality? Would one then be forced to defend natural asexuality because it was natural? Could one claim that it carried deep human meaning?

The response to this challenge broaches the ontological meaning of sexual reproduction. For it is impossible, I submit, for there to have been human life—or even higher forms of animal life—in the absence of sexuality and sexual reproduction. We find asexual reproduction only in the lowest forms of life: bacteria, algae, fungi, some lower invertebrates. Sexuality brings with it a new and enriched relationship to the world. Only sexual animals can seek and find complementary others with whom to pursue a goal that transcends their own existence. For a sexual being, the world is no longer an indifferent and largely homogeneous otherness, in part edible, in part dangerous. It also contains some very special and related and complementary beings, of the same kind but of opposite sex, toward whom one reaches out with special interest and intensity. In higher birds and mammals, the outward gaze keeps a lookout not only for food and predators, but also for prospective mates; the beholding of the many-splendored world is suffused with desire for union, the animal antecedent of human eros and the germ of sociality. Not by accident is the human animal both the sexiest animal—whose females do not go into heat but are receptive throughout the estrous cycle and whose males must therefore have greater sexual appetite and energy in order to reproduce successfully—and also the most aspiring, the most social, the most open, and the most intelligent animal.

The soul-elevating power of sexuality is, at bottom, rooted in its strange connection to mortality, which it simultaneously accepts and tries to overcome. Asexual reproduction may be seen as a continuation of the activity of self-preservation. When one organism buds or divides to become two, the original being is (doubly) preserved, and nothing dies. Sexuality, by contrast, means perishability and serves replacement; the two that come together to generate one soon will die. Sexual desire in human beings as in animals, thus serves an end that is partly hidden from, and finally at odds with, the self-serving individual. Whether we know it or not, when we are sexually active we are voting with our genitalia for our own demise. The salmon swimming upstream to spawn and die tell the universal story: Sex is bound up with death, to which it holds a partial answer in procreation.

Through children, a good common to both husband and wife, male and female achieve some genuine unification (beyond the mere sexual "union," which fails to do so). The two become one through sharing generous (not needy) love for this third being as good. Flesh of their flesh, the child is the parents' own commingled being externalized, and given a separate and persisting existence. Unification is enhanced also by their commingled work of rearing. Providing an opening to the future beyond the grave, carrying not only our seed but also our names, our ways and our hopes that they will surpass us in goodness and happiness, children are a testament to the possibility of transcendence. Gender duality and sexual desire, which first draws our love upward and outside of ourselves, finally provide for the partial overcoming of the confinement and limitation of perishable embodiment altogether.

Human procreation, in sum, is not simply an activity of our rational wills. It is a more complete activity precisely because it engages us bodily, erotically, and spiritually, as well as rationally. There is wisdom in the mystery of nature that has joined the pleasure of sex, the inarticulate longing for union, the communication of the loving embrace, and the deep-seated and only partly articulate desire for children in the very activity by which we continue the chain of human existence and participate in the renewal of human possibility. Whether or not we know it, the severing of procreation from sex, love and intimacy is inherently dehumanizing, no matter how good the product.

We are now ready for the more specific objections.

The Perversities of Cloning

First, an important if formal objection: Any attempt to clone a human being would constitute an unethical experiment upon the resulting child-to-be. As the animal experiments (frog and sheep) indicate, there are grave risks of mishaps and deformities. Moreover, because of what cloning means, one cannot presume a future cloned child's consent to be a clone, even a healthy one. Thus ethically speaking, we cannot even get to know whether or not human cloning is feasible.

I understand, of course, the philosophical difficulty of trying to compare a life with defects against nonexistence. Several bioethicists, proud of their philosophical cleverness, use this conundrum to embarrass claims that one can injure a child in its conception, precisely because it is only thanks to that complained-of conception that the child is alive to complain. But common sense tells us that we have no reason to fear such philosophisms. For we surely know that people can harm and even maim children in the very act of conceiving them, say, by paternal transmission of the AIDS virus, maternal transmission of heroin dependence or, arguably, even by bringing them into being as bastards, or with no capacity or willingness to look after them properly. And we believe that to do this intentionally, or even negligently, is inexcusable and clearly unethical.

Cloning creates serious issues of identity and individuality. The cloned person may experience concerns about his distinctive identity not only because he will be in genotype and appearance identical to another human being, but, in this case, because he may also be twin to the person who is his "father" or "mother"—if one can still call them that. What would be the psychic burdens of being the "child" or "parent" of your twin? The cloned individual, moreover, will be saddled with a genotype that has already lived. He will not be fully a surprise to the world.

People are likely always to compare his performances in life with that of his alter ego. True, his nurture and his circumstance in life will be different; genotype is not exactly destiny. Still, one must also expect parental and other efforts to shape this new life after the original—or at least to view the child with the original version always firmly in mind. Why else did they clone from the star basketball player, mathematician and beauty queen—or even dear old dad—in the first place?

Since the birth of Dolly, there has been a fair amount of doublespeak on this matter of genetic identity. Experts have rushed in to reassure the public that the clone would in no way be the same person, or have any confusions about his or her identity; as previously noted, they are pleased to point out that the clone of Mel Gibson would not be Mel Gibson. Fair enough. But one is short-changing the truth by emphasizing the additional importance of the intrauterine environment, rearing, and social setting: genotype obviously matters plenty. That, after all, is the only reason to clone, whether human beings or sheep. The odds that clones of Wilt Chamberlain will play in the NBA are, I submit, infinitely greater than they are for clones of Willie Shoemaker.

Curiously, this conclusion is supported, inadvertently, by the one ethical sticking point insisted on by friends of cloning: no cloning without the donor's consent. Though an orthodox liberal objection, it is in fact quite puzzling when it comes from people (such as Ruth Macklin) who also insist that genotype is not identity or individuality, and who deny that a child could reasonably complain about being made a genetic copy. If the clone of Mel Gibson would not be Mel Gibson, why should Mel Gibson have grounds to object that someone had been made his clone? We already allow researchers to use blood and tissue samples for research purposes of no benefit to their sources: my falling hair, my expectorations, my urine and even my biopsied tissues are "not me" and not mine. Courts have held that the profit gained from uses to which scientists put my discarded tissues do not legally belong to me. Why, then, no cloning without consent—including, I assume, no cloning from the body of someone who just died? What harm is done the donor, if genotype is "not me"? Truth to tell, the only powerful justification for objecting is that genotype really does have something to do with identity, and everybody knows it. If not, on what basis could Michael Jordan object that someone cloned "him" from cells, say, taken from a "lost" scraped-off piece of his skin? The insistence on donor consent unwittingly reveals the problem of identity in all cloning.

Troubled psychic identity (distinctiveness), based on all-too-evident genetic identity (sameness), will be made much worse by the utter confusion of social identity and kinship ties. For, as already noted, cloning radically confounds lineage and social relations, for "offspring" as for "parents." As bioethicist James Nelson has pointed out, a female child cloned from her "mother" might develop a desire for a relationship to her "father," and might understandably seek out the father of her "mother," who is after all also her biological twin sister. Would "grandpa," who thought his paternal duties concluded, be pleased to discover that the clonant looked to him for paternal attention and support?

Social identity and social ties of relationship and responsibility are widely connected to, and supported by, biological kinship. Social taboos on incest and adultery everywhere serve to keep clear who is related to whom (and especially which child belongs to which parents), as well as to avoid confounding the social identity of parent-and-child (or brother-and-sister) with the social identity of lovers, spouses, and co-parents. True, social identity is altered by adoption (but as a matter of the best interest of already living children: we do not deliberately produce children for adoption). True, artificial insemination and *in vitro* fertilization with donor sperm, or whole embryo donation, are in some way forms of "prenatal adoption"—a not altogether unproblematic practice. Even here, though, there is in each case (as in all sexual reproduction) a known male source of sperm and a known single female source of egg—a genetic father and a genetic mother—should anyone care to know (as adopted children often do) who is genetically related to whom.

In the case of cloning, however; there is but one "parent." The usually sad situation of the "single-parent child" is here deliberately planned, and with a vengeance. In the case of self-cloning, the "offspring" is, in addition, one's twin; and so the dreaded result of incest—to be parent to one's sibling—is here brought about deliberately, albeit without any act of coitus. Moreover, all other relationships will be confounded. What will father, grandfather, aunt, cousin, sister mean? Who will bear what ties and what burdens? What sort of social identity will someone have with one whole side—"father's" or "mother's"—necessarily excluded? It is no answer to say that our society, with its high incidence of divorce, remarriage, adoption, extramarital childbearing and the rest, already confounds lineage and confuses kinship and responsibility for children (and everyone else), unless one also wants to argue that this is, for children, a preferable state of affairs.

Human cloning would also represent a giant step toward turning begetting into making, procreation into manufacture (literally, something "handmade"), a process already begun with *in vitro* fertilization and genetic testing of embryos. With cloning, not only is the process in hand, but the total genetic blueprint of the cloned individual is selected and determined by the human artisans. To be sure, subsequent development will take place according to natural processes; and the resulting children will still be recognizably human. But we here would be taking a major step into making man himself simply another one of the man-made things. Human nature becomes merely the last part of nature to succumb to the technological project, which turns all of nature into raw material at human disposal, to be homogenized by our rationalized technique according to the subjective prejudices of the day. How does begetting differ from making? In natural procreation, human beings come together, complementarily male and female, to give existence to another being who is formed, exactly as we were, by what we are: living, hence perishable, hence aspiringly erotic, human beings. In clonal reproduction, by contrast, and in the more advanced forms of manufacture to which it leads, we give existence to a being not by what we are but by what we intend and design. As with any product of our making, no matter how excellent, the artificer stands above it, not as an equal but as a superior, transcending it by his will and creative prowess. Scientists who clone animals make it perfectly clear that they are engaged in instrumental making; the animals are, from the start, designed as means to serve rational human purposes. In human cloning, scientists and prospective parents would be adopting the same technocratic mentality to human children: human children would be their artifacts.

Such an arrangement is profoundly dehumanizing, no matter how good the product. Mass-scale cloning of the same individual makes the point vividly; but the violation of human equality, freedom, and dignity are present even in a single planned clone. And procreation dehumanized into manufacture is further degraded by commodification, a virtually inescapable result of allowing baby-making to proceed under the banner of commerce. Genetic and reproductive biotechnology companies are already growth industries, but they will go into commercial orbit once the Human Genome Project nears completion. Supply will create enormous demand. Even before the capacity for human cloning arrives, established companies will have invested in the harvesting of eggs from ovaries obtained at autopsy or through ovarian surgery, practiced embryonic genetic alteration, and initiated the stockpiling of prospective donor tissues. Through the rental of surrogate-womb services, and through the buying and selling of tissues and embryos, priced according to the merit of the donor, the commodification of nascent human life will be unstoppable.

Finally, and perhaps most important, the practice of human cloning by nuclear transfer—like other anticipated forms of genetic engineering of the next generation—would enshrine and aggravate a profound and mischievous misunderstanding of the meaning of having children and of the parent-child relationship. When a couple now chooses to procreate, the partners are saying yes to the emergence of new life in its novelty, saying yes not only to having a child but also, tacitly, to having whatever child this child turns out to be. In accepting our finitude and opening ourselves to our replacement, we are tacitly confessing the limits of our control. In this ubiquitous way of nature, embracing the future by pro-creating means precisely that we are relinquishing our grip, in the very activity of taking up our own share in what we hope will be the immortality of human life and the human species. This means that our children are not our children: they are not our property, not our possessions. Neither are they supposed to live our lives for us, or anyone else's life but their own. To be sure, we seek to guide them on their way, imparting to them not just life but nurturing, love, and a way of life; to be sure, they bear our hopes that they will live fine and flourishing lives, enabling us in small measure to transcend our own limitations. Still, their genetic distinctiveness and independence are the natural foreshadowing of the deep truth that they have their own and never-before-enacted life to live. They are sprung from a past, but they take an uncharted course into the future.

Ban the Cloning of Humans

What, then, should we do? We should declare that human cloning is unethical in itself and dangerous in its likely consequences. In so doing, we shall have the backing of the overwhelming majority of our fellow Americans, and of the human race, . . . The president's call for a moratorium on human cloning has given us an important opportunity. In a truly unprecedented way, we can strike a blow for the human control of the technological project, for wisdom, prudence, and human dignity. The prospect of human cloning, so repulsive to contemplate, is the occasion for deciding whether we shall be slaves of unregulated progress, and ultimately its artifacts, or whether we shall remain free human beings who guide our technique toward the enhancement of human dignity. If we are to seize the occasion, we must, as the late Paul Ramsey wrote, raise the ethical questions with a serious and not a frivolous conscience. A man of frivolous conscience announces that there are ethical quandaries ahead that we must urgently consider before the future catches up with us. By this he often means that we need to devise a new ethics that will provide the rationalization for doing in the future what men are bound to do because of new actions and interventions science will have made possible. In contrast a man of serious conscience means to say in raising urgent ethical questions that there may be some things that men should never do. The good things that men do can be made complete only by the things they refuse to do.

Journal/Discussion Questions

✍ *Kass describes a feeling of repugnance toward cloning. What are your feelings toward cloning? Were they affected in any way by reading Kass's article?*

1. What effects does Kass claim cloning has on a sense of individuality? Do you agree with Kass's argument? Explain.
2. Kass claims that cloning is dehumanizing. What does he mean by "dehumanizing"? Do you agree with his analysis? State your reasons.

Ronald Bailey
"The Twin Paradox: What Exactly Is Wrong with Cloning People?"*

Ronald Bailey, a contributing editor of Reason Magazine, *is a writer and television producer in Washington, D.C. His books include* Ecoscam: The False Prophets of Ecological Apocolypse *(1994) and* The True State of the Planet *(1995).*

In this article, Ronald Bailey challenges those who would dismiss cloning as unethical, arguing that upon closer examination he maintains that there are few good arguments against cloning per se. Maintaining that environment plays as essential a role as genetics in determining identity, Bailey claims that clones would be unique and would be just as entitled to rights as any other human being.

As You Read, Consider This:

1. What arguments does Bailey consider against cloning? What is his reply to each of them?
2. What do you think Bailey's views in general are about prediction and regulation? How do they affect his position in this article?

By now everyone knows that Scottish biotechnologists have cloned a sheep. They took a cell from a 6-year-old sheep, added its genes to a hollowed out egg from another sheep, and placed it in the womb of yet another sheep, resulting in the birth of an identical twin sheep that is six years younger than its sister. This event was followed up by the announcement that some Hawaiian scientists had cloned mice. The researchers say that in principle it should be possible to clone humans. That prospect has apparently frightened a lot of people, and quite a few of them are calling for regulators to ban cloning since we cannot predict what the consequences of it will be.

President Clinton rushed to ban federal funding of human cloning research and asked privately funded researchers to stop such research at least until the National Bioethics Advisory Commission issues a report on the ethical implications of human cloning. The commission, composed of scientists, lawyers, and ethicists, was appointed last year to advise the federal government on the ethical questions posed by biotechnology research and new medical therapies. But Sen. Christopher Bond (R-MO) wasn't waiting around for the commission's recommendations; he'd already made up his mind. Bond introduced a bill to ban the federal funding of human cloning or human cloning research. "I want to send a clear signal," said the senator, "that this is something we cannot and should not tolerate. This type of research on humans is morally reprehensible."

Carl Feldbaum, president of the Biotechnology Industry Organization, hurriedly said that human cloning should be immediately banned. Perennial Luddite Jeremy Rifkin grandly pronounced that cloning "throws every convention, every historical tradition, up for grabs." At the putative opposite end of the political spectrum conservative columnist George Will chimed in: "What if the great given—a human being is a product of the union of a man and woman—is no

* Ronald Bailey, "The Twin Paradox: What Exactly Is Wrong with Cloning People?" *Reason Magazine,* 1997.

longer a given?" In addition to these pundits and politicians, a whole raft of bioethicists declared that they, too, oppose human cloning. Daniel Callahan of the Hastings Center said flat out: "The message must be simple and decisive: The human species doesn't need cloning." George Annas of Boston University agreed: "Most people who have thought about this believe it is not a reasonable use and should not be allowed . . . This is not a case of scientific freedom vs. the regulators."

Given all of the brouhaha, you'd think it was crystal clear why cloning humans is unethical. But what exactly is wrong with it? Which ethical principle does cloning violate? Stealing? Lying? Coveting? Murdering? What? Most of the arguments against cloning amount to little more than a reformulation of the old familiar refrain of Luddites everywhere: "If God had meant for man to fly, he would have given us wings. And if God had meant for man to clone, he would have given us spores." Ethical reasoning requires more than that.

What would a clone be? Well, he or she would be a complete human being who happens to share the same genes with another person. Today, we call such people identical twins. To my knowledge no one has argued that twins are immoral. Of course, cloned twins would not be the same age. But it is hard to see why this age difference might present an ethical problem—or give clones a different moral status. "*You* should treat all clones like you would treat all monozygous [identical] twins or triplets," concludes Dr. H. Tristam Engelhardt, a professor of medicine at Baylor and a philosopher at Rice University. "That's it." It would be unethical to treat a human clone as anything other than a human being. If this principle is observed, he argues, all the other "ethical" problems for a secular society essentially disappear. John Fletcher, a professor of biomedical ethics in the medical school at the University of Virginia, agrees: "I don't believe that there is any intrinsic reason why cloning should not be done."

Let's take a look at a few of the scenarios that opponents of human cloning have sketched out. Some argue that clones would undermine the uniqueness of each human being. "Can individuality, identity and dignity be severed from genetic distinctiveness, and from belief in a person's open future?" asks George Will. Will and others have apparently fallen under the sway of what Fletcher calls "genetic essentialism." Fletcher says polls indicate that some 30 percent to 40 percent of Americans are genetic essentialists, who believe that genes almost completely determine who a person is. But a person who is a clone would live in a very different world from that of his genetic predecessor. With greatly divergent experiences, their brains would be wired differently. After all, even twins who grow up together are separate people—distinct individuals with different personalities and certainly no lack of Will's "individuality, identity and dignity."

In addition, a clone that grew from one person's DNA inserted in another person's host egg would pick up "maternal factors" from the proteins in that egg, altering its development. Physiological differences between the womb of the original and host mothers could also affect the clone's development. In no sense, therefore, would or could a clone be a "carbon copy" of his or her predecessor. What about a rich jerk who is so narcissistic that he wants to clone himself so that he can give all his wealth to himself? First, he will fail. His clone is simply not the same person that he is. The clone may be a jerk too, but he will be his own individual jerk. Nor is Jerk Sr.'s action unprecedented. Today, rich people, and regular people too, make an effort to pass along some wealth to their children when they die. People will their estates to their children not only because they are connected by bonds of love but also because they have genetic ties. The principle is no different for clones.

Senator Bond and others worry about a gory scenario in which clones would be created to provide spare parts, such as organs that would not be rejected by the predecessor's immune system. "The creation of a human being should not be for spare parts or as a replacement," says Bond. I agree. The simple response to this scenario is: Clones are people. You must treat them like people. We don't forcibly take organs from one twin and give them to the other. Why would we do that in the case of clones?

The technology of cloning may well allow biotechnologists to develop animals that will grow human-compatible organs for transplant. Cloning is likely to be first used to create animals that produce valuable therapeutic hormones, enzymes, and proteins. But what about cloning exceptional human beings? George Will put it this way: "Suppose a cloned Michael Jordan, age 8, preferred violin to basketball? Is it imaginable? If so, would it be tolerable to the cloner?" Yes, it is imaginable, and the cloner would just have to put up with violin recitals. Kids are not commercial property—slavery was abolished some time ago. We all know about Little League fathers and stage mothers who push their kids, but given the stubborn nature of individuals, those parents rarely manage to make kids stick forever to something they hate. A ban on cloning wouldn't abolish pushy parents.

One putatively scientific argument against cloning has been raised. As a National Public Radio commentator who opposes cloning quipped, "Diversity isn't just politically correct, it's good science." Sexual reproduction seems to have evolved for the purpose of staying ahead of ever-mutating pathogens in a continuing arms race. Novel combinations of genes created through sexual reproduction help immune systems devise defenses against rapidly evolving germs, viruses, and parasites. The argument against cloning says that if enough human beings were cloned, pathogens would likely adapt and begin to get the upper hand, causing widespread disease. The analogy often cited is what happens when a lot of farmers all adopt the same corn hybrid. If the hybrid is highly susceptible to a particular bug, then the crop fails. That warning may have some validity for cloned livestock, which may well have to live in environments protected from infectious disease. But it is unlikely that there will be millions of clones of one person. Genomic diversity would still be the rule for humanity. There might be more identical twins, triplets, etc., but unless there are millions of clones of one person, raging epidemics sweeping through hordes of human beings with identical genomes seem very unlikely. But even if someday millions of clones of one person existed, who is to say that novel technologies wouldn't by then be able to control human pathogens? After all, it wasn't genetic diversity that caused typhoid, typhus, polio, or measles to all but disappear in the United States. It was modern sanitation and modern medicine. There's no reason to think that a law against cloning would make much difference anyway. "It's such a simple technology, it won't be banable," says Engelhardt. "That's why God made offshore islands, so that anybody who wants to do it can have it done." Cloning would simply go underground and be practiced without legal oversight. This means that people who turned to cloning would not have recourse to the law to enforce contracts, ensure proper standards, and hold practitioners liable for malpractice.

Who is likely to be making the decisions about whether human cloning should be banned? When President Clinton appointed the National Bioethics Advisory Commission last year his stated hope was that such a commission could come up with some sort of societal consensus about what we should do with cloning. The problem with achieving and imposing such a consensus is that Americans live in a large number of disparate moral communities. "If you call up the Pope in Rome, do you think he'll hesitate?" asks Engelhardt. "He'll say, 'No, that's not the way that

Christians reproduce.' And if you live Christianity of a Roman Catholic sort, that'll be a good enough answer. And if you're fully secular, it won't be a relevant answer at all. And if you're in-between, you'll feel kind of generally guilty."

Engelhardt questions the efficacy of such commissions:

"Understand why all such commissions are frauds. Imagine a commission that really represented our political and moral diversity. It would have as its members Jesse Jackson, Jesse Helms, Mother Teresa, Bella Abzug, Phyllis Schafly. And they would all talk together, and they would never agree on anything . . . Presidents and Congresses rig—manufacture fraudulently—a consensus by choosing people to serve on such commissions who already more or less agree . . . Commissions are created to manufacture the fraudulent view that we have a consensus."

Unlike Engelhardt, Fletcher believes that the National Bioethics Advisory Commission can be useful, but he acknowledges that "all of the commissions in the past have made recommendations that have had their effects in federal regulations. So they are a source eventually of regulations." The bioethics field is littered with ill-advised bans, starting in the mid-1970s with the two-year moratorium on recombining DNA and including the law against selling organs and blood and Clinton's recent prohibition on using human embryos in federally funded medical research. As history shows, many bioethicists succumb to the thrill of exercising power by saying no. Simply leaving people free to make their own mistakes will get a bioethicist no perks, no conferences, and no power. Bioethicists aren't the ones suffering, the ones dying, and the ones who are infertile, so they do not bear the consequences of their bans. There certainly is a role for bioethicists as advisers, explaining to individuals what the ramifications of their decisions might be. But bioethicists should have no ability to stop individuals from making their own decisions, once they feel that they have enough information.

Ultimately, biotechnology is no different from any other technology—humans must be allowed to experiment with it in order to find its best uses and, yes, to make and learn from mistakes in using it. Trying to decide in advance how a technology should be used is futile. The smartest commission ever assembled simply doesn't have the creativity of millions of human beings trying to live the best lives that they can by trying out and developing new technologies. So why is the impulse to ban cloning so strong? "We haven't gotten over the nostalgia for the Inquisition," concludes Engelhardt. "We are people who are postmodernist with a nostalgia for the Middle Ages. We still want the state to have the power of the Inquisition to enforce good public morals on everyone, whether they want it or not."

Journal/Discussion Questions

✍ *In contrast to Kass, Bailey seems to experience no feelings of repugnance about cloning. How does his article affect your own feelings about this issue?*

1. Much of Bailey's argument turns on the equivalent of twins and clones. In what ways are twins and clones the same? In what ways do they differ? How do these differences affect Bailey's arguments?
2. Bailey claims that "Trying to decide in advance how a technology should be used is futile." Do you agree or disagree with this claim? Why?

Richard A. McCormick
"Should We Clone Humans? Wholeness, Individuality, Reverence"

Richard A. McCormick, S.J., is a Catholic moral theologian and philosopher who specializes in biomedical ethics. His earlier work includes How Brave a New World.

In contrast to those who maintain that decisions about human cloning and genetic manipulation are personal matters of individual autonomy, McCormick argues that they are profoundly social issues. He proposes three fundamental values—wholeness, individuality, and reverence—to serve as guides in decision making in this area.

As You Read, Consider This:

1. McCormick claims that the assumption that "anything that helps overcome infertility is morally appropriate" is "frighteningly myopic." What does he mean by this? Do you agree?
2. What, according to McCormick, is the moral status of the pre-embryo?

The cloning of human embryos by Dr. Jerry L. Hall at George Washington University Medical Center last month has set off an interesting ethical debate. Should it be done? For what purposes? With what controls? It is not surprising—though I find it appalling—that some commentators see the entire issue in terms of individual autonomy. Embryos belong to their producers, they argue, and it is not society's business to interfere with the exercise of people's privacy (see comments in the *New York Times,* October 26 [1993]).

One's approach to cloning will vary according to the range of issues one wants to consider. For example, some people will focus solely on the role of cloning in aiding infertile couples—and they will likely conclude that there is nothing wrong with it. The scarcely hidden assumption is that anything that helps overcome infertility is morally appropriate. That is, I believe, frighteningly myopic.

Human cloning is an extremely social matter, not a question of mere personal privacy. I see three dimensions to the moral question: the wholeness of life, the individuality of life, and respect for life.

Wholeness. Our society has gone a long way down the road of positive eugenics, the preferential breeding of superior genotypes. People offhandedly refer to "the right to a healthy child." Implied in such loose talk is the right to discard the imperfect. What is meant, of course, is that couples have a claim to reasonably available means to ensure that their children are born healthy. We have pre-implementation diagnosis for genetic defects. We have recently seen several cases of "wrongful life" where the child herself or himself is the plaintiff. As a member of the ethics committee of the American Fertility Society, I regularly receive brochures from sperm banks stating the donors' race, education, hobbies, height, weight and eye color. We are rapidly becoming a pick-and-choose society with regard to our prospective children. More than a few couples withhold acceptance of their fetuses pending further testing. This practice of eugenics raises a host of problems: What qualities are to be maximized? What defects are intolerable? Who decides? But the critical flaw in "preferential breeding" is the perversion of our attitudes: we begin to value the person in terms of the particular trait he or she was programmed to have. In short, we reduce the whole to a part. People who do that are in a moral wilderness.

Individuality. Uniqueness and diversity (sexual, racial, ethnic, cultural) are treasured aspects of the human condition, as was sharply noted by a study group of the National Council of Churches in 1984 (Genetic Engineering: Social and Ethical Consequences). Viewed theologically, human beings, in their enchanting, irreplaceable uniqueness and with all their differences, are made in the image of God. Eugenics schemes that would bypass, downplay or flatten human diversities and uniqueness should be viewed with a beady eye. In the age of the Genome Project it is increasingly possible to collapse the human person into genetic data. Such reductionism could shatter our wonder at human individuality and diversity at the very time that, in other spheres of life, we are emphasizing it.

Life. Everyone admits that the pre-embryo (preimplanted embryo) is human life. It is living, not dead. It is human, not canine. One need not attribute personhood to such early life to claim that it demands respect and protection.

Two considerations must be carefully weighed as we try to discern our obligations toward pre-embryonic life. The first consideration is for the potential of the pre-embryo. Under favorable circumstances, the fertilized ovum will move through developmental individuality and then progressively through functional, behavioral, psychic and social individuality. In viewing the first stage, one cannot afford to blot out subsequent stages. It retains its potential for personhood and thus deserves profound respect. This is a weighty matter for the believer who sees the human person as a member of Gods family and the temple of the Spirit. Interference with such a potential future cannot be a light undertaking.

The second consideration concerns our own human condition. I would gather these concerns under the notion of "uncertainty." There is uncertainty about the extent to which enthusiasm for human research can be controlled. That is, if we concluded that pre-embryos need not be treated in all circumstances as persons, would we little by lithe extend this to embryos? Would we gradually trivialize the reasons justifying pre-embryo manipulation? These are not abstract worries; they have become live questions.

Furthermore, there is uncertainty about the effect of pre-embryo manipulation on personal and societal attitudes toward nascent human life in general. Will there be further erosion of our respect? I say "further" because of the widespread acceptance and practice of abortion. There is grave uncertainty about our ability to say no and backtrack when we detect abuses, especially if they have produced valuable scientific and therapeutic data or significant treatment. Medical technology ("progress") has a way of establishing irreversible dynamics.

Because the pre-embryo does have intrinsic potential and because of the many uncertainties noted above, I would argue that the pre-embryo should be treated as a person. These obligations, may be prima facie—to use W.D. Ross's phrase—and subject to qualifications. But when we are dealing with human life, the matter is too important to be left to local or, regional criteria and controls. We need uniform national controls. Without them, our corporate reverence for life, already so deeply compromised, will be further eroded.

In sum, human cloning is not just another technological step to be judged in terms of its effects on those cloned. What frightens me above all is what human cloning would do to all of us—to our sense of the wholeness, individuality and sanctity of human life. These are intertwined theological concerns of the first magnitude.

Journal/Discussion Questions

✍ *McCormick expresses his concerns as "theological." Do you think these concerns are limited only to those who share his religious beliefs? Discuss.*

1. "Preferential breeding," as McCormick calls it, undermines the value of wholeness. Explain his reasoning for this claim. In what ways do you agree with him? Disagree? Should wholeness be an important value?
2. To what extent do advances in cloning threaten diversity? Do you think that diversity is an important value in this context? Explain.
3. McCormick maintains that the preembryo should be treated as a person. What support does he offer for this claim? Do you agree or disagree? Why?

Concluding Discussion Questions

Where Do You Stand Now?

Instructions

You have already answered the following questions in your moral problems self-quiz at the beginning of this book. Now that you have studied the material in this section, take a moment to answer the same questions again.

	Strongly Agree	*Agree*	*Undecided*	*Disagree*	*Strongly Disagree*	*Chapter 2: Cloning and Reproductive Technologies*
6.	❑	❑	❑	❑	❑	*In vitro* fertilization is morally wrong.
7.	❑	❑	❑	❑	❑	Any procedure that helps infertile couples to have children is good.
8.	❑	❑	❑	❑	❑	Surrogate mothers should never have to give up their babies if they don't want to do so.
9.	❑	❑	❑	❑	❑	Surrogate motherhood should be illegal.
10.	❑	❑	❑	❑	❑	Genetic manipulation of embryos should be forbidden.

Compare your answers to the present self-quiz with the answers to the initial self-quiz. How, if at all, have your answers changed? How have the *reasons* for your answers changed?

Journal/Discussion Questions

✍ *If you were going to have a baby, to what extent would you want to select its characteristics in advance? Which characteristics, if any, would you not want to consciously select? Physical characteristics? Physical and mental capabilities? Personality traits? Sex? Sexual orientation?*

1. In light of the readings in this chapter, what new issues about reproductive technologies were most interesting to you? Which ones do you think will be most difficult for us as a society to resolve?
2. Should there be any limits on couples who wish to use artificial means to have children? Should there be any limits on individuals who wish to do so?
3. Should society regulate the practice of surrogacy? In what ways? How should it deal with surrogate mothers who change their minds?

For Further Reading

Web Resources

The Reproductive Technologies page of Ethics Updates (http://ethics.acusd.edu) contains numerous resources relating to reproductive technologies and cloning. This includes the Ian Wilmut articles, court decisions, and reports of the National Bioethics Advisory Committee.

Journals

The *Hastings Center Reports, BioEthics, Kennedy Institute of Ethics, Journal of Medicine and Philosophy, Biomedical Ethics Reviews,* and *Law, Medicine & Health Care* for discussion of issues relating specifically to biomedical ethics. Some of the best articles in the *Hastings Center Reports* have been gathered together in *Life Choices: A Hastings Center Introduction to Bioethics,* edited by Joseph H. Howell and William Frederick Sale (Washington, DC: Georgetown University Press, 1995).

Review Articles and Reports

There are a number of helpful bibliographies available on issues relating to *reproductive technologies;* see Mary Carrington Coutts, "Human Gene Therapy," *Scope Note 24* (Washington, DC: Georgetown University, 1994); and Walters, LeRoy, and Kahn, Tamar Joy, eds., *Bibliography of Bioethics,* Vols. 1–19 (Washington, DC: Kennedy Institute of Ethics, Georgetown University). For a review of some of the moral issues raised by new reproductive technologies, see Helen Bequaert Holmes, "Reproductive Technologies," *Encyclopedia of Ethics,* edited by Lawrence C. Becker and Charlotte B. Becker (New York: Garland, 1992), Vol. II, pp. 1083–1089.

There have been a number of national commissions, both here and in England, that have prepared reports and policy recommendations on these issues. In the United States, the National Bioethics Advisory Commission reports, which are available on-line at *http://bioethics.gov/pubs.html,* contain extensive resources and provide an excellent point of departure for those interested in the current state of these issues; see especially the Commission's Report on Cloning. Also see Mary Warnock, *A Question of Life: The Warnock Report on Human Fertilization and Embryology* (Oxford: Basil Blackwell, 1985); Jonathan Glover et al., *Fertility and the Family: The Glover Report on Reproductive Technologies to the European Commission* (London: Fourth Estate, 1989); American Fertility Society, Ethics Committee, "Ethical Considerations of the New Reproductive Technologies," in *Fertility and Sterility,* Vol. 46, No. 3, supplement 1 (1986) and *Fertility and Sterility,* Vol. 53, No. 6, supplement 2 (1990). For a religious response to the Warnock report, see Oliver O'Donovan, *Begotten or Made?* (Oxford: Clarendon Press, 1984). For a survey of results of such reports, see LeRoy Walters, "Ethical Aspects of the New Reproductive Technologies," *Annals of the New York Academy of Sciences,* No. 541 (1988), pp. 646–664.

Anthologies and Books

There are a number of excellent anthologies available in the area of reproductive technologies. Among the general anthologies on issues in bioethics, see the excellent *Contemporary Issues in Bioethics,* edited by Tom L. Beauchamp and LeRoy Walters, Fifth Edition (Belmont, CA: Wadsworth, 1999); for an excellent selection of both philosophical and non-philosophical authors, see *Genetic Engineering: Opposing Viewpoints* (San Diego: Greenhaven Press, 1994) and Carol Levine, ed., *Taking Sides: Clashing View on Controversial Bioethical Issues* (Guilford, CN: Dushkin, 1995). On the issue of the family, see especially *Kindred Matters: Rethinking the Philosophy of the Family,* edited by Diana Tietjens Meyers, Kenneth Kipnis, and Cornelius F. Murphy, Jr. (Ithaca: Cornell University Press, 1993).

One of the principal areas of concern in regard to genetic screening is *sex selection.* See Mary Anne Warren, *Gendercide: The Implications of Sex Selection* (Totowa, NJ: Rowman and Allanheld, 1985); and her "IVF and Women's Interests: An Analysis of Feminist Concerns," *Bioethics* 2, No. 1 (1988), pp. 37–57; for a review on recent feminist work in this and related areas, see Anne Donchin, "The Growing Feminist Debate Over the New Reproductive Technologies," *Hypatia,* Vol. 4, No. 3 (1989), pp. 136–149 (also see several other related articles in this volume); and Helen Bequaert Holmes, "Sex Preselection: Eugenics for Everyone?" *Biomedical Ethics Reviews—1985,* edited by J. Humber and R. Almeder (Clifton, NJ: Humana Press, 1985). Also see Michelle Stanworth, *Reproductive Technologies: Gender, Motherhood, and Medicine* (Minneapolis, MN: University of Minnesota Press, 1987).

For some excellent resources in regard to questions of *genetic engineering,* see *Ethical Issues in the New Reproductive Technologies,* edited by Richard Hull (Belmont, CA: Wadsworth, 1990); Kenneth D. Alpern, *The Ethics of Reproductive Technology* (New York: Oxford University Press); Sherill Cohen and Nadine Taub, eds., *Reproductive Laws for the 1990s* (Clifton, NJ: Humana Press, 1989); Ruth F. Chadwick, ed., *Ethics, Reproduction, and Genetic Control* (London: Croom Helm, 1987); Elaine Baruch, et al., *Test Tube Women: What Future for Motherhood?* (London: Pandora, 1984) contains essays mostly against new reproductive technologies; Clifford Grobstein's *From Chance to Purpose: An appraisal of External Human Fertilization* (Reading, MA: Addison-Wesley, 1981) and his later *Science and the Unborn: Choosing Human Futures* (New York: Basic Books, 1988); Joseph Fletcher's *The Ethics of Genetic Control: Ending Reproductive Roulette* (Buffalo, NY: Prometheus Books, 1988) strongly presents the case in favor of genetic manipulation, while Gena Corea's *The Mother Machine: Reproductive Technologies from Artificial Insemination to Artificial Wombs* (New York: Harper and Row, 1985) gives a strong presentation of arguments against such manipulation. For a well-argued and balanced approach to these issues, see Glenn McGee, *The Perfect Baby: A Pragmatic Approach to Genetics* (Totowa, NJ: Rowman & Littlefield, 1997). Also see the anthology, *The Future of Human Reproduction,* edited by John Harris and Søren Holm (New York: Oxford, 1998).

Key Essays

On the issue of *genetic engineering,* see the issue of *The Hastings Center Report,* Vol. 24, No. 2 (March 1994), with articles by Joseph Palca, "A Word to the Wise; on the Approval of *in vitro* Fertilization Research"; John A. Robertson, "The question of human cloning"; and Richard A.

McCormick, "Blastomere separation: some concerns; embryo splitting as a treatment to *in vitro* fertilization." For a good collection of essays on the status of the fetus, see *Biomedical Ethics Reviews: Bioethics and the Fetus: Medical, Moral, and Legal Issues,* edited by James M. Humber and Robert Almeder (Clifton, NJ: Humana Press, 1991) and Peter Singer et al., eds., *Embryo Experimentation* (New York: Cambridge University Press). For a critique of the philosophical viability of the notion of the *pre-embryo,* see A.A. Howsepian, "Who or What Are We?" *Review of Metaphysics,* Vol. 45, No. 3 (March 1992), pp. 483–502, which replied to Richard McCormick's "Who or What Is the Pre-Embryo?" in the *Kennedy Institute of Ethics Journal,* Vol. 1 (1991), pp. 1–15; Alan Holland, "A Fortnight of My Life Is Missing: A Discussion of the Status of the Human 'Pre-Embryo,' " *Applied Philosophy,* edited by Brenda Almond and Donald Hill (London: Routledge, 1991), pp. 299–311.

Cloning

There are a number of excellent books on cloning. Among the best anthologies are: *Clones and Clones: Facts and Fantasies about Human Cloning,* edited by Martha C. Nussbaum and Cass R. Sunstein (New York: Norton, 1998); Glenn McGee, The Human Cloning Debate (Berkeley: Berkeley Hills Books, 1998); *Cloning: For and Against,* edited by M. L. Rantala and Arthur J. Milgram (Chicago: Open Court, 1999); *Flesh of My Flesh: The Ethics of Cloning Humans. A Reader,* edited by Gregory E. Pence (Totowa, NJ: Rowman & Littlefield, 1998); *Human Cloning: Religious Responses,* edited by Ronald Cole-Turner (Louisville, KY: Westminster John Knox Press, 1997). Also see Leon R. Kass and James Q. Wilson, *The Ethics of Human Cloning* (Washington, DC: The AEI Press, 1998).

CHAPTER 3

Euthanasia

Videotape:

ABCNEWS

Topic: Mercy or Homicide? The Strange Case of Dr. Jack Kevorkian

Source: ABC *Nightline* (November 23, 1998)

Anchors: John Donvan, Forrest Sawyer

NARRATIVE ACCOUNTS

Anonymous
"It's Over, Debbie"

The author of this essay remains anonymous; at the time this was written, he or she was a gynecology resident. After the publication of this essay in The Journal of the American Medical Association, *unsuccessful attempts were made to indict the resident for murder.*

This article describes an actual instance of euthanasia by a physician who at that time was a resident in gynecology. The case of Debbie, as it has come to be known, is discussed in several selections later in this chapter.

The call came in the middle of the night. As a gynecology resident rotating through a large, private hospital, I had come to detest telephone calls, because invariably I would be up for several hours and would not feel good the next day. However, duty called, so I answered the phone. A nurse informed me that a patient was having difficulty getting rest, could I please see her. She was on 3 North. That was the gynecologic-oncology unit, not my usual duty station. As I trudged along, bumping sleepily against walls and corners and not believing I was up again, I tried to imagine what I might find at the end of my walk. Maybe an elderly woman with an anxiety reaction, or perhaps something particularly horrible.

I grabbed the chart from the nurses' station on my way to the patient's room, and the nurse gave me some hurried details: a twenty-year-old girl named Debbie was dying of ovarian cancer. She was having unrelenting vomiting apparently as the result of an alcohol drip administered for sedation. Hmmm, I thought. Very sad. As I approached the room I could hear loud, labored breathing. I entered and saw an emaciated, dark-haired woman who appeared much older than twenty. She was receiving nasal oxygen, had an IV, and was sitting in bed suffering from what was obviously severe air hunger. The chart noted her weight at eighty pounds. A second woman, also dark-haired but of middle age, stood at her right, holding her hand. Both looked up as I entered. The room seemed filled with the patient's desperate effort to survive. Her eyes were hollow, and she had suprasternal and intercostal retractions with her rapid inspirations. She had not eaten or slept in two days. She had not responded to chemotherapy and was being given supportive care only. It was a gallows scene, a cruel mockery of her youth and unfulfilled potential. Her only words to me were, "Let's get this over with."

I retreated with my thoughts to the nurses' station. The patient was tired and needed rest. I could not give her health, but I could give her rest. I asked the nurse to draw 20 mg. of morphine sulfate into a syringe. Enough, I thought, to do the job. I took the syringe into the room and told the two women I was going to give Debbie something that would let her rest and to say good-bye. Debbie looked at the syringe, then laid her head on the pillow with her eyes open, watching what was left of the world. I injected the morphine intravenously and watched to see if my calculations would be correct. Within seconds her breathing slowed to a normal rate, her eyes closed, and her features softened as she seemed restful at last. The older woman stroked the hair of the now-sleeping patient. I waited for the inevitable next effect of depressing the respiratory drive. With clocklike certainty, within four minutes the breathing rate slowed even more, then became irregular, then ceased. The dark-haired woman stood erect and seemed relieved.

It's over, Debbie.

Journal/Discussion Questions

✍ *As you develop your own position on the morality and legality of euthanasia, in what ways does this article help you to develop your own thinking?*

1. If you had been the resident in this situation, what would you have done? Why?
2. One of the major issues in euthanasia is the question of informed consent. Do you think the resident had informed consent? What more, if anything, should have been done to insure informed consent?
3. If you were the district attorney for the city in which this took place, would you seek to charge the resident with a crime? Why or why not?

Timothy E. Quill, M.D.
"Death and Dignity: A Case of Individualized Decision Making"

Timothy Quill, M.D., specializes in internal medicine, has had experience as a hospice director, and is an associate professor of medicine and psychiatry at the University of Rochester School of Medicine and Dentistry. His book, Death and Dignity: Making Choices and Taking Charge *argues in favor of physician-assisted euthanasia.*

In sharp contrast to the previous selection, this piece depicts a strong and long relationship between a physician and his patient. As the patient, Diane, confronts her terminal cancer, she decides that she does not want extraordinary medical care. Her doctor, Timothy Quill, must then face crucial issues about how willing he is to help to alleviate Diane's suffering and support her choice to die.

Diane was feeling tired and had a rash. A common scenario, though there was something subliminally worrisome that prompted me to check her blood count. Her hematocrit was 22, and the white-cell count was 4.3 with some metamyelocytes and unusual white cells. I wanted it to be viral, trying to deny what was staring me in the face. Perhaps in a repeated count it would disappear. I called Diane and told her it might be more serious than I had initially thought—that the test needed to be repeated and that if she felt worse, we might have to move quickly. When she pressed for the possibilities, I reluctantly opened the door to leukemia. Hearing the word seemed to make it exist. "Oh, shit!" she said. "Don't tell me that." Oh, shit! I thought, I wish I didn't have to.

Diane was no ordinary person (although no one I have ever come to know has been really ordinary). She was raised in an alcoholic family and had felt alone for much of her life. She had vaginal cancer as a young woman. Through much of her adult life, she had struggled with depression and her own alcoholism. I had come to know, respect, and admire her over the previous eight years as she confronted these problems and gradually overcame them. She was an incredibly clear, at times brutally honest, thinker and communicator. As she took control of her life, she developed a strong sense of independence and confidence. In the previous 3½ years, her hard work had paid off. She was completely abstinent from alcohol, she had established much deeper connections with her husband, college-age son, and several friends, and her business and her artistic work were blossoming. She felt she was really living fully for the first time.

Not surprisingly, the repeated blood count was abnormal, and detailed examination of the peripheral-blood smear showed myelocytes. I advised her to come into the hospital, explaining that we needed to do a bone marrow biopsy and make some decisions relatively rapidly. She came to the hospital knowing what we would find. She was terrified, angry, and sad. Although we knew the odds, we both clung to the thread of possibility that it might be something else.

The bone marrow confirmed the worst: acute myelomonocytic leukemia. In the face of this tragedy, we looked for signs of hope. This is an area of medicine in which technological intervention has been successful, with cures 25 percent of the time—long-term cures. As I probed the costs of these cures, I heard about induction chemotherapy (three weeks in the hospital, prolonged neutropenia, probable infectious complications, and hair loss; 75 percent of patients respond, 25 percent do not). For the survivors, this is followed by consolidation chemotherapy (with similar side effects; another 25 percent die, for a net survival of 50 percent). Those still alive, to have a reasonable chance of long-term survival, then need bone marrow transplantation (hospitalization for two months and whole-body irradiation, with complete killing of the bone marrow, infectious complications, and the possibility for graft-versus-host disease—with a survival of approximately 50 percent, or 25 percent of the original group). Though hematologists may argue over the exact percentages, they don't argue about the outcome of no treatment—certain death in days, weeks, or at most a few months.

Believing that delay was dangerous, our oncologist broke the news to Diane and began making plans to insert a Hickman catheter and begin induction chemotherapy that afternoon. When I saw her shortly thereafter, she was enraged at his presumption that she would want treatment, and devastated by the finality of the diagnosis. All she wanted to do was go home and be with her family. She had no further questions about treatment and in fact had decided that she wanted none. Together we lamented her tragedy and the unfairness of life. Before she left, I felt the need to be sure that she and her husband understood that there was some risk in delay, that the problem was not going to go away, and that we needed to keep considering the options over the next several days. We agreed to meet in two days.

She returned in two days with her husband and son. They had talked extensively about the problem and the options. She remained very clear about her wish not to undergo chemotherapy and to live whatever time she had left outside the hospital. As we explored her thinking further, it became clear that she was convinced she would die during the period of treatment and would suffer unspeakably in the process (from hospitalization, from lack of control over her body, from the side effects of chemotherapy, and from pain and anguish). Although I could offer support and my best effort to minimize her suffering if she chose treatment, there was no way I could say any of this would not occur. In fact, the last four patients with acute leukemia at our hospital had died very painful deaths in the hospital during various stages of treatment (a fact I did not share with her). Her family wished she would choose treatment but sadly accepted her decision. She articulated very clearly that it was she who would be experiencing all the side effects of treatment and that odds of 25 percent were not good enough for her to undergo so toxic a course of therapy, given her expectations of chemotherapy and hospitalization and the absence of a closely matched bone marrow donor. I had her repeat her understanding of the treatment, the odds, and what to expect if there were no treatment. I clarified a few misunderstandings, but she had a remarkable grasp of the options and implications.

I have been a longtime advocate of active, informed patient choice of treatment or nontreatment, and of a patient's right to die with as much control and dignity as possible. Yet there was something about her giving up a 25 percent chance of long-term survival in favor of almost certain death that disturbed me. I had seen Diane fight and use her considerable inner resources to overcome alcoholism and depression, and I half expected her to change her mind over the next week. Since the window of time in which effective treatment can be initiated is rather narrow, we met several times that week. We obtained a second hematology consultation and talked at length about the meaning and implications of treatment and nontreatment. She talked to a psychologist she had seen in the past. I gradually understood the decision from her perspective and became convinced that it was the right decision for her. We arranged for home hospice care (although at that time Diane felt reasonably well, was active, and looked healthy), left the door open for her to change her mind, and tried to anticipate how to keep her comfortable in the time she had left.

Just as I was adjusting to her decision, she opened up another area that would stretch me profoundly. It was extraordinarily important to Diane to maintain control of herself and her own dignity during the time remaining to her. When this was no longer possible, she clearly wanted to die. As a former director of a hospice program, I know how to use pain medicines to keep patients comfortable and lessen suffering. I explained the philosophy of comfort care, which I strongly believe in. Although Diane understood and appreciated this, she had known of people lingering in what was called relative comfort, and she wanted no part of it. When the time came, she wanted to take her life in the least painful way possible. Knowing of her desire for independence and her decision to stay in control, I thought this request made perfect sense. I acknowledged and explored this wish but also thought that it was out of the realm of currently accepted medical practice and that it was more than I could offer or promise. In our discussion, it became clear that preoccupation with her fear of a lingering death would interfere with Diane's getting the most out of the time she had left until she found a safe way to ensure her death. I feared the effects of a violent death on her family, the consequences of an ineffective suicide that would leave her lingering in precisely the state she dreaded so much, and the possibility that a family member would be forced to assist her, with all the legal and personal repercussions that would follow. She discussed this at length with her family. They believed that they should respect her choice. With this in mind, I told Diane that information was available from the Hemlock Society that might be helpful to her.

A week later she phoned me with a request for barbiturates for sleep. Since I knew that this was an essential ingredient in a Hemlock Society suicide, I asked her to come to the office to talk things over. She was more than willing to protect me by participating in a superficial conversation about her insomnia, but it was important to me to know how she planned to use the drugs and to be sure that she was not in despair or overwhelmed in a way that might color her judgment. In our discussion, it was apparent that she was having trouble sleeping, but it was also evident that the security of having enough barbiturates available to commit suicide when and if the time came would leave her secure enough to live fully and concentrate on the present. It was clear that she was not despondent and that in fact she was making deep, personal connections with her family and close friends. I made sure that she knew how to use the barbiturates for sleep, and also that she knew the amount needed to commit suicide. We agreed to meet regularly, and she promised to meet with me before taking her life, to ensure that all other avenues had been exhausted. I wrote the prescription with an uneasy feeling about the boundaries I was exploring—spiritual, legal, professional, and personal. Yet I also felt strongly that I was setting her free to get the most out of the time she had left, and to maintain dignity and control on her own terms until her death.

The next several months were very intense and important for Diane. Her son stayed home from college, and they were able to be with one another and say much that had not been said earlier. Her husband did his work at home so that he and Diane could spend more time together. She spent time with her closest friends. I had her come into the hospital for a conference with our residents, at which she illustrated in a most profound and personal way the importance of informed decision making, the right to refuse treatment, and the extraordinarily personal effects of illness and interaction with the medical system. There were emotional and physical hardships as well. She had periods of intense sadness and anger. Several times she became very weak, but she received transfusions as an outpatient and responded with marked improvement of symptoms. She had two serious infections that responded surprisingly well to empirical courses of oral antibiotics. After three tumultuous months, there were two weeks of relative calm and well-being, and fantasies of a miracle began to surface.

Unfortunately, we had no miracle. Bone pain, weakness, fatigue, and fevers began to dominate her life. Although the hospice workers, family members, and I tried our best to minimize the suffering and promote comfort, it was clear that the end was approaching. Diane's immediate future held what she feared the most—increasing discomfort, dependence, and hard choices between pain and sedation. She called up her closest friends and asked them to come over to say good-bye, telling them that she would be leaving soon. As we had agreed, she let me know as well. When we met, it was clear that she knew what she was doing, that she was sad and frightened to be leaving, but that she would be even more terrified to stay and suffer. In our tearful good-bye, she promised a reunion in the future at her favorite spot on the edge of Lake Geneva, with dragons swimming in the sunset.

Two days later her husband called to say that Diane had died. She had said her final good-byes to her husband and son that morning, and asked them to leave her alone for an hour. After an hour, which must have seemed an eternity, they found her on the couch, lying very still and covered by her favorite shawl. There was no sign of struggle. She seemed to be at peace. They called me for advice about how to proceed. When I arrived, her husband and son were quiet. We talked about what a remarkable person she had been. They seemed to have no doubts about the course she had chosen or about their cooperation, although the unfairness of her illness and the finality of her death were overwhelming to us all.

I called the medical examiner to inform him that a hospice patient had died. When asked about the cause of death, I said, "acute leukemia." He said that was fine and that we should call a funeral director. Although acute leukemia was the truth, it was not the whole story. Yet any mention of suicide would have given rise to a police investigation and probably brought the arrival of an ambulance crew for resuscitation. Diane would have become a "coroner's case," and the decision to perform an autopsy would have been made at the discretion of the medical examiner. The family or I could have been subject to criminal prosecution, and I to professional review, for our roles in support of Diane's choices. Although I truly believe that the family and I gave her the best care possible, allowing her to define her limits and directions as much as possible, I am not sure the law, society, or the medical profession would agree. So I said "acute leukemia" to protect all of us, to protect Diane from an invasion into her past and her body, and to continue to shield society from the knowledge of the degree of suffering that people often undergo in the process of dying. Suffering can be lessened to some extent, but in no way eliminated or made benign, by the careful intervention of a competent, caring physician, given current social constraints.

Diane taught me about the range of help I can provide if I know people well and if I allow them to say what they really want. She taught me about life, death, and honesty and about taking charge and facing tragedy squarely when it strikes. She taught me that I can take small risks for people that I really know and care about. Although I did not assist in her suicide directly, I helped indirectly to make it possible, successful, and relatively painless. Although I know we have measures to help control pain and lessen suffering, to think that people do not suffer in the process of dying is an illusion. Prolonged dying can occasionally be peaceful, but more often the role of the physician and family is limited to lessening but not eliminating severe suffering.

I wonder how many families and physicians secretly help patients over the edge into death in the face of such severe suffering. I wonder how many severely ill or dying patients secretly take their lives, dying alone in despair. I wonder whether the image of Diane's final aloneness will persist in the minds of her family, or if they will remember more the intense, meaningful months they had together before she died. I wonder whether Diane struggled in that last hour, and whether the Hemlock Society's way of death by suicide is the most benign. I wonder why Diane, who gave so much to so many of us, had to be alone for the last hour of her life. I wonder whether I will see Diane again, on the shore of Lake Geneva at sunset, with dragons swimming on the horizon.

Journal/Discussion Questions

✍ *Have you ever known anyone in a situation similar to Diane's? How did they deal with it? How would you have dealt with it?*

1. Do you think that Dr. Quill made the right decision in this case? Why or why not? How would you have responded to Diane's decision?
2. Do you think physicians should ever be allowed to assist patients in ending their own lives? What guidelines, if any, would you propose for physicians who face this choice?

An Introduction to the Moral Issues

As we consider the details of the issue of euthanasia, it is helpful to begin by realizing the pervasiveness of the issue. Increasingly, people die in a medical context—often a hospital—that is unfamiliar to them and populated primarily by strangers. Currently, 85 percent of Americans die in some kind of health-care facility (this includes not only hospitals, but nursing homes, hospices, etc.); of this group, 70 percent (which is equivalent to almost 60 percent of the population as a whole) choose to withhold some kind of life-sustaining treatment.[1] It is highly likely that each of us will eventually face that same decision about ourselves; it is even more likely that we will indirectly be involved in that decision as family members and loved ones face death.

Dying in a hospital is particularly difficult, for there is nothing within medicine itself—which is tenaciously committed to winning every possible battle with death, even though there is no hope of ever winning the war—that helps physicians to let go, to allow an individual to die peacefully. There are certainly many physicians who show great wisdom in dealing with this issue (the selection from Dr. Quill is a good example of this), but their wisdom flows primarily from their character as persons rather than from their medical knowledge. Medical knowledge alone does not tell us when to let go, and medical practice—perhaps quite rightly—is often committed to fighting on and on, no matter what the odds. Yet this means that each of us as patients must face this question squarely.

What Are We Striving For?

Before we begin to consider some of the intricate conceptual issues posed by euthanasia, it is important to ask ourselves what our goal is in this area. In our discussion of abortion, almost everyone would agree that our ultimate goal was to have a society in which there were no unwanted pregnancies; at that point, abortion would disappear as a moral issue. Obviously, in the case of euthanasia, things are much different. Clearly, we are not striving for a society in which there are no unwanted deaths. That would not only be impossible, but also—at least from a population point of view—undesirable. We cannot do away with death or avoid it.

Given this basic fact, our goal in this area presumably centers around *how we die,* not whether we die. The word "euthanasia" comes from the Greek, *eu,* which means "good" or "well," and the Greek word for death, *thanatos.* In its broadest sense, euthanasia is about dying well. How do we do this?

The first, and most obvious, point is that dying well is intimately linked to living well. It is highly unlikely that we will die well if we have not been able to live well. Those who die surrounded by loved ones and at peace with themselves are those who have lived lives filled with love and who have come to peace with their lives; their lives are, in a certain fundamental sense, complete and not marred by unresolved fundamental regrets. It is very different, I think, for those who have not found love or peace in their lives; their deaths are often characterized by loneliness and a sense of incompleteness, a grasping for what could have been. Much of what needs to be said about euthanasia is not about death, but about life. A good life is the best preparation for a good death. Unfortunately, even a good life is no guarantee of a good death; chance can always intervene to make one's death untimely, unbearably painful, or uncharacteristically lonely.

There is a second, and much narrower, sense of euthanasia: a (relatively) painless death free from the pain and the intrusion of medical attempts to sustain life. Most of the philosophical discussion has centered around this second sense of euthanasia, but some of the difficulties that arise in this second and narrower sense of euthanasia can be reduced if it is placed within the context of this wider sense of euthanasia. All too often, we try through medical means to help an individual to die well, when in actuality all that is within reach medically is to help the person to die painlessly and quickly. A quick and painless death is not the same thing as a good death, but sometimes it is the best we can do.

Some Initial Distinctions

Recent discussions of euthanasia have been dominated by several important distinctions—and by disagreement over exactly how the distinctions are to be drawn and what significance they should have. The three most important of these are the distinction between active and passive euthanasia, voluntary and involuntary euthanasia, and assisted and unassisted euthanasia. Let's consider each of these in turn.

Active versus Passive Euthanasia

The distinction between active and passive euthanasia seems, on the surface, easy enough. *Active euthanasia* occurs in those instances in which someone takes active means, such as a lethal injection, to bring about someone's death; *passive euthanasia* occurs in those instances in which someone simply refuses to intervene in order to prevent someone's death. In a hospital setting, a DNR (do not resuscitate) order is one of the most common means of passive euthanasia.

How do we draw the line between killing and letting die?

Conceptual clarity. This distinction has been attacked in at least two ways. First, some have attacked the *conceptual clarity* of the distinction, arguing that the line between active and passive is much more blurred than one might initially think. One reason this distinction becomes conceptually slippery, especially in regard to the notion of passive euthanasia, is that it is embedded in a background set of assumptions about what constitutes normal care and what the normal duties of care givers are. In typical hospital settings, there is a distinction between ordinary and extraordinary care. At one end of the spectrum, giving someone food and water is clearly ordinary care; at the other end of the spectrum, giving someone an emergency heart and lung transplant to save that person's life is clearly extraordinary care. Refusing to give food and water seems to be different than refusing to perform a transplant. Both are passive, but one involves falling below the expectations of normal care while the other does not. Typically, DNRs would fall somewhere in the middle ground on this scale. The source of this bit of conceptual slipperiness comes from that we need to distinguish between two levels on passive euthanasia: (1) refusing to provide extraordinary care, and (2) refusing to provide any life-sustaining care at all. Just as in daily life we would distinguish between the person who refuses to jump into a turbulent sea to save a drowning child and the person who refuses to reach into a bathtub to save a baby drowning there, so, too, in medical contexts we must distinguish between refusing to take extraordinary means to prevent death and refusing to provide normal care (such as nutrition and hydration) to sustain life.

There is at least a second reason why this distinction is conceptually slippery, especially in regard to the notion of active euthanasia. As we have already seen in our discussion of abortion, philosophers distinguish between the intended consequences of an action and the unintended (but foreseeable) consequences of an action. This distinction is crucial to the principle of the double effect, which under certain specifiable conditions morally permits an individual to perform an action that would otherwise not be allowed. Many Catholic ethicians, for example, would argue that a physician might be morally permitted to perform a surgical procedure such as a hysterectomy to remove a cancerous uterus even if this results in the death of a fetus, as long as the intention was not to kill the fetus, the cause was serious, and there was no other means to that end. Similarly, physicians might give certain terminal patients pain-killers in large dosages, realizing that such dosages might cause death but having no other way of alleviating the patient's extreme pain.

Moral significance. In addition to attacking the conceptual clarity of the active/passive distinction, some ethicists have attacked the *moral significance* of this distinction. The standard view is that active euthanasia is morally much more questionable than passive euthanasia, since it involves actively choosing to bring about the death of a human being. Critics of the moral significance of this distinction have argued that active euthanasia is often more compassionate than passive euthanasia and morally preferable to it. The typical type of case they adduce is one in which (1) there is no doubt that the patient will die soon, (2) the option of passive euthanasia causes significantly more pain for the patient (and often the family as well) than active euthanasia and does nothing to enhance the remaining life of the patient, and (3) passive measures will not bring about the death of the patient. Certain types of cancers are not only extremely painful, but also very resistant to pain-killing medications in dosages that still permit patients to be aware of themselves and those around them. It is not uncommon for situations to occur in which patients will undoubtedly die (within several days, if not hours) and in which their remaining time will be filled either with extreme pain or unconsciousness resulting from pain medication. Removal of life-support may not bring about the death of such patients if their heart and respiratory systems have not been seriously compromised. In such situations, passive euthanasia seems to be *crueler* than active euthanasia and therefore morally less preferable.

Voluntary, Nonvoluntary, and Involuntary Euthanasia

The second crucial distinction in discussion of euthanasia is among voluntary, nonvoluntary, and involuntary euthanasia. Voluntary euthanasia occurs when the individual chooses to die; nonvoluntary euthanasia occurs when the individual's death is brought about (either actively or passively) without the individual's choosing to die; involuntary euthanasia occurs when the individual's death is brought about against the individual's wishes. Several points need to be made about this distinction.

The distinction between nonvoluntary and involuntary. Involuntary euthanasia covers those cases in which an individual does not want to be euthanized; nonvoluntary euthanasia refers to those in which the individual cannot make an expressed choice at all. The former class of cases is clearly troubling: the individual wishes to live and someone else intentionally terminates that individual's life. Most would say that this is simply murder. The latter class of cases is more common and morally more ambiguous. How do we treat those individuals, usually terminally ill and unable to choose (due to coma or some other medical condition), who may be in great pain and who have never clearly expressed their wishes about euthanasia in the past? Similarly, infants are unable to express their wishes about this (or any other) matter. If euthanasia is employed in such cases, it is involuntary, but not in the same sense as it is involuntary when the patient has expressed a clear wish not to be euthanized. Thus, we get the following type of division:

Euthanasia
- Voluntary: Patient makes the choice
- Nonvoluntary: Patient is unable to choose
- Involuntary: Against the patient's wishes

The morally most troubling of these cases will be those of involuntary euthanasia where the patient is unable to choose.

Assisted versus Unassisted Euthanasia

The final important distinction in the discussion of euthanasia centers about the fact that many instances of euthanasia occur when an individual is no longer physically able to carry out the act. Assistance becomes necessary, either to perform the action at all or at least to die in a relatively painless and nonviolent way. Several important points need to be noted about this distinction.

The following chart helps us to see the ways in which these basic distinctions relate to one another, the types of acts they designate, and their current legal status in the United States:

Euthanasia: Some Fundamental Distinctions

	Passive	Active: Not Assisted	Active: Assisted
Voluntary	Currently legal; often contained in living wills	Equivalent to suicide for the patient	Equivalent to suicide for the patient; possibly equivalent to murder for the assistant
Nonvoluntary: Patient not able to choose	Sometimes legal, but only with court permission	Not possible	Equivalent to either suicide or being murdered for the patient; legally equivalent to murder for the assistant
Involuntary: Against patient's wishes	Not legal	Not possible	Equivalent to being murdered for the patient; equivalent to murder for the assistant

Equipped with these distinctions, let's now turn to a consideration of the fundamental moral issues raised by euthanasia, looking first at the justifications that have been offered for and against euthanasia and then considering the three most typical types of cases: defective newborns, adults with profoundly diminished lives, and those in the final and painful phase of a terminal illness.

Euthanasia As the Compassionate Response to Suffering

One of the principal moral motives that moves us toward euthanasia is compassion: we see needless suffering, whether in ourselves or others, we want to alleviate or end it, and euthanasia is the only means of doing so. The paradigmatic situation here is that of a patient who is near death, who is in great pain that is not responsive to medication, and who has made an informed choice to die. At that juncture, those who care about the patient simply want the patient's suffering to end—there seems to be no point in further suffering, for there is no hope of recovery—and euthanasia becomes the way of ending it.

Is euthanasia a proper way to express one's compassion for the suffering of the dying?

It is important to understand the *intention* contained in this kind of response. The direct intention is not to kill the patient; neither is it a utilitarian intention concerning the reduction of the overall amount of suffering; nor is it an egoistic intention that simply seeks to be rid of an annoying relative. Rather, the direct intention is simply to stop the patient's pointless suffering. In passive euthanasia, the means is the withholding or withdrawal of life-sustaining treatment; in active euthanasia, the means for ending that suffering is some action—such as a lethal injection—that brings about the death of the patient. There are certainly situations in which passive euthanasia would not quickly end the suffering; patients may continue to live, sometimes for days, in great agony once life-support has been removed. In such cases, active euthanasia offers the only avenue for ending the pain. It is precisely this type of response that has come to be known as "mercy killing." If any situation justifies active euthanasia, this would seem to be it.

Some cases of compassionate euthanasia can be viewed as an instance of the principle of double effect, but only when the intention was still to relieve pain. If a physician was administering increasingly large doses of pain medication which eventually and foreseeably resulted in the patient's death, this could be covered under the principle of the double effect as long as the intention throughout was to relieve the patient's pain. It's not clear, however, whether this is really euthanasia; it seems better described as a last-ditch, high-risk attempt to alleviate the patient's suffering.

There is a sense in which the motivation and justification of compassionate euthanasia may appear to be utilitarian, or at least consequentialist, in character: the concern is with eliminating pointless suffering. It asks what good comes from the suffering and what bad comes from the termination of the suffering. But there are two ways in which the motivation for this response is not utilitarian in the standard sense. First, it is concerned principally, perhaps even exclusively, with the welfare of the patient, not with the *overall* welfare. Second, it is not a *calculated* response in the way in which classical utilitarianism is; rather, it is a response from the heart, a compassionate response that seeks to eliminate the pointless suffering of someone we care about. It arises, not out of calculation, but out of care.

The adjective "pointless" is crucial here for two reasons. First, it indicates that euthanasia is not a proper response to *all* suffering, only to that suffering which serves no purpose. Generally, suffering that results in the patient's getting better (or at least improving to some minimally acceptable level) is not seen as pointless. Second, it helps explain part of the disagreement in our own society about the morality of euthanasia. Our views on euthanasia will depend in part on our background assumptions about the nature and purpose of suffering. Once again, we see that there are at least two distinct traditions here. On the one hand, many in our society hold that suffering always has a purpose—usually a purpose that God can discern, even if we mere mortals cannot. It may build character, purify an individual, provide an example to others, provide retribution, or serve some part in a larger plan beyond our grasp. On this view, even the suffering in the final stage of a terminal illness serves some purpose, although we may not be able to say what it is. On the other hand, many others in our society believe that suffering is simply an unqualified evil that should be eradicated whenever possible. Suffering, on this view, is always pointless in itself, even if it is sometimes unavoidable for the sake of some other goal such as recovering from an illness. These two views on suffering will be discussed in more detail in the next section.

This compassionate response may not be limited just to cases of extreme pain in terminally ill patients; it may extend, at least in respect to passive euthanasia, to cases of extreme physical debility or to cases of Alzheimer's where the individual's personal identity has long ago been lost. The principal criterion here would seem to be the individual's wish no longer to be alive under such conditions—whether that wish is currently expressed or had been expressed clearly at an earlier point in life. Again, the focus here is on what the person wants and what is in the person's best interest.

The Sanctity of Life and the Right to Die

There are very few villains in the debate over euthanasia, but there are disagreements about the interpretation and relative place of certain fundamental values and rights. One of the most prominent areas of conflict centers around the relationship between the sanctity of life and the right to die.

The Sanctity of Life

Human life, many of us believe, is sacred. In its original form, this belief is a religious one; the sanctity of life is an indication that life is a gift from God and therefore cannot be ended by human hand without violating God's law or rejecting God's love. Moreover, in its original form—one sees this most clearly in Buddhism, but also in other religious traditions—this belief encompasses *all* life, not just human life. In this form, it is not only a tradition that encompasses pacifism and opposes capital punishment, abortion, and euthanasia, but also one that respects the lives of animals and the living environment as a whole. Life is a sacred gift from God, and it is not the proper role of human beings to take it away from anyone. Respect for life, in the words of one Catholic bishop, is a "seamless garment" which covers the entire fabric of living creation. No distinction is drawn about the quality of life. All life is to be respected, loved, and cared for. It is this tradition that leads to the compassion of the Buddha and of Mother Theresa.

Followers of this tradition do not support either active or passive euthanasia in the sense discussed here. However, they certainly are committed to the broader sense of "dying well" and spiritual discipline is often part of that commitment. Their alternative to active or passive euthanasia in the Western sense is not neglect, but compassion and love and ministering to the sick, the infirm, and the dying.

The Right to Die

Those who argue that human beings have a right to die usually differ from those who stress the sanctity of life on two principal points. First, and more importantly, they do not see life as a gift from God which cannot be disposed of at will; instead, they often see life ontologically as an accident and almost always morally as the possession of an individual. The dominant metaphor here is of life as property rather than gift. In this tradition, each person is seen as *owning* his or her own life, and owners are allowed to do whatever they want with their property. Second, respect for life in this tradition entails allowing the proper owner—that is, the individual—to decide for himself or herself whether to continue living. Notice that this tradition does not deny respect for life; rather, it has a different view of the source of life and of who holds proper dominion over life.

Those in this tradition respond quite differently to illnesses that profoundly reduce the quality of an individual's life or produce great and needless pain. Their focus is on reducing suffering, maintaining a minimal threshold of quality for the individual's life, and encouraging individuals to make their own decisions about the termination of their own life. The focus is thus on the quality of life and individual autonomy. The types of cases that those in this tradition point to are usually cases in which individuals want to die in order to end their suffering but are kept alive against their own wishes because a family member, the court, or in some cases the administrators of health care facilities—ever fearful of suits and federal investigations—are unwilling to let them die.

Yet there is also an irony in this tradition, for its emphasis on technology and control helps to create the very problem which it then seeks to solve through euthanasia. Just as it prolongs life through technology, it then must figure out how to end life technologically. Active euthanasia for the chronically ill and slowly dying rarely arises as an issue in nontechnological societies because, prior to the introduction of modern, high-tech medicine, people either died or got better.

The Conflict of Traditions

It is important to understand the nature of this disagreement—and it is especially important to avoid certain easy ways of misunderstanding it. This is not a conflict between those who respect life and those who do not, nor is it a conflict between those who are indifferent to suffering and those who seek to eliminate it. Rather, it is a conflict between two types of traditions, both of which respect life and both of which encourage compassion and the reduction of suffering. The differences between them center around how they understand life and what they accept as legitimate ways of reducing suffering.

How do we respond to such a conflict? Certainly one common response is to look for a winner, marshaling arguments in support of one tradition and against the other. My own inclination, however, is quite different. I think that we are better off as a society precisely because both of these traditions are present and vital. Each keeps the other in check, as it were. The sanctity of life tradition continually reminds us of our own frailty, of the fact that we are not masters of the universe; it checks our inclination toward *hubris.* The right to die tradition, on the other hand, stresses the importance of reducing suffering in the world and increasing individual autonomy. I think our moral world would be impoverished if we had only one of these traditions. Let's see how this works out in practice.

The Value of Life and the Cost of Caring

In the *Groundwork of a Metaphysics of Morals,* Immanuel Kant drew a crucial moral distinction between rational beings and mere things.[2] Everything, Kant maintains, has either a *price* or a *dignity.* Mere things always have a price, that is, an equivalent value of some kind (usually a monetary one); they can be exchanged one for the other. Rational beings, however, have dignity, for the value of a human being is such that it is beyond all calculations of price; they cannot be exchanged, one for the other. In drawing this distinction, Kant articulated a moral insight which remains powerful today: the belief that human life is priceless and that we therefore ought not to put a price tag on it. Human life is to be preserved at all costs, for the value of human life is beyond that of any costs. Indeed, this may well be one of the motivations in critical care situations when the full arsenal of medicine's skill and technology is brought to bear on a frail, old, dying person in order to prolong his or her life for a few days, weeks, or even months. We cannot put a price tag on human life, the Kantian inside us says. There is something morally odious about thinking that a human life can be traded for something else.

Many of us find that Kant's insight strikes a resonant chord in our moral lives, but that there is another, potentially dissonant note in all of this. Costs *do* matter, as utilitarians such as Richard Brandt make clear, although there is much disagreement about the kinds of costs and how much they matter. We can see this on both the personal level and on the level of social policy. On the personal level, individuals and families struggle with this issue. Imagine a family, such as the one given in the case study at the beginning of this chapter, with a member who requires costly and continual medical care that goes well beyond insurance; family resources—emotional as well as financial—may be drained in the attempt to continue care. Here costs are not simply monetary, but also emotional and spiritual. Financial costs are not limited simply to restrictions on the family vacation, but may extend into areas such as education that directly affect the welfare of the children in the family. Similarly, emotional and spiritual costs to the family may be quite high, although these costs may be more evenly distributed over the range of options.

On the social policy level, we recognize that an amazingly large percentage of our health care dollars are spent on persons during the final weeks of their lives, and ethicists such as Daniel Callahan have maintained that we ought not to spend our money and resources in this way. Although firmly opposing active euthanasia, Callahan maintains that we should respect the natural life span and we should not use intrusive means—such as respirators and feeding tubes—to keep the elderly alive. Here we have some degree of passive involuntary euthanasia, at least for those who lack the private financial resources to pay for continued extraordinary care. This raises the specter of involuntary passive euthanasia for all but the rich. Of course, this is only an inequity if we believe that a longer life under such conditions is better than a shorter one.

Slippery Slopes

Even among those who are not opposed to euthanasia in principle, there are serious reservations about the possibility that legalizing euthanasia could lead to abuses. Once the door is opened even a little, the danger is that more will be permitted—either through further legalization or because of objectionable but common abuses which, while not permitted by the new proposal, could not be effectively curbed—than we originally wanted. History makes us cautious. Euthanasia of the physically and mentally handicapped was part of Hitler's plan, and by some estimates as many as 200,000 handicapped people were killed as part of the Nazi eugenics program. Not surprisingly, many are watching the Netherlands very carefully now, for active euthanasia has been tolerated there for a number of years and legalized in 1994.

Undervalued Groups

Would the legalization of euthanasia open the door to further abuses?

The slippery slope argument has an added dimension when placed within a social context of discrimination. In a society in which the lives of certain classes of people are typically undervalued, legalized euthanasia could become a further instrument of discrimination. The classes discriminated against may vary from society to society, and the classes may be based on race, ethnicity, gender, social orientation, religious beliefs, social class, age, or some other characteristic. However the classes are determined, the point remains the same: legalized euthanasia would be more likely to encourage the early deaths of members of those classes that are discriminated against in society. For this argument to work, it must either presuppose that euthanasia is bad in itself or else that it would encourage certain morally unjustified kinds of euthanasia such as involuntary euthanasia. The latter line of argument seems to be plausible, namely, that the legalization of voluntary euthanasia would result in undue pressure on certain segments of society to "choose" euthanasia when they did not really want to do so.

There is certainly no shortage of undervalued groups in the United States. Some groups are racially constituted: some Native Americans and some African Americans feel that their people have been treated in ways that have genocidal overtones. For them, it is extremely important that they have especially strong guarantees that they will not be the objects of euthanasia disproportionately. Similar issues exist for the poor and the homeless, but they are often less able to advance their own interests in public forums. Finally, and perhaps most pervasively, the elderly in the United States (and elsewhere as well) form a group that is highly undervalued. Several factors contribute to this. First, our society tends to value youth rather than age, aggressive problem-solving intelligence and new ideas rather than the wisdom of long experience. Second, our society tends to value work, and the elderly are often retired and no longer able to be productive. Third, our society tends to be highly mobile, and as a result elderly parents often live in a different location from their children; extended, loving families are hard to find. Fourth, as the percentage of the entire population that is over sixty-five grows, this will put increasing pressure on our social welfare resources; the possibility of increasing resentment toward the aged by younger generations in our society is certainly great.

Moral Pluralism

Any satisfactory proposal for liberalizing the euthanasia laws must contain adequate provisions to prevent it from sliding down the slope to unacceptable practices. It is here that a pluralistic approach has much to recommend itself, for by encouraging both traditions it provides a check on each. Just as pro-choice forces will try to minimize cases in which people are kept alive and suffering against their will, so too, pro-life forces will try to insure that euthanasia is used only in cases where everyone wants it. It is precisely the tension between traditions that helps to reduce the likelihood that one will slide down the slope.

Endnotes

1. Miles, S., and Gomez, C., *Protocols for Elective Use of Life-Sustaining Treatment.* (New York: Springer-Verlag, 1988). Cited in Margaret Battin, "Euthanasia: The Way We Do It, the Way They Do It," *Journal of Pain and Symptom Management,* 6, no. 5, 298–305.
2. Immanuel Kant, *The Moral Law: Kant's Groundwork of the Metaphysic of Morals,* trans. and anal. by H.J. Paton (London: Hutchinson University Library, 1969), pp. 96–97.

Journal/Discussion Questions

✍ *Under what conditions, if any, would you want others to withhold medical treatment from you? To withhold fluids and nutrition? To actively terminate your life?*

✍ *Write your own living will, including in it all instructions and requests you think are relevant.*

The Arguments

John Hardwig
"Is There a Duty to Die?"*

John Hardwig is professor of philosophy at East Tennessee State University. He has published widely in the area of ethics.

Hardwig maintains that modern medicine and American individualistic culture have uncouraged us to think that we have an almost unlimited right to live and to health care. Hardwig argues that there are circumstances in which we have a duty to die, and that this will become a more common scenario as a result of the advances of modern medicine and technology.

As You Read, Consider This:

1. Under what circumstances, according to Hardwig, do we have a duty to die?
2. How does Hardwig deal with the case of someone who has a duty to die but does not want to die?
3. What does Hardwig mean by "the individualistic fantasy"?

When Richard Lamm made the statement that old people have a duty to die, it was generally shouted down or ridiculed. The whole idea is just too preposterous to entertain. Or too threatening. In fact, a fairly common argument against legalizing physician-assisted suicide is that if it were legal, some people might somehow get the idea that they have a duty to die. These people could only be the victims of twisted moral reasoning or vicious social pressure. It goes without saying that there is no duty to die.

But for me the question is real and very important. I feel strongly that I may very well some day have a duty to die. I do not believe that I am idiosyncratic, morbid, mentally ill, or morally perverse in thinking this. I think many of us will eventually face precisely this duty. But I am first of all concerned with my own duty. I write partly to clarify my own convictions and to prepare myself. Ending my life might be a very difficult thing for me to do.

This notion of a duty to die raises all sorts of interesting theoretical and metaethical questions. I intend to try to avoid most of them because I hope my argument will be persuasive to those holding a wide variety of ethical views. Also, although the claim that there is a duty to die would

* *The Hastings Center Report,* 27, no. 2 (March 13, 1997), pp. 34–42.

ultimately require theoretical underpinning, the discussion needs to begin on the normative level. As is appropriate to my attempt to steer clear of theoretical commitments, I will use "duty," "obligation," and "responsibility" interchangeably, in a pre-theoretical or preanalytic sense.[1]

Circumstances and a Duty to Die

Do many of us really believe that no one ever has a duty to die? I suspect not. I think most of us probably believe that there is such a duty, but it is very uncommon. Consider Captain Oates, a member of Admiral Scott's expedition to the South Pole. Oates became too ill to continue. If the rest of the team stayed with him, they would all perish. After this had become clear, Oates left his tent one night, walked out into a raging blizzard, and was never seen again.[2] That may have been a heroic thing to do, but we might be able to agree that it was also no more than his duty. It would have been wrong for him to urge—or even to allow—the rest to stay and care for him.

This is a very unusual circumstance—a "lifeboat case"—and lifeboat cases make for bad ethics. But I expect that most of us would also agree that there have been cultures in which what we would call a duty to die has been fairly common. These are relatively poor, technologically simple, and especially nomadic cultures. In such societies, everyone knows that if you manage to live long enough, you will eventually become old and debilitated. Then you will need to take steps to end your life. The old people in these societies regularly did precisely that. Their cultures prepared and supported them in doing so.

Those cultures could be dismissed as irrelevant to contemporary bioethics; their circumstances are so different from ours. But if that is our response, it is instructive. It suggests that we assume a duty to die is irrelevant to us because our wealth and technological sophistication have purchased exemption for us . . . except under very unusual circumstances like Captain Oates's.

But have wealth and technology really exempted us? Or are they, on the contrary, about to make a duty to die common again? We like to think of modern medicine as all triumph with no dark side. Our medicine saves many lives and enables most of us to live longer. That is wonderful, indeed. We are all glad to have access to this medicine. But our medicine also delivers most of us over to chronic illnesses and it enables many of us to survive longer than we can take care of ourselves, longer than we know what to do with ourselves, longer than we even are ourselves.

The costs—and these are not merely monetary of prolonging our lives when we are no longer able to care for ourselves—are often staggering. If further medical advances wipe out many of today's "killer diseases"—cancers, heart attacks, strokes, ALS, AIDS, and the rest—then one day most of us will survive long enough to become demented or debilitated. These developments could generate a fairly widespread duty to die. A fairly common duty to die might turn out to be only the dark side of our life-prolonging medicine and the uses we choose to make of it.

Let me be clear. I certainly believe that there is a duty to refuse life-prolonging medical treatment and also a duty to complete advance directives refusing life-prolonging treatment. But a duty to die can go well beyond that. There can be a duty to die before one's illnesses would cause death, even if treated only with palliative measures. In fact, there may be a fairly common responsibility to end one's life in the absence of any terminal illness at all. Finally, there can be a duty to die when one would prefer to live. Granted, many of the conditions that can generate a duty to die also seriously undermine the quality of life. Some prefer not to live under such conditions. But even those who want to live can face a duty to die. These will clearly be the most controversial and troubling cases; I will, accordingly, focus my reflections on them.

The Individualistic Fantasy

Because a duty to die seems such a real possibility to me, I wonder why contemporary bioethics has dismissed it without serious consideration. I believe that most bioethics still shares in one of our deeply embedded American dreams: the individualistic fantasy. This fantasy leads us to imagine that lives are separate and unconnected, or that they could be so if we chose. If lives were unconnected, things that happened in my life would not or need not affect others. And if others were not (much) affected by my life, I would have no duty to consider the impact of my decisions on others. I would then be free morally to live my life however I please, choosing whatever life and death I prefer for myself. The way I live would be nobody's business but my own. I certainly would have no duty to die if I preferred to live.

Within a health care context, the individualistic fantasy leads us to assume that the patient is the only one affected by decisions about her medical treatment. If only the patient were affected, the relevant questions when making treatment decisions would be precisely those we ask: What will benefit the patient? Who can best decide that? The pivotal issue would always be simply whether the patient wants to live like this and whether she would consider herself better off dead.[3] "Whose life is it, anyway?" we ask rhetorically.

But this is morally obtuse. We are not a race of hermits. Illness and death do not come only to those who are all alone. Nor is it much better to think in terms of the bald dichotomy between "the interests of the patient" and "the interests of society" (or a third-party payer), as if we were isolated individuals connected only to "society" in the abstract or to the other, faceless members of our health maintenance organization.

Most of us are affiliated with particular others and most deeply, with family and loved ones. Families and loved ones are bound together by ties of care and affection, by legal relations and obligations, by inhabiting shared spaces and living units, by interlocking finances and economic prospects, by common projects and also commitments to support the different life projects of other family members, by shared histories, by ties of loyalty. This life together of family and loved ones is what defines and sustains us; it is what gives meaning to most of our lives. We would not have it any other way. We would not want to be all alone, especially when we are seriously ill, as we age, and when we are dying.

But the fact of deeply interwoven lives debars us from making exclusively self-regarding decisions, as the decisions of one member of a family may dramatically affect the lives of all the rest. The impact of my decisions upon my family and loved ones is the source of many of my strongest obligations and also the most plausible and likeliest basis of a duty to die. "Society," after all, is only very marginally affected by how I live, or by whether I live or die.

A Burden to My Loved Ones

Many older people report that their one remaining goal in life is not to be a burden to their loved ones. Young people feel this, too: when I ask my undergraduate students to think about whether their death could come too late, one of their very first responses always is, "Yes, when I become a burden to my family or loved ones." Tragically, there are situations in which my loved ones would be much better off—all things considered, the loss of a loved one notwithstanding—if I were dead.

The lives of our loved ones can be seriously compromised by caring for us. The burdens of providing care or even just supervision twenty-four hours a day, seven days a week are often overwhelming.[4] When this kind of caregiving goes on for years, it leaves the caregiver exhausted, with no time for herself or life of her own. Ultimately, even her health is often destroyed. But it can also be emotionally devastating simply to live with a spouse who is increasingly distant, uncommunicative, unresponsive, foreign, and unreachable. Other family members' needs often go unmet as the caring capacity of the family is exceeded. Social life and friendships evaporate, as there is no opportunity to go out to see friends and the home is no longer a place suitable for having friends in.

We must also acknowledge that the lives of our loved ones can be devastated just by having to pay for health care for us. One part of the recent SUPPORT study documented the financial aspects of caring for a dying member of a family. Only those who had illnesses severe enough to give them less than a 50 percent chance to live six more months were included in this study. When these patients survived their initial hospitalization and were discharged about one-third required considerable caregiving from their families; in 20 percent of cases a family member had to quit work or make some other major lifestyle change; almost one-third of these families lost all of their savings; and just under 30 percent lost a major source of income.[5]

If talking about money sounds venal or trivial, remember that much more than money is normally at stake here. When someone has to quit work, she may well lose her career. Savings decimated late in life cannot be recouped in the few remaining years of employability, so the loss compromises the quality of the rest of the caregiver's life. For a young person, the chance to go to college may be lost to the attempt to pay debts due to an illness in the family, and this decisively shapes an entire life.

A serious illness in a family is a misfortune. It is usually nobody's fault; no one is responsible for it. But we face choices about how we will respond to this misfortune. That's where the responsibility comes in and fault can arise. Those of us with families and loved ones always have a duty not to make selfish or self-centered decisions about our lives. We have a responsibility to try to protect the lives of loved ones from serious threats or greatly impoverished quality, certainly an obligation not to make choices that will jeopardize or seriously compromise their futures. Often, it would be wrong to do just what we want or just what is best for ourselves; we should choose in light of what is best for all concerned. That is our duty in sickness as well as in health. It is out of these responsibilities that a duty to die can develop.

I am not advocating a crass, quasi-economic conception of burdens and benefits, nor a shallow, hedonistic view of life. Given a suitably rich understanding of benefits, family members sometimes do benefit from suffering through the long illness of a loved one. Caring for the sick or aged can foster growth, even as it makes daily life immeasurably harder and the prospects for the future much bleaker. Chronic illness or a drawn-out death can also pull a family together, making the care for each other stronger and more evident. If my loved ones are truly benefiting from coping with my illness or debility, I have no duty to die based on burdens to them.

But it would be irresponsible to blithely assume that this always happens, that it will happen in my family, or that it will be the fault of my family if they cannot manage to turn my illness into a positive experience. Perhaps the opposite is more common: a hospital chaplain once told me that he could not think of a single case in which a family was strengthened or brought together by what happened at the hospital.

Our families and loved ones also have obligations, of course—they have the responsibility to stand by us and support us through debilitating illness and death. They must be prepared to make significant sacrifices to respond to an illness in the family. I am far from denying that. Most of us are aware of this responsibility and most families meet it rather well. In fact, families deliver more than 80 percent of the long-term care in this country, almost always at great personal cost. Most of us who are a part of a family can expect to be sustained in our time of need by family members and those who love us.

But most discussions of an illness in the family sound as if responsibility were a one-way street. It is not, of course. When we become seriously ill or debilitated, we, too, may have to make sacrifices. To think that my loved ones must bear whatever burdens my illness, debility, or dying process might impose upon them is to reduce them to means to my well-being. And that would be immoral. Family solidarity, altruism, bearing the burden of a loved ones misfortune, and loyalty are all important virtues of families, as well. But they are all also two-way streets.

Objections to a Duty to Die

To my mind, the most serious objections to the idea of a duty to die lie in the effects on my loved ones of ending my life. But to most others, the important objections have little or nothing to do with family and loved ones. Perhaps the most common objections are: (1) there is a higher duty that always takes precedence over a duty to die; (2) a duty to end one's own life would be incompatible with a recognition of human dignity or the intrinsic value of a person; and (3) seriously ill, debilitated, or dying people are already bearing the harshest burdens and so it would be wrong to ask them to bear the additional burden of ending their own lives.

These are all important objections; all deserve a thorough discussion. Here I will only be able to suggest some moral counterweights—ideas that might provide the basis for an argument that these objections do not always preclude a duty to die.

An example of the first line of argument would be the claim that a duty to God, the giver of life, forbids that anyone take her own life. It could be argued that this duty always supersedes whatever obligations we might have to our families. But what convinces us that we always have such a religious duty in the first place? And what guarantees that it always supersedes our obligations to try to protect our loved ones?

Certainly, the view that death is the ultimate evil cannot be squared with Christian theology. It does not reflect the actions of Jesus or those of his early followers. Nor is it clear that the belief that life is sacred requires that we never take it. There are other theological possibilities.[6] In any case, most of us—bioethicists, physicians, and patients alike—do not subscribe to the view that we have an obligation to preserve human life as long as possible. But if not, surely we ought to agree that I may legitimately end my life for other-regarding reasons, not just for self-regarding reasons.

Secondly, religious considerations aside, the claim could be made that an obligation to end one's own life would be incompatible with human dignity or would embody a failure to recognize the intrinsic value of a person. But I do not see that in thinking I had a duty to die I would necessarily be failing to respect myself or to appreciate my dignity or worth. Nor would I necessarily be failing to respect you in thinking that you had a similar duty. There is surely also a sense in which we fail to respect ourselves if in the face of illness or death, we stoop to choosing just what is best for ourselves. Indeed, Kant held that the very core of human dignity is the ability to act on a self-imposed moral law, regardless of whether it is in our interest to do so.[7] We shall return to the notion of human dignity.

A third objection appeals to the relative weight of burdens and thus, ultimately, to considerations of fairness or justice. The burdens that an illness creates for the family could not possibly be great enough to justify an obligation to end one's life—the sacrifice of life itself would be a far greater burden than any involved in caring for a chronically ill family member.

But is this true? Consider the following case:

An 87-year-old woman was dying of congestive heart failure. Her APACHE score predicted that she had less than a 50 percent chance to live for another six months. She was lucid, assertive, and terrified of death. She very much wanted to live and kept opting for rehospitalization and the most aggressive life-prolonging treatment possible. That treatment successfully prolonged her life (though with increasing debility) for nearly two years. Her 55-year-old daughter was her only remaining family, her caregiver, and the main source of her financial support. The daughter duly cared for her mother. But before her mother died, her illness had cost the daughter all of her savings, her home, her job, and her career.

This is by no means an uncommon sort of case. Thousands of similar cases occur each year. Now, ask yourself which is the greater burden:

(a) To lose a 50 percent chance of six more months of life at age 87?

(b) To lose all your savings, your home, and your career at age 55?

Which burden would you prefer to bear? Do we really believe the former is the greater burden? Would even the dying mother say that (a) is the greater burden? Or has she been encouraged to believe that the burdens of (b) are somehow morally irrelevant to her choices?

I think most of us would quickly agree that (b) is a greater burden. That is the evil we would more hope to avoid in our lives. If we are tempted to say that the mother's disease and impending death are the greater evil, I believe it is because we are taking a "slice of time" perspective rather than a "lifetime perspective."[8] But surely the lifetime perspective is the appropriate perspective when weighing burdens. If (b) is the greater burden, then we must admit that we have been promulgating an ethic that advocates imposing greater burdens on some people in order to provide smaller benefits for others just because they are ill and thus gain our professional attention and advocacy.

A whole range of cases like this one could easily be generated. In some, the answer about which burden is greater will not be clear. But in many it is. Death or ending your own life is simply not the greatest evil or the greatest burden.

This point does not depend on a utilitarian calculus. Even if death were the greatest burden (thus disposing of any simple utilitarian argument), serious questions would remain about the moral justifiability of choosing to impose crushing burdens on loved ones in order to avoid having to bear this burden oneself. The fact that I suffer greater burdens than others in my family does not license me simply to choose what I want for myself, nor does it necessarily release me from a responsibility to try to protect the quality of their lives.

I can readily imagine that, through cowardice, rationalization, or failure of resolve, I will fail in this obligation to protect my loved ones. If so, I think I would need to be excused or forgiven for what I did. But I cannot imagine it would be morally permissible for me to ruin the rest of my partner's life to sustain mine or to cut off my sons' careers, impoverish them, or compromise the quality of their children's lives simply because I wish to live a little longer. This is what leads me to believe in a duty to die.

Who Has a Duty to Die?

Suppose, then, that there can be a duty to die. Who has a duty to die? And when? To my mind, these are the right questions, the questions we should be asking. Many of us may one day badly need answers to just these questions.

But I cannot supply answers here, for two reasons. In the first place, answers will have to be very particular and contextual. Our concrete duties are often situated, defined in part by the myriad details of our circumstances, histories, and relationships. Though there may be principles that apply to a wide range of cases and some cases that yield pretty straightforward answers, there will also be many situations in which it is very difficult to discern whether one has a duty to die. If nothing else, it will often be very difficult to predict how one's family will bear up under the weight of the burdens that a protracted illness would impose on them. Momentous decisions will often have to be made under conditions of great uncertainty.

Second and perhaps even more importantly, I believe that those of us with family and loved ones should not define our duties unilaterally, especially not a decision about a duty to die. It would be isolating and distancing for me to decide without consulting them what is too much of a burden for my loved ones to bear. That way of deciding about my moral duties is not only atomistic, it also treats my family and loved ones paternalistically. They must be allowed to speak for themselves about the burdens my life imposes on them and how they feel about bearing those burdens.

Some may object that it would be wrong to put a loved one in a position of having to say, in effect, "You should end your life because caring for you is too hard on me and the rest of the family." Not only will it be almost impossible to say something like that to someone you love, it will carry with it a heavy load of guilt. On this view, you should decide by yourself whether you have a duty to die and approach your loved ones only after you have made up your mind to say good-bye to them. Your family could then try to change your mind, but the tremendous weight of moral decision would be lifted from their shoulders.

Perhaps so. But I believe in family decisions. Important decisions for those whose lives are interwoven should be made together, in a family discussion. Granted, a conversation about whether I have a duty to die would be a tremendously difficult conversation. The temptations to be dishonest could be enormous. Nevertheless, if I am contemplating a duty to die, my family and I should, if possible, have just such an agonizing discussion. It will act as a check on the information, perceptions, and reasoning of all of us. But even more importantly, it affirms our connectedness at a critical juncture in our lives and our life together. Honest talk about difficult matters almost always strengthens relationships.

However, many families seem unable to talk about death at all, much less a duty to die. Certainly most families could not have this discussion all at once, in one sitting. It might well take a number of discussions to be able to approach this topic. But even if talking about death is impossible, there are always behavioral clues—about your caregiver's tiredness, physical condition, health, prevailing mood, anxiety, financial concerns, outlook, overall well-being, and so on. And families unable to talk about death can often talk about how the caregiver is feeling, about finances, about tensions within the family resulting from the illness, about concerns for the future. Deciding whether you have a duty to die based on these behavioral clues and conversation about them honors your relationships better than deciding on your own about how burdensome you and your care must be.

I cannot say when someone has a duty to die. Still, I can suggest a few features of one's illness, history, and circumstances that make it more likely that one has a duty to die. I present them here without much elaboration or explanation.

1. A duty to die is more likely when continuing to live will impose significant burdens—emotional burdens, extensive caregiving, destruction of life plans, and, yes, financial hardship—on your family and loved ones. This is the fundamental insight underlying a duty to die.
2. A duty to die becomes greater as you grow older. As we age, we will be giving up less by giving up our lives, if only because we will sacrifice fewer remaining years of life and a smaller portion of our life plans. After all, it's not as if we would be immortal and live forever if we could just manage to avoid a duty to die. To have reached the age of, say, seventy-five or eighty years without being ready to die is itself a moral failing, the sign of a life out of touch with life's basic realities.[9]
3. A duty to die is more likely when you have already lived a full and rich life. You have already had a full share of the good things life offers.
4. There is greater duty to die if your loved ones' lives have already been difficult or impoverished, if they have had only a small share of the good things that life has to offer (especially if through no fault of their own).
5. A duty to die is more likely when your loved ones have already made great contributions—perhaps even sacrifices—to make your life a good one. Especially if you have not made similar sacrifices for their well-being or for the well-being of other members of your family.
6. To the extent that you can make a good adjustment to your illness or handicapping condition, there is less likely to be a duty to die. A good adjustment means that smaller sacrifices will be required of loved ones and there is more compensating interaction for them. Still, we must also recognize that some diseases—Alzheimer or Huntington chorea—will eventually take their toll on your loved ones no matter how courageously, resolutely, even cheerfully you manage to face that illness.
7. There is less likely to be a duty to die if you can still make significant contributions to the lives of others, especially your family. The burdens to family members are not only or even primarily financial, neither are the contributions to them. However, the old and those who have terminal illnesses must also bear in mind that the loss their family members will feel when they die cannot be avoided, only postponed.
8. A duty to die is more likely when the part of you that is loved will soon be gone or seriously compromised. Or when you soon will no longer be capable of giving love. Part of the horror of cementing disease is that it destroys the capacity to nurture and sustain relationships, taking away a person's agency and the emotions that bind her to others.
9. There is a greater duty to die to the extent that you have lived a relatively lavish lifestyle instead of saving for illness or old age. Like most upper middle-class Americans, I could easily

have saved more. It is a greater wrong to come to your family for assistance if your need is the result of having chosen leisure or a spendthrift lifestyle. I may eventually have to face the moral consequences of decisions I am now making.

These, then, are some of the considerations that give shape and definition to the duty to die. If we can agree that these considerations are all relevant, we can see that the correct course of action will often be difficult to discern. A decision about when I should end my life will sometimes prove to be every bit as difficult as the decision about whether I want treatment for myself.

Can the Incompetent Have a Duty to Die?

Severe mental deterioration springs readily to mind as one of the situations in which I believe I could have a duty to die. But can incompetent people have duties at all? We can have moral duties we do not recognize or acknowledge, including duties that we never recognized. But can we have duties we are unable to recognize? Duties when we are unable to understand the concept of morality at all? If so, do others have a moral obligation to help us carry out this duty? These are extremely difficult theoretical questions. The reach of moral agency is severely strained by mental incompetence.

I am tempted to simply bypass the entire question by saying that I am talking only about competent persons. But the idea of a duty to die clearly raises the specter of one person claiming that another—who cannot speak for herself—has such a duty. So I need to say that I can make no sense of the claim that someone has a duty to die if the person has never been able to understand moral obligation at all. To my mind, only those who were formerly capable of making moral decisions could have such a duty.

But the case of formerly competent persons is almost as troubling. Perhaps we should simply stipulate that no incompetent person can have a duty to die, not even if she affirmed belief in such a duty in an advance directive. If we take the view that formerly competent people may have such a duty, we should surely exercise extreme caution when claiming a formerly competent person would have acknowledged a duty to die or that any formerly competent person has an unacknowledged duty to die. Moral dangers loom regardless of which way we decide to resolve such issues.

But for me personally, very urgent practical matters turn on their resolution. If a formerly competent person can no longer have a duty to die (or if other people are not likely to help her carry out this duty), I believe that my obligation may be to die while I am still competent, before I become unable to make and carry out that decision for myself. Surely it would be irresponsible to evade my moral duties by temporizing until I escape into incompetence. And so I must die sooner than I otherwise would have to. On the other hand, if I could count on others to end my life after I become incompetent, I might be able to fulfill my responsibilities while also living out all my competent or semi-competent days. Given our society's reluctance to permit physicians, let alone family members, to perform aid-in-dying, I believe I may well have a duty to end my life when I can see mental incapacity on the horizon.

There is also the very real problem of sudden incompetence—due to a serious stroke or automobile accident, for example. For me, that is the real nightmare. If I suddenly become incompetent, I will fall into the hands of a medical-legal system that will conscientiously disregard my moral beliefs and do what is best for me, regardless of the consequences for my loved ones. And that is not at all what I would have wanted!

Social Policies and a Duty to Die

The claim that there is a duty to die will seem to some a misplaced response to social negligence. If our society were providing for the debilitated, the chronically ill, and the elderly as it should be, there would be only very rare cases of a duty to die. On this view, I am asking the sick and debilitated to step in and accept responsibility because society is derelict in its responsibility to provide for the incapacitated.

This much is surely true: there are a number of social policies we could pursue that would dramatically reduce the incidence of such a duty. Most obviously, we could decide to pay for facilities that provided excellent long-term care (not just health care!) for all chronically ill, debilitated, mentally ill, or demented people in this country. We probably could still afford to do this. If we did, sick, debilitated, and dying people might still be morally required to make sacrifices for their families. I might, for example, have a duty to forgo personal care by a family member who knows me and really does care for me. But these sacrifices would only rarely include the sacrifice of life itself. The duty to die would then be virtually eliminated.

I cannot claim to know whether in some abstract sense a society like ours should provide care for all who are chronically ill or debilitated. But the fact is that we Americans seem to be unwilling to pay for this kind of long-term care, except for ourselves and our own. In fact, we are moving in precisely the opposite direction—we are trying to shift the burdens of caring for the seriously and chronically ill onto families in order to save costs for our health care system. As we shift the burdens of care onto families, we also dramatically increase the number of Americans who will have a duty to die.

I must not, then, live my life and make my plans on the assumption that social institutions will protect my family from my infirmity and debility. To do so would be irresponsible. More likely, it will be up to me to protect my loved ones.

A Duty to Die and the Meaning of Life

A duty to die seems very harsh, and often it would be. It is one of the tragedies of our lives that someone who wants very much to live can nevertheless have a duty to die. It is both tragic and ironic that it is precisely the very real good of family and loved ones that gives rise to this duty. Indeed, the genuine love, closeness, and supportiveness of family members is a major source of this duty: we could not be such a burden if they did not care for us. Finally, there is deep irony in the fact that the very successes of our life-prolonging medicine help to create a widespread duty to die. We do not live in such a happy world that we can avoid such tragedies and ironies. We ought not to close our eyes to this reality or pretend that it just doesn't exist. We ought not to minimize the tragedy in any way.

And yet, a duty to die will not always be as harsh as we might assume. If I love my family, I will want to protect them and their lives. I will want not to make choices that compromise their futures. Indeed, I can easily imagine that I might want to avoid compromising their lives more than I would want anything else. I must also admit that I am not necessarily giving up so much in giving up my life: the conditions that give rise to a duty to die would usually already have compromised the quality of the life I am required to end. In any case, I personally must confess that at age fifty-six, I have already lived a very good life, albeit not yet nearly as long a life as I would like to have.

We fear death too much. Our fear of death has led to a massive assault on it. We still crave after virtually any life-prolonging technology that we might conceivably be able to produce. We still too often feel morally impelled to prolong life—virtually any form of life—as long as possible. As if the best death is the one that can be put off longest.

We do not even ask about meaning in death, so busy are we with trying to postpone it. But we will not conquer death by one day developing a technology so magnificent that no one will have to die. Nor can we conquer death by postponing it ever longer. We can conquer death only by finding meaning in it.

Although the existence of a duty to die does not hinge on this, recognizing such a duty would go some way toward recovering meaning in death. Paradoxically, it would restore dignity to those who are seriously ill or dying. It would also reaffirm the connections required to give life (and death) meaning. I close now with a few words about both of these points.

First, recognizing a duty to die affirms my agency and also my moral agency. I can still do things that make an important difference in the lives of my loved ones. Moreover, the fact that I still have responsibilities keeps me within the community of moral agents. My illness or debility has not reduced me to a mere moral patient (to use the language of the philosophers). Though it may not be the whole story, surely Kant was onto something important when he claimed that human dignity rests on the capacity for moral agency within a community of those who respect the demands of morality.

By contrast, surely there is something deeply insulting in a medicine and an ethic that would ask only what I want (or would have wanted) when I become ill. To treat me as if I had no moral responsibilities when I am ill or debilitated implies that my condition has rendered me morally incompetent. Only small children,[7] the demented or insane, and those totally lacking in the capacity to act are free from moral duties. There is dignity, then, and a kind of meaning in moral agency, even as it forces extremely difficult decisions upon us.

Second, recovering meaning in death requires an affirmation of connections. If I end my life to spare the futures of my loved ones, I testify in my death that I am connected to them. It is because I love and care for precisely these people (and I know they care for me) that I wish not to be such a burden to them. By contrast, a life in which I am free to choose whatever I want for myself is a life unconnected to others. A bioethics that would treat me as if I had no serious moral responsibilities does what it can to marginalize, weaken, or even destroy my connections with others.

But life without connection is meaningless. The individualistic fantasy, though occasionally liberating, is deeply destructive. When life is good and vitality seems unending, life itself and life lived for yourself may seem quite sufficient. But if not life, certainly death without connection is meaningless. If you are only for yourself, all you have to care about as your life draws to a close is yourself and your life. Everything you care about will then perish in your death. And that—the end of everything you care about—is precisely the total collapse of meaning. We can, then, find meaning in death only through a sense of connection with something that will survive our death.

This need not be connections with other people. Some people are deeply tied to land (for example, the family farm), to nature, or to a transcendent reality. But for most of us, the connections that sustain us are to other people. In the full bloom of life, we are connected to others in many ways—through work, profession, neighborhood, country, shared faith and worship, common leisure pursuits, friendship. Even the guru meditating in isolation on his mountain top is connected to a long tradition of people united by the same religious quest.

But as we age or when we become chronically ill, connections with other people usually become much more restricted. Often, only ties with family and close friends remain and remain important to us. Moreover, for many of us, other connections just don't go deep enough. As Paul Tsongas has reminded us, "When it comes time to die, no one says, 'I wish I had spent more time at the office.' "

If I am correct, death is so difficult for us partly because our sense of community is so weak. Death seems to wipe out everything when we can't fit it into the lives of those who live on. A death motivated by the desire to spare the futures of my loved ones might well be a better death for me than the one I would get as a result of opting to continue my life as long as there is any pleasure in it for me. Pleasure is nice, but it is meaning that matters.

I don't know about others, but these reflections have helped me. I am now more at peace about facing a duty to die. Ending my life if my duty required might still be difficult. But for me, a far greater horror would be dying all alone or stealing the futures of my loved ones in order to buy a little more time for myself. I hope that if the time comes when I have a duty to die, I will recognize it, encourage my loved ones to recognize it, too, and carry it out bravely.

Acknowledgments

I wish to thank Mary English, Hilde Nelson, Jim Bennett, Tom Townsend, the members of the Philosophy Department at East Tennessee State University, and anonymous reviewers of the *Report* for many helpful comments on earlier versions of this paper. In this paper, I draw on material in John Hardwig, "Dying at the Right Time; Reflections on (Un)Assisted Suicide" in *Practical Ethics,* edited by H. LaFollette (London: Blackwell, 1996), with permission.

Endnotes

1. Given the importance of relationships in my thinking, "responsibility"—rooted as it is in "respond"—would perhaps be the most appropriate word. Nevertheless, I often use "duty" despite its legalistic overtones, because Lamm's famous statement has given the expression "duty to die" a certain familiarity. But I intend no implication that there is a law that grounds this duty, nor that someone has a right corresponding to it.
2. For a discussion of the Oates case, see Tom L. Beauchamp, "What Is Suicide?" in *Ethical Issues in Death and Dying,* edited by Tom L. Beauchamp and Seymour Perlin (Englewood Cliffs, NJ: Prentice-Hall, 1978).
3. Most bioethicists advocate a "patient-centered ethics"—an ethics which claims only the patients' interests should be considered in making medical treatment decisions. Most health care professionals have been trained to accept this ethic and to see themselves as patient advocates. For arguments that a patient-centered ethics should be replaced by a family-centered ethics, see John Hardwig, "What About the Family?" *Hastings Center Report* 20, no. 2 (1990): 5–10; Hilde L. Nelson and James L. Nelson, *The Patient in the Family* (New York: Routledge, 1995).

4. A good account of the burdens of caregiving can be found in Elaine Brody, *Women in the Middle: Their Parent-Care Years* (New York: Springer, 1990). Perhaps the best article-length account of these burdens is Daniel Callahan, "Families as Caregivers; the Limits of Morality" in *Aging and Ethics: Philosophical Problems in Gerontology,* edited by Nancy Jecker (Totowa, NJ: Humana Press, 1991).
5. Kenneth E. Covinsky et al., "The Impact of Serious Illness on Patients' Families," *Journal of the American Medical Association* 272 (1994): 1839–1844.
6. Larry Churchill, for example, believes that Christian ethics takes us far beyond my present position: "Christian doctrines of stewardship prohibit the extension of one's own life at a great cost to the neighbor. . . . And such a gesture should not appear to us a sacrifice, but as the ordinary virtue entailed by a just, social conscience." Larry Churchill, *Rationing Health Care in America* (South Bend, IN: Notre Dame University Press, 1988), p. 112.
7. Kant, as is well known, was opposed to suicide. But he was arguing against taking your life out of self-interested motives. It is not clear that Kant would or we should consider taking your life out of a sense of duty to be wrong. See Hilde L. Nelson, "Death with Kantian Dignity," *Journal of Clinical Ethics* 7 (1996): 215–221.
8. Obviously, I owe this distinction to Norman Daniels. Norman Daniels, *Am I My Parents' Keeper? An Essay on Justice Between the Young and the Old* (New York: Oxford University Press, 1988). Just as obviously, Daniels is not committed to my use of it here.
9. Daniel Callahan, The *Troubled Dream of Life* (New York: Simon & Schuster, 1993).

Journal/Discussion Questions

✍ *Can you ever imagine a circumstance in which you personally would feel that you had a duty to die? What would you do?*

1. What is the fundamental insight that underlies Hardwig's claim that we may have a duty to die in certain circumstances?
2. What specific circumstances would increase the likelihood that a person would have a duty to die, according to Hardwig? Do you agree with his analysis?
3. How does Hardwig answer the question of whether the incompetent have a duty to die? Do you agree with him? Explain.
4. How does Hardwig see the relationship between the duty to die and questions about the meaning of life?

James Rachels
"Active and Passive Euthanasia"

James Rachels is one of the most prominent of contemporary moral philosophers, especially in the area of applied ethics. His books include Created from Animals: the Moral Implications of Darwinism, The Elements of Moral Philosophy, *and* The End of Life: the Morality of Euthanasia.

This article, originally published in a medical journal and directed toward physicians, was the first major challenge to the moral significance of the distinction between active and passive euthanasia.

As You Read, Consider This:

1. Why, according to Rachels, is active euthanasia morally preferable to passive euthanasia in some cases?
2. What, according to Rachels, is the difference between killing and letting die?

The distinction between active and passive euthanasia is thought to be crucial for medical ethics. The idea is that it is permissible, at least in some cases, to withhold treatment and allow a patient to die, but it is never permissible to take any direct action designed to kill the patient. This doctrine seems to be accepted by most doctors, and it is endorsed in a statement adopted by the House of Delegates of the American Medical Association on December 4, 1973:

> The intentional termination of the life of one human being by another—mercy killing—is contrary to that for which the medical profession stands and is contrary to the policy of the American Medical Association.
>
> The cessation of the employment of extraordinary means to prolong the life of the body when there is irrefutable evidence that biological death is imminent is the decision of the patient and/or his immediate family. The advice and judgment of the physician should be freely available to the patient and/or his immediate family.

However, a strong case can be made against this doctrine. In what follows I will set out some of the relevant arguments, and urge doctors to reconsider their views on this matter.

To begin with a familiar type of situation, a patient who is dying of incurable cancer of the throat is in terrible pain, which can no longer be satisfactorily alleviated. He is certain to die within a few days, even if present treatment is continued, but he does not want to go on living for those days since the pain is unbearable. So he asks the doctor for an end to it, and his family joins in the request.

Suppose the doctor agrees to withhold treatment, as the conventional doctrine says he may. The justification for his doing so is that the patient is in terrible agony, and since he is going to die anyway, it would be wrong to prolong his suffering needlessly. But now notice this. If one simply withholds the treatment, it may take the patient longer to die, and so he may suffer more than he would if more direct action were taken and a lethal injection given. This fact provides strong reason for thinking that, once the initial decision not to prolong his agony has been made, active euthanasia is actually preferable to passive euthanasia, rather than the reverse. To say otherwise is to endorse the option that leads to more suffering rather than less, and is contrary to the humanitarian impulse that prompts the decision not to prolong his life in the first place.

Part of my point is that the process of being "allowed to die" can be relatively slow and painful, whereas being given a lethal injection is relatively quick and painless. Let me give a different sort of example. In the United States about one in 600 babies is born with Down's syndrome. Most of these babies are otherwise healthy—that is, with only the usual pediatric care, they will proceed to an otherwise normal infancy. Some, however, are born with congenital defects such as intestinal obstructions that require operations if they are to live. Sometimes, the parents and the doctor will decide not to operate, and let the infant die. Anthony Shaw describes what happens then:

> . . . When surgery is denied [the doctor] must try to keep the infant from suffering while natural forces sap the baby's life away. As a surgeon whose natural inclination is to use the scalpel to fight off death, standing by and watching a salvageable baby die is the most emotionally exhausting experience I know. It is easy at a conference, in a theoretical discussion, to decide that such infants should be allowed to die. It is altogether different to stand by in the nursery and watch as dehydration and infection wither a tiny being over hours and days. This is a terrible ordeal for me and the hospital staff—much more so than for the parents who never set foot in the nursery.[1]

I can understand why some people are opposed to all euthanasia, and insist that such infants must be allowed to live. I think I can also understand why other people favor destroying these babies quickly and painlessly. But why should anyone favor letting "dehydration and infection wither a tiny being over hours and days"? The doctrine that says that a baby may be allowed to dehydrate and wither, but may not be given an injection that would end its life without suffering, seems so patently cruel as to require no further refutation. The strong language is not intended to offend, but only to put the point in the clearest possible way.

My second argument is that the conventional doctrine leads to decisions concerning life and death made on irrelevant grounds.

Consider again the case of the infants with Down's syndrome who need operations for congenital defects unrelated to the syndrome to live. Sometimes, there is no operation, and the baby dies, but when there is no such defect, the baby lives on. Now, an operation such as that to remove an intestinal obstruction is not prohibitively difficult. The reason why such operations are not performed in these cases is, clearly, that the child has Down's syndrome and the parents and doctor judge that because of that fact it is better for the child to die.

But notice that this situation is absurd, no matter what view one takes of the lives and potentials of such babies. If the life of such an infant is worth preserving, what does it matter if it needs a simple operation? Or, if one thinks it better that such a baby should not live on, what difference does it make that it happens to have an unobstructed intestinal tract? In either case, the matter of life and death is being decided on irrelevant grounds. It is the Down's syndrome, and not the intestines, that is the issue. The matter should be decided, if at all, on that basis, and not be allowed to depend on the essentially irrelevant question of whether the intestinal tract is blocked.

What makes this situation possible, of course, is the idea that when there is an intestinal blockage, one can "let the baby die," but when there is no such defect there is nothing that can be done, for one must not "kill" it. The fact that this idea leads to such results as deciding life or death on irrelevant grounds is another good reason why the doctrine should be rejected.

One reason why so many people think that there is an important moral difference between active and passive euthanasia is that they think killing someone is morally worse than letting someone die. But is it? Is killing, in itself, worse than letting die? To investigate this issue, two cases may be considered that are exactly alike except that one involves killing whereas the other involves letting someone die. Then, it can be asked whether this difference makes any difference to the moral assessments. It is important that the cases be exactly alike, except for this one difference, since otherwise one cannot be confident that it is this difference and not some other that accounts for any variation in the assessments of the two cases. So, let us consider this pair of cases:

In the first, Smith stands to gain a large inheritance if anything should happen to his six-year-old cousin. One evening while the child is taking his bath, Smith sneaks into the bathroom and drowns the child, and then arranges things so that it will look like an accident.

In the second, Jones also stands to gain if anything should happen to his six-year-old cousin. Like Smith, Jones sneaks in planning to drown the child in his bath. However, just as he enters the bathroom Jones sees the child slip and hit his head, and fall face down in the water. Jones is delighted; he stands by, ready to push the child's head back under if it is necessary, but it is not necessary. With only a little thrashing about, the child drowns all by himself, "accidentally," as Jones watches and does nothing.

Now Smith killed the child, whereas Jones "merely" let the child die. That is the only difference between them. Did either man behave better, from a moral point of view? If the difference between killing and letting die were in itself a morally important matter, one should say that Jones's behavior was less reprehensible than Smith's. But does one really want to say that? I think not. In the first place, both men acted from the same motive, personal gain, and both had exactly the same end in view when they acted. It may be inferred from Smith's conduct that he is a bad man, although that judgment may be withdrawn or modified if certain further facts are learned about him—for example, that he is mentally deranged. But would not the very same thing be inferred about Jones from his conduct? And would not the same further considerations also be relevant to any modification of this judgment? Moreover, suppose Jones pleaded, in his own defense, "After all, I didn't do anything except just stand there and watch the child drown. I didn't kill him; I only let him die." Again, if letting die were in itself less bad than killing, this defense should have at least some weight. But it does not. Such a "defense" can only be regarded as a grotesque perversion of moral reasoning. Morally speaking, it is no defense at all.

Now, it may be pointed out, quite properly, that the cases of euthanasia with which doctors are concerned are not like this at all. They do not involve personal gain or the destruction of normal, healthy children. Doctors are concerned only with cases in which the patient's life is of no further use to him, or in which the patient's life has become or will soon become a terrible burden. However, the point is the same in these cases: The bare difference between killing and letting die does not, in itself, make a moral difference. If a doctor lets a patient die, for humane reasons, he is in the same moral position as if he had given the patient a lethal injection for humane reasons. If his decision was wrong—if, for example, the patient's illness was in fact curable—the decision would be equally regrettable no matter which method was used to carry it out. And if the doctor's decision was the right one, the method used is not in itself important.

The AMA policy statement isolates the crucial issue very well; the crucial issue is "the intentional termination of the life of one human being by another." But after identifying this issue, and forbidding "mercy killing," the statement goes on to deny that the cessation of treatment is the intentional termination of a life. This is where the mistake comes in, for what is the cessation of treatment, in these circumstances, if it is not "the intentional termination of the life of one human being by another." Of course it is exactly that, and if it were not, there would be no point to it.

Many people will find this judgment hard to accept. One reason, I think, is that it is very easy to conflate the question of whether killing is, in itself, worse than letting die, with the very different question of whether most actual cases of killing are more reprehensible than most actual cases of letting die. Most actual cases of killing are clearly terrible (think, for example, of all the murders reported in the newspapers), and one hears of such cases every day. On the other hand, one hardly ever hears of a case of letting die, except for the actions of doctors who are motivated by humanitarian reasons. So one learns to think of killing in a much worse light than of letting die. But this does not mean that there is something about killing that makes it in itself worse than letting die, for it is not the bare difference between killing and letting die that makes the difference in these cases. Rather, the other factors—the murderer's motive of personal gain, for example, contrasted with the doctor's humanitarian motivation—account for different reactions to the different cases.

I have argued that killing is not in itself any worse than letting die; if my contention is right, it follows that active euthanasia is not any worse than passive euthanasia. What arguments can be given on the other side? The most common, I believe, is the following:

"The important difference between active and passive euthanasia is that, in passive euthanasia, the doctor does not do anything to bring about the patient's death. The doctor does nothing, and the patient dies of whatever ills already afflict him. In active euthanasia, however, the doctor does something to bring about the patient's death: he kills him. The doctor who gives the patient with cancer a lethal injection has himself caused his patient's death; whereas if he merely ceases treatment, the cancer is the cause of the death."

A number of points need to be made here. The first is that it is not exactly correct to say that in passive euthanasia the doctor does nothing, for he does do one thing that is very important: he lets the patient die. "Letting someone die" is certainly different, in some respects, from other types of action—mainly in that it is a kind of action that one may perform by way of not performing certain other actions. For example, one may let a patient die by way of not giving medication, just as one may insult someone by way of not shaking his hand. But for any purpose of moral assessment, it is a type of action nonetheless. The decision to let a patient die is subject to moral appraisal in the same way that a decision to kill him would be subject to moral appraisal: it may be assessed as wise or unwise, compassionate or sadistic, right or wrong. If a doctor deliberately let a patient die who was suffering from a routinely curable illness, the doctor would certainly be to blame for what he had done, just as he would be to blame if he had needlessly killed the patient. Charges against him would then be appropriate. If so, it would be no defense at all for him to insist that he didn't "do anything." He would have done something very serious indeed, for he let his patient die.

Fixing the cause of death may be very important from a legal point of view, for it may determine whether criminal charges are brought against the doctor. But I do not think that this notion can be used to show a moral difference between active and passive euthanasia. The reason why it is considered bad to be the cause of someone's death is that death is regarded as a great evil—and so it is. However, if it has been decided that euthanasia—even passive euthanasia—is desirable in a given case, it has also been decided that in this instance death is no greater an evil than the patient's continued existence. And if this is true, the usual reason for not wanting to be the cause of someone's death simply does not apply.

Finally, doctors may think that all of this is only of academic interest—the sort of thing that philosophers may worry about but that has no practical bearing on their own work. After all, doctors must be concerned about the legal consequences of what they do, and active euthanasia is clearly forbidden by the law. But even so, doctors should also be concerned with the fact that the law is forcing upon them a moral doctrine that may well be indefensible, and has a considerable effect on their practices. Of course, most doctors are not now in the position of being coerced in this matter, for they do not regard themselves as merely going along with what the law requires. Rather, in statements such as the AMA policy statement that I have quoted, they are endorsing this doctrine as a central point of medical ethics. In that statement, active euthanasia is condemned not merely as illegal but as "contrary to that for which the medical profession stands," whereas passive euthanasia is approved. However, the preceding considerations suggest that there is really no moral difference between the two, considered in themselves (there may be important moral differences in some cases in their consequences, but, as I pointed out, these differences may make active euthanasia, and not passive euthanasia, the morally preferable option). So, whereas doctors may have to discriminate between active and passive euthanasia to satisfy the law, they should not do any more than that. In particular, they should not give the distinction any added authority and weight by writing it into official statements of medical ethics.

Endnote

1. A. Shaw, "Doctor, Do We Have a Choice?" *The New York Times Magazine* (January 30, 1972): 54.

Journal/Discussion Questions

✍ *Rachels maintains that active euthanasia is sometimes justified on the basis of a desire to alleviate suffering, and that it is more humane than passive euthanasia. What limits are there on compassionate action? Can compassion ever be a legitimate reason for ending someone's life?*

1. Rachels offers two principal arguments against the distinction between active and passive euthanasia. What are these arguments?
2. What objections to his position does Rachels consider? Are you convinced by his replies to those objections? Can you think of any objections that Rachels does not consider? What are they?
3. Rachels claims that "killing is not in itself any worse than letting die." What support does he offer for this claim? Do you agree? Why or why not?

Richard Doerflinger
"Assisted Suicide: Pro-Choice or Anti-Life?"

Richard Doerflinger is associate director of the Office for Pro-Life Activities of the National Conference of Catholic Bishops, Washington, DC.

In this article, Doerflinger argues that respect for life is incompatible with assisting in active euthanasia. He argues, furthermore, that liberalization of the euthanasia laws is dangerous, because it could combine with other factors at work in society to threaten the value of individual lives.

As You Read, Consider This:

1. On what basis does Doerflinger claim that arguments in favor of assisted suicide presuppose a viewpoint on the value of life?
2. What, according to Doerflinger, are the two kinds of slippery slope arguments? Why is this distinction crucial for understanding the euthanasia issue?

The intrinsic wrongness of directly killing the innocent, even with the victim's consent, is all but axiomatic in the Jewish and Christian worldviews that have shaped the laws and mores of Western civilization and the self-concept of its medical practitioners. This norm grew out of the conviction that human life is sacred because it is created in the image and likeness of God, and called to fulfillment in love of God and neighbor.

With the pervasive secularization of Western culture, norms against euthanasia and suicide have to a great extent been cut loose from their religious roots to fend for themselves. Because these norms seem abstract and unconvincing to many, debate tends to dwell not on the wrongness of the act as such but on what may follow from its acceptance. Such arguments are often described as claims about a "slippery slope," and debate shifts to the validity of slippery slope arguments in general.

Since it is sometimes argued that acceptance of assisted suicide is an outgrowth of respect for personal autonomy, and not lack of respect for the inherent worth of human life, I will outline how autonomy-based arguments in favor of assisting suicide do entail a statement about the value of life. I will also distinguish two kinds of slippery slope argument often confused with each other, and argue that those who favor social and legal acceptance of assisted suicide have not adequately responded to the slippery slope claims of their opponents.

Assisted Suicide versus Respect for Life

Some advocates of socially sanctioned assisted suicide admit (and a few boast) that their proposal is incompatible with the conviction that human life is of intrinsic worth. Attorney Robert Risley has said that he and his allies in the Hemlock Society are "so bold" as to seek to "overturn the sanctity of life principle" in American society. A life of suffering, "racked with pain," is "not the kind of life we cherish."[1]

Others eschew Risley's approach, perhaps recognizing that it creates a slippery slope toward practices almost universally condemned. If society is to help terminally ill patients to commit suicide because it agrees that death is objectively preferable to a life of hardship, it will be difficult to draw the line at the seriously ill or even at circumstances where the victim requests death.

Some advocates of assisted suicide therefore take a different course, arguing that it is precisely respect for the dignity of the human person that demands respect for individual freedom as the noblest feature of that person. On this rationale a decision as to when and how to die deserves the respect and even the assistance of others because it is the ultimate exercise of self-determination—"ultimate" both in the sense that it is the last decision one will ever make and in the sense that through it one takes control of one's entire self. What makes such decisions worthy of respect is not the fact that death is chosen over life but that it is the individual's own free decision about his or her future.

Thus Derek Humphry, director of the Hemlock Society, describes his organization as "pro-choice" on this issue. Such groups favor establishment of a constitutional "right to die" modeled on the right to abortion delineated by the U.S. Supreme Court in 1973. This would be a right to choose whether or not to end one's own life, free of outside government interference. In theory, recognition of such a right would betray no bias toward choosing death.

Life versus Freedom

This autonomy-based approach is more appealing than the straightforward claim that some lives are not worth living, especially to Americans accustomed to valuing individual liberty above virtually all else. But the argument departs from American traditions on liberty in one fundamental respect.

When the Declaration of Independence proclaimed the inalienable human rights to be "life, liberty, and the pursuit of happiness," this ordering reflected a long-standing judgment about their relative priorities. Life, a human being's very earthly existence, is the most fundamental right because it is the necessary condition for all other worldly goods including freedom; freedom in turn makes it possible to pursue (without guaranteeing that one will attain) happiness. Safeguards against the deliberate destruction of life are thus seen as necessary to protect freedom and all other human goods. This line of thought is not explicitly religious but is endorsed by some modem religious groups:

> The first right of the human person is his life. He has other goods and some are more precious, but this one is fundamental—the condition of all the others. Hence it must be protected above all others.[2]

On this view suicide is not the ultimate exercise of freedom but its ultimate self-contradiction: A free act that by destroying life, destroys all the individual's future earthly freedom. If life is more basic than freedom, society best serves freedom by discouraging rather than assisting self-destruction. Sometimes one must limit particular choices to safeguard freedom itself, as when American society chose over a century ago to prevent people from selling themselves into slavery even of their own volition.

It may be argued in objection that the person who ends his life has not truly suffered loss of freedom, because unlike the slave he need not continue to exist under the constraints of a loss of freedom. But the slave does have some freedom, including the freedom to seek various means of liberation or at least the freedom to choose what attitude to take regarding his plight. To claim that a slave is worse off than a corpse is to value a situation of limited freedom less than one of no freedom whatsoever, which seems inconsistent with the premise of the "pro-choice" position. Such a claim also seems tantamount to saying that some lives (such as those with less than absolute freedom) are objectively not worth living, a position that "pro-choice" advocates claim not to hold.

It may further be argued in objection that assistance in suicide is only being offered to those who can no longer meaningfully exercise other freedoms due to increased suffering and reduced capabilities and lifespan. To be sure, the suffering of terminally ill patients who can no longer pursue the simplest everyday tasks should call for sympathy and support from everyone in contact with them. But even these hardships do not constitute total loss of freedom of choice. If they did, one could hardly claim that the patient is in a position to make the ultimate free choice about suicide. A dying person capable of making a choice of that kind is also capable of making less monumental free choices about coping with his or her condition. This person generally faces a bewildering array of choices regarding the assessment of his or her past life and the resolution of relationships with family and friends. He or she must finally choose at this time what stance to take regarding the eternal questions about God, personal responsibility, and the prospects of a destiny after death.

In short, those who seek to maximize free choice may with consistency reject the idea of assisted suicide, instead facilitating all choices *except* that one which cuts short all choices.

In fact proponents of assisted suicide do not consistently place freedom of choice as their highest priority. They often defend the moderate nature of their project by stating, with Derek Humphry, that "we do not encourage suicide for any reason except to relieve unremitting suffering." It seems their highest priority is the "pursuit of happiness" (or avoidance of suffering) and not "liberty" as such. Liberty or freedom of choice loses its value if one's choices cannot relieve suffering and lead to happiness; life is of instrumental value insofar as it makes possible choices that can bring happiness.

In this value system, choice as such does not warrant unqualified respect. In difficult circumstances, as when care of a suffering and dying patient is a great burden on family and society, the individual who chooses life despite suffering will not easily be seen as rational, thus will not easily receive understanding and assistance for this choice.

In short, an unqualified "pro-choice" defense of assisted suicide lacks coherence because corpses have no choices. A particular choice, that of death, is given priority over all the other choices it makes impossible, so the value of choice as such is not central to the argument.

A restriction of this rationale to cases of terminal illness also lacks logical force. For if ending a brief life of suffering can be good, it would seem that ending a long life of suffering may be better. Surely the approach of the California "Humane and Dignified Death Act"—where consensual killing of a patient expected to die in six months is presumably good medical practice, but killing the same patient a month or two earlier is still punishable as homicide—is completely arbitrary.

Slippery Slopes, Loose Cannons

Many arguments against sanctioning assisted suicide concern a different kind of "slippery slope": Contingent factors in the contemporary situation may make it virtually inevitable in practice, if not compelling at the level of abstract theory, that removal of the taboo against assisted suicide will lead to destructive expansions of the right to kill the innocent. Such factors may not be part of euthanasia advocates' own agenda; but if they exist and are beyond the control of these advocates, they must be taken into account in judging the moral and social wisdom of opening what may be a Pandora's box of social evils.

To distinguish this sociological argument from our dissection of the conceptual *logic* of the rationale for assisted suicide, we might call it a "loose cannon" argument. The basic claim is that socially accepted killing of innocent persons will interact with other social factors to threaten lives that advocates of assisted suicide would agree should be protected. These factors at present include the following:

The Psychological Vulnerability of Elderly and Dying Patients

Theorists may present voluntary and involuntary euthanasia as polar opposites; in practice there are many steps on the road from dispassionate, autonomous choice to subtle coercion. Elderly and disabled patients are often invited by our achievement-oriented society to see themselves as useless burdens on younger, more vital generations. In this climate, simply offering the option of "self-deliverance" shifts a burden of proof, so that helpless patients must ask themselves why they are not availing themselves of it. Society's offer of death communicates the message to certain patients that they *may* continue to live if they wish but the rest of us have no strong interest in their survival. Indeed, once the choice of a quick and painless death is officially accepted as rational, resistance to this choice may be seen as eccentric or even selfish.[3]

The Crisis in Health Care Costs

The growing incentives for physicians, hospitals, families, and insurance companies to control the cost of health care will bring additional pressures to bear on patients. Curt Garbesi, the Hemlock Society's legal consultant, argues that autonomy-based groups like Hemlock must "control the public debate" so assisted suicide will not be seized upon by public officials as a cost-cutting device. But simply basing one's own defense of assisted suicide on individual autonomy does not solve the problem. For in the economic sphere also, offering the option of suicide would subtly shift burdens of proof.

Adequate health care is now seen by at least some policymakers as a human right, as something a society owes to all its members. Acceptance of assisted suicide as an option for those requiring expensive care would not only offer health care providers an incentive to make that option seem attractive—it would also demote all other options to the status of strictly private choices by the individual. As such they may lose their moral and legal claim to public support—in much the same way that the U.S. Supreme Court, having protected abortion under a constitutional "right of privacy," has quite logically denied any government obligation to provide public funds for this strictly private choice. As life-extending care of the terminally ill is increasingly seen as strictly elective, society may become less willing to appropriate funds for such care, and economic pressures to choose death will grow accordingly.

Legal Doctrines on "Substituted Judgment"

American courts recognizing a fundamental right to refuse life-sustaining treatment have concluded that it is unjust to deny this right to the mentally incompetent. In such cases the right is exercised on the patient's behalf by others, who seek either to interpret what the patient's own wishes might have been or to serve his or her best interests. Once assisted suicide is established as a fundamental right, courts will almost certainly find that it is unjust not to extend this right to those unable to express their wishes. Hemlock's political arm, Americans Against Human Suffering, has underscored continuity between "passive" and "active" euthanasia by offering the Humane and Dignified Death Act as an amendment to California's "living will" law, and by including a provision for appointment of a proxy to choose the time and manner of the patient's death. By such extensions our legal system would accommodate nonvoluntary, if not involuntary, active euthanasia.

Expanded Definitions of Terminal Illness

The Hemlock Society wishes to offer assisted suicide only to those suffering from terminal illnesses. But some Hemlock officials have in mind a rather broad definition of "terminal illness."

Derek Humphry says "two and a half million people alone are dying of Alzheimer's disease."[4] At Hemlock's 1986 convention, Dutch physician Pieter Admiraal boasted that he had recently broadened the meaning of terminal illness in his country by giving a lethal injection to a young quadriplegic woman—a Dutch court found that he acted within judicial guidelines allowing euthanasia for the terminally ill, because paralyzed patients have difficulty swallowing and could die from aspirating their food at any time.

The medical and legal meaning of terminal illness has already been expanded in the United States by professional societies, legislatures, and courts in the context of so-called passive euthanasia. A Uniform Rights of the Terminally Ill Act proposed by the National Conference of Commissioners on Uniform State Laws in 1986 defines a terminal illness as one that would cause the patient's death in a relatively short time if life-preserving treatment is not provided—prompting critics to ask if all diabetics, for example, are "terminal" by definition. Some courts already see comatose and vegetative states as "terminal" because they involve an inability to swallow that will lead to death unless artificial feeding is instituted. In the Hilda Peter case, the New Jersey Supreme Court declared that the traditional state interest in "preserving life" referred only to "cognitive and sapient life" and not to mere "biological" existence, implying that unconscious patients are terminal, or perhaps as good as dead, so far as state interests are concerned. Is there any reason to think that American law would suddenly resurrect the older, narrower meaning of "terminal illness" in the context of active euthanasia?

Prejudice against Citizens with Disabilities

If definitions of terminal illness expand to encompass states of severe physical or mental disability, another social reality will increase the pressure on patients to choose death: long-standing prejudice, sometimes bordering on revulsion, against people with disabilities. While it is seldom baldly claimed that disabled people have "lives not worth living," able-bodied people often say they could not live in a severely disabled state or would prefer death. In granting Elizabeth Bouvia a right to refuse a feeding tube that preserved her life, the California Appeals Court bluntly stated that her physical handicaps led her to "consider her existence meaningless" and that "she cannot be faulted for so concluding." According to disability rights expert Paul Longmore, in a society with such attitudes toward the disabled, "talk of their 'rational' or 'voluntary' suicide is simply Orwellian newspeak"[5]

Character of the Medical Profession

Advocates of assisted suicide realize that most physicians will resist giving lethal injections because they are trained, in Garbesi's words, to be "enemies of death." The California Medical Association firmly opposed the Humane and Dignified Death Act, seeing it as an attack on the ethical foundation of the medical profession.

Yet California appeals judge Lynn Compton was surely correct in his concurring opinion in the *Bouvia* case, when he said that a sufficient number of willing physicians can be found once legal sanctions against assisted suicide are dropped. Judge Compton said this had clearly been the case with abortion, despite the fact that the Hippocratic Oath condemns abortion as strongly as it condemns euthanasia. Opinion polls of physicians bear out the judgment that a significant number would perform lethal injections if they were legal.

Some might think this division or ambivalence about assisted suicide in the medical profession will restrain broad expansions of the practice. But if anything, Judge Compton's analogy to our experience with abortion suggests the opposite. Most physicians still have qualms about abortion, and those who perform abortions on a full-time basis are not readily accepted by their colleagues as paragons of the healing art. Consequently, they tend to form their own professional societies, bolstering each other's positive self-image and developing euphemisms to blunt the moral edge of their work.

Once physicians abandon the traditional medical self-image, which rejects direct killing of patients in all circumstances, their new substitute self-image may require ever more aggressive efforts to make this killing more widely practiced and favorably received. To allow killing by physicians in certain circumstances may create a new lobby of physicians in favor of expanding medical killing.

The Human Will to Power

The most deeply buried yet most powerful driving force toward widespread medical killing is a fact of human nature: Human beings are tempted to enjoy exercising power over others; ending another person's life is the ultimate exercise of that power. Once the taboo against killing has been set aside, it becomes progressively easier to channel one's aggressive instincts into the destruction of life in other contexts. Or as James Burtchaell has said: "There is a sort of virginity about murder; once one has violated it, it is awkward to refuse other invitations by saying, 'But that would be murder!' "[6]

Some will say assisted suicide for the terminally ill is morally distinguishable from murder and does not logically require termination of life in other circumstances. But my point is that the skill and the instinct to kill are more easily turned to other lethal tasks once they have an opportunity to exercise themselves. Thus Robert Jay Lifton has perceived differences between the German "mercy killings" of the 1930s and the later campaign to annihilate the Jews of Europe, yet still says that "at the heart of the Nazi enterprise . . . is the destruction of the boundary between healing and killing."[7] No other boundary separating these two situations was as fundamental as this one, and thus none was effective once it was crossed. As a matter of historical fact, personnel who had conducted the "mercy killing" program were quickly and readily recruited to operate the killing chambers of the death camps.[8] While the contemporary United States fortunately lacks the anti-Semitic and totalitarian attitudes that made the Holocaust possible, it has its own trends and pressures that may combine with acceptance of medical killing to produce a distinctively American catastrophe in the name of individual freedom.

These "loose cannon" arguments are not conclusive. All such arguments by their nature rest upon a reading and extrapolation of certain contingent factors in society. But their combined force provides a serious case against taking the irreversible step of sanctioning assisted suicide for any class of persons, so long as those who advocate this step fail to demonstrate why these predictions are wrong. If the strict philosophical case on behalf of "rational suicide" lacks coherence, the pragmatic claim that its acceptance would be a social benefit lacks grounding in history or common sense.

Endnotes

1. Presentation at the Hemlock Society's Third National Voluntary Euthanasia Conference, "A Humane and Dignified Death," September 2–27, 1986, Washington, DC. All quotations from Hemlock Society officials are from the proceedings of this conference unless otherwise noted.
2. Vatican Congregation for the Doctrine of the Faith, *Declaration on Procured Abortion* (1974), para. 11.
3. I am indebted for this line of argument to Dr. Eric Chevlen.
4. Denis Herbstein, "Campaigning for the Right to Die," *International Herald Tribune,* 11 September 1986.
5. Paul K. Longmore, "Elizabeth Bouvia, Assisted Suicide, and Social Prejudice," *Issues in Law and Medicine* 3:2 (1987), 168.
6. James T. Burtchaell, *Rachel Weeping and Other Essays on Abortion* (Kansas City: Andrews & McMeel, 1982), 188.
7. Robert Jay Lifton, *The Nazi Doctors: Medical Killing and the Psychology of Genocide* (New York: Basic Books, 1986), 14.
8. Yitzhak Rad, *Belzec, Sobibor, Treblinka* (Bloomington, IN: Indiana University Press, 1987), 11, 16–17.

Journal/Discussion Questions

✍ *Doerflinger's analysis takes place within the larger context of a Christian worldview. Do you share this worldview? Do you agree with Doerflinger's conclusions about euthanasia?*

1. According to Doerflinger, the prohibition against killing the innocent is grounded in the Judeo-Christian conviction that life is sacred. Do you think that the religious belief that human life is sacred necessarily leads to the conclusion that voluntary euthanasia is always morally wrong? Do other religious traditions permit euthanasia? Discuss.
2. Doerflinger argues that proponents of euthanasia claim that liberty is their highest value, but this claim is misleading. Why, according to Doerflinger, is it misleading?
3. In the "loose cannon" argument, Doerflinger maintains that legalizing euthanasia will interact with seven other factors in our society in ways that are ultimately harmful. What are these other factors? How plausible do you think each of these seven arguments is? Which of the seven factors do you think is the greatest threat?
4. Doerflinger sees euthanasia as related to "the human will to power." What does he mean by this? Are you convinced by his analysis? Discuss.

Gregory S. Kavka
"Banning Euthanasia"

Gregory Kavka is the author of Hobbesian Moral and Political Theory *and* Moral Paradoxes of Nuclear Deterrence *as well as numerous articles in moral and political philosophy. He died of cancer in 1994 at the age of 46.*

In the following article, Kavka maintains that it is wrong to prevent people from rescuing others in great suffering, and that banning voluntary euthanasia does precisely this, for it prevents some people (usually physicians) from rescuing someone else (usually a patient) from great suffering.

As You Read, Consider This:

1. What is the basic moral principle that Kavka's argument rests on?
2. On what basis does Kavka prevent his argument from justifying (assisted) suicide in general?

Recently, the Dutch Parliament has made active voluntary euthanasia "quasi-legal" in the Netherlands by voting to formally protect from prosecution physicians who carry it out under strict and clearly defined guidelines.[1] Yet, with the failure of Proposition 161 in the November 1992 election in California, active voluntary euthanasia remains illegal in all fifty states of the United States. Indeed, the legislature of the state of Michigan has recently passed a law specifically designed to prevent retired Pathologist Jack Kevorkian (or any of his followers) from euthanizing patients by assisting them in committing suicide.[2]

In this paper, I will present a simple, but novel, moral argument for legalizing active voluntary euthanasia. In brief, I argue that banning active voluntary euthanasia, by forbidding it either in law or in professional codes of medical practice, is very morally wrong because it prevents some people from rescuing others from great suffering. Spelled out more fully, my argument rests on some general, but highly plausible, factual claims combined with a simple and attractive moral principle. Below, I set out the argument by presenting its factual and moral elements in turn, explaining its conclusion, and defending it from some important objections.

The Argument

Factual Premises

The factual premisses of my argument concern, respectively, those who may wish to be euthanized and those (especially some physicians) who might be willing to euthanize them. First, it is evident that there are some people who are in such great suffering due to irreversible and adverse medical circumstances that they wish to have their lives ended very soon, even though they are aware that—in their own case—this can be done only by active euthanasia (e.g., a fatal injection). This is merely to say that there are some patients who would want active euthanasia if it were available to them.[3] Second, banning active voluntary euthanasia—by law or codes of medical ethics—

deters some people (in particular, some physicians) from actively euthanizing some people who want to have their lives ended in this manner.[4] In other words, if medical codes and laws were liberalized to allow active voluntary euthanasia, there would be more physicians who would make this option available to more patients. Putting these two simple assertions together yields the main conclusion of the factual component of my argument: *Banning active voluntary euthanasia prevents some people (physicians) from rescuing some others (patients) from great suffering in a manner in which these others wish to be rescued.*

The Moral Principle

The case of the evil Colonel. Turning to the moral component of my argument, let us begin our inquiry by imagining a non-medical situation in which a person's only release from great suffering is death. An evil Colonel is the unrestrained ruler of his military district in some backward country, and he is greatly angered at some unfortunate Private (e.g., for not showing the Colonel sufficient respect). He begins to slowly and agonizingly torture the Private to death over a period of weeks, making no bones of his aim of inflicting maximum suffering ending in death. After only a few hours of torture, the Private (even during intervals between the torture sessions) begs repeatedly to be killed immediately by any means rather than have the torture go on. The only one—besides the heartless Colonel—in a position to save him from weeks of torture (without sharing his fate) is the Water Boy who periodically brings water for the Private to drink. In the kitchen, he slips a fatal dose of poison in the cup of water he is about to take to the prisoner. (The poison will kill the prisoner in a short time, but is not likely to be discovered—the Colonel is not the type to ask for an autopsy when a prisoner drops dead during torture.) The Cook in the kitchen sees what the Water Boy is doing and stops him by threatening to tell the Colonel if the Water Boy delivers the poison to the Private.

It is clear that in this situation the Cook has acted wrongly, very wrongly. He has eliminated the Private's only real hope of rescue from weeks of agonizing torture. His conduct is not, of course, as wrongful as that of the Colonel, but that is hardly to say anything in its favor. It is also worth noting that what the Cook does is *much worse* than merely allowing torture to go forward without intervening. Suppose, for example, that the Water Boy had declined to poison the water even though he was certain he could do so without risk of detection. Whether, in that case, he acts wrongly in failing to rescue the Private is, perhaps, a difficult question to answer. But the Cook does not merely fail to rescue, he prevents a rescue-in-progress from taking place. That this is much worse is evident when we consider the parallel case of aiding the world's starving poor. Philosophers have extensively debated the issue of whether citizens in wealthy nations are failing to live up to their obligations if they do not provide aid to the world's starving poor.[5] But it is not debatable that it would be very wrong to prevent others who are willing to provide such aid from doing so. No one, for example, would regard a law preventing U.S. citizens or charities from providing aid to the world's starving poor as anything but iniquitous. Clearly, however bad it is to fail to rescue someone in dire need, it is worse to actively intervene to prevent someone else from rescuing them.

These considerations flowing from our hypothetical torture case suggest the following moral principle: *It is very wrong to prevent someone from rescuing someone else from great suffering (in a manner in which the latter person wishes to be rescued).* It is this principle which explains what the Cook has done wrong. He has prevented one person, the Water Boy, from rescuing another, the

Private, from great suffering, the Colonel's torture, in a manner in which the Private—in his constant pleading for an early death—wishes to be rescued.

Combining this simple moral principle with the earlier factual claim that banning active voluntary euthanasia prevents some people from rescuing others from great suffering in a manner in which the latter wish to be rescued immediately yields the conclusion that *banning active voluntary euthanasia is very wrong.*[6] And it is wrong for one of the same reasons that torture is wrong: it involves acting in such a way as to insure that people experience great suffering that they would not experience, save for the actor's intervention.[7] (The Private's continued great suffering, past the point at which the Water Boy would have poisoned him absent the Cook's threat, is the result of the interventions of both the Colonel and the Cook.) Of course, if banning active voluntary euthanasia is very wrong, as this argument indicates, legislators and physicians' organizations should act forthwith to remove their blanket bans on it.

Note, however, that the argument allows for the legitimacy of strict restrictions on the practice of active euthanasia, to insure both the voluntariness of the patient's choice and the presence of great suffering brought on by a medical condition. The Dutch rules, for example, state that "the request for euthanasia must come from a patient who is doing so voluntarily, who is mentally competent, has a hopeless disease without prospect for improvement, and is undergoing unbearable physical or mental suffering."[8] Such restrictions conflict with neither the spirit nor the letter of my argument. It is only in those cases in which considerations concerning the patient's well being (i.e., ending of great suffering from a hopeless medical condition) and her autonomous choices concur in recommending early death as the best course of action, that my argument implies we may not prevent physicians from pursuing this course. It is an argument for legalizing active voluntary euthanasia, *not* for allowing suicide (or assisted suicide) *in general.*

Notice, however, that my argument does *not* require that the patient be in terminal condition. Why not? Because if it is wrong to prevent a terminal patient being relieved of a short period of great suffering, it is at least as wrong to prevent non-terminal patients being relieved of longer periods of great suffering. Intuitively, we tend to recoil from this conclusion. If, for example, you survey a large class of undergraduates, you typically find a large majority in favor of euthanasia for the terminally ill who are suffering, and a large majority against euthanasia for patients suffering from horrible chronic conditions that are not terminal.[9] You can bring out the tension between these two beliefs by simply asking them "Which is worse, suffering for a short time or suffering for a long time?"[10] The same point can be made by considering a variation of our earlier torture case in which the Colonel plans to extend the Private's torture over months and years. The Cook's interference with the Water Boy's rescue-by-poisoning plan would be even more reprehensible in this case than in the case described earlier. For it would doom the Private to a much longer period of extreme misery.

Objections and Replies

First objection. Having set out my main argument, and having clarified the sorts of restrictions on active voluntary euthanasia it supports, I proceed to defend the argument by answering six objections to it. The first objection says that it is permissible—even obligatory—to stop someone from being rescued from great suffering if they will die as the result of the "rescue." Thus, for example, if someone is suffering greatly from a painful but life-saving medical procedure, and an onlooker attempts to interrupt the proceedings to stop the patient's pain, it would be correct for you to subdue the onlooker so that the procedure may continue.

This objection establishes that some rescues to prevent great suffering may be permissibly prevented on the grounds that the rescue would result in the sufferer's death. But it fails to establish that such prevention is permissible whenever the rescue would kill the sufferer. For consider our earlier example of the Private being tortured by the Colonel. The Water Boy's rescue-by-poisoning would kill the Private, yet we judge the Cook's interference with this rescue to be wrong in full knowledge of this fact, because the rescue is in the Private's interest and has his consent. And clearly the physician who provides a fatal injection to a patient suffering horribly from an irreversible medical condition is acting in a situation parallel to that of the Water Boy, rather than that of the onlooker who attempts to disrupt a painful life-saving procedure.

This reply may not satisfy the objector. For he may believe in absolute deontological prohibitions against certain kinds of actions, including deliberately (or intentionally) killing the innocent. Even if there are such absolute prohibitions, it does not follow immediately that they should be enshrined in, or enforced by, law. For example, while deceitful betrayal of a close friend, or blasphemy against the true deity, are kinds of acts that may always be wrong, it might be unwise and harmful to legally punish such acts. Still, the prohibition on deliberately killing the innocent might be regarded as so central to social life that it must be enshrined in law.

But is there any such absolute prohibition? Supposing so has wildly counterintuitive implications concerning a class of cases I call Extra Death cases. In such cases, deliberately killing an innocent person is the only way to prevent that person and other innocent persons from being killed. In such cases, if we refrain from killing, innocent people will die that we could have saved, and no innocent people will be saved. A common case of this sort arises fairly frequently if—at least for the sake of argument—we regard the human fetus as a person. When an abortion can save the mother's life, but both mother and fetus will die if one is not performed, we have an Extra Death case. The fetus perishes whatever is done, but aborting saves the mother. Yet the absolute prohibition view says—quite implausibly—that we must not abort, that we must sacrifice the mother's life, even though the fetus cannot benefit.[11]

Would it help to modify the absolute prohibition view to allow killing the innocent when other lives are saved and the victim consents? It does make the view more plausible, but only at the cost of undermining the objection to my argument. Suppose, for example, that the modified doctrine allows physicians to kill a terminal patient, with her consent, to allow her still healthy kidneys to be transplanted to save the lives of two of her children who each need one of her kidneys to live. If this is so, it would seem arbitrary to deny the permissibility of the same action to save her children the sufferings involved in a lifetime of kidney-dialysis. But if she may be killed, with her consent, to prevent the great suffering of others, it would be outrageous to suppose that she could not be killed, with her consent, to prevent her own great suffering. Thus, the objection based on an absolute prohibition on deliberately killing the innocent leads to a painful dilemma for its supporters: either they accept the highly implausible implications of their view in Extra Death cases, or they allow for reasonable modifications in their absolutism and end up unable to condemn voluntary euthanasia. We may leave them impaled on the horns of this dilemma and move on.

Second objection. A second objection notes that my argument implicitly (and wrongly) assumes that early death may benefit a person in great suffering. Despite rejection of this assumption by some writers on euthanasia,[12] I feel safe in relying on it. Can we deny that the dead victims of torture would have been better off if they had died earlier in the horrible process? Can we deny that some of those who endure the "natural tortures" imposed by painful and debilitating illnesses without hope of recovery would benefit from an early death? If we do deny this, if we hold that early death harms all patients, then we must oppose passive as well as active euthanasia, a position that few would be willing to accept.

Third objection. Another implicit assumption of my argument—that death is the only alternative to great suffering—leads to a third objection. In my torture cases, I have stipulated that the Private may be rescued from torture only by death. Otherwise, if—for example—the cavalry is on the way to capture the Colonel, the Water Boy is wrong to poison the Private and the Cook is right to stop him. But, continues the objection, in the real world, the cavalry is on the way for suffering patients, in the form of better medical treatment for pain. Thus, active euthanasia is no longer justified, because it is no longer needed.[13]

To the extent that improved pain management techniques make life bearable and worth continuing for the afflicted, the urgency of legalizing active voluntary euthanasia is reduced. But no one is supposing that now, or in the near future, all the afflicted will be successfully treated by these techniques. Pain-killers do not address all of the sufferings of the afflicted: the disabilities, the mental anguish, the loss of the enjoyments of normal life, the loss of independence, and so on.[14] And even if all significant physical pain could be eliminated short of death *in principle* (an unrealistic prospect in any case), real suffering patients actually being relieved of their physical pains by an overburdened and imperfect medical system is too much to expect. For those whose sufferings remain untreatable, or untreated, death may remain the only way *in fact* in their own case to relieve their suffering. If and when pain management techniques overcome the need for voluntary euthanasia, patients will stop requesting it. In the meantime, it is wrong to deprive those who do request it of their only practical succor from great suffering by preventing willing physicians from euthanizing them under appropriate safeguards.

Fourth objection. Perhaps the most likely objection to my argument that it is wrong to ban active voluntary euthanasia is the claim that regardless of the beneficial effects such acts of euthanasia may have for particular patients, legalizing euthanasia would have bad effects on society as a whole. Various possible negative effects are often cited in this context, including negative effects on the morale of medical personnel, and reduction of incentives to manage pain. But the most common, and significant objection of this form is a slippery slope argument: if we legalize active voluntary euthanasia, this will eventually lead to the legalization of other, more objectionable, forms of euthanasia, to the great detriment of society.

Now to succeed, slippery slope arguments must establish two things: first, that following policy A is likely to lead to later policy or effect B, and that B is socially harmful or morally odious. In other words, we should not adopt A, because we will then slide down the slippery slope *and end up at an undesirable place.* But there are two different possible long-range effects of legalizing active voluntary euthanasia—the legalization of active *non-voluntary* euthanasia (e.g., of the permanently comatose and others who cannot express their will) and the legalization of active *involuntary* euthanasia (e.g., of those who do not want to die but are pressured into saying that they do, or are killed against their wishes to economize on medical costs). Legalization of active non-voluntary euthanasia might well follow from the legalization of active voluntary euthanasia, but it is unclear that this is undesirable if there are appropriate restrictions and safeguards. Active involuntary euthanasia, on the other hand, is clearly undesirable—tantamount to murder, we might say without much exaggeration. But it seems highly unlikely, in a civilized society, that its legalization would result from legalizing active voluntary euthanasia. So legalizing active voluntary euthanasia has one purported "slippery slope" effect that is bad (i.e., legalized active involuntary euthanasia), and one that is likely (i.e., legalized non-voluntary euthanasia), but none that is both bad and likely. Hence, the slippery slope argument against active voluntary euthanasia apparently fails.[15]

The objection to legalization of active voluntary euthanasia based on bad social consequences—whether or not it is formulated as a slippery slope argument—fails for a more general reason. Preventing patients who wish to be euthanized from being rescued from their great sufferings, in order to benefit society, would unfairly sacrifice their vital individual interests to the end of collective benefit. Most philosophers find strict utilitarian moral theory unacceptable for precisely this reason—it allows, indeed requires, the well-being of individuals to be sacrificed to promote group good.[16] This is especially outrageous when the individual losses are large, concrete, certain, and fall on some of society's least fortunate members (e.g., those in the most hopeless and painful medical conditions), while the group gains are indirect, diffuse, and speculative. And this is precisely the situation as regards the banning of active voluntary euthanasia.

Fifth objection. But perhaps the worry of opponents of legalizing euthanasia is not about social harm, but the harm to individuals who might be euthanized against their wills. And even if a slide down the slippery slope to *legalized* involuntary euthanasia is unlikely, it is more plausible to claim that once any form of euthanasia is legalized, safeguards will inevitably be abused so that many patients end up being killed against their wills. Indeed, critics of legalized euthanasia have contended that the Dutch experience validates this claim, with statistics indicating that about 140 patients a year in the Netherlands are actively euthanized without being consulted, even though they were competent to be consulted and to give or withhold consent.[17] The implication is that some of these people would not have consented, and hence were killed against their wills.

Others have interpreted the Dutch data differently. They point out that these "unconsulted competent" patients were all in a hopeless terminal condition, a significant fraction of them had previously expressed a desire for early life-termination, that families were consulted in nearly all cases, and that life expectancy was less than a day for more than half these patients, and less than a week for eighty-seven per cent of them.[18] Thus, one knowledgeable observer writes, "There is no evidence of any patient being put to death *against* his or her implied wish."[19] It has also been observed that there are characteristics of the American legal system that would make involuntary euthanasia less likely here than in Holland if voluntary euthanasia were legalized,[20] and that there are a number of institutional safeguards that can be instituted to prevent involuntary euthanasia from occurring in a significant number of cases.[21] In light of this, it seems that to oppose legalizing euthanasia in the United States one must either (1) take a quite pessimistic view of our legal and medical systems' capacities to enact, heed and enforce such safeguards, or (2) must consider it more important to save a few imminently terminal patients from unwanted earlier deaths than to save very many times that number of patients from great, unwanted, and unnecessary suffering. In my view, we should not be so cynical about our institutions, or so convinced of the great value of life irrespective of its quality for the person whose life it is, as to endorse either of these attitudes.

Sixth objection. A final objection to my argument is that—contrary to my conclusion—laws prohibiting active voluntary euthanasia are morally permissible because as individuals have no right to be euthanized, society has no obligation to allow euthanasia. The astute deontological ethicist F.M. Kamm presents a version of this argument in the following passage:

> Yet even if it is permissible to perform voluntary active euthanasia, we are not obligated to do so, and so even the person who requests it does not have a right to active euthanasia. And even though many people are willing to kill someone for his own good, many others are not. . . . Although many people who wish to be actively euthanized may not get their wish if we do not permit active euthanasia, they also will not have their rights violated, nor will we fail in our duties to them if there is a law prohibiting active euthanasia.[22]

Now I would agree that individuals have no *unconditional* right to be actively euthanized—that is, a right to be actively euthanized even if no one volunteers to perform this service for them. And this is so for the very reason that Kamm suggests: some people object to performing active euthanasia, and no one who so objects should be obligated to do so. But it does not follow that individuals lack the *conditional* right to be actively euthanized, (under appropriate circumstances) provided there are volunteers who are willing to supply this service. This can readily be seen by considering the right to marry. This is clearly not a right to be married regardless of whether anyone wants to marry you, but a conditional right to marry if a volunteer can be found. The fact that some people (indeed most) would not wish to marry you in no way implies that you lack this conditional right. But this conditional right to marry would be violated, or negated, by a law banning marriage, as the conditional right to be actively euthanized by a willing volunteer is violated by laws banning active euthanasia. Thus, Kamm's argument that we may permissibly ban active euthanasia turns out to be a *non sequitur,* apparently brought on by failure to note in this context the important moral difference between failing to rescue someone from suffering and preventing a willing third-party from carrying out such a rescue. Even lacking an unconditional right to be rescued, we may possess a right that third parties not interfere with (or prevent) our rescue by a willing party.

Of course, even the conditional right to be actively euthanized has been challenged. Leon Kass writes,

> Even if we . . . merely allow those to practice it [active voluntary euthanasia] who are freely willing, our society would be drastically altered. For unless the state accepts the job of euthanizer, which God forbid that it should, it would thus surrender its monopoly on the legal use of lethal force, a monopoly it holds and needs if it is to protect innocent life, its first responsibility.[23]

How are we to understand this argument? If the state's "first responsibility" of protecting innocent life is understood to include protecting a suffering patient from active euthanasia at his own request, Kass' argument begs the question by assuming what is to be proved: that the state should prevent voluntary active euthanasia. But if protecting innocent life does not include this sort of protection, an argument is needed why the state's surrendering authority over this particular use of lethal force (e.g., to physicians) would undermine its effective exercise of its right to use force to protect innocent life in other contexts. Are we to suppose that legalizing active voluntary euthanasia will undermine the efforts of the police and courts to deter and punish crime, or of the armed forces to defend the state in just wars? If so, Kass owes us an argument to that effect.

In closing, I should note that the success of my argument does not strictly depend on asserting possession of an individual right to be actively euthanized, even the conditional right to be actively euthanized at your request if conditions are appropriate and there is a willing volunteer. Rather, my argument establishes that it is morally wrong for the state (and medical groups) to prevent physicians from rescuing patients from great suffering at the patients' request by blanket bans on active euthanasia. My argument does not assert that this is wrong because of some right the patient has, but rather because it is wrong to make a person undergo great, unwanted, and unnecessary suffering if we can prevent that suffering by merely standing aside and letting a willing volunteer rescue that person from it.

Acknowledgments

An earlier version of this paper was presented to the Moral and Political Philosophy Society of Orange County (MAPPS) and to the Liberty Society of Irvine. I am grateful to members of those groups, and to Jefferson McMahan, for helpful comments. Ronald B. Miller and Kurt Norlin provided useful references.

Endnotes

1. "Dutch Parliament Approves Law Permitting Euthanasia," *New York Times,* International Edition, February 10, 1993, Section A, p. 5.
2. "Dr. Kevorkian's Death Wish," *Newsweek,* March 8, 1993, pp. 46–48. In this paper, I treat assisted suicide of those facing a life not worth living because of their medical condition as a special case of voluntary euthanasia.
3. It would be hard for opponents of legalizing active voluntary euthanasia to reject this premise. If it were false, legalization would not have a significant practical effect for want of any volunteers.
4. Again, opponents of active voluntary euthanasia would have to acknowledge the truth of this premise or admit that laws banning active voluntary euthanasia have only a symbolic function.
5. Aiken, William, and LaFollette, Hugh, eds. *World Hunger and Moral Obligation* (Englewood Cliffs: Prentice Hall, 1977).
6. Since a legal ban prevents rescue from great suffering in *many* cases, it is presumably much worse than preventing rescue from suffering in a single instance, other things being equal.
7. There is another possible difference between preventing rescue from human torture and preventing rescue from the "natural torture" endured by some patients. Torture, unlike a patient's suffering, may be thought of as a bad with two components—the natural evil of the patient's horrible experience, and the moral evil of its deliberate infliction by the torturer. It might therefore be thought that, other things being equal, it is more important to prevent torture inflicted by people than torture inflicted by nature. If so, it would perhaps be worse to prevent the prevention of torture in a particular instance (e.g., stop the Water Boy from poisoning the Private) than to prevent the prevention of natural suffering in a particular instance (e.g., by restraining a Dr. Kevorkian from assisting a patient in committing suicide). Whether this argument works, however, depends on whether you think the moral evil created by the

Colonel is diminished if the Private drops dead of poison before the Colonel is finished with him. I am inclined to doubt that it is.

Jefferson McMahan has suggested to me the following additional argument (which he attributes to Thomas Scanlon) that it is not more important to stop harms caused by evil people than by natural events. If it were, then we should choose to rescue nineteen people from suffering (or death) caused by evil people rather than save twenty others from equal suffering (or death) caused by natural disaster. But, faced with such a choice, and all other things being equal, it seems clear we should save the greater number.

8. "Dutch Parliament Approves Law Permitting Euthanasia," *op. cit.*
9. I owe this point to Virginia Warren.
10. Favoring euthanasia only in terminal cases could make sense if accompanied by certain empirical background assumptions, e.g., suffering is much worse in the terminal stages of illness, non-terminal patients may be saved by new miracle cures.
11. For an example of an otherwise well-argued deontological view that founders on its failure to recognize and address the Extra Death problem, see Charles Fried, *Right and Wrong* (Cambridge, MA: Harvard University Press, 1978). The various attempts of supporters of the Doctrine of Double Effect to get around this problem face an unsolved dilemma: if they allow sufficient "redescription" in this sort of case so that the fetus' death turns out unintended (hence permissible), similar redescriptions will vitiate the bite of the Doctrine so that it cannot proscribe what its supporters want it to proscribe, e.g., civilian bombing in warfare.
12. Leon R. Kass ("Is There a Right to Die?" *Hastings Center Report* 23 [January–February, 1993], 42) writes: "[W]e cannot serve the patient's good by deliberately eliminating the patient."
13. An argument of this form is suggested in Alexander Morgan Capron, "At Law—Even in Defeat, Proposition 161 Sounds a Warning," *Hastings Center Report* 23 (January–February, 1993), 32–34.
14. While 46 percent of patients in the Netherlands requesting euthanasia gave "pain" as a reason for their request, an equal percentage mentioned "unworthy dying," and a greater number (57 percent) mentioned "loss of dignity." See Paul J. Van Der Maas et al., "Euthanasia and Other Medical Decisions Concerning the End of Life," *The Lancet* 338 (Sept. 14, 1991): 669–674, at 672.
15. For a more detailed reply to the Slippery Slope argument, along somewhat similar lines, see Dan Brock, "Voluntary Active Euthanasia," *Hastings Center Report* 22 (1992), 10–22.
16. See, for example, John Rawls, *A Theory of Justice* (Cambridge, MA: Harvard University Press, 1971), pp. 22–27.
17. Richard Fenigsen, "The Report of the Dutch Governmental Committee on Euthanasia," *Issues in Law and Medicine* 7 (1991), 339–344, at 342.
18. Chris Ciesielski-Carlucci, "The Termination of Life without Request in the Netherlands," *VES News* (May 1993), London, forthcoming.
19. Margaret P. Battin, "Seven (More) Caveats Concerning the Discussion of Euthanasia in the Netherlands," *American Philosophical Association Newsletter on Philosophy and Medicine* 92 (1993), 76–80, at 78.

20. Gary Seay, review of Carlos Gomez, *Regulating Death: Euthanasia and the Case of the Netherlands, American Philosophical Association Newsletter on Medicine and Philosophy* 92 (1993): 89–92, at 91.
21. Margaret Battin, "Voluntary Euthanasia and the Risks of Abuse: Can We Learn Anything from the Netherlands," *Law, Medicine, and Health Care* 20 (1992), 133–143.
22. F.M. Kamm, *Creation and Abortion: A Study in Moral and Legal Philosophy* (New York: Oxford University Press, 1992), p. 35.
23. "Is There a Right to Die?" p. 42.

Journal/Discussion Questions

✍ *Kavka's objection to banning euthanasia centers, in part, on the claim that it is wrong to prevent someone from rescuing someone else from great suffering. The focus, in other words, in on rescuing someone from suffering. Presuming you were qualified to do so (e.g., that you were a physician), how would you respond to a request from someone in great and terminal pain to save that person from further suffering through euthanasia? What would the moral issues be for you?*

1. According to Kavka, people do not have to be in terminal condition in order to justifiably request euthanasia. Why not? Do you agree?
2. Some opponents of euthanasia maintain that human life is sacred and that we therefore must never intentionally kill any human being. How does Kavka reply to supporters of this position? Do you agree or disagree with his reply? Explain.
3. How does Kavka deal with the "slippery slope" objection to legalizing euthanasia? Are you convinced by his reply?

Daniel Callahan
"Pursuing a Peaceful Death"

A cofounder of The Hastings Center, Daniel Callahan has been a major voice in biomedical ethics for the past thirty years. His books include Abortion: Law, Choice, and Morality, Abortion: Understanding Differences, *edited with Sidney Callahan,* Setting Limits: Medical Goals in an Aging Society *and* The Troubled Dream of Life: Living with Mortality. *He has a particular interest in the relationship of ethics and culture, and of the way in which problems require not only careful rational analysis, but also a feel for culture, for one's own understanding of the world, and for the way we are individually and socially shaped by the technologies and artifacts of our society.*

Recognizing that modern medicine has made dying much more difficult than before, Callahan considers some of the ways in which this may deform the process of dying. He then sketches out what a "good death" would involve, and argues that medicine should see one of its tasks as helping people to die well.

As You Read, Consider This:

1. How does Callahan define a "peaceful death"? What things would you add or subtract from his list of characteristics?
2. What does Callahan mean by "medical futility"? What role does this notion play in his argument?

On the face of it, one might be forgiven for thinking that death at the hands of modern technological medicine should be a far more benign, sensitive event than it was in earlier times. Do we not have a much greater biological knowledge, thus enabling more precise prognoses of death? Do we not have more powerful analgesics, thereby enhancing the capacity to control pain?

Do we not possess more sophisticated machines, capable of better managing organs gone awry? Do we not have greater psychological knowledge, suitable to relieve the anxieties and suffering of an anticipated death? Do we not, adding all that up, have at hand exactly what we need to enhance the possibility of a peaceful death?

The answer in each case is yes and no. Yes, we do have much more knowledge than we did prior to modern medicine. But no, that knowledge has not made death a more peaceful event, either in reality or in anticipation. The enhanced biological knowledge and technological skill have served to make our dying all the more problematic: harder to predict, more difficult to manage, the source of more moral dilemmas and nasty choices, and spiritually more productive of anguish, ambivalence, and uncertainty. In part this is because, with the advent of modern medicine, the earlier superstructure of meaning and ritual was dismantled, thus setting death adrift in a world of uncertain value and import. But also in part it is because modern medicine brought with it a stance toward death that is ambivalent about its necessity and inevitability.

In response to that ambivalence, without knowing it, without using quite that language, we have come to feel only now the loss of what the late French historian Philippe Aries called a "tame" death.[1] By that he meant a death that was tolerable and familiar, affirmative of the bonds of community and social solidarity, expected with certainty and accepted without crippling fear. That kind of human ending, common to most people throughout history until recently, Aries contrasted with the "wild" death of technological medicine. The latter death—which began to occur in the nineteenth century—is marked by undue fear and uncertainty, by the presence of medical powers not quite within our mastery, by a course of decline that may leave us isolated and degraded. It is wild because it is alien from and outside of the cycle of life, because modern technologies make its course highly uncertain, and because it seems removed from a full, fitting presence in the life of the community.

The technologies of that death, ever more clever in their ability to sustain failing organs, provide a set of tools that endlessly sustain our ambivalence and allow it to be played out in tortuous detail. Precisely because they have opened up new possibilities in the ancient struggle with our mortality, those technologies have made our understanding of that mortality all the more difficult. To confound us more, they have misled us into thinking we have a greater dominance over our mortality than was earlier the case.

What can be done to gain a better way of thinking about medical technology and our human mortality? How can that technology be made to serve a peaceful death, not to be its enemy? What can be done to bring about a change? I want to try to make plausible a different way of thinking about the use of technology and then suggest some ways of implementing it. The change I propose can be put very simply, however strange and odd it may sound. We should begin backward. Death should be seen as the necessary and inevitable end point of medical care.

Death As the End Point of Medical Care

In considering its appropriate goals, medicine should, so to speak, simultaneously work backward as well as forward. Medicine now characteristically works forward only, looking to promote the good of life, both to lengthen life and improve its quality. Death is reluctantly admitted into the realm of medicine as the limit to achieving those ends, but that limit is itself uncertain at its boundary, not readily located. Thus also is the termination of treatment judged to be a lesser moral evil, because the quality of life cannot be sustained at the level at which, ideally, medicine would like to sustain it.

What if, however we began our thinking with death? What if we asked how medicine should conduct itself to promote both a good life and a peaceful death? What if medicine once and for all accepted death as a limit that cannot be overcome and used that limit as an indispensable focal point in thinking about illness and disease? The reality of death as a part of our biological life would be seen, not as a discordant note in the search for health and well-being, but as a foreseeable endpoint of its enterprise, and its pacification as a proper goal of medicine from the outset. What if the aim of scientific medicine was not an endless struggle against death, with the fight against disease as the token of that struggle, but helping humans best live a mortal, not immortal, life?

These questions are almost naive. But I see no evidence that they are deeply and persistently asked in modern medicine. If they were, then death would have to be taken seriously, allowed an honored role in the ideals of medicine, not treated as only a necessary evil and a temporary scientific failure. The acceptance, management, and understanding of death would become as fully a part of the mainline enterprise of medicine as the pursuit of health. It would not be necessary even to conceive of a hospice movement, a separate system of caring for the dying; that would be taken for granted as central to the enterprise of medicine itself, not a specially constructed sideshow, out of sight of the main tent.

If the ordinary goal of medicine is the preservation or restoration of health, death should be the understood and expected ultimate outcome of that effort, implicitly and inherently there from the start. The only question is when and how, not whether. Medicine's pursuit of health should be leavened by its need when health fails, as it must, to prepare the way for as peaceful a death as possible. If death is part of the human life cycle, then care for the dying body must be integral to the ends of medicine.

Death is, to sharpen the point, that to which medical care should be oriented from the outset in the case of all serious, potentially life-threatening illnesses, or of a serious decline of mental and physical capacities as a result of age or disease. Of each serious illness—especially with the elderly—a question should be asked and a possibility entertained: could it be that this illness is the one that either will be fatal or, since some disease must be fatal, should soon be allowed to be fatal? If so, then a different strategy toward it should come immediately into play, an effort to work toward a peaceful death rather than fight for a cure.

What am I saying that is different from the present stance of medicine? At present, medicine takes as its task only the pursuit of health, or the preservation of a decent quality of life, with death as the accidental result of illnesses and diseases thought to be avoidable and contingent, even though in fact still fatal. Death is what happens when medicine fails, and is thus outside its proper scientific scope. That is why, I surmise, a great medical classic, *Cecil Textbook of Medicine,* a primary guide for physicians, refers in only twenty-five of its twenty-three hundred pages to death (and only in five to pain).[2] For a book filled with accounts of lethal diseases and ways to treat them, there is a strikingly scant discussion—three pages only of treatment for those in the terminal phase of disease. It tells what to do to hold off death, but not what is to be done when that is not possible. That omission is a stark example of the way death is kept beyond the borders of medicine, an unwelcome, unwanted, unexpected, and ultimately accidental intruder. What if, by contrast, every section of that book dealing with potentially fatal diseases had a part dealing with the care of those dying from the disease? The care of the dying cancer patient is not identical with the care of a person dying from congestive heart disease or kidney failure. But this could never be guessed from reading standard treatment textbooks.

An incorporation of that approach in textbooks and clinical training would make clear, in the most direct way, that this disease may be, sometimes voluntarily and sometimes not, the cause of death—death, which must come to all and is thus no accident. Then the physician's task would become that of accepting a particular illness as the likely cause of death, opening the way for a peaceful death by choosing that combination of treatment and palliation of the accepted condition most likely to make it possible. The objective here would be exactly the opposite of technological brinkmanship, which goes as far as possible with aggressive treatment, stopping only when it is useless to go further. In the task of allowing a peaceful death, brinkmanship would be repudiated from the outset. Active treatment to cure disease and stop death from coming would stop well short of its technical possibilities, at that point when a peaceful death could be most assured and best managed. The worry that a patient might die sooner than technologically necessary would be actively balanced by anxiety that a patient might die later than was compatible with a peaceful death.

Deforming Our Dying

A peaceful death can be understood both positively and negatively. I will begin with the latter, specifying some ways in which our dying can be deformed. If we can better discern some of the ways that happens, the ideal of a peaceful death can be given greater substance. Our dying can be deformed in three ways: by deforming the process of dying, by deforming the dying self, and by deforming the community of the living.

Deforming the Process of Dying

The process of dying is deformed when it is subject to the violence of technological attenuation, drawn out and unduly extended by medical interventions, directly or indirectly. Technological brinkmanship is the most common way of creating the deformity—that is, pushing aggressive treatment as far as it can go in the hope that it can be stopped at just the might moment if it turns out to be futile. That brinkmanship and the gamble it represents can both save life and ruin dying; that is the dilemma it poses. The most obvious kind of technological violence comes when a particular course of treatment—some forms of chemotherapy for cancer, or cardiopulmonary resuscitation for a dying person—itself directly imposes the violence.

Less noticed, but bound to become increasingly important, is the violence done when the cure of one disease sets the stage for the advent of another, perhaps even more cruel than the death one has just averted. Consider, for instance, the person cured of cancer at seventy-five who is set up for the enhanced risk, by virtue of age alone, of the onset of a fatal case of Alzheimer's disease at eighty, or for an excessively long period of severe frailty. We increase the likelihood of spending our declining years helpless, demented, and incontinent if medicine saves our lives long enough to help us avert all of the lethal diseases that stand in the way of that (not so splendid) final outcome.

We may of course gain some extra good years before that happens, and for some it will not happen at all. I only want to underscore the gamble implicit here, a kind of technological Russian roulette with one's last years of life. We must reckon whether it is a good or bad gamble, and how much we are prepared to accept a deformed dying as a result. Increasing frailty and bodily decline are themselves part of the aging process, the wasting away that ordinarily precedes death in old age. There is no inherent evil in the dependency that withering can bring. My complaint is instead directed against a kind of medicine that drives us toward technological brinkmanship and thus needlessly exacerbates and attenuates the withering in destructive ways, genuinely deforming the process of dying. The process of dying is deformed when, through overconfidence in our power to manage technology and to manage our own ambivalence toward death, we fail to take account of what an overzealous medicine can do.

The process of dying is also deformed when there is an extended period of a loss of consciousness well before we are actually dead. It is deformed when there is an exceedingly and unduly long period of debility and frailty before death. It is deformed when there is a lengthy period of pain and suffering prior to death. Note the words I have used: "extended," "exceedingly," "unduly," and "lengthy." By these I mean to say that death may well and unavoidably be preceded by some pain and suffering, some loss of consciousness, some debility and frailty, but that we human beings have generated our own miseries when we allow technology to create a situation that produces exceedingly long periods of those evils. I offer no precise definition of "exceedingly." Frailty and debility can be tolerated for longer periods of time than straight pain and suffering, and a few days even of unconsciousness might be tolerable.

It is when those evils go on and on that a problem, a desperate one, arises. Left unattended, the biological process of dying would not ordinarily lead to such deformities, even if it will happen in some minority of cases. That is something we can know from the dying of other biological organisms, especially higher animals, and from the historical record of human death itself before our modern era, where an extended period of dying was the exception rather than the rule. Our contemporary deformities of dying, it is then fair to say, ordinarily arise only as the result of human medical intervention.

Deforming the Dying Self

The most obvious way the dying self can be deformed is by allowing the fear of death, or the fear of what dying may do to our ideal self, itself to corrupt the self. Obsessions with a loss of control, or with a diminishment of the idealized optimal self, or with the prospect of pain, are other ways this can happen. That is to turn our dying into an occasion of unrelenting self-pity and self-castigation: I can never be again what I once was, I do not want to be what I now am, and I do not want to be what I will become as my death draws even closer.

Some delicacy is in order in trying to make this point. It is understandable that we should not want to lose all control or to become less of a self than we once were, or that we should fear pain. Anxiety, even terror, is to be expected as we approach our death, both because of the physical threats of dying and because of the challenge to our sense of self-worth and self-coherence. It is the preoccupation with those evils that introduces the potential deformity, the feeling that we cannot be worthy human beings if they are our fate, and an inability to think of anything but our losses, our failures, our diminution.

Deforming the Community of the Living

Just as we can harm the self, our sense of self-worth, in responding to the threat of death, so too, can we do harm to others. If the horror of death—or, more likely, of illness, decline, and dying together—yields social policies designed to relieve that suffering at all costs, then the community of the living is put at risk. A society that takes the relief of the ordinary burdens of life (of which death is surely one) as a goal to be pursued with singular dedication must ultimately fail, putting its members in harm's way even as it does so.

This can happen when the pursuit of health and the avoidance of death become an excessively high priority, gained at the cost of ignoring other social evils. It can happen when the medical community comes to believe it must, as the price of relieving suffering, be prepared to kill or assist in suicide, thus distorting its oldest and most central traditions. It can happen when, as a community ideal, a life that includes any suffering is rejected as intolerable. It can happen when a life thought "not worth living" (the Nazi expression) is one marked by suffering, a less than ideal self, and a failure to make adequate contributions to society.

The possibility of a peaceful death will, then, require as a minimal condition that death not be deformed, either individually or socially. But more will be required to enhance its possibility.

Defining a Peaceful Death

It is not difficult, just listening to the way people talk about the kind of death they would like, to gain a decent sense of what they would count as a peaceful death. I could try to do that, but I would prefer to put it in my own voice, recognizing that there may be individual variations:

- I want to find some meaning in my death or, if not a full meaning, a way of reconciling myself to it. Some kind of sense must be made of my mortality.
- I hope to be treated with respect and sympathy, and to find in my dying a physical and spiritual dignity.
- I would like my death to matter to others, to be seen in some larger sense as an evil, a rupturing of human community, even if they understand that my particular death might be preferable to an excessive and prolonged suffering, and even if they understand death to be part of the biological nature of the human species.
- If I do not necessarily want to die in the public way that marked the era of a tame death, with strangers coming in off the streets, I do not want to be abandoned, psychologically ejected

from the community, because of my impending death. I want people to be with me, at hand if not in the same room.

- I do not want to be an undue burden on others in my dying, though I accept the possibility that I may be some burden. I do not want the end of my life to be the financial or emotional ruination of another life.
- I want to live in a society that does not dread death—at least an ordinary death from disease at a relatively advanced age—and that provides support in its rituals and public practices for comforting the dying and, after death, their friends and families.
- I want to be conscious very near the time of my death, and with my mental and emotional capacities intact. I would be pleased to die in my sleep, but I do not want a prolonged coma prior to my death.
- I hope that my death will be quick, not drawn out.
- I recoil at the prospect of a death marked by pain and suffering, though I would hope to bear it well if that is unavoidable.

There is a difference between this desired peaceful death and Philippe Aries's tame death. Technological advances make it possible to manage better those conditions that could not, in the past, be made amenable to a tame death, especially the degenerative diseases of aging. We can, that is, have both the advantages of the older tame death and, with the help of technology, many improvements in contemporary death.

The most evident characteristic of a peaceful death as I have outlined it is the way it blends personal, medical, and social strands. Whatever meaning we find in our dying and death must come from within ourselves, though we may and probably will of course draw upon religious and other traditions for important help. We could also reasonably look to the larger society for public practices, rituals, and attitudes that can provide a more comforting context for the acceptance of death. A modified return to special symbols of mourning, such as black armbands for men and dark clothes for women, as well as the enhancement of groups organized for grieving spouses, or religious services, would be examples of the possibilities here. As for the relief of pain, there we can look to medical practice, and even expect from that practice some help with suffering, a more subtle condition stemming in part from an interior perception of the significance of dying and from the kind of external support we are given in the face of our anxieties.

Could a peaceful death be assured every patient? No. Medicine cannot now and probably never will be able to avert all pain and suffering or ensure a tranquil course of illness. No society could wholly overcome the fear of death or the rending of community that is death. No one can be confident that fear, anguish, or a sense of pointlessness and futility will not be one's lot, even if one has lived the kind of life most conducive to reducing that possibility. Since no one can give us, as our own, a meaning to our dying and death, we must find that for ourselves; some of us will never find it.

Since there can be no guarantee that a peaceful death will be ours, some store of courage must be available. If I am correct in my surmise that the obsessively feared loss of control of our dying is itself part of the problem—a fear that we will not be either ourselves or in command of ourselves—then one way to resist the force of this fear is to be willing to accept some loss of control. The price of obsession is undue fear. Relief can be sought in a willingness to live with, and die with, less than perfection here. Yet if we can understand that there is a middle way, then the possibility of a peaceful death can be greatly enhanced. It is at least as likely that we could create the possibility of a peaceful death for a majority of people by changing our medical attitudes and expectations as by the more violent course of euthanasia and assisted suicide, and with far less loss of other values in the process.

Medical Futility

The general orientation and resource allocation priorities of the health care system can make a considerable difference, albeit indirectly for the most part, in the care of the dying. Of more direct and immediate impact will be the aggregate effect of what clinicians at the bedside come to consider futile or marginally useful treatment. As a concept, futility has both medical and moral dimensions.[3] Its medical feature is that of a probability that a particular treatment for a particular person will not be efficacious, that is, it will not return the patient to good health or sustain the patient in any medically viable way. The moral feature is a judgment that some forms of medical treatment, with either a low or no probability of success, should be morally judged to be useless. Taken together, then, a judgment of medical futility is medical insofar as it relies on judgments of probability of medical outcome, and moral in that it relies upon judgments about whether the pursuit of low-probability outcomes is morally required.

There is already considerable pressure from physicians to be allowed to make judgments of medical futility on their own, without having to ask patients or their families. Their goal is not to avoid a doctor-patient interaction, but to be spared the pressure of unrealistic patient demands. It is one thing, they say, to be asked by patients or their families to stop treatment; that is acceptable. It is still another to be asked to provide treatment of a kind physicians think futile or useless; that they take to be unacceptable, a threat to their professional integrity.

Their instinct is correct and reasonable. Physicians ought not to be required to perform procedures or provide treatment that they believe will do no good. Yet it would be arbitrary to allow physicians unilaterally to make those judgments, given the fights of patients to be informed of their situation. It would be better if the standards here were established collectively, by joint bodies of lay people and physicians.

This might best be done in individual hospitals, where joint medical-lay panels could help establish an institutional policy sensitive to local needs and values. It should not, I believe, be done with individual patients on a case-by-case basis. Judgments of futility could then be made, and treatment denied, but on the basis of consensual norms and publicly visible policies.[4] The development of such policies would, of course, have a potentially significant impact on the options available to patients. Some general societal standards would come to replace unlimited patient choice.

What would be the pertinence of such a development for the termination of treatment? It would be valuable if in coming years some consensus were achieved about futile treatment. Futility needs, however, to be understood in two senses: futile because no benefit whatever can be achieved from treatment, and futile because, given resource limitations, the treatment is economically unjustifiable. Thus we must have a general social agreement on the right of physicians to withhold medical treatment from persons in the persistent vegetative state, and an agreement on the forms of medical treatment that would be considered futile for those faced with imminent death from an acute or chronic illness or from the slow death of dementia.

A standard of futility compatible with the goal of avoiding an unnecessarily painful or extended death would be most valuable. The test of futility could be twofold: first, an inability to arrest more than momentarily (by a few days or weeks) a downward, deteriorating course; and second, the probability, should that kind of effort be made, that a peaceful death would become increasingly unlikely. At that point, curative medical treatment has indeed become futile and ought to be stopped. The standard is thus one that looks to the possibility of sustaining life in some decent fashion, but also and simultaneously to the choices necessary for enhancing the possibility of a peaceful death.

The most difficult but impending problem of futility judgments is whether to embody them in public policy. As matters now stand, it is customary for both federal and private health care plans to provide reimbursement for the care of those in a persistent vegetative state; families and medical staffs that want medical treatment to be continued for these patients can be reimbursed for its cost. Should financial support continue in the future? I believe that, in principle, it should not. Ideally speaking, it makes no sense in light of budget restraints or humane public policy to use medical technology to sustain for an extended period the life of someone who will almost certainly never return to consciousness.

The temptation here is to adopt an either-or approach. If we consider the patient alive, then we think we should provide the patient with all those forms of health care that we would provide any other live person; or if we simply consider the patient as dead, even if not legally so, we think we should stop all care. The problem, however, is that we as a society remain uncertain about the status of patients who manage to combine, in a bewildering way, elements of both life and death. An appropriate compromise, I believe, would be to provide minimal nursing care but not the extended artificial nutrition and hydration that many institutions now routinely provide—probably because of public disagreement about the moral status of someone in that condition.

My guess is that increasingly few people will for long believe that this form of "life" merits being called human. It is a moribund life sustained by technological artifact in the face of a biological condition crying out to come to an end, as in nature it ordinarily would. Yet as long as disagreement persists, it would be unwise to stop treatment precipitately or high-handedly. That could seem to bespeak an indifference to the important convictions of some people, convictions not without some merit. But every effort should slowly be made to change those convictions so that a social consensus could build to form the basis of new policy that would refuse reimbursement for patients in that condition. A softer, perhaps more tolerable alternative would be to assign a low priority to such treatment, to help assure it would not capture resources that could be better spent on more needy patients with a chance of real recovery or amelioration of their condition.

A peaceful death should have both an individual and a public face. For the individual it can bring life to a fitting close, marked by connection to the self through reason and self-consciousness, and by connection to others through dying within the circle of human companionship and caring. But death should also have a peaceful public face. The control and management of death, understood as an unavoidable part of life, should not consume an undue share of resources, as if keeping death at bay represented society's most important goal. People should have a chance to live a healthy life, avoid premature death, and then die without that technological brinkmanship that knows no boundaries in the war against mortality.

I would define a peaceful death in a public context as a death that, on the one hand, rejected a disproportionate share of resources which, through a kind of economic violence, threatened other societal goods such as education and housing; and, on the other hand, rejected euthanasia and assisted suicide as still other forms of violence, though medical and social rather than economic.

What about family burdens as a form of quasi-domestic violence? It is not improper for people to worry about being a burden on their families or to wish they could spare them undue emotional and financial hardship. We can readily recognize the possibility of taking down with us, in a parallel destruction, those family members whose devotion—economic or emotional or both—is pressed too far. It is hard to see how a death that impoverishes a family, or destroys the later years of an elderly spouse, or wrecks the family life of a dutiful child caring for an elderly parent, can be called entirely peaceful.

At the same time, however, it is right and proper that we bear one another's illness and dying. We should not only be willing to care for others; no less important, we should allow them to care for us if there is no moral or humane way to avoid that burden. We do not need a medical system and a set of moral values that will impose upon families the drain of extended illness and death, especially when that has been brought about not by natural forces but by an excessive application of life-sustaining technologies. We should be willing to bear what nature and human mortality bring to us. But there is no reason why we should have to bear artificially extended deaths. A patient should reject them for the sake of the family's welfare after he or she is gone. And when a patient is incompetent and death on the way, family members should not be forced, through guilt or a confusion about killing and allowing to die, to believe that a termination of treatment is wrongful killing. It is not killing at all.

Endnotes

1. Philippe Aries, *The Hour of Our Death,* trans. Helen Weaver (New York: Alfred A. Knopf, 1981), pp. 5–28; see also Philippe Aries, *Western Attitudes Toward Death,* trans. Patricia M. Ranum (Baltimore: Johns Hopkins University Press, 1974).
2. James R. Wyngaarden, Lloyd H. Smith, and J. Claude Bennett, eds., *Cecil Textbook of Medicine,* 19th ed. (Philadelphia: W.B. Saunders, 1992).
3. See Lawrence J. Schneiderman, Nancy S. Jecker, and Albert R. Jonsen, "Medical Futility: Its Meaning and Ethical Implications," *Annals of Internal Medicine* 112, no. 12 (1990): 949–954; John D. Lantos et al., "The Illusion of Futility in Medical Practice," *American Journal of Medicine* 87 (July 1980), 81–84; Tom Tomlinson and Howard Brody, "Futility and the Ethics of Resuscitation," JAMA 264, no. 10 (1990), 1276–1280; Stuart J. Youngner, "Who Defines Futility?" JAMA 260, no. 14 (1988), 2094–2095.
4. See Daniel Callahan, "Medical Futility, Medical Necessity: The Problem-Without-A-Name," *Hastings Center Report* 21, no. 4 (1991), 30–35.

Journal/Discussion Questions

✍ *What kind of death do you want to have? What do you think will be the greatest barriers to dying in the way you want?*

1. To what extent, according to Callahan, has modern medicine changed the ways in which we die? In what ways has dying been deformed? Why has this given rise to a *moral* problem?
2. How would Callahan's suggestions change the way in which physicians today typically treat dying patients? Discuss.

CONCLUDING DISCUSSION QUESTIONS

Where Do You Stand Now?

Instructions

You have already answered the following questions in your moral problems self-quiz at the beginning of this book. Now that you have studied the material in this section, take a moment to answer the same questions again.

	Strongly Agree	Agree	Undecided	Disagree	Strongly Disagree	*Chapter 3: Euthanasia*
11.	❑	❑	❑	❑	❑	Euthanasia is always morally wrong.
12.	❑	❑	❑	❑	❑	Euthanasia should be illegal at least under almost all circumstances.
13.	❑	❑	❑	❑	❑	The principal moral consideration about euthanasia is the question of whether the person freely chooses to die or not.
14.	❑	❑	❑	❑	❑	Actively killing someone is always morally worse than just letting them die.
15.	❑	❑	❑	❑	❑	Sometimes we have a duty to die.

Compare your answers to the present self-quiz with the answers to the initial self-quiz. How, if at all, have your answers changed? How have the *reasons* for your answers changed?

Journal/Discussion Questions

✍ *Under what conditions, if any, would you want others to withhold medical treatment from you? To withhold fluids and nutrition? To actively terminate your life?*

✍ *Review the living will you wrote at the beginning of this chapter (p. 149). What changes, if any, would you make in it after reading this chapter?*

1. You have now read, thought, and discussed a number of aspects of the morality of the euthanasia decision. How have your views *changed* and developed? Has your understanding changed of the reasons supporting other positions that are different from your own? What issue(s) remain unresolved for you at this point?

2. What, in the readings is this section, was the most thought-provoking idea you encountered? In what ways did it prompt you to reconsider some of your previous beliefs?
3. In light of the preceding readings, what do you think is the single most compelling reason for legalizing euthanasia? What do you think is the single most compelling reason for *not* doing so? If euthanasia were to be legalized, what do you think would be the most important safeguard that should accompany it?

FOR FURTHER READING

Web Resources

For Web-based resources, including the major Supreme Court decisions on end-of-life decisions, see the Euthanasia page of *Ethics Updates (http://ethics.acusd.edu).* Among the resources are: the Amicus Brief. Assisted Suicide: The Brief by Ronald Dworkin, Thomas Nagel, Robert Nozick, John Rawls, Thomas Scanlon, and Judith Jarvis Thomson; Frances M. Kamm's "A Right to Choose Death" in the *Boston Review;* Peter Unger's *Living High and Letting Die;* Robert Young's "Voluntary Suicide"; *Stanford Encyclopedia of Philosophy;* and links to several important documentaries on end-of-life decisions.

Journals

In addition to the standard journals in ethics mentioned in Chapter 1, see *The Hastings Center Reports, The Journal of Medicine and Philosophy, Bioethics,* and *The Kennedy Institute of Ethics Journal.*

Anthologies

There are several very helpful *anthologies* that deal with euthanasia. *Beneficent Euthanasia,* edited by Marvin Kohl (Buffalo: Prometheus Books, 1975) contains a very good range of pieces; *Ethical Issues Relating to Life and Death,* edited by John Ladd (New York: Oxford University Press, 1979); *Euthanasia: The Moral Issues,* edited by Robert M. Baird and Stuart E. Rosenbaum (Buffalo: Prometheus Books, 1989) contains a nice balance of philosophical and popular pieces; *Euthanasia: Opposing Viewpoints,* edited by Carol Wekesser (San Diego: Greenhaven Press, 1995) also contains a good balance of philosophical and popular pieces, all in relatively short segments. Also see, *Voluntary Euthanasia,* edited by A.B. Downing and Barbara Smoker (London: Peter Owen, 1986), which includes a number of important essays, including an exchange between Yale Kamisar and Glanville Williams; and *The Dilemmas of Euthanasia,* edited by J.A. Behnke and Sissela Bok (New York, 1975); and *Suicide and Euthanasia,* edited by Baruch Brody (Dordrecht: Kluwer); *Euthanasia Examined,* edited by John Keown (Cambridge: Cambridge University Press, 1995). On cross-cultural perspectives, see especially *Ethnic Variations in Dying, Death, and Grief,* edited by Donald P. Irish et al. (Philadelphia: Taylor & Francis, 1993).

On the distinction between *killing and letting die,* see *Killing and Letting Die,* edited by Bonnie Steinbock and Alastair Norcross, 2nd ed. (New York: Fordham University Press, 1994), which contains virtually all the major essays on this topic; it also contains an excellent bibliography.

Review Articles

For an excellent survey of the philosophical issues (and a very helpful annotated bibliography), see Marvin Kohl, "Euthanasia," *Encyclopedia of Ethics,* edited by Lawrence C. Becker and Charlotte B. Becker (New York: Garland, 1992), pp. 335–339.

Journal Articles

The "Symposium on Physician-Assisted Suicide" in *Ethics,* Vol. 109, 3 (April, 1999) contains excellent articles by Judith Jarvis Thomson, Dan W. Brock, Paul J. Weithman, Gerald Dworkin, F.M. Kamm, J. David Velleman, and Ezekiel J. Emanuel. The *distinction between active and passive euthanasia* was seriously questioned in our selection from James Rachels, "Active and Passive Euthanasia," *New England Journal of Medicine,* Vol. 292, No. 2 (January 9, 1975), pp. 78–80. Rachels position has been criticized by a number of philosophers, including Tom L. Beauchamp, "A Reply to Rachels on Active and Passive Euthanasia," in *Social Ethics,* First Edition, edited by Thomas A. Mappes and Jane S. Zembaty (New York: McGraw-Hall, 1977), pp. 67–76; Thomas D. Sullivan, "Active and Passive Euthanasia: An Impertinent Distinction?" in *Social Ethics,* 4th ed., edited by Thomas A. Mappes and Jane S. Zembaty (New York: McGraw-Hall, 1992), pp. 115–121; Rachels' reply to Sullivan in variously reprinted, including in Mappes and Zembaty's *Social Ethics,* 4th ed., pp. 121–131. Also see Bonnie Steinbock, "The Intentional Termination of Life," *Ethics in Science and Medicine,* Vol. 6, No. 1 (1979), pp. 59–64.

Among the important philosophical essays, see Philippa Foot, "Euthanasia," reprinted in her *Virtues and Vices* (Berkeley: University of California Press, 1978), pp. 33–61; Judith Jarvis Thomson's "Killing, Letting Die, and the Trolley Problem," and "The Trolley Problem," reprinted in her *Rights, Restitution, and Risk,* edited by William Parent (Cambridge: Harvard University Press, 1986), pp. 78–93, 94–116; in "Euthanasia: A Christian View," *Philosophic Exchange,* Vol. 2, No. 2 (1975), pp. 43–52, R.M. Hare develops a version of the Golden Rule argument against euthanasia.

Books

Among the *philosophical books devoted primarily to euthanasia and decisions at the end of life,* see especially James Rachels, *The End of Life: The Morality of Euthanasia* (New York: Oxford University Press, 1986); Fred Feldman, *Confrontations with the Reaper: A Philosophical Study of the Nature and Value of Death* (New York: Oxford University Press, 1992); Jay F. Rosenberg, *Thinking Clearly about Death* (Englewood Cliffs, NJ: Prentice-Hall, 1983); Marvin Kohl, *The Morality of Killing: Sanctity of Life, Abortion, and Euthanasia* (New York, Humanities Press, 1974); Kenneth L. Vaux, *Death Ethics: Religious and Cultural Values in Prolonging and Ending Life* (Philadelphia: Trinity Press International, 1992); Daniel Callahan, *Setting Limits: Medical Goals in an Aging Society* (New York: Simon and Schuster, 1987); and Margaret Battin, *The Least Worst Death: Essays in Bioethics on the End of Life* (New York: Oxford, 1994); Peter Singer, *Rethinking Life and Death* (New York: St. Martin's Press, 1994). For a superb *multimedia CD-ROM presentation* of a particularly difficult case in voluntary assisted euthanasia, see *A Right to Die: The Dax Cowart Case* (Routledge, 1999), by Robert Cavalier, Preston Covey, and David Anderson. The multimedia resources bring home the tragic reality of Dax's situation.

On the more general issue of *death,* see *The Metaphysics of Death,* edited by John Martin Fischer (Stanford: Stanford University Press, 1993); Herbert Fingarette, *Death: Philosophical Soundings* (Chicago: Open Court, 1996).

Among the more *popular literature* on euthanasia, see Derek Humphrey's *Final Exit: The Practicalities of Self-deliverance and Assisted Suicide for the Dying* (Eugene, OR: Hemlock Society, 1991). Perhaps the most (in)famous public figure in this area is Jack Kevorkian; see *Prescription—Medicide: The Goodness of Planned Death* (Buffalo, NY: Prometheus Books, 1991). For a much more moderate voice, see C. Everett Koop, *The Right to Live, the Right to Die* (Wheaton, IL: Tyndale House, 1976). In *Death and Dignity: Making Choices and Taking Charge* (New York: W.W. Norton, 1993), Timothy E. Quill, MD argues, at least in part on the basis of his experience as a hospice director, in favor of physician-assisted euthanasia; for an interesting contrast, see *Euthanasia Is Not the Answer: A Hospice Physician's View,* by David Cundiff. (Totowa, NJ: Humana Press, 1992), Ira Byock, *Dying Well* (New York: Riverhead, 1997), and M. Scott Peck, *Denial of the Soul: Spiritual and Medical Perspectives on Euthanasia and Mortality* (New York: Harmony Books, 1997).

On the *Nazi euthanasia program,* see most recently Michael Burleigh's *Death and Deliverance* (Cambridge: Cambridge University Press, 1994) as well as Robert Jay Lifton's *The Nazi Doctors* (New York: Basic Books, 1986).

Suicide

There are a number of excellent *anthologies* of selections dealing solely with the issue of suicide. These include: *On Suicide,* Introduction by Robert Coles, edited by John Miller (San Francisco: Chronicle Books, 1992); and *Essays in Self-Destruction,* edited by Edwin S. Shneidman (New York: J. Aronson, 1967). For a more strictly philosophical approach, see the anthologies *Suicide, the Philosophical Issues,* edited by M. Pabst Battin and David J. Mayo (New York: St. Martin's Press, 1980) and *Suicide: Right or Wrong?* edited by John Donnelly (Buffalo: Prometheus Press, 1990) for excellent selections of philosophical works on suicide.

A. Alvarez's *The Savage God: A Study of Suicide* (New York, Random House, 1972) is a classic study. On the effects of *depression,* see especially William Styron, *Darkness Visible* (New York: Random House, 1990).

Among contemporary *philosophical approaches to suicide,* see the interesting contrast between the Kantian approach of Thomas E. Hill, Jr., "Self-Regarding Suicide: A Modified Kantian View," *Autonomy and Self-Respect* (Cambridge: Cambridge University Press, 1991), pp. 85–103 and the utilitarian perspective of Richard Brandt, "The Morality and Rationality of Suicide," in his *Morality, Utilitarianism, and Rights* (Cambridge: Cambridge University Press, 1992), pp. 315–335. For an excellent longer study, see Margaret Pabst Battin, *Ethical Issues in Suicide* (Englewood Cliffs, NJ: Prentice-Hall, 1982).

CHAPTER 4

Punishment and the Death Penalty

Videotape:

Topic: Crime and Justice: Judgment at Midnight

ABCNEWS *Source:* ABC *Nightline* (January 21, 1999)

Anchor: Ted Koppel

NARRATIVE ACCOUNT

Helen Prejean, C.S.J.
"Crime Victims on the Anvil of Pain"

Sister Helen Prejean, C.S.J., is a native of Louisiana, a member of the Sisters of St. Joseph of Medaille, and a spiritual counselor both to inmates on death row and to the families of their victims. Her book and the movie based on it, Dead Man Walking: An Eyewitness Account of the Death Penalty in the United States *quickly became one of the most influential works questioning the morality of the death penalty.*

In the following newspaper article from 1988, Helen Prejean tries to do justice both to her firm conviction that the death penalty is wrong and her compassion for those who have lost a family member to a violent crime. She describes, briefly but graphically, the pain of both and the effects of their pain on her.

As You Read, Consider This:

1. Do you think that Sister Prejean perceives the death row inmates clearly? The families of the victims?
2. What moves you about Sister Prejean's account of her ministry to death row inmates and to the families of their victims?

I stand outside the door and take a deep breath. It's my first meeting with the New Orleans Chapter of Parents of Murdered Children, a support group for people whose children have met violent deaths.

Vernon Harvey, my nemesis of sorts, waits for me on the other side of the door. His stepdaughter, Faith, was murdered by Robert Lee Willie. I was Robert's spiritual adviser. Both of us witnessed Robert's execution in the electric chair.

Prior to the execution, both of us had appeared at the Pardon Board hearing—he, urging Robert's death; I, pleading for his life. He was furious at me.

"You should be helping victims' families," he had told me.

Finally, at his urging I was coming to this meeting.

People ask me how I got involved in all this. Good question. I ask it of God sometimes when I pray.

For 20 years I did what most other Catholic nuns were doing—teaching the young, conducting religious education programs in a suburban church parish. But in 1981 I moved into a steamy public housing project in New Orleans and for the first time in my life tasted the struggle of those who live on the "underside of history."

One day a friend in prison ministry asked me to become a pen pal to someone on death row. "Sure," I said, having no idea what lay in store for me. I wrote to Elmo Patrick Sonnier, then I became his spiritual adviser, then I watched him die in the electric chair. I became a strong advocate for death row inmates and their families.

I am with Elmo Patrick Sonnier in the death house. The guards are in his cell, shaving his head, his left ankle. . . .

He returns to the metal door where I sit on the other side. His body sags in the chair. He looks naked, stripped. He smokes cigarettes and drinks black coffee.

I've known him for two years. As a child he alternated between divorced parents and he was out on his own by the time he was 16. He had done his share of settling life's challenges with his fists, but never anything like Nov. 5, 1977, when he and his brother killed a teen-age couple. The fathers of the victims will be there to witness his execution.

He's talking non-stop . . . snatches from the past . . . how good it felt to go hunting when the weather was cool . . . driving 18 wheelers . . . "thank you for your love . . . please take care of my Mama . . ."

We pray together. "God, just give me the strength to make that last walk." He starts to shiver. A guard puts a denim jacket over his shoulders.

It's midnight. "Time to go, Sonnier," the warden says.

We walk to the electric chair, my hand on his shoulder as I read from the Bible. We stop. I look up and see the chair. The guards are leading me away. "Pray for me, Pat." He turns around. "I will, Sister Helen, I will."

His last words . . . he looks at the parents of the murdered teen-agers. "Forgive me for what me and my brother did."

He sits in the chair. The guards move quickly, strapping his arms, his legs. He finds my face among the witnesses. "I love you," he says.

I turn the doorknob and enter the room where the Parents of Murdered Children are meeting. Vernon comes over to greet me. His eyes say, "You're coming around—at last."

The meeting begins. The motto of the group is "Give sorrow words."

—"Laura was stabbed by my son's best friend one week before her 12th birthday. Her skiing outfit is still hanging in the closet . . . five years now. I just can't give it away."

—"When my child was killed, it took over a week to find her body. The police treated us like we were the criminals. They brushed us off whenever we phoned."

—"I got to witness the son of a b— fry who killed our daughter. The chair is too quick. I hope he's burning in hell."

—"I'm beginning to let my anger go. I put John's picture on the Christmas tree. My Christmas angel, I call him."

—"Friends avoid us. If you try to bring up your child's death, they change the subject."

I leave the meeting stunned by the pain I have been allowed to touch. On the anvil of that pain I forge a new commitment to expend my energies for victims' families as well as death row inmates.

Now I work on a task force to see that victims' families get state-allotted funds for counseling, unemployment compensation, funeral expenses. Only a handful of sheriff's offices in Louisiana bother to appoint the personnel to administer these funds. Related, I think, to a mind-set prevalent in our criminal justice system: big on recrimination; short on healing.

As I see it, the death penalty is just another killing (and a highly selective one at that; two-thirds of all executions happen in four southern states). Obviously executions don't do anything for the criminal, and, from what I've seen, they don't do much for victims' families either.

Our need to protect ourselves from killers is real. When I walk to my car at night I glance often over my shoulder. I know now that really bad things can happen to really good people. But surely in 1988 we who purport to be the most civilized of societies can find a way to incapacitate dangerous criminals without imitating their tragic, violent behavior.

Journal/Discussion Questions

✍ *Sister Prejean's reactions to both the death row inmates and to the families of their victims are probably different from our own—certainly the combination is most unusual, for she seems able to appreciate the humanity of both without idealizing either. Do you think that her perceptions are correct? If they are different from your own and you think they are correct, what makes it difficult for you fully to perceive the humanity of these murderers? Of their victims?*

1. How does Sister Prejean reconcile her commitment to the death row inmates and to the families of their victims? Does this have more moral force than if she were just committed to one or the other alone? Why?
3. Why is Sister Prejean opposed to the death penalty? What does she suggest as an alternative?

An Introduction to the Moral Issues

In the mid-1990s, we have seen increasing calls to "get tough" in regard to punishment, particular punishment for crimes of violence and punishment for repeat offenders. Eager to capitalize on public fear, politicians have proposed increasingly stringent penalties for particular crimes of violence and for those who have been convicted of crimes in the past. Yet all of this remains troubling, for it is not clear that things are getting any better. We punish more and more in America, but it doesn't seem that our society is safer or that criminals are really deterred by the threat of punishment. Indeed, the United States currently has more individuals in prison today that any other industrialized country, and there seems to be little end in sight.

Justifications of Punishment

Punishment needs justification. The very idea of punishment is that we impose something unpleasant—perhaps even painful or horrible, such as hanging or electrocution—on people against their will. On what basis do we claim the right to do something that odious? It is to this question that justifications of punishment are directed.

Justifications of punishment generally fall into one of two types: *backward-looking* justifications, which essentially see punishment as retribution for a past offense, and *forward-looking* accounts, which see the justification of punishment in some future state of affairs (such as reduction of crime or even rehabilitation of the criminal) that it may bring about. Of the forward-looking accounts, the most common is a deterrence model, which sees the justification of punishment to be located primarily in the ways in which it deters future crime. Rehabilitative models, which see punishment as being more properly replaced by rehabilitation, are also forward-looking, but there is some dispute about whether they genuinely involve punishment. So, too, are models of punishment that see that justification of punishment as being in the type of society that it produces.

In addition to distinguishing between backward-looking and forward-looking accounts of the justification of punishment, we can also distinguish between accounts of punishment in general as an institution (i.e., why are we justified in punishing *at all*?), accounts of the justification of particular punishments (i.e., why is this particular punishment justified for this particular *type* of offense), and justifications of specific instances of punishment (i.e., why is this *particular* individual given this *particular* sentence?). As we shall see, the justification of punishment in general need not be the same as the justification of particular punishments. In this context, we will not be concerned with any specific instances of punishment.

Retributivism: An Eye for an Eye

Retributivist accounts of punishment see it essentially as a kind of paying-back, a retribution for past offenses. A person has been wronged, and the state is justified in inflicting on the wrongdoer the same degree of pain or suffering that the wrongdoer inflicted on the victim. With this comes some rough principle of proportionality, which came to be associated with the Old Testament maxim of "an eye for an eye, a tooth for a tooth," the *lex talionis.* As we shall see, there are difficulties in interpreting this maxim too literally, but the power of the metaphor is obvious once one acknowledges that it is a metaphor and not a literal guide to behavior. Punishment, retributivists claim, must fit the crime.

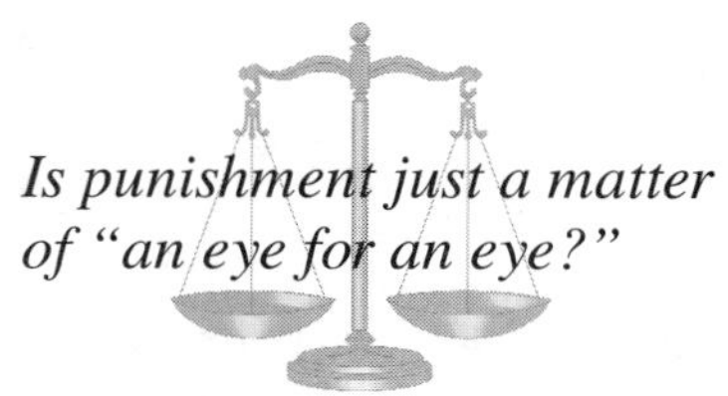

Is punishment just a matter of "an eye for an eye?"

Retributivism as revenge. The crudest account of retributivist justifications of punishment sees them simply as a more or less disguised version of revenge. Friedrich Nietzsche, for example, maintained that revenge was at the heart of the modern notion of punishment. Some have criticized and rejected retributivist accounts of punishment because of this link between retributivism and revenge. Retributivism, they claim, is simply our primitive desire to hit back dressed up in moral clothing.

Defenders of retributivism can respond with two types of replies. On the one hand, they can admit the link between retributivism and revenge but deny that this is grounds for rejecting retributivism. Revenge, they can argue, is a fundamental moral impulse of human beings that places a check on external aggression. Without the desire for revenge, we would be willing accomplices in our own victimization. Revenge, in other things, is not such a bad thing after all, and is certainly not sufficient grounds for rejecting retributivism.

On the other hand, retributivists can argue that retribution is not about revenge, or at least not in any exclusive sense or in any morally shallow sense. Retribution, they argue, is about something more: about balancing the scales of justice, about safeguarding the rights of victims, and about changing perpetrators. Let's look briefly at each of these claims.

The scales of justice. Several different reasons have been advanced in support of this general claim of retributivism. First, underlying some retributivist thought is a metaphor of *moral balance* which is closely associated with the notion of justice. Punishment resets the moral scales, as it were, of society after they have been upset through an offense. Think, for example, of the punishment of Nazis who ran the death camps. Such punishment was often seen as balancing the scales of justice, and many felt it was morally odious for such actions to go unpunished.

The rights of victims. Some retributivists have taken a somewhat different tact: *victims,* they argue, have a right to see that the perpetrators suffer their just desserts. Clearly it would be anarchy if victims were to take this task upon themselves, so punishment becomes the proper domain of the state. Indeed, the very idea of having rights in a particular state is that the state guarantees those rights, by preventing others from violating them when possible and punishing violators.

The effect on perpetrators. Finally, some retributivists focus on the effect that punishment should have on those who perpetrate offenses. First, punishment should bring about some kind of insight. The Kantian account of this insight is that, by willing the crime (e.g., a theft), the perpetrator wills that the maxim behind it (that one person is entitled to appropriate another person's property without permission) be a universal law; thus the perpetrator is in effect willing that others are equally entitled to take the perpetrator's property. What's fair for one is fair for all. Others have argued that perpetrators should experience the pain, suffering, etc. that they have inflicted on their victims. Indeed, there is something profoundly moral about this which has nothing to do with revenge *per se*. Many, including Josiah Royce, have argued that the essence of the moral point of view is the realization that the suffering of others is of equal value to one's own suffering. Think, for example, of punishments of drunk drivers that require them to ride with paramedics to the scenes of auto accidents, to visit victims of other drunk drivers in hospital and rehabilitation facilities, to talk to families who have lost loved ones in accidents caused by drunk drivers. From a moral point of view, such punishments are best understood as programs that help perpetrators understand the real and potential pain and suffering that their offenses can cause.

Second, punishment should "wipe the slate clean." Again, this is part of the balance metaphor insofar as once the scales are back in correct balance, there is nothing leftover to be an object of resentment. Yet this is also a corollary of the intended effect of punishment on perpetrators: if they realize how wrong their deeds were, then they have made a kind of moral progress which entitles them to full reinstatement in the moral community. Many thinkers, not just retributivists, have argued that perpetrators give up their membership in the moral community through their crimes, and it is in part the insights gained through their own punishment—as well as the suffering endured—that entitle them to reinstatement in the moral community.

Criticisms of retributivism. When strict retributivists are asked to justify the institution of punishment, they are at something of a disadvantage. In order to justify something like the institution of punishment, we have to point to something else—and that something else is usually consequentialist and forward-looking in character. Retributivists often seem stuck with simply saying, "Well, it's just *right* that criminals should be punished." If they go further and maintain that it's right because . . . , then what follows the "because" is usually a forward-looking consequentialist concern. It may be that it's right because without punishment society would run amok, or it may be right because it teaches people important lessons about society, but in any case the "because" clause usually turns out to be a forward-looking one.

Second, critics of strict retributivism argue that the *lex talionis,* the law of "an eye for an eye, a tooth for a tooth," is much less simple than it would appear. If someone is convicted of torture, do we then torture that person as a punishment? If someone is convicted of rape, are they to be raped in return? What do we do with someone who has hijacked a bus? Plagiarized a term paper? Desecrated a historical monument? Robbed a bank? The *lex talionis,* in other word, appears to offer literal guidance on punishment, but on closer inspection it can only be interpreted as metaphorical.

Finally, some critics of strict retributivism maintain that it can lead to individual punishments in particular cases that are cruel or that do not serve the ends of justice. Think, for example, of those who committed serious but undetected crimes in their youth and then led exemplary lives, only to have their crime uncovered in old age. Strict retributivists would seem to be committed to punishment that is equally severe, whether the crime is discovered minutes after its commission or decades later. It may be possible to temper this with some degree of mercy, but mercy has no necessary place in the retributivist's world.

Deterrence

One of the principal forward-looking justifications of punishment is its deterrent effect. There are two aspects to such deterrence. The first, and more immediate, is the deterrent effect on the perpetrators who are convicted: punishment deters them from committing such crimes again. The second level of deterrence is more general: punishment of perpetrators deters others, those who have not committed such crimes but may be inclined to do so, from committing them. Common to both is the simple claim that punishment deters crime, and it is upon this that its justification rests.

There is much to be said for forward-looking justifications of the institution of punishment as a whole. Indeed, we do not have to stop with deterrence of further crimes in our forward-looking justifications, for we can then point out why such deterrence would be valuable to society: the greater sense of public safety, the elimination of societal resources destroyed through crime, etc. Overall, the forward-looking claim is a clearly utilitarian one: societies that have the institution of punishment are better than those that do not. Overall, punishment makes society a better place in which to live.

Normative and empirical considerations. Notice that deterrence-based justifications of punishment contain both normative and empirical premises. In order to justify punishment on the basis of its deterrent effect, we really need two types of premises. First, we need an *empirical claim* that punishment does in fact deter. Second, we need a *normative claim* that deterrence (or a society with deterrence) is good. Thus our argument looks like this:

Empirical Premise:	Punishment reduces crime.
Normative Premise:	Reducing crime is good.
Conclusion:	Punishment is good.

Obviously, neither of these premises is controversial, at least in its most general form. Although there is a lot of controversy about the deterrent effects of particular punishments, it seems uncontroversially true that overall punishment reduces crime. Similarly, it is uncontroversially true that reducing crime is good. However, when we look more closely, problems begin to emerge.

Paths to deterrence. The potential difficulties with this argument begin to emerge when we look more closely at the premises. The empirical premise about the deterrent effect of punishment is generally true, but as it stands it only refers to punishment in general, not particular punishments. Moreover, it leaves open the possibility that something else may also reduce crime, perhaps even more effectively. Some candidates for other general societal factors that reduce crime may include a strong moral education, strong family support, the reduction of physical and sexual abuse in childhood, reduction of dependency on drugs and alcohol, and the reduction of poverty and discrimination; some, more specifically crime-related factors include increased funding for community policing, more intensive parole programs, and more research on factors that reduce the occurrence of crime. Clearly, we do not want to say that *only* punishment reduces crime. The question then becomes whether punishment is the best means or—presuming that we do not want to consider these as mutually exclusive alternatives—what the proper mixture should be between punishment and other means of reducing crime.

Punishment and prevention. These considerations have a particular relevance when we are thinking of punishment in general as an institution and the distribution of resources in society. There is an interesting analogy here between crime and lung cancer. Punishment is one of the ways that society seeks to reduce crime, but it is often a last-ditch effort. Just as surgery, radiation, and chemotherapy may be effective therapies against lung cancer, so too imprisonment (and perhaps even the death penalty) may be effective responses to crime, but there is a sense in which they all come too late. They arrive on the scene after the event has happened and the damage has been done. Preventive approaches are far more effective, but much less visible—and thus it may be much harder to obtain funding for them. It makes good sense to spend more of our resources on reducing the causes of cancer—such as smoking and environmental factors—than on developing increasingly effective surgical and therapeutic techniques for curing existing cases of cancer. Similarly, when we consider how we want to distribute our total resources as a society in regard to crime, it makes good sense to concentrate on changing the conditions that give rise to criminal behavior rather than focusing primarily on punishing that behavior once it has occurred. Increasingly severe punishments do not provide the most effective long-term answer to the question of crime. The answer is not to punish crime more severely and more often after it happens, but to support those changes that will reduce the occurrence of crime in the first place.

Conflicting goods. Although the normative premise looks uncontroversial, it too needs at least additional precision. Reducing crime is clearly good, but it is not the *only* good that we strive for, and we must insure that in seeking to reduce crime we do not impinge upon other, perhaps even more important rights and goods. Reducing crime is good, but so too is respecting individual rights, and these two goods often come into conflict. We could easily reduce the level of crime by more extensive surveillance of citizens, by restrictive curfews, by permitting police searches and seizures at will, by outlawing the possession of any weapons, and the like. However, we don't do these things because they conflict with individual rights to liberty, and the preservation of those rights is a good that we strive to realize. We can accept the premise that reducing crime is good, but we must not overlook the fact that it is not the only good.

Disproportionate punishments. One of the greatest potential dangers of deterrence-based models of punishment is that they seem to open the door to justifying punishment, or a severity of punishment, disproportionate to the offense. Recall, for example, the case of Michael Fay, who was sentenced to caning (and also to prison and to fines) for various acts of vandalism in Singapore. Many Americans were outraged at the severity of the sentence, but officials in Singapore pointed out that the penalty was their standard penalty, that everyone knows what the penalties are (including Mr. Fay), and that their society has an amazingly low incident of crime as a result. In other words, they said, this punishment deters, so what's wrong with it? Indeed, many Americans agreed, perhaps indicating their discontent with the American criminal justice system rather than their allegiance to Singapore's.

The philosophical issue here is an important one. If the *only* justification for punishment is deterrence, then it would seem to follow that the more a punishment deters, the more justified it is. Let's furthermore presume that punishments that are inevitable, swift, and public are more likely to deter than punishments that are not. A department store that is bothered by shoplifting, for example, may want to have surveillance equipment, roving undercover police, and roving magistrates to arrest shoplifters, try them on the spot, and then impose a swift, certain, severe, and public punishment such as cutting off a hand for first offenders, cutting off the other hand for second offenders.

This would, one suspects, reduce the amount of shoplifting—indeed, it would probably reduce even the *appearance* of shoplifting—but our immediate reply to such a proposal would presumably be twofold. First, we would say that such punishment violates the shoplifter's rights. But doesn't all punishment do so? Indeed, the whole idea of punishment is to do something to offenders that they don't like—otherwise it wouldn't be punishment. Second, we would say that such punishment is disproportionate to the offense. But proportionality is really a retributivist concept. For the strict deterrence theorist, proportionality just isn't an issue.

Punishing the innocent. In the most extreme cases, deterrence seems to justify punishing the innocent if doing so would result in a significant deterrent effect. The acceptability of this practice seems to follow from a pure deterrence theory. If the sole justification of punishment is deterrence, and if in a particular case punishing an innocent person—whom the public thought was guilty—would have a significant deterrent effect, then punishing an innocent person in that context would be justified. Imagine, for example, that a distinguished diplomat from a foreign country with nuclear capabilities is killed in mysterious circumstances. The United States authorities do not know who killed the diplomat, but they realize that an international incident—perhaps culminating in a nuclear attack—could occur if someone is not arrested immediately. Determined to avoid such a thing, officials arrange the arrest of an innocent man—who in fact is only months from death by cancer—whose generalized guilt is so great that he can be enticed into confessing to the crime. He is then executed, and the crisis is avoided.

In discussing these kinds of cases, which he calls *telishment,* John Rawls points out that they can only be justified from a utilitarian perspective if we consider them as individual cases. However, if we asked whether we could justify a rule permitting telishment from a utilitarian standpoint, we clearly could not do so. Rule utilitarian justifications are not subject to the same potential abuses as act utilitarian ones are.

Rehabilitation

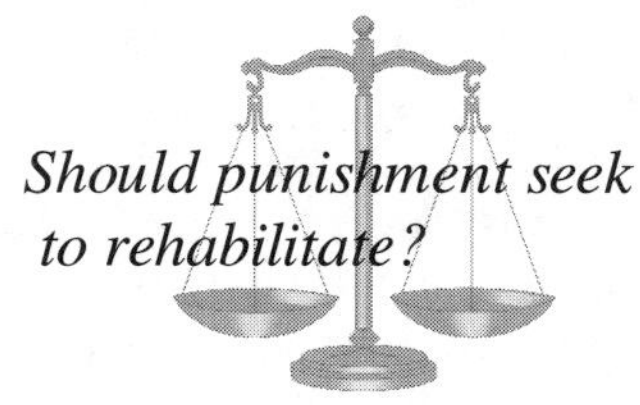
Should punishment seek
to rehabilitate?

Typically, retributivist models of punishment see moral agents as autonomous agents who have chosen to do something wrong. Deterrence models are largely indifferent to questions about the autonomy of offenders; they are only concerned with preventing crime in the future. Rehabilitation models typically begin with a different model of the moral agent, one that sees offenders as having in some sense diminished moral capacity—often due to societal factors—and thus more in need of rehabilitation than punishment.

Although most Americans are not enthusiastic about rehabilitative models of punishment, they are distressed because their prisons often seem to do more harm than good: inexperienced criminals emerge hardened and more inclined than ever toward a life of crime. Prisons seem to be a training school for criminals, an intensive internship program in criminal values and techniques.

Although they deter the criminals from committing (at least most of) their usual crimes while in prison, those criminals often return to the streets tougher, meaner, and more skilled in crime than when they entered prison.

One of the difficulties of rehabilitation as a goal of punishment is that it makes punishment more open-ended, which in some cases can result in a longer period of loss of freedom for the offender. Furthermore, some kinds of rehabilitation treat offenders as though they were not fully responsible moral and legal agents. Such programs are also very expensive to administer, and they seem to offer criminals positive opportunities not always available to the general citizen. Finally, it is far from clear that such programs work often enough to justify their expense.

Reconciliation and Healing

Unfortunately, there has been no shortage in recent years (or at virtually any other time in human history, for that matter) of horrible, systematic violations of human rights by governments and their representatives. Think of the Nazi persecution of Jews and others, of the human rights violations in Latin America, of the horrors of apartheid in South Africa. When societies begin to come to terms with such offenses, they face a difficult challenge, for they must both punish and heal. Sometimes these seem like incompatible goals. Punishment seems divisive, while reconciliation seems to demand that offenders be allowed to go free without punishment.

Consider South Africa. After many decades of brutal torture and murder on the part of the South African government against the indigenous population (and their sympathizers), the white South African government relinquished power, allowing a majority government by blacks and persons of mixed race. As a society, South Africa faced a crucial question. Should it attempt to punish all those guilty of torture and murder over the years, or should it set aside such considerations of justice in order to avoid the divisiveness of such trials and their accompanying punishments? Nelson Mandela, the first black president of South Africa, set the tone for the new government by inviting his jailer of thirty years to attend his inauguration. In doing so, Mr. Mandela sent a clear message that he would pursue a path of reconciliation rather than retribution. This is an extremely morally demanding path, for it is important to note that it is most morally demanding on those who have suffered the most. Those who have suffered, the victims and their families, have a morally understandable desire for retribution. Yet it is often precisely the divisiveness generated by such trials that threatens the often fragile social fabric of a new regime. The danger of ignoring retribution is twofold. First, those who have suffered will feel that they have not been avenged properly. Second, it can be interpreted as sending a message that possible future acts of political oppression will be unpunished as well. Some countries, most notably in Latin America, have tried to find a middle ground here by holding investigative hearings intended to establish an accurate public record of abuses—thereby recognizing the suffering of victims—but have not pursued punishment for the offenders in the interests of national reconciliation.

A corresponding issue exists on the individual level. Those who have been wronged have to face the issue of how to put the crime "behind them." Punishment alone rarely brings healing, but for many it is the precondition for healing. The families of murder victims, for example, often await the execution of the murderer as a necessary step in their healing process. For others, the road to healing is through mercy and forgiveness. In their eyes, punishment may be justified, but it may nonetheless not be the best course of action.

Mixed Justifications

Some philosophers, most notably John Rawls, have argued that retributivist and consequentialist accounts of punishment can be combined, and that each has distinctive strengths in particular areas and that the combination avoids the weaknesses each typically have. The general strategy in such approaches has been to distinguish between the justification of punishment as an institution in general and the justification of particular punishments. They then consider the liabilities associated with each of the two major approaches to punishment, the retributivist and the deterrence-based theories. Typically, retributivist justifications of the *institution* of punishment are weak and open to the charge that punishment is simply revenge dressed up in legal clothing. Similarly, deterrence-based (and consequentialist in general) justifications of particular punishments run the risks of disproportionate punishment and punishment of the innocent when such punishment is the best deterrent. On the other hand, each of these positions is seen as having a unique strength. Retributivism contains a doctrine of proportionality that seems appropriate in determining the nature and severity of particular punishments. Similarly, consequentialist theories are certainly correct in saying that the overall justification for punishing at all is that it has good effects for society as a whole, especially in terms of deterrence. Thus, in order to avoid the difficulties associated with each position and retain the benefits of each, mixed justifications typically argue that the institution of punishment in terms of its benefit to society as a whole, while the severity of particular punishments is justified on the basis of a retributivist's principle of proportionality.

Although there is much to recommend such mixed theories, the principal drawback seems to be precisely their mixed character. Just as physics is continually searching for a Grand Unified Theory that explains everything in terms of a few simple principles that apply everywhere, so, too, philosophers want a theory that illuminates the continuity of our moral experience. Mixed theories fail to do that, and their failure raises the suspicion that we are employing theories in an ad hoc manner—that is, applying them when they yield the results we want, and ignoring them when they do not. However, the whole idea of a theory is that it is *not* ad hoc, that it applies uniformly. We still seem to lack a grand unified theory of punishment.

The Limits of Punishment

In light of these considerations, we can formulate at least some of the general restrictions that ought to be imposed on punishment in general. Some of these are general considerations following from the nature of law, others derive specifically from our preceding discussion.

Public notice of offenses. First, and most uncontroversially, we clearly are not entitled to punish people if we do not tell them in advance that something is an offense. Laws must be publicly proclaimed, and that is a fundamental principle of all law, not just criminal law.

Authority to punish. Second, punishment can only be administered by those who are legally entitled to do so. Part of being a member of a state is that we cede to the state certain powers, including the power to punish. On the retributivist view, when the state punishes someone who has committed a crime against me, it does so in my name.

Guilt. Third, we should punish *only* the guilty. Whatever utilitarian justification might be given for intentionally punishing the innocent, telishment is not permissible.

Reasonable doubt. Fourth, we should punish only when we have a reasonable degree of certitude that they are guilty. The greater the potential severity of the punishment, the greater the level of certitude.

Equitable administration. Fifth, we should punish *all* the guilty in the same way—or at least punishment must also be administered equitably, that is, certain groups ought not to be treated differently on irrelevant grounds. This is a basic requirement of justice. In the United States, this is particularly an issue in regard to race, and especially in regard to the death penalty and African Americans, which will be discussed below.

Proportionality. Sixth, the punishment must be proportional to the offense. To hang pickpockets, for example, is to punish disproportionately.

"Cruel and unusual." Seventh, some punishments, even if they are proportional to the offense, are too cruel ever to be used. Some people have committed truly heinous crimes—the torture, mutilation, and killing of infants and young children is the most obvious example—and they *deserve* the same suffering in return. However, for us to administer this suffering would be to debase ourselves. Such punishments are too cruel, too inhumane for us to administer without damaging ourselves.

Punishment and social conditions that give rise to crimes. Like cancer and other diseases, crime is best dealt with through preventive measures before it occurs. When confronted by an increase in crime, we must respond not only with short-term answers (such as imprisonment), but also with long-term answers that address the root conditions that give rise to crime.

Punishment and Imagination

There are, as we have seen, many possible purposes of punishment, but certainly one of the legitimate purposes is to bring the perpetrator back into the moral community. Crime is a rupture in the moral fabric of society, and punishment attests to the nature and seriousness of that rupture. What often seems missing in punishment is a realization on the part of perpetrators of the consequences of their deeds. We often want to say, as a society (and especially on behalf of the victims) to perpetrators: "Look, *this* is what you did—this is the horror, and the pain, and the suffering, and perhaps even the death, that you have caused." Only when they realize the depth of the harm that they have caused will they change, and only when they have changed in this way are they worthy of being readmitted into the moral community.

Punishment may be a means of helping criminals to realize what they have done. Certainly this motivation is compatible with the *lex talionis*—an eye for an eye—insofar as, by imposing on perpetrators the same harm they have imposed on their victims, perpetrators may come to understand what they have done to someone else. It may also be compatible with deterrence-based accounts of punishment insofar as realizing the harm one has inflicted may serve to deter a person from committing the same crime again.

One of the principal difficulties that faces us in structuring punishment is that we often lack imagination. We are unable to devise new ways of helping criminals to see the true consequences of their crimes for others. There is no necessary correlation between sitting in prison for years and realizations of this kind. However, programs of punishment that bring offenders face-to-face with the consequences of their misdeeds offer some hope of effecting the type of change of heart that heralds genuine rehabilitation.

Capital Punishment

If punishment in general is problematic, capital punishment is especially so. The United States is one of the few major industrialized countries in the world to practice capital punishment, and one of an even smaller group that permits the death penalty for crimes committed by minors.

A Life for a Life

Advocates of the death penalty often invoke the *lex talionis,* the law of "an eye for an eye, a tooth for a tooth," as their justification for the death penalty. If we take that law literally, then it becomes "a death for a death." It is, however, more helpful to take this law metaphorically as one of proportionality: our harshest punishment for our worst crimes. This is in fact the way in which it has been interpreted in the United States, where the death penalty is reserved for aggravated murder and a handful of other, similarly egregious crimes.

Yet the legitimacy of this metaphorical interpretation raises interesting questions. Why don't we take the *lex talionis* literally? Why shouldn't a torturer be tortured as punishment? Why shouldn't a rapist endure the agony of being raped as punishment? Why shouldn't someone who has raped, tortured, and killed a person be punished in the same way? As we reflect on these questions, we discover that capital punishment isn't the worst possible punishment—there are other punishments, such as torture and rape and mutilation, which are worse *in some way.* When we try to specify the exact way in which they are worse, we get an interesting answer. They aren't worse in the sense that they are more final, that they destroy more possibilities. Clearly the death penalty is the worst in this respect, since it eliminates any further possibilities for the person being executed. Rather, it is worse in the sense that it is *crueler.* If we ranked punishments along a continuum according to their *level of cruelty,* we might get something like this:

When are we justified in killing someone as punishment?

Punishments: Scale of Cruelty

Monetary Fines ➪ Day Service ➪ Imprisonment ➪ Execution ➪ Rape and Torture

This is a different scale than we might get if we ranked punishments according to the *extent to which they destroyed a person's future possibilities.* Then we might get something like this:

Punishments: Scale of Destruction of Life Possibilities

Monetary Fines ➪ Day Service ➪ Imprisonment ➪ Rape and Torture ➪ Execution

The metaphorical interpretation of the *lex talionis* comes into play when the literal interpretation results in a punishment that is too far to the right on the cruelty scale. Clearly, everyone admits that some punishments are too cruel. The issue then becomes one of drawing the line: at what point do we say that the literal interpretation of the *lex talionis* results in a punishment that is too cruel? The claim of opponents of the death penalty is that the line should be drawn before execution; advocates of the death penalty draw the line after execution.

We now can see that there is a sense in which the death penalty is the worst possible punishment (it completely destroys all future life possibilities) and a sense in which it isn't the worst (other punishments may be crueler). While literal interpretations of the *lex talionis* would seem to justify crueler punishments such as torture for convicted torturers, we are barred from such punishments because of their cruelty; yet the death penalty seems acceptable for the most heinous of crimes because it is the worst possible punishment in another sense.

The Sanctity of Life

Opponents of the death penalty are often motivated by a moral concern for the sanctity of life. We can distinguish three versions of this concern. First, the *strong version,* such as we find among Quakers and Buddhists, maintains an absolute prohibition on the taking of *any* human life. It is thus opposed to the death penalty because it involves intentionally killing a human being, just as it would be opposed to war and even killing in self-defense. Second, the *moderate version,* which we find in many religious traditions, is opposed to any taking of *innocent* human life. This version would also be opposed to practices such as active euthanasia as well as the death penalty. It would be opposed to the death penalty insofar as its administration inevitably involves inadvertently executing innocent people occasionally. Finally, the *weak version* of this view maintains that any practice involving the intentional killing of other human beings must have an extremely strong justification—and that the justification of the death penalty instead of life imprisonment simply isn't strong enough to warrant its use.

For those who support the strong or moderate versions of the sanctity of life, the potential deterrent effect of capital punishment is not really an issue. In their eyes, even if capital punishment deters more effectively than alternative punishments, it still is not justified, for it involves the intentional taking of a human life.

Hope and the Possibility of Change

Opponents of the death penalty are often motivated by another, less articulated concern. For many of them, the death penalty is a sign of giving up, a sign that we have concluded—at least in this particular instance—that there is nothing salvageable about this criminal, that there is nothing that redeems this person's life and justifies his (and it is almost always "his," not "hers") continued existence. Sometimes this is part of a larger religious worldview that sees hope for all human beings, no matter what their situation; sometimes it is part of a purely humanistic worldview that sees human beings as fundamentally good at the core and only brutalized and deformed through external influences.

For those who share this belief, in whatever form, the death penalty is an act of breaking faith with ourselves, with our humanity, an act of despair from people who no longer know what else to do.

The Effect of the Death Penalty: Deterrence or Brutalization?

What effect does the death penalty have? Two competing and incompatible claims have been advanced in answer to this question. On the one hand, some have argued that it has a deterrence effect, that is, that it reduces the number of potential future crimes for which it is a punishment. On the other hand, others have argued that it results in what has been called the *brutalization effect,* that is, that the number of capital crimes actually *increases* as a result of executions.

The empirical findings. There are two distinct issues here: an empirical one and a normative one. The *empirical question* is in the domain of social scientists, and their answer is by no means univocal. This is hardly surprising, given the complexity of the issue. One not only has to show that the death penalty deters, but that it deters more effectively than alternative punishments such as life imprisonment. Moreover, even if the death penalty as presently administered doesn't deter more effectively than the alternatives, there is still the question of whether it might be a more effective deterrent if it were administered differently (more often, more quickly, etc.)

The empirical findings on the effects of capital punishment have been mixed. They range between two extremes. On the one hand, some researchers have argued that the death penalty was responsible for saving seven or eight lives (of innocent potential victims) per year in the United States while it was being used.[1] On the other hand, others have claimed that the number of capital offenses goes up immediately following an execution.[2] One of the more interesting studies has compared *contiguous states,* such as North and South Dakota, where one has the death penalty and the other does not, but which in many other respects are similar. If the death penalty were an effective deterrent, one would expect that the rate of capital crimes would decline in the state with the death penalty, but this has not been the case.

The argument from common sense. Some theorists have argued that we need not be bothered by these contradictory findings; all we need to do is to reflect for a moment, and common sense will give us the answer to our question about the deterrent effects of capital punishment. When prisoners are given a choice between life in prison and the death penalty, they inevitably choose life in prison. We don't find "lifers" trying to get their sentence changed to death; on the other hand, we find there are plenty of prisoners on death row who are trying to get their sentences changed to life in prison. Common sense and a moment's reflection tell us that virtually everyone considers execution to be worse than life in prison. And if everyone considers it to be worse, then they will be more deterred by it than by a life sentence.

The common sense argument, at least in its initial version, falls short of the mark in at least two respects. First, granting the premises of the argument, we still have an additional question: Do potential criminals, when contemplating a capital offense, think that they will receive the death penalty rather than life in prison? For deterrence to work, it must be effective *before* the crime is committed, and the argument from common sense does not assure us that it is. Second, the argument ignores any other factors as influencing the situation. (This is a problem with hypothetical examples in general: often we only discover in them the factors that we wanted to be there in the first place; real life cases are messier, more surprising, and consequently more instructive.) For example, it ignores the possibility that potential criminals might feel that since the state kills (through executions), it's okay for them to kill.

If the death penalty deters,
is it thereby justified?

The moral issue. The *moral issue* on which deterrence turns is distinct from the empirical question: If it turns out that capital punishment deters significantly more effectively than alternative punishments, then ought we to employ it? After all, the death penalty is the intentional killing of another human being—in the eyes of some, murder by the state. It is certainly consistent to say that capital punishment deters and still be opposed to it because it violates the sanctity of human life (as we have already seen), because of the high probability that some innocent people will be executed, or because it is administered in our society in an unavoidably arbitrary manner.

Deterrence and publicity. If capital punishment is justified in terms of its deterrent effect, then it would seem to follow that it should be administered in such a way as to maximize its potential as a deterrent. If we are executing criminals in order to deter other (potential) criminals from committing the same crime, then shouldn't we execute them in such a way as to have the greatest possible impact on anyone else who might commit such a crime? Two possible changes might increase the deterrent effect.

First, as mentioned above, punishments that are administered quickly and surely are, all other things being equal, more likely to be effective deterrents than punishments that are administered long after the fact and sporadically. In capital punishment cases, every effort should be made to hasten the judicial process and the execution if the point of such punishment is deterrence.

Second, the more vivid the realization of the consequences, the more effectively they influence behavior. In the case of capital punishment, this would seem to justify public, televised executions, presuming that they increase the deterrent effect of capital punishment. Indeed, if deterrence is the justification for such punishment, then it seems to be wasting an individual's execution if the government does not maximize its potential deterrent effects. Of course, this would have to be done in a way that properly shelters children, etc., and at the same time is most likely to reach those most likely to commit capital crimes.

The Irrevocability of Capital Punishment

One of the common objections to capital punishment is that it is irrevocable: once an innocent person is executed, there is no way to bring that person back to life again. Yet when we reflect on this argument, we see that it is not stated very precisely, for *all* punishment (except, perhaps, monetary fines, which can be returned with interest) is in a very real sense irrevocable. Twenty years in prison cannot be given back to someone who was falsely convicted. The real issue is that there is no way of even attempting to compensate for the injustice when someone has been executed, since the person is no longer alive to receive the compensation.

The Demand for Certitude

The high stakes in capital punishment create an additional demand in terms of the level of certitude required to carry out the punishment. Precisely because there is no way to undo a mistake in capital punishment, we must be more certain than would otherwise be required that we are in fact executing the guilty party.

In evaluating this argument, we can again look at two distinct issues. The first is an empirical one. How often do mistakes get made? One recent estimate claimed that in the United States since 1900, fifty-seven innocent persons—or, more precisely, persons whose innocence can be *proved* in retrospect—have been executed.[3] The further claim is that, if this number can be shown to have been innocent, how many more were innocent that we did not know about? This is a difficult empirical matter, but it seems reasonable to conclude that at least some times, innocent persons are executed, even if we are not certain how many. This situation is exacerbated by the increase in executions in recent years and by the Supreme Court decisions that exclude the uncovering of new evidence of innocence as a basis for reconsideration of a case. However, DNA tests have offered new, scientific evidence that has helped to exonerate a number of inmates on death row. Since capital punishment again became legal in 1976, 82 convicts—one out of every seven waiting to be executed—have been exonerated.[4]

The second issue raised by this argument is a normative one. If capital punishment results in the taking of innocent life, at what point do we say that this invalidates its use? Those who oppose the taking of any innocent life at all would say that capital punishment ought to be abandoned if it results in the taking of even one innocent life. Utilitarians, in contrast, would be concerned about the numbers. They would ask how many innocent lives are apt to be lost as opposed to alternative punishments (such as life in prison without parole)? However, the calculations here become tricky, because presumably the utilitarian has to calculate the total number of innocent lives saved, not just innocent lives on death row. At that juncture, deterrence becomes relevant, since effective deterrence also saves innocent lives—the lives of potential victims. Imagine if utilitarians were faced with a choice between two alternatives.

Alternative # 1: No capital punishment; life imprisonment instead

- Saves 8 innocent lives of prisoners per decade
- Saves no innocent lives of potential victims over Alternative #2

Alternative # 2: Capital punishment

- Costs 8 innocent lives of prisoners per decade
- Saves 20 innocent lives of potential victims per decade

If the numbers worked out this way (and these numbers are purely hypothetical), and if everything else is equal (and it never is in real life), then the utilitarian would have to be in favor of capital punishment, even though it costs the lives of some innocent persons, because it costs fewer innocent lives *overall.*

Interestingly, there is little that retributivists have to contribute to this discussion. Their concern is exclusively with justified punishment, and there is nothing internal to retributivism itself that provides us with moral guidance about mistakes. Obviously, no moral system *espouses* mistakes.

Racial Bias

There is little doubt that the death penalty in the United States is administered in a way that exhibits racial bias, although that does not mean that the individuals who reach these judgments are intentionally racist. The bias is most evident when dealing with African Americans, and two aspects of it are especially noteworthy. First, if the murderer is an African-American male, he is somewhat more likely than his Caucasian counterpart to receive the death penalty. Second, and much more significantly, if the *victim* is Caucasian, the murderer is much more likely to receive the death penalty than if he is Caucasian. The race of the victim is the most significant racial factor, and African-Americans who kill Caucasians are the most likely to receive the death penalty.

The subtlety of racial bias. Several factors need to be noted about the influence of race on sentences of death, and the first of these is an appreciation of the various levels on which such bias can be influential. Long before a jury begins to deliberate on a case, numerous decisions are made which contribute to the final decision. The extent of public and political pressure for a public verdict in a case (as opposed to plea bargaining), the zeal (or lack thereof) with which law enforcement investigators pursue their inquiries, and the extent to which the prosecution is willing to look for and identify special circumstances (which justify asking for the death penalty) are but a few of the factors that influence whether juries are even presented with a case in which the death penalty is permitted and requested.

The empirical evidence. What empirical evidence is available for the claim that the death penalty is administered in a racially biased way? The consensus[5] seems to be that the *race of the victim* is a very significant factor in a prosecutor's decision to seek the death penalty: prosecutors are four times more likely to seek the death penalty in cases in which African Americans kill Caucasians than in cases in which African Americans kill African Americans. Nor is this the only significant factor. Obviously, it makes a major difference which state the murder was committed in, since only some states permit capital punishment; furthermore, 50 percent of all executions occur in two states (Florida and Texas). Furthermore, prosecutors in rural counties are more likely to seek the death penalty than their counterparts in large urban areas. Both the race of the victim and where the murder is committed are important factors in prosecutors' decisions to seek the death penalty.

The reply of death penalty supporters. Advocates of the use of the death penalty, such as Ernest van den Haag, have an interesting reply to such claims of bias. They are willing to admit, at least on occasion, that there is some arbitrariness in the administration of the death penalty, but they have a reply that is at least initially plausible. Imagine a dozen cars speeding on the freeway, and a police officer pulls one over and gives its driver a ticket. We can hardly claim that the driver does not deserve the ticket because there were others who were also speeding who got away? Clearly the fact that some of the guilty are not punished does not mean that we should refrain from punishing those that we have caught. Similarly, though there may be some perpetrators of capital offenses who are not convicted of them, that does not mean we are not entitled to execute those who are properly convicted. The fact that the death penalty is administered somewhat arbitrarily does not mean that it should not be used at all. If anything, it only means that we should try to execute more people, all offenders who deserve it.

Are the criteria for capital crimes clear and well-justified? Opponents of the death penalty say that such analogies are misleading in at least three respects. First, the criteria for speeding are clear and well-defined, and the means for determining whether someone is violating the speed limit are relatively well-established. The criteria for capital offenses are much vaguer and much harder to apply consistently. Although legislatures have attempted to specify the aggravating circumstances that transform a simple murder into a capital offense, many—including most recently Justice Harry A. Blackmun—have concluded that, despite extensive guidelines, the United States has simply failed to reduce the arbitrariness with which the death penalty is applied.

Are people who do not deserve the death penalty executed? Second, the speeding analogy suggests that the police arrest only those who are actually speeding. However, in regard to the death penalty, there is reasonable evidence—as mentioned above—that some innocent persons are executed.

Is the death penalty sought for morally suspect reasons? Finally, the speeding example suggests that it was a matter of pure chance that some drivers were arrested while others got away. However, we would be more suspicious if the police arrested only speeding drivers with, say, red hair or Chicago Bulls bumper stickers. In the case of the death penalty, it appears that it is administered in a systematically uneven way that treats those who kill whites more harshly than those who kill blacks. Such a pattern of discrimination becomes a part of a much larger societal pattern of discrimination that ought to be opposed in its various manifestations. Thus when it is said that the death penalty is administered in an arbitrary manner, that does not mean it is applied randomly—there is a pattern to its application.

Two senses of justice. Telling though these replies may seem, many still feel that the execution of criminals who have perpetrated particularly heinous crimes is right. Isn't it, after all, simply a matter of *justice* that those who have committed especially gruesome murders be executed, no matter what might happen to other offenders?

There is a sense in which this is true, and an examination of that sense reveals two distinct meanings of justice. First, there is what Joel Feinberg has called noncomparative justice, which is simply a matter of dessert, of what one deserves. But there is also a second, comparative sense of justice, which involves treating everyone (in a given class) the same. It is in this sense that the administration of the death penalty is unjust: there are insufficient morally relevant reasons why it is applied in some cases and not in others.

Diversity and Consensus

As always in this book, each of us has to come to a considered, reflective judgment that weighs complex and competing claims. Indeed, that's the very nature of the problems selected for this book—the easy problems have been omitted, since we need little help in resolving them. We can, however, draw some conclusions which may provide part of the common ground we need here to reach a societal consensus on the issue of the death penalty.

First, many people on both sides of this debate agree that the *empirical evidence about the deterrent effect of capital punishment is inconclusive.* There is no incontrovertible evidence that the death penalty is a more effective deterrent than life imprisonment, but neither is there clear evidence that it is not. Moreover, this remains such an empirically tricky question to settle that there is little likelihood that there will be an indisputable empirical answer to the question of the death penalty's deterrent effect.

Second, most people agree that human life is sacred or at least extremely valuable (for those who do not frame the issue in religious terms), but this shared belief leads to opposite conclusions. For some, it leads to a prohibition against capital punishment because it involves the intentional taking of human life. For others, it leads to support of the death penalty as either the proper penalty for violating the sanctity of life or as the deterrent most likely to preserve the sanctity of innocent life.

Third, almost everyone would agree that a society in which capital crimes do not occur is better than one in which they occur and are punished. Our long-range focus needs to be on reducing the number of crimes that could be classified as capital, and the most effective long-term use of our resources is toward that end. It is an empirical question what will most effectively promote that goal—some suggestions include more community-based policing, more rehabilitation in and out of prison, more programs that reduce drug and alcohol use (which are often associated with crime), more programs that strengthen family and community values, and more research into which programs are most effective in reducing crime—and it is a question well worth pursuing.

Finally, I would hope—and this is a personal hope rather than a statement of societal consensus—that many will agree that capital punishment, no matter how deserved it is on the basis of the crime (and surely there are crimes which justify it), is unworthy of us. It diminishes us, the ones in whose name it is administered. And it is, finally, an act of despair, a declaration that the person to be executed is beyond hope, beyond redemption. This may in fact be a realistic assessment of that individual, but there is moral merit in living in the area between realism and hope.

Endnotes

1. See Isaac Ehrlich, "The Deterrent Effect of Capital Punishment: A Question of Life or Death," *American Economic Review,* Vol. 65 (June, 1975), pp. 397–417; also see the discussion of this issue below in Jeffrey Reiman's "Justice, Civilization, and the Death Penalty," and the bibliography in his footnote 35.
2. W. Bowers and G. Pierce in "Deterrence or Brutalization: What is the Effect of Executions?" *Crime & Delinquency* 26 (1980), 453–484.
3. See especially, the study by Hugo A. Bedeau and M.L. Radelet, "Miscarriages of Justice in Potentially Capital Cases," *Stanford Law Review,* Vol. 40 (1987), pp. 21–179.
4. Caitlin Lovinger, "Death Row's Living Alumni," *The New York Times,* Week in Review, August 22, 1999, p. 4.
5. See, for example, Raymond Paternoster, "Race of the Victim and Location of Crime: The Decision to Seek the Death Penalty in South Carolina," *Journal of Criminal Law and Criminology,* Vol. 74 (1983), pp. 754–785 and S.R. Gross, "Race and Death: The Judicial Evaluation of Discrimination in Capital Sentencing," U.C. Davis Law Review, Vol. 18 (1985), pp. 1275–1325 and Gross's *Death and Discrimination: Racial Disparities in Capital Sentencing* (Boston: Northeastern University Press, 1989); also see W. Bowers and G. Pierce, "Arbitrariness and Discrimination under Post-*Furman* Capital Statutes," Crime & Delinquency, Vol. 26 (1980), pp. 563–635.

THE ARGUMENTS

David Gelernter
"What Do Murderers Deserve? The Death Penalty in Civilized Societies"

David Gelernter, a professor of computer science at Yale, was letter-bombed in June 1993 and nearly lost his life. He is the author, most recently, of Drawing Life: Surviving the Unabomber *and* Machine Beauty: Elegance and the Heart of Technology. *He is at work on a novel, portions of which have appeared in* Commentary *(August 1997 and January 1998).*

Gelernter argues that capital punishment is not only permissible, but in a certain sense it is a characteristic of a civilized society that finds murder intolerable. It is part of our communal response to an intolerable action.

As Your Read, Consider This:

1. Murder, Gelernter tells us, always involves "messing in other people's problems." Why is this true? What significance does it have?
2. What role, according to Gelernter, do the emotions play in making decisions about the death penalty?

No civilized nation ever takes the death penalty for granted; two recent cases force us to consider it yet again. A Texas woman, Karla Faye Tucker, murdered two people with a pickaxe, was said to have repented in prison, and was put to death. A Montana man, Theodore Kaczynski, murdered three people with mail bombs, did not repent, and struck a bargain with the Justice Department; he pleaded guilty and will not be executed. (He also attempted to murder others and succeeded in wounding some, myself included.) Why did we execute the penitent and spare the impenitent? However we answer this question, we surely have a duty to ask it.

And we ask it—I do, anyway—with a sinking feeling, because in modern America, moral upside-downness is a specialty of the house. To eliminate race prejudice we discriminate by race. We promote the cultural assimilation of immigrant children by denying them schooling in English. We throw honest citizens in jail for child abuse, relying on testimony so phony any child could see through it. Orgasm studies are okay in public high schools but the Ten Commandments are not. We make a point of admiring manly women and womanly men. None of which has anything to do with capital punishment directly, but it all obliges us to approach any question about morality in modern America in the larger context of this country's desperate confusion about elementary distinctions.

Why execute murderers? To deter? To avenge? Supporters of the death penalty often give the first answer, opponents the second. But neither can be the whole truth. If our main goal were deterring crime, we would insist on public executions—which are not on the political agenda, and not an item that many Americans are interested in promoting. If our main goal were vengeance, we would allow the grieving parties to decide the murderer's fate; if the victim had no family or friends to feel vengeful on his behalf, we would call the whole thing off.

In fact, we execute murderers in order to make a communal proclamation: that murder is intolerable. A deliberate murderer embodies evil so terrible that it defiles the community. Thus the late social philosopher Robert Nisbet: "Until a catharsis has been effected through trial, through the finding of guilt and then punishment, the community is anxious, fearful, apprehensive, and above all, contaminated."

Individual citizens have a right and sometimes a duty to speak. A community has the right, too, and sometimes the duty. The community certifies births and deaths, creates marriages, educates children, fights invaders. In laws, deeds, and ceremonies it lays down the boundary lines of civilized life, lines that are constantly getting scuffed and needing renewal.

When a murder takes place, the community is obliged, whether it feels like it or not, to clear its throat and step up to the microphone. Every murder demands a communal response. Among possible responses, the death penalty is uniquely powerful because it is permanent and can never be retracted or overturned. An execution forces the community to assume forever the burden of moral certainty; it is a form of absolute speech that allows no waffling or equivocation. Deliberate murder, the community announces, is absolutely evil and absolutely intolerable, period.

Of course, we could make the same point less emphatically if we wanted to—for example, by locking up murderers for life (as we sometimes do). The question then becomes: is the death penalty overdoing it? Should we make a less forceful proclamation instead?

The answer might be yes if we were a community in which murder was a shocking anomaly and thus in effect a solved problem. But we are not. Our big cities are full of murderers at large. "One can guesstimate," writes the criminologist and political scientist John J. DiIulio, Jr., "that we are nearing or may already have passed the day when 500,000 murderers, convicted and undetected, are living in American society."

DiIulio's statistics show an approach to murder so casual as to be depraved. We are reverting to a pre-civilized state of nature. Our natural bent in the face of murder is not to avenge the crime but to shrug it off, except in those rare cases when our own near and dear are involved. (And even then, it depends.)

This is an old story. Cain murders Abel and is brought in for questioning: where is Abel, your brother? The suspect's response: how should I know? "What am I, my brother's keeper?" It is one of the very first statements attributed to mankind in the Bible; voiced here by an interested party, it nonetheless expresses a powerful and universal inclination. Why mess in other people's problems? And murder is always, in the most immediate sense, someone else's problem, because the injured party is dead.

Murder in primitive societies called for a private settling of scores. The community as a whole stayed out of it. For murder to count, as it does in the Bible, as a crime not merely against one man but against the whole community and against God—that was a moral triumph that is still basic to our integrity, and that is never to be taken for granted. By executing murderers, the community reaffirms this moral understanding by restating the truth that absolute evil exists and must be punished.

Granted (some people say), the death penalty is a communal proclamation; it is nevertheless an incoherent one. If our goal is to affirm that human life is more precious than anything else, how can we make such a declaration by destroying life?

But declaring that human life is more precious than anything else is not our goal in imposing the death penalty. Nor is the proposition true. The founding fathers pledged their lives (and fortunes and sacred honor) to the cause of freedom; Americans have traditionally believed that some things are more precious than life. ("Living in a sanitary age, we are getting so we place too high a value on human life—which rightfully must always come second to human ideas." Thus E.B. White in 1938, pondering the Munich pact ensuring "peace in our time" between the Western powers and Hitler.) The point of capital punishment is not to pronounce on life in general but on the crime of murder.

Which is not to say that the sanctity of human life does not enter the picture. Taking a life, says the Talmud (in the course of discussing Cain and Abel), is equivalent to destroying a whole world. The rabbis used this statement to make a double point: to tell us why murder is the gravest of crimes, and to warn against false testimony in a murder trial. But to believe in the sanctity of human life does not mean, and the Talmud does not say it means, that capital punishment is ruled out.

A newer objection grows out of the seemingly random way in which we apply capital punishment. The death penalty might be a reasonable communal proclamation in principle, some critics say, but it has become so garbled in practice that it has lost all significance and ought to be dropped. DiIulio writes that "the ratio of persons murdered to persons executed for murder from 1977 to 1996 was in the ballpark of 1,000 to 1"; the death penalty has become in his view "arbitrary and capricious," a "state lottery" that is "unjust both as a matter of Judeo-Christian ethics and as a matter of American citizenship."

We can grant that, on the whole, we are doing a disgracefully bad job of administering the death penalty. After all, we are divided and confused on the issue. The community at large is strongly in favor of capital punishment; the cultural elite is strongly against it. Our attempts to speak with assurance as a community come out sounding in consequence like a man who is fighting off a choke-hold as he talks. But a community as cavalier about murder as we are has no right to back down. That we are botching things does not entitle us to give up.

Opponents of capital punishment tend to describe it as a surrender to our emotions—to grief, rage, fear, blood lust. For most supporters of the death penalty, this is exactly false. Even when we resolve in principle to go ahead, we have to steel ourselves. Many of us would find it hard to kill a dog, much less a man. Endorsing capital punishment means not that we yield to our emotions but that we overcome them. (Immanuel Kant, the great advocate of the death penalty precisely on moral grounds, makes this point in his reply to the anti-capital-punishment reformer Cesare Beccaria—accusing Beccaria of being "moved by sympathetic sentimentality and an affectation of humanitarianism.") If we favor executing murderers it is not because we want to but because, however much we do not want to, we consider ourselves obliged to.

Many Americans, of course, no longer feel that obligation. The death penalty is hard for us as a community above all because of our moral evasiveness. For at least a generation, we have urged one another to switch off our moral faculties. "Don't be judgmental!" We have said it so many times, we are starting to believe it.

The death penalty is a proclamation about absolute evil, but many of us are no longer sure that evil even exists. We define evil out of existence by calling it "illness"—a tendency Aldous Huxley anticipated in his novel *Brave New World* (1932) and Robert Nisbet wrote about in 1982: "America has lost the villain, the evil one, who has now become one of the sick, the disturbed. . . . America has lost the moral value of guilt, lost it to the sickroom."

Our refusal to look evil in the face is no casual notion; it is a powerful drive. Thus we have (for example) the terrorist Theodore Kaczynski, who planned and carried out a hugely complex campaign of violence with a clear goal in mind. It was the goal most terrorists have: to get famous and not die. He wanted public attention for his ideas about technology; he figured he could get it by attacking people with bombs.

He was right. His plan succeeded. It is hard to imagine a more compelling proof of mental competence than this planning and carrying out over decades of a complex, rational strategy. (Evil, yes; irrational, no; they are different things.) The man himself has said repeatedly that he is perfectly sane, knew what he was doing, and is proud of it.

To call such a man insane seems to me like deliberate perversity. But many people do. Some of them insist that his thoughts about technology constitute "delusions," though every terrorist holds strong beliefs that are wrong, and many nonterrorists do, too. Some insist that sending bombs through the mail is ipso facto proof of insanity—as if the twentieth century had not taught us that there is no limit to the bestiality of which sane men are capable.

Where does this perversity come from? I said earlier that the community at large favors the death penalty, but intellectuals and the cultural elite tend to oppose it. This is not (I think) because they abhor killing more than other people do, but because the death penalty represents absolute speech from a position of moral certainty, and doubt is the black-lung disease of the intelligentsia—an occupational hazard now inflicted on the culture as a whole.

American intellectuals have long differed from the broader community—particularly on religion, crime and punishment, education, family, the sexes, race relations, American history, taxes and public spending, the size and scope of government, art, the environment, and the military. (Otherwise, I suppose, they and the public have been in perfect accord.) But not until the late 60s and 70s were intellectuals finally in a position to act on their convictions. Whereupon they attacked the community's moral certainties with the enthusiasm of guard dogs leaping at throats.* The result is an American community smitten with the disease of intellectual doubt—or, in this case, self-doubt.

The failure of our schools is a consequence of our self-doubt, of our inability to tell children that learning is not fun and they are required to master certain topics whether they want to or not. The tortured history of modern American race relations grows out of our self-doubt: we passed a civil-rights act in 1964, then lost confidence immediately in our ability to make a race-blind society work, racial preferences codify our refusal to believe in our own good faith. During the late stages of the cold war, many Americans laughed at the idea that the American way was morally superior or the Soviet Union was an "evil empire"; some are still laughing. Within their own community and the American community at large, doubting intellectuals have taken refuge (as doubters often do) in bullying, to the point where many of us are now so uncomfortable at the prospect of confronting evil that we turn away and change the subject.

Returning then to the penitent woman and the impenitent man: the Karla Faye Tucker case is the harder of the two. We are told that she repented of the vicious murders she committed. If that

* I have written about this before in "How the Intellectuals Took Over (And What to Do About It)," *Commentary,* March 1997.

is true, we would still have had no business forgiving her, or forgiving any murderer. As Dennis Prager has written apropos this case, only the victim is entitled to forgive, and the victim is silent. But showing mercy to penitents is part of our religious tradition, and I cannot imagine renouncing it categorically.

Why was Cain not put to death, but condemned instead to wander the earth forever? Among the answers given by the rabbis in the Midrash is that he repented. The moral category of repentance is so important, they said, that it was created before the world itself. I would therefore consider myself morally obligated to think long and hard before executing a penitent. But a true penitent would have to have renounced (as Karla Faye Tucker did) all legal attempts to overturn the original conviction. If every legal avenue has been tried and has failed, the penitence window is closed. Of course, this still leaves the difficult problem of telling counterfeit penitence from the real thing, but everything associated with capital punishment is difficult.

As for Kaczynski, the prosecutors who accepted the murderer's plea-bargain say they got the best outcome they could, under the circumstances, and I believe them. But I also regard this failure to execute a cold-blooded impenitent terrorist murderer as a tragic abdication of moral responsibility. The tragedy lies in what, under our confused system, the prosecutors felt compelled to do. The community was called on to speak unambiguously. It flubbed its lines, shrugged its shoulders, and walked away.

Which brings me back to our moral condition as a community. I can describe our plight better in artistic than in philosophical terms. The most vivid illustrations I know of self-doubt and its consequences are the paintings and sculptures of Alberto Giacometti (who died in 1966). Giacometti was an artist of great integrity; he was consumed by intellectual and moral self-doubt, which he set down faithfully. His sculpted figures show elongated, shriveled human beings who seem corroded by acid, eaten-up to the bone, hurt and weakened past fragility nearly to death. They are painful to look at. And they are natural emblems of modern America. We ought to stick one on top of the Capitol and think it over.

In executing murderers, we declare that deliberate murder is absolutely evil and absolutely intolerable. This is a painfully difficult proclamation for a self-doubting community to make. But we dare not stop trying. Communities may exist in which capital punishment is no longer the necessary response to deliberate murder. America today is not one of them.

Journal/Discussion Questions

✍ *Gelernter sees American society as plagued by self-doubt. Do you agree with this analysis? Discuss.*

1. How would Gelernter reply to Sr. Helen Prejean's objections to the death penalty?

2. How does Gelernter think we should react to murders who genuinely repent after the murder? Do you agree? Why?

Jeffrey H. Reiman
"Justice, Civilization, and the Death Penalty"

Jeffrey Reiman is professor of philosophy and justice at the American University in Washington, D.C. He is the author of several books, including The Rich Get Richer and the Poor Get Prison *and* Justice and Modern Moral Philosophy.

This article stakes out an interesting position. In contrast to most abolitionists, Reiman admits that the death penalty may well be a just punishment for murder. However, he still argues against the death penalty in states such as ours, maintaining that abolition of the death penalty is part of the process of becoming more civilized.

As You Read, Consider This:

1. What, according to Reiman, is the heart of the retributivist position? How does it differ from sheer revenge?
2. What is the difference between retributivism in general and proportional retributivism?
3. What, according to Reiman, makes the death penalty so horrible? Should horribleness be part of some punishments? Why or why not?

On the issue of capital punishment, there is as clear a clash of moral intuitions as we are likely to see. Some (now a majority of Americans) feel deeply that justice requires payment in kind and thus that murderers should die; and others (once, but no longer, nearly a majority of Americans) feel deeply that the state ought not be in the business of putting people to death. Arguments for either side that do not do justice to the intuitions of the other are unlikely to persuade anyone not already convinced. And, since, as I shall suggest, there is truth on both sides, such arguments are easily refutable, leaving us with nothing but conflicting intuitions and no guidance from reason in distinguishing the better from the worse. In this context, I shall try to make an argument for the abolition of the death penalty that does justice to the intuitions on both sides. . . .

Just Deserts and Just Punishments

In my view, the death penalty is a just punishment for murder because the *lex talionis,* an eye for an eye, and so on, is just, although, as I shall suggest at the end of this section, it can only be rightly applied when its implied preconditions are satisfied. The *lex talionis* is a version of retributivism. Retributivism—as the word itself suggests—is the doctrine that the offender should be paid back with suffering he deserves because of the evil he has done, and the *lex talionis* asserts that injury equivalent to that he imposed is what the offender deserves. But the *lex talionis* is not the only version of retributivism. Another, which I shall call "proportional retributivism," holds that what retribution requires is not equality of injury between crimes and punishments, but "fit" or proportionality, such that the worst crime is punished with the society's worst penalty, and so on, though the society's worst punishment need not duplicate the injury of the worst crime. Later, I shall try to show how a form of proportional retributivism is compatible with acknowledging the justice of the *lex talionis.* Indeed, since I shall defend the justice of the *lex talionis,* I take such compatibility as a necessary condition of the validity of any form of retributivism. . . .

I think that we can see the justice of the *lex talionis* by focusing on the striking affinity between it and the *golden rule.* The *golden rule* mandates "Do unto others as you would have others do unto you," while the *lex talionis* counsels "Do unto others as they have done unto you." It would not be too far-fetched to say that the *lex talionis* is the law enforcement arm of the golden rule, at least in the sense that if people were actually treated as they treated others, then everyone would necessarily follow the golden rule because then people could only willingly act toward others as they were willing to have others act toward them. This is not to suggest that the *lex talionis* follows from the golden rule, but rather that the two share a common moral inspiration: the equality of persons. Treating others as you would have them treat you means treating others as equal to you, because adopting the golden rule as one's guiding principle implies that one counts the suffering of others to be as great a calamity as one's own suffering, that one counts one's right to impose suffering on others as no greater than their right to impose suffering on one, and so on. This leads to the *lex talionis* by two approaches that start from different points and converge.

I call the first approach "Hegelian" because Hegel held (roughly) that crime upsets the equality between persons and retributive punishment restores that equality by "annulling" the crime. As we have seen, acting according to the golden rule implies treating others as your equals. Conversely, violating the golden rule implies the reverse: Doing to another what you would not have that other do to you violates the equality of persons by asserting a right toward the other that the other does not possess toward you. Doing back to you what you did "annuls" your violation by reasserting that the other has the same right toward you that you assert toward him. Punishment according to the *lex talionis* cannot heal the injury that the other has suffered at your hands, rather it rectifies the indignity he has suffered, by restoring him to equality with you.

"Equality of persons" here does not mean equality of concern for their happiness, as it might for a utilitarian. On such a (roughly) utilitarian understanding of equality, imposing suffering on the wrongdoer equivalent to the suffering he has imposed would have little point. Rather, equality of concern for people's happiness would lead us to impose as little suffering on the wrongdoer as was compatible with maintaining the happiness of others. This is enough to show that retributivism (at least in this "Hegelian" form) reflects a conception of morality quite different from that envisioned by utilitarianism. Instead of seeing morality as administering doses of happiness to individual recipients, the retributivist envisions morality as maintaining the relations appropriate to equally sovereign individuals. A crime, rather than representing a unit of suffering added to the already considerable suffering in the world, is an assault on the sovereignty of an individual that temporarily places one person (the criminal) in a position of illegitimate sovereignty over another (the victim). The victim (or his representative, the state) then has the right to rectify this loss of standing relative to the criminal by meting out a punishment that reduces the criminal's sovereignty in the degree to which he vaunted it above his victim's. It might be thought that this is a duty, not just a right, but that is surely too much. The victim has the right to forgive the violator without punishment, which suggests that it is by virtue of having the right to punish the violator (rather than the duty), that the victim's equality with the violator is restored.

I call the second approach "Kantian" since Kant held (roughly) that, since reason (like justice) is no respecter of the sheer difference between individuals, when a rational being decides to act in a certain way toward his fellows, he implicitly authorizes similar action by his fellows toward him. A version of the golden rule, then, is a requirement of reason: acting rationally, one always acts as he would have others act toward him. Consequently, to act toward a person as he has acted toward others is to treat him as a rational being, that is, as if his act were the product of a rational decision. From this, it may be concluded that we have a duty to do to offenders what they have done, since this amounts to according them the respect due rational beings. Here too, however, the assertion of a duty to punish seems excessive, since, if this duty arises because doing to people what they have done to others is necessary to accord them the respect due rational beings, then we would have a duty to do to all rational persons *everything*—good, bad, or indifferent—that they do to others. The point rather is that, by his acts, a rational being *authorizes* others to do the same to him, he doesn't compel them to. Here too, then, the argument leads to a right, rather than a duty, to exact the *lex talionis.* And this is supported by the fact that we can conclude from Kant's argument that a rational being cannot validly complain of being treated in the way he has treated others, and where there is no valid complaint, there is no injustice, and where there is no injustice, others have acted within their rights. It should be clear that the Kantian argument also rests on the equality of persons, because a rational agent only implicitly authorizes having done to him action similar to what he has done to another, if he and the other are similar in the relevant ways.

The "Hegelian" and "Kantian" approaches arrive at the same destination from opposite sides. The "Hegelian" approach starts from the victim's equality with the criminal, and infers from it the victim's right to do to the criminal what the criminal has done to the victim. The "Kantian" approach starts from the criminal's rationality, and infers from it the criminal's authorization of the victim's right to do to the criminal what the criminal has done to the victim. Taken together, these approaches support the following proposition: The equality and rationality of persons implies that an offender deserves and his victim has the right to impose suffering on the offender equal to that which he imposed on the victim. This is the proposition I call the *retributivist principle,* and I shall assume henceforth that it is true. This principle provides that the *lex talionis* is the criminal's just desert and the victim's (or as his representative, the state's) right. Moreover, the principle also indicates the point of retributive punishment, namely, it affirms the equality and rationality of persons, victims and offenders alike. And the point of this affirmation is, like any moral affirmation, to make a statement, to the criminal, to impress upon him his equality with his victim (which earns him a like fate) and his rationality (by which his actions are held to authorize his fate), and to the society, so that recognition of the equality and rationality of persons becomes a visible part of our shared moral environment that none can ignore in justifying their actions to one another. . . .

The truth of the retributivist principle establishes the justice of the *lex talionis,* but, since it establishes this as a right of the victim rather than a duty, it does not settle the question of whether or to what extent the victim or the state should exercise this right and exact the *lex talionis.* This is a separate moral question because strict adherence to the *lex talionis* amounts to allowing criminals, even the most barbaric of them, to dictate our punishing behavior. It seems certain that there are at least some crimes, such as rape or torture, that we ought not try to match. And this is not merely a matter of imposing an alternative punishment that produces an equivalent amount of suffering, as, say, some number of years in prison that might "add up" to the harm caused by a rapist or a torturer. Even if no amount of time in prison would add up to the harm caused by a torturer, it still seems that we ought not torture him even if this were the only way of making him suffer as much as he has made his victim suffer. Or, consider someone who has committed several murders in cold blood. On the *lex talionis,* it would seem that such a criminal might justly be brought to within an inch of death and then revived (or to within a moment of execution and then reprieved) as many times as he has killed (minus one), and then finally executed. But surely this is a degree of cruelty that would be monstrous.

Since the retributivist principle establishes the *lex talionis* as the victim's right, it might seem that the question of how far this right should be exercised is "up to the victim." And indeed, this would be the case in the state of nature. But once, for all the good reasons familiar to readers of John Locke, the state comes into existence, public punishment replaces private, and the victim's right to punish reposes in the state. With this, the decision as to how far to exercise this right goes to the state as well. To be sure, since (at least with respect to retributive punishment) the victim's right is the source of the state's right to punish, the state must exercise its right in ways that are faithful to the victim's right. Later, when I try to spell out the upper and lower limits of just punishment, these may be taken as indicating the range within which the state can punish and remain faithful to the victim's right.

I suspect that it will be widely agreed that the state ought not administer punishments of the sort described above even if required by the letter of the *lex talionis,* and thus, even granting the justice of *lex talionis,* there are occasions on which it is morally appropriate to diverge from its requirements. We must, of course, distinguish such morally based divergence from that which is based on practicality. Like any moral principle, the *lex talionis* is subject to "ought implies can." It will usually be impossible to do to an offender exactly what he has done—for example, his offense will normally have had an element of surprise that is not possible for a judicially imposed punishment, but this fact can hardly free him from having to bear the suffering he has imposed on another. Thus, for reasons of practicality, the *lex talionis* must necessarily be qualified to call for doing to the offender *as nearly as possible* what he has done to his victim. When, however, we refrain from raping rapists or torturing torturers, we do so for reasons of morality, not of practicality. And, given the justice of the *lex talionis,* these moral reasons cannot amount to claiming that it would be *unjust* to rape rapists or torture torturers. Rather the claim must be that, even though it would be just to rape rapists and torture torturers, other moral considerations weigh against doing so. . . .

The implication of this is that there is a range of just punishments that includes some that are just though they exact less than the full measure of the *lex talionis.* What are the top and bottom ends of this range? I think that both are indicated by the retributivist principle. The principle identifies the *lex talionis* as the offender's desert and since, on retributive grounds, punishment beyond what one deserves is unjust for the same reasons that make punishment of the innocent unjust, the *lex talionis* is the upper limit of the range of just punishments. On the other hand, if the retributivist principle is true, then denying that the offender deserves suffering equal to that which he imposed amounts to denying the equality and rationality of persons. From this it follows that we fall below the bottom end of the range of just punishments when we act in ways that are incompatible with the *lex talionis* at the top end. That is, we fall below the bottom end and commit an injustice to the victim when we treat the offender in a way that is no longer compatible with sincerely believing that he deserves to have done to him what he has done to his victim. Thus, the upper limit of the range of just punishments is the point after which more punishment is unjust to the offender, and the lower limit is the point after which less punishment is unjust to the victim. In this way, the range of just punishments remains faithful to the victim's right which is their source.

This way of understanding just punishment enables us to formulate proportional retributivism so that it is compatible with acknowledging the justice of the *lex talionis:* If we take the *lex talionis* as spelling out the offender's just deserts, and if other moral considerations require us to refrain from matching the injury caused by the offender while still allowing us to punish justly, then surely we impose just punishment if we impose the closest morally acceptable approximation to the *lex talionis.* Proportional retributivism, then, in requiring that the worst crime be punished by the society's worst punishment and so on, could be understood as translating the offender's just desert into its nearest equivalent in the society's table of morally acceptable punishments. Then the two versions of retributivism (*lex talionis* and proportional) are related in that the first states what just punishment would be if nothing but the offender's just desert mattered, and the second locates just punishment at the meeting point of the offender's just deserts and the society's moral scruples. And since this second version only modifies the requirements of the *lex talionis* in light of other moral considerations, it is compatible with believing that the *lex talionis* spells out the offender's just deserts, much in the way that modifying the obligations of promisers in light of other moral considerations is compatible with believing in the binding nature of promises.

Proportional retributivism so formulated preserves the point of retributivism and remains faithful to the victim's right which is its source. Since it punishes with the closest morally acceptable approximation to the *lex talionis,* it effectively says to the offender, you deserve the equivalent of what you did to your victim and you are getting less only to the degree that *our* moral scruples limit us from duplicating what you have done. Such punishment, then, affirms the equality of persons by respecting as far as is morally permissible the victim's right to impose suffering on the offender equal to what he received, and it affirms the rationality of the offender by treating him as authorizing others to do to him what he has done though they take him up on it only *as far as is morally permissible.* Needless to say, the alternative punishments must in some convincing way be comparable in gravity to the crimes which they punish, or else they will trivialize the harms those crimes caused and be no longer compatible with sincerely believing that the offender deserves to have done to him what he has done to his victim and no longer capable of impressing upon the criminal his equality with the victim. If we punish rapists with a small fine or a brief prison term, we do an injustice to their victims, because this trivializes the suffering rapists have caused and thus is incompatible with believing that they deserve to have done to them something comparable to what they have done to their victims. If, on the other hand, instead of raping rapists we impose on them some grave penalty, say a substantial term of imprisonment, then we do no injustice even though we refrain from exacting the *lex talionis.*

To sum up, I take the *lex talionis* to be the top end of the range of just punishments. When, because we are simply unable to duplicate the criminal's offense, we modify the *lex talionis* to call for imposing on the offender as nearly as possible what he has done, we are still at this top end, applying the *lex talionis* subject to "ought implies can." When we do less than this, we still act justly as long as we punish in a way that is compatible with sincerely believing that the offender deserves the full measure of the *lex talionis,* but receives less for reasons that do not underline this belief. If this is true, then it is not unjust to spare murderers as long as they can be punished in some other suitably grave way. I leave open the question of what such an alternative punishment might be, except to say that it need not be limited to such penalties as are currently imposed. For example, though rarely carried out in practice, a life sentence with no chance of parole might be a civilized equivalent of the death penalty—after all, people sentenced to life imprisonment have traditionally been regarded as "civilly dead." . . .

I take it then that the justice of the *lex talionis* implies that it is just to execute murderers, but not that it is unjust to spare them as long as they are systematically punished in some other suitably grave way. Before developing the implications of this claim, a word about the implied preconditions of applying the *lex talionis* is in order. . . .

Since I believe that the vast majority of murders in America are a predictable response to the frustrations and disabilities of impoverished social circumstances,[7] and since I believe that that impoverishment is a remediable injustice from which others in America benefit, I believe that we have no right to exact the full cost of murders from our murderers until we have done everything possible to rectify the conditions that produce their crimes. But these are the "Reagan years," and not many—who are not already susceptible—will be persuaded by this sort of argument. This does not, in my view, shake its validity; but I want to make an argument whose appeal is not limited to those who think that crime is the result of social injustice. I shall proceed then, granting not only the justice of the death penalty, but also, at least temporarily, the assumption that our murderers are wholly deserving of dying for their crimes. If I can show that it would still be wrong to execute murderers, I believe I shall have made the strongest case for abolishing the death penalty.

Civilization, Pain, and Justice

As I have already suggested, from the fact that something is justly deserved, it does not automatically follow that it should be done, since there may be other moral reasons for not doing it such that, all told, the weight of moral reasons swings the balance against proceeding. The same argument that I have given for the justice of the death penalty for murderers proves the justice of beating assaulters, raping rapists, and torturing torturers. Nonetheless, I believe, and suspect that most would agree, that it would not be right for us to beat assaulters, rape rapists, or torture torturers, *even though it were their just deserts*—and even if this were the only way to make them suffer as much as they had made their victims suffer. Calling for the abolition of the death penalty, though it be just, then, amounts to urging that as a society we place execution in the same category of sanction as beating, raping, and torturing, and treat it as something it would also not be right for us to do to offenders, *even if it were their just deserts.*

To argue for placing execution in this category, I must show what would be gained therefrom; and to show that, I shall indicate what we gain from placing torture in this category and argue that a similar gain is to be had from doing the same with execution. I select torture because I think the reasons for placing it in this category are, due to the extremity of torture, most easily seen—but what I say here applies with appropriate modification to other severe physical punishments, such as beating and raping. First, and most evidently, placing torture in this category broadcasts the message that we as a society judge torturing so horrible a thing to do to a person that we refuse to do it even when it is deserved. Note that such a judgment does not commit us to an absolute prohibition on torturing. No matter how horrible we judge something to be, we may still be justified in doing it if it is necessary to prevent something even worse. Leaving this aside for the moment, what is gained by broadcasting the public judgment that torture is too horrible to inflict even if deserved?

I think the answer to this lies in what we understand as civilization. In *The Genealogy of Morals,* Nietzsche says that in early times "pain did not hurt as much as it does today."[8] The truth in this puzzling remark is that progress in civilization is characterized by a lower tolerance for one's own pain and that suffered by others. And this is appropriate, since, via growth in knowledge, civilization brings increased power to prevent or reduce pain and, via growth in the ability to communicate and interact with more and more people, civilization extends the circle of people with whom we empathize. If civilization is characterized by lower tolerance for our own pain and that of others, then publicly refusing to do horrible things to our fellows both signals the level of our civilization *and, by our example, continues the work of civilizing.* And this gesture is all the more powerful if we refuse to do horrible things to those who deserve them. I contend then that the more things we are able to include in this category, the more civilized we are and the more civiliz*ing.* Thus we gain from including torture in this category, and if execution is especially horrible, we gain still more by including it.

Needless to say, the content, direction, and even the worth of civilization are hotly contested issues, and I shall not be able to win those contests in this brief space. At a minimum, however, I shall assume that civilization involves the taming of the natural environment and of the human animals in it, and that the overall trend in human history is toward increasing this taming, though the trend is by no means unbroken or without reverses. On these grounds, we can say that growth in civilization generally marks human history, that a reduction in the horrible things we tolerate doing to our fellows (even when they deserve them) is part of this growth, and that once the work of civilization is taken on consciously, it includes carrying forward and expanding this reduction.

This claim broadly corresponds to what Emile Durkheim identified, nearly a century ago, as "two laws which seem . . . to prevail in the evolution of the apparatus of punishment." The first, the law of quantitative change, Durkheim formulates as:

> *The intensity of punishment is the greater the more closely societies approximate to a less developed type—and the more the central power assumes an absolute character.*

And the second, which Durkheim refers to as the law of qualitative change,

> *Deprivations of liberty, and of liberty alone, varying in time according to the seriousness of the crime, tend to become more and more the normal means of social control.*[9]

Several things should be noted about these laws. First of all, they are not two separate laws. As Durkheim understands them, the second exemplifies the trend toward moderation of punishment referred to in the first. Second, the first law really refers to two distinct trends, which usually coincide but do not always. That is, moderation of punishment accompanies both the movement from less to more advanced types of society and the movement from more to less absolute rule. Normally these go hand in hand, but where they do not, the effect of one trend may offset the effect of the other. Thus, a primitive society without absolute rule may have milder punishments than an equally primitive but more absolutist society. This complication need not trouble us, since the claim I am making refers to the first trend, namely, that punishments tend to become milder as societies become more advanced; and that this is a trend in history is not refuted by the fact that it is accompanied by other trends and even occasionally offset by them. Moreover, I shall lose this article with a suggestion about the relation between the intensity of punishment and the justice of society, which might broadly be thought of as corresponding to the second trend in Durkheim's first law. Finally, and most important for our purposes, is the fact that Durkheim's claim that punishment becomes less intense as societies become more advanced is a generalization that he supports with an impressive array of evidence from historical societies from pre-Christian times to the time in which he wrote—and this in turn supports my claim that the reduction in the horrible things we do to our fellows is in fact part of the advance of civilization.

Against this it might be argued that many things grow in history, some good, some bad, and some mixed, and thus the fact that there is some historical trend is not a sufficient reason to continue it. Thus, for example, history also brings growth in population, but we are not for that reason called upon to continue the work of civilization by continually increasing our population. What this suggests is that in order to identify something as part of the work of civilizing, we must show not only that it generally grows in history, but that its growth is, on some independent grounds, clearly an advance for the human species—that is, either an unmitigated gain or at least consistently a net gain. And this implies that even trends which we might generally regard as advances may in some cases bring losses with them, such that when they did it would not be appropriate for us to lend our efforts to continuing them. Of such trends we can say that they are advances in civilization except when their gains are outweighed by the losses they bring—and that we are only called upon to further these trends when their gains are *not* outweighed in this way. It is clear in this light that increasing population is a mixed blessing at best, bringing both gains and losses. Consequently, it is not always an advance in civilization that we should further, though at times it may be.

What can be said of reducing the horrible things that we do to our fellows even when deserved? First of all, given our vulnerability to pain, it seems clearly a gain. Is it however an unmitigated gain? That is, would such a reduction ever amount to a loss? It seems to me that there are two conditions under which it would be a loss, namely, if the reduction made our lives more dangerous, or if not doing what is justly deserved were a loss in itself. Let us leave aside the former, since, as I have already suggested and as I will soon indicate in greater detail, I accept that if some horrible punishment is necessary to deter equally or more horrible acts, then we may have to impose the punishment. Thus my claim is that reduction in the horrible things we do to our fellows is an advance in civilization *as long as our lives are not thereby made more dangerous,* and that it is only then that we are called upon to extend that reduction as part of the work of civilization. Assuming then, for the moment, that we suffer no increased danger by refraining from doing horrible things to our fellows when they justly deserve them, does such refraining to do what is justly deserved amount to a loss?

It seems to me that the answer to this must be that refraining to do what is justly deserved is only a loss where it amounts to doing an injustice. But such refraining to do what is just is not doing what is unjust, unless what we do instead falls below the bottom end of the range of just punishments. Otherwise, it would be unjust to refrain from torturing torturers, raping rapists, or beating assaulters. In short, I take it that if there is no injustice in refraining from torturing torturers, then there is no injustice in refraining to do horrible things to our fellows generally, when they deserve them, as long as what we do instead is compatible with believing that they do deserve them. And thus that if such refraining does not make our lives more dangerous, then it is no loss, and given our vulnerability to pain, it is a gain. Consequently, reduction in the horrible things we do to our fellows, when not necessary to our protection, is an advance in civilization that we are called upon to continue once we consciously take upon ourselves the work of civilization.

To complete the argument, however, I must show that execution is horrible enough to warrant its inclusion alongside torture. Against this it will be said that execution is not especially horrible since it only hastens a fate that is inevitable for us. I think that this view overlooks important differences in the manner in which people reach their inevitable ends. I contend that execution is especially horrible, and it is so in a way similar to (though not identical with) the way in which torture is especially horrible. I believe we view torture as especially awful because of two of its features, which also characterize execution: intense pain and the spectacle of one human being completely subject to the power of another. This latter is separate from the issue of pain since it is something that offends us about unpainful things, such as slavery (even voluntarily entered) and prostitution (even voluntarily chosen as an occupation). Execution shares this separate feature, since killing a bound and defenseless human being enacts the total subjugation of that person to his fellows. I think, incidentally, that this accounts for the general uneasiness with which execution by lethal injection has been greeted. Rather than humanizing the event, it seems only to have purchased a possible reduction in physical pain at the price of increasing the spectacle of subjugation—with no net gain in the attractiveness of the death penalty. Indeed, its net effect may have been the reverse.

In addition to the spectacle of subjugation, execution, even by physically painless means, is also characterized by a special and intense psychological pain that distinguishes it from the loss of life that awaits us all. Interesting in this regard is the fact that although we are not terribly squeamish about the loss of life itself, allowing it in war, self-defense, as a necessary cost of progress, and so on, we are, as the extraordinary hesitance of our courts testifies, quite reluctant to execute. I think this is because execution involves the most psychologically painful features of deaths. We normally regard death from human causes as worse than death from natural causes, since a humanly caused shortening of life lacks the consolation of unavoidability. And we normally regard death whose coming is foreseen by its victim as worse than sudden death, because a foreseen death adds to the loss of life the terrible consciousness of that impending loss. As a humanly caused death whose advent is foreseen by its victim, an execution combines the worst of both.

Thus far, by analogy with torture, I have argued that execution should be avoided because of how horrible it is to the one executed. But there are reasons of another sort that follow from the analogy with torture. Torture is to be avoided not only because of what it says about what we are willing to do to our fellows, but also because of what it says about us who are willing to do it. To torture someone is an awful spectacle not only because of the intensity of pain imposed, but because of what is required to be able to impose such pain on one's fellows. The tortured body cringes, using its full exertion to escape the pain imposed upon it—it literally begs for relief with its muscles as it does with its cries. To torture someone is to demonstrate a capacity to resist this begging, and that in turn demonstrates a kind of hard-heartedness that a society ought not parade.

And this is true not only of torture, but of all severe corporal punishment. Indeed, I think this constitutes part of the answer to the puzzling question of why we refrain from punishments like whipping, even when the alternative (some months in jail versus some lashes) seems more costly to the offender. Imprisonment is painful to be sure, but it is a reflective pain, one that comes with comparing what is to what might have been, and that can be temporarily ignored by thinking about other things. But physical pain has an urgency that holds body and mind in a fierce grip. Of physical pain, as Orwell's Winston Smith recognized, "you could only wish one thing: that it should stop."[10] Refraining from torture in particular and corporal punishment in general, we both refuse to put a fellow human being in this grip and refuse to show our ability to resist this wish. The death penalty is the last corporal punishment used officially in the modern world. And it is corporal not only because administered via the body, but because the pain of foreseen, humanly administered death strikes us with the urgency that characterizes intense physical pain, causing grown men to cry, faint, and lose control of their bodily functions. There is something to be gained by refusing to endorse the hardness of heart necessary to impose such a fate.

By placing execution alongside torture in the category of things we will not do to our fellow human beings even when they deserve them, we broadcast the message that totally subjugating a person to the power of others *and* confronting him with the advent of his own humanly administered demise is too horrible to be done by civilized human beings to their fellows even when they have earned it. Too horrible to do, and too horrible to be capable of doing. And I contend that broadcasting this message loud and clear would in the long run contribute to the general detestation of murder and be, to the extent to which it worked itself into the hearts and minds of the populace, a deterrent. In short, refusing to execute murderers though they desire it both reflects and continues the taming of the human species that we call civilization. Thus, I take it that the abolition of the death penalty, though it is a just punishment for murder, is part of the civilizing mission of modern states. . . .

Conclusion: History, Force, and Justice

I believe that, taken together, these arguments prove that we should abolish the death penalty though it is a just punishment for murder. Let me close with an argument of a different sort. When you see the lash fall upon the backs of Roman slaves, or the hideous tortures meted out in the period of the absolute monarchs, you see more than mere cruelty at work. Surely you suspect that there is something about the injustice of imperial slavery and royal tyranny that requires the use of extreme force to keep these institutions in place. That is, for reasons undoubtedly related to those that support the second part of Durkheim's first law of penal evolution, we take the amount of force a society uses against its own people as an inverse measure of its justness. And though no more than a rough measure, it is a revealing one nonetheless, because when a society is limited in the degree of force it can use against its subjects, it is likely to have to be a juster society since it will have to gain its subjects' cooperation by offering them fairer terms than it would have to, if it could use more force. From this we cannot simply conclude that reducing the force used by our society will automatically make our society more just—but I think we can conclude that it will have this tendency, since it will require us to find means other than force for encouraging compliance with our institutions, and this is likely to require us to make those institutions as fair to all as possible. Thus I hope that America will pose itself the challenge of winning its citizens' cooperation by justice rather than force, and that when future historians look back on the twentieth century, they will find us with countries like France and England and Sweden that have abolished the death penalty, rather than with those like South Africa and the Soviet Union and Iran that have retained it—with all that this suggests about the countries involved.

Acknowledgment

This paper is an expanded version of my opening statement in a debate with Ernest van den Haag on the death penalty at an Amnesty International conference on capital punishment, held at John Jay College in New York City, on October 17, 1983. I am grateful to the Editors of *Philosophy and Public Affairs* for very thought-provoking comments, to Hugo Bedau and Robert Johnson for many helpful suggestions, and to Ernest van den Haag for his encouragement.

Endnotes

1. Ernest van den Haag and John P. Conrad, *The Death Penalty: A Debate* (New York: Plenum Press, 1983). Unless otherwise indicated, page references in the text and notes are to this book.

2. "As a general rule, a man is undone by *waiting* for capital punishment well before he dies. Two deaths are inflicted on him, the first being worse than the second, whereas he killed but once" (Albert Camus, "Reflections on the Guillotine," in *Resistance, Rebellion and Death* [New York: Knopf, 1969], p. 205. Based on interviews with the condemned men on Alabama's death row, Robert Johnson presents convincing empirical support for Camus' observation, in *Condemned to Die: Life Under Sentence of Death* (New York: Elsevier, 1981).
3. Hegel writes that "The sole positive existence which the injury [i.e., the crime] possesses is that it is the particular will of the ciminal [i.e., it is the criminal's intention that distinguishes criminal injury from, say, injury due to an accident]. Hence to injure (or penalize) this particular will as a will determinately existent is to annul the crime, which otherwise would have been held valid, and to restore the right." (G.W.F. Hegel, *The Philosophy of Right,* trans. T.M. Knox [Oxford Clarendon Press, 1962; originally published in German in 1821], p. 69; see also p. 331n). I take this to mean that the right is a certain equality of sovereignty between the wills of individuals, crime disrupts that equality by placing one will above others, and punishment restores the equality by annulling the illegitimate ascendance. On these grounds, as I shall suggest below, the desire for revenge (strictly limited to the desire "to even the score") is more respectable than philosophers have generally allowed. And so Hegel writes that "The annulling of crime in this sphere where right is immediate [i.e., the condition prior to conscious morality] is principally revenge, which is just in its content in so far as it is retributive" (ibid., p. 73).
4. Kant writes that "any underserved evil that you inflict on someone else among the people is one that you do to yourself. If you vilify him, you vilify yourself; if you steal from him, you steal from yourself; if you kill him, you kill yourself." Since Kant holds that "If what happens to someone is also willed by him, it cannot be a punishment," he takes pains to distance himself from the view that the offender wills his punishment. "The chief error contained in this sophistry," Kant writes, "consists in the confusion of the criminal's [that is, the murderer's] own judgment (which one must necessarily attribute to his reason) that he must forfeit his life with a resolution of the will to take his own life" (Immanuel Kane, *The Metaphysical Elements of Justice, Part I of The Metaphysics of Morals,* trans. J. Ladd [Indianapolis: Bobbs-Merrill, 1965; originally published in 1797], pp. 101, 105–106). I have tried to capture this notion of attributing a judgment to the offender rather than a resolution of his will with the term "authorizes."
5. "Even if a civil society were to dissolve itself by common agreement of all its members . . . , the last murderer remaining in prison must first be executed, so that everyone will duly receive what his actions are worth" (Kant, ibid., p. 102).
6. Kant, *Metaphysical Elements of Justice,* p. 104; see also p. 133.
7. "In the case of homicide, the empirical evidence indicates that poverty and poor economic conditions are systematically related to higher levels of homicide" (Richard M. McGahey, "Dr. Ehrlich's Magic Bullet: Economic Theory, Econometrics, and the Death Penalty," *Crime & Delinquency* 26, no. 4 [October 1980], 502). Some of that evidence can be found in Peter Passell, "The Deterrent Effect of the Death Penalty: A Statistical Test," *Stanford Law Review* (November 1975), 61–80.
8. Friedrich Nietzsche, *The Birth of Tragedy and The Genealogy of Morals* (New York: Doubleday, 1956), pp. 199–200.

9. Emile Durkheim, "Two Laws of Penal Evolution," *Economy and Society* 2 (1973), 285 and 294; italics in the original. This essay was originally published in French in *Année Sociologique* 4 (1899–1900).
10. George Orwell, *1984* (New York: New American Library, 1983; originally published in 1949), p. 197.

Journal/Discussion Questions

✍ *Have you ever known someone who experienced the murder of a close family member? How did this affect their feelings about capital punishment? How does this relate to Reiman's Kantian and Hegelian analyses of retributivism?*

1. Reiman's position is an unusual one in that it accepts the justice of the death penalty but still argues for its abolition. In what ways does it differ from your own? Did reading his article prompt you to reconsider any elements of your own position?
2. What, according to Reiman, is the difference between the *lex talionis* and proportional retributivism? Why is this distinction important to his argument?
3. What is the *retributivist principle?* What are its Kantian and Hegelian foundations? How is it related to the Golden Rule?
4. Why, according to Reiman, should we refrain from raping rapists and torturing torturers? Why should we refrain from executing murderers?
5. Reiman considers the "common sense" argument that capital punishment deters. What objections does he raise to it? Are those objections convincing?

Walter Berns
"The Morality of Anger"

Walter Berns is John M. Olin University Professor at Georgetown University.

In this selection, which is drawn from his For Capital Punishment: Crime and the Morality of the Death Penalty, *Berns argues in favor of the moral force of anger and its place in punishment.*

As You Read, Consider This:

1. Compare and contrast Berns's reactions to Simon Wiesenthal and your reactions. Do they indicate any differences in your positions on the death penalty and the general purpose of punishment?
2. In what ways, according to Berns, is anger connected to punishment and to justice?

Until recently, my business did not require me to think about the punishment of criminals in general or the legitimacy and efficacy of capital punishment in particular. In a vague way, I was aware of the disagreement among professionals concerning the purpose of punishment—whether it was intended to deter others, to rehabilitate the criminal, or to pay him back—but like most laymen I had no particular reason to decide which purpose was right or to what extent they may all have been right. I did know that retribution was held in ill repute among criminologists and jurists—to them, retribution was a fancy name for revenge, and revenge was barbaric—and, of course, I knew that capital punishment had the support only of policemen, prison guards, and some local politicians, the sort of people Arthur Koestler calls "hanghards" (Philadelphia's Mayor Rizzo comes to mind). The intellectual community denounced it as both unnecessary and immoral. It was the phenomenon of Simon Wiesenthal that allowed me to understand why the intellectuals were wrong and why the police, the politicians, and the majority of the voters were right: We punish criminals principally in order to pay them back, and we execute the worst of them out of moral necessity. Anyone who respects Wiesenthal's mission will be driven to the same conclusion.

Of course, not everyone will respect that mission. It will strike the busy man—I mean the sort of man who sees things only in the light cast by a concern for his own interests—as somewhat bizarre. Why should anyone devote his life—more than thirty years of it!—exclusively to the task of hunting down the Nazi war criminals who survived World War II and escaped punishment? Wiesenthal says his conscience forces him "to bring the guilty ones to trial." But why punish them? What do we hope to accomplish now by punishing SS Obersturmbannführer Adolf Eichmann or SS Obersturmbannführer Franz Stangl or someday—who knows?—Reichsleiter Martin Bormann? We surely don't expect to rehabilitate them, and it would be foolish to think that by punishing them we might thereby deter others. The answer, I think, is clear: We want to punish them in order to *pay them back*. We think they must be made to pay for their crimes with their lives and we think that we, the survivors of the world they violated, may legitimately exact that payment because we, too, are their victims. By punishing them, we demonstrate that there are laws that bind men across generations as well as across (and within) nations, that we are not simply isolated individuals, each pursuing his selfish interests and connected with others by a mere contract to live and let live. To state it simply, Wiesenthal allows us to see that it is right, morally right, to be angry with criminals and to express that anger publicly, officially, and in an appropriate manner, which may require the worst of them to be executed.

Modern civil-libertarian opponents of capital punishment do not understand this. They say that to execute a criminal is to deny his human dignity; they also say that the death penalty is not useful, that nothing useful is accomplished by executing anyone. Being utilitarians, they are essentially selfish men, distrustful of passion, who do not understand the connection between anger and justice, and between anger and human dignity.

Anger is expressed or manifested on those occasions when someone has acted in a manner that is thought to be unjust, and one of its origins is the opinion that men are responsible, and should be held responsible for what they do. Thus, as Aristotle teaches us, anger is accompanied not only by the pain caused by the one who is the object of anger, but by the pleasure arising from the expectation of inflicting revenge on someone who is thought to deserve it. We can become angry with an inanimate object (the door we run into and then kick in return) only by foolishly attributing responsibility to it, and we cannot do that for long, which is why we do not think of returning later to revenge ourselves on the door. For the same reason, we cannot be more than momentarily angry with any one creature other than man; only a fool and worse would dream of taking revenge on a dog. And, finally, we tend to pity rather than to be angry with men who—because they are insane, for example—are not responsible for their acts. Anger, then, is a very human passion not only because only a human being can be angry, but also because anger acknowledges the humanity of its objects: it holds them accountable for what they do. And in holding particular men responsible, it pays them the respect that is due them as men. Anger recognizes that only men have the capacity to be moral beings and, in so doing, acknowledges the dignity of human beings. Anger is somehow connected with justice, and it is this that modern penology has not understood; it tends, on the whole, to regard anger as a selfish indulgence.

Anger can, of course, be that; and if someone does not become angry with an insult or an injury suffered unjustly, we tend to think he does not think much of himself. But it need not be selfish, not in the sense of being provoked only by an injury suffered by oneself. There were many angry men in America when President Kennedy was killed; one of them—Jack Ruby—took it upon himself to exact the punishment that, if indeed deserved, ought to have been exacted by the law. There were perhaps even angrier men when Martin Luther King, Jr., was killed, for King, more than anyone else at the time, embodied a people's quest for justice; the anger—more, the "black rage"—expressed on that occasion was simply a manifestation of the great change that had occurred among black men in America, a change wrought in large part by King and his associates in the civil rights movement: the servility and fear of the past had been replaced by pride and anger, and the treatment that had formerly been accepted as a matter of course or as if it were deserved was now seen for what it was, unjust and unacceptable. King preached love, but the movement he led depended on anger as well as love, and that anger was not despicable, being neither selfish nor unjustified. On the contrary, it was a reflection of what was called solidarity and may more accurately be called a profound caring for others, black for other blacks, white for blacks, and, in the world King was trying to build, American for other Americans. If men are not saddened when someone else suffers, or angry when someone else suffers unjustly, the implication is that they do not care for anyone other than themselves or that they lack some quality that befits a man. When we criticize them for this, we acknowledge that they ought to care for others. If men are not angry when a neighbor suffers at the hands of a criminal, the implication is that their moral faculties have been corrupted, that they are not good citizens.

Criminals are properly the objects of anger, and the perpetrators of terrible crimes—for example, Lee Harvey Oswald and James Earl Ray—are properly the objects of great anger. They have done more than inflict an injury on an isolated individual; they have violated the foundations of trust and friendship, the necessary elements of a moral community, the only community worth living in. A moral community, unlike a hive of bees or a hill of ants, is one whose members are expected freely to obey the laws and, unlike those in a tyranny, are trusted to obey the laws. The criminal has violated that trust, and in so doing has injured not merely his immediate victim but the community as such. He has called into question the very possibility of that community by suggesting that men cannot be trusted to respect freely the property, the person, and the dignity of those with whom they are associated. If, then, men are not angry when someone else is robbed, raped, or murdered, the implication is that no moral community exists, because those men do not care for anyone other than themselves. Anger is an expression of that caring, and society needs men who care for one another, who share their pleasures and their pains, and do so for the sake of the others. It is the passion that can cause us to act for reasons having nothing to do with selfish or mean calculation; indeed, when educated it can become a generous passion, the passion that protects the community or country by demanding punishment for its enemies. It is the stuff from which heroes are made.

A moral community is not possible without anger and the moral indignation that accompanies it. Thus the most powerful attack on capital punishment was written by a man, Albert Camus, who denied the legitimacy of anger and moral indignation by denying the very possibility of a moral community in our time. The anger expressed in our world, he said, is nothing but hypocrisy. His novel *Létranger* (variously translated as *The Stranger* or *The Outsider*) is a brilliant portrayal of what Camus insisted is our world, a world deprived of God, as he put it. It is a world we would not choose to live in and one that Camus, the hero of the French Resistance, disdained. Nevertheless, the novel is a modern masterpiece, and Meursault, its antihero (for a world without anger can have no heroes), is a murderer.

He is a murderer whose crime is excused, even as his lack of hypocrisy is praised, because the universe, we are told, is "benignly indifferent" to how we live or what we do. Of course, the law is not indifferent; the law punished Meursault and it threatens to punish us if we do as he did. But Camus the novelist teaches us that the law is simply a collection of arbitrary conceits. The people around Meursault apparently were not indifferent; they expressed dismay at his lack of attachment to his mother and disapprobation of his crime. But Camus the novelist teaches us that other people are hypocrites. They pretend not to know what Camus the opponent of capital punishment tells: namely, that "our civilization has lost the only values that, in a certain way, can justify that penalty . . . [the existence of] a truth or a principle that is superior to man." There is no basis for friendship and no moral law; therefore, no one, not even a murderer, can violate the terms of friendship or break that law; and there is no basis for the anger that we express when someone breaks that law. The only thing we share as men, the only thing that connects us one to another, is a "solidarity against death," and a judgment of capital punishment "upsets" that solidarity. The purpose of human life is to stay alive.

Like Meursault, Macbeth was a murderer, and like *Létranger,* Shakespeare's *Macbeth* is the story of a murder; but there the similarity ends. As Lincoln said, "Nothing equals *Macbeth.*" He was comparing it with the other Shakespearean plays he knew, the plays he had "gone over perhaps as frequently as any unprofessional reader . . . *Lear, Richard Third, Henry Eighth, Hamlet*"; but I think he meant to say more than that none of these equals *Macbeth.* I think he meant that no other literary work equals it. "It is wonderful," he said. *Macbeth* is wonderful because, to say nothing more here, it teaches us the awesomeness of the commandment "Thou shalt not kill."

What can a dramatic poet tell us about murder? More, probably, than anyone else, if he is a poet worthy of consideration, and yet nothing that does not inhere in the act itself. In *Macbeth,* Shakespeare shows us murders committed in a political world by a man so driven by ambition to rule that world that he becomes a tyrant. He shows us also the consequences, which were terrible, worse even than Macbeth feared. The cosmos rebelled, turned into chaos by his deeds. He shows a world that was not "benignly indifferent" to what we call crimes and especially to murder, a world constituted by laws divine as well as human, and Macbeth violated the most awful of those laws. Because the world was so constituted, Macbeth suffered the torments of the great and the damned, torments far beyond the "practice" of any physician. He had known glory and had deserved the respect and affection of king, countrymen, army, friends, and wife; and he lost it all. At the end he was reduced to saying that life "is a tale told by an idiot, full of sound and fury, signifying nothing"; yet, in spite of the horrors provoked in us by his acts, he excites no anger in us. We pity him; even so, we understand the anger of his countrymen and the dramatic necessity of his death. *Macbeth* is a play about ambition, murder, tyranny; about horror, anger, vengeance, and perhaps more than any other of Shakespeare's plays, justice. Because of justice, Macbeth has to die, not by his own hand—he will not "play the Roman fool, and die on [his] sword"—but at the hand of the avenging Macduff. The dramatic necessity of his death would appear to rest on its *moral* necessity. Is that right? Does this play conform to our sense of what a murder means? Lincoln thought it was "wonderful."

Surely Shakespeare's is a truer account of murder than the one provided by Camus, and by truer I mean truer to our moral sense of what a murder is and what the consequences that attend it must be. Shakespeare shows us vengeful men because there is something in the souls of men—then and now—that requires such crimes to be revenged. Can we imagine a world that does not take its revenge on the man who kills Macduff's wife and children? (Can we imagine the play in which Macbeth does not die?) Can we imagine a people that does not hate murderers? (Can we imagine a world where Meursault is an outsider only because he does not *pretend* to be outraged by murder?) Shakespeare's poetry could not have been written out of the moral sense that the death penalty's opponents insist we ought to have. Indeed, the issue of capital punishment can be said to turn on whether Shakespeare's or Camus' is the more telling account of murder.

There is a sense in which punishment may be likened to dramatic poetry. Dramatic poetry depicts men's actions because men are revealed in, or make themselves known through, their actions; and the essence of a human action according to Aristotle, consists in its being virtuous or vicious. Only a ruler or a contender for rule can act with the freedom and on a scale that allows the virtuousness or viciousness of human deeds to be fully displayed. Macbeth was such a man, and in his fall, brought about by his own acts, and in the consequent suffering he endured, is revealed the meaning of morality. In *Macbeth* the majesty of the moral law is demonstrated to us; as I said it teaches us the awesomeness of the commandment Thou shalt not kill. In a similar fashion, the punishments imposed by the legal order remind us of the reign of the moral order; not only do they remind us of it, but by enforcing its prescriptions, they enhance the dignity of the legal order in the eyes of moral men, in the eyes of those decent citizens who cry out "for gods who will avenge injustice." That is especially important in a self-governing community, a community that gives laws to itself.

If the laws were understood to be divinely inspired or, in the extreme case, divinely given, they would enjoy all the dignity that the opinions of men can grant and all the dignity they require to ensure their being obeyed by most of the men living under them. Like Duncan in the opinion of Macduff, the laws would be "the Lord's anointed," and would be obeyed even as Macduff obeyed the laws of the Scottish kingdom. Only a Macbeth would challenge them, and only a Meursault would ignore them. But the laws of the United States are not of this description; in fact, among the proposed amendments that became the Bill of Rights was one declaring not that all power comes from God, but rather "that all power is originally vested in, and consequently derives from the people"; and this proposal was dropped only because it was thought to be redundant: the Constitution's preamble said essentially the same thing, and what we know as the Tenth Amendment reiterated it. So Madison proposed to make the Constitution venerable in the minds of the people, and Lincoln, in an early speech, went so far as to say that a "political religion" should be made of it. They did not doubt that the Constitution and the laws made pursuant to it would be supported by "enlightened reason," but fearing that enlightened reason would be in short supply, they sought to augment it. The laws of the United States would be obeyed by some men because they could hear and understand "the voice of enlightened reason," and by other men because they would regard the laws with that "veneration which time bestows on everything."

Supreme Court justices have occasionally complained of our habit of making "constitutionality synonymous with wisdom." But the extent to which the Constitution is venerated and its authority accepted depends on the compatibility of its rules with our moral sensibilities; despite its venerable character, the Constitution is not the only source of these moral sensibilities. There was even a period, before slavery was abolished by the Thirteenth Amendment, when the Constitution was regarded by some very moral men as an abomination: Garrison called it "a covenant with death and an agreement with Hell," and there were honorable men holding important political offices and judicial appointments who refused to enforce the Fugitive Slave Law even though its constitutionality had been affirmed. In time this opinion spread far beyond the ranks of the original abolitionists until those who held it composed a constitutional majority of the people, and slavery was abolished.

But Lincoln knew that more than amendments were required to make the Constitution once more worthy of the veneration of moral men. That is why, in the Gettysburg Address, he made the principle of the Constitution an inheritance from "our fathers." That it should be so esteemed is especially important in a self-governing nation that gives laws to itself, because it is only a short step from the principle that the laws are merely a product of one's own will to the opinion that the only consideration that informs the law is self-interest; and this opinion is only one remove from lawlessness. A nation of simple self-interested men will soon enough perish from the earth.

It was not an accident that Lincoln spoke as he did at Gettysburg or that he chose as the occasion for his words the dedication of a cemetery built on a portion of the most significant battlefield of the Civil War. Two and a half years earlier, in his First Inaugural Address, he had said that Americans, north and south, were not and must not be enemies, but friends. Passion had strained but must not be allowed to break the bonds of affection that tied them one to another. He closed by saying this: "The mystic chords of memory, stretching from every battlefield, and patriot grave, to every living heart and hearthstone, all over this broad land, will yet swell the chorus of the Union, when again touched, as surely they will be, by the better angels of our nature." The chords of memory that would swell the chorus of the Union could be touched, even by a man of Lincoln's stature, only on the most solemn occasions, and in the life of a nation no occasion is more solemn than the burial of the patriots who have died defending it on the field of battle. War is surely an evil, but as Hegel said, it is not an "absolute evil." It exacts the supreme sacrifice, but precisely because of that it can call forth such sublime rhetoric as Lincoln's. His words at Gettysburg serve to remind Americans in particular of what Hegel said people in general needed to know, and could be made to know by means of war and the sacrifices demanded of them in wars: namely, that their country is something more than a "civil society" the purpose of which is simply the protection of individual and selfish interests.

Capital punishment, like Shakespeare's dramatic and Lincoln's political poetry (and it is surely that, and was understood by him to be that), serves to remind us of the majesty of the moral order that is embodied in our law, and of the terrible consequences of its breach. The law must not be understood to be merely a statute that we enact or repeal at our will, and obey or disobey at our convenience—especially not the criminal law. Wherever law is regarded as merely statutory, men will soon enough disobey it, and will learn how to do so without any inconvenience to themselves. The criminal law must possess a dignity far beyond that possessed by mere statutory enactment or utilitarian and self-interested calculations. The most powerful means we have to give it that dignity is to authorize it to impose the ultimate penalty. The criminal law must be made awful, by which I mean inspiring or commanding "profound respect or reverential fear." It must remind us of the moral order by which alone we can live as *human* beings, and in America, now that the Supreme Court has outlawed banishment, the only punishment that can do this is capital punishment.

The founder of modern criminology, the eighteenth-century Italian Cesare Beccaria, opposed both banishment and capital punishment because he understood that both were inconsistent with the principle of self-interest, and self-interest was the basis of the political order he favored. If a man's first or only duty is to himself, of course he will prefer his money to his country he will also prefer his money to his brother. In fact, he will prefer his brother's money to his brother, and a people of this description, or a country that understands itself in this Beccarian manner, can put the mark of Cain on no one. For the same reason, such a country can have no legitimate reason to execute its criminals, or, indeed, to punish them in any manner. What would be accomplished by punishment in such a place? Punishment arises out of the demand for justice, and justice is demanded by angry, morally indignant men; its purpose is to satisfy that moral indignation and thereby promote the law-abidingness that, it is assumed, accompanies it. But the principle of self-interest denies the moral basis of that indignation.

Not only will a country based solely on self-interest have no legitimate reason to punish; it may have no need to punish. It may be able to solve what we call the crime problem by substituting a law of contracts for a law of crimes. According to Beccaria's social contract, men agree to yield their natural freedom to the "sovereign" in exchange for his promise to keep the peace. As it becomes more difficult for the sovereign to fulfill his part of the contract, there is a demand that he be made to pay for his nonperformance. From this comes compensation or insurance schemes embodied in statutes whereby the sovereign (or state), being unable to keep the peace by punishing criminals, agrees to compensate its contractual partners for injuries suffered at the hands of criminals, injuries the police are unable to prevent. The insurance policy takes the place of law enforcement and the *posse comitatus,* and John Wayne and Gary Cooper give way to Mutual of Omaha. There is no anger in this kind of law, and none (or no reason for any) in the society. The principle can be carried further still. If we ignore the victim (and nothing we do can restore his life anyway), there would appear to be no reason why—the worth of a man being his price, as Beccaria's teacher, Thomas Hobbes, put it—coverage should not be extended to the losses incurred in a murder. If we ignore the victim's sensibilities (and what are they but absurd vanities?), there would appear to be no reason why—the worth of a woman being *her* price—coverage should not be extended to the losses incurred in a rape. Other examples will no doubt suggest themselves.

This might appear to be an almost perfect solution to what we persist in calling the crime problem, achieved without risking the terrible things sometimes done by an angry people. A people that is not angry with criminals will not be able to deter crime, but a people fully covered by insurance has no need to deter crime: they will be insured against all the losses they can, in principle, suffer. What is now called crime can be expected to increase in volume, of course, and this will cause an increase in the premiums paid, directly or in the form of taxes. But it will no longer be necessary to apprehend, try, and punish criminals, which now costs Americans more than $1.5 billion a month (and is increasing at an annual rate of about 15 percent), and one can buy a lot of insurance for $1.5 billion. There is this difficulty, as Rousseau put it: To exclude anger from the human community is to concentrate all the passions in a "self-interest of the meanest sort, and such a place would not be fit for human habitation.

When, in 1976, the Supreme Court declared death to be a constitutional penalty, it decided that the United States was not that sort of country; most of us, I think, can appreciate that judgment.

We want to live among people who do not value their possessions more than their citizenship, who do not think exclusively or even primarily of their own rights, people whom we can depend on even as they exercise their rights, and whom we can trust, which is to say, people who, even in the absence of a policeman, will not assault our bodies or steal our possessions, and might even come to our assistance when we need it, and who stand ready, when the occasion demands it, to risk their lives in defense of their country. If we are of the opinion that the United States may rightly ask of its citizens this awful sacrifice, then we are also of the opinion that it may rightly impose the most awful penalty, if it may rightly honor its heroes, it may rightly execute the worst of its criminals. By doing so, it will remind its citizens that it is a country worthy of heroes.

Journal/Discussion Questions

✍ *Consider your reaction to the bombing of the Federal Building in Oklahoma City. To what extent does Berns's analysis shed light on your feelings? What shortcomings does his analysis have in light of your own experience?*

1. Berns sees the function of punishment to be in part one of "paying back." What, precisely, are we paying the criminal back for?
2. Why, according to Berns, is it important to stay in touch with our anger about criminals and their crimes? Do you agree? What are the dangers of this position?

CONCLUDING DISCUSSION QUESTIONS

Where Do You Stand Now?

Instructions

You have already answered the following questions in your moral problems self-quiz at the beginning of this book. Now that you have studied the material in this section, take a moment to answer the same questions again.

	Strongly Agree	*Agree*	*Undecided*	*Disagree*	*Strongly Disagree*	*Chapter 4: Punishment and the Dealth Penalty*
16.	❑	❑	❑	❑	❑	The purpose of punishment is primarily to pay back the offender.
17.	❑	❑	❑	❑	❑	The purpose of punishment is primarily to deter the offender and others from committing future crimes.
18.	❑	❑	❑	❑	❑	Capital punishment is always morally wrong.
19.	❑	❑	❑	❑	❑	The principal moral consideration about capital punishment is the question of whether it is administered arbitrarily or not.
20.	❑	❑	❑	❑	❑	The principal moral consideration about capital punishment is that it doesn't really deter criminals.

Compare your answers to the present self-quiz with the answers to the initial self-quiz. How, if at all, have your answers changed? How have the *reasons* for your answers changed?

Journal/Discussion Questions

✍ *Imagine that you are on a jury. You have just found a young adult guilty of a particularly heinous rape/torture/murder of a small child. The defendant appears to be unrepentant. Now you are being asked to consider sentencing. The prosecution is asking for the death penalty, while the defense is requesting a sentence of life imprisonment. How would you vote? What factors would you consider? What would be the major stumbling block to changing your mind and voting the other way?*

Given your answers to these questions, how does your position fit in with the positions and issues discussed in this chapter?

1. You have now read, thought, and discussed a number of aspects of punishment in general and the use of the death penalty

in particular. How have your views *changed* and developed? Has your understanding changed of the *reasons* supporting other positions that are different from your own? If so, in what way(s)? What idea had the greatest impact on your thinking about punishment? About the death penalty? Why?

2. Imagine that a close family member was murdered. How, if at all, would this affect your views on punishment? On capital punishment? Presuming that the murderer were caught, what would you like punishment to accomplish?
3. Imagine that you are a new member of the Senate, and that you have just been given an assignment to the Senate committee that is responsible for recommendations about criminal punishment on the state and local levels as well as nationally. Your committee is asked to determine (a) what aspects of our current punishment practices are in need of revision and (b) what changes you would recommend for the future. At the first meeting of the committee, the committee chair asks each member to state their initial general views on these two issues. What would your response be?

FOR FURTHER READING

Web Resources

For Web-based resources, including the major Supreme Court decisions on the death penalty, see the Punishment & Death Penalty page of *Ethics Updates (http://ethics.acusd.edu).* Among the resources are extensive statistical information about the use of the death penalty in America, John Stuart Mill's speech in favor of capital punishment, John Rawls' "Two Concepts of Rules," and works by Hugo Bedeau.

Punishment

There are a number of excellent *anthologies on punishment,* many of which contain articles on the death penalty in particular. See *Punishment and the Death Penalty: The Current Debate,* edited by Robert M. Baird and Stuart E. Rosenbaum (Buffalo, NY: Prometheus Books, 1995); *Punishment: A Philosophy and Public Affairs Reader,* edited by A. John Simmons, Marshall Cohen, Joshua Cohen, and Charles R. Beitz (Princeton: Princeton University Press, 1995); *Philosophy of Punishment,* edited by Robert M. Baird and Stuart E. Rosenbaum (Buffalo, NY: Prometheus Books, 1988); *Punishment: Selected Readings,* edited by Joel Feinberg and Hyman Gross (Encino, CA: Dickenson, 1975); *Philosophical Perspectives on Punishment,* edited by Gertrude Ezorsky (Albany: State University of New York Press, 1972); *The Philosophy of Punishment: A Collection of Papers,* edited by H.B. Acton (New York: St. Martin's Press, 1969); *Theories of Punishment,* edited by Stanley E. Grupp (Bloomington: Indiana University Press, 1971). In contrast to such comparatively modern problems as abortion and *in vitro* fertilization, punishment has been a theme for philosophers for centuries.

The anthology by Ezorsky contains an excellent selection of *classical sources* as well as contemporary authors. Also see Plato's *Laws,* Jeremy Bentham's *An Introduction to the Principles of Morals and Legislation* (Oxford: Blackwell, 1967), especially Chapter 13, Section 2; Immanuel Kant, *The Metaphysical Elements of Justice, Part I of The Metaphysics of Morals,* translated by John Ladd (Indianapolis: Bobbs-Merrill, 1965); and G.W.F. Hegel, *The Philosophy of Right,* translated by T.M. Knox (Oxford: Clarendon Press, 1962).

Among the influential *contemporary articles and books,* see especially Jeffrie G. Murphy, "Marxism and Retribution," *Philosophy and Public Affairs* 2, no. 3 (Spring 1973), 217–243, in which he argues in favor of a retributivist view of punishment that is compatible with the Marxist tradition; also see his *Retribution, Justice and Therapy* (Dordrecht: Reidel, 1979). Edmund L. Pincoffs, *The Rationale of Legal Punishment* (New York: Humanities Press, 1966) is an eloquent defense of a retributivist view of punishment. Also see Ernest van den Haag, *Punishing Criminals* (New York: Basic Books, 1975). John Cottingham, "Punishment," *The Encyclopedia of Ethics,* edited by Lawrence C. Becker and Charlotte B. Becker (New York: Garland, 1992), Vol. II, pp. 1053–1055 and Stanley I. Benn, "Punishment," *The Encyclopedia of Philosophy,* Vol. 7, ed. Paul

Edwards (New York: Macmillan, 1967), pp. 29–36 both offer excellent surveys of the major issues about punishment. Among the noteworthy articles, see Andrew von Hirsch, "Doing Justice: The Principle of Commensurate Deserts," and Hyman Gross, "Proportional Punishment and Justifiable Sentences," in *Sentencing,* eds. H. Gross and A. von Hirsch (New York: Oxford University Press, 1981), pp. 243–256 and 272–283, respectively, offer perspicuous discussions of retributivism and punishment. Also see Michael Davis, "How to Make the Punishment Fit the Crime," *Ethics,* Vol. 93 (July 1983), pp. 744 ff. and Herbert Morris, "Persons and Punishment," *The Monist* 52, no. 4 (October 1968), 475–50l, which argues that criminals have a natural, inalienable, and absolute right to be punished that derives from their fundamental right to be treated as a person. For a detailed and nuanced discussion of the issue of retributivism in punishment, see Marvin Henberg, *Retribution: Evil for Evil in Ethics, Law, and Literature* (Philadelphia: Temple University Press, 1990).

Capital Punishment

Among the many *books and anthologies on the death penalty,* see the selections and exchanges in Hugo Adam Bedau, *The Death Penalty in America,* 3rd ed. (New York: Oxford University Press, 1982); Ernest van den Haag and John P. Conrad, *The Death Penalty: A Debate* (New York: Plenum Press, 1983). Also see Walter Berns, *For Capital Punishment: Crime and the Morality of the Death Penalty* (New York: Basic Books, 1979); Charles Black, *Capital Punishment: The Inevitability of Caprice and Mistake,* 2nd ed. (New York: W.W. Norton, 1976); Robert Johnson, *Condemned to Die: Life Under Sentence of Death* (New York: Elsevier, 1981); Jeffrey H. Reiman, *The Rich Get Richer and the Poor Get Prison: Ideology, Class, and Criminal Justice,* 2nd ed. (New York: John Wiley, 1984); Stephen Nathanson, *An Eye for an Eye: The Morality of Punishing by Death* (Totowa, NJ: Rowman & Littlefield, 1987); and *The Death Penalty: Opposing Viewpoints,* edited by Carol Wekesser (San Diego: Greenhaven Press, 1991) contains a good balance of short pieces. For an excellent debate on this issue, see Louis P. Pojman and Jeffrey Reiman, *The Death Penalty: For and Against* (Lanthan: Rowman & Littlefield, 1998).

Among the many helpful *articles* on capital punishment, see Hugo Adam Bedau's excellent overview, analysis, and bibliography in "Capital Punishment," *The Encyclopedia of Ethics,* edited by Lawrence C. Becker and Charlotte B. Becker (New York: Garland, 1992), Vol. I, pp. 122–125; Stanley I. Benn, "Punishment," *The Encyclopedia of Philosophy* 7, ed. Paul Edwards (New York: Macmillan, 1967), p. 32 ff.; and Richard Wasserstrom, "Capital Punishment as Punishment: Some Theoretical Issues and Objections," *Midwest Studies in Philosophy,* Vol. 7, pp. 473–502, who raises a number of objections to capital punishment, not because it is capital, but because it is punishment.

On the *inhumanity of the death penalty,* Michael Davis has recently argued in "The Death Penalty, Civilization, and Inhumaneness," *Social Theory and Practice,* Vol. 16, No. 2 (Summer 1990), pp. 245–259, that the "argument from inhumaneness" advanced by Reiman and Bedau lacks an adequate account of inhumaneness. Jeffrey Reiman replied to Davis in "The Death Penalty, Deterrence, and Horribleness: Reply to Michael Davis," *Social Theory and Practice,* Vol. 16, No. 2 (Summer 1990), pp. 261–272. Also see Thomas A. Long, "Capital Punishment—'Cruel and Unusual'?" *Ethics,* Vol. 83 (April 1973), pp. 214–223 and the reply by Robert S. Gerstein, "Capital Punishment—'Cruel and Unusual': A Retributivist Response," Ethics, Vol. 85 (October 1974), pp. 75–79.

On the *irrevocability of capital punishment,* see Michael Davis, "Is The Death Penalty Irrevocable?" *Social Theory and Practice,* Vol. 10 (Summer 84), pp. 143–156, argues that there is no morally significant sense in which the death penalty is more irrevocable than life imprisonment; the death penalty is only distinctive in regard to the more modest claim about what we can do to correct error in application.

On the *arbitrariness of the death penalty,* see especially Christopher Meyers, in "Racial Bias, the Death Penalty, and Desert," *Philosophical Forum,* (Winter 1990–1991) pp. 139–148, supports *McCleskey v. Kemp* (1987), in which the Supreme Court ruled that racial bias was not sufficient ground for overturning a death sentence, as long as punishment is seen as retribution and as long as defendants do not receive more punishment than they deserve; Brian Calvert, in "Retribution, Arbitrariness and the Death Penalty," *Journal of Social Philosophy,* Vol. 23, No. 3 (Winter 92), pp. 140–165, which argues that the administration of the death penalty is arbitrary because there is not a sufficiently clear distinction in kind between murders that deserve execution and murders that deserve life imprisonment. On class bias in the criminal justice system, see especially Jeffrey Reiman, *The Rich Get Richer and the Poor Get Poorer,* 5th ed. (Boston: Allyn & Bacon, 1998).

On the *deterrent effect of the death penalty,* see Ernest Van Den Haag, "Deterrence and the Death Penalty: A Rejoinder," *Ethics,* Vol. 81 (October 1970), pp. 74–75; Hugo Adam Bedau, "A Concluding Note," *Ethics,* Vol. 81, (October 1970) p. 76; Michael Davis, "Death, Deterrence, and the Method of Common Sense," *Social Theory and Practice,* Vol. 7, (Summer 1981), pp. 145–178, uses what he calls the "method of common sense" to show that the death penalty is the most effective humane deterrent available to us. Steven Goldberg, "On Capital Punishment," *Ethics,* Vol. 85 (October 1974), pp. 67–74, argues in favor of capital punishment for its deterrent effect on potential criminals and George Schedler, "Capital Punishment and Its Deterrent Effect," *Social Theory and Practice,* Vol. 4 (Fall 76), pp. 47–56 refutes the "innocent people" argument. David A. Conway, "Capital Punishment and Deterrence: Some Considerations in Dialogue Form," *Philosophy & Public Affairs* 3, no. 4 (Summer 1974), pp. 433 ff.

On *mercy and the death penalty,* see Kathleen Dean Moore, *Pardons, Justice, Mercy, and the Public Interest* (New York: Oxford, 1989). For a personal memoir about his decisions, see Edmund G. (Pat) Brown, with Dick Adler, *Public Justice, Private Mercy. A Governor's Education on Death Row* (New York: Weidenfeld & Nicolson, 1989). On the relationship between retribution and mercy, see Marvin Henberg, *Retribution: Evil for Evil in Ethics, Law, and Literature* (Philadelphia: Temple University Press, 1990). Martha Minow's *Between Vengeance and Forgiveness: Facing History after Genocide and Mass Violence* (Boston: Beacon, 1998) is an excellent consideration of these issues in a different context than our domestic one.

On alternatives to punishment, see David C. Anderson, *Sensible Justice. Alternatives to Prison* (New York: The New Press, 1998) and Elliott Currie, *Crime and Punishment in America* (New York: Metropolitan Books, 1998).

PART TWO

Matters of Diversity and Equality

Conceptualizing the Issues

In the following four chapters, a wide range of issues—hate crimes, harassment, stereotyping, hate speech, welfare, to name but a few—will be raised. These issues often cut across the boundaries of the four chapters that deal with race, gender, sexual orientation, and economic inequality.

It is possible to approach each of these issues separately, one at a time. In fact, the public discussion of these issues often occurs precisely in this fashion, with pundits and politicians singling out specific problems for comment.

There is another way of approaching these issues that places the particular issues within a larger context. Let me suggest that we ask ourselves five questions.

1. **What would the ideal society look like in regard to each of these issues?** Consider, first of all, the issue of race. What would the ideal society look like in regard to race? Would race be as unimportant as, say, eye color? Would race be important to identity, but not an object of discrimination? Would each race, as separatists urge, try to maintain its own identity? Similar questions could be asked about gender, sexual orientation, and economic status.

2. **What would the minimally acceptable society look like in regard to each of these issues?** Again, consider race. Even if we were not able to achieve ideal racial conditions of harmony and understanding, we might still say that certain conditions must be met for a society to be morally acceptable at all. Hate crimes, for example, would have to be abolished; job discrimination should be eliminated.

3. **What is the present condition of society in regard to this issue?** For example, when you consider issues about affirmative action, one of the questions to answer is what is the actual condition of minority groups in our society today? This is an empirical question, and the social sciences are the disciplines that attempt to provide us with answers to this question.

4. **How do we best get from the actual condition to the minimally acceptable condition of society?** This presumes that, at least in some respects, the present situation does not meet minimal expectations. This question is also, at least in significant measure, an empirical question about

what works, about what is effective, in moving from one condition to another. Generally speaking, this is the realm of law and rights, the area of minimal requirements that must be guaranteed to all. It is also the area in which the least amount of compromise and tolerance is present.

5. **Finally, how do we get from the minimally acceptable state of society to the ideal one?** Once we move beyond the moral minimum to a consideration of the ideals toward which we are striving, we realize two things. First, there is more room for legitimate differences in regard to ideals. Reasonable people of good will can differ widely on these. Second, as a result of the first difference, the means of reaching the ideal state are generally persuasive rather than coercive. We seek to convince others of our ideals rather than to force them to comply. Public debate, education, and incentive programs are but a few of the possible means of getting to this ideal state.

The following diagram will help to visualize these five questions and their relationship to one another:

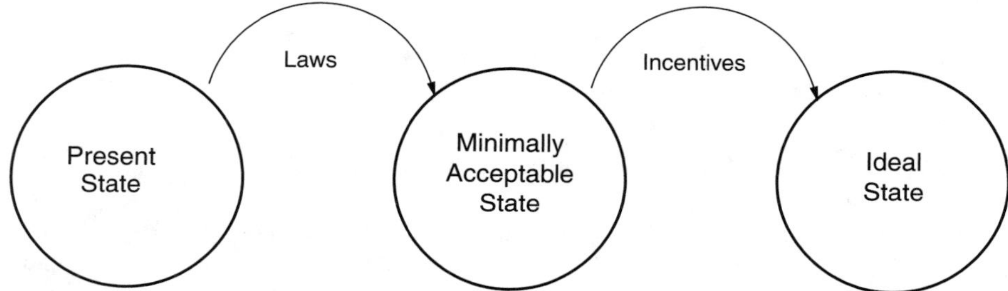

In each chapter of this section, this general framework has been converted to a specific questionnaire to help you to conceptualize your own stance on these issues and also to help to bring into focus both the similarities and the differences between your vision of society and the vision of your classmates.

CHAPTER 5

Race and Ethnicity

Videotape:

Topic: A Murder in Mississippi

ABCNEWS *Source:* ABC *Nightline* (May 29, 1998)

Anchors: John Donvan, Ted Koppel

NARRATIVE ACCOUNT

Studs Turkel
"Race: How Blacks and Whites Think and Feel about the American Obsession"

Studs Turkel, a longtime Chicagoan and host for the past thirty-five years of a talk show on WFMT radio in Chicago, is the author of several oral histories, including Working *and* The Good War. *This interview is drawn from his book,* Race: How Blacks and Whites Think and Feel about the American Obsession.

This selection, entitled "Clarence Page: 'It's a Boy!'" is a 1990 interview by Studs Turkel with Clarence Page, a columnist of the Chicago Tribune *and member of its editorial board. Mr. Page won the Pulitzer Prize for Commentary. He frequently appears as a television commentator. Except for a four-year absence, when he worked for the Chicago CBS station, he has been with the newspaper twenty years. He was the second black reporter ever hired by the* Tribune *as a full-time employee.*

When I broke in here as a police reporter, I learned a new phrase, "cheap it out." News out of black neighborhoods were viewed as cheap news. [Laughs.] If I got a tip on a double homicide, they'd say, "Oh, South Side. Cheap it out." Some old-timers still use the phrase. It was demeaning to me to see how this double standard worked.

If I was going to survive and make it as a reporter, I had to understand how news judgment was made. I got to be an assistant city editor. But it was so demoralizing to be a lonely voice around a big table of fellows who were largely suburban white male. Trying to sell them on the idea of a South Side homicide being as important as a North Side homicide was as incomprehensible as my speaking Martian. Eventually I decided I didn't want to be management anymore. I'd fight my battles elsewhere.

You could say there's a triple standard in black, white, and Hispanic news; rich, poor, and middle-class. One of my white colleagues said, "News is what happens near the news editor's house." That's why it's so important to have a multicultural newsroom.

The double standard is still there. A fire death in the inner city is not worth a fire death in the outer city. [Laughs.] Isn't that an interesting phrase, "inner city"? So is the word "underclass." When I say underclass to a black person, he tends to think of a specific pathological group with a specific set of problems. When I use the word with a white person, chances are better than even that he'll think black. Whites tend to generalize about blacks. We do the same thing, in a lot of ways. I may be doing it at this moment. All of us learn racial generalizations early on and it sticks with us. It frustrates me as a journalist.

I am optimistic. It comes from being around long enough to have seen things worse than they are. Twenty years ago, I was the only black person here. We have quite a few now—not enough, but a lot more than we used to.

I was in high school when the Voting Rights Act was passed. Segregation didn't bend with its passage. When we got a black mayor elected in Chicago, I saw a low-intensity race war break out. The young blacks find white people not nearly as enlightened as they expected. They find out how lonely it is to walk into a predominantly white newsroom. You're dealing with the same questions as a new arrival in town, as well as with some extra ones.

I learned that if it's dark out and I see a white friend, don't approach him too quickly. Don't startle him because the first thing he's going to see is a black man. I have startled people without meaning to. If I'm walking with a group of black males down the street, I'm aware that a white guy passing by might be scared. I imagine those black kids in Central Park were well aware of just how intimidating their presence was. To a large degree, they acted out what was expected of them.

If you expect a kid to be a thug, he's going to be one, nine times out of ten. If you have low expectations, he'll meet them. Today, our society has low expectations of young black males.

When I wake up in the morning and see my pregnant wife beside me, I know from ultrasound we'll probably have a boy. A young black male. How different I think as the father of a young black male than if I were a white father of a white male. There's a certain level of expectations society has of my kid different from the other one. If he's a teen-aged boy walking down the street wearing Adidas basketball shoes, jeans, and a troop jacket, he's regarded differently from a white teen-ager in Adidas basketball shoes, jeans, and a troop jacket. They wear the same outfit, yet are looked upon so differently.

I think of moving to the suburbs because of the schools. But I think: "Where will I be welcome? Where will I be possibly burned out?" In 1990, I think about that. If I were to move into a predominantly white suburb, the first thing that crosses their mind is not the Pulitzer Prize, it's "a black family in our neighborhood." Even among the most liberal white families, the question is: Is it bad for my property values?

What else do I think of when I wake up in the morning? Getting to work. I hope the weather's nice, because if it's bad, a taxi will pass me by and pick up a white person halfway down the block. It happens to me all the time. I'm dressed in a suit, tie, carry a briefcase. Just like the white guy who got the cab. I'm a member of the *Tribune* editorial board, right? I dress the role, right? Just getting to work, I think about that.

I'm conscious of how I'm dressed because I want this cabdriver to see that I'm not a welfare recipient. The average white guy may go out there in dirty blue jeans and expect the taxi to stop just like that. And it will. It will stop for him more quickly than for me, three-piece suit and everything.

When I'm on the El, I see people reacting certain ways. I've got prejudices, too, because I've dealt with pickpockets and purse-snatchers. I have formed a profile in my mind of such a potential thief: a young black male. I don't want to project that image to others, but I'm thinking it.

Black people are more afraid of crime than whites. They've got reason to be. We are victims of it more often. I've experienced a mugging, I've had a gun pointed at me, and a knife, and I've given over my wallet. I've had to deal with high-crime neighborhoods a lot. My family has experienced crime.

If you are Bernard Goetz with a gun in your pocket, I don't want you to feel intimidated. He shot four individuals, two of whom were going through the motions of intimidating him. Another was sitting on the bench, not even close to him, the one Goetz shot and paralyzed. He fell on the floor and played dead. Goetz looked at him and said, "You're not hurt so bad, here's another." So he pierced his spine and paralyzed the kid for life. This kid didn't even have a record. Because he was black and with the group, Goetz generalized. He shot them all.

The kid was from a middle-class home. He was eleven when his father died. His mother, now a single mom, low-income, moves back to the Bronx from which they had escaped. His life changed over night. What would happen to my wife and child if I died? What happens to people who are a paycheck away from poverty? This is something white folks don't think about when they see this new class of black folks getting into the mainstream. They don't think how many of us are only a paycheck away from poverty.

I don't worry about it as much as I used to. I'm finally starting to get comfortable with the fact that I'm not going to fall back out of the middle class. It took me years. Often, I wished I had the cavalier attitude of some of my white peers who grew up middle class.

When my wife told me she was half white, I asked her what she considered herself. She said, "I was raised by my mother to think I was mixed and I still think of myself that way. But society says I'm black, so I go along with it."

Black people are already a rainbow coalition, because even if you're black and Asian, you're black.

I'm always wondering what other people think of me. Even now. What they think of why I am where I am. Am I where I am because I'm black? It used to be: Would I be further advanced if I were white? Nowadays, people wonder: Am I being advanced because I'm black?

Now that I won the Pulitzer Prize, I wonder if people wonder if I won it because I'm non-white. [Laughs.] My predecessors, who deserved it, who toiled in the vineyards longer than I—did the judges feel obliged to give it to me? I have aspired to a new level of insecurity.

In my younger, single days, I'd go to these Rush Street bars just to spite them. I'd better explain. There are bars on the street that still have a reputation of giving young black people a hard time. We've learned to be sensitive about going where we're welcome and where we're not.

It didn't matter if I was a professional, they'd always give me the once-over and say, "You can't come in wearing jeans." I looked past the door and saw most of the guys in jeans. "You haven't got enough IDs." I always had a bunch of them with me.

Things have improved a lot. Kids who are fresh off the campus are a lot more comfortable with whites than my generation was. But the discomfort level is still there. You don't see any more of a black-white mix than you did twenty years ago.

Know what the problem is? We black folks didn't live up to the expectations of the white folks who helped us out during the civil-rights movement. They didn't live up to our expectations either, because we were expecting more of white folks than this.

We didn't live up to the expectations Jews had of us. They expected blacks, once Jim Crow was beaten, to aspire toward success the way Jews did: education. Blacks decided to aspire the way the Irish did: City Hall. Politics.

Black-Jewish tensions have been considerably overblown by the media. The coverage of Louis Farrakhan says it all. Among the great many black people, he's rated as useful and entertaining. An educated clown. People will fill Madison Square Garden and watch him for his entertainment value. How many have joined his movement? Very few. He can say anything and the media will rush out there.

When I worked for Channel 2, they chartered a plane and flew me and a crew to Indianapolis to cover a routine Farrakhan speech. We had to put it on the air that night. It was his usual stuff, nothing extraordinary. I know why they sent me down there. They were hoping he'd say something outrageous. This is their thing.

Naturally, Farrakhan welcomes all this attention. What respect he has from black people comes to anybody who stands up to white folks and tells it like it is. My wife was thrilled when I took her to see him. She heard so much about him as entertaining. Did she become a follower? No. There is a side of us as black people that resents the way we are ignored as individuals, the way mainstream America insults us. In a way, Farrakhan is feeding off that sentiment.

I wake up in the morning, watch the news, and hear of a heinous crime. "I hope he's not black" is the first thought that crosses my mind. Before I even see the picture on TV. A lot of black folks are the same way. When I was a kid, my uncle used to say, "Please, Lord, don't let it be black."

A white backlash is the last thing that worries us now. We've always had a backlash, but never called it that. Why should we worry about it now? The truth is we don't fear white people anymore. We don't have the kind of fear our fathers and grandfathers had.

Our lives are still controlled by white people, and that's still on our minds. Malcolm X once put the question: Why do the media never refer to all-white neighborhoods as segregated? An all-black neighborhood is always referred to as segregated. Why? Because they know who's doing the segregating. Black people didn't segregate themselves. An all-white neighborhood is never referred to as a ghetto, yet the youngsters who grow up there are socially deprived of the benefits that come from a pluralistic society. Many grow up socially disabled.

So when I wake up in the morning and see my pregnant wife and the odds are overwhelming it's going to be a boy, a young black male. . . . [Trails off:]*

Journal/Discussion Questions

✍ *Reflect on your own reactions to this interview. To what extent does your own race and ethnicity shape those reactions?*

1. Truth is often found, not just in general theories, but in the details of everyday life. What aspects of this interview surprised you? What details revealed truths not generally acknowledged?
2. Do you agree with Mr. Page about the extent of racism in our own society today? Discuss.

* It was a boy.

AN INTRODUCTION TO THE MORAL ISSUES

The issues of race and ethnic identity have always been central to American society, yet at the same time our American identity as a "melting pot" has in part been forged on the basis of denying this as the principal basis of our identity.

Recall our threefold structure for analyzing these issues: the problem, the ideal, and the means for going from one to the other. We will begin by considering the facts of racism, turn to a consideration of the various ideals, and then discuss which means offer the most hope of moving us from actual situation toward the ideal. But first, a few words about a basic distinction.

Race and Ethnicity

What is the difference between race and ethnicity?

Although distinct concepts, race and ethnicity are obviously related to one another. Generally, anthropologists see *race* as a physical characteristic. They recognize the existence of three or four major racial groups: Caucasoid, Negroid, Mongoloid, and sometimes Australoid. (The U.S. Census Bureau, on the other hand, recognizes four races, adding Native American—which anthropologists consider as part of Mongoloid—to the first three.) *Ethnicity,* on the other hand, refers primarily to social and cultural forms of identification and self-identification. There are many more ethnic identities than racial ones. The English, French, Italians, Germans, and Poles all share a common race, but they consider themselves ethnically different.

Several points should be noted about these concepts. First, race inevitably has a socially constituted meaning, and it is at this point the distinction between race and ethnicity is somewhat less clear-cut. Whatever race is, it isn't *just* a physical characteristic. Second, although we have a clear term to denote discrimination based on race (namely, racism), we lack a corresponding term to indicate discrimination based on ethnicity. However, ethnically based discrimination (witness the atavistic conflicts of Eastern Europe) is often of the same structure as racism, and sometimes masquerades as racially based when it is actually ethnically grounded. Third, it is worth noting that, at least in the United States, we tend to think of racial categories as mutually exclusive. In forms asking about race, we are usually asked to "check one of the following: white, black, Asian or American Indian." However, some of us are either remotely (i.e., back at least two generations) or recently (i.e., our parents or grandparents) of mixed race. Forms that allow individuals to acknowledge the plurality of their racial and ethnic identities would not only be more accurate, but also less polarizing for society as a whole.

The Facts of Racism

Racism has been a pervasive and disturbing fact of American society. The very founding of the United States is inextricably bound up with the racism that characterized our treatment of Native Americans and, soon thereafter, with the racism that helped to make slavery possible. The legacy, and in some cases the continuing reality, of that racism is still with us today. Most Americans in their forties and older grew up in a world where racial discrimination was still legally sanctioned. African-Americans (and others as well) were *legally* denied access to schools, jobs, neighborhoods, churches, clubs, and the voting booth well into the middle 1960s. Although such discrimination continues to some extent today, it is no longer done under the sanction of law.

The word *racism* is both descriptive and evaluative. As a *descriptive* term, it refers to certain attitudes and actions that (a) single out certain people on the basis of their racial—or, in some cases, ethnic—heritage and (b) disadvantage them in some way on this basis. (The second element, disadvantaging someone on the basis of race, has to be present or else simple categorization—such as one finds in a census—would be racist.) College admissions policies that excluded African-Americans on the basis of their race would be a clear example of racism. Yet *racism* also has an *evaluative* element: it conveys a negative value judgment that racism is morally objectionable, evil. The evaluative element may refer primarily to the *intention* behind the practice or to the *consequences* of such a practice.

This distinction between intention and consequence also provides part of the foundation for a distinction between *overt racism* and *institutional racism.* Gertrude Ezorsky, for example, sees overt racist action as grounded in "the agent's racial bias against the victim or in a willingness to oblige the racial prejudice of others" (*Racism and Justice,* p. 249). In the case of institutional racism, no negative value judgment is made about the agents' intentions. Their actions might not be intended to harm a particular racial group at all, although this may be an unintended consequence. The negative value judgment is reserved primarily for the *consequences* of such actions and policies.

It is important, both morally and politically, to distinguish between government-sanctioned racism and racism that occurs without such official endorsement. When our government enacts racist laws—such as separate schooling, housing—then it acts in our name as citizens, and it seems reasonable to argue that we as citizens are under an obligation to those who have been wronged. On the other hand, when an individual restaurant owner illegally discriminates against a potential patron on the basis of race, it does not seem that we as citizens are under the same kind of obligation to those who have been wronged because the restaurant owner was not acting in our names. Virtually all ethnic minorities have been subject to unfair treatment at one time or another in American history, but only a few—most notably, Native Americans, African Americans, and Japanese-Americans—have been the object of governmentally-sanctioned discrimination. The government would seem to have a special obligation in those cases in which groups have been wronged, not just by individuals, but by the government itself. Furthermore, we as citizens may be obligated to compensate wronged groups because such discrimination was done in our name.

Compensatory Programs

How do we respond morally to the fact of racism in our society and the role that it has played in our history? One response has been to suggest that we owe *compensation* to those who have been wronged. Compensatory programs, which seek to indemnify previously wronged individuals or groups, are essentially backward-looking; they seek to determine who has been wronged in the past and to make up for it in the present and future. Here the issue of governmental sanction assumes special importance. Insofar as racist discrimination was legally required in the past, it was done in our name as citizens. Consequently, we as citizens have a debt to compensate such discrimination. We do not have the same debt in the case of illegal discriminatory acts by individuals. In those cases, racist individuals may owe a debt of compensation to those they have discriminated against; but since they did not discriminate in our name, we are not under the same compensatory debt merely as citizens.

Presumably compensatory programs are limited in scope to a repayment of the debt incurred by the wrong. There is a strong case, for example, that the United States as a whole owes a compensatory debt to many Native American tribes for the various ways in which those tribes have been mistreated by the U. S. government. Moreover, the death of those who have been wronged does not nullify the compensatory debt. It makes both moral and legal sense to compensate the descendants of those who have been wronged or the group as a whole, even if those who were originally wronged are now dead.

Similarly, compensatory programs do not necessarily demand that the current recipients be in a negative condition. Consider, for example, the Japanese-Americans who were wrongfully incarcerated during World War II. It is certainly possible that we might conclude that they should be compensated for the wrong imposed upon them by our government, even if they have subsequently achieved economic success. This is little different, some would argue, from repaying a debt: the obligation to repay is not diminished by the fact that the person to whom the debt is owed has just won the lottery.

It is important to realize the morally symbolic value of such programs, which is often as important as any monetary value. When we commit ourselves as a country to compensate those who have been wronged by us as a country—the case of the indemnification of Japanese Americans interned in detention camps is an example of this—we are acknowledging our guilt as a country and stating our willingness to rectify the harm that we have caused. There is, as it were, a totaling of the public moral ledger that is often important in the process of moral reconciliation. When those who have been harmed feel that the perpetrators (a) genuinely recognize that they have done wrong, and (b) are genuinely trying to make up for the actual harm they caused, then it becomes much easier for the victims to put the wrong behind them and heal the moral rift between themselves and the perpetrators.

Such compensatory programs are different, at least in their moral logic, from future-oriented programs—whether equal rights approaches or affirmative action programs—that seek to create some future goal of equality. Similarly, because compensatory programs are essentially backward-looking, differing ideals of the place of race and ethnicity in society are irrelevant to them. In future-oriented programs, on the other hand, the ideals we are striving to realize are of paramount importance. Let us now turn to a consideration of such future-oriented programs, beginning first with a consideration of the ideals that they may be striving to implement.

Ideals of the Place of Race in Society

What, precisely, is our ideal in regard to the place of race and ethnicity in our society? Several possible models suggest themselves, ranging from strongly separatist models to highly assimilationist ones. The ideal to which we are committed will have important implications for the means we choose for eradicating racism. Let's briefly consider each type of ideal.

Separatist Models

Despite claims about being a "melting pot," the United States has a long history of racial—and, often, ethnic—separatism. Sometimes separatism is imposed from outside the group, sometimes it comes from within. Racial separatism was often imposed in laws against Native Americans, African-Americans, and (during World War II) Japanese and Japanese-Americans. The intent of such legislation was both to keep the races separate and to maintain the supremacy of the white race in particular.

Why do some groups find separatism an attractive option in the United States?

Separatism has often been a comparatively attractive option for comparatively small groups whose culture would easily be obliterated by the larger culture of the society if it were not protected in some way. Some Native American tribes (members of the Acoma Pueblo, for example) have chosen to maintain a largely separate life, sheltered from the intrusions of outsiders, as a way of preserving their own identity. Separatist groups may be constituted along strictly ethnic lines—the major eastern cities of the United States often contained numerous ethnic neighborhoods in which residents could easily go about their day-to-day affairs without having to know English—and sometimes on the basis of religious commitments. The Amish and the Mennonites, for example, have long been committed to a largely separatist view of their place in American society as a whole, and many major religions exhibit a separatist current in monasteries, cloistered convents, and the like. Similarly, some utopian communities have preferred a separatist model of their place in society. Typically, most of these groups ask little from the larger world around them except to be left alone.

Clearly, there is no moral justification for *imposing* separatism on others, and such attempts are almost always conjoined with either overt or covert beliefs in the racial supremacy of those in control. Self-imposed separatism is a morally more ambiguous matter, and key to its evaluation are the questions of what the proponents of separatism propose to preserve and why they want to preserve it. Moreover, we must recognize that separatism is usually a matter of degree. Only a few are at the far extreme of not wanting to share anything—language, products, transportation—with the surrounding society.

The strongest argument in support of self-imposed racial or ethnic separatism is what we can call *the identity argument*. It maintains that a firm sense of one's race and ethnicity is a necessary component of one's identity as a person, and that this sense of racial and ethnic identity can be preserved only through separatism. These issues are often discussed under the heading of "the politics of identity" or "the politics of recognition," and this has been a principal concern for many racial and ethnic groups that fear their identities will be lost through immersion in the larger society.

Critics of such separatist models maintain that, while some degree of separatism may be workable, strongly separatist models threaten to undermine the sense in which we have a national identity at all. Moreover, some argue that some separatists are inconsistent: they both want to be left alone by the larger society and at the same time be provided with the benefits of that larger society.

Assimilationist Models

The "melting pot" metaphor of American society suggests a model of American society that is primarily assimilationist. Differences are largely obliterated, melted down, and the result is a homogeneous nation of citizens. Indeed, this seems to have occurred with most immigrant groups from western and eastern Europe. Many whose ethnic background is European identify themselves primarily as American and only secondarily—and sometimes not at all—in terms of their ethnic European background. Traditional liberalism in the United States has been strongly committed to an assimilationist model, at least within the political realm.

The tension between separatist and assimilationist models comes out in various areas of daily life and public policy. For example, one of the principal issues in publicly funded education is whether it should seek to encourage such assimilation or whether it should seek to encourage the preservation and development of racial and ethnic identity.

Pluralistic Models

Somewhere between these two extremes is a middle ground that both respects diversity and at the same time tries to establish the minimal conditions necessary to a common life—a shared political life even if not a shared community. The principal thrust of a pluralistic model is to suggest, first, that there are certain minimal conditions necessary to the establishment of a common life; second, that specific groups may maintain a partially separate identity without negating that common life; and, third, that the identity of any given individual is constituted through both participation in the common life and through identification with any number of specific groups.

What model of race and ethnicity do pluralists support?

Pluralists do not even need to posit that different groups in society exhibit some fundamental agreement with one another. Consider an analogous issue: pacifism. I am not a pacifist. I do not believe that all killing of human beings is wrong, but I am glad that I live in a society in which some people are pacifists. Their presence reminds me of a truth, albeit a partial truth, that human life is of inestimable importance and ought not to be destroyed if that can be avoided. On the other hand, I am glad that I do not live in a society in which everyone is a pacifist. Not only would I feel morally lonely in such a world, but I would fear that it would lack the resilience to defend itself in the face of aggressive evil if faced with such a challenge. The tension between pacifists and nonpacifists is a good thing for our society as a whole and for each of us as individuals, and our lives would be diminished if we did not have one of these two opposing groups. Nor are these opposing groups without common ground. They both respect life—or, at least, most of both groups do most of the time. No one advocates indiscriminate killing, and those who defend killing at all usually do so through an appeal to some core values, including the value of innocent life (which can be preserved through self-defense or whose loss can be avenged through capital punishment).

So, too, with racial and ethnic pluralism. Our world is richer for the diversity of our traditions, and there is no need to make everyone be like us. Indeed, I can feel that our world is a better place precisely because there are people who are *not* like me. The diversity of racial and ethnic traditions is a source of richness for the society as a whole, providing a wealth of possibilities far beyond the scope of any single ethnic tradition. That wealth of possibilities becomes especially important whenever we need help, whenever we run out of possibilities dealing with a specific issue, for we can then turn to the wisdom of other ethnic traditions to discover new and potentially better ways of dealing with that issue.

Finally, we should note that pluralism is multidimensional in the following sense. Pluralists would typically not only favor a diversity of ethnic traditions, but would also maintain that we as individuals are members of a wide range of communities, many of which may have little or nothing to do with race and ethnicity. There are many lines of affiliation in which ethnicity plays no role: computer hackers, smokers, people who hate to fly. Pluralists typically see a plurality of identities within the individual, not just within society as a whole.

Multiculturalism, Separatism, and Pluralism

Descriptive multiculturalism. In the past decade, multiculturalism has become a buzz word whose meaning is far from clear. All too often, it becomes a political rallying cry for both its opponents and proponents. At its most innocuous, *multicultural* is simply a descriptive term referring to societies that contain more than one cultural tradition within themselves. On this definition of *multicultural,* many societies are multicultural. Yet there is a second, more normative meaning of *multicultural* that sets forth an *ideal* of how societies should treat the various cultural traditions in their midst.

What is multiculturalism?

Separatist multiculturalism. There is no single, normative sense of the ideal of multiculturalism, but for the purposes of analysis we can distinguish two currents that run through contemporary discussions of multiculturalism. One ideal of multiculturalism is separatist in character. It sees racial or ethnic identity as the principal—or at least omnipresent—component of personal identity, and it emphasizes racial and ethnic affiliations. *Who you are* is constituted, first and foremost, by your race and ethnicity; consequently, you are first and foremost *the same* as those who have the same race or ethnicity and *different from* anyone who does not share that race or ethnicity. Identity is constituted by race and ethnicity, and races and ethnicities are mutually exclusive. If you're one race and ethnicity, you're not the other. This seems, at least to me, to emphasize the ways in which races and ethnicities are different, to accentuate what sets them apart and to deemphasize what they have in common.

Pluralistic multiculturalism. There is a second sense of multiculturalism which is more closely affiliated with pluralism. This strain of multiculturalism sees racial and ethnic diversity as good, but (a) does not see racial and ethnic identities as necessarily exclusive and (b) sees individual identity as only partially constituted by racial or ethnic affiliations. Let's consider each of these two points.

First, in this pluralistic model of multiculturalism, an individual may have several racial or ethnic affiliations and affirming one need not be done at the expense of affirming the others. One may, for example, be African-American and Jewish, and affirming one identity does not entail denying the other identity.

Second, in the pluralistic model of multiculturalism, one's principal identity may not have much to do with one's race or ethnicity. One's principal identity may be religious—one may be a Baha'i or a Pentecostal or a Buddhist, and one's sense of self may be primarily constituted along that axis. Or one's primary identity may be constituted through parenting, job, avocation, or any number of other factors. Identity, in other words, is a more widely varied and richly textured thing than separatist multiculturalism would suggest.

Pluralistic multiculturalism, in other words, is not committed either to belief that racial and ethnic identities are mutually exclusive or to the belief the personal identities are necessarily primarily constituted along racial or ethnic lines.

Pluralistic multiculturalism also allows us to recognize that race and ethnicity may not even be the principal issues in some disputes. For example, the moral issue about separatist groups in the United States may not actually be primarily along the separatist/assimilationist axis, but rather along a quite different axis that sometimes overlaps with the issue of separatist: the group's attitude toward outside groups. To the extent that group identity is tied up with hatred or oppression of other groups, then we are morally justified in objecting to that particular aspect of the group's identity. Although such hatred and oppression are perhaps more characteristic of separatist groups simply because it would be inconsistent to advocate assimilation of groups one hates or oppresses, there is nothing intrinsic to separatism that entails hatred or oppression of other groups. *Lawrence A. Blum's* article, *"Philosophy and the Values of a Multicultural Community,"* provides an insightful discussion of the minimal values we should encourage in multicultural communities.

The Means to Our Ideals

Let's imagine, simply for the sake of discussion, that we have general agreement about our actual situation and about the ideal condition toward which we are striving. The question that then presents itself is how we are to move from one to the other. In general, we can distinguish several kinds of approaches. First, *equal rights approaches* seek to insure that previously discriminated against groups are henceforth treated in a scrupulously fair manner. Such approaches seek to eliminate discrimination in the future, but are often unable to significantly reduce the cumulative and continuing effects of past patterns of discrimination. Second, *affirmative action approaches* attempt to provide some kind of special support, consideration, or advantage to groups that have previously been discriminated against. These have the advantage of seeking to undo the residual effects of past discrimination, but they run the risk of being viewed as further discrimination. Finally, *special protection approaches* provide selected groups with stronger-than-usual protection of the law in specific areas relating to their identity as a group. Regulations banning hate speech, for example, give extra protection of law to certain groups. Such approaches stand midway between equal rights approaches and affirmative action approaches, providing more than extra protection but less than affirmative action in protection of certain groups.

Equal Rights Approaches

Since *Brown v. Board of Education* in 1954, the United States has increasingly committed itself to equal rights for all citizens, regardless of race. The Civil Rights Act of 1964 extended and deepened this commitment, and there are few today who would argue publicly that some citizens ought to be denied their civil rights on the basis of race or discriminated against because of race. Such a commitment was implicit in our Constitution and is increasingly central to our identity as a nation.

It is important to note, however, that there is often a huge gulf between commitment to the general principle of equal rights and commitment to the specific means of insuring such equality. This is particularly the case where there are existing, often deeply ingrained patterns of discrimination. To what extent does the government take an active role in (a) discouraging such attitudes of discrimination and (b) punishing acts of discrimination? Consider, for example, the issue of discrimination in housing. Is the cause of equal rights in this area adequately served by simply passing a law forbidding such discrimination? Should special enforcement agencies be established?

Affirmative Action Programs

Four senses of affirmative action. Affirmative action is a notoriously slippery term, and it is important to define precisely what we mean when we use it. There are several possible senses of the term. If we consider it just within the context of hiring potential employees, we can distinguish four senses, two of which are weak, the other two of which are strong.

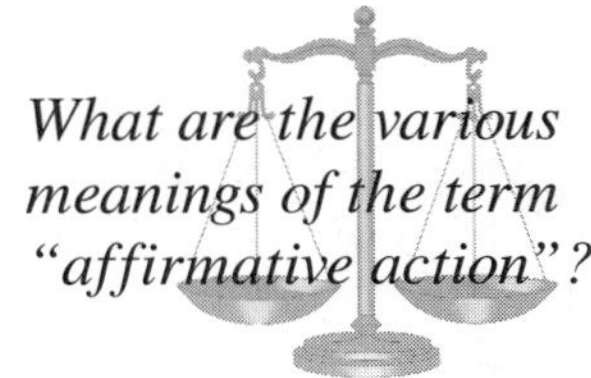

What are the various meanings of the term "affirmative action"?

Weak senses of affirmative action:

1. Encouraging the largest possible number of minority applications in the applicant pool, and then choosing the best candidates regardless of gender, race, and so on.
2. When the two best candidates are equally qualified and one is a minority candidate, choosing the minority candidate.

Strong senses of affirmative action:

3. From a group of candidates, all of whom are qualified, choosing the minority candidate over better-qualified nonminority ones.
4. Choosing an unqualified minority candidate over a qualified nonminority one.

The third and fourth alternatives involve choosing a minority candidate over a better qualified nonminority one. Almost no one *advocates* the fourth alternative, although critics sometimes claim that support for the third alternative in theory leads, in practice, to the fourth alternative. Many are willing to support the third alternative. Proponents of affirmative action often argue that the first two types of affirmative action, although commendable, are often insufficient to break the cycle of past discrimination and that a more active program—that is, the third type of program—is necessary if affirmative action is to achieve its goal.

Forward-looking defenses of strong affirmative action programs usually contain three crucial elements. First, they need some criterion for determining when racist discrimination exists in a particular area. Second, they need to show that affirmative action programs are the best means of achieving the desired equality. Finally, they need to deal with the objection that merit, not race, should determine who gets jobs and admissions to educational institutions. Let's look at each of these three elements.

Equality, equal representation, and quotas. The general goal of affirmative action programs is a discrimination-free society. The question immediately arises about how we determine when we have reached a discrimination-free society, when we have achieved genuine equality of opportunity. One commonly proposed indicator that we have reached this goal is the proportional representation of racial groups in various types of jobs. If there is proportional representation of whites, blacks, Asians, and Native Americans among physicians, for example, this is taken as evidence that we have genuine equality of opportunity and that there is no racism at work here. Conversely, lack of proportional representation is taken as *prima facie* evidence of racism, and it is this course of reasoning that leads so easily to quotas. Critics of this argument maintain that lack of proportional representation might be due to numerous other factors besides racism. Inequality of outcome, they argue, does not necessarily entail inequality of opportunity.

The best means to achieving equality. Second, defenders of affirmative action must show that such programs are the only—or at least the best, the most efficient, or the speediest—way of reaching the goal of equality in society. If, they argue, we are committed to a society in which all professions are equally accessible to all groups, and if one of the conditions of accessibility is that a significant number of one's own group *already* be represented in that profession, then some type of active intervention would seem to be necessary in order to change the composition of that profession. Strong affirmative action is seen as the only way of breaking the circle of disadvantage. Presumably, once proportional representation is achieved, then the need for such programs will diminish.

Such forward-looking justifications of strong affirmative action assume, however, that affirmative action programs will have the intended consequences—and only those consequences. This is an empirical claim and open to much dispute. Part of the dispute over affirmative action during the past decade has been an empirical one. What are the *actual* consequences of affirmative action programs? Critics of such programs point out that affirmative action programs have had unintended and undesirable consequences that undermine their effectiveness. They have stigmatized minorities in professions shaped by such programs, undermining the accomplishments of those minority persons who have succeeded without the help of affirmative action programs. Moreover, advocates of such programs have underestimated the degree of resentment such programs have created among nonminorities, especially white males. Finally, some have maintained that such programs foster a culture of dependency and victimhood that is ultimately not beneficial to anyone.

The critique of meritocracy. Since the most common objection to affirmative action programs of the third type is that the job should go to the most qualified candidate, the defense of type three programs is often supplemented with an attack on both the theory and the practice of meritocracy. The *theory* of meritocracy (i.e., jobs should always go to the most qualified) is attacked in two ways. First, one may argue that merit is only one among many possibly relevant criteria that can be used when giving people jobs or admitting people to schools. After all, don't many colleges and universities have strong affirmative action programs for recruiting student athletes in money-making sports such as college football? Second, one can enlarge the notion of merit and qualification to include other factors (such as race, ethnicity, or gender) not usually included. For example, if one wants to increase the number of role models of physicians for African-Americans, then race might become a relevant qualification for medical school. The *practice* of meritocracy is also often attacked, and here the argument is that institutions do not in fact live up to their own professed standards of meritocratic neutrality. Colleges and universities may, for example, give special consideration to the children of their alums; employers may give jobs to relatives; superficially neutral requirements such as letters of recommendation may actually be part of an insiders' network, often an "old boys' network." The significance of these various attacks is to undermine the claim that a position either should or even usually does go to the most qualified candidate.

Extended senses of affirmative action. Affirmative action programs are not limited to employment and admissions requirements. School busing programs that are designed to achieve racial balance in city schools are affirmative action programs, and we can draw a parallel distinction between equal rights approaches and affirmative action programs. Equal rights approaches would prohibit any school district from rejecting any otherwise qualified applicant on the basis of race or ethnicity. The limitation of such approaches, however, is that schools then continue to perpetuate the racial divisions of historically segregated neighborhoods, neighborhoods that may still be economically segregated in ways that reflect earlier patterns of racial segregation. Busing then becomes a way of acting affirmatively to establish racial balance in schools that otherwise would not be so balanced.

In awarding government contracts, the government often provides financial incentives to firms that either are minority-owned or who subcontract a certain percentage of their work to minority-owned businesses. This, too, is an extended form of affirmative action, one which the Supreme Court has said must now be subject to strict scrutiny.

In American society today, affirmative action programs are the focus of tremendous controversy. As the readings in this section show, this is not simply a division between those in favor of racial equality and those opposed to it. It is a far more complex problem, with both black and white advocates of racial equality on both sides of the question and with charges of racism being leveled against both proponents and opponents of strong affirmative action.

Special Protection Programs

In recent years, some attempts have been made to provide special protection to particular groups on the basis of race. Such programs do not qualify as affirmative action programs, but they clearly go beyond simple equal rights guarantees. Consider two examples: interracial adoptions and hate speech laws.

Interracial adoption. As the number of interracial adoptions began to increase in the 1960s, the National Association of Black Social Workers urged in 1972 that "Black children should be placed only with black families whether for foster care or for adoption, because black children in white homes are cut off from the healthy development of themselves as black people." Many local child welfare agencies soon developed guidelines that forbid interracial adoptions, even when this resulted in many children not being adopted. The principal rationale was that children need to be in the same-race family to develop a sense of their racial identity, and that the government is committed to fostering the development of that sense of identity. Some African-Americans go further, arguing that such adoptions are a form of racial genocide, and that the government must provide special protection to them as a result.

Hate speech. Another area in which attempts at special protection have been made is hate speech. Advocates of such protection maintain that racist speech is often deeply damaging to minorities, and that the government ought to provide special protection to them against such speech. This special protection has been criticized on three grounds. First, it severely limits the right of free speech, which has a very strong constitutional foundation in the United States. In the eyes of the critics of such restrictions, it is not clear that the possible benefits outweigh the accompanying loss of freedom. Second, such restrictions are usually framed in such a way as to protect minorities in particular from such speech, but in the interests of equality shouldn't such protection be extended to all races and ethnicities? Yet in the past when it has existed, hate speech laws have typically been used to oppress racial minorities rather than protect them. Finally, there is a disturbingly large element of vagueness in such legislation. Precisely what counts as "hate speech" and what doesn't?

Common Ground

As a nation, we have clearly committed ourselves to a society in which racism is not to be tolerated. We certainly sometimes fail to live up to this commitment, some of us may not share the commitment, and some may even view some of the remedies (such as affirmative action) as further instances of the problem (i.e., racism), but virtually no one advocates a society in which basic human rights are distributed differentially according to race.

Some in our society, even if they don't advocate unequal civil rights, do advocate hatred of other racial and ethnic groups. Few, however, truly believe that other groups should hate *them.* Their racially based hatred, in other words, is not something that they are willing to universalize. Nor is it something that we have to condone.

The elimination, or at least reduction, of inequalities caused by racial and ethnic discrimination is a complex matter, and here we find, even among people of good will who are committed to eradicating the legacy of racism in our society, there is deep disagreement about how this can best be accomplished. Certain programs, most notably strong affirmative action programs, have elicited great controversy and resentment. If there is a common ground here, it is probably to be found in searching for other means that promote the same goal with fewer liabilities.

Race and Ethnicity Questionnaire: Developing an Overview

1. What is the actual state of American society today in regard to race and ethnicity?
   a. Overall, the actual state of race and ethnicity in American society is:
      i. Excellent
      ii. Very good
      iii. Good
      iv. Poor
      v. Terrible
   b. List three important facts that support your evaluation.
   c. What are the three most important issues in regard to race and ethnicity today?
2. What are the minimum conditions necessary for a just society in regard to race and ethnicity? List at least three characteristics or conditions.
3. What are the ideal conditions necessary for a just society in regard to race and ethnicity? List at least three characteristics or conditions.
4. How should we get from the actual state to the minimally acceptable state? List specific ways of getting from the actual state of society to the minimal conditions listed above.
5. How should we get from the actual state to the ideal state? List specific ways of getting from the actual state of society to the ideal conditions listed above.

The Arguments

Bernard R. Boxill
"Equality, Discrimination, and Preferential Treatment"

Bernard Boxill is a professor of philosophy at the University of North Carolina at Chapel Hill. He works in social and political philosophy and African American philosophy. He is the author of Blacks and Social Justice, *and is currently finishing a book,* Boundaries and Justice, *on international ethics and distributive justice.*

In this article, Bernard Boxill presents the case for preferential treatment. He distinguishes between backward-looking arguments and forward-looking arguments, and examines the egalitarian principles upon which they are based.

As You Read, Consider This:

1. What, according to Boxill, is the difference between backward-looking arguments for preferential treatment and forward-looking ones?
2. In what way do arguments for preferential treatment depend on egalitarian principles?
3. What are the principal objections to backward-looking arguments according to Boxill? How does he reply to those objections?
4. What are the principal objections to forward-looking arguments according to Boxill? How does he reply to those objections?

Looking back on the United States Supreme Court's 1954 decision against segregated schools, and the civil rights revolution it started, many people in the late twentieth century began to hope that America's sense of fair play had finally gained the upper hand over prejudice and racism. They were therefore bitterly disappointed when, more than thirty years after that historic decision, a wave of racial incidents swept major American universities. They were aware, of course, that racism persisted; they would have been saddened, but not surprised to hear of comparable or even worse incidents in some rural backwater in the deep South. But these incidents had happened in the North, and in traditional bastions of enlightenment and liberalism like the universities of Massachusetts, Michigan, Wisconsin, as well as Dartmouth, Stanford, and Yale. What had caused the setback?

According to some pundits, the blame should be placed on preferential treatment. Writing in *Commentary,* for example, Charles Murray maintained that preferential treatment promotes racism because it maximizes the likelihood that blacks hired for a job, or admitted to a university, will be less capable than the whites beside them; and, he warned ominously that the recent racial incidents were only a thin leading edge of what we may expect in the coming years.[1]

The advocates of preferential treatment reply that although preferential treatment may provoke immediate animosity it will in the long run lead to a racially and sexually harmonious society. Many also maintain that it is justified because it helps to compensate those who have been wrongly harmed by racist and sexist practices and attitudes. This essay is an attempt to evaluate these claims.

As the preceding paragraph suggests, there are two main kinds of argument for preferential treatment. The first, forward-looking argument, justifies preferential treatment because of its supposed good consequences. The second, backward-looking argument, justifies preferential treatment as compensation for past wrongful injuries. In this section I will briefly describe these arguments and the egalitarian principles they rely on. Let us begin with the backward-looking argument.

The most plausible version of the backward-looking argument relies on the principle of equal opportunity. The controlling idea of this principle is that the positions in a society should be distributed on the basis of a fair competition among individuals. It has two parts, both necessary to capture that idea. The first is that positions should be awarded to individuals with the qualities and abilities enabling them best to perform the functions expected of those filling the positions. Thus it requires that individuals be evaluated for positions strictly on the basis of their qualifications for those positions. The second is that individuals should have the same chances to acquire the qualifications for desirable positions. At a minimum this requires that elementary and secondary schools provide everyone with the same advantages whether they are rich or poor, black or white, male of female, handicapped or whole.

Most societies routinely violate both parts of the equal opportunity principle. In most societies, for example, people are frequently ruled out of consideration for positions simply because they are handicapped, or aged, or female, or members of a racial minority. And in most societies these violations of the first part of the equal opportunity principle are compounded by violations of the second part of the equal opportunity principle. Schools for the rich are usually better than schools for the poor; schools for whites are usually better than schools for blacks; talented girls are steered away from careers in engineering, architecture, and the physical sciences; and the handicapped are more or less generally ignored.

Advocates of the backward-looking argument for preferential treatment maintain that violations of the equal opportunity principle are seriously unjust, and that those who have been harmed by these violations normally deserve compensation. In particular, they argue that preferential treatment is justified as a convenient means of compensating people who have been systematically denied equal opportunities on the basis of highly visible characteristics like being female or black.

Let us now consider the forward-looking argument. Advocates of this argument believe that preferential treatment will not only help to equalize opportunities by breaking down racial and sexual stereotypes, but will also have deeper and more important egalitarian consequences. To understand what these consequences are it is necessary to see that the equal opportunity principle has limitations as an egalitarian principle.

If we relied exclusively on the equal opportunity principle to distribute positions, we would tend to put the more talented in the more desirable positions. Since these positions usually involve work which is intrinsically more satisfying than the work other positions involve, our practice would tend to do more to satisfy the interests of the more talented in having satisfying work than to satisfy the like interests of the less talented. Further, because the more desirable positions generally pay better than the less desirable positions, use of the equal opportunity principle to distribute positions would also enable the more talented more fully to satisfy their other interests than the less talented, insofar at least as satisfying these other interests costs money.

In general then, exclusive reliance on the equal opportunity to distribute positions would tend to give greater weight to satisfying the interests of the more talented than to satisfying the like interest of the less talented. This violates the general principle of equal consideration of interests which forbids giving any person's interests greater or lesser weight than the like interests of any other person. This principle does not presuppose any factual equality among individuals, for example, that they are equal in intelligence or rationality or moral personality. Consequently, it is not contradicted by the fact that some people are more talented than others, and it does not have to be withdrawn because of that fact. It is a fundamental moral principle. It says that whatever the differences between people are, equal weight ought to be given to their like interests.

The principle of equal consideration of interests is the moral basis of the principle of equal opportunity. That principle has a limited place in egalitarian theories because it helps to implement the principle of equal consideration of interests. For, although it tends to give greater weight to the interests of the more talented in having satisfying work, it also tends to get talent into positions where it can better serve everyone's interests. This defense of the equal opportunity principle is, however, only partial. Although it justifies some reliance on the equal opportunity principle to match talent and occupational position, it does not justify the higher incomes which normally go with the more desirable positions. Admirers of the market often argue, of course, that such incomes are necessary to encourage the talented to acquire the qualifications required for the more desirable positions; but this is not very compelling given that these positions are already usually the most intrinsically satisfying in the society.

Advocates of the forward-looking argument for preferential treatment believe that it will help implement the principle of equal consideration of interests in addition to helping to equalize opportunities. Most societies don't come close to implementing either principle. They deny equal opportunities to certain individuals and give far less weight to satisfying the interests of those individuals than to satisfying the exactly similar interests of other individuals. For example, the interests of the aged in finding rewarding employment are routinely treated as being intrinsically less important than the similar interests of younger people, and for this reason they are often denied rewarding employment, even when they are the best qualified. The interests of the handicapped are more often downgraded in violation of the second part of the equal opportunity principle, as are the interests of women and the members of racial minorities. Such individuals are normally not given the same chance to acquire qualifications for desirable positions as men or those in the dominant racial group. If those favoring the forward-looking argument are right, preferential treatment will gradually abolish these violations of the equal opportunity principle, and help to usher in a society in which equal consideration is given to the like interests of all.

We have now sketched the two main arguments for preferential treatment and the egalitarian principles which are supposed to justify them. We must now see how these arguments are worked out in detail, and whether they can stand up to criticism. I will examine them mainly as they apply to preferential treatment for women and black people, but they can be applied to other cases where preferential treatment seems justified. In section (ii) I will examine the backward-looking argument, in section (iii) the forward-looking argument.

The Backward-Looking Argument

Perhaps the most common objection made against preferential treatment is that distinctions based on race or sex are invidious. Especially in America, critics tend to brandish Justice Harlan's dictum, "Our Constitution is color-blind . . ."

Justice Harlan's point was that the American Constitution forbids denying a citizen any of the rights and privileges normally accorded to other citizens on account of his or her color or race. The critics argue that the color-blind principle, Justice Harlan's dictum appeals to, and the similar sex-blind principle follow from the equal opportunity principle if we assume that citizens have rights to be evaluated for desirable positions solely on the basis of their qualifications for these positions, and that neither color, nor sex is normally a qualification for a position. If they are right, preferential treatment violates the equal opportunity principle because it violates the color-blind and sex-blind principles.

Preferential treatment certainly seems to violate the first part of the equal opportunity principle. It may, for example, require that a law school refuse admission to a white male and admit instead a woman or black who on most standards seems less qualified. But we must not forget the second part of the equal opportunity principle, that everyone must have an equal chance to acquire qualifications. Unless it is satisfied, the competition for places will not be fair. And in the case under discussion the second part of the equal opportunity principle may very well not be satisfied. Whites generally go to better schools than blacks, and society supports a complex system of expectations and stereotyping which benefits white males at the expense of blacks and women. So preferential treatment need not make the competition for desirable places and positions unfair. On the contrary, by compensating women and blacks for being denied equal chances to acquire qualifications, it may make that competition more fair.

In America the objection is often made that if blacks deserve compensation for being unjustly discriminated against, so also do Italians, Jews, Irish, Serbo-Croatians, Asians, and practically every ethnic group in America, since these groups too have been unjustly discriminated against. The implication is that since the society obviously cannot meet all these claims for compensation, it has no good reason to meet black claims for compensation.

I find no merit in this objection. In America, at least, discrimination against blacks has historically been far more severe than discrimination against other racial and ethnic groups. Further, while various European ethnic groups were certainly discriminated against, they also profited from the severer discrimination against blacks since they immigrated to America to take the jobs native blacks were denied because of their race. So, the claim that many other ethnic groups besides blacks have been discriminated against falls short of its goal. If society can only meet some claims for compensation, it should meet the most pressing claims, and blacks appear to have the most pressing claims.

This argument is compelling if we focus our attention on certain segments of the black population, especially the black underclass. The black underclass is characterized by alarming and unprecedented rates of joblessness, welfare dependence, teenage pregnancies, out-of-wedlock births, female-headed families, drug abuse and violent crime. But most blacks are not in the underclass. In particular, many if not most of the blacks who benefit from preferential treatment have middle-class origins. To be preferentially admitted to law school or medical school, a black or woman must usually have attended a good college, and earned good grades, and this gives those from the middle and upper classes a decided advantage over those from the lower socio-economic classes. This fact has raised many eyebrows.

Some critics complained that it showed that the typical beneficiaries of preferential treatment have no valid claim for compensation. They evidently assumed that middle- and upper-class blacks and women are unscathed by racist or sexist attitudes. This assumption is unjustified. Because of the civil rights victories, most forms of racial and sexual discrimination are illegal, and potential discriminators are likely to be wary of indulging their prejudices against blacks and women who have the money and education to make them pay for their illegality. But it does not follow that middle-class blacks and women are unscathed by racist and sexist attitudes. These attitudes do not support only discrimination. As I noted earlier, they support an elaborate system of expectations and stereotyping which subtly but definitely reduces the chances of women and blacks to acquire qualifications for desirable positions.

A somewhat more serious objection, stemming from the facts about the middle-class origins of the beneficiaries of preferential treatment, is that preferential treatment does not compensate those who most deserve compensation. The objection itself can be easily dismissed. As long as preferential treatment compensates those who deserve compensation, the fact that it does not compensate those who most deserve compensation is hardly an argument against it. The objection does, however, raise a serious difficulty since the society may not be able to compensate all those who deserve compensation. In that case, present programs of preferential treatment which benefit mainly middle-class blacks and women may have to be scrapped to make way for other programs which compensate those who more deserve it. Besides the underclass, the main candidate is the "working poor."

Recent commentators have complained that in the hullabaloo about the underclass, society has forgotten the "working poor." The schools their children attend may be only slightly better than the schools black children in the underclass attend. If so, present programs of preferential treatment may be particularly unfair. Because they compensate for the disadvantages of race and sex, but tend to ignore the disadvantages of class, they are apt to discriminate against white males from the "working poor" and in favor of middle or even upper-class blacks or women whose opportunities are already much better.

Fortunately, blacks, women, and the "working poor" need not quarrel among themselves over who most deserves compensation. Although each of these groups has probably profited from discrimination against the other two, preferential treatment need not compensate one of them at the expense of the others. Conceivably, it can compensate all of them at the expense of white middle-class males.

The members of this group have profited from discrimination against the members of the other groups, but have escaped all systematic discrimination, as well as the disadvantages of a lower-class education.

There is, however, a serious difficulty with viewing preferential treatment as compensation. Insofar as its beneficiaries have been denied equal opportunities, they deserve compensation; but it is not clear what compensation they deserve. Perhaps this will be clear for specific violations of the first part of the equal opportunity principle. If a firm denies a woman a job because of her sex, she deserves that job as compensation whenever it becomes available, even if others are at that time better qualified. In violations of the second part of the equal opportunity principle, it will be more difficult to determine what compensation those who have been wronged deserve. In particular it is far from clear that the compensation they deserve is desirable places and positions.

Let us consider this difficulty as it applies to the middle-class beneficiaries of preferential treatment. In that case the stock answer to the difficulty is that, were it not for racial and sexual discrimination and stereotyping, the middle-class blacks and women who receive preferential treatment for desirable places and positions would have been the best qualified candidates for these places and positions. Unfortunately, however, it must contend with the equally stock objection that were it not for the past history of racial and sexual discrimination and stereotyping, the middle-class blacks and women who receive preferential treatment for desirable places and positions would probably not even exist, let alone be best qualified for any places and positions.

The point this objection makes cannot be gainsaid. Racial and sexual discrimination and stereotyping have radically changed the face of society. Had they never existed, the ancestors of middle-class blacks and women receiving preferential treatment would almost certainly never have met, which implies that the middle-class blacks and women receiving preferential treatment would almost certainly never have existed. But the objection may be irrelevant. The proposal is not to imagine a world without a history of racial and sexual discrimination and stereotyping; it is to imagine a world without racial and sexual discrimination and stereotyping in the present generation. In such a world, most of the middle-class blacks and women receiving preferential treatment would certainly exist; and the argument is that they would be the most qualified for the places and positions they receive in the present world because of preferential treatment.

Unfortunately, this won't quite do. In the alternative world we are asked to imagine, most of the middle-class blacks and women who receive preferential treatment would probably be much better qualified than they are in our present world, for they would not have to contend with any racial or sexual discrimination and stereotyping. It does not follow, however, that they would be the *most* qualified for the places and positions they receive because of preferential treatment. Present programs of preferential treatment have forward-looking aims. They try to break down racial and sexual stereotypes by hastening the day when the races and sexes are represented in desirable positions in proportion to their numbers. This aim may not be consistent with a policy of benefiting only those who would be the most qualified for the places and positions they receive were there no racial or sexual discrimination and stereotyping.

It may seem that this difficulty can be met if we assume that the races and sexes are equally talented. Given this assumption it may seem to follow that in a world without racial or sexual discrimination, the races and sexes will be represented in desirable positions in proportion to their numbers, and accordingly that the blacks and women who receive preferential treatment for desirable places and positions would be the most qualified for these places and positions were there no racial or sexual discrimination. Both inferences, however, forget the complication of class.

Take first this complication as it applies to race. The black middle class is much smaller relative to the total black population than is the white middle class relative to the total white population. Those who compete for the desirable positions in society are drawn overwhelmingly from the middle classes; many in the lower socio-economic classes are excluded by their relatively poor education. Consequently, even if the races are equally talented, and there were no racial discrimination, the numbers of blacks in desirable positions would still be disproportionately small, and less than the number benefited by programs of preferential treatment.

A weaker, but still significant version of this difficulty affects the argument for women. Since women are half the middle class, and half the population, perhaps we can argue that preferential treatment benefits women who would have been the most qualified for the positions it awards them, were there no sexual discrimination. It does not follow, however, that they deserve preferential treatment. The force of the appeal to a world without sexual discrimination and stereotyping is that, as far as possible, compensation should give people what they would have received in a world without injustice. Sexual discrimination is not, however, the only injustice. It is also an injustice that poor children are badly educated compared to rich children. In the absence of that injustice it is far from clear that were there no sexual discrimination and stereotyping the middle-class white women receiving preferential treatment would have been the most qualified for the positions it awards them.

I conclude that the forward-looking aims of preferential treatment outstrip its backward-looking justification. Present programs of preferential treatment with their forward-looking aims cannot be justified solely on the backward-looking ground that they are compensation for violations of the equal opportunity principle.

The Forward-Looking Argument

As we saw earlier, the forward-looking aims of preferential treatment are to help make opportunities more equal, and ultimately, to enable society to give more equal consideration to the like interests of its members. A plausible case can be made for the claim that preferential treatment can help to make opportunities more equal. Suppose, for example, that the culture and traditions of a society lead its members to the firm conviction that women cannot be engineers. Since engineering is a rewarding and well-paid profession, and many women have the talent to excel at it, preferential treatment to encourage more women to become engineers may help to break the stereotype and equalize opportunities.

These possible consequences of preferential treatment may not be enough to justify it if, as some critics object, it violates the rights of white males to be evaluated for positions solely on the basis of their qualifications. This objection follows from the color-blind and sex-blind principles, which in turn follow from the equal opportunity principle if we assume that the qualifications for positions can never include color or sex, but must be things like scores on aptitude tests, and grades and university diplomas. I will argue, however, that this assumption is false, and consequently that the color-blind and sex-blind principles must sometimes be relaxed. The crucial premise in my argument is the point made earlier that applications of the equal opportunity principle must be framed so as to serve the principle of equal consideration of interests.

Suppose that a state establishes a medical school, but most of the school's graduates practice in cities, so that people in rural areas do not get adequate medical care. And suppose it was found that applicants for medical school from rural areas are more likely upon graduation to practice in these areas than applicants from urban areas. If the state gave equal weight to the interests of rural and urban people in receiving medical treatment, it seems that it could justifiably require the medical school to begin considering rural origins as one of the qualifications for admission. This could cause some applicants from urban areas to be denied admission to medical school who would otherwise have been admitted; but I do not see how they could validly complain that this violated their rights; after all, the medical school was not established in order to make them doctors, but in order to provide medical services for the community.

A similar example shows how race could conceivably be among the qualifications for admission to medical school. Thus suppose that people in the black ghettos do not get adequate medical care because not enough doctors choose to practice there; and suppose it was found that black doctors are more likely than white doctors to practice in black ghettos; as in the previous case, if the state gave equal weight to the interests of black and white people in receiving medical treatment, it could easily be justified in requiring medical schools to begin considering being black as a qualification for admission.

Critics sometimes object that some white doctors are more likely to practice in black ghettos than some black doctors. Although what they say is undeniable, it do not invalidate the case for considering race a qualification for admission to medical school. Practically all policies awarding places and positions must rely on generalizations which everyone knows are not true in every case. For example, no reasonable person suggests that universities should abandon their policy of awarding places partly on the basis of test scores, although these scores do not, of course, infallibly predict success and failure in university.

The implication of this discussion is that what counts as qualification for a position is ultimately determined by the principle of equal consideration of interests. In particular, the qualifications for a position are the qualities and abilities a person needs in order to perform adequately the functions expected of anyone filling the position, and thereby to enable society to give more equal weight to the like interests of all. So conceived, color and sex may be among the qualifications for positions. Although this implies that the color-blind and sex-blind principles are not always acceptable, it does not challenge the equal opportunity principle. It allows that people have rights to be evaluated for positions strictly on the basis of their qualifications for these positions. What it denies is that preferential treatment necessarily violates these rights of white males.

Although preferential treatment need not violate anyone's rights, the forward-looking argument may be open to other sorts of objection. In particular, it depends on factual claims about the consequences of preferential treatment. Skeptics challenge these claims. They claim, for example, that preferential treatment powerfully encourages the belief that women and blacks cannot compete against white males without special help. This was the point of Charles Murray's criticism of preferential treatment cited in the beginning of this essay. But even if the skeptics are mistaken, and preferential treatment is justifiable on purely forward-looking grounds, the backward-looking considerations favoring it remain significant. People have like interests in being acknowledged to have equal moral standing. When, as in the United States, a society has systematically excluded the members of a racial minority from the moral and political community, and in word and deed denied their equal moral standing, it does not acknowledge that equality simply by awarding them benefits, even if the benefits are generous. It must admit that they are owed these benefits because of their past treatment. In such cases especially, programs based on preferential treatment are an important means to achieving an egalitarian society.

Endnotes

1. Justice Harlan's comment may be found in: Bell, D.A., Jr., ed. *Civil Rights: Leading Cases* (Boston: Little, Brown and Co., 1980). See *Plessy v. Ferguson,* 1986.
2. Murray, C. "The coming of custodial democracy," *Commentary, 86* (1988), 20–26.

Further Reading

Books

Boxill, B.R. *Blacks and Social Justice* (Totowa, NJ: Rowman and Allenheld, 1984).

Clark, K. *Dark Ghetto* (New York: Harper and Row, 1965).

Fishkin, J.S. *Justice, Equal Opportunity, and the Family* (New Haven: Yale University Press, 1983).

Fullinwider, R.K. *The Reverse Discrimination Controversy* (Totowa, NJ: Rowman and Littlefield, 1980).

Goldman, A.H. *Justice and Reverse Discrimination* (Princeton: Princeton University Press, 1979).

Singer, P. *Practical Ethics* (Cambridge: Cambridge University Press, 1979).

Wilson, W.J. *The Truly Disadvantaged* (Chicago: University of Chicago Press, 1988).

Articles

Blackstone, W. Reverse Discrimination and Compensatory Justice. *Social Theory and Practice,* 3(1975), 258–271.

Boxill, B.R. The Morality of Reparations, *Social Theory and Practice,* 2 (1972), 113–124.

———, The Morality of Preferential Hiring, *Philosophy and Public Affairs,* 7 (1978), 246–268.

McGary, H., Jr. Justice and Reparations, *Philosophical Forum,* 9 (1977–1978), 250–263.

———, Reparations, Self-Respect and Public Policy, *Ethical Theories and Social Issues,* edited by David Goldberg (New York: Holt, Rinehart and Winston, 1989).

Nagel, T. Equal Treatment and Compensatory Discrimination, *Philosophy and Public Affairs,* 2 (1973), 348–363.

Wasserstrom, R.A. Racism, sexism, and preferential treatment: An approach to the topics, *UCLA Law Review,* 24(1977), 581–622.

———, "The university and the case for preferential treatment." *American Philosophical Quarterly,* 13 (1976), 165–170.

Journal/Discussion Questions

✍ *Have you ever benefited from, or been disadvantaged by, affirmative action? If so, how did you analyze the moral issues involved?*

1. In reading Boxill's article, what arguments did you encounter that you hadn't thought about before? Were you convinced by those arguments?
2. Critically evaluate Boxill's assessment of backward-looking arguments.
3. Critically evaluate Boxill's assessment of forward-looking arguments.

Louis Pojman
"Why Affirmative Action Is Immoral"

Louis Pojman is a philosopher who has published extensively in the area of ethics, including books on abortion, the death penalty, equality, environmental ethics, and the Danish philosoher Søren Kierkegaard.

Pojman chronicles his own changing views on the morality of affirmative action, concentrating on two arguments which he initially found convincing: the level playing field argument, and the compensation argument.

As You Read, Consider This:

1. Pojman distinguishes between procedural affirmative action and preferential affirmative action. What, according to Pojman, is the difference between these two? On what basis does he oppose procedural affirmative action?
2. What are Pojman's objections to the level playing field argument?
3. What are Pojman's objections to the compensation argument?

> The state shall not discriminate against, or grant preferential treatment to, any individual or group on the basis of race, sex, color, ethnicity, or national origin in the operation of public employment, public education, or public contracting (*California Civil Rights Initiative,* Proposition 209).

When affirmative action was first proposed in the early 1960s, as a civil rights activist and member of CORE, I supported it. The shackled runner metaphor, set forth by President Lyndon Johnson in his 1965 Howard University speech, seemed to make moral sense. An opportunity gap existed between White and Black societies which greatly handicapped Blacks. This was my *forward-looking* reason for supporting affirmative action. But I had a *backward-looking* argument, as well. America owed compensation to Blacks who had been hideously oppressed in our society. The reasons that caused me to change my mind on this issue will be discussed in this paper, in which I will argue that *preferential* affirmative action is immoral. I have given comprehensive critiques of affirmative action (henceforth AA) elsewhere, and space prevents a repetition of that material.[1] In this short paper I limit my arguments to AA regarding race, since if any group deserves AA it is African-Americans. Also I concentrate on university admittance and hiring, since these are the areas with which I am most familiar.

First some definitional preliminaries: By *Affirmative Action* I refer to preferential treatment based on race, gender or ethnicity. We might call this *Preferential Affirmative Action* as opposed to *Procedural Affirmative Action,* which requires that special attention be given to insure that everything reasonable is done to recruit and support equally qualified minorities and women. I support *Procedural Affirmative Action* even to the point of allowing the properties in question to function as tie-breakers. In my experience, however, *Procedural Affirmative Action* tends to slip into *Preferential Affirmative Action.* Bureaucracies in general cannot be trusted to abide by the rules, hence the present need to eliminate AA altogether. Recall how race-norming procedures and AA admittance policies were kept secret for years. In the early 1990s, the University of Delaware withdrew Linda Gottfriedson's fellowship because she exposed the practice of race-norming. If and when we are committed to fair evaluations, *Procedural Affirmative Action* will be morally acceptable.

Let me turn to the two arguments that once persuaded me of the soundness of *Preferential Affirmative Action,* which I now believe to be unsound.

The Level Playing Field Argument

This is a version of President Johnson's Howard University "Shackled Runner" speech. Here is how Mylan Engel puts the argument:

> Consider a race, say a hundred yard dash. Mr. White starts at the 50 yard mark, while Mr. Black starts at the 0 yard mark. The gun goes off and sure enough Mr. White wins. Now very few people would think that sort of race was fair. . . . They certainly wouldn't think that Mr. White deserved significant economic gain for beating Mr. Black in such a race. Now, it seems to me that a similar sort of argument can be made in defense of strong AA. One need not appeal to compensation for past injustices, etc. The fact is that many white males have an unfair head start in the education and employment game. Consider a statistic reported on NPR today: 27% of Blacks and Latinos currently are living below the poverty line (the poverty line is now $16,400 for a family of four), whereas only 11% of (non-Asian) whites are living below the poverty line. And at each level above the poverty line, there is a disproportionate number of whites. The economic advantage experienced by whites is that more whites can afford to send their children to exclusive college preparatory private schools, and even those whites who can't afford to send their children to private schools, still have a better chance of living in a wealthy school district with better public schools. So, by the time the Young Mr. Whites and the Young Mr. Blacks are ready to start the university application process, more often than not, the young Mr. Whites already have the equivalent of a 50 or at least a 25-yard head start in the college application game.[2]

First of all, more should be done for poor families and poor neighborhoods, as well as poor schools. Economic disparities between the rich and the poor should be reduced. Programs, such as the East German youth program and President Clinton's Youth Corps, which has unfortunately foundered, in which every American youth gives 2 years to national service, either in the military or in community service, much of which would be geared toward improving the lot of the economically and educationally disadvantaged. The reward would be free college or grad school tuition or job/career training.

Secondly, I gradually came to see that the Level Playing Field Argument could best support a class-based approach to AA, rather than a race-based one. On current poverty statistics, 74 percent of Blacks and Hispanics are not living in poverty and 11 percent of Whites are, so this kind of AA would cut across racial and gender lines. I am sympathetic to class-based AA. The question is: what kind of help should be given?

Financial assistance would seem to be the best kind. Candidates would be accepted into universities on the basis of their qualifications, but would then be assisted according to need.[3] There is nothing new about this kind of program, it has traditionally been used (Pell Grants, etc.). Tie breakers could be used too. If Mr. Poor and Mr. Rich both had similar scores, it would be reasonable to take the disadvantage into consideration and award a place to Mr. Poor.

Engel points out, as an objection to this argument, that AA actually harms the very people it seeks to help, especially by stigmatizing them with the label "AA admittee" = "inferior student." But isn't the point that AA admittees are often not equipped to handle the rigors of the top schools? So we are doubly harming them. Even Bok and Bowen's new book *The Shape of the River,* which advocates AA in college admittance, concedes that blacks with identical SAT scores as whites get (on average) lower grades. The Center for Civil Rights has shown that in every state university examined (Michigan, North Carolina, Washington, etc.), Black admittance rates are based on much lower SAT scores and their failure and drop out rates are usually more than double those of whites. So AA actually is counterproductive, contributing to harming those it would help. Moreover, some schools have had to lower their standards to accommodate less qualified Blacks. While I was teaching at the University of Mississippi, a strong AA program was implemented. The Math Department had to switch to a high school algebra text in order to teach that course. The Affirmative Action handbook stated that any qualified minority (and female) candidate had a presumptive claim on any open academic position in the university. Sidney Hook relates an incident where a Religious Studies Department was instructed by an accrediting association to drop the requirements of Hebrew and Greek, since it was discouraging members of minorities groups to major in that discipline.

It gradually dawned on me that affirmative action was guilty of enacting the Peter Principle, which states that we should promote people to positions beyond their present abilities, where they will very likely fail. So Black students with SATs of 1150 are admitted to Harvard or Berkeley, from which they drop out or fail, whereas they would have done very well at a first rate state university or less prestigious small college.

My own experience is that of a poor teen-ager who started off at mediocre Morton High and Morton Jr. College in Cicero, Illinois, and who worked his way up to Columbia University and Union Seminary, then fellowships to the University of Copenhagen, and finally to Oxford University. I didn't get into Oxford until my 30s and would have failed had I gone right out of high school or junior college. I saw my community college, not as a stigma, but as an opportunity to improve myself so that I might be worthy of a more rigorous challenge.

Furthermore, it isn't Mr. Rich who is likely to be affected by AA. It's Mr. Poor-but-talented-White who is likely to be harmed. Mr. Rich has had such support, coaching and early advantages that he's on his way to success. Neither Mr. Poor Black nor Mr. Poor White is normally helped by AA. Mr. and Miss Middle Class Black is the main beneficiary.

There is another problem with the Level Playing Filed Argument. It supposes that if everything were just, we'd have equal results in every area of life. But why should we expect this? Anyone who is familiar with Irish, Italian and Jewish ethnic patterns in New York City can attest to the fact that people from different ethnic communities (with the same economic status) turn out very differently: the Irish and Italian tended to go into the fire department and police force; the Jews into academics, science and technology. There is evidence that Ashkanazy Jews have on average higher intelligence (measured in terms of academic ability, at least) than other ethnic groups. Both genetically and culturally differences exist between people and may exist between groups. This point may be uncomfortable to egalitarians, but, as philosophers, we should be concerned with the evidence, which, at least, gives us no reason to think that every group has the same average abilities.[4]

There is one other argument that caused me to give up the Leveling Argument. It can function as a disincentive to responsible parenting. If you and I both have the same economic opportunities but you save your money and dedicate your life to producing two excellent children with the best advantages, whereas I gamble, drink, spend enormous amounts of money on expensive cars, and neglect my 10 children, why should your two better qualified children be denied admission to Yale simply because my children are more needy (or are Black)? This seems to me to be a disincentive to good parenting as well as a denial of the merit attained by the better qualified. AA programs aren't fine grained enough to sort out these nuances.[5]

In conclusion, while many Middle Class Blacks and other minorities may be helped by AA policies, these policies do little to help the truly disadvantaged. The Leveling Argument is unsound. But even if it were sound, since it is basically a utilitarian argument, other considerations of justice could still override it. I turn to the second argument that once led me to support AA.

The Compensation Argument for Preferential Affirmative Action

The argument goes like this: historically Blacks have been wronged and severely harmed by Whites. Therefore white society should compensate Blacks for the injury caused them. Reverse discrimination in terms of preferential hiring, contracts, and scholarships seemed a fitting way to compensate for the past wrongs.[6] I was a member of Riverside Church in New York City when at a Sunday service in May of 1969, James Foreman pushed aside the minister and issued the Black Manifesto, demanding $500 million from the American religious establishment for reparations to Blacks. Foreman's disruption caused me to reassess my support of this argument, and gradually I began to realize that it involves a distorted notion of compensation.

Normally, we think of compensation as owed by a specific person A to another person B whom A has wronged in a specific way C. For example, if I have stolen your car and used it for a period of time to make business profits that would have gone to you, it is not enough that I return your car. I must pay you an amount reflecting your loss and my ability to pay. If I have made $5,000 and only have $10,000 in assets, it would not be possible for you to collect $20,000 in damages—even though that is the amount of loss you have incurred.

Sometimes compensation is extended to groups of people who have been unjustly harmed by the greater society. For example, the United States government has compensated the Japanese-Americans who were interred during the Second World War, and the West German government has paid reparations to the survivors of Nazi concentration camps. But here specific individuals have been identified who were wronged in an identifiable way by the government of the nation in question.

On the face of it, demands by Blacks for compensation do not fit the usual pattern. Southern states with Jim Crow laws could be accused of unjustly harming blacks, but it is hard to see that the United States government was involved in doing so. Much of the harm done to Blacks was the result of private discrimination, rather than state action. So the Germany/US analogy doesn't hold. Furthermore, it is not clear that all blacks were harmed in the same way or whether some were *unjustly* harmed or harmed more than poor Whites and others (e.g., Jews, Poles, short people). Finally, even if identifiable blacks were harmed by identifiable social practices, it is not clear that most forms of

Affirmative Action are appropriate to restore the situation. The usual practice of a financial payment, as I noted earlier, seems more appropriate than giving a high level job to someone unqualified or only minimally qualified, who, speculatively, might have been better qualified had he not been subject to racial discrimination. If John is the star tailback of our college team with a promising professional future, and I accidentally (but culpably) drive my pick-up truck over his legs, and so cripple him, John may be due compensation, but he is not due the tailback spot on the football team.

Still, there may be something intuitively compelling about compensating members of an oppressed group who are minimally qualified. Suppose that the Hatfields and the McCoys are enemy clans and some youths from the Hatfields go over and steal diamonds and gold from the McCoys, distributing it within the Hatfield economy. Even though we do not know which Hatfield youths did the stealing, we would want to restore the wealth, as far as possible, to the McCoys. One way might be to tax the Hatfields, but another might be to give preferential treatment in terms of scholarships and training programs and hiring to the McCoys.

This is perhaps the strongest argument for Affirmative Action, and it may well justify some weaker versions of AA, but it is doubtful whether it is sufficient to justify strong versions with quotas and goals and time tables in skilled positions. There are at least three reasons for this. First, we have no way of knowing how many people of any given group would have achieved some given level of competence had the world been different. Secondly, the normal criterion of competence is a strong prima facie consideration when the most important positions are at stake. There are three reasons for this: (1) treating people according to their merits respects them as persons, as ends in themselves, rather than as means to social ends (if we believe that individuals possess a dignity which deserves to be respected, then we ought to treat that individual on the basis of his or her merits, not as a mere instrument for social policy); (2) society has given people expectations that if they attain certain levels of excellence they will be rewarded appropriately; and (3) filling the most important positions with the best qualified is the best way to ensure efficiency in job-related areas and in society in general. These reasons are not absolutes. They can be overridden.[7] But there is a strong presumption in their favor, so that a burden of proof rests with those who would override them.

The third reason against using affirmative action to compensate has to do with the arbitrariness of using preferential treatment in a market-driven process. Take the hiring of professors according to affirmative action guidelines. Should we hire (or admit into professional schools) minimally qualified AA candidates over better qualified candidates because they have suffered injustice as *individuals* or because they belong to a *group* that has suffered. If it is because they have suffered injustice, then it is irrelevant that they are members of minority groups. We should treat them as individuals and compensate them accordingly. So race and gender are really irrelevant. What counts is the injustice done to them. But if we reward them because they are members of an oppressed group, then we may do injustice by not rewarding individuals of other groups who have suffered injustice. Poor coal miners of West Virginia, railroad workers who worked under oppressive conditions to build the transcontinental railroads, short people, ugly people, people from abusive homes, and so forth all deserve some compensation from a society that has dealt them a raw deal. But hiring or admitting to special professional schools is arbitrary compensation in that it compensates only a few of the oppressed, and, generally, not the worst off. It compensates the best off Blacks and women, many who come from relatively wealthy families, leaving the truly disadvantaged, impoverished Blacks and Whites, males and females, in the same situation they already were in.[8]

At this point we face the objection that "innocent" White males have enormously profited from racism and sexism, so that while some of the above has merit, it doesn't acquit White males altogether. Preferential treatment to previously oppressed people may still be justified, all things considered. We turn to this argument.

The Argument for Compensation from Those Who Innocently Benefitted from Past Injustice

Young White males as innocent beneficiaries of unjust discrimination against blacks and women have no grounds for complaint when society seeks to level the tilted field. They may be innocent of oppressing blacks, other minorities, and women, but they have unjustly benefited from that oppression or discrimination. So it is perfectly proper that less qualified women and blacks be hired before them.

The operative principle is: He who knowingly and willingly benefits from a wrong must help pay for the wrong. Judith Jarvis Thomson puts it this way: "Many [white males] have been direct beneficiaries of policies which have down-graded blacks and women . . . and even those who did not directly benefit . . . had, at any rate, the advantage in the competition which comes of the confidence in one's full membership [in the community], and of one's right being recognized as a matter of course."[9] That is, white males obtain advantages in self-respect and self-confidence deriving from a racist/sexist system which denies these to blacks and women.

Here is my response to this argument: As I noted in the previous section, compensation is normally individual and specific. If A harms B regarding X, B has a right to compensation from A in regards to X. If A steals B's car and wrecks it, A has an obligation to compensate B for the stolen car, but A's son has no obligation to compensate B. Suppose A is unable to compensate B himself but he could steal C's car (roughly similar to B's). A has no right to steal C's car to compensate A. Furthermore, if A dies or disappears, B has no moral right to claim that society compensate him for the stolen car, though if he has insurance, he can make such a claim to the insurance company. Sometimes a wrong cannot be compensated, and we just have to make the best of an imperfect world.

Recently (mid-September, 1998), an umpire called what would have been Mark McGwire's 66th home run of the season a ground-rule double on the grounds that a fan caught the ball before it made it to the stands. A replay showed that the ball had already cleared the stands, so that it was a home run. The commissioner of baseball refused to overrule the umpire's decision. Two days later Sammy Sosa hit two home runs, thus tying McGwire for the home run lead. McGwire was the victim of an unintended injustice (if the fact that it was an honest mistake bothers you, suppose the umpire did it on purpose). Should Sosa give up one of his home runs in order to rectify the injustice to McGwire? Morally, McGwire deserves to hold the record for home runs, but according to the rules, he has a right only to a tie at this point.

Suppose my parents, divining that I would grow up to have an unsurpassable desire to be a basketball player, bought an expensive growth hormone for me. Unfortunately, a neighbor stole it and gave it to little Michael, who gained the extra 13 inches—my 13 inches—and shot up to an enviable 6 feet 6 inches. Michael, better known as Michael Jordan, would have been a runt like me but for his luck. As it is he profited from the injustice, and excelled in basketball, as I would have done had I had my proper dose.

Do I have a right to the millions of dollars that Jordan made as a professional basketball player—the unjustly accused innocent beneficiary of my growth hormone? I have a right to something from the neighbor who stole the hormone, and it might be kind of Jordan to give me free tickets to the Bull's basketball games, and remember me in his will. As far as I can see, however, he does not owe me anything, either legally or morally.

Suppose further that Michael Jordan and I are in high school together and we are both qualified to play basketball, only he is far better than I. Do I deserve to start in his position because I would have been as good as he is had someone not cheated me as a child? Again, I think not. But if being the lucky beneficiary of wrongdoing does not entail that Jordan (or the coach) owes me anything in regard to basketball, why should it be a reason to engage in preferential hiring in academic positions or highly coveted jobs? If minimal qualifications are not adequate to override excellence in basketball, even when the minimality is a consequence of wrongdoing, why should they be adequate in other areas?

Affirmative Action Requires Discrimination against a Different Group

Here is the third reason why I changed my mind on AA. Weak or procedural AA weakly discriminates against new minorities, mostly innocent young White males, and strong or preferential Affirmative Action strongly discriminates against these new minorities. As I argued earlier, this discrimination is unwarranted, since, even if some compensation to Blacks were indicated, it would be unfair to make innocent white males bear the whole brunt of the payments. Recently I had this experience. I knew a brilliant young philosopher, with outstanding publications in first level journals, who was having difficulty getting a tenure-track position. For the first time in my life I offered to make a phone call on his behalf to a university to which he had applied. When I reached the Chair of the Search Committee, he offered that the committee was under instructions from the Administration to hire a woman or a Black. They had one of each on their short-list, so they weren't even considering the applications of White males. At my urging he retrieved my friend's file, and said, "This fellow looks far superior to the two candidates we're interviewing, but there's nothing I can do about it." Cases like this come to my attention regularly. In fact, it is poor White youth who become the new pariahs on the job market. The children of the wealthy have little trouble getting into the best private grammar schools and, on the basis of superior early education, into the best universities, graduate schools, managerial and professional positions. Affirmative Action simply shifts injustice, setting Blacks, Hispanics, Native Americans, Asians and women against young White males, especially ethnic and poor white males. It makes no more sense to discriminate in favor of a rich Black or female who had the opportunity of the best family and education available against a poor White, than it does to discriminate in favor of White males against Blacks or women. It does little to rectify the goal of providing equal opportunity to all.

At the end of his essay supporting Affirmative Action, Albert Mosley points out that other groups besides Blacks have been benefited by AA, "women, the disabled, the elderly."[10] He's correct in including the elderly, for through powerful lobbies, such as the AARP, they do get special benefits, including Medicare, and may sue on the grounds of being discriminated against due to *Ageism,* prejudice against older people. Might this not be a reason to reconsider Affirmative

Action? Consider the sheer rough percentages of those who qualify for some type of AA programs.

Group	*Percentage in Population*
1. Women	52
2. Blacks	12
3. Hispanics	9
4. Native Americans	2
5. Asian-Americans	4
6. Physically and Mentally Disabled	10
7. Welfare recipients	6
8. The Elderly	25 (est. Adults over 60)
9. Italians (in New York City)	3
Total	123

The Office of Federal Contract Compliance (OFCC) includes as protected categories not only Blacks but "all persons of Mexican, Puerto Rican, Cuban or Spanish origin or ancestry." The Small Business Administration adds Eskimos and Aleuts. Federal contracting programs include the following groups as meriting preferential treatment: People from Burma, Thailand, Malaysia, Indonesia, Singapore, Brunei, Japan, China, Taiwan, Laos, Cambodia, Vietnam, Korea, the Philippines, U.S. Trust Territory of the Pacific Islands, Republic of the Marshall Islands, federated States of Micronesia, the Commonwealth of the Northern Mariana Islands, Guam, Samoa, Macao, Hong Kong, Fiji, Tonga, Kiribati, Tuvalu, Mauru, India, Pakistan, Bangladesh, Sri Lanka, Bhutan, the Maldives Islands, and Nepal.[11] Recent immigrants from these countries sometimes are awarded contracts in preference to lower bids by White male owned firms. Recently, it has been proposed that homosexuals be included in oppressed groups deserving Affirmative Action.[12] At Northeastern University in 1996 the faculty governing body voted to grant homosexuals Affirmative Action status at this university. How many more percentage points would this add? Several authors have advocated putting all poor people on the list.[13] And if we took handicaps seriously, would we not add ugly people, obese people, people who stammer, color-blind people, people with genetic liabilities, and, especially, short people, for which there is ample evidence of discrimination? How about left-handed people (about 9% of the population), they can't play short-stop or third base and have to put up with a right-handedly biased world. The only group not on the list is that of White males. Are they, especially healthy, middle-class young White males, becoming the new "oppressed class"? Should we add them to our list?

Respect for persons entails that we treat each person as an end in himself or herself, not simply as a means to be used for social purposes. What is wrong about discrimination against Blacks is that it fails to treat Black people as individuals, judging them instead by their skin color not their merit. What is wrong about discrimination against women is that it fails to treat them as individuals, judging them by their gender, not their merit. What is equally wrong about *Affirmative Action* is that it fails to treat White males with dignity as individuals, judging them by *both their race and gender,* instead of their merit. *Current Strong Affirmative Action is both racist and sexist.*

Conclusion

Let me sum up my discussion. The goal of the Civil Rights movement and of moral people everywhere has been justice for all, for a color-blind society, where people will not be judged by their race or gender but by their moral character and abilities. The question is: How best to get there? Civil rights legislation removed the unjust legal barriers, opening the way towards equal opportunity, but it did not tackle other factors, causes that result in unjust discrimination. Procedural Affirmative Action aims at encouraging minorities and women to strive for excellence in all areas of life, without unduly jeopardizing the rights of other groups, such as White males and Asians. The problem of Procedural Affirmative Action is that it easily slides into Preferential Affirmative Action where quotas, "goals and time-tables," "equal results,"—in a *word reverse discrimination*—prevail and are forced onto groups, thus promoting mediocrity, inefficiency, and resentment. My argument has been that, if we are serious about attaining a color-blind society, with a large amount of opportunity for all, we should shape our lives and our institutions in ways that make that more likely. AA vitiates that goal by setting up a new class of pariah, young White males, depriving them of the opportunities that they merit. Furthermore, AA frequently aims at the higher levels of society—universities and skilled jobs, but, if we want to improve our society, the best way to do it is to concentrate on families, children, early education, and the like, so that all are prepared to avail themselves of opportunity. Affirmative Action, on the one hand, is arbitrary, compensating a few of the better-off members of AA groups, and doing nothing for the truly disadvantaged, and on the other hand, is doubly arbitrary in exacting a penalty from unlucky talented young white males, who themselves may have been victims of oppression, while leaving better-off members of society untouched by its policies.

In addition to the arguments I have offered, Affirmative Action, rather than unite people of good will in the common cause of justice, tends to balkanize us into segregation-thinking. Professor Derrick Bell of Harvard Law School recently said that the African-American Supreme Court Judge Clarence Thomas, in his opposition to Affirmative Action, "doesn't think black."[14] Does Bell really claim that there is a standard and proper "Black" (and presumably a White) way of thinking? Ideologues like Bell, whether radical Blacks like himself, or Nazis who advocate "think Aryan," both represent the same thing: cynicism about rational debate, the very antithesis of the quest for impartial truth and justice. People of good will, who believe in reason to resolve our differences will oppose this kind of balkanization of ethnic groups.

Martin Luther said that humanity is like a man mounting a horse who always tends to fall off on the other side of the horse. This seems to be the case with Affirmative Action. Attempting to redress the discriminatory iniquities of our history, our well-intentioned social engineers now engage in new forms of discriminatory iniquity and thereby think that they have successfully mounted the horse of racial harmony. They have only fallen off on the other side of the issue.[15]

Endnotes

1. See "The Moral Status of Affirmative Action" in *Public Affairs Quarterly,* vol. 6:2 (1992) and "The Case against Strong Affirmative Action" in *International Journal for Applied Philosophy,* vol. 12 (1998).

2. Mylan Engel, Correspondence, September 24, 1998.
3. Objective measures, such as SAT and ACT scores, along with high school grade point average, have considerable validity. The charge of being prejudicial has been adequately refuted. Actually, they predict better for Blacks than for Whites. Wherever possible recommendations and personal interviews should be used to supplement these measures.
4. Also, many Haitian and Latinos are recent immigrants to the USA (sometimes illegally so). Why should they be given preference over young white males? Why should the university be made to carry the heavy burden of leveling society when people come to our land voluntarily? Note too that poor Blacks and Hispanics typically have larger families than Whites and middle-class Blacks. If the poor are to be given special benefits, don't procreative responsibilities go along with them?
5. Many people think that it is somehow unjust if one community (or family) spends more money or resources on its children's education than another. A few years ago the New Jersey legislature passed a bill prohibiting communities from spending more than the average amount of money on its children's public education, lest inequalities emerge. But, if we believe that parents should have considerable freedom on how they use their resources, why is disparity unjust? Suppose you choose to have only 2 children and make enormous sacrifices for their education and upbringing (say 40 units on each child) and I (with similar resources) have 10 children and spend less total resources to all 10 (averaging 5 units on each child). Why, should society have to make up the difference between what is spent on the 10 children. Surely, such supplementary aid, beyond a certain minimal limit, is a disincentive to be a responsible parent. Yet we don't want the children to suffer either. This may be a prima facie reason to require licenses for parenting (which has its own serious problems).
6. For a good discussion of this argument see B. Boxill, "The Morality of Reparation" in *Social Theory and Practice* 2:1(1972) and Albert G. Mosley in his and Nicholas Capaldi, *Affirmative Action; Social Justice or Unfair Preference?* (Totawa, NJ: Rowman and Littlefield, 1996), pp. 23–27.
7. Merit sometimes may be justifiably overridden by need, as when parents choose to spend extra earnings on special education for their disabled child rather than for their gifted child. Sometimes we may override merit for utilitarian purposes. For example, suppose you are the best shortstop on a baseball team but are also the best catcher. You'd rather play shortstop, but the manager decides to put you at catcher because, while your friend can do an adequate job at short, no one else is adequate at catcher. It's permissible for you to be assigned the job of catcher. Probably, some expression of appreciation would be due you.
8. I am indebted to Robert Simon's "Preferential Hiring" *Philosophy and Public Affairs* 3 (1974) for helping me to formulate this argument.
9. Judith Jarvis Thomson, "Preferential Hiring" in Marshall Cohen, Thomas Nagel, and Thomas Scanlon, eds., *Equality and Preferential Treatment* (Princeton: Princeton University Press, 1977).
10. Albert Mosley, *op. cit.,* p. 53.
11. For a discussion of these figures, see Terry Eastland, *Ending Affirmative Action* (New York: Basic Books, 1996), p. 5Sf and 140f.
12. J. Sartorelli, "The Nature of Affirmative Action, Anti-Gay Oppression, and the Alleviation of Enduring Harm" *International Journal of Applied Philosophy* (vol. 11. No. 2, 1997).

13. For example, Iddo Landau, "Are You Entitled to Affirmative Action?" *International Journal of Applied Philosophy* (vol. 11. No. 2, 1997) and Richard Kahlenberg "Class Not Race" (*The New Republic* April 3, 1995).
14. See L. Gordon Crovitz, "Borking Begins, but Mudballs Bounce Off Judge Thomas, " *The Wall Street Journal,* July 17, 1991. Have you noticed the irony in this mudslinging at Judge Thomas? The same blacks and whites who oppose Judge Thomas, as not the best person for the job, are themselves the strongest proponents of Affirmative Action, which embraces the tenet that minimally qualified Blacks and women should get jobs over White males.
15. Some of the material in this essay appeared in "The Moral Status of Affirmative Action" *Public Affairs Quarterly,* vol. 6:2 (1992). I have not had space to consider all the objections to my position or discuss the issue of freedom of association which, I think, should be given much scope in private but not in public institutions. Barbara Bergmann (*In Defense of Affirmative Action* (New York: Basic Books, 1996, pp. 122–125)) and others argue that we already offering preferential treatment for athletes and veterans, especially in university admissions, so, being consistent, we should provide it for women and minorities. My answer is that I am against giving athletic scholarships, and I regard scholarships to veterans as a part of a contractual relationship, a reward for service to one's country. But I distinguish entrance programs from actual employment. I don't think that veterans should be afforded special privilege in hiring practices, unless it be as a tie breaker.

I should also mention that my arguments from merit and respect apply more specifically to public institutions than private ones, where issues of property rights and freedom of association carry more weight.

Journal/Discussion Questions

1. What is it that convinced Pojman to change his mind on affirmative action? What is you evaluation of this argument? Do you agree with Pojman? Explain.
2. How does Pojman think that the legitimate goals of affirmative action should be accomplished in our society?

Lawrence A. Blum
"Philosophy and the Values of a Multicultural Community"

Lawrence Blum is a professor of philosophy at the University of Massachusetts, Boston. He is the author of numerous articles and books in ethics, including Friendship, Altruism and Morality *and* Moral Perception and Particularity, *a collection of his recent essays.*

What values are desirable in a multiracial, multicultural campus? In this essay, Blum explores three values he considers crucial in such a community: opposition to racism, multiculturalism, and a sense of community, connection, or common humanity.

As You Read, Consider This:

1. How does Blum define "racism" and "racist"? Is there anything controversial about his definitions?
2. How is multiculturalism different from mere opposition to racism? What, exactly, is the relationship between multiculturalism and ethnocentrism?

Many philosophers are wary about recent calls for greater cultural diversity in university curricula, especially demands that non-Western traditions and modes of thought be given significant recognition. Philosophy departments are often among the last to institute such changes and to join interdisciplinary efforts at implementing this diversity. But I will argue that attention to multiculturalism should be seen as a boon to philosophy.

Philosophy can come into the educational debate over cultural diversity in two places. One concerns philosophy as a specific intellectual discipline among others, and the way diversity is to be explained, justified, and incorporated within its courses. The other is philosophy as contributing to the overall exploration of the issues of multiculturalism as they apply not only to course content but to the classroom and the university as multiracial and multicultural communities of learning. Important as the first is, we should not confine ourselves to a narrow disciplinary focus but should see philosophy as having its role to play in creating what the recent Carnegie Foundation Report "Campus Life: In Search of Community" expressed as a community which is, among other things, just, caring, open, and civil.[1] Taking this role seriously can also show how philosophy can expand to include issues of race, culture, and ethnicity into many courses in ethics, social, and political philosophy, and perhaps other areas of philosophy as well. I would like to begin such an exploration of philosophy and multicultural community today.

I will discuss three distinct values desirable in a multiracial, multicultural campus. They are: (1) opposition to racism, (2) multiculturalism, (3) sense of community, connection, or common humanity. These values are seldom clearly distinguished, and are often entirely run together, defeating clear thought about the real goals and possibilities of multicultural communities.[2] Failure to make these distinctions blinds us both to possible tensions among these distinct values and to the raising of the question of how best to realize them all so as to minimize that tension.

1. Opposition to Racism

The notion of "racism" is highly charged emotionally, and the term is used in contemporary parlance in a number of ways. There has been a well-documented increase in what are unquestionably racist incidents on campus, but also frequent yet more controversial *charges* of racism for any number of remarks and behavior. I want to suggest that the core meaning of "racism" is connected with the *domination* or *victimization* of some groups by others, and with the notion of the subordinate groups as inferior or less worthy than the dominant group. I will call an act or reaction "racist" if it expresses a notion of a member of a different racial group as being inferior.[3]

On this view the following phenomena, often called "racist" by many students, are not (necessarily, or usually) racist: (1) Departure from pure meritocratic justice: Affirmative action programs which prefer a minority student with lower test scores to a Caucasian student with higher ones. (2) Minority exclusiveness: Black students sitting together in the college dining room, thereby making it uncomfortable for whites to join them. (3) Stereotyping: A white student's unthinkingly assuming that a Latino student is from a lower socio-economic background than his own.

None of these actions express beliefs of superiority toward other groups; this is why they should not (I suggest) be called "racist." This does not mean that these actions and policies cannot be criticized as violating some other moral value appropriate to multiracial communities, especially college communities. My point is precisely that there are several values relevant to a multiracial community—values which are distinct from one another.

While all racism is bad, on the definition of racism as dominance-attitude, not all manifestations of racism are *equally* bad. To oversimplify a complex issue here, racist attitudes which lend support to an existing structure of racism in which the possessor of the racist attitude is a member of a dominant group are worse than racist attitudes of a member of a subordinate group toward a member of a dominant group, for the latter do not support an existing structure of domination. For example beliefs and doctrines of Caucasian inferiority to people of color are genuinely racist and worthy of condemnation. Yet these manifestations of racism toward whites are not as bad, dangerous, or condemnable as doctrines of white superiority to people of color (or attitudes expressing those doctrines), since the latter, and not the former, play a role in supporting actual structures of domination. The source of the value asymmetry here is that racism supporting existing subordination invokes and reinforces the social weight of this structure of dominance, bringing it down against its victim, and thus (other things being equal) more deeply shames and harms its victim than does subordinate-to-dominant racism, which does not carry that social and historical resonance. (The different force of the formally similar expressions "honkie" and "nigger" illustrates this point.)[4]

This asymmetry helps clarify the frequent mutual incomprehension between white and non-white students concerning racism. Many black students tend to think of racism solely as a phenomenon of whites against blacks or other non-whites. White students by contrast tend to equate—and condemn equally—all attitudes of racial insult, exclusion, or differentiation, by any racial group toward any other.

Aside from the point made earlier that some of what these white students call "racism" is not actually racism (according to my account), each group holds part of the truth. The non-white students see that the core and most socially dangerous phenomenon of racism is the actual, historical domination or victimization of one group by another, and attitudes of superiority (whether conscious or not) which directly support that domination. Many white students fail entirely to see this, not acknowledging—or not acknowledging the significance of—continuing subordinate status (in the United States) of people of color.

The white students, on the other hand, are correct to see clearly that *all* manifestations of racial contempt and superiority are worthy of condemnation, precisely because they are the *sorts* of attitudes which do underpin racial subordination. The non-white students' attitude has the effect of entirely letting non-whites off the hook for objectionable attitudes of superiority or contempt toward other groups.[5]

To state briefly what is involved in learning to oppose racism, and in embodying that value in an educational community: There is a philosophical component involved in understanding why racism is wrong, involving among other things learning how racism damages its victims; but learning the psychological, sociological, economic, and historical dynamics of racism and of resistance to it are essential as well. Public condemnation of racism on the campus is also essential.

2. Multiculturalism

Like "racism," this is a term of great currency and imprecise usage. I will use it to encompass the following two components: (a) understanding and valuing one's own cultural heritage, and (b) having respect for and interest in the cultural heritage of members of groups other than one's own. Note that condition (b) takes multiculturalism beyond what is often referred to as "cultural pluralism"—a situation in which different groups are each turned inward into their own group, valuing and learning about their own cultural heritage but being indifferent to that of others. While the idea of cultural pluralism perhaps contains the notion of tolerance for and recognition of the right of others to pursue their own cultural exploration and learning, "multiculturalism" as I am understanding it goes beyond this to encompass a positive interest in and respect for other cultures.

Often the initial association with "cultural diversity" or "multiculturalism"—for example when implying a policy to diversify the curriculum—is as (1) giving non-Caucasian students an understanding of and validation of their own cultural heritages (and thereby also broadening the sense of inclusion in the university's intellectual enterprise), and (2) expanding Caucasian students' intellectual horizons and reducing their ethnocentrism. Yet these two albeit crucial goals do not comprise the whole of what I mean by "multiculturalism." For in addition, my definition implies that members of *every* group (whites and non-whites alike) be involved in overcoming their own ethnocentrism, one possible curricular implication being that every student ought to study, say, two cultures other than her own.

Bypassing for this short presentation further difficulties regarding the definition of multiculturalism (e.g., what constitutes a "culture," which cultures should count for curricular and non-curricular attention, how respect for different cultures is consistent with criticism of them), I want to focus on how what I have called *multiculturalism* is a distinct value from what I have called *opposition to racism,* yet how both are essential in a multiracial community. First, each involves looking at the same group through distinct lenses. From the viewpoint of anti-racism, groups are divided into dominant and subordinate. From an anti-racist perspective, to study for example Native Americans or African Americans involves looking at the way these groups have been oppressed, undermined, damaged, and the like by white America, at the beliefs and policies which have supported this mistreatment, and at the subordinate group's resistance to this subordination. It is to study subordinate groups primarily in their role as victims and resisters.

By contrast, to learn about cultural groups from a multicultural perspective involves studying the group's customs, rituals, language, systems of thought and religion, forms of cultural expression, accomplishments and contributions to the wider societies of which they are a part, and the like. The contrast resides not so much in distinct aspects of the groups in question focused on by the multicultural *versus* the anti-racist perspective; for subordinate groups' forms of cultural expressions are often so intimately bound up with their oppressed status and history that no simple delineation is possible. (Consider for example Afro-American music, Jewish humor.) The point is that both anti-racism and multiculturalism bring an analytical perspective on the study of cultural groups that the other lacks.

"Multiculturalism" is the preferred rubric of many educators.[6] But multiculturalism without anti-racism projects a world (or society) of cultural groups, each with its own way of life, forms of cultural expression, accomplishments and the like, all existing on something like an equal level. While this sense of equality—to teach and learn informed respect for every culture—may be appropriately (if only roughly) seen as an appropriate aspiration taken purely by itself, it obscures the fact that in our world and our society some of these cultures have been subordinated, undermined, and mistreated by other ones. It is as if one could just affirm that each group is equal, without taking into account the fact that in the world they are not treated as equal; it is this lack of equality that the anti-racist perspective keeps before us.

At the same time, the anti-racist perspective is also by itself incomplete. First, seeing a culture in terms of its victimization—or even its victimization and its resistance to that victimization—is only a partial perspective on that culture, omitting (or omitting important dimensions of) cultural expression and accomplishment. Second, the value perspective of anti-racism is itself only partial. To see that racism is wrong—and to firmly believe that it is wrong—is not the same as, and does not even require, actually having a positive appreciation for the culture of the subordinate group. In fact it is possible to be genuinely anti-racist while knowing little about the cultures of different groups that have been discriminated against. For example, many European, Christian, rescuers of Jews during the Nazi occupation expressed a fully anti-racist outlook in attempting their noble and dangerous rescue efforts; but few had genuine respect for Jews as a distinct cultural/religious group.[7]

While I have been arguing for the distinctness of anti-racism and multiculturalism as goals and values, they are also, or can be, mutually supportive. Learning to value a different culture can certainly help to bring home to a student the wrongness of that culture's mistreatment (even if the student were already in agreement on the abstract point that racism is wrong). It can awaken students for whom opposition to racism does not run very deep to the humanity of others—in its particular manifestation in the culture being studied. Both anti-racism and multiculturalism involve taking those outside one's own group seriously. Though they do so in different ways, both have the power to combat egoism and ethnocentrism.

3. Sense of Community, Connection, or Common Humanity

In addition to exemplifying the values of opposition to racism and multiculturalism, one also wants the college community to constitute and to foster a cross-racial sense of connection or community. At first glance, this might not seem a distinct value. For isn't opposition to racism grounded in a sense of common humanity? Isn't racism wrong because it violates that common humanity? And doesn't the mutual respect involved in multiculturalism also express a sense of community?

But a sense of (cross-racial) community is, I want to argue, a distinct value. For a genuinely anti-racist individual does not necessarily have a sense of connection to those of another race, even while she or he regards those others as equals. For this sense of community can be negated not only by regarding others as *inferior* but simply by experiencing them as "other," as apart from, distant from, oneself, as persons one does not feel comfortable with because they are not members of one's own group.

It seems clear that many college students do not feel a genuine or full sense of cross-racial community, even though these same students are not racist in the sense defined here; they do not regard the other groups as inferior. Yet to be a genuine *community,* and not just a collection of people seeing each other as equals, a learning community must embody more than anti-racism.

There are ways of teaching and learning about racism which may fail to create, or even to hinder, a cross-racial sense of community. These ways reinforce a "we/they" consciousness in both the white and the non-white students; for example, never mentioning whites who stood against racism but projecting simply a (not really incorrect, but only partial) image of racism as "white oppressing black." It is undoubtedly true that learning about racism and why it is wrong has the inherent potentiality to undermine or strain this sense of connection. And classes on this subject might find ways within the pedagogical structure of the class to meliorate that effect—for example, by having cross-racial groups work on class projects. Ultimately, however, such classes are necessary to help reconstruct or create a sense of community at a more informed level. Without a firm anti-racist component, any sense of cross-racial community will fail to involve true equals.

A sense of (cross-racial) connection is distinct from multiculturalism as well, even though multiculturalism teaches respect for others. The more minimal condition of valuing one's own culture and tradition goes nowhere toward creating a sense of cross-racial community, and its inward-turning can serve to undermine that connection (though at the same time for some minority students this aspect of multiculturalism might be a necessary condition for their being able to experience a sense of connection with white students—from a base of cultural self-respect).

Even including the second condition of multiculturalism (respect for other cultures) does not guarantee a sense of community. For there are ways of presenting other cultures which can simultaneously promote a sense of respect yet of distance from members of that culture—for example, placing too much emphasis on the self-enclosed, self-coherent, and differentness of each culture. Such a presentation would be *intellectually* deficient in not recognizing the multiplicity within each culture, its changes over time, its influences from other cultures, and (in most cases) values or elements it shares with other cultures. But my point here is that this intellectual error also has the unfortunate moral effect of helping to create or perpetuate among students a sense of distance between members of different cultures.

Recognizing these potentially divisive or distancing effects of both anti-racism and multiculturalism has been one source of opposition to both of them. "Why don't we just emphasize commonalities among our students, and reinforce them through a curriculum emphasizing a common Western and national tradition," say some (for example, occasionally in the "Point of View" column of the *Chronicle of Higher Education*). But ignoring both racism and genuinely culturally distinct sources of identity will not make these go away. Moreover, as I have tried to argue, both anti-racism and multiculturalism represent distinct and worthy goals, which an educational community must uphold and institutionalize. Any sense of community in the absence of a recognition of these values will in any case be a false and deceptive one.

What is necessary, I suggest, is to take seriously the three distinct goals, to recognize that it may not always be possible to realize all simultaneously, but to search for ways—in the curriculum, the classroom, and the organization of life on campus—to minimize the conflict among them, and to teach those values in ways that do mutually enhance one another to the greatest extent possible.

What I have presented here is a mere sketch of a nest of complex philosophical and value issues concerning multiracial college classrooms and communities. Philosophy should not cede the discussion of these issues to social scientists, historians, and literature teachers, as we have tended to do. There is clarificatory and constructive work to be done here to which philosophy brings a necessary perspective. That work needs to be done in various courses in moral, social, and political philosophy, as well as in contributions to campus-wide debate.

Endnotes

1. Carnegie Foundation for the Advancement of Teaching, *Campus Life: In Search of Community* (1990).
2. For example, the excellent Carnegie study mentioned above takes up racial/cultural issues primarily in its "A Just Community" chapter, misleadingly implying a conceptual unity to the distinct issues of access and retention, ignorance of groups and traditions other than one's own, outright discrimination, and minority in-group exclusiveness.
3. To simplify, I will continue to use the language of "dominant/subordinate," though this bypasses not insignificant differences among the terms "subordination," "victimization," "exploitation," "oppression," being "dominated," being "discriminated against," being "mistreated," being an "object of injustice"—all of which terms are used in this context.
4. This too-brief account of moral asymmetries in manifestations of racism is spelled out in my (unpublished) talk in the "Ethics and Society" Lecture Series, Stanford University, April 1990.
5. Note that the forgoing analysis does not concern racism of one subordinate or vulnerable group toward another—e.g., Koreans toward blacks, or blacks toward Jews. This complex matter is discussed in the manuscript mentioned in the previous note.
6. Cf. the excellent article defending multicultural education, but in distinction from and even denial of the anti-racist perspective by Diane Ravitch, "Diversity and Democracy: Multicultural Education in America," *American Educator*, Spring 1990.
7. On this see the L. Blum "Altruism and the Moral Value of Rescue: Resisting Persecution, Racism, and Genocide," in L. Baron, L. Blum, D. Krebs, P. Oliner, S. Oliner, and Z. Smolenska, *Embracing the Other: Philosophical, Psychological, and Historical Perspectives on Altruism* (New York: NYU Press, 1992).

Journal/Discussion Questions

✍ *As a college student, you are involved in a community that is probably multiracial and multicultural. What are the most important values for people on your campus? How does this relate to Blum's values?*

1. Blum says that "not all manifestations of racism are *equally* bad." What makes some manifestations of racism worse than others?
2. What does Blum mean by *multiculturalism*? What is the difference between *multiculturalism* and *opposition to racism*? Why does each perspective need to be complemented by the other?
3. Some critics of multiculturalism ask, "Why don't we just emphasize commonalities among our students, and reinforce them through a curriculum emphasizing a common Western and national tradition?" How does Blum reply to this question? In what ways do you agree with his reply? Disagree?
4. What other values, if any, do you think are essential to a multicultural community?

Concluding Discussion Questions

Where Do You Stand Now?

Instructions:

You have already answered the following questions in your moral problems self-quiz at the beginning of this book. Now that you have studied the material in this section, take a moment to answer the same questions again.

	Strongly Agree	*Agree*	*Undecided*	*Disagree*	*Strongly Disagree*	*Chapter 5: Race and Ethnicity*
21.	❑	❑	❑	❑	❑	African Americans are still often discriminated against in employment.
22.	❑	❑	❑	❑	❑	Affirmative action helps African Americans and other minorities.
23.	❑	❑	❑	❑	❑	Racial separatism is wrong.
24.	❑	❑	❑	❑	❑	Hate speech should be banned.
25.	❑	❑	❑	❑	❑	We should encourage the development of racial and ethnic identity.

Compare your answers to the present self-quiz with the answers to the initial self-quiz. How, if at all, have your answers changed? How have the *reasons* for your answers changed?

Journal/Discussion Questions

✍ *In light of the readings in this chapter, would you change the way in which you understand any of your personal experiences in regard to issues of race or ethnicity?*

1. Do you think that their racially based injustices still occur in our society? If so, how do you think these can best be rectified and eliminated in the future?
2. What is your vision of a future ideal society in the United States in regard to the issues of race and ethnicity? How does that ideal relate to some of the ideals we have seen in this chapter? How do you think we can best move toward your ideal? What are the greatest possible objections to your ideal?

For Further Reading

Web Resources

For Web-based resources, including the major Supreme Court decisions on race and affirmative action, see the Race and Ethnicity page of *Ethics Updates (http://ethics.acusd.edu).*

Review Article

Bernard R. Boxill's "Racism and Related Issues," *Encyclopedia of Ethics,* edited by Lawrence and Charlotte Becker (New York: Garland, 1992), Vol. II, pp. 1056–1059 provides an excellent overview of work on race and related issues.

Racism

There is an extensive and often powerful *literature dealing with the prevalence of racism in our society.* Derrick Bell's *Faces at the Bottom of the Well: The Permanence of Racism* (New York: Basic Books, 1992) provides a penetrating look at the pervasiveness of racism in the United States today. Patricia J. Williams's *The Alchemy of Race and Rights* (Cambridge: Harvard University Press, 1991) is part autobiography, part feminist legal philosophy, and part cultural critique. Cornel West's *Race Matters* (Boston: Beacon Press, 1993) and his *Prophetic Thought in Postmodern Times* (Monroe, Maine: Common Courage Press, 1993) are both well-argued analyses by one of the foremost contemporary African-American thinkers. Shelby Steele's *The Content of Our Character: A New Vision of Race in America* (New York: Harper Collins, 1990) offers a much more conservative interpretation of these phenomena. Stephen L. Carter's *Reflections of an Affirmative Action Baby* (New York: Basic Books, 1991) stresses the ambiguity of affirmative action for African Americans. *Lure and Loathing: Essays on Race, Identity, and the Ambivalence of Assimilation,* edited by Gerald Early (New York: Penguin Press, 1993) contains a number of insightful autobiographical essays on the ambivalence toward assimilation experienced by many contemporary African-Americans. Naomi Zack's *Race and Mixed Race* (Philadelphia: Temple University Press, 1993), *Thinking about Race* (Wadsworth, 1998), and *American Mixed Race: The Culture of Diversity* (Roman & Littlefield, 1995) offer a perceptive analysis of many of the issues surrounding mixed race in our society.

Several excellent *anthologies* contain shorter selections on these issues. See, especially, *Racism in America: Opposing Viewpoints,* edited by William Dudley (San Diego, CA.: Greenhaven Press, 1991), which contains an excellent selection of largely popular pro-and-con pieces on a number of topics related to racism; *Taking Sides: Race and Ethnicity,* 3rd ed., edited by Richard C. Monk (Guilford, CN: Dushkin, 1998), which treats a wide range of issues relating to ethnicity as well as race; *Race, Class, and Gender in the United States,* Third Edition, edited by Paula S. Rothenberg (New York: St. Martin's Press, 1995), which is a gold mine of eloquent selections; *Bigotry, Prejudice, and*

Hatred: Definitions, Causes, and Solutions, edited by Robert M. Baird and Stuart E. Rosenbaum (Buffalo: Prometheus Books, 1993), which contains an number of excellent philosophical selections; and *Anatomy of Racism,* edited by David Theo Goldberg (Minneapolis: University of Minnesota Press, 1990), which contains pieces by Appiah, Outlaw, Fanon, Barthes, Kristeva, Said, Goldberg, and Gates. The transcript of a two-day conference on "Race and Racism" is printed in *Salmagundi,* Nos. 104–105 (Fall 1994–Winter 1995), pp. 3–155; this consists of a round-table discussion including Orlando Patterson, Christopher Lasch, Dinesh D'Souza, Anthony Appiah, Jean Elshtain, David Rieff, Michelle Moody-Adams, Norman Birnbaum, and Gerald Early. Also see *Women of Color in U.S. Society,* edited by Maxine Baca Zinn and Bonnie Thornton Dill (Philadelphia: Temple University Press, 1994), a collection of 16 essays, largely from social scientific standpoints.

Among the specifically *philosophical approaches to racism* and related issues, see the issue of *Philosophia,* Vol. 8, Nos. 2–3 (November 1978) that contains several articles on racism, including Marcus George Singer, "Some Thoughts on Race and Racism," pp. 153–183; Kurt Baier, "Merit and Race," pp. 121–151; and Peter Singer, "Is Racial Discrimination Arbitrary?" pp. 185–203; also see the double issue of *Philosophical Forum,* Vol. 9, Nos. 2–3 (1977–1978), entitled "Philosophy and the Black Experience" and the triple issue, "African-American Perspectives and Philosophical Traditions," Vol. XXIV, Nos. 1–3 (Fall–Spring 1992–1993). See Kwama Anthony Appiah, "Illusions of Race," *In My Father's House: Africa in the Philosophy of Culture* (New York: Oxford University Press, 1992), pp. 28–46, for a discussion of the slipperiness of the concept of race.

On the relationship between *racism* and *sexism,* see Richard A. Wasserstrom, "On Racism and Sexism," in *Today's Moral Problems,* Third Edition, edited by Richard A. Wasserstrom (New York: Macmillan, 1985), pp. 1–28; and Laurence Thomas, "Sexism and Racism: Some Conceptual Differences," *Ethics,* Vol. 90 (January 1980), pp. 239–247.

Claims of racially based differences in *intelligence* have been frequent over the ages. In recent times, see Arthur Jenson, "How Much Can We Boost I.Q. and Scholastic Achievement?" *Harvard Educational Review,* Vol. 39, No. 1 (1969), pp. 1–123; William Schockley, "Dysgenecs, Geniticity, and Raciology," *Phi Delta Kappan* (January 1972), pp. 297–307; and, most recently, Charles Murray and Richard Herrnstein, *The Bell Curve* (New York: Free Press, 1994). Equally common have been strong critiques of such connections, including Steven Jay Gould, *Ever Since Darwin* (New York: W.W. Norton, 1977) and Ashley Montagu, *Man's Most Dangerous Myth: The Fallacy of Race,* 4th ed. (Cleveland: World, 1964).

Multiculturalism

Some of the initial articles on multiculturalism are to be found in *Debating P.C.,* edited by Paul Berman (New York: Laurel, 1992) and *Culture Wars: Opposing Viewpoints,* edited by Fred Whitehead (San Diego: Greenhaven Press, 1994). For perceptive comments on these issues, see Henry Louis Gates, Jr., *Loose Cannons: Notes on the Culture Wars* (New York: Oxford University Press, 1993). Among the critics of multiculturalism are Arthur M. Schlesinger, Jr., *The Disuniting of America* (New York: W.W. Norton, 1992), William J. Bennett, *The De-Valuing of America* (New York: Summit Books, 1992), Dinesh D'Souza, *Illiberal Education: The Politics of Race and Sex on Campus* (New York: Vintage, 1992), and Robert Hughes, *Culture of Complaint* (New York: Oxford University Press, 1993).

For an excellent discussion of the philosophical and political dimensions of multiculturalism, see Amy Gutmann, "The Challenge of Multiculturalism in Political Ethics," *Philosophy and Public*

Affairs, Vol. 22, No. 3 (1993), pp. 171–206 and the essays in *Defending Diversity: Contemporary Philosophical Perspectives on Pluralism and Multiculturalism,* edited by Lawrence Foster and Patricia Herzog (Amherst, MA: University of Massachusetts Press, 1994). For a philosophically sophisticated account of the question of identity within this context, see Charles Taylor, *Multiculturalism and "The Politics of Recognition,"* with commentary by Amy Gutman, Steven C. Rockefeller, Michael Walzer, and Susan Wolf (Princeton: Princeton University Press, 1992). On the issue of identity, also see the papers by Anthony Appiah and others at the APA Symposium on Gender, Race, and Ethnicity, *Journal of Philosophy,* Vol. 87, No. 10 (October 1990), pp. 493–499. Also see the articles on multiculturalism and philosophy that appeared in *Teaching Philosophy,* Vol. 14, No. 2 (June 1991). See, more recently, Will Kymlicka, *Multicultural Citizenship: A Liberal Theory of Minority Rights* (New York: Oxford, 1995) and K. Anthony Appiah and Amy Gutmann, *Color Conscious: The Political Morality of Race* (Princeton, NJ: Princeton University Press, 1996).

The issue of *banning hate speech* has received a lot of attention in the past decade. Some of the most influential essays are gathered together in Mari J. Matsuda, et al., *Words That Wound: Critical Race Theory, Assaultive Speech, and the First Amendment* (Boulder, Colorado: Westview Press, 1993) and Henry Louis Gates, Jr., et al., *Speaking of Race, Speaking of Sex, Hate Speech, Civil Rights, and Civil Liberties,* with an Introduction by Ira Glesser (New York: New York University Press, 1994); also see Gates's "Let Them Talk: Why Civil Liberties Pose No Threat to Civil Rights," *The New Republic,* Vol. 209, Nos. 12–13 (September 20, 1993), p. 37 ff. Andrew Altman, "Liberalism and Campus Hate Speech: A Philosophical Examination," *Ethics,* Vol. 103, No. 2 (January 1993), pp. 302–317. Also see, Catharine A. MacKinnon, *Only Words* (Cambridge: Harvard University Press, 1993). More recently, see James B. Jacobs and Kimberly Potter, *Hate Crimes: Criminal Law and Identity Politics* (New York: Oxford, 1998) and Andrew Sullivan, "What's So Bad About Hate?" *New York Times Magazine* (September 26, 1999), pp. 50 ff.

Affirmative Action

There are a number of excellent *anthologies* dealing with the issue of affirmative action. These include *Social Justice and Preferential Treatment,* edited by William T. Blackstone and Robert Heslep (Athens: University of Georgia Press, 1976), *Equality and Preferential Treatment,* edited by Marshall Cohen, Thomas Nagel, and Thomas Scanlon (Princeton: Princeton University Press, 1977); *Affirmative Action and the University: A Philosophical Inquiry,* edited by Steven M. Cahn (Philadelphia: Temple University Press, 1993); *Reverse Discrimination,* edited by Barry R. Gross (Buffalo: Prometheus Books, 1977); *Equal Opportunity,* edited by Norman E. Bowie (Boulder: Westview Press, 1988); *Discrimination, Affirmative Action, and Equal Opportunity: An Economic and Social Perspective,* co-edited by W.E. Block and M.A. Walker (Vancouver, B.C., Canada: Fraser Institute, 1981), which includes contributions by Gary Becker, Thomas Sowell, and Kurt Vonnegut, Jr.; *Racial Preference and Racial Justice: The New Affirmative Action Controversy,* edited by Russell Nieli (Washington, DC: Ethics and Public Policy Center, 1991); and, most recently, *Debating Affirmative Action: Race, Gender, Ethnicity, and the Politics of Inclusion,* edited and with an introduction by Nicolaus Mills (New York: Delta, 1994).

Among *books* arguing one side of this issues, see especially Bernard R. Boxill, *Blacks and Social Justice* (Totowa, NJ: Rowman & Allanheld, 1984); Gertrude Ezorsky, *Racism and Justice: The Case for Affirmative Action* (Ithaca: Cornell University Press, 1991); *The Reverse Discrimination Controversy: A Moral and Legal Analysis,* by Robert K. Fullinwider (Totowa, NJ: Rowman and

Littlefield, 1980); *Affirmative Discrimination: Ethnic Inequality and Public Policy,* by Nathan Glazer (New York: Basic Books, 1975); *Out of Order: Affirmative Action and the Crisis of Doctrinaire Liberalism,* by Nicholas Capaldi (Buffalo, NY: Prometheus Books, 1985); *Invisible Victims: White Males and The Crisis of Affirmative Action,* by Frederick R. Lynch (New York: Greenwood Press, 1989); *Justice and Reverse Discrimination,* by Alan H. Goldman (Princeton, NJ: Princeton University Press, 1979); Barry R. Gross, *Discrimination in Reverse: Is Turnabout Fair Play?* (New York: New York University Press, 1978); Michael Rosenfeld, *Affirmative Action and Justice: A Philosophical and Constitutional Inquiry* (New Haven: Yale University Press, 1991); and Iris Marion Young, *Justice and the Politics of Difference* (Princeton: Princeton University Press, 1990), especially the chapter on "Affirmative Action and the Myth of Merit," pp. 192–225.

Among the many important *philosophical articles* on this set of topics, see W. Blackstone, "Reverse Discrimination and Compensatory Justice," *Social Theory and Practice,* Vol. 3 (1975), pp. 258–271; Bernard R. Boxill's "The Morality of Reparations," *Social Theory and Practice,* Vol. 2 (1972), pp. 113–124 and "The Morality of Preferential Hiring," *Philosophy and Public Affairs,* Vol. 7 (1978), pp. 246–268; H. McGary, Jr., "Justice and Reparations," *Philosophical Forum,* Vol. 9 (1977–1978), pp. 250–263; Thomas Nagel, "Equal Treatment and Compensatory Discrimination," *Philosophy and Public Affairs,* Vol. 2 (1973), pp. 348–363; and Thomas E. Hill, Jr., "The Message of Affirmative Action" *Social Philosophy and Policy,* Vol. 8 (Spring 1991), pp. 108–129.

CHAPTER 6

Gender

Videotape:

Topic: Men, Women, and Sex in the Workplace
ABCNEWS *Source:* ABC *Nightline* (February 10, 1998)
Anchors: Dave Marash, Forrest Sawyer

EXPERIENTIAL ACCOUNT

Frances Conley and Elizabeth L'Hommedieu
"Walking Out on the Boys"

One of the first board-certified female neurosurgeons in the United States, Frances Conley was a tenured professor of surgery at Stanford Medical School. She submitted her resignation because of the cumulative effects of sexism. She later withdrew her resignation after disciplinary action was taken against one of her male colleagues. Elizabeth L'Hommedieu conducted the interview for Time *magazine.*

In this interview, Dr. Conley discusses some of the instances of "gender insensitivity" that led her to submit her resignation to Stanford Medical School and some of the ways in which such sexism might be mitigated.

Q. After 16 years as a professor at Stanford, you resigned abruptly, charging what you called "gender insensitivity" on the part of male colleagues. Most people interpreted that to mean sexual harassment. Were you sexually harassed?

A. I am not talking about sexual harassment. I think harassment is too volatile a term. Sexism is one way of describing it. It is a pervasive attitude problem. The examples I can give will seem trivial, but they are real, and they do affect a person who has a professional life. If I am in an operating room, I have to be in control of the team that is working with me. That control is established because people respect who I am and what I can do. If a man walks into the operating room and says, "How's it going, honey?" what happens to my control? It disappears because every woman who is working in that room with me has also been called "honey" by this same guy, and it means all of a sudden I don't have the status of a surgeon in control of the case being done. I have suddenly become a fellow "honey."

Q. Surely there is more to it than being called "honey." Are there any other examples?

A. When I was younger I would be repeatedly asked to bed by fellow doctors. This would always happen in front of an audience. It was always done for effect. Another common example is that if I have a disagreement with my male counterparts, I generally tend to get the label of being "difficult" because I am suffering from PMS syndrome or because I am "on the rag." That is a gender-identification problem. You can't say that to a male counterpart who disagrees with you. These men tend to use the female image and those things that are perceived by society as making women inferior, i.e., the fact that we are different biologically, and they make that the focus of their dealing with me. I define that as sexism. It is not sexual harassment. I have had male doctors run their hands up my leg, never in an operating room, but in meetings. It is always done for an audience. Two months ago, I stood up to leave a meeting of all men and me, and as I stood up one of them said to me, "Gee, I can see the shape of your breasts, even through your white coat." I am sorry, but to me that is not right.

Q. Why wouldn't men do this to you simply because you are an attractive woman?

A. I have analyzed it, and I believe it's because they cannot see me as a peer. They have to establish a relationship that makes me inferior to them. The one they can immediately grab onto is a sexual relationship where the man is supposed to be dominant and the woman subservient.

Q. You've said twice now that these sexist remarks are made in front of an audience. Why would that be?

A. They have to show their peers that they do not accept this woman as an equal.

Q. You have been a surgeon for 25 years. Why did you tolerate this kind of treatment for so long?

A. In order for a female to get taken into the club, which is necessary in order to get cases and to get trained, you have to become a member. I decided that I would go along because I wanted to get to where I wanted to be. I really wanted to be a neurosurgeon. I thought I could be a good neurosurgeon. Had I made an issue of some of the things that were happening during the time that I was a resident, I wouldn't have gotten to where I am.

Q. How pervasive do you think this kind of treatment of female doctors is?

A. The vast majority of men that I have worked with—and there have been a lot of them—are wonderful, warm, supportive human beings who make me feel good about me when I am with them. It is just a few bad apples, but those bad apples can make you feel pretty small.

Q. Are all the "bad apples" concentrated in the Stanford neurosurgery department?

A. No, they are not. I would say they are much more concentrated in the surgery department across all specialties rather than in, say, pediatric medicine or anesthesia.

Q. What do you think you have accomplished by resigning?

A. First, I will be able to rebuild myself and regain my self-dignity. When I resigned, I had not intended to make a statement. As it turned out, I did, because I wrote a letter to a local newspaper, and that does make a statement. Many media people said, "You are so naive." I really had not anticipated the reaction to the editorial I wrote. I have been amazed. It is like an abscess that has been festering for years. It's been getting bigger and bigger. What I did was throw a scalpel at it and opened it. Now there is pus running all over the floor. What I have done, I hope, is help others open up a dialogue about this. If we can get men and women to start talking to one another about what gender insensitivity means, then we will have accomplished a great deal.

Q. The day after you resigned, you attended a student-faculty senate meeting at which one student described a teacher's using a sex doll to "spice up" a lecture, and another student said her breasts had been fondled. This must have struck a chord with you.

A. I think the thing that hit me the most was realizing that these were medical students complaining, and they are having these kinds of problems in their learning place, where they are supposed to be free to learn and to train to become professionals. This is a pervasive, global problem for women who are trying to get into professional careers. I think the reason it is coming out is because of the critical numbers. Since close to 50% of Stanford's medical classes can be women, when you do something in a class that is sexist in nature, you're offending not four people but 40.

Q. Stanford President Donald Kennedy has just brought disciplinary charges of sexual harassment and professional misconduct against a male cardiology professor. The charges are based on complaints that two female medical students filed with the university several months prior to your resignation. Do you think your resignation played a part in the university's decision to take action?

A. No. I do not believe that my situation influenced this decision. I know nothing about this case. I have enough faith in the people who run the university to feel that they are doing what is right regardless of whether or not I have made a flap. I do not think that Kennedy or any other people would have taken my resignation into account.

Q. You have said that the structure of medicine was set up for men by men. How do you think medicine would differ were it to be set up by women?

A. It would be far less dictatorial. It would be management by committee—by teamwork. Uniformly, my operating room is a team, and I believe this to be true of most women's O.R.s. The people who work with me are respected, professional, and do a job. We are all doing a job to reach a common goal, and that is to take good care of that patient. I think the nurses feel as if they have tremendous self-worth when they are in my O.R. There are lots of pleases and lots of thank yous. My operating room is a happy environment.

Q. Where does Stanford President Donald Kennedy stand on all this?

A. I have spoken with Kennedy, and I think he is very supportive. I am not sure he was aware that the gender-relationship problems were quite as significant as they are, and I think he has been most surprised by that. I know he has been getting an earful, because I have been getting copies of many letters that have been sent to him.

Q. You have said that with so many more females in medical schools across the country, their environments must change. What steps would you suggest?

A. One is to raise the level of consciousness about this type of behavior so that the consciousness is ongoing. The second is to be sure that the appointments that are made to executive positions are made with a great deal of care as to what that person's feelings are and how they relate not only to women but also to minorities, nurses, and secretaries. It has to be an environment where people are respected for being people—where every person has self-worth and dignity. There would also be value in having more women in higher administrative positions in medical schools, where the decisions are being made.

Q. What has been your husband's reaction to your resignation?

A. He has been very supportive of it, primarily because he has been very aware of my unhappiness. He, too, has been flabbergasted by the supportive response and feels that it should have come out a long time ago.

Q. How has he handled all your private complaints over the years?

A. He has always let me be a very independent person, and that has been terribly important for me so that I could develop as a professional the way I wanted to. I think at times he has been distressed by my complaints. He will occasionally make sniping comments at people whom he thinks have been demeaning to me, but he hasn't wanted to jeopardize that which I have done. He has been very careful not to be actively entered into the situation, but he has always been phenomenally supportive of me.

Journal/Discussion Questions

✍ *If you had been in Dr. Conley's place, how would you have dealt with this problem?*

1. How does Conley distinguish between "gender insensitivity" and "sexual harassment"?
2. If you were the dean of Stanford Medical School, how would you have dealt with this issue in your school?

An Introduction to the Moral Issues

As we turn to a consideration of the issue of gender, we discover that a wide range of moral issues presents itself. Some have to do with equality and the various ways in which women have been denied equality in our society: sex discrimination, sexist language, sexual harassment, rape, pornography, hate speech, and reproductive rights. Others have to do with issues of diversity: not only diverse ideals of the place of gender in society but also the issue of whether women have a distinctive moral voice. In this introduction, we shall survey these issues, seeking to illuminate what is at stake in each of these areas and highlighting the questions each of us must answer in regard to this issue. Then we shall turn to a discussion of competing models of the place of gender in society, and conclude with a discussion of the means of remedying some of the problems discussed here. First, however, let's take a quick look at the ways in which the issue of gender is similar to, and different from, ethnicity.

Gender and Ethnicity

In what ways do issues of gender differ from those of ethnicity?

The issue of gender raises a number of issues of diversity and equality that echo those encountered in our discussion of race and ethnicity, but there are also a number of important differences. Principal among these is that there is no natural attraction among the races in the same way that there is between the sexes and that there is nothing comparable to procreation, childbirth, and child rearing that binds the races together in the way that males and females are brought together for these purposes. Nor is separatism as viable an option as it is for races and ethnicities. There have never been purely male or female countries in the way in which we have countries that are composed predominantly of one racial group or another, nor did we ever have male and female neighborhoods in cities in the way in which we have had ethnic neighborhoods. Finally, there is another important difference between racially based discrimination and gender-based discrimination: there are more indirect ways in which men suffer from discrimination against women who are in their family (wife, daughters, and other relatives) than there are ways in which one race suffers from discrimination against other races.

Yet the types of discrimination that women and racial minorities have suffered show striking similarities, and the remedies proposed to rectify these injustices also overlap in important ways. Although non-African-American women were not enslaved in the way in which both African-American males and females were, women not only lacked the vote until the twentieth century, but also lacked legal standing in other respects as well. Often unable to own property when married or to testify in court on their own behalf, women lacked many of the protections of the law accorded to white males. Even after achieving political equality through the vote, women often lacked legal protections when discriminated against and are still battling for economic equality.

Defining the Problems: Issues of Sexism

Sexism is a notoriously difficult term to define precisely, but its overall elements are clear. It refers to both *attitudes* and *behavior.* Sexist attitudes are attitudes that see individuals, solely because of their gender, as being less than their male or female counterparts. For example, although both are equally competent, Jane is seen by her employer as less competent than her coworker John; the employer is exhibiting a sexist attitude. If the employer then goes ahead and, on the basis of this distorted perception, promotes John but does not promote Jane, then the employer is behaving in a sexist manner. Sexist *attitudes* refer to our perceptions and feelings; sexist *behavior* to our actions.

Overt and Institutional Sexism

Just as we did with racism, we can distinguish between overt and institutional sexism. *Overt sexism* is the intentional discrimination against a person because of that person's gender. For example, if a person is denied a job because that person is a male or female, that is an act of overt sexism. In contrast to this, *institutional sexism* occurs when a person is (perhaps unintentionally) discriminated against because of factors that pertain to that person's gender. For example, in some college sports such as basketball and football, women may be underrepresented if teams were open to both male and female applicants; if athletic scholarship money was given only to those who made the team, the indirect result would be that far fewer women would receive athletic scholarships than men. Although there may be no intent to discriminate in athletic scholarships against women, the net result might be precisely such institutional sexism.

Sexist Language

One of the more contentious areas of discussion in regard to sexism is language. There are two distinct aspects to this issue: (1) the gendered structure of our language and (2) its specific vocabulary. In regard to linguistic structure, many have pointed out that English, like many other languages, is gendered; we often are forced by our language to identify a person as either male or female, even when we don't know the person's gender. Since the masculine gender is the default gender in cases where we don't know, we usually supply the masculine pronouns and adjectives. It is very awkward to say, "The pioneer rode on his or her wagon." Instead, we usually say, "The pioneer rode on his wagon," thereby giving the false impression that the only pioneers were men. Advocates of a gender-neutral language have tried, with only partial success, to encourage us to use language in gender-neutral ways. This demands that we pay attention to our use of language, but that is usually something good. With some degree of care, it is usually possible to reformulate our language in gender-neutral ways. I have often used plural constructions in this book precisely for this reason.

Sexist vocabulary abounds in our language. Sometimes it is rooted in differential perceptions: a man is seen as "assertive," a woman behaving in exactly the same way is perceived as "aggressive."

Sometimes the specific words tell us a lot. Obscene, transitive verbs describing sexual intercourse (e.g., "screw") are usually used in such a way as to place women as the direct object and are usually synonymous in English with "to harm or to hurt." This suggests a view of sexual intercourse that few of us would commend. Sexist language is often used to exert power. In the interview with Dr. Frances Conley, we see some of the ways in which her male colleagues used sexist language to intimidate and establish their own superior position of power.

Although it is easy to parody some attempts to eliminate sexist language, the point underlying such attempts is both clear and commendable. When we respect and care about someone, we speak both to them and about them in ways that manifest that respect and concern. In the final analysis, we try to avoid sexist language because we care about persons and respect them, and such language is incompatible with such caring and respect. If, on the other hand, we do not care for and respect others, our sexist language only solidifies and exacerbates that lack of caring and respect. The language is not the root problem, but the symptom of something deeper that has gone wrong. But just as it is valuable in medicine to reduce symptoms of disease, so too, there is a value in reducing sexist language, even though such reductions are far from a cure for the underlying ailment.

Sex Discrimination

Discrimination based on gender has certainly diminished over the years, but it still remains an important issue in American society. Although the Equal Rights Amendment was never ratified by the required number of states, there are a number of legal guarantees available to individuals, especially women, who are the objects of sex discrimination. Moreover, numerous affirmative action programs have helped to increase the representation of women in places where they had previously been discriminated against.

Overt job discrimination. Overt discrimination, where a woman is denied a job or promotion solely because she is a woman or is paid less than her male counterpart in the same job, has decreased significantly in recent years. In the 1960s, women made 59 cents for every dollar earned by men. In 1990, this figure was 72 cents, and, for younger women during that year, it was 80 cents. How much of this remaining discrepancy is due to discrimination and how much is due to other factors (women, on the average, work fewer hours per week than their male counterparts, many have fewer years of work experience than men of the same age, some leave the job force earlier when the family no longer needs the second income, etc.) is unclear, but it is clear that the relative position of women to men in the marketplace—although still subordinate—is definitely improving. Those who are discriminated against in these ways have legal recourse, even without the ERA, and there is an increasingly wide consensus in American society that we ought not to discriminate against people on the basis of gender. Although we may fail to live up to our ideals in this area, clearly equal pay for equal work has become one of our accepted ideals.

Comparable worth. One of the more subtle ways in which sex discrimination occurs is when predominantly female occupations are paid less than comparable occupations whose employees are predominantly male. Examples come easily enough to mind: plumbers and truck drivers versus cleaning staff and secretaries. Although intuitively this seems true (at least to me), there are two significant problems in translating this intuition into something more concrete and effective. First, the notion of "comparable," although intuitively plausible, is very difficult to make precise. Second, many (especially market conservatives) are very wary of intervening in the market to regulate wages.

Legal protection: theory and implementation. Finally, it is important to note that it is often insufficient simply to pass legislation prohibiting something like sex discrimination unless there is a monitoring and enforcement structure to implement the legislation. Often, the impact of the legislation can be undermined if there is insufficient funding for its implementation.

Sexual Harrassment

Harassment in general consists of using undue and unwelcome *means*—usually short of outright violence—to pressure someone to some *end,* usually to do something that the harrassee does not want to do. Thus there are two crucial components of harassment: the means and the end. Workers might try to force a fellow worker to quit by pouring coffee in his locker, letting the air out of his car's tires, calling him on the phone repeatedly in the middle of the night. Such actions would be the means of harassment, while the end would be forcing the other worker to quit.

Sexual harassment is usually sexual in two senses: (1) the *end* is usually to pressure someone (usually a woman) to have sexual intercourse with the harasser; and (2) the *means* to this end are usually things such as repeated sexual innuendoes, unwanted fondling, showing pictures, and so on. Sometimes, however, the means may be comparatively unrelated to sex; they may be threats about losing one's job, a promotion, a raise, or something else that the harasser controls. Sometimes, too, the end may not even really be sexual: it may simply be about power. In the interview with Dr. Frances Conley, she speculates that her male harassers were primarily concerned with establishing their own dominance.

Several points need to be made about sexual harassment. First, most of us would agree that the less harassment in society, the better. This applies to all types of harassment, not just sexual harassment. Second, we are particularly wary of harassment of those who are most vulnerable to the intimidation of harassment: individuals of little power (usually women, often financially vulnerable) who have something (sex) that the harasser wants. Third, it is sometimes difficult to make judgments about incidents of harassment, especially when dealing with a single incident in isolation and without witnesses. However, in practice, harassment is often repeated and often done in front of other people. Fourth, sometimes appropriate expressions of sexual interest may cross the line into sexual harassment, either due to the insensitivity of the harasser or to the oversensitivity of the harrassee.

What can we do to reduce sexual harassment in our society?

Given these general points about harassment, the central question facing us as a society in this regard is the extent to which we want actively to discourage sexual harassment, to provide special protection to those who may be victimized by it, and to punish those who harass. Sexual harassment can be discouraged through educational programs (beginning in schools, continuing on the job), the media, and the like. This is by no means limited to government initiatives; individuals can decide to provide appropriate models for dealing with harassment in their personal and public lives, in their business dealings, and so on. Potential victims can be afforded special protection through tough antiharassment laws and through vigorous prosecution of those laws. Yet again, this is not simply a matter of legislation. Individuals can speak out against harassment when they witness it, even though it does not directly affect them. Companies can have strong internal policies against it, and it can be a serious factor in personnel decisions. Finally, we can pass strong legislation at various levels of government that discourage and punish sexual harassment.

Rape

One of the ways in which women's experience of the world differs from men's is that it includes the possibility of rape as a much more omnipresent and real threat. Indeed, except for the unusual circumstances of homosexual rape in prisons, men are virtually free from this threat in their everyday lives. Women, however, encounter it lurking in the corners of their everyday world: a deserted parking lot late at night, a seldom-used staircase in an office building, getting one's keys out in order to open the front door of one's apartment.

No one defends rape, so that is hardly a moral issue. However, many things may contribute indirectly toward taking rape less seriously than we should—pornography, media depictions of violence against women—and certainly one of the moral issues is the extent to which these should be regulated in order to reduce the climate of violence toward women. Moreover, there are issues of conflicting rights in rape trials—the victim's right to protection versus the defendant's right to a strong defense—that bear directly on how women can bring charges of rape against an individual without having the trial itself become another ordeal of violation. Finally, there are important issues of definition. Date rape, for example, raises important issues about the definition of consent. Some feminists go further and see rape as a metaphor—indeed, almost a literal description—for typical interactions between men and women, but there is a danger in such claims. If many things that do not involve forced sexual intercourse are seen as rape, then the danger is that standard instances of rape will be taken less seriously.

For women to be as safe from rape as men, special measures seem appropriate in at least three areas. First, we should do whatever we can, consistent with the rights of free speech, to reduce the climate of violence against women. The focus here need not be on government restrictions, although those may have their place. A refusal to patronize things that advocate such violence (particular movies, rap music groups, authors, etc.) does not deny the right of free speech, it simply asserts the right to be opposed to the content of some free speech as morally wrong. Similarly, a personal willingness to stand up and speak out individually when one encounters such violence is crucial. Second, our criminal justice system must insure that accusers are not treated like criminals and that trials do not repeat the victim's violation. Much has been done in this area with teams specially trained to handle rape cases, but much remains to be done. If my house is burglarized, the principal issue is not whether I locked the front door securely enough; similarly, in rape cases the principal issue should not be the consent of the victim. Finally, if the purpose of punishment is (at least in part) deterrence, then every effort needs to be made to punish offenders in ways that minimize the chance of recurrence.

Pornography

Supporters of increased respect for women find the issue of pornography particularly troubling. On the one hand, it is clear that most pornography that depicts women does so in ways that debase women and that often make them the objects of violence. Such depictions, many believe, contribute to an atmosphere of disrespect toward women and implicitly sanction violence toward women. On the other hand, most supporters of women's rights consider the right to free speech to be fundamental to our society, and as a result they are very wary of legislation that restricts freedom of speech. Indeed, they realize that there is no shortage of persons who are willing to censor feminist ideas and that encouraging restrictions in the case of pornography may well open the door to censorship of their own views. Furthermore, they realize that proposals to ban pornography often ally them politically with conservatives whom they oppose in many other respects.

Some feminists, most notably Catharine MacKinnon, have argued that sometimes words are like deeds, and that the case for banning pornography rests in part on its status as an offensive action. Yet many have argued that it is dangerous to blur the distinction between words and deeds in the way that MacKinnon suggests. To do so extends the concept of an offensive action too far, and the net result is that everything gets trivialized. If uttering a sexist epithet is viewed as an act of rape, then violent rape by a stranger would seem to be in the same category as sexist slurs. Both are objectionable, but they are so different in degree that it seems misleading to lump them into a single category.

Reproductive Rights

One of the more controversial areas in regard to the status of women in society is the issue of reproductive rights. This encompasses a range of issues, including contraception and abortion and the responsibility of fathers.

Pregnancy Control

Advocates of women's rights maintain that one of the most important of women's rights is the right to choose whether and when to bear children. This right, they argue, can never be implemented unless women and girls of childbearing age have adequate access to reliable information about birth control and adequate access to the technology of birth control and, finally, the opportunity to use the means of birth control that they choose. This involves organizations and sometimes schools providing information, often at an early age when the risk of pregnancy is high, to all, but especially to females. It also involves providing contraceptive means (birth control pills, etc.) if requested. Finally, it involves discouraging any sexual relationships in which girls and women are not allowed to use the birth control means of their choice.

Opponents of such proposals often see them as conflicting with parental authority and as encouraging sexual behavior that they—that is, the opponents—would like to discourage. This is particularly an issue for parents with teen-age daughters, where issues of parental rights often conflict with adolescent rights. There is much greater agreement that adult women ought to be able to exert the level of control over pregnancy that they feel is appropriate.

Abortion

Some feminists see abortion solely as an issue of women's rights, and they maintain that no woman ought to be forced to bear a child against her will. Whether the pregnancy resulted involuntarily, accidentally, or even by choice, strong advocates of women's reproductive rights maintain that a woman should be free to choose to terminate the pregnancy if she wishes. We have discussed this issue at length in Chapter 1.

Women's Moral Voice

Do women speak in a different moral voice than men? If so, is it equal, better, or worse than men's?

During the 1970s, while doing work on the psychology of moral development that originally had nothing to do with gender issues, Carol Gilligan gradually came to realize that the dominant psychological framework for understanding moral development (developed by Lawrence Kohlberg)[1] failed to illuminate women's psychological development in a satisfactory way. Indeed, trying to categorize females' responses to moral dilemmas within Kohlberg's framework, which was originally developed solely with male subjects in mind, was like trying to fit round pegs into square holes. Gilligan became increasingly interested in articulating the distinctive characteristics of females' moral experiences, and a series of her essays appeared in 1982 in the volume *In a Different Voice* (Harvard University Press). The book quickly struck a resonant chord with many scholars in a wide range of disciplines, and soon there was an extensive discussion of women's "voices" not only in morality, but in literature, religion, the natural sciences, the social sciences, and the arts. Gilligan argues that whereas men typically think of moral issues in terms of rights, justice, fairness, and duty, women are much more likely to think of these same issues in terms of connectedness, caring, compromise, and interpersonal responsibility. Although the exact relationship between these two voices in Gilligan's view (are they separate but equal, complementary, antithetical, or is one superior to the other?) is unclear, her work has provoked a tremendous amount of research and speculation on gender differences, especially within the moral realm.

While many find Gilligan's work refreshing and liberating, others are disturbed by the ways in which her characterization of women's moral voices seems to echo a traditional stereotype of women as concerned more with feelings than rules, more concrete than abstract, more sympathetic than just. There are two issues here: First, there are *empirical* questions about the accuracy of Gilligan's findings. These are the domain of moral psychologists. Second, there are *normative* questions about the validity of each of these voices, and those questions fall primarily in the realm of moral philosophy.

Models of the Place of Gender in Society

Just as we saw that there was disagreement about the role of race in society, so too, we find that there is a significant degree of disagreement about precisely what the role of gender ought to be in society. The fundamental question that we face here is how we envision a future ideal society in regard to gender. Would it be one in which men and women occupy relatively traditional roles such as were common a generation ago? Is it one in which all references to gender have been banished, a unisex society? Is it one in which we still have some traditional roles but individuals—whether male or female—are free to choose whatever roles they want? Let's turn to a closer consideration of each of these three models of the place of gender in society.

The Traditional Model

Advocates of the traditional model of gender roles see the place of women as primarily in the home and the place of men as primarily in the workplace. Even within the home, the husband is seen as head of the family and the wife is viewed as subservient to him. For a man, his home is his castle; for his wife, the home is all too often something to be cleaned and a place of unpaid work. In the workplace, traditionalists usually—either explicitly in earlier times, or now implicitly—advocate a gender-based division of labor in which women occupy only low-paying (maids), menial (cleaning women), subservient (secretaries), and child-related (elementary school teachers) jobs that typically receive less pay than their male counterparts.

Critics of the traditional model argue that it places women in an inferior position in the home and in the workplace as well. Women's work in the home is unpaid, and their labor in the workplace is underpaid. Moreover, women's options are most severely limited in this model, and they are especially limited from jobs that bring wealth and power. Moreover, in an age when man are freer to divorce their wives in midlife and marry younger women after their family is grown, and in an age when all too many fathers ignore child support, women are especially vulnerable to financial abandonment in middle age. In a society that is reluctant to hire middle-aged people, especially those without a strong employment history, such women face great challenges when they try to return to the workforce. Some critics of this model also add that the model is also injurious to men, forcing them into an emotionally constricting gender-based stereotype that denies them the joys of close relationships and places the burdens of financial support squarely on their shoulders.

Defenders of the traditional model center around the necessity of this model for a strong family life and the importance of strong family life for society as a whole. Although talk about family values is often vague and misleading, there is clearly a sound point here: the most effective juncture for dealing with many widespread social problems is before they begin, and the best time to do this is when children are young and in the home. We shall return to a discussion of this topic below when we consider gender roles and the family.

The Androgynous Model

At the other extreme from the traditional model, some have advocated a model of society in which gender would be as irrelevant as, for example, eye color presently is. Just as eye color makes no difference in job selection, salary, voting, child care, or anything else remotely similar, so, too—according to the androgynous model—gender should make no differences in these things either. Defenders of androgyny differ about how extensive the domain of the androgynous ought to be. The most extreme position, *strong androgyny,* maintains that sex- and gender-based distinctions ought to be eliminated whenever possible in all areas of life. *Weak androgyny* maintains that gender-based discrimination ought to be eliminated in the public realm (i.e., the workplace and the political realm), but in the private realm of personal relationships it may be unobjectionable.

Among the objections raised to androgyny, three stand out. First, many argue that strong androgyny is impossible. There are simply too many differences between men and women for it to be possible to fit all into the same inevitably constricting mold. Indeed, recent research—which is quickly echoed in pop psychology and therapy—seems to suggest that there are many differences, including in areas such as communication styles. Trying to cram everyone into a single model would undo the progress we have made in understanding and appreciating our differences. The merit of this claim will be discussed below in the section of the nature-nurture controversy. Second, many claim that, even if strong androgyny were possible, it is hardly desirable. Just as we seek to encourage diversity and difference in society as a whole, so too, such critics argue, we should try to encourage diversity and difference in the domain of gender. Finally, some have argued that strong androgyny is part of a larger view that sees men primarily as oppressors and women primarily as victims.

Some defenders of strong androgyny reply to such criticisms by defending a weaker version of their position, which simply seeks to abolish sex-based stereotyping and prohibit, at least within the realm of work and politics, discrimination based on gender. At the juncture, androgyny comes increasingly close to the next model, which emphasizes the importance of freedom of choice for all persons.

The Maximal Choice Model

Finally, many have argued in favor of a model that seeks to eliminate any gender-based restrictions on individual choice. In contrast to advocates of strict androgyny, supporters of the maximal choice model do not seek a unisex society. They are willing to accept that men and women may typically develop different personality traits and that there might even be typical differences in behavior. However, they stress the centrality of establishing a society that promotes *freedom of choice,* so that individuals can make whatever choices they want in both public and private life irrespective of their gender. Gender-based discrimination in the workplace and in the political realm would be abolished, and equally qualified men and women would have equal accessibility to any job, profession, or office they desire. Similarly, within the family, men and women would be equally free to occupy any combination of roles traditionally associated with either men or women.

Criticisms of this model come from both sides. Traditionalists maintain that this model leads to great confusion in roles for everyone, and that social coherence is reduced as a result. Strong androgynists claim that, unless freedom of choice is reinforced with a strong restructuring of gender-based societal roles and expectations, the "freedom" is illusory: People will be subtly shifted into roles that correspond to the majority's expectations. Only a more radical form of androgyny will establish the social order necessary to insure genuine freedom of choice.

The Nature-Nurture Controversy

Obviously, the choice of models in this realm will depend in part on the extent to which a choice is possible. Some have argued that choice is limited by human nature, and that nature fixes (at least to some extent) our gender roles. Others have claimed that these roles are established primarily (perhaps even exclusively) through nurture and are thus open to change. Advocates of change support the nurture side of this controversy, while advocates of the status quo (or, in some cases, an idealized version of it) support the nature side of the debate.

Although this controversy obviously cannot be settled here, it is important to distinguish three questions when evaluating arguments in this area. First, to what extent do differences between the sexes actually exist? This is an empirical question best answered through careful research, especially in the natural and social sciences. Second, if differences do exist, what is their basis? Are they genetically based, "hard-wired" differences that remain unaffected by environmental changes or are they part of our "software" that can be reprogrammed through changes in child rearing, education, and the like? This is also an empirical question, but a more difficult one since it is asking about the *causes* of certain empirical conditions, not simply whether the empirical conditions exist. Third, whether there are differences or not, we must ask whether there *ought* to be differences and, if so, what those differences ought to be.

Gender Roles and the Family

If we genuinely treat men and women equally, what happens to the family?

The place of gender in the family is one of the most difficult and controversial areas in which to seek common ground. As we indicated above in the discussion of the traditional model of gender roles, women pay a high price in their lives for their commitment to family—often a higher price than their male counterparts. As women have sought more equal access to the rewards of the workplace and more equal distribution of the responsibilities of home and family life, many men and women have been forced to rethink the ideal of the family and the way in which responsibilities have been apportioned by gender.

As Susan Moller Okin shows in the selection from her "Justice, Gender, and the Family," we would have to reorganize the family significantly if we were to make the family a just institution. In particular, responsibilities for the home and for children would have to be distributed evenly, and this entails a significant restructuring of roles. Such restructuring need not conflict with important social values, but it certainly involves a significant reordering of priorities and responsibilities for men.

How Should We Try to Realize Our Ideal Society?

We have seen that, once we are concerned about gender equality, we must face a wide range of issues. Some of these are relatively specific: gender discrimination in employment, sexual harassment, and pornography. Some are more global in character: whether there are distinctive moral voices for men and women, what kind of gender roles we want to endorse in society.

As we develop a position on each of these issues, we must also ask how we can best move toward realizing that position. We have seen that, in regard to specific issues, some mixture of legislation and individual and group initiative seems to offer the best hope of a more just society.

Just as we did in regard to issues of race and ethnicity, we can distinguish among (1) *strict equality legislation,* that seeks to insure that women are not treated any differently than men; (2) *special protection legislation,* which seeks to provide special protections to people (usually women) in especially vulnerable situations such as rape or sexual harassment; and (3) *affirmative action legislation,* which seeks to remedy inequalities through various types of affirmative action programs that are basically like those developed for race.

Yet it is important to see these specific issues within the larger context of our ideal for the place of gender in society, for it is our ultimate vision of the role of gender in society that guides our decisions on particular issues. What kind of a relationship do we envision between men and women in the future?

Endnotes

1. Lawrence Kohlberg, *The Philosophy of Moral Development* (San Francisco: Harper & Row, 1981).
2. Christina Hoff Sommers, *Who Stole Feminism?* (New York: Simon and Schuster, 1994).

The Arguments

Catharine MacKinnon
"What Is Sexual Harassment?"

Catharine MacKinnon, a professor at the Law School of the University of Michigan, pioneered the development of the legal concept of sexual harassment. Her book, Sexual Harassment of Working Women, *pioneered the application of civil rights law to sexual harassment. She was co-counsel in the first sexual harassment case heard by the Supreme Court. Her other books include* Toward a Feminist Theory of the State, Only Words, *and, with Andrea Dworkin,* In Harm's Way.

In this short interview, MacKinnon outlines the main components of sexual harassment.

As You Read, Consider This:

1. How exactly does MacKinnon define sexual harassment? To what extent is it subjective? To what extent is it objective?
2. Why is sexual harassment often so difficult to prove?

Q: What is sexual harassment?

A: In its broadest definition, it is sexual pressure that you are not in a position to refuse. In its verbal form, it includes a working environment that is saturated with sexual innuendoes, propositions, advances. Other forms include leering, for example, at a woman's breasts while she talks, or staring up her skirt while she is bending over to get files. In its physical form, it includes unwanted sexual touching and rape.

Q: When was sexual harassment first recognized as a legal concept?

A: There were earlier cases, but the breakthrough occurred in 1977 when the Court of Appeals for the District of Columbia decided that Paulette Barnes was discriminated against when her government job was abolished in retaliation for her refusal to grant sexual favors to her boss. The Barnes case established that sexual harassment is sex discrimination under the Civil Rights Act. The 1986 Supreme Court case not only ratified the Barnes result but recognized as well that sexual harassment also encompasses a sexually hostile working environment.

Q: How does a woman prove she has been subjected to harassment?

A: A woman may have kept records or confided in friends, or she may have exhibited behavior—she may act upset, for example—consistent with having been aggressed against sexually. But the primary evidence is what the woman says happened.

Q: But if all she has is her word, isn't she in a very difficult position?

A: Unfortunately, yes. It is very difficult for a woman to go up against a man's denial. Based on my experience with complaints at all levels, the rule of thumb is that it takes at least three women who are victims to counteract the simple stonewalling of a man. In matters of sexual abuse, women have one-third of a man's credibility, at best.

Q: It must be hard, then, for a woman to come forward with complaints of sexual harassment?

A: It was clearly difficult for Anita Hill. It should be noted that most of the women who have brought forward claims that have advanced the laws of sexual harassment have been black. Because racism is often sexualized, black women have been particularly clear in identifying this behavior as a violation of their civil rights.

Q: Do you think Professor Hill's appearance before the Judiciary Committee will encourage other women to come forward?

A: I don't know how many women will want to be subjected to the kind of brutal cross-examination Professor Hill withstood with such grace. Still, I think more women will see that Anita Hill did survive and will understand that what she did she did for all women. They will see that if they come forward with these kinds of allegations, they will not only survive but change the world for women, like she did.

Journal/Discussion Questions

✍ *Have you ever been involved in, or witnessed, an incident of sexual harassment? How well does MacKinnon's definition apply to that incident?*

1. What is MacKinnon's definition of sexual harassment? Do you agree with it? Is it too narrow or too broad?
2. What are the issues surrounding the question of proving sexual harassment? Develop and defend your own position on this issue.

Linda L. Peterson
"The Reasonableness of the Reasonable Woman Standard"*

Linda Peterson, who teaches at the University of San Diego, specializes in medieval philosopy and in ethics. In this article, she addresses what is perhaps the most vexing question in regard to sexual harassment. What standard should be used in judging whether something is harassment or not? Should we define this according to what any reasonable person would consider to be harassment? Or should it be what any reasonable woman would consider to be harassment?

As You Read, Consider This:

1. What major court case exemplifies the reasonable person standard? What case exemplifies the reasonable women standard?
2. Why does Peterson claim that the reasonable person standard is not acceptable?
3. What are the principal objections to the reasonable woman standard?

* *Public Affairs Quarterly,* Volume 13, Number 2 (April, 1999), pp. 141–158.

In sexual harassment litigation, there is often agreement between opposing parties about the non-moral characterization of the behavior of the alleged offender(s). The pivotal point of contention almost invariably centers on whether or not the behavior at issue can be characterized as "offensive," "objectionable," "intimidating," "harmful," and so on. Recent court decisions in this area of law are underwritten by a common presupposition: *viz.*, the appropriateness or inappropriateness of these morally laden descriptions of the relevant behavior must be relativized to some standard of assessment or point of view.

Yet there is no commonly endorsed position about what that point of view should be. Some decisions rely on the perspective or point of view of the ostensibly genderless "reasonable person." The "Reasonable Person Standard" (hereafter RPS) is supposed to represent the most objective and unbiased perspective that it is possible to take.[1] Appeal to this standard dates back as far as 1837.[2] The "reasonable man of ordinary prudence" is a mythical creature whose point of view is supposed to mirror prevailing cultural norms: "He is a personification of a community ideal of reasonable behavior, determined by the jury's social judgment."[3]

As the number of sexual harassment lawsuits has increased, some courts have shifted to the "Reasonable Woman Standard"[4] (hereafter RWS). The adoption of this perspectival framework by these courts has been motivated by the belief that women tend to assess behavior differently from men.[5] The same behavior under the non-moral description may be seen as "harassing" from the point of view of the hypothetical "reasonable woman," while not being seen to be an instance of harassment from the point of view of the alleged harasser(s).

While the perspective of the "reasonable person" is commonly held to be "objective," the perspective of the "reasonable woman" is typically characterized as "subjective."[6] Unfortunately, there seems to be no consensus about what is meant by the terms "objective" and "subjective" as applied to these standards of assessment. In what follows, I assess arguments presented by legal scholars and jurists in their debate over the acceptability of the RWS. In reviewing such arguments, I find the term "subjective" being used in a variety of different senses. My position, ultimately, is that the most commonly advanced arguments based on the supposed subjectivity of the RWS are flawed in any sense of the term. Finally, I contend that the subjective/objective dichotomy cannot be applied to a critique of the relative merits of the RPS over the RWS in a nonquestion-begging way.

I. The RPS vs. the RWS in Application

I will begin by synopsizing two landmark cases for sexual harassment law. These cases clearly illustrate the manner in which the two standards of assessment have profoundly influenced the outcome of sexual harassment claims.

Rabidue v. Osceola Refining Co. and the RPS

Plantiff, Vivien Rabidue, alleged that, during her term of employment at Osceola, she was repeatedly subjected to verbal and other forms of abuse and harassment by her supervisor, Douglas Henry. Rabidue was the only woman working in a supervisory position for the refining company. In 1986, her case was decided by the United States Court of Appeals for the Sixth Circuit. The majority opinion characterized defendant Henry as follows:

> . . . an extremely vulgar and crude individual who customarily made obscene comments about women generally, and, on occasion, directed such obscenities to the plaintiff. Management was aware of Henry's vulgarity, but had been unsuccessful in curbing his offensive personality traits during the time encompassed by this controversy. The plaintiff and Henry, on the occasions when their duties exposed them to each other, were constantly in a confrontation posture. The plaintiff, as well as other female employees, were annoyed by Henry's vulgarity.[7]

Henry was reported to have said of Rabidue: "All that bitch needs is a good lay." Further, defendant Henry referred to Rabidue as a "fat ass," and also used the words "cunt" and "whore."[8] Offensive photos of women were displayed within the workplace environment. One such photo featured a man with a golf club standing over a naked woman with a golf ball between her breasts. The plaintiff alleged that she had been made the brunt of sexual jokes and insults on the part of her supervisor. Dissenting Judge J. Keith wrote of plaintiff Rabidue:

> [She] was the only woman in a salaried management position; she was denied similar wage benfits as her male peers; the male she alleged charges against was not fired because his computer expertise was needed; and the plaintiff was the one who was reprimanded and eventually fired.[9]

Yet the majority in this case found against the plaintiff, who was described, in their opinion, as "capable, independent, ambitious, aggressive, intractable, and opinionated."[10] The majority appealed to what was described as "the perspective of a reasonable person's reaction to a similar environment under like or similar circumstances."[11] Apparently, in their judgment, Rabidue's own perspective and assessment of her supervisor and the working environment at Osceola did not fit that of the "reasonable person." In finding against Rabidue, the court maintained that:

> . . . in the absence of conduct which would interfere with that hypothetical reasonable individual's work performance and affect seriously the psychological well-being of that reasonable person under like circumstances, a plaintiff may not prevail on asserted charges . . . regardless of whether the plaintiff was actually offended by the defendant's conduct. . . . In the case at bar, the record effectively disclosed that Henry's obscenities, although annoying, were not so startling as to have affected seriously the psyches of the plaintiff or other female employees.[12]

Further, according to the majority opinion, the environment at Osceola was consistent with what is acceptable from the point of view of society at large. Displays deemed offensive by Rabidue, following the majority opinion, need to be considered "in the context of a society that condones and publicly features and commercially exploits open displays of written and pictorial erotica at the newsstands, on prime-time television, at the cinema, and in other public places."[13]

Ellison v. Brady and the RWS

Plaintiff, Kerry Ellison, worked as an agent for the Internal Revenue Service. Her coworker, Sterling Gray, developed an obsessional attraction to her and repeatedly asked her out. Ellison refused his requests for social engagements, but Gray persisted, writing a note and two love letters. In her *Whittier Law Review* synopsis of *Ellison v. Brady,* Tracy Treger observes that Gray's written communications with Ellison were "neither lewd nor obscene."[14] Treger further remarks that the objectionable conduct in the Ellison case was "not nearly as egregious as the conduct in ... other cases that found actionable harassment."[15]

Yet, in 1991, the United States Court of Appeals for the Ninth Circuit found for plaintiff Ellison. In deeming the alleged harassing conduct to be actionable under Title VII of the Civil Rights Act of 1964, the Ellison majority appealed to the RWS, while rejecting the RPS as being unduly biased toward the perspective of men. The court held that the RPS fails to take into account the manner in which women are acculturated in our society. From the point of view of the RWS, the court maintained, it is understandable that behavior that might strike men as innocuous and unobjectionable could be perceived as frightening and threatening from a woman's perspective.[16]

In the sections to follow, I consider the ethical implications of appeals to the RPS, as in the Rabidue case, as opposed to appeals to the RWS, as in the Ellison case. I will begin by stating some arguments against the RWS based on its ostensible subjectivity.

II. Objections to the Use of a Subjective Standard in Sexual Harassment Cases

The supposed objectivity of the RPS is said to reside in the appeal of this standard to what is generally accepted within the society or community as a whole. In her review of the history of sexual harassment law, legal scholar Coralie Whitcomb notes that the courts have developed a "dual test" to be used in determining whether a workplace environment is hostile:

1. Does the behavior offend some community standard of what is acceptable? (objective test)
2. Was the behavior offensive (unwelcome) to the individual? (subjective test)[17]

Regarding the employment of these tests, Whitcomb observes:

> When definitions of actionable conduct for sexual harassment complaints are debated, the discussion utilizes an objective approach. It is in this arena where the 'reasonable person test' has been used to decide whether a so called 'reasonable person' would consider the behavior to be sufficiently severe or pervasive to alter the conditions of employment and create an abusive work environment.[18]

Commenting on the U.S. Supreme Court's view of the "unwelcomeness test," legal scholar Caroline Forrell notes: "The Court requires the plaintiff, in addition to proving that the environment is objectively abusive, to show that *she perceived it as abusive.*" [Emphasis mine][19] In the Ellison case, the plaintiff's individual perceptions of the Gray's behavior carried a great deal of weight with the court in their determination that the behavior was abusive. Objections to emphasis on the alleged victim's point of view, in such cases, underwrite the following arguments against the RWS.

Prioritizing Perspectives: The Unfairness Charge

From a purely moral standpoint, unless some version of radical subjectivism is true, it is obvious that "perceived by some individual as abusive" does not automatically yield "is abusive." Let us suppose that the alleged harasser in the Ellison case, Sterling Gray, did not see his behavior as abusive. To grant the plaintiff's point of view a privileged status simply because the plaintiff is a woman seems, *prima facie,* unfair.

Further, suppose we accept the court's opinion that plaintiff Ellison's point of view derives from her acculturation as a woman in this society. If the gender acculturation hypothesis is extended, then, to Gray's point of view, it seems that he could not help seeing his behavior differently from the way it was seen by Ellison, given that his point of view was the culmination of a different acculturation process. Since there are two different acculturation processes culminating in two opposing points of view, there needs to be some way of determining which point of view is decisive. Granting the plaintiff's subjective perspective priority over that of the alleged harasser because it is the result of a different acculturation process seems, *ceteris paribus,* unfair to the accused. Accordingly, it appears that fairness requires an appeal to some objective standard to use as a prioritization or ranking principle for the disparate perspectives.

Stereotyping and Gender-Essentialism

As a landmark case for sexual harassment law, the Ellison case set the stage for the use of the RWS in other cases alleging harassment leading to a hostile working environment. There is skepticism among feminist legal scholars, however, about what sort of precedent the Ellison case sets. The Ellison decision is based on acknowledgement that Kerry Ellison was irritated and annoyed by Gray's written love messages to her. But the fact that Ellison was annoyed does not necessarily indicate that other similarly situated women would be annoyed as well. Yet insofar as the Ellison case is able to function as a precedent in the legal arena, the implication is that her point of view *does* reflect the perspective of women generally.

The assumptions underlying the latter conclusion are two-fold. The first is that it makes sense to attribute some perspective or point of view to women as a group. This is the assumption that *gender-essentialism* is true, *viz.,* that there is some generic outlook—some common framework of beliefs, desires, expectations, values, etc.—shared by all persons who are of the same sex. Legal scholar Angela Harris equates "gender-essentialism" as applied to women, with "the notion that a unitary 'essential' women's experience can be isolated and described independently of race, class, sexual orientation, and other realities of experience."[20] The second assumption follows straightforwardly from the first. If all women, inherently, share a common point of view, then it makes sense to take any particular woman's point of view as representative of women generally.

Of course, apart from the essentialist presupposition, this sort of inferential leap would seem to be an instance of the fallacy of hasty generalization. And, indeed, many feminists take the inference from a particular woman's point of view to what all women want, need, desire, and so on, to be fallacious in just that way. The assumption that all women share a singular point of view ignores significant differences among women relating to (*e.g.,* age, relative affluence or poverty, health, sexual orientation, ethnicity).[21]

The Proliferation of Subjective Standards

The law is supposed to apply equally and uniformly to all. But, some legal scholars reason, the uniformity of the law is undercut by the application of a subjective standard for women. If the law allows the particular point of view of an individual, *qua woman,* to have privileged status and to be regarded as exemplifying the perspective of all women, then uniformity requires that there should be standards linked to other non-gender based characteristics as well. But this would lead, inevitably, to an unmanageable proliferation of standards. Tracy Treger puts this argument as follows:

> Although a particular woman may react differently than a man to the same incident of harassment, a new standard is not warranted. If the court were correct in thinking that we need a reasonable woman standard, then a similar argument would show that the reasonable person standard in such areas as torts should be replaced by a variety of standards—reasonable blind person, reasonable elderly person, reasonable baby-boomer, etc.[22]

This criticism is clearly linked to the argument stated in the previous section relating to gender-essentialism and stereotyping. The argument, fully spelled out, runs as follows. Gender-essentialism (which takes off from subjectivity at the individual level) leads to gender-stereotyping. And gender-stereotyping leads to stereotyping on the basis of other characteristics, which will lead eventually to so many diverse characteristic-based standards that there will be a return to focus on individual subjectivity. Obviously, if each alleged victim's point of view were regarded as decisive in settling harassment disputes, there would be as many subjective standards as there are plaintiffs.

Subjective Standards as Perpetuating Discrimination

Some critics hold that the RWS will harm women in that it will perpetuate sex discrimination. Suppose one woman is seen as being particularly vulnerable, sensitive and in need of special treatment. If this individual's personal point of view is taken to represent women generally, then all women will be seen as hypersensitive, overly vulnerable and in need of being treated with kid gloves. According to an opinion of the Michigan Supreme Court, "courts utilizing the reasonable woman standard pour into the standard stereotypical assumptions of women which infer women are sensitive, fragile, and in need of a more protective standard."[23] And, in their *amicus curiae* opinion as conveyed to the Michigan court, the University of Michigan Women and Law Clinic maintained that the support the RWS provides some women as individuals will contravene and undermine women's interests at the group level:

> [Women will be seen as] a weaker, less able group in need of protection. In effect, distinguishing women for special protection puts them back in the disadvantaged position which led to the need for special protection in the first place.[24]

Thus, following this line of criticism, the RWS is likely to have the opposite of its intended effect. Designed, originally, to insure equal treatment of women in the workplace, this argument holds that it is likely, instead, to perpetuate sex-discrimination and gender-bias. At bottom, the claim is that the RWS promotes the mistaken view that women are emotionally and psychologically more vulnerable than men. And this mistaken view, RWS critics maintain, will be compounded by a further mistake, *viz.*, the assumption that women are less capable of handling the rigors of demanding employment roles. Accordingly, following this line of criticism, the RWS will lead to women being denied hiring and promotional opportunities to which equal treatment under the law entitles them.

III. Analysis of the term "Subjective" as Applied to the RWS

The pivotal assumption underlying each of the foregoing arguments against the RWS is that it is a *subjective* standard of assessment and, therefore, objectionable. A review of the debate over the RWS shows the term "subjective" to be used in three different senses. In this section, I analyze each of these senses and discuss the implications of using "subjective" in each sense, respectively.

Subjectivity as Mind-Dependence

In claiming that the subjective test for abusiveness relies on the particular woman's *perceptions* of behavior, legal scholars are using the term "subjective" in the same way that philosophers use it when they refer to Cartesian subjectivity. In the *Meditations,* Descartes introduces skepticism about the existence of a mind-independent correlate to the individual's perceptions *via* the "Dreaming Argument."[25] Descartes indicates that, based on a purely phenomenological inventory of one's perceptions, there seems to be no criterion by which to differentiate veridical (waking) perceptions from non-veridical (dreaming) perceptions. A subject might believe her perceptions to be causally linked to mind-independent objects, but, if she is dreaming, she is deceived in believing this.

Likewise, in sexual harassment cases where the individual's perceptions are considered relevant, the following problem arises. The same subjective states (taken in the Cartesian sense) of the alleged victim are compatible with both (a) the presence of an objectively real harm, and (b) the absence of an objectively real harm. Thus, a kind of moral skepticism about the objectivity of the alleged victim's perception is introduced—the moral analogue of the metaphysical skepticism about the objectivity of perceptions generated by Descartes. The upshot is that the alleged victim's perceptions are regarded as possibly delusional. It is possible, then, that the alleged victim is like a hypochrondriac whose somatic perceptions are not linked to any objectively real pathological process. The "victim" may perceive herself as being harmed when there is no objective warrant for this perception.

Legal scholar Coralie Whitcomb appeals to the Cartesian sense of "subjective" in her critique of standards such as the RWS. She uses the term "subjective" defined as pertaining to "experience or knowledge conditioned by merely personal characteristics of mind or by particular states of mind. . . . "[26] In the Ellison case, the district court (whose decision was subsequently overturned by the Ninth Circuit Court of Appeals) refused to adopt a gender-based standard of assessment. The district court's decision in this case was based on the assumption that Ellison's perceptions of Gray's behavior were, in fact, illusory. The district court concluded that Ellison's perceptions of harm had no objective correlate, and that the defendant's behavior was, in reality, "isolated and genuinely trivial."[27] In refusing to adopt a gender-based standard, the district court declined to base its decision on what it took to be Ellison's subjective mental states.

Subjectivity as Idiosyncracy within a Group

On this rendering of the term "subjective," the causal linkage between the subject's perceptions and the behavior of the alleged harasser is not questioned. Instead, it is taken for granted that the relevant behavior *is* offensive and harmful to the victim. But the effects the behavior produced in the victim are regarded as being the result of a possibly anomalous or atypical causal process. Granted that certain actions produced a certain effect in the plaintiff (as Gray's sending messages offended and harassed Ellison), there is still the issue of whether or not the plaintiff's response is idiosyncratic. It could be that the majority of women would respond differently to the same behavior. Given this view of the victim's subjective assessment, the victim is not being viewed as possibly delusional. She is not the analogue of the hypochondriac. Instead, she is seen as being like a person who responds atypically to the injection of a drug. Her response is taken to be objectively grounded; the causal chain productive of the response is seen to be clear and real. It is just that her response is so unusual as to make it unreasonable that any employer should be expected to have taken precautions to avoid it. The Michigan Supreme Court, for example, viewed the RWS to be subjective in this latter sense. In refusing to adopt the RWS in a case of alleged harassment, the court claimed that:

> [T]he alternative to an objective standard would be to accept all plaintiffs' subjective evaluations of conduct, thereby imposing upon an employer liability for behavior that, for idiosyncratic reasons, is offensive to an employee.[28]

Commenting on the Sixth Circuit Court of Appeals decision in *Rabidue v. Osceola Refining Co.,* legal scholar Nancy Ehrenreich remarks that the court viewed plaintiff Rabidue as being an "unreasonable idiosyncratic woman"—an "overly sensitive, obnoxious woman, incapable of getting along with others. . . . "[29] On Ehrenreich's view of the Rabidue court's decision, the court viewed the defendant's behavior as *harmful,* but the gravity of the harm was "minimized" *via* emphasis on the idiosyncracy of the victim's response. Ehrenreich comments:

> Through emphasizing the plaintiff's 'abrasiveness' and minimizing the harmfulness of the harasser's conduct, the court subtly suggested that something was wrong with Rabidue for having been offended by Henry's behavior.[30]

Criticisms of the ostensible subjectivity of the RWS based on this construal of "subjective" take off from the assumption that the law is not intended to protect the idiosyncratic, anomalous, and atypical person.

"Subjectivity" as Negatively Defined

A third sense of "subjective" accords the term no positive significance, but rather defines "subjective" as "whatever is not objective." In this sense of "subjective," the RWS is held to be *subjective* because it is not *objective* in the way that the RPS allegedly is. Recall that the RPS is supposedly objective in that it takes into account the perspective or point of view of the society as a whole. A standard, then, that does not take prevailing social norms into account is held to be "subjective." According to some of its detractors, the RWS is subjective in that, unlike the "objective" and "unbiased" RPS, the RWS takes only the perspective or point of view of a certain segment of society into account, *viz.,* the perspective of its female members.

IV. Response to Criticisms of the RWS

The arguments against the RWS stated above can be divided into two categories: (1) utilitarian arguments concluding to negative consequences deriving from the RWS, and (2) a deontological, rights-based argument regarding the alleged unfairness of the RWS.

The three consequentialist arguments all rely on the claim that the RWS is subjective, either in the Cartesian sense or in the sense in which subjectivity is equated with idiosyncracy. The unfairness objection relies on the negative construal of the assumed subjectivity of the RWS. I will respond to the consequentialist arguments first.

Arguments Against Generalizing from the Individual's Point of View

The three arguments concluding to negative consequences deriving from the RWS are all intimately related. Gender stereotyping, on the assumption that gender-essentialism is true, is said to lead to unequal treatment of women. Further, the process in which essentialism and stereotyping combine to generate a special standard for women, it is argued, will lead to a similar process occurring in the case of other characteristics (*e.g.,* age and ethnicity) which will eventually lead to an unwieldy proliferation of subjective standards. The way to call a halt to the production of negative consequences, it is contended, is to avoid using any subjective standard (*e.g.,* the RWS) and use only the supposedly objective and gender-neutral RPS.

Now suppose the RWS is regarded as being subjective in the Cartesian sense. Seen in this way, the standard allows the actions of the alleged harasser to be judged according to the subjective perceptions of the individual woman, even while it is acknowledged that those perceptions are *not necessarily grounded in any objective harm.* If the standard is regarded as subjective in this sense, then it would inevitably run interference with itself. For a court would then be in the very odd position of simultaneously endorsing the following competing claims: (1) the subject's perceptions are relevant to the determination of the appropriateness or inappropriateness of the defendant's behavior, and (2) the subject's perceptions are acknowledged to be possibly delusional.

Further, insofar as the subject's perceptions are seen to be purely subjective or "private" in the Cartesian sense, it is impossible, simultaneously, to see them as indicative or reflective of the perspective of women as a group. For, on the Cartesian sense of "subjective," there is no bridge from individual subjectivity to the hypothesis of inter-subjective agreement or consensus. Taking "subjective" in this sense, gender-essentialism and sterotyping are blocked from the outset.

Legal scholar Caroline Forrell makes this latter point in the following passage.[31]

> The purely subjective standard has the advantage of avoiding claims of stereotyping and essentialism because the plaintiff's perceptions are not measured against a universalizing external standard. If the decision maker believes that the plaintiff found the environment to be hostile, sexual harassment is established.[32]

The situation is the same where "subjective," as applied to an individual woman's perspective, is used to characterize that perspective as "atypical" or "idiosyncratic," as opposed to "normal" or "commonly held." A court that adopts the RWS while viewing it as subjective in this sense will hold, simultaneously, that (1) a particular woman's point of view is relevant to the determination of the status of the defendant's behavior, and (2) the particular point of view in question is not representative of women as a group. Clearly, the simultaneous endorsement of these claims is not inconsistent. Still, it is clear that it will be impossible to generalize from an individual perspective that is acknowledged, at the outset, to be anomalous. Hence, on this construal of "subjective" as applied to the RWS, the possibility of stereotyping resulting from gender-essentialism is vitiated.

Ultimately, none of the consequentialist arguments are effective in opposing the RWS on either sense of "subjective" in which an individual's subjective point of view is supposed to be the basis for generalizing about what holds true for women as a group.

The Unfairness Objection

This objection to the RWS does not rest on the assumption that negative consequences will follow on generalizing from a particular individual's point of view. Instead, this objection takes off from the presupposition that the RWS is subjective in what I have called the "negative sense," *viz.*, it fails to capture the prevailing perspective of society as a whole.

To see that the unfairness objection rests on this construal of "subjective" as applied to the RWS, consider how the objection gets raised in response to the Ellison case. In deciding this case by appeal to the RWS, the court gave plaintiff Ellison's point of view priority over Gray's perspective. The court's rationale for appealing to the RWS, as opposed to the RPS, was that the RPS fails to take into account the way in which women are acculturated. For a woman in our society, the fears of being stalked, assaulted and raped form an everpresent backdrop that conditions her experiences, even when she does not perceive any immediate or imminent threat of harm. The Ellison court, taking into account such conditioning elements of women's experiences, reasoned that the plaintiff's perceptions of Gray's behavior as threatening are understandable. In taking into account the broader issue of the socialization of women in our society, the court did not limit its focus of attention to a single individual's subjective point of view.

On the other hand, it is important to note that the court's finding that Ellison's response is *understandable,* as framed in the context of broader culture-based issues, does *not* entail that the court saw her response as necessarily reflective of the way *all* women would respond in a similar situation. Given that all women are subject to similar acculturating influences, it does not follow that those influences will inevitably culminate in every woman responding to a particular kind of situation in exactly the same way. The Ellison court can consistently hold that (1) Ellison's particular response to Gray's advances is not necessarily indicative of any consensus among women as a group, and (2) her response is, nonetheless, reasonable given the way in which women, as a group, are socialized. Thus this court's opinion need not be construed as an instance of gender-essentializing and stereotypical universalizing from an individual woman's subjective responses.

The charge that the Ellison court's appeal to the RWS is unfair arises out of the assumption that focusing on what is unique about women's experiences is to fail to take into account the objective perspective of society as a whole. What, according to this objection, does fairness require? To adjudicate between competing perspectives, some principle of prioritization is required. If it is unjust to prioritize on the basis of a non-moral characteristic, such as sex, then some other ranking principle needs to be found. In his dissenting opinion in the Ellison case, Judge Stevens opposed the application of the RWS, advocating the RPS as an unbiased standard. In her review of the rationale for Judge Stevens' dissent, Coralie Whitcomb observes:

> Judge Stevens returned to the 157-year-old standard of the reasonable man used in the law of torts. He explained that such a standard usually refers to an average adult person, regardless of gender, and was the standard that Title VII presupposed. . . . Judge Stephens concluded by holding that "a gender neutral standard would greatly contribute to the clarity of this and future cases in the area."[33]

Accordingly, the dissenting judge in this case advocates using, as a ranking principle, the standard that putatively reflects generally held beliefs and norms in society at large, *viz.,* the RPS.

Clearly Judge Steven's way of resolving the fairness issue works only on the assumption that the RPS really is unbiased and gender-neutral. If it is not unbiased and gender-neutral, then the RPS has no claim to objectivity over the ostensible subjectivity of the RWS. I take up the problem about genderless standards in the next section.

V. Subjectivity and Objectivity vs. Gender-Bias and Gender-Neutrality

My position is that, given that sexist attitudes and norms continue to permeate our workplace environments and courts of law, there is no reason to believe that a gender-neutral standard of assessment exists. The opinion of the Rabidue court, which was supposed to be the result of applying an unbiased, gender-neutral standard (the RPS), was manifestly biased toward the perspective of the males in the Osceola Refining Co. workplace. Further, if there is no gender-neutral standard, it makes no sense to characterize the RWS as "subjective" insofar as it is ostensibly and nominally gender-biased. For "subjective" is a correlative term that carries significance only in contrast with what can be seen to be "objective." In the absence of any objective standard, there is no subjective standard either.

Caroline Forrell makes the following comment about the alleged gender-neutrality of the RPS:

> I view the need for the reasonable woman standard as transitional. When society evolves to the point where men and women are equal in fact, as well as in theory, the balance in power will most likely result in widespread support for women's perspectives. At such a point in time, if it ever comes, the reasonable person standard would be truly gender-neutral and would be appropriate even in cases involving sexually based injuries.[34]

I agree with Forrell regarding the claim that there is, at present, no gender-neutral standard of assessment. I disagree, however, with the idea that a genderless or gender-neutral standard is the *desideratum.* I hold that a genderless standard of assessment is unacceptable for the following two reasons.

To begin with, even in a utopian society that is virtually free of sexism, a genderless standard could not be used to make determinations about *inherently gendered* legal and moral issues. Allegations of sexual harassment are inherently gendered. In order to be in a position to make an adequate evaluation of such allegations, one needs to be able to stand in the shoes of the allegedly oppressed party. A genderless standard takes the perspective of a genderless person—whatever that might be. Suppose a jurist or jury were required to adopt this perspective. Imagine, for example, that you have no gender, nor any sexual characteristics whatsoever. Now try to determine what it would be like to be fondled, pinched, grabbed, called a "whore," a "bitch," and so on.

The ideal of a genderless standard is based on a myth about what it takes to be the best possible evaluator. The best evaluative posture is supposedly the dispassionate, neutral, disembodied stance, completely divorced from lived experience. The ideal evaluator is supposed to be separated and uninvolved. Yet the dispassionate, uninvolved, remote stance is, on the contrary, the worst possible evaluative stance. For it is impossible for one who assumes that stance to take seriously what it is like to be victimized and oppressed.

Secondly, the presumption of gender-neutrality is often a cover for gender-bias. This was the case in the Rabidue court's attempt to achieve objectivity *via* use of the RPS. Of the court's decision, Tracy Treger writes:

> In *Rabidue,* the Sixth Circuit began by using a reasonable person standard. But in its attempt to maintain objectivity, that court disregarded the most relevant factor, gender, and focused on the norms of work environments generally. The court noted that: "[I]n some work environments, humor and language are rough hewn and vulgar. Sexual jokes, sexual conversations and girlie magazines abound." Given that such conduct was the workplace norm, the court held that the environment was not unreasonably offensive.[35]

Treger sees the Rabidue court as ignoring gender. Insofar as the court desired to adopt a gender-neutral perspective, this is clearly what the Sixth Circuit saw itself as doing. But the fact that the court ignored or perspectively eliminated the plaintiff's gender does not entail that it achieved a genderless stance. The court's decision, in the Rabidue case, reeks of gender-bias. The working environment at Osceola Refining is *not* commonplace in our culture. "Girlie magazines" do not abound in banks, hospitals, car dealerships, real estate offices, and other businesses where the public is routinely encountered. The Sixth Circuit's opinion is apparently based on the observation that the working environment at Osceola is normative for that company. But that observation, apart from its obvious triviality, fails to address the salient issue, *viz.,* whether the environment in question is oppressive to women.

In its attempt to place the Osceola environment in a broader social context, as is required by the RPS, the Sixth Circuit claimed that what Vivien Rabidue saw as oppressive is really just the norm for the society in which we live. The court referred to displays of erotica in the media—on newsstands, on television, in movie theatres, and so on.[36] In alluding to the extent to which our society advocates freedom of expression and tolerates open displays of pornography, the court implicitly pits the defendant's freedom of expression against the plaintiff's entitlement to work in an environment free of oppression.[37]

What the court failed to take into account in this case, is that the right to freedom of expression in the workplace is not absolute. At best, it is a *prima facie* entitlement, if that. One cannot, as a rule, use one's workplace as a forum for expressing political support for a candidate. Nor is it standardly acceptable to wear political hats and buttons to work to manifest one's party affiliation. Nor is one allowed to express oneself by dressing in any way one sees fit. Nor is the freedom of sexual expression preserved in the typical workplace environment. An employee in a brokerage firm or bank, for example, would not be allowed to fondle and caress clients, to make obscene or sexually suggestive remarks to clients, and so on.

The right of employees to freedom of expression, in our society, is not allowed to contravene the interests of the employer in profit maximization. Companies, such as Osceola, that permit sexist displays and behavior to permeate the workplace environment do so because the presence of women in the workplace is not seen as vital to their interest in profit maximization. If the goal of profit maximization could not be achieved in an environment alienating to women, the employees' supposed entitlement to indulge in such displays and behavior would be tolerated neither by the employers nor by the courts. It is only in companies where women are viewed as fungible and inessential members of the workforce that such hostile environments are tolerated.

VI. Conclusion

In the end, the subjective/objective dichotomy is out of place as a way of characterizing standards for assessing acceptable conduct in the workplace. Given that there is no purely objective and unbiased perspectival construct from which to assess sexual harassment allegations, there is no warrant for characterizing the RWS as subjective. To do so is to make a distinction without a difference.

Some legal scholars have suggested replacing the RWS with the Golden Rule. Tracy Treger, for example, makes this suggestion: "A better approach, perhaps, is to encourage sensitivity toward *all* fellow employees in the work environment—a type of 'do unto others' policy."[38] But, as feminist moral psychologist, Carol Gilligan, observes, the Golden Rule has a built-in reflexivity. One is enjoined to treat others in the manner in which one wants to be treated oneself. The recommended procedure is to think about what one wants for oneself and generalize from there. Ultimately, this does not encourage a person to take seriously the idea that another person might want to be treated differently.[39]

In adjudicating cases of intractable perspectival conflict between sexual harassment litigants, the law has to have a starting point. Given that a perspective of pure neutrality is unattainable, the RWS, which prompts assessment of the facts from the point of view of the alleged victim's lived experience, is a good place to start.

Endnotes

1. W. Page Keeton, *Prosser and Keaton On Torts,* 5th ed., Ch. 5, Section 32, "The Reasonable Person."
2. *Ibid.,* p. 174.
3. *Ibid.,* p. 175.
4. For examples of courts relying on the "Reasonable Woman Standard" see *Yates v. Avco Corp.,* 819 F.2d, 630, 637 and *Ellison v. Brady,* 924 F.2d 872, 879 (9th Cir. 1991). For decisions relying on the "Reasonable Person Standard" see *Rabidue v. Osceola Refining Co.,* 805 F.2d 611 (6th Cir., 1986) and *Radtke v. Everett,* 501 N.W.2d 155 (Mich. 1993).
5. See, *e.g.,* Paul P. Dumont, "*Radtke v. Everett:* An Analysis of the Michigan Supreme Court's rejection of the Reasonable Woman/Victim Standard: Treating Perspectives That Are Different as Though They Were Exactly Alike," *Golden Gate Univ. Law Review,* Vol. 27, 1997. See p. 256: "The RWS, which is premised on the theory that males and females perceive sexual

behavior differently, deems actionable that conduct which offends and intimidates a reasonable woman, including sexual conduct which some males may not find objectionable."

6. See Caroline Forrell, "Essentialism, Empathy and the Reasonable Woman," *University of Illinois Law Review,* Fall, 1994, n. 4. See p. 772 re. the long-standing tradition of holding the RPS to be objective. Re. the ostensible objectivity of the RPS vs. the "subjectivity" of the RWS, see Paul P. Dumont, *op. cit.,* pp. 269 and 273.
7. *Rabidue,* 805 F.2d at 615. For a detailed synopsis and analysis of this case, see Caroline Forrrell, *op. cit.,* pp. 794–795.
8. *Rabidue, ibid.,* p. 624.
9. *Ibid.,* pp. 623–624.
10. *Ibid.,* p. 615. See Caroline Forrell, *op. cit.,* for an excellent analysis and synopsis of the majority and dissenting opinions, pp. 793–796. Forrell notes that, for the majority in this case, Rabidue's "personality made her complaints less serious and genuine." See also Coralie Whitcomb's synopsis and critique of Rabidue in, "Sexual Harassment: Does Implementation of a Reasonable Woman Standard Forecast the Return to the Reasonable Man Standard?" *Glendale Law Review,* Winter/Summer, 1995 14n 1–2, pp. 129–148.
11. *Ibid.,* p. 620.
12. *Ibid.,* pp. 620–623.
13. *Rabidue,* 805 F .2d, 623.
14. "The Reasonable Woman? Unreasonable!!!: Ellison v. Brady," in *Whittier Law Review,* Fall, 1993, 14 n. 3, p. 681.
15. *Ibid.*
16. See Paul Dumont, *op. cit.,* p. 265.
17. Whitcomb, *op. cit.,* p. 133.
18. *Ibid.,* pp. 133–134.
19. Forrell, *op. cit.,* p. 792. Forrell cites Harris v. Forklift Sys., Inc., 114 S. Ct. 367, 370, 371 (1993).
20. Angela P. Harris, "Race and Essentialism in Feminist Legal Theory," *Stanford Law Review,* 42, 581, 585, 1990. Tracy Treger, *op. cit.,* cites Harris' definition and, herself, defines "gender-essentialism" as "the belief that all women perceive conduct from a singular feminine perspective to the exclusion of all other views." See p. 683.
21. See Treger, *op. cit.,* and Harris, *op. cit.*
22. Treger, *op. cit.,* p. 683.
23. Radtke v. Everett, 501 N.W.2d, 167. See Paul Dumont, *op. cit.,* critique of the Radtke case.
24. *Ibid.,* p. 167.
25. See *Meditation I,* "Concerning Things That Can be Doubted."
26. Whitcomb, *op. cit.,* p. 144, fn. 101.
27. *Ellison v. Brady,* 924 F2d, 876.
28. *Radtke v. Everett,* 501 N.W. 2d.

29. Nancy S. Ehrenreich, "Pluralist Myths and Powerless Men: The Ideology of Reasonableness in Sexual Harassment Law," *The Yale Law Journal* 99, No. 6. (April, 1990): 1177–1234.
30. *Ibid.*
31. Forrell, *op. cit.,* p. 801. Forrell also notes that, though some feminists endorse the purely subjective standard, she sees focussing on the individual woman as "troubling" for a number of reasons. She defends a gender-based standard of assessment, but does not see such a standard as being subjective in what I refer to as the "Cartesian sense." I also agree with Forrell on this latter point.
32. *Ibid.*
33. Coralie Whitcomb, *op. cit.,* p. 143. Ref. to *Ellison v. Brady,* 924 F.2d, 884, 885.
34. Forrell, *op. cit.,* p. 783, see fn. 62.
35. Treger, *op. cit.,* p. 687. It should be noted that Treger, ultimately, opposes the RWS, in spite of her criticisms of the RPS as applied by the Rabidue court.
36. See quote of Rabidue court's opinion on this issue, Section I.1 above. *Rabidue,* 805 F .2d, 623.
37. Nancy Ehrenreich sees Rabidue's freedom as being in conflict with the defendant's. See *op. cit.,* p. 250, "Conflicting Liberties."
38. Treger, *op. cit.,* p. 693.
39. Carol Gilligan, "Remapping the Moral Domain: New Images of Self in Relationship," in *Mapping the Moral Domain,* eds. Gilligan, Ward and Taylor. (Cambridge: Harvard Univ. Press, 1988), p. 7. See also Caroline Forell, *op. cit.,* p. 814. Forell writes: "If the golden rule applies, then *who* applies the standard is all that really matters. If men can only be expected to do unto others as they would have others do unto them, the reasonable woman standard does not serve any useful purpose. After all, the reasonable woman standard is meant to highlight the fact that men find some conduct enjoyable that women find harmful. The reasonable woman standard will make a difference only when men understand that conduct they view as enjoyable, or at least as harmless, can be perceived by other people as harmful and demeaning."

Journal/Discussion Questions

1. What does Peterson mean by "gender essentialism?" What role does this concept play in the development of her argument?
2. Peterson distinguishes several senses of "subjective." What are these? What role do they play in her argument?
3. What difference, in practice, would it make if sexual harassment was judged on the basis of the reasonable woman standard instead of the reasonable person standard?

Susan Moller Okin
"Justice, Gender, and the Family"

Susan Moller Okin, a professor of political science at Stanford University, is the author of Women in Western Political Thought.

This selection is the concluding chapter of Professor Okin's Justice, Gender, and the Family, *in which she addresses the question of how we can make the family a more just institution that reduces the vulnerability of women and children and at the same time respects individual freedom of choice. Okin adopts a Rawlsian approach, asking what policies we would agree to about marriage, family, and related responsibilities if we did not know in advance whether we would find ourselves in the position of men or women. From this standpoint (which Rawls calls the original position), we can envision a society in which gender plays a much smaller role.*

As You Read, Consider This:

1. What is Okin's view of "a just society" in regard to gender? How does this differ from your own view?
2. How would everyday family life as you have known it change in light of Okin's suggestions?

The family is the linchpin of gender, reproducing it from one generation to the next. As we have seen earlier in *Justice, Gender, and the Family,* family life as typically practiced in our society is not just, either to women or to children. Moreover, it is not conducive to the rearing of citizens with a strong sense of justice. In spite of all the rhetoric about equality between the sexes, the traditional or quasi-traditional division of family labor still prevails. Women are made vulnerable by constructing their lives around the expectation that they will be primary parents; they become more vulnerable within marriages in which they fulfill this expectation, whether or not they also work for wages; and they are most vulnerable in the event of separation or divorce, when they usually take over responsibility for children without adequate support from their ex-husbands. Since approximately half of all marriages end in divorce, about half of our children are likely to experience its dislocations, often made far more traumatic by the socioeconomic consequences of both gender-structured marriage and divorce settlements that fail to take account of it. I have suggested that, for very important reasons the family *needs* to be a just institution, and have shown that contemporary theories of justice neglect women and ignore gender. How can we address this injustice?

This is a complex question. It is particularly so because we place great value on our freedom to live different kinds of lives, there is no current consensus on many aspects of gender, and we have good reason to suspect that many of our beliefs about sexual difference and appropriate sex roles are heavily influenced by the very fact that we grew up in a gender-structured society. All of us have been affected, in our very psychological structures, by the fact of gender in our personal pasts, just as our society has been deeply affected by its strong influence in our collective past. Because of the lack of shared meanings about gender, it constitutes a particularly hard case for those who care deeply about both personal freedom and social justice. The way we divide the labor and responsibilities in our personal lives seems to be one of those things that people should be free to work out for themselves, but because of its vast repercussions it belongs clearly within the scope of things that must be governed by principles of justice. Which is to say, in the language of political and moral theory, that it belongs both to the sphere of "the good" and to that of "the right."

I shall argue here that any just and fair solution to the urgent problem of women's and children's vulnerability must encourage and facilitate the equal sharing by men and women of paid and unpaid work, of productive and reproductive labor. We must work toward a future in which all will be likely to choose this mode of life. A just future would be one without gender. In its social structures and practices, one's sex would have no more relevance than one's eye color or the length of one's toes. No assumptions would be made about "male" and "female" roles; childbearing would be so conceptually separated from child rearing and other family responsibilities that it would be a cause for surprise, and no little concern, if men and women were not equally responsible for domestic life or if children were to spend much more time with one parent than the other. It would be a future in which men and women participated in more or less equal numbers in every sphere of life, from infant care to different kinds of paid work to high-level politics. Thus it would no longer be the case that having no experience of raising children would be the practical prerequisite for attaining positions of the greatest social influence. Decisions about abortion and rape, about divorce settlements and sexual harassment, or about any other crucial social issues would not be made, as they often are now, by legislatures and benches of judges overwhelmingly populated by men whose power is in large part due to their advantaged position in the gender structure. If we are to be at all true to our democratic ideals, moving away from gender is essential. Obviously, the attainment of such a social world requires major changes in a multitude of institutions and social settings outside the home, as well as within it.

Such changes will not happen overnight. Moreover, any present solution to the vulnerability of women and children that is just and respects individual freedom must take into account that most people currently live in ways that are greatly affected by gender, and most still favor many aspects of current, gendered practices. Sociological studies confirm what most of us already infer from our own personal and professional acquaintances: there are no currently shared meanings in this country about the extent to which differences between the sexes are innate or environmental, about the appropriate roles of men and women, and about which family forms and divisions of labor are most beneficial for partners, parents, and children.[1] There are those, at one extreme, for whom the different roles of the two sexes, especially as parents, are deeply held tenets of religious belief. At the other end of the spectrum are those of us for whom the sooner all social differentiation between the sexes vanishes, the better it will be for all of us. And there are a thousand varieties of view in between. Public policies must respect people's views and choices. But they must do so only insofar as it can be ensured that these choices do not result, as they now do, in the vulnerability of women and children. Special protections must be built into our laws and public policies to ensure that, for those who choose it, the division of labor between the sexes does not result in injustice. In the face of these difficulties—balancing freedom and the effects of past choices against the needs of justice—I do not pretend to have arrived at any complete or fully satisfactory answers. But I shall attempt here to suggest some social reforms, including changes in public policies and reforms of family law, that may help us work toward a solution to the injustices of gender.

Marriage has become an increasingly peculiar contract, a complex and ambiguous combination of anachronism and present-day reality. There is no longer the kind of agreement that once prevailed about what is expected of the parties to a marriage. Clearly, at least in the United States, it is no longer reasonable to assume that marriage will last a lifetime, since only half of current marriages are expected to. And yet, in spite of the increasing legal equality of men and women and the highly publicized figures about married women's increased participation in the labor force, many couples continue to adhere to more or less traditional patterns of role differentiation. As a recent article put it, women are "out of the house but not out of the kitchen."[2] Consequently, often working part-time or taking time out from wage work to care for family members, especially children, most wives are in a very different position from their husbands in their ability to be economically self-supporting. This is reflected, as we have seen, in power differentials between the sexes within the family. It means also, in the increasingly common event of divorce, usually by mutual agreement, that it is the mother who in 90 percent of cases will have physical custody of the children. But whereas the greater need for money goes one way, the bulk of the earning power almost always goes the other. This is one of the most important causes of the feminization of poverty, which is affecting the life chances of ever larger numbers of children as well as their mothers. The division of labor within families has always adversely affected women, by making them economically dependent on men. Because of the increasing instability of marriage, its effects on children have now reached crisis proportions.

Some who are critical of the present structure and practices of marriage have suggested that men and women simply be made free to make their own agreements about family life, contracting with each other, much as business contracts are made.[3] But this takes insufficient account of the history of gender in our culture and our own psychologies, of the present substantive inequalities between the sexes, and, most important, of the well-being of the children who result from the relationship. As has long been recognized in the realm of labor relations, justice is by no means always enhanced by the maximization of freedom of contract, if the individuals involved are in unequal positions to start with. Some have even suggested that it is consistent with justice to leave spouses to work out their own divorce settlement.[4] By this time, however, the two people ending a marriage are likely to be far more unequal. Such a practice would be even more catastrophic for most women and children than is the present system. Wives in any but the rare cases in which they as individuals have remained their husbands' socioeconomic equals could hardly be expected to reach a just solution if left "free" to "bargain" the terms of financial support or child custody. What would they have to bargain *with?*

There are many directions that public policy can and should take in order to make relations between men and women more just. In discussing these, I shall look back to some of the contemporary ways of thinking about justice that I find most convincing. I draw particularly on Rawls's idea of the original position and Walzer's conception of the complex equality found in separate spheres of justice, between which I find no inconsistency. I also keep in mind critical legal theorists' critique of contract, and the related idea, suggested earlier, that rights to privacy that are to be valuable to all of us can be enjoyed only insofar as the sphere of life in which we enjoy them ensures the equality of its adult members and protects children. Let us begin by asking what kind of arrangements persons in a Rawlsian original position would agree to regarding marriage, parental and other domestic responsibilities, and divorce. What kinds of policies would they agree to for other aspects of social life, such as the workplace and schools, that affect men, women, and children and relations among them? And let us consider whether these arrangements would satisfy Walzer's separate spheres test—that inequalities in one sphere of life not be allowed to overflow into another. Will they foster equality within the sphere of family life? For the protection of the privacy of a domestic sphere in which inequality exists is the protection of the right of the strong to exploit and abuse the weak.

Let us first try to imagine ourselves, as far as possible, in the original position, knowing neither what our sex nor any other of our personal characteristics will be once the veil of ignorance is lifted.* Neither do we know our place in society or our particular conception of the good life. Particularly relevant in this context, of course, is our lack of knowledge of our beliefs about the characteristics of men and women and our related convictions about the appropriate division of labor between the sexes. Thus the positions we represent must include a wide variety of beliefs on these matters. We may, once the veil of ignorance is lifted, find ourselves feminist men or feminist women whose conception of the good life includes the minimization of social differentiation between the sexes. Or we may find ourselves traditionalist men or women whose conception of the good life, for religious or other reasons, is bound up in an adherence to the conventional division of labor between the sexes. The challenge is to arrive at and apply principles of justice having to do with the family and the division of labor between the sexes that can satisfy these vastly disparate points of view and the many that fall between.

There are some traditionalist positions so extreme that they ought not be admitted for consideration, since they violate such fundamentals as equal basic liberty and self-respect. We need not, and should not, that is to say, admit for consideration views based on the notion that women are inherently inferior beings whose function is to fulfill the needs of men. Such a view is no more admissible in the construction of just institutions for a modern pluralist society than is the view, however deeply held, that some are naturally slaves and others naturally and justifiably their masters. We need not, therefore, consider approaches to marriage that view it as an inherently and desirably hierarchical structure of dominance and subordination. Even if it were conceivable that a person who did not know whether he or she would turn out to be a man or a woman in the society being planned would subscribe to such views, they are not admissible. Even if there were no other reasons to refuse to admit such views, they must be excluded for the sake of children, for everyone in the original position has a high personal stake in the quality of childhood. Marriages of dominance and submission are bad for children as well as for their mothers, and the socioeconomic outcome of divorce after such a marriage is very likely to damage their lives and seriously restrict their opportunities.

With this proviso, what social structures and public policies regarding relations between the sexes, and the family in particular, could we agree on in the original position? I think we would arrive at a basic model that would absolutely minimize gender. I shall first give an account of some of what this would consist in. We would also, however, build in carefully protective institutions for those who wished to follow gender-structured modes of life. These, too, I shall try to spell out in some detail.

* I say so far as possible because of the difficulties already pointed out in Chapter 5 of *Justice, Gender, and the Family.* Given the deep effects of gender on our psychologies, it is probably more difficult for us, having grown up in a gender-structured society, to imagine not knowing our sex than anything else about ourselves. Nevertheless, this should not prevent us from trying.

Moving Away from Gender

First, public policies and laws should generally assume no social differentiation of the sexes. Shared parental responsibility for child care would be both assumed and facilitated. Few people outside of feminist circles seem willing to acknowledge that society does not have to choose between a system of female parenting that renders women and children seriously vulnerable and a system of total reliance on day care provided outside the home. While high quality day care, subsidized so as to be equally available to all children, certainly constitutes an important part of the response that society should make in order to provide justice for women and children, it is only one part.[5] If we start out with the reasonable assumption that women and men are equally parents of their children, and have equal responsibility for both the unpaid effort that goes into caring for them and their economic support, then we must rethink the demands of work life throughout the period in which a worker of either sex is a parent of a small child. We can no longer cling to the by now largely mythical assumption that every worker has "someone else" at home to raise "his" children.

The facilitation and encouragement of equally shared parenting would require substantial changes.[6] It would mean major changes in the workplace, all of which could be provided on an entirely (and not falsely) gender-neutral basis. Employers must be required by law not only completely to eradicate sex discrimination, including sexual harassment, they should also be required to make positive provision for the fact that most workers, for differing lengths of time in their working lives, are also parents, and are sometimes required to nurture other family members, such as their own aging parents. Because children are borne by women but can (and, I contend, should) be raised by both parents equally, policies relating to pregnancy and birth should be quite distinct from those relating to parenting. Pregnancy and childbirth, to whatever varying extent they require leave from work, should be regarded as temporarily disabling conditions like any others, and employers should be mandated to provide leave for all such conditions.[7] Of course, pregnancy and childbirth are far more than simply "disabling conditions," but they should be treated as such for leave purposes, in part because their disabling effects vary from one woman to another. It seems unfair to mandate, say, eight or more weeks of leave for a condition that disables many women for less time and some for much longer, while not mandating leave for illnesses or other disabling conditions. Surely a society as rich as ours can afford to do both.

Parental leave during the postbirth months must be available to mothers and fathers on the same terms, to facilitate shared parenting; they might take sequential leaves or each might take half-time leave. All workers should have the right, without prejudice to their jobs, seniority, benefits, and so on, to work less than full-time during the first year of a child's life, and to work flexible or somewhat reduced hours at least until the child reaches the age of seven. Correspondingly greater flexibility of hours must be provided for the parents of a child with any health problem or disabling condition. The professions whose greatest demands (such as tenure in academia or the partnership hurdle in law) coincide with the peak period of child rearing must restructure their demands or provide considerable flexibility for those of their workers who are also participating parents. Large-scale employers should also be required to provide high-quality on-site day care for children from infancy up to school age. And to ensure equal quality of day care for all young children, direct government subsidies (not tax credits, which benefit the better-off) should make up the difference between the cost of high-quality day care and what less well-paid parents could reasonably be expected to pay.

There are a number of things that schools, too, must do to promote the minimization of gender. As Amy Gutmann has recently noted, in their present authority structures (84 percent of elementary school teachers are female, while 99 percent of school superintendents are male), "schools do not simply reflect, they perpetuate the social reality of gender preferences when they educate children in a system in which men rule women and women rule children." She argues that, since such sex stereotyping is "a formidable obstacle" to children's rational deliberation about the lives they wish to lead, sex should be regarded as a relevant qualification in the hiring of both teachers and administrators, until these proportions have become much more equal.[8]

An equally important role of our schools must be to ensure in the course of children's education that they become fully aware of the politics of gender. This does not only mean ensuring that women's experience and women's writing are included in the curriculum, although this in itself is undoubtedly important.[9] Its political significance has become obvious from the amount of protest that it has provoked. Children need also to be taught about the present inequalities, ambiguities, and uncertainties of marriage, the facts of workplace discrimination and segregation, and the likely consequences of making life choices based on assumptions about gender. They should be discouraged from thinking about their futures as *determined* by the sex to which they happen to belong. For many children, of course, personal experience has already "brought home" the devastating effects of the traditional division of labor between the sexes. But they do not necessarily come away from this experience with positive ideas about how to structure their own future family lives differently. As Anita Shreve has recently suggested, "the old home economics courses that used to teach girls how to cook and sew might give way to the new home economics: teaching girls *and boys* how to combine working and parenting."[10] Finally, schools should be required to provide high-quality after-school programs, where children can play safely, do their homework, or participate in creative activities.

The implementation of all these policies would significantly help parents to share the earning and the domestic responsibilities of their families, and children to grow up prepared for a future in which the significance of sex difference is greatly diminished. Men could participate equally in the nurturance of their children, from infancy and throughout childhood, with predictably great effects on themselves, their wives or partners, and their children. And women need not become vulnerable through economic dependence. In addition, such arrangements would alleviate the qualms many people have about the long hours that some children spend in day care. If one parent of a preschooler worked, for example, from eight to four o'clock and the other from ten to six o'clock, a preschool child would be at day care for only six hours (including nap time), and with each one or both of her or his parents the rest of the day. If each parent were able to work a six-hour day, or a four-day week, still less day care would be needed. Moreover, on-site provision of day care would enable mothers to continue to nurse, if they chose beyond the time of their parental leave.[11]

The situation of single parents and their children is more complicated, but it seems that it too, for a number of reasons, would be much improved in a society in which sex difference was accorded an absolute minimum of social significance. Let us begin by looking at the situation of never-married mothers and their children. First, the occurrence of pregnancy among single teenagers, which is almost entirely unintended, would presumably be reduced if girls grew up more assertive and self-protective, and with less tendency to perceive their futures primarily in terms of motherhood. It could also be significantly reduced by the wide availability of sex education and contraception.[12] Second, the added weight of responsibility given to fatherhood in a gender-free society would surely give young men more incentive than they now have not to incur the results of careless sexual behavior until they were ready to take on the responsibilities of being parents. David Ellwood has outlined a policy for establishing the paternity of all children of single mothers at the time of birth, and for enforcing the requirement that their fathers contribute to their support throughout childhood, with provision for governmental backup support in cases where the father is unable to pay. These proposals seem eminently fair and sensible, although the minimum levels of support suggested ($1,500 to $2,000 per year) are inadequate, especially since the mother is presumed to be either taking care of the child herself or paying for day care (which often costs far more than this) while she works.[13]

Third, never-married mothers would benefit greatly from a work structure that took parenthood seriously into account, as well as from the subsidization of high-quality day care. Women who grew up with the expectation that their work lives would be as important a part of their futures as the work lives of men would be less likely to enter dead-ended, low-skilled occupations, and would be better able to cope economically with parenthood without marriage.

Most single parenthood results, however, not from single mothers giving birth, but from marital separation and divorce. And this, too, would be significantly altered in a society not structured along the lines of gender. Even if rates of divorce were to remain unchanged (which is impossible to predict), it seems inconceivable that separated and divorced fathers who had shared equally in the nurturance of their children from the outset would be as likely to neglect them, by not seeing them or not contributing to their support, as many do today. It seems reasonable to expect that children after divorce would still have two actively involved parents, and two working adults economically responsible for them. Because these parents had shared equally the paid work and the family work, their incomes would be much more equal than those of most divorcing parents today. Even if they were quite equal, however, the parent without physical custody should be required to contribute to the child's support, *to the point where the standards of living of the two households were the same.* This would be very different from the situation of many children of divorced parents today, dependent for both their nurturance and their economic support solely on mothers whose wage work has been interrupted by primary parenting.

It is impossible to predict all the effects of moving toward a society without gender. Major current injustices to women and children would end. Men would experience both the joys and the responsibilities of far closer and more sustained contact with their children than many have today. Many immensely influential spheres of life—notably politics and the professional occupations—would for the first time be populated more or less equally by men and women, most of whom were also actively participating parents. This would be in great contrast to today, when most of those who rise to influential positions are either men who, if fathers, have minimal contact with their children, or women who have either forgone motherhood altogether or hired others as full-time caretakers for their children because of the demands of their careers. These are the people who make policy at the highest levels—policies not only *about* families and their welfare and about the education of children, but about the foreign policies, the wars and the weapons that will determine the future or the lack of future for all these families and children. Yet they are almost all people who gain the influence they do in part by never having had the day-to-day experience of nurturing a child. This is probably the most significant aspect of our gendered division of labor, though the least possible to grasp. The effects of changing it could be momentous.

Protecting the Vulnerable

The pluralism of beliefs and modes of life is fundamental to our society, and the genderless society I have just outlined would certainly not be agreed upon by all as desirable. Thus when we think about constructing relations between the sexes that could be agreed upon in the original position, and are therefore just from all points of view, we must also design institutions and practices acceptable to those with more traditional beliefs about the characteristics of men and women, and the appropriate division of labor between them. It is essential, if men and women are to be allowed to so divide their labor, as they must be if we are to respect the current pluralism of beliefs, that society protect the vulnerable. Without such protection, the marriage contract seriously exacerbates the initial inequalities of those who entered into it and too many women and children live perilously close to economic disaster and serious social dislocation; too many also live with violence or the continual threat of it. It should be noted here that the rights and obligations that the law would need to promote and mandate in order to protect the vulnerable need not—and should not—be designated in accordance with sex, but in terms of different functions or roles performed. There are only a minute percentage of "househusbands" in this country, and a very small number of men whose work lives take second priority after their wives'. But they can quite readily be protected by the same institutional structures that can protect traditional and quasi-traditional wives, so long as these are designed without reference to sex.

Gender-structured marriage, then, needs to be regarded as a currently necessary institution (because still chosen by some) but one that is socially problematic. It should be subjected to a number of legal requirements, at least when there are children.[14]* Most important, there is no need for the division of labor between the sexes to involve the economic dependence, either complete or partial, of one partner on the other. Such dependence can be avoided if both partners have *equal legal entitlement* to all earnings coming into the household. The clearest and simplest way of doing this would be to have employers make out wage checks equally divided between the earner and the partner who provides all or most of his or her unpaid domestic services. In many cases, of course, this would not change the way couples actually manage their finances; it would simply codify what they already agree on—that the household income is rightly shared, because in a real sense jointly earned. Such couples recognize the fact that the wage-earning spouse is no more supporting the homemaking and child-rearing spouse than the latter is supporting the former; the form of support each offers the family is simply different. Such couples might well take both checks, deposit them in a joint account, and really share the income, just as they now do with the earnings that come into the household.

In the case of some couples, however, altering the entitlement of spouses to the earned income of the household as I have suggested *would* make a significant difference. It would make a difference in cases where the earning or higher-earning partner now directly exploits this power, by refusing to make significant spending decisions jointly, by failing to share the income, or by psychologically or physically abusing the non-earning or low-earning partner, reinforced by the notion that she (almost always the wife) has little option but to put up with such abuse or to take herself

*I see no reason why what I propose here should be restricted to couples who are legally married. It should apply equally to "common law" relationships that produce children, and in which a division of labor is practiced.

and her children into a state of destitution. It would make a difference, too, in cases where the higher-earning partner indirectly exploits this earning power in order to perpetuate the existing division of labor in the family. In such instances considerable changes in the balance of power would be likely to result from the legal and societal recognition that the partner who does most of the domestic work of the family contributes to its well-being just as much, and therefore rightly *earns* just as much, as the partner who does most of the workplace work.

What I am suggesting is *not* that the wage-working partner pay the homemaking partner for services rendered. I do not mean to introduce the cash nexus into a personal relationship where it is inappropriate. I have simply suggested that since both partners in a traditional or quasi-traditional marriage work, there is no reason why only one of them should get paid, or why one should be paid far more than the other. The equal splitting of wages would constitute public recognition of the fact that the currently unpaid labor of families is just as important as the paid labor. If we do *not* believe this, then we should insist on the complete and equal sharing of both paid and unpaid labor, as occurs in the genderless model of marriage and parenting described earlier. It is only if we *do* believe it that society can justly allow couples to distribute the two types of labor so unevenly. But in such cases, given the enormous significance our society attaches to money and earnings, we should insist that the earnings be recognized as equally earned by the two persons. To call on Walzer's language, we should do this in order to help prevent the inequality of family members in the sphere of wage work to invade their domestic sphere.

It is also important to point out that this proposal does not constitute unwarranted invasion of privacy or any more state intervention into the life of families than currently exists. It would involve only the same kind of invasion of privacy as is now required by such things as registration of marriages and births, and the filing of tax returns declaring numbers and names of dependents. And it *seems* like intervention in families only because it would alter the existing relations of power within them. If a person's capacity to fulfill the terms of his or her work is dependent on having a spouse at home who raises the children and in other ways sustains that worker's day-to-day life, then it is no more interventionist to pay both equally for their contributions than only to pay one.

The same fundamental principle should apply to separation and divorce to the extent that the division of labor has been practiced within a marriage. Under current divorce laws, as we have seen, the terms of exit from marriage are disadvantageous for almost all women in traditional or quasi-traditional marriages. Regardless of the consensus that existed about the division of the family labor, these women lose most of the income that has supported them *and* the social status that attached to them because of their husband's income and employment, often at the same time as suddenly becoming single parents, and prospective wage workers for the first time in many years. This combination of prospects would seem to be enough to put most traditional wives off the idea of divorcing even if they had good cause to do so. In addition, since divorce in the great majority of states no longer requires the consent of both spouses, it seems likely that wives for whom divorce would spell economic and social catastrophe would be inhibited in voicing their dissatisfactions or needs within marriage. The terms of exit are very likely to affect the use and the power of voice in the ongoing relationship. At worst, these women may be rendered virtually defenseless in the face of physical or psychological abuse. This is not a system of marriage and divorce that could possibly be agreed to by persons in an original position in which they did not know whether they were to be male or female, traditionalist or not. It is a fraudulent contract, presented as beneficial to all but in fact to the benefit only of the more powerful.

For all these reasons, it seems essential that the terms of divorce be redrawn so as to reflect the gendered or nongendered character of the marriage that is ending, to a far greater extent than they do now.[15] The legal system of a society that allows couples to divide the labor of families in a traditional or quasitraditional manner *must* take responsibility for the vulnerable position in which marital breakdown places the partner who has completely or partially lost the capacity to be economically self-supporting. When such a marriage ends, it seems wholly reasonable to expect a person whose career has been largely unencumbered by domestic responsibilities to support financially the partner who undertook these responsibilities. This support, in the form of combined alimony and child support, should be far more substantial than the token levels often ordered by the courts now. *Both postdivorce households should enjoy the same standard of living.* Alimony should not end after a few years, as the (patronizingly named) "rehabilitative alimony" of today does; it should continue for at least as long as the traditional division of labor in the marriage did and, in the case of short-term marriages that produced children, until the youngest child enters first grade and the custodial parent has a real chance of making his or her own living. After that point, child support should continue at a level that enables the children to enjoy a standard of living equal to that of the noncustodial parent. There can be no reason consistent with principles of justice that some should suffer economically vastly more than others from the breakup of a relationship whose asymmetric division of labor was mutually agreed on.

I have suggested two basic models of family rights and responsibilities, both of which are currently needed because this is a time of great transition for men and women and great disagreement about gender. Families in which roles and responsibilities are equally shared regardless of sex are far more in accord with principles of justice than are typical families today. So are families in which those who undertake more traditional domestic roles are protected from the risks they presently incur. In either case, justice as a whole will benefit from the changes. Of the two, however, I claim that the genderless family is more just, in the three important respects that I spelled out at the beginning of this book: it is more just to women; it is more conducive to equal opportunity both for women and for children of both sexes; and it creates a more favorable environment for the rearing of citizens of a just society. Thus, while protecting those whom gender now makes vulnerable, we must also put our best efforts into promoting the elimination of gender.

The increased justice to women that would result from moving away from gender is readily apparent. Standards for just social institutions could no longer take for granted and exclude from considerations of justice much of what women now do, since men would share in it equally. Such central components of justice as what counts as productive labor, and what count as needs and deserts, would be greatly affected by this change. Standards of justice would become humanist, as they have never been before. One of the most important effects of this would be to change radically the situation of women as citizens. With egalitarian families, and with institutions such as workplaces and schools designed to accommodate the needs of parents and children, rather than being based as they now are on the traditional assumption that "someone else" is at home, mothers would not be virtually excluded from positions of influence in politics and the workplace. They would be represented at every level in approximately equal numbers with men.

In a genderless society, children, too, would benefit. They would not suffer in the ways that they do now because of the injustices done to women. It is undeniable that the family in which each of us grows up has a deeply formative influence on us—on the kind of persons we want to be as well as the kind of persons we are.[16] This is one of the reasons why one cannot reasonably leave the family out of "the basic structure of society," to which the principles of justice are to apply. Equality of opportunity to become what we want to be would be enhanced in two important ways by the development of families without gender and by the public policies necessary to support their development. First, the growing gap between the economic well-being of children in single-parent and those in two-parent families would be reduced. Children in single-parent families would benefit significantly if fathers were held equally responsible for supporting their children, whether married to their mothers or not; if more mothers had sustained labor force attachment; if high-quality day care were subsidized; and if the workplace were designed to accommodate parenting. These children would be far less likely to spend their formative years in conditions of poverty, with one parent struggling to fulfill the functions of two. Their life chances would be significantly enhanced.

Second, children of both sexes in gender-free families would have (as some already have) much more opportunity for self-development free from sex role expectations and sex-typed personalities than most do now. Girls and boys who grow up in highly traditional families, in which sex difference is regarded as a determinant of everything from roles, responsibilities, and privileges to acceptable dress, speech, and modes of behavior, clearly have far less freedom to develop into whatever kind of person they want to be than do those who are raised without such constraints. It is too early for us to know a lot about the developmental outcomes and life choices of children who are equally parented by mothers and fathers, since the practice is still so recent and so rare. Persuasive theories such as Chodorow's, however, would lead us to expect much less differentiation between the sexes to result from truly shared parenting.[17] Even now, in most cases without men's equal fathering, both the daughters and the sons of wage-working mothers have been found to have a more positive view of women and less rigid views of sex roles; the daughters (like their mothers) tend to have greater self-esteem and a more positive view of themselves as workers, and the sons, to expect equality and shared roles in their own future marriages.[18] We might well expect that with mothers in the labor force and with fathers as equal parents, children's attitudes and psychologies will become even less correlated with their sex. In a very crucial sense, their opportunities to become the persons they want to be will be enlarged.

Finally, it seems undeniable that the enhancement of justice that accompanies the disappearance of gender will make the family a much better place for children to develop a sense of justice. We can no longer deny the importance of the fact that families are where we first learn, by example and by how we are treated, not only how people do relate to each other but also how they *should*. How would families not built on gender be better schools of moral development? First, the example of co-equal parents with shared roles, combining love with justice, would provide a far better example of human relations for children than the domination and dependence that often occur in traditional marriage. The fairness of the distribution of labor, the equal respect, and the interdependence of his or her parents would surely be a powerful first example to a child in a family with equally shared roles. Second, as I have argued, having a sense of justice requires that we be able to empathize, to abstract from our own situation and to think about moral and political issues from the points of view of others. We cannot come to either just principles or just specific decisions by thinking, as it were, as if we were nobody, or thinking from nowhere; we must, therefore, learn to think from the point of view of others, including others who are different from ourselves.

To the extent that gender is de-emphasized in our nurturing practices, this capacity would seem to be enhanced, for two reasons. First, if female primary parenting leads, as it seems to, to less distinct ego boundaries and greater capacity for empathy in female children, and to a greater tendency to self-definition and abstraction in males, then might we not expect to find the two capacities better combined in children of both sexes who are reared by parents of both sexes? Second, the experience of *being* nurturers, throughout a significant portion of our lives, also seems likely to result in an increase in empathy, and in the combination of personal moral capacities, fusing feelings with reason, that just citizens need.[19]

For those whose response to what I have argued here is the practical objection that it is unrealistic and will cost too much, I have some answers and some questions. Some of what I have suggested would not cost anything, in terms of public spending, though it would redistribute the costs and other responsibilities of rearing children more evenly between men and women. Some policies I have endorsed, such as adequate public support for children whose fathers cannot contribute, may cost more than present policies, but may not, depending on how well they work.[20] Some, such as subsidized high-quality day care, would be expensive in themselves, but also might soon be offset by other savings, since they would enable those who would otherwise be full-time child carers to be at least part-time workers.

All in all, it seems highly unlikely that the *long-term* costs of such programs—even if we count only monetary costs, not costs in human terms—would outweigh the long-term benefits. In many cases, the cycle of poverty could be broken—and children enabled to escape from, or to avoid falling into, it—through a much better early start in life.[21] But even if my suggestions would cost, and cost a lot, we have to ask: How much do we care about the injustices of gender? How much do we care that women who have spent the better part of their lives nurturing others can be discarded like used goods? How ashamed are we that one-quarter of our children, in one of the richest countries in the world, live in poverty? How much do we care that those who raise children, *because* of this choice, have restricted opportunities to develop the rest of their potential, and very little influence on society's values and direction? How much do we care that the family, our most intimate social grouping, is often a school of day-to-day injustice? How much do we *want* the just families that will produce the kind of citizens we need if we are ever to achieve a just society?

Endnotes

1. See *Justice, Gender, and the Family,* chap. 3, pp. 67–68.
2. "Women: Out of the House But Not Out of the Kitchen," *New York Times,* February 24, 1988, pp. Al, C10.
3. See, for example, Marjorie Maguire Schultz, "Contractual Ordering of Marriage: A New Model for State Policy," *California Law Review 70,* no. 2 (1982); Lenore Weitzman, *The Marriage Contract: Spouses, Lovers, and the Law* (New York: The Free Press, 1981), parts 3–4.
4. See, for example, David L. Kirp, Mark G. Yudof, and Marlene Strong Franks, *Gender Justice* (Chicago: University of Chicago Press, 1986), pp. 183–185. Robert H. Mnookin takes an only slightly less laissez-faire approach, in "Divorce Bargaining: The Limits on Private Ordering," *University of Michigan Journal of Law Reform* 18, no. 4 (1985).
5. It seems reasonable to conclude that the effects of day care on children are probably just as variable as the effects of parenting—that is to say, very widely variable depending on the quality of the day care and of the parenting. There is no doubt that good out-of-home day care is expensive—approximately $100 per half-time week in 1987, even though child-care workers are

now paid only about two-thirds as much per hour as other comparably educated women workers (Victor Fuchs, *Women's Quest for Economic Equality* [Cambridge: Harvard University Press, 1988], pp. 137–138). However, it is undoubtedly easier to control its quality than that of informal "family day care." In my view, based in part on my experience of the excellent day-care center that our children attended for a total of seven years, good-quality day care must have small-scale "home rooms" and a high staff-to-child ratio, and should pay staff better than most centers now do. For balanced studies of the effects of day care on a poor population, see Sally Provence, Audrey Naylor, and June Patterson, *The Challenge of Day Care* (New Haven: Yale University Press, 1977); and, most recently, Lisbeth B. Schorr (with Daniel Schorr), *Within Our Reach—Breaking the Cycle of Disadvantage* (New York: Anchor Press, Doubleday, 1988), chap. 8.

6. Much of what I suggest here is not new; it has formed part of the feminist agenda for several decades, and I first made some of the suggestions I develop here in the concluding chapter of *Women in Western Political Thought* (Princeton: Princeton University Press, 1979). Three recent books that address some of the policies discussed here are Fuchs, *Women's Quest,* chap. 7; Philip Green, *Retrieving Democracy: In Search of Civic Equality* (Totowa, NJ: Rowman and Allanheld, 1985), pp. 96–108; and Anita Shreve, *Remaking Motherhood: How Working Mothers Are Shaping Our Children's Future* (New York: Fawcett Columbine, 1987), pp. 173–178. In Fuchs's chapter he carefully analyzes the potential economic and social effects of alternative policies to improve women's economic status, and concludes that "child-centered policies" such as parental leave and subsidized day care are likely to have more of a positive impact on women's economic position than "labor market policies" such as anti-discrimination, comparable pay for comparable worth, and affirmative action have had and are likely to have. Some potentially very effective policies, such as on-site day care and flexible and/or reduced working hours for parents of young or "special needs" children, seem to fall within both of his categories.

7. The dilemma faced by feminists in the recent California case *Guerra v. California Federal Savings and Loan Association,* 107 S. Ct. 683 (1987) was due to the fact that state law mandated leave for pregnancy and birth that it did *not* mandate for other disabling conditions. Thus to defend the law seemed to open up the dangers of discrimination that the earlier protection of women in the workplace had resulted in. (For a discussion of this general issue of equality versus difference, see, for example, Wendy W. Williams, "The Equality Crisis: Some Reflections on Culture, Courts, and Feminism," *Women's Rights Law Reporter* 7, no. 3 [1982].) The Supreme Court upheld the California law on the grounds that it treated workers equally in terms of their rights to become parents.

8. Amy Gutmann, *Democratic Education* (Princeton: Princeton University Press, 1987), pp. 112–115; quotation from pp. 113–114. See also Elisabeth Hansot and David Tyack, "Gender in American Public Schools: Thinking Institutionally," *Signs* 13, no. 4 (1988).

9. A classic text on this subject is Dale Spender, eds., *Men's Studies Modified: The Impact of Feminism on the Academic Disciplines* (Oxford: Pergamon Press, 1981).

10. Shreve, *Remaking Motherhood,* p. 237.

11. Although 51 percent of infants are breast-fed at birth, only 14 percent are entirely breast-fed at six weeks of age. Cited from P. Leach, *Babyhood* (New York: Alfred A. Knopf, 1983), by

Sylvia Ann Hewlett, in *A Lesser Life: The Myth of Women's Liberation in America* (New York: Morrow, 1986), p. 409, note 34.

Given this fact, it seems quite unjustified to argue that lactation *dictates* that mothers be the primary parents, even during infancy.

12. In Sweden, where the liberalization of abortion in the mid-1970s was accompanied by much expanded birth-control education and information and reduced-cost contraceptives, the rates of both teenage abortion and teenage birth decreased significantly. The Swedish teenage birth-rate was by 1982 less than half what it had been in the 1970s. Mary Ann Glendon, *Abortion and Divorce in Western Law* (Cambridge: Harvard University Press, 1987), p. 23 and note 65. Chapter 3 of Schorr's *Within Our Reach* gives an excellent account of programs in the United States that have proven effective in reducing early and unplanned pregnancies. Noting the strong correlation between emotional and economic deprivation and early pregnancy, she emphasizes the importance, if teenagers are to have the incentive not to become pregnant, of their believing that they have a real stake in their own futures, and developing the aspirations and self-assertiveness that go along with this. As Victor Fuchs points out, approximately two-thirds of unmarried women who give birth are twenty or older (*Women's Quest,* p. 68). However, these women are somewhat more likely to have work skills and experience, and it seems likely that many live in informal "common law marriage" heterosexual or lesbian partnerships, rather than being *in fact* single parents.
13. David Ellwood, *Poor Support: Poverty in the American Family* (New York: Basic Books, 1988), pp. 163–174. He estimates that full-time day care for each child can be bought for $3,000 per year, and half-time for $1,000. He acknowledges that these estimated costs are "modest." I think they are unrealistic, unless the care is being provided by a relative or close friend. Ellwood reports that, as of 1985, only 18 percent of never-married fathers were ordered to pay child support, and only 11 percent actually paid any (p. 158).
14. Mary Ann Glendon has set out a "children first" approach to divorce (Glendon, *Abortion and Divorce,* pp. 94ff.); here I extend the same idea to ongoing marriage, where the arrival of a child is most often the point at which the wife becomes economically dependent.
15. My suggestions for protecting traditional and quasi-traditional wives in the event of divorce are similar to those of Lenore Weitzman in *The Divorce Revolution: The Unexpected Social and Economic Consequences for Women and Children in America* (New York: The Free Press, 1985), chap. 11, and Mary Ann Glendon in *Abortion and Divorce,* chap. 2. Although they would usually in practice protect traditional wives, the laws should be gender-neutral so that they would equally protect divorcing men who had undertaken the primary functions of parenting and homemaking.
16. Here I paraphrase Rawls's wording in explaining why the basic structure of society is basic. "The Basic Structure as Subject," *American Philosophical Quarterly* 14, no. 2 (1977): 160.
17. See chap. 6, note 58 in *Justice, Gender, and the Family.*
18. Shreve, *Remaking Motherhood,* chaps. 3–7.
19. See, for example, Sara Ruddick, "Maternal Thinking," *Feminist Studies* 6, no. 2 (1980); Diane Ehrensaft, "When Women and Men Mother," in *Mothering: Essays in Feminist Theory,* ed. Joyce Trebilcot (Totowa, NJ: Rowman and Allanheld, 1984); Judith Kegan Gardiner, "Self Psychology as Feminist Theory," *Signs* 12, no. 4 (1987), esp. 778–780.

20. David Ellwood estimates that "if most absent fathers contributed the given percentages, the program would actually save money" (*Poor Support,* p. 169).
21. Schorr's *Within Our Reach* documents the ways in which the cycle of disadvantage can be effectively broken, even for those in the poorest circumstances.

Journal/Discussion Questions

✍ *In what ways did gender play a role in your own family as you were growing up? If you become a parent, what changes—if any—would you like to see in regard to the place of gender in your family?*

1. Okin argues that "A just future would be one without gender. In its social structures and practices, one's sex would have no more relevance than one's eye color or the length of one's toes." How does this compare to your vision of a just future? In what ways do you agree? Disagree? Explain.
2. In a gender neutral society, what changes does Okin foresee in the workplace? Do you think such changes would be a good thing? Why or why not?
3. How, according to Okin, would elementary school education change in a gender-neutral society? Do you think that elementary school education in today's society perpetuates sexism and roles based on gender? Ideally, how would you like to see children educated in regard to gender?
4. In discussing single parenthood and divorce, Okin suggests that "the parent without physical custody should be required to contribute to the child's support, *to the point where the standards of living of the two households were the same.*" Do you agree or disagree? Discuss your reasons.

Concluding Discussion Questions

Where Do You Stand Now?

Instructions

You have already answered the following questions in your moral problems self-quiz at the beginning of this book. Now that you have studied the material in this section, take a moment to answer the same questions again.

	Strongly Agree	*Agree*	*Undecided*	*Disagree*	*Strongly Disagree*	*Chapter 6: Gender*
26.	❑	❑	❑	❑	❑	Women's moral voices are different from men's.
27.	❑	❑	❑	❑	❑	Women are still discriminated against in the workplace.
28.	❑	❑	❑	❑	❑	Sexual harassment should be illegal.
29.	❑	❑	❑	❑	❑	Affirmative action helps women.
30.	❑	❑	❑	❑	❑	Genuine equality for women demands a restructuring of the traditional family.

Compare your answers to the present self-quiz with the answers to the initial self-quiz. How, if at all, have your answers changed? How have the *reasons* for your answers changed?

Journal/Discussion Questions

✍ *Do you think the fact that you are a male or female has influenced your attitude toward any of the readings or ideas you encountered in this chapter? Discuss.*

1. What do you see as the ideal role of sex and gender in society? What do you think are the greatest liabilities associated with your view? The greatest assets? How does your view of this ideal relate to the views of the authors in this section?
2. Do you think that women are still discriminated against in today's society? Discuss the evidence for your position. If discrimination still exists, how should we as a society respond to it?
3. The issue of raising children is a central concern to many people, and is particularly troublesome to those who want to insure equality between the sexes. Discuss the potential conflict between child-raising and sex equality and explain how you think our society should deal with this issue. Relate your position to those presented in this chapter.

For Further Reading

Web Resources

For Web-based resources, including the major Supreme Court decisions on gender issues, see the Gender and Sexism page of *Ethics Updates* (http://ethics.acusd.edu). Among the resources are the Glass Ceiling Report and RealVideo of lectures by Carol Gilligan.

Journals

In addition to the standard journals in ethics discussed in the Appendix, there are several excellent journals devoted to issues of feminism. *Signs* is one of the oldest, and is a genuinely interdisciplinary journal devoted to issues relating to women; *Hypatia* is a philosophy journal created by members of the Society of Women in Philosophy; also see *Feminist Studies* and *differences: A Journal of Feminist Cultural Studies.*

Review Articles; Overviews

For an excellent overview of feminist ethics, see Alison M. Jaggar, "Feminist Ethics," *Encyclopedia of Ethics,* edited by Lawrence C. Becker and Charlotte B. Becker (New York: Garland Publishing, 1992), Vol. I, pp. 361–370; Jane Grimshaw, "The Idea of a Female Ethic," *A Companion to Ethics,* edited by Peter Singer (Oxford: Blackwell, 1991), pp. 491–499. For an excellent overview of various positions, see Rosemarie Tong, *Feminist Thought: A More Comprehensive Introduction* (Boulder, CO: Westview Press, 1998) and *Feminist Frameworks,* edited by Alison M. Jaggar and Paula S. Rothenberg, 2nd ed. (New York: McGraw-Hill, 1984).

Anthologies, Articles, and Books

There are a number of excellent anthologies on feminism and ethics, including Eva Feder Kittay and Diana Meyer's *Women and Moral Theory* (Savage, MD: Rowman & Littlefield, 1987); *Feminism and Political Theory,* edited by Cass R. Sunstein (Chicago: University of Chicago Press, 1990); Claudia Card's *Feminist Ethics* (Lawrence, KS: University of Kansas Press, 1991), which contains an excellent bibliography; *Explorations in Feminist Ethics,* edited by Eva Browning Cole and Susan Coultrap-McQuin (Bloomington, IN: Indiana University Press, 1992), which also has an excellent bibliography; *Ethics: A Feminist Reader,* edited by Elizabeth Frazer, Jennifer Hornsby, and Sabina Lovibond (Oxford: Blackwell, 1992); *Women and Values. Readings in Recent Feminist Philosophy,* 2nd ed., edited by Marilyn Pearsall (Belmont, CA: Wadsworth, 1993). For a lively, representative selection of contemporary articles on feminism, see *Feminism: Opposing Viewpoints,* edited by Carol Wekesser (San Diego, CA: Greenhaven Press, 1995). Also see Martha C. Nussbaum's excellent *Sex and Social Justice* (New York: Oxford, 1999) as well as *Women, Culture and Development: A Study of Human Capabilities,* edited by Martha Nussbaum and Jonathan Glover (New York: Oxford, 1995).

Rita C. Manning, *Speaking from the Heart: A Feminist Perspective on Ethics* (Savage, MD: Rowman and Littlefield, 1992) is one of many excellent defenses of feminist perspectives in ethics. For a critical look at some elements in contemporary feminism, see Katie Roiphe, *The Morning After: Sex, Fear, and Feminism* (Boston: Little, Brown, 1993) and Christina Hoff Sommers, *Who Stole Feminism?* (New York: Simon and Schuster, 1994).

Gender and Moral Voices

Carol Gilligan's *In a Different Voice* (Cambridge: Harvard University Press, 1982) has had a profound impact in a wide range of disciplines; her more recent work is to be found in a collection of essays that she co-edited with Janie Victoria Ward and Jill McLean Taylor, *Mapping the Moral Domain* (Cambridge: Center for the Study of Gender, Education and Human Development, 1988) and in *Meeting at the Crossroad,* by Lyn Mikel Brown and Carol Gilligan (Cambridge: Harvard University Press, 1992). Nel Noddings's *Caring* (Berkeley: University of California Press, 1984) and, more recently, her book *Women and Evil* (Berkeley: University of California Press, 1989) have also been influential in articulating a distinctive moral voice for women.

Several journal exchanges are also of particular relevance here, most of which have appeared in *Ethics:* the Kohlberg-Flanagan exchange on "Virtue, Sex, and Gender" *Ethics,* Vol. 92, No. 3 (April 1982), pp. 499–532; Lawrence Blum's "Gilligan and Kohlberg: Implications for Moral Theory" *Ethics,* Vol. 98, No. 3 (April 1988), pp. 472–491; and the symposium on "Feminism and Political Theory," Ethics, Vol. 99, No. 2 (January 1989). Owen Flanagan's *Varieties of Moral Personality* (Cambridge: Harvard University Press, 1991) contains several excellent chapters (esp. Chapters 9–11) on this issue. Blum's essay, along with his previously unpublished "Gilligan's 'Two Voices' and the Moral Status of Group Identity," are both to be found in his *Moral Perception and Particularity* (New York: Cambridge University Press, 1994). Also see the essays in Part III of Claudia Card's anthology *Feminist Ethics,* cited above.

Pornography and Hate Speech

For a survey of the ethical issues surrounding pornography, as well as an excellent bibliography, see Donald VanDeVeer, "Pornography," *Encyclopedia of Ethics,* edited by Lawrence C. Becker and Charlotte B. Becker (New York: Garland Publishing, 1992), Vol. II, pp. 991–993. See the now classic pieces in *Take Back the Night,* edited by Laura Lederer (New York: William Morrow, 1980). For strong statements of opposition to pornography, see Andrea Dworkin, *Pornography: Men Possessing Women* (New York: Perigree Books, 1983), Catharine A. MacKinnon, *Only Words* (Cambridge: Harvard University Press, 1993). For a representative selection of philosophical positions on this issue, see *Pornography and Censorship,* edited by David Copp and Susan Wendell (Buffalo: Prometheus Books, 1983).

The issue of banning hate speech has received a lot of attention in the past decade. Some of the most influential essays are gathered together in Mari J. Matsuda, et al., *Words That Wound: Critical Race Theory, Assaultive Speech, and the First Amendment* (Boulder, CO: Westview Press, 1993) and Henry Louis Gates, Jr., et al., *Speaking of Race, Speaking of Sex, Hate Speech, Civil*

Rights, and Civil Liberties, with an Introduction by Ira Glesser (New York: New York University Press, 1994); also see Gates's "Let Them Talk: Why Civil Liberties Pose No Threat to Civil Rights," *The New Republic,* Vol. 209, No. 12–13 (September 20, 1993), p. 37 ff. Andrew Altman, "Liberalism and Campus Hate Speech: A Philosophical Examination," *Ethics,* Vol. 103, No. 2 (January 1993), pp. 302–317. On the more general issue of sexist language, see *Sexist Language: A Modern Philosophical Analysis,* edited by Mary Vetterling-Braggin (n.p.: Littlefield, Adams and Co., 1981).

Sexual Harassment

See the review article "Sexual Abuse and Harassment" by Naomi Scheman in *Encyclopedia of Ethics,* edited by Lawrence C. Becker and Charlotte B. Becker (New York: Garland Publishing, 1992), Vol. II, pp. 1139–1141. Also see Catharine MacKinnon, *Sexual Harassment of Working Women* (New Haven: Yale University Press, 1979) for a view of sexual harassment as sex discrimination. Also see the excellent anthology, *Sexual Harassment: Confrontations and Decisions,* edited by Edmund Wall (Buffalo: Prometheus Books, 1992).

Affirmative Action

For a general bibliography of affirmative action, see the references mentioned in the bibliography for the chapter on race and ethnicity. For a perceptive analysis of the ways in which certain practices result in sex discrimination, see Mary Anne Warren, "Secondary Sexism and Quota Hiring," *Philosophy and Public Affairs,* Vol. 6 (1977), pp. 240–261. In addition, see *Justice, Gender, and Affirmative Action,* by Susan D. Clayton and Faye J. Crosby (Ann Arbor: University of Michigan Press, 1992).

CHAPTER 7

Sexual Orientation

Videotape:

Topic: Man Apparently Killed Because He Was Gay
ABCNEWS *Source:* ABC *Nightline* (March 10, 1999)
Anchor: Sam Donaldson

Experiential Accounts

André Dubus
"A Quiet Siege: The Death and Life of a Gay Naval Officer"

André Dubus's most recent work is Broken Vessels, *a collection of essays (David Godine).*

In this essay, Dubus recounts the story of the Commander of the Air Group (CAG) aboard the carrier USS Ranger in the early 1960s. Dubus shows the way in which a naval investigation into the Commander's sexual orientation led to his suicide, and also shows the way in which his sexual orientation was largely irrelevant to his life as an officer.

He was a Navy pilot in World War II and in Korea, and when I knew him in 1961 for a few months before he killed himself he was the Commander of the Air Group aboard the USS Ranger, an aircraft carrier, and we called him by the acronym CAG. He shot himself with his .38 revolver because two investigators from the Office of Naval Intelligence came aboard ship while we were anchored off Iwakuni in Japan and gave the ship's captain a written report of their investigation of CAG's erotic life. CAG was a much-decorated combat pilot, and his duty as a commander was one of great responsibility. The ship's executive officer, also a commander, summoned CAG to his office, where the two investigators were, and told him that his choices were to face a general court-martial or to resign from the Navy. Less than half an hour later CAG was dead in his stateroom. His body was flown to the United States; we were told that he did not have a family, and I do not know where he was buried. There was a memorial service aboard ship, but I do not remember it; I only remember a general sadness like mist in the passageways.

I did not really know him. I was a first lieutenant then, a career Marine; two years later I would resign and become a teacher. On the Ranger I was with the Marine detachment; we guarded the planes' nuclear weapons stored belowdecks, ran the brig, and manned one of the antiaircraft gun mounts. We were fifty or so enlisted men and two officers among a ship's crew of about 3,000 officers and men. The Air Group was not included in the ship's company. They came aboard with their planes for our seven-month deployment in the western Pacific. I do not remember the number of pilots and bombardier-navigators, mechanics and flight controllers, and men who worked on the flight deck, but there were plenty of all, and day and night you could hear planes catapulting off the front of the deck and landing on its rear.

The flight deck was 1,052 feet long, the ship weighed 81,000 tons fully loaded, and I rarely felt its motion. I came aboard in May for a year of duty, and in August we left our port in San Francisco Bay and headed for Japan. I had driven my wife and three young children home to Louisiana, where they would stay during the seven months I was at sea, and every day I longed for them. One night on the voyage across the Pacific I sat in the wardroom drinking coffee with a lieutenant commander at one of the long tables covered with white linen. The wardroom was open all night because men were always working. The lieutenant commander told me that Soviet submarines tracked us, they recorded the sound of our propellers and could not be fooled by the sound of a decoy ship's propellers, and that they even came into San Francisco Bay to do this; our submarines did the same with Soviet carriers. He said that every time we tried in training exercises to evade even our own submarines we could not do it, and our destroyers could not track and stop them. He said, "So if the whistle blows we'll get a nuclear fish up our ass in the first thirty minutes. Our job is to get the birds in the air before that. They're going to Moscow."

"Where will they land afterward?"

"They won't. They know that."

The voyage to Japan was five or six weeks long because we did not go directly to Japan; the pilots flew air operations. Combat units are always training for war, but these men who flew planes, and the men in orange suits and ear protectors who worked on the flight deck during landings and takeoffs, were engaging in something not at all as playful as Marine field exercises generally were. They were imperiled. One pilot told me that from his fighter-bomber in the sky the flight deck looked like an aspirin tablet. On the passage to Japan I became friendly with some pilots, drinking coffee in the wardroom, and I knew what CAG looked like because he was CAG. He had dark skin and alert eyes, and he walked proudly. Then in Japan I sometimes drank with young pilots. I was a robust twenty-five-year-old, one of two Marine officers aboard ship, and I did not want to be outdone at anything by anyone. But I could not stay with the pilots; I had to leave them in the bar, drinking and talking and laughing, and make my way back to the ship to sleep and wake with a hangover. Next day the pilots flew; if we did not go to sea, they flew from a base on land. Once I asked one of them how he did it.

"The pure oxygen. Soon as you put on the mask, your head clears."

It was not simply the oxygen, and I did not understand any of these wild, brave, and very efficient men until years later when I read Tom Wolfe's *The Right Stuff.*

It was on that same tour that I saw another pilot die. I worked belowdecks with the Marine detachment but that warm gray afternoon the entire ship was in a simulated condition of war, and my part was to stand four hours of watch in a small turret high above the ship. I could move the turret in a circular way by pressing a button, and I looked through binoculars for planes or ships in the 180-degree arc of our port side. On the flight deck planes were taking off; four could do this in quick sequence. Two catapults launched planes straight off the front of the ship, and quickly they rose and climbed. The third and fourth catapults were on the port side where the flight deck angled sharply out to the left, short of the bow. From my turret I looked down at the ship's bridge and the flight deck. A helicopter flew low near the ship, and planes were taking off. On the deck were men in orange suits and ear protectors; on both sides of the ship, just beneath the flight deck, were nets for these men to jump into, to save themselves from being killed by a landing plane that veered or skidded or crashed. One night I'd inspected a Marine guarding a plane on the flight deck; we had a sentry there because the plane carried a nuclear bomb. I stepped from a hatch into the absolute darkness of a night at sea and into a strong wind that lifted my body with each step. I was afraid it would lift me off the deck and hurl me into the sea, where I would tread water in that great expanse and depth while the ship went on its way; tomorrow they would learn that I was missing. I found the plane and the Marine; he stood with one arm around the cable that held the wing to the deck.

In the turret I was facing aft when it happened: men in orange were at the rear of the flight deck, then they sprinted forward, and I rotated my turret toward the bow and saw a plane in the gray sea and an orange-suited pilot lying facedown in the water, his parachute floating beyond his head, moving toward the rear of the ship. The plane had dropped off the port deck and now water covered its wing, then its cockpit, and it sank. The pilot was behind the ship; his limbs did not move, his face was in the sea, and his parachute was filling with water and starting to sink. The helicopter hovered low and a sailor on a rope descended from it; he wore orange, and I watched him coming down and the pilot floating and the parachute sinking beneath the waves. There was still some length of parachute line remaining when the sailor reached the pilot; he grabbed him; then the parachute lines tightened their pull and drew the pilot down. There was only the sea now beneath the sailor on the rope.

Then he ascended.

I shared a stateroom with a Navy lieutenant, an officer of medical administration, a very tall and strong man from Oklahoma. He had been an enlisted man, had once been a corpsman aboard a submarine operating off the coast of the Soviet Union, and one night their periscope was spotted, destroyers came after them, and they dived and sat at the bottom and listened by sonar to the destroyers' sonar trying to find them. He told me about the sailor who had tried to save the pilot. In the dispensary they gave him brandy, and the sailor wept and said he was trained to do that job, and this was his first time, and he had failed. Of course he had not failed. No man could lift another man attached to a parachute filled with water. Some people said the helicopter had not stayed close enough to the ship while the planes were taking off. Some said the pilot was probably already dead; his plane dropped from the ship, and he ejected himself high into the air, but not high enough for his parachute to ease his fall. This was all talk about the mathematics of violent death; the pilot was killed because he flew airplanes from a ship at sea.

He was a lieutenant commander, and I knew his face and name. As he was being catapulted, his landing gear on the left side broke off and his plane skidded into the sea. He was married; his widow had been married before, also to a pilot who was killed in a crash. I wondered if it was her bad luck to meet only men who flew; years later I believed that whatever in their spirits made these men fly also drew her to them.

I first spoke to CAG at the officers' club at the Navy base in Yokosuka. The officers of the Air Group hosted a party for the officers of the ship's company. We wore civilian suits and ties, and gathered at the club to drink. There were no women. The party was a matter of protocol, probably a tradition among pilots and the officers of carriers; for us young officers it meant getting happily drunk. I was doing this with pilots at the bar when one of them said, "Let's throw CAG into the pond."

He grinned at me, as I looked to my left at the small shallow pond with pretty fish in it; then I looked past the pond at CAG, sitting on a soft leather chair, a drink in his hand, talking quietly with two or three other commanders sitting in soft leather chairs. All the pilots with me were grinning and saying yes, and the image of us lifting CAG from his chair and dropping him into the water gave me joy, and I put my drink on the bar and said, "Let's go."

I ran across the room to CAG, grabbed the lapels of his coat, jerked him up from his chair, and saw his drink spill onto his suit; then I fell backward to the floor, still holding his lapels, and pulled him down on top of me. There was no one else with me. He was not angry yet, but I was a frightened fool. I released his lapels and turned my head and looked back at the laughing pilots. Out of my vision the party was loud, hundreds of drinking officers who had not seen this, and CAG sounded only puzzled when he said, "What's going on?"

He stood and brushed at the drink on his suit, watching me get up from the floor. I stood not quite at attention but not at ease either. I said, "Sir, I'm Marine Lieutenant Dubus. Your pilots fooled me." I nodded toward them at the bar, and CAG smiled. "They said, 'Let's throw CAG into the pond.' But, sir, the joke was on me."

He was still smiling.

"I'm very sorry, sir."

"That's all right, Lieutenant."

"Can I get the Commander another drink, sir?"

"Sure," he said, and told me what he was drinking, and I got it from the bar, where the pilots were red-faced and happy, and brought it to CAG, who was sitting in his chair again with the other commanders. He smiled and thanked me, and the commanders smiled; then I returned to the young pilots and we all laughed.

Until a few months later, on the day he killed himself, the only words I spoke to CAG after the party were greetings. One night I saw him sitting with a woman in the officers' club, and I wished him good evening. A few times I saw him in the ship's passageways; I recognized him seconds before the features of his face were clear: he had a graceful, athletic stride that dipped his shoulders. I saluted and said, "Good morning, sir" or "Good afternoon, sir." He smiled as he returned my salute and greeting, his eyes and voice mirthful, and I knew that he was seeing me again pulling him out of his chair and down to the floor, then standing to explain myself and apologize. I liked being a memory that gave him sudden and passing amusement.

On a warm sunlit day we were anchored off Iwakuni, and I planned to go with other crew members on a bus to Hiroshima. I put on civilian clothes and went down the ladder to the boat that would take us ashore. I was not happily going to Hiroshima; I was going because I was an American, and I felt that I should look at it and be in it. I found a seat on the rocking boat, then saw CAG in civilian clothes coming down the ladder. There were a few seats remaining, and he chose the one next to me. He asked me where I was going, then said he was going to Hiroshima, too. I was relieved and grateful; while CAG was flying planes in World War II, I was a boy buying savings stamps and bringing scrap metal to school. On the bus he would talk to me about war, and in Hiroshima I would walk with him and look with him, and his seasoned steps and eyes would steady mine. Then from the ship above us the officer of the deck called down, "CAG?"

CAG turned and looked up at him, a lieutenant junior grade in white cap and short-sleeved shirt and trousers.

"Sir, the executive officer would like to see you."

I do not remember what CAG said to me. I only remember my disappointment when he told the boat's officer to go ashore without him. All I saw in CAG's face was the look of a man called from rest back to his job. He climbed the ladder, and soon the boat pulled away.

Perhaps when I reached Hiroshima CAG was already dead; I do not remember the ruins at ground zero or what I saw in the museum. I walked and looked, and stood for a long time at a low arch with an open space at the ground, and in that space was a stone box that held the names of all who died on the day of the bombing and all who had died since because of the bomb. That night I ate dinner ashore, then rode the boat to the ship, went to my empty room, climbed to my upper bunk, and slept for only a while, till the quiet voice of my roommate woke me: "The body will be flown to Okinawa."

I looked at him standing at his desk and speaking into the telephone.

"Yes. A .38 in the temple. Yes."

I turned on my reading lamp and watched him put the phone down. He was sad, and he looked at me. I said, "Did someone commit suicide?"

"CAG."

"CAG?"

I sat up.

"The ONI investigated him."

Then I knew what I had not known I knew, and I said, "Was he a homosexual?"

"Yes."

My roommate told me the executive officer had summoned CAG to his office, shown him the report, and told him that he could either resign or face a general court-martial. Then CAG went to his room. Fifteen minutes later the executive officer phoned him; when he did not answer, the executive officer and the investigators ran to his room. He was on his bunk, shot in the right temple, his pilot's .38 revolver in his hand. His eyelids fluttered; he was unconscious but still alive, and he died from bleeding.

"They ran?" I said. "They ran to his room?"

Ten years later one of my shipmates came to visit me in Massachusetts; we had been civilians for a long time. In my kitchen we were drinking beer, and he said, "I couldn't tell you this aboard ship, because I worked in the legal office. They called CAG back from that boat you were on because he knew the ONI was aboard. His plane was on the ground at the base in Iwakuni. They were afraid he was going to fly it and crash into the sea and they'd lose the plane."

All 3,000 of the ship's crew did not mourn. Not every one of the hundreds of men in the Air Group mourned. But the shock was general and hundreds of men did mourn, and each morning we woke to it, and it was in our talk in the wardroom and in the passageways. In the closed air of the ship it touched us, and it lived above us on the flight deck and in the sky. One night at sea a young pilot came to my room; his face was sunburned and sad. We sat in desk chairs, and he said, "The morale is very bad now. The whole Group. It's just shot."

"Did y'all know about him?"

"We all knew. We didn't care. We would have followed him into hell." Yes, they would have followed him; they were ready every day and every night to fly with him from a doomed ship and follow him to Moscow, to perish in their brilliant passion.

Journal/Discussion Questions

✍ *Do you know people who have had to conceal their sexual orientation? Discuss the moral issues that surround this situation.*

1. One of the interesting aspects of this essay is the way in which the CAG's sexual orientation is irrelevant to his position as Air Group Commander. In what ways is sexual orientation simply a personal matter? A private matter? In what ways is it public?
2. Discuss the moral issues raised by this story.

David Firestone
"Murder Reveals Double Life of Being Gay in the Rural South"

David Firestone is a correspondent for The New York Times.

"If he was gay or not," Billy Jack Gaither's mother said, "that still didn't give them no right to kill him." There's no disagreement on that issue. What this selection prompts us to ask, however, is what we should do in a world in which these kinds of things still happen. It shows us why gays often conceal their sexual orientation and raises important questions about whether and how they should be protected from those who are filled with hate.

Sylacauga, Alabama. March 5, 1999. The closets that gay people build in small, severe towns like this one are thick and difficult to penetrate, and Billy Jack Gaither's was locked even tighter than most.

Until the day two weeks ago when he was beaten to death and burned, Mr. Gaither, who was 39, lived with his disabled parents in their white clapboard house, tending to their needs, cooking dinner and cleaning up, singing in the choir of his Baptist church. His parents swear they had no idea he was gay, and his father, Marion Gaither, is still half in denial, desperately pointing out that his son once had a girlfriend in Birmingham whom he almost married.

But the small group of gay residents in this central Alabama city of 13,000 knew Billy Jack Gaither as one of their own, sharing their fears of public knowledge. A friend who grew up with him and used to accompany him on the nearly 40-mile trip northwest to the gay bars of Birmingham said Mr. Gaither would have probably escaped Sylacauga, like most gay people who grow up here, but was too devoted to his parents to contemplate leaving. The friend, who did not want to be identified for fear of losing business, said Mr. Gaither had never wanted to hurt his deeply religious, Baptist parents by revealing the nature of his sexuality.

Now his parents and the rest of Sylacauga have found out about Mr. Gaither, and in the worst possible way. On Thursday, officials charged two local men with Mr. Gaither's murder, saying the two had said they became angered after he made a sexual advance at one of them.

The murder is being called another signpost of hate, like the deaths of Matthew Shepard, killed in Wyoming last year because he was gay, and James Byrd Jr., the black man dragged to his death behind a truck last year in Jasper, Tex.

The Coosa County Sheriff's report said the men, Steven E. Mullins and Charles M. Butler Jr., had known Mr. Gaither and met him on the night of Feb. 19 at a local nightclub, the Frame. They then locked him in the trunk of his car and drove to a deserted boat dock where they bludgeoned him to death with an ax handle, then heaved his body onto a pyre of burning tires, the report said. His remains were found the next day on the banks of Peckerwood Creek, which churches use for baptizing.

Mr. Gaither's parents had barely absorbed the horror of his gruesome death before they were forced to learn the motive for his murder, and the secret life that he had led for so long. They knew him as the kindest of their four boys, the one who read his big illustrated Bible every night before going to bed, who never came home late on those rare occasions when he did go with friends to one of the local bars (all of them straight).

"If he was gay, he sure never showed it," his mother, Lois Gaither, said this morning. "He never flaunted himself as being gay or talked about it. And whether he was or not, it don't make me love him any less. He was my young'un."

She added, in a kind of rueful acknowledgment of the truth, "Whatever he did, he never brought it home."

But Marion Gaither, debilitated by multiple heart attacks and a stroke, sat on the couch near his wife, holding his forehead in his hands, shaking his head at all references to his son's sexuality. When a television news report came on saying his son was killed because he was gay, Mr. Gaither shouted out: "If he was gay. If he was gay."

A tour of the house, however, gave a glimpse of the separate world that Billy Jack Gaither lived in. He had decorated his room with a large collection of Scarlett O'Hara dolls and other figurines from "Gone With the Wind," for which he hunted at flea markets on weekends. A large picture of Clark Gable kissing Vivian Leigh hung over his bedroom fireplace; pink chiffon curtains fluttered around antique etchings of antebellum women in hoop skirts.

The rest of the house, which his parents also allowed him to decorate, was more conventional. In the living room he hung a painting of the Last Supper, next to another of Jesus praying in the garden; between them was a golden plaque of the Ten Commandments.

The two rooms, one for the outside world, the other for himself, seemed to illustrate the traditional dichotomy of small-town Southern gay life. Billy Jack Gaither's friend said there were about 100 gay people in town, but none were open about their sexual orientation. Though there had never been a violent incident like this one against a gay person, the friend said, there was plenty of evidence that homosexuality was not appreciated.

Not long ago, he said, citing one example, a group of downtown merchants hung up a series of flags on light poles to spruce up the image of the central business district. The merchants were not aware that one flag used a rainbow symbol sometimes employed by gay groups, but a local church recognized the symbol and began a strident campaign to remove it, saying that its presence promoted a gay life style in Sylacauga. The flag quickly came down.

Those gay people who have not moved out of town occasionally travel together to gay bars in Birmingham or Montgomery, the friend said. He said Mr. Gaither occasionally went on such trips, and was known to have had at least two short-term relationships with other men, whom he would meet out of town.

Sylacauga, with more than 70 churches in its boundaries, is not unlike most rural Southern towns in its conservatism and religious beliefs. It is industrial rather than agricultural, with many people working in one of the factories that ring Sylacauga. Mr. Gaither operated a computer terminal at the Russell Corporation, an athletic wear manufacturer, in nearby Alexander City. He dropped out of Sylacauga High School in the 11th grade, but later got his equivalency diploma and joined the Marines for a year before getting an honorable discharge because of high blood pressure, his parents said.

David W. White, the Birmingham coordinator for the Gay and Lesbian Alliance of Alabama, said Mr. Gaither had frequented a Birmingham bar called the Tool Box, one of five gay bars in the city. Many gay people from surrounding small towns drive to Birmingham for companionship, he said, because the slightest indication of homosexuality in a town like Sylacauga would invite harassment, or worse.

"I would consider it difficult to live anywhere in Alabama other than Birmingham," Mr. White said. "Even in Birmingham, I would never in a public place grab my partner's hand and walk down the street. It would literally be a death wish in the state of Alabama. You would almost be inciting violence to do something like that."

Until now, Mr. Gaither's friend said, gay people in town have been more concerned about harassment and the loss of jobs or business than about violence. That all changed with Mr. Gaither's murder.

"We're all looking over our shoulders now," said the friend, who carefully closed the doors of his office before even discussing the subject. "You know, Mullins lived just two miles from here."

Mr. Mullins, who shaved his head, was known around town for wearing Ku Klux Klan T-shirts and making racist comments, but Mr. Gaither's friend said gay residents had not been aware of him or Mr. Butler as someone to fear. Mr. Mullins and Mr. Butler are being held in the Coosa County jail in lieu of $500,000 bond each; their case will be handed to a grand jury on March 17.

Although the two men could face execution if they are convicted of capital murder, they cannot be charged with a hate crime, because Alabama's hate-crime statute covers only crimes committed due to race, religion, ethnicity and disability, but not sexual orientation. Mr. White and other advocates of gay rights said the murder would increase the pressure on the Alabama Legislature to broaden the statute. Mr. Shepard's death led to similar calls for hate-crime legislation that would apply to gays.

President Clinton was explicit in comparing the two cases today in offering his prayers to Mr. Gaither's friends and family.

"In times like this, the American people pull together and speak with one voice, because the acts of hatred that led to the deaths of such innocent men are also acts of defiance against the values our society holds most dear," Mr. Clinton said in a statement.

Mrs. Gaither put it somewhat differently.

"If he was gay or not," she said, "that still didn't give them no right to kill him."

Journal/Discussion Questions

✍ *One of the most striking things about this incident is the level of hatred, a hatred that has nothing to do specifically with the individual who was killed. Have you ever seen this kind of hatred? Where do you think it comes from? How can it be eliminated or reduced?*

An Introduction to the Moral Issues

Let's begin by considering what type of discrimination occurs against gays and lesbians in contemporary American society. Then we shall turn to a discussion of the arguments advanced against homosexuality, the competing ideals of the place of sexual orientation in society, and the means for attaining those ideals.

Discrimination against Gays and Lesbians

What types of discrimination do gays and lesbians experience in our society?

Discrimination against gays and lesbians differs in several ways from the previous two types of discrimination we have considered: racism and sexism. One of the principal reasons for this is that sexual orientation is generally much less apparent than either race or sex. Because they are less easily identifiable, gays and lesbians are less likely to be subject to certain kinds of discrimination. Homosexuals have not formally been denied voting rights as women and African-Americans have been, apparently do not suffer from a lower level of income than their heterosexual counterparts, and have not usually encountered restrictions on their individual right to hold property. In these ways, they are not in need of the same kinds of affirmative action programs that have been defended for racial minorities and women.

Despite these differences which favor gays and lesbians, they are discriminated against in ways that would not be tolerated today if such discrimination were directed against racial minorities or women. They are not permitted to serve openly in the military; they are not permitted to marry one another, with both the emotional and financial costs that such prohibitions incur; they are often discriminated against in child-related matters such as child custody during divorces, adoption, foster parenting, Big Brothers, the Boy Scouts, and the like. Consider, for example, the financial costs of not being permitted to marry. When a husband dies, his estate may pass to his wife without taxes; when a gay person's life-partner dies, transferred assets are heavily taxed.

Moreover, gays and lesbians—and their families—usually experience a very painful process when they begin to let their sexual orientation become public. Again, there is nothing comparable for racial minorities or for women. Announcements of one's race or gender rarely come as surprises to one's family and loved ones in the way that revealing one's sexual orientation often does.

Finally, it is important to realize that some gays and lesbians experience discrimination because of the radical character of their beliefs and "lifestyles." Here it is difficult to draw the line, but it would seem that at least part of the criticism and opposition they experience is directed primarily against their radicalness, not their gayness.

Let's now turn to a consideration of two specific areas of discrimination—gays and lesbians in the military, and homosexual marriage—and the more general issue raised by these particular problems, the issue of protection for gay rights.

Gays and Lesbians in the Military

After he was elected in 1992, President Clinton attempted to lift the ban against homosexuals in the military and thereby ignited a heated debate about whether open homosexuals should be officially allowed to serve in the armed forces. Various arguments were advanced against lifting the ban, many of which centered around the effect on heterosexual military personnel "unit cohesion" and "combat effectiveness." Interestingly, some of the same arguments advanced against gays could also be advanced against women in the armed forces, and many of the arguments about the possibility of sexual harassment and unwanted sexual attention—if taken seriously—could certainly provide a welcome amount of protection for many women in the military.

Homosexual Marriage

Presently in the United States, only marriages for heterosexuals are recognized by law. Some gay rights supporters have advocated the legalization of gay and lesbian marriages. Because they cannot be legally married, committed gay and lesbian couples are often denied the emotional and financial supports that a legally sanctioned marriage provides. Making a lifelong commitment is often difficult under any circumstances, and it becomes more so when one's commitment has no legal standing. This has particularly been a source of anguish for gays since the onset of AIDS, when gays have cared for dying partners but have not been given the recognition of one who has lost a spouse. Some of the obstacles they face include denial of hospital visitation rights, challenges to durable power of attorney by blood-related family, the denial of rights to pass property without taxation, and challenges to the wills of the deceased by blood families. Other gay rights advocates have argued that marriage does not provide the path to liberation that Andrew Sullivan and others have claimed.

Gay and Lesbian Civil Rights

The more general issue raised by a number of supporters of gay rights is whether it ought to be legal to discriminate against people simply because of their sexual orientation. Should landlords be allowed to turn down potential tenants because of sexual orientation? Should schools and day-care centers be allowed to fire (or refuse to hire) individuals because they are gay or lesbian? Some advocates of gay and lesbian rights maintain that discrimination against individuals because of sexual orientation should be banned, just as we have banned such discrimination when based on race or gender.

Arguments against Homosexuality

Opponents of homosexuality and of equal rights for homosexuals advance several different kinds of arguments in support of their position. These can be classified into three main types: (a) *religious arguments,* which usually proceed from some prohibitions against homosexuality in religious texts;

(b) *intrinsic arguments,* that is, arguments asserting that there is something intrinsically immoral about homosexuality; and (c) *extrinsic arguments,* arguments that claim that homosexuality ought to be prohibited because of factors usually associated with, but not necessary to, homosexuality. Let's examine each of these three types of arguments.

Religious Arguments

Religious arguments against homosexuality tend to be of two types, and those two types generally overlap. The first type of argument is narrowly *textual*—that is, it maintains that the tradition's religious text(s) condemn homosexuality, therefore it is wrong. The second type is what we can call a *tradition* argument. It maintains that a given religious tradition and worldview, taken as a whole, are incompatible with homosexuality. Let's consider each of these.

Is religion compatible with homosexuality?

Textual arguments. Religious arguments against homosexuality often appeal to some specific passage in the Bible, the Koran, or whatever religious text is central to that tradition, and then interpret that passage as a condemnation of homosexuality. The structure of such arguments is simple: x (in this case, x = homosexuality) is wrong because it is condemned by God, and we know that God condemns it because he says so in our religious text.

Two difficulties are often raised in regard to such arguments. First, is the passage actually being interpreted correctly? Here issues of translation and context are crucial, and such texts are often open to multiple interpretations. Second, do we—and ought we to—do everything espoused by that text. There are often many things our religious texts tell us to do that believers in fact reject. For example in the New Testament, Mark 16 encourages believers to "pick up serpents" if they believe, but few Christians do so or believe that they ought to do so. There is, in other words, a selectivity about textual arguments, at least taken in isolation, that makes them suspicious.

Tradition arguments. The second, and often more thoughtful, kind of argument against homosexuality is one which asks "What are we, as a community and a tradition, all about?" Once having established the elements central to that tradition's identity, it then asks whether homosexuality is compatible with that tradition. This type of argument is much broader in scope and potentially much more subtle and textured. Instead of asking whether a specific kind of act is compatible with a selected religious text, this type of argument asks whether a particular religious tradition and way of life are compatible with a gay or lesbian life. Religious traditions show a wide range of variance on this issue, including the 1963 Quaker position that homosexual activity within a monogamous relationship is "natural" for some individuals and as much a gift of the Spirit as heterosexuality.

Notice that tradition arguments are not narrowly focused on the compatibility between a given religious tradition and the specific acts of gay or lesbian sex. Rather, they ask about the compatibility between their tradition and a *gay life.* This is a much broader question, made all the more complex by the fact that the term "a gay life" covers a wide range of different types of lives. We shall return to this issue in our discussion of the difference between intrinsic and extrinsic arguments.

The act and the agent. Finally, it is important to note that some religiously-based opposition to homosexuality distinguishes between (a) being a homosexual and (b) homosexual acts, and often reserves its condemnation—in the spirit of Augustine, who said to "Love the sinner, and hate the sin"—for homosexual acts while maintaining that *being* a homosexual does not exclude a person from the religious community in question. Within these traditions, celibate gays and lesbians are welcomed into full membership in the community.

Many gays and lesbians reply to such a distinction by maintaining that their sexual orientation is so central to their identity as persons that to deny it through celibacy would be tantamount to denying a fundamental dimension of their identity as persons. It is, in other words, a distinction without a difference.

Intrinsic Arguments

Those who argue that there is something intrinsically immoral about homosexuality usually say that it is "unnatural" or that it thwarts the "natural" purpose of sex, which is procreation. Let's consider each of these arguments.

The argument from nature. Outside of a religious tradition, one of the arguments most frequently advanced against homosexuality is that it "goes against nature." This is an interesting argument, and much turns on the meaning of "nature." For the argument to work, two premises must be established: (1) that homosexuality is in fact "unnatural" in the required sense, and (2) that we ought not to do something that is "unnatural." Let's consider each of these claims in order.

First, in what sense, if any, is homosexuality "unnatural"? If we look just at the species of human beings, then we get two possible answers. Homosexuality is unnatural in the sense that it does not conform to the sexual orientation of the majority of human beings; however, homosexuality is natural in the sense that it is normal that a small percentage of human beings are (probably genetically, i.e., naturally) homosexual in their orientation. Edward Wilson, the sociobiologist, has argued in *On Human Nature* that homosexuality in a certain percentage of the population is a normal condition that benefits humanity as a whole. Certainly, for homosexuals, their sexual orientation seems completely "natural" to them. Indeed, it would seem reasonable to argue that heterosexuality is natural for heterosexuals and homosexuality is natural for homosexuals. Furthermore, is homosexuality more "unnatural" than celibacy, a value and way of life highly esteemed by many religious and ethical traditions? If heterosexual sex is taken as the paradigm case of normalcy, the danger is that too little will count as normal in the end.

Yet there are a lot of things—such as war and death—that may be "natural," yet they would hardly qualify as good. This brings us to our second point: the words "natural" and "unnatural" must have some *normative* force if they are to generate a conclusion about the moral unacceptability of homosexuality. In other words, what is "unnatural" must be linked to what is bad or morally evil. Here the terrain becomes more difficult. On what basis can we say that the natural is good, especially if things like violence and death are natural? The only way is to say that not everything that is statistically normal—and "natural" in this sense—is natural in the sense of being morally good. Yet how do we make this judgment? In particular, how do we make it in a way that would show that homosexuality is unnatural in the moral sense? Traditionally, this has been done through an appeal to God's purpose in nature, but this again brings us back to religious arguments.

Sex and procreation. The other way that the argument from nature establishes the moral sense of nature is through claiming that there are purposes in nature which provide the basis for the moral sense of the natural. In particular, one of our natural purposes is procreation, and advocates of this position maintain that homosexuality breaks an essential link between sex and procreation. This, they claim, is what makes homosexuality morally objectionable.

In what sense, if any, is the purpose of sex procreation? What implications does this have for your views about gay and lesbian sexuality?

The difficulty with this argument is that, if it proves anything at all, it probably proves too much. If the argument were sound, it would seem to show that all sexual acts not aimed toward procreation (or at least in principle open to it) are immoral. In fact, this is the position that some—particularly Catholics—hold, but it seems to commit its adherents to condemning masturbators, people who practice birth control, and gays and lesbians equally.

Extrinsic Arguments

Some opponents of homosexuality argue against it because of factors often (though perhaps erroneously) associated with it. For example, some might argue that gay relationships are not to be encouraged, since they tend not to be permanent in the way that heterosexual relationships (allegedly) are. Yet one has to be careful in assessing such arguments for at least two reasons. First, because homosexuality is often still condemned in our society, it is difficult to obtain reliable empirical data on such issues. Second, some of these alleged extrinsic factors might in fact be due to the very discrimination that gays and lesbians would like to see eliminated. For example, it is undoubtedly more difficult to maintain long-term committed relationships without the support of the law and one's family. To criticize gays and lesbians for (allegedly) not having committed relationships, and to then deny them the support of legally-sanctioned relationships, is to beg the question.

An interesting extrinsic argument is often raised in the discussion of homosexuals in the military. If the presence of gays in the military makes heterosexual soldiers uncomfortable, is that an acceptable reason for banning gays? (Certainly we would not agree to this principle if we substituted race for sexual orientation.) Clearly, other people's reactions are something that is completely extrinsic to homosexuality.

Drawing the line between intrinsic and extrinsic factors. It is easy to find clear-cut cases of both extrinsic and intrinsic arguments. For example, some have advocated banning homosexuals from positions requiring a security clearance, since they may be more subject to blackmail than their heterosexual counterparts. But this is clearly an extrinsic argument, and it only has force in a society that discriminates against gays and lesbians. (Of course, it also further contributes to that discrimination.) Eliminate the discrimination, and the possibility for blackmail evaporates. Nothing intrinsic to homosexuality makes it susceptible to blackmail. On the other hand, being erotically attracted to someone of the same sex is intrinsic to being gay or lesbian, and arguments against such attraction would be applicable to all cases of homosexuality.

Is Homosexuality a Matter of Choice?

Researchers remain uncertain about what the causes of homosexuality are. Some believe that the ultimate cause will turn out to be genetic, while others think it will center around early childhood experiences. Few believe that it is a matter of unimpeded adult choice, such as one might choose whether and how to part one's hair or what type of career to pursue. Most testimony indicates that sexual orientation is set, whatever the causes, by the time a person starts to be sexually aware. Sexual orientation, in other words, does not appear to be a *choice* in any significant sense.

This question is morally relevant for at least two reasons. First, we usually do not hold people responsible for things that they do not choose. It seems unjust to many people to condemn people for being homosexual if those people had no choice at all in their sexual orientation. Second, many people fear that interactions with gay persons may cause others to become gay. This is particularly an issue when gay adults are around children—as parents, foster parents, teachers, scout leaders, and the like. If sexual orientation is unaffected by such interactions, this issue may diminish in importance.

Is Sexual Orientation Exclusively Either Heterosexual or Homosexual?

Finally, it is important to note that much of the contemporary discussion of these issues rests on the presumption that there is a sharp dividing line between, on the one hand heterosexuals and, on the other hand, gays and lesbians. The picture becomes more complex if, as some have suggested, sexual orientation may be bisexual. This has been argued in two quite distinct senses. First, some maintain that some individuals are naturally bisexual, just as some are naturally either heterosexual or homosexual. Second, a few theorists have argued that both sexual orientations are present in everyone to some degree, and that individuals are distinguished by the degree to which one orientation holds ascendancy over the other.

Models of the Place of Sexual Orientation in Society

When we envision the ideal society as we would like to see it, what place does sexual orientation have in it? Is it a society composed solely of heterosexuals, or at least one in which homosexuals are not tolerated as members in good standing? Is it a society in which gays and lesbians are not discriminated against, but whose presence is also not stressed in any way? Or is it a society in which difference is celebrated and encouraged?

Our picture here is a complex one, because we actually have two separate—and sometimes conflicting—factors at work as individuals develop their own position on this issue. First, there is the issue of the morality of homosexuality, which is part of an individual's overall views on sexual morality. Second, there is the issue of societal rights and governmental protection of those rights. Here the issue is the extent to which government ought to be involved in legislating matters of sexual morality.

Let's consider how both of these factors intersect to form the major positions in this ongoing societal debate.

The Traditional Model

Many conservatives espouse an ideal of society that has no room for gays and lesbians. In some versions, simply being homosexual is enough to eliminate a person from the community. In other versions, gays and lesbians would be allowed to have their sexual orientation, but not to engage in homosexual acts. They would, in other words, be sentenced to a life of involuntary chastity.

Defenders of conservative models offer two kinds of arguments. First, some maintain that homosexuality is intrinsically evil, and that therefore it should not be tolerated. Many defenders of this position cite religious sources as the foundation of their belief, while others appeal to some version of the "unnaturalness" argument discussed above. Second, some conservatives maintain that homosexuality contradicts important social and moral values—such as the value of family life—and should not be tolerated for that reason. Here the focus is not on homosexual *acts,* but on the *values* of homosexuals.

What arguments support the traditional model of sexuality?

Critics of the traditional model offer several replies. First, many defenders of homosexuality argue that it is not unnatural, a point we have already discussed above. Second, they point out that even if one believed something was unnatural and thus evil, it doesn't automatically follow that one is in favor of banning it. Many might think smoking cigarettes is bad, but that doesn't mean it should be completely banned. Third, they argue that it is consistent to support certain key social values, such as the value of family life, and yet not require that *everyone* live out that value in the same way. Many religious orders forbid their members from marrying, yet their presence is not seen in society as contradicting the value of family life. Fourth, many gays and lesbians support family life, and in some cases would even like to have the option of marriage open to them.

Perhaps the most telling reply to supporters of the traditional model is one that does not address their specific arguments, but rather the plight of individuals who are ostracized from society simply on the basis of who they are. If the traditional model were to prevail, gays and lesbians would be excluded from presenting themselves honestly in society simply because of their sexual orientation, not because of any specific, nonsexual actions or values. Where can these people go? They can either pretend they are straight, and thus gain some acceptance, or stand by their sexual orientation and be excluded from society. They must choose, in other words, between acceptance through denial of their own identity or exclusion as a result of affirming their sexual identity. A model of society that excludes a significant group in this way seems to be both a cruel and an unjust model.

The Liberal Model

There is no single "liberal" position on the issue of gay and lesbian rights. However, there are two principal currents in the liberal tradition that discourage discrimination against homosexuals: the emphasis on individual autonomy and the importance of the right to privacy.

Autonomy arguments. Liberals characteristically believe that individual liberty is a very high priority, and consequently many hold that individuals should be free to have and express whatever sexual orientation they wish. In some versions of liberalism, this right is virtually absolute, limited only in those instances when its exercise infringes on someone else's autonomy, while other versions of liberalism believe that such rights may be restricted for other reasons as well.

Privacy arguments. Many liberals place a high value on the right to privacy, and see a person's sexual orientation as protected from public scrutiny by that right to privacy. A person's sexual orientation, they argue, is no one else's business, especially not the government's business. Privacy arguments are particularly important in regard to the issue of whether the state may forbid certain kinds of sexual acts between consenting adults in private.

The difference between toleration, acceptance, and support. Liberal positions differ in the degree to which they are supportive of gay and lesbian rights. We can distinguish three levels here.

- *Tolerance:* Gays and lesbians should not be discriminated against, but they also should not be encouraged. The "don't ask, don't tell" policy of the military may fall into this category, although many gays and lesbians see it as less than tolerant. Also in this category are people who believe homosexuality is bad but who also believe sexual morality shouldn't be legislated. Supporters of this position would be in favor of abolishing laws that forbid homosexual acts between consenting adults in private.

How strongly should society support gay rights?

- *Acceptance:* Gays and lesbians should be allowed to express their sexual orientation openly to the same extent that heterosexuals are allowed to express their sexual orientation openly, and should not be discriminated against because of it. This would include support for legal protection against discrimination based on sexual orientation.
- *Endorsement:* Gay and lesbian sexual orientation and lifestyles should be presented as an option that is as valid and valuable as heterosexual orientation and lifestyles. This may include presenting gay and lesbian families as models in public school curricula, legally sanctioning gay marriages, and so on.

Within the liberal tradition, there is a wide variation in the level of support for gay and lesbian rights.

The Polymorphous Model

Finally, some in our society—and this includes some heterosexuals and some homosexuals—see sexuality as centered purely around pleasure, and they see no necessary link between sexuality and either procreation or intimacy. Whatever brings pleasure is good, and pleasure may come in many forms—that is, it may be polymorphus. Advocates of this view of sexuality hold that people should be allowed to engage in whatever kind of sexual activity they want and with whomever they want.

Diversity and Consensus

Although there is relatively little common ground between the most extreme positions on this issue, there is the possibility of some reasonable consensus in the following way.

It seems reasonable that we, as a society, may want to encourage certain fundamental moral values in society. Although such encouragement need not take the form of legislating morality (in the sense of attempting to force people to hold particular moral values through legislative fiat), and although it need not deny individual freedom or the right to privacy (we can discourage something without outlawing it), we may indeed decide to encourage certain values (such as honesty, long-lasting commitment, monogamy, etc.) in our society as a whole, including both heterosexuals and homosexuals. We may further want to discourage certain values and their associated behaviors (such as treating people merely as sexual objects, anonymous sex, etc.), again for everyone, regardless of sexual orientation. The focus, in other words, for finding common ground is not on sexual orientation, but on values.

We can see how this could be applied to issues such as homosexuals in the military and to gay and lesbian marriages. Traditionally, the military has stood for certain values—patriotism, loyalty to one's unit, discipline, and so on—that could be affirmed for both homosexuals and heterosexuals. Indeed, this is in fact almost exactly the situation we have seen for decades (if not centuries). The gays and lesbians in the military have been committed first and foremost to military values, and have often served with great distinction, as the selection from André Dubus, "The Death and Life of a Gay Naval Officer," illustrates. The only difference would be to allow them to acknowledge their sexual orientation while still retaining their commitment to the values of the military.

A similar approach can be taken to the question of gay and lesbian marriages. It seems reasonable that society as a whole would want to encourage certain values such as commitment, individual caring, intimacy, and the like. Insofar as marriage is one of the institutions which helps to support these values, extending this to include gays and lesbians would seem reasonable, for it gives them the opportunity to participate in a highly important societal institution.

THE ARGUMENTS

Barry Goldwater
"Job Protection for Gays"

Barry Goldwater was the former senator from Arizona, and the author of several books, including The Conscience of a Conservative. *The present article appeared in 1994.*

Former Senator Goldwater argues that equal job protection for gays is a necessary part of his conservative political philosophy. Conservatives, he argues, have long stood for a separation of church and state and for the principle that individuals ought to be able to live their lives as they wish, without government intrusion, as long as they do not hurt other people. Gays, he maintains, do not hurt others, and consequently there is no basis for discriminating against them.

As You Read, Consider This:

1. Goldwater argues for his position on the basis of *conservative* principles. Does his presentation of the conservative position seem accurate? How would members of the religious right challenge his vision of conservativism?
2. Why, according to Goldwater, is it in our national *economic* best interest to eliminate job discrimination against gays?

Last year, many who opposed lifting the ban on gays in the military gave lip service to the American ideal that employment opportunities should be based on skill and performance. It's just that the military is different, they said. In civilian life, they'd never condone discrimination.

Well, now's their chance to put up or shut up.

A bipartisan coalition in Congress has proposed legislation to protect gays against job discrimination. Congress is waking up to a reality already recognized by a host of Fortune 500 companies, including AT&T, Marriott and General Motors. These businesses have adopted policies prohibiting discrimination based on sexual orientation because they realize that their employees are their most important asset.

America is now engaged in a battle to reduce the deficit and to compete in a global economy. Job discrimination excludes qualified individuals, lowers work-force productivity and eventually hurts us all. Topping the new world order means attracting the best and creating a workplace environment where everyone can excel. Anything less makes us a second-rate nation. It's not just bad—it's bad business.

But job discrimination against gays and lesbians is real, and it happens every day. Cracker Barrel, a national restaurant chain, adopted a policy of blatant discrimination against employees suspected of being gay. Would anyone tolerate policies prohibiting the hiring of African Americans, Hispanics or women?

Today, in corporate suites and factory warehouses, qualified people live in fear of losing their livelihood for reasons that have nothing to do with ability. In urban and rural communities, hatred and fear force good people from productive employment to the public dole—wasting their talents and the taxpayers' money.

Gays and lesbians are a part of every American family. They should not be shortchanged in their efforts to better their lives and serve their communities. As President Clinton likes to say, "If you work hard and play by the rules, you'll be rewarded"—and not with a pink slip just for being gay.

It's time America realized that there was no gay exemption in the right to "life, liberty, and the pursuit of happiness" in the Declaration of Independence. Job discrimination against gays—or anybody else—is contrary to each of these founding principles.

Some will try to paint this as a liberal or religious issue. I am a conservative Republican, but I believe in democracy and the separation of church and state. The conservative movement is founded on the simple tenet that people have the right to live life as they please, as long as they don't hurt anyone else in the process. No one has ever shown me how being gay or lesbian harms anyone else. Even the 1992 Republican platform affirms the principle that "bigotry has no place in our society."

I am proud that the Republican Party has always stood for individual rights and liberties. The positive role of limited government has always been the defense of these fundamental principles. Our party has led the way in the fight for freedom and a free-market economy, a society where competition and the Constitution matter—and sexual orientation shouldn't.

Now some in our ranks want to extinguish this torch. The radical right has nearly ruined our party. Its members do not care enough about the Constitution, and they are the ones making all the noise. The party faithful must not let it happen. Anybody who cares about real moral values understands that this isn't about granting special rights—its about protecting basic rights.

It is for this reason that more than 100 mayors and governors, Republicans and Democrats, have signed laws and issued orders protecting gays and lesbians. In fact, nearly half the states have provided some form of protection to gays in employment. But of course many others have not, including my own state of Arizona.

It's not going to be easy getting Congress to provide job protection for gays. I know that firsthand. The right wing will rant and rave that the sky is falling. They've said that before—and we're still here. Constitutional conservatives know that doing the right thing takes guts and foresight, but that's why we're elected, to make tough decisions that stand the test of time.

My former colleagues have a chance to stand with civil rights leaders, the business community and the 74 percent of Americans who polls show favor protecting gays and lesbians from job discrimination. With their vote they can help strengthen the American work ethic and support the principles of the Constitution.

Journal/Discussion Questions

✍ *Have you ever experienced—either first-hand or as a direct observer—discrimination against gays or lesbians in a work setting? Describe the incident and discuss what you perceive to be the motivations of the participants.*

1. Imagine that you have been asked by your senator to help draft legislation to protect gays and lesbians from job discrimination. How would you word such legislation? What arguments would you outline in support of it? What objections would you expect to hear to it? How would you reply to such objections?

Martha Nussbaum
"Gay Rights"

Martha Nussbaum is the Ernst Freund Professor of Law and Ethics at the University of Chicago, holding appointments in the Law School, Philosophy Department, and Divinity School, Associate in Classics. She is the author of numerous books and articles in philosophy, including The Fragility of Goodness, The Therapy of Desire, For Love of Country, Cultivating Humanity, *and* Sex and Social Justice.

Nussbaum looks at five rights that are at issue in the contemporary discussion of gay rights, the rights to: (1) protection from violence; (2) consensual adult sexual relations; (3) nondiscrimination in housing, employment, and education; (4) military service; and (5) custody and adoption of children.

As You Read, Consider This:

1. In each of the five areas of rights that Nussbaum considers, what justification does she offer for the rights claims she discusses?

> Now in my own cases when I catch a guy like that I just pick him up and take him into the woods and beat him until he can't crawl. I have had seventeen cases like that in the last couple of years. I tell that guy if I catch him doing that again I will take him out to the woods and I will shoot him. I tell him that I carry a second gun on me just in case I find guys like him and that I will plant it in his hand and say that he tried to kill me and that no jury will convict me.
>
> (Police officer in a large industrial city in the US, being interviewed about his treatment of homosexuals; Westley, 'Violence and the Police,' quoted in Comstock, 1991, pp. 90–95)

Whose rights are we talking about when we talk about "gay rights," and what are the rights in question? I shall take on, first, the surprisingly difficult task of identifying the people. Next, I shall discuss a number of the most important rights that are at issue, including: (1) the right to be protected against violence and, in general, the right to the equal protection of the law; (2) the right to have consensual adult sexual relations without criminal penalty; (3) the right to nondiscrimination in housing, employment and education; (4) the right to military service; (5) the right to marriage and/or its legal benefits; (6) the right to retain custody of children and/or to adopt.

Whose Rights?

. . . let us define gays, lesbians and bisexuals, the class of persons with a "homosexual or bisexual orientation" (now the most common formulation in nondiscrimination law), as those who stably and characteristically desire to engage in sexual conduct with a member or members of the same sex (whether or not they also desire sexual conduct with the opposite sex) and let us adopt a difficult-to-ascertain but not impossibly broad definition of same-sex conduct, namely that it is bodily conduct intended to lead to orgasm on the part of one or both parties. Notice, then, that we are talking about the rights both of people who frequently perform these acts and also of those who desire to but don't.

What Rights?

The Right to Be Protected against Violence

Gays, lesbians and bisexuals are targets of violence in America. Twenty-four percent of gay men and ten percent of lesbians, in a recent survey, reported some form of criminal assault because of their sexual orientation during the past year (as compared to general population assault rates in a comparable urban area of 4 percent for women and 6 percent for men). A Massachusetts study found that 21 percent of lesbian and gay students, compared to 5 percent of the entire student body, report having been physically attacked. An average of five recent U.S. noncollege surveys on anti-gay/lesbian violence show that thirty-three percent of those surveyed had been chased or followed, 23 percent had had objects thrown at them, 18 percent had been punched, hit, kicked or beaten, 16 percent had been victims of vandalism or arson, 7 percent had been spat on, and 7 percent had been assaulted with a weapon (data from Comstock, 1991, pp. 31–55). To live as a gay or lesbian in America is thus to live with fear. As one might expect, such violence is not unknown in the military. Most famous, but not unique, was the 1992 death of navy radioman Allen Schindler at the hands of three of his shipmates who, unprovoked, stalked and then fatally beat him—and later blamed their crime on the presence of gays in the military.

Who are the perpetrators? They are more likely than average assault perpetrators are to be strangers to their victims. Ninety-four percent of them are male (as compared with 87 percent for comparable crimes of violence); 46 percent are under twenty-two years of age (as compared with 29 percent for comparable crimes); 67 percent are white. They do not typically exhibit what are customarily thought of as criminal attitudes. Many conform to or are models of middle-class respectability (Comstock, 1991, pp. 91–92). The arresting officer in a Toronto incident in which five youths beat a forty-year-old gay man to death remarked, "If you went to [a shopping mall] and picked up any group of young males about the same age as these boys—that is what they were like." Average (Comstock, 1991, p. 93). The data suggest that gay-beatings, including the most lethal, are often in essence 'recreational': groups of adolescent men, bored and intoxicated, seek out gays not so much because they have a deep-seated hatred of them as because they recognize that this is a group society has agreed to dislike and not to protect fully (Comstock, 1991, p. 94). A California perpetrator of multiple anti-gay beatings, interviewed by Comstock, cited as reasons for his acts: boredom, the desire for adventure, a belief in the wrongness of homosexuality and, finally, attraction to the men he and his friends attacked. He told Comstock that [we] were probably attacking something within ourselves (Comstock, 1991, pp. 171–172).

Physical assaults are crimes as defined by the laws of every state in the U.S. In that sense, the right to be protected against them is a right that gays and lesbians have already. But there is ample evidence that the police often fail to uphold these rights. They may indeed actively perpetrate violence against gays, in unduly violent behavior during vice arrests, etc. Such violence is illegal if it exceeds the requirements of arrest, but it is widely practiced. Even more common is the failure of police to come promptly to the aid of gays and lesbians who are being assaulted. A Canadian study finds that in 56 percent of cases in which gays sought police protection the behavior of the responding officers was "markedly unsatisfactory" (Comstock, 1991, pp. 151–162).

In numerous U.S. jurisdictions, moreover, killers of gays have successfully pleaded "reasonable provocation," alleging that the revulsion occasioned by a (noncoercive and nonviolent) homosexual advance, or even by witnessing gay sexual acts, justified a homicidal response; there is no corresponding tradition of a "heterosexual advance" defense. In a 1990 Pennsylvania case in which a drifter murdered two lesbians whom he saw making love in the woods, the court refused to allow this defense, saying that the law "does not recognize homosexual activity between two persons as legal provocation sufficient to reduce an unlawful killing . . . from murder to voluntary manslaughter" (*Commonwealth v. Carr*). This is, however, the exception rather than the rule (Mison, 1992).

There is a good case for linking rights involving protection against violence to other facets of gay experience as yet not universally recognized. As long as no laws protect gays against discrimination in other areas of life and guarantee their equal citizenship, as long as their sex acts can be criminalized, as long they are disparaged as second-class citizens, we may expect the rights they do have to go on being underenforced, and violence against them to remain a common fact.

My discussion of violence has not addressed the emotional violence done to lesbians and gay people by the perception that they are hated and despised. This issue too can be addressed by law and public policy; for by enacting non-discrimination laws (such as the law recently enacted in my home state of Massachusetts, which forbids discrimination against lesbian and gay students in the school system) one can begin to alter the behavior that causes this harm. Perhaps eventually one may alter attitudes themselves.

The Right to Have Consensual Adult Sexual Relations without Criminal Penalty

Consensual sexual relations between adult males were decriminalized in Britain in 1967. In the US, five states still criminalize only same-sex sodomy, while eighteen statutes (including the Uniform Code of Military Justice) criminalize sodomy for all. Five state sodomy laws have recently been judicially repealed, and, in addition, a Massachusetts law prohibiting "unnatural and lascivious act[s]." (But Massachusetts still has another law prohibiting "crime against nature," *Symposium*, 1993, p. 1774.) These laws are rarely enforced, but such enforcement as there is highly selective, usually against same-sex conduct. Penalties are not negligible: the maximum penalty for consensual sodomy in Georgia is twenty years' imprisonment.

Although sodomy laws are, as I have argued, both under and over-inclusive for same-sex conduct, it is frequently assumed that sodomy defines gay or lesbian sexual life. Thus the laws, in addition to their use in targeting the consensual activities of actual sodomites, can also be used to discriminate against gay and lesbian individuals who have never been shown to engage in the practices in question—as when Robin Shahar lost her job in the Georgia Attorney General's office for announcing a lesbian marriage. It was claimed that she could not be a reliable enforcer of the stare's sodomy statute (*Shahar v. Bowers*). (All heterosexual intercourse outside marriage is criminal "fornication" in Georgia, and yet there is no evidence that Bowers ever denied employment to heterosexual violators of either that law or the sodomy law.)

The case against sodomy laws is strong. Rarity of enforcement creates a problem of arbitrary and selective police behavior. Although neither all nor only homosexuals are sodomites, the laws are overwhelmingly used to target them; and the fact that some of their acts remain criminal is closely connected with the perception that they are acceptable targets of violence and with other social exclusions as well. For example, "[t]here is . . . a natural reluctance to appoint to judicial positions people who have committed hundreds or even thousands of criminal acts" (Posner, 1992, p. 311)—unjustified as this reluctance may be, and also arbitrary, given that the judiciary is no doubt full of heterosexual perpetrators of sodomy and criminal fornication. (Laumann shows that the frequency of both oral and anal sex among heterosexuals increases with level of education, Laumann et al., 1994.)

Most important, such adult consensual sexual activity does no harm. There is thus no public benefit to offset the evident burdens these laws impose. As Judge Posner concludes, such laws "express an irrational fear and loathing of a group that has been subjected to discrimination" (1992, p. 346). We have no need of such laws in a country all too full of incitements to violence.

Should the age of consent be the same for same-sex as for opposite-sex activity? I am inclined to think that, in current American and European nations, 16 is a reasonable age for both. The biggest problem with age of consent law generally is the failure to discriminate between the act of two 15-year-olds and an act between a 30-year-old and a 15-year-old. In both same and opposite-sex relations, the law should (and often does) address itself to this issue.

The Right to Be Free from Discrimination in Housing, Employment and Education

Gays, lesbians and bisexuals suffer discrimination in housing and employment. Many U.S. states and local communities have responded to this situation by adopting non-discrimination laws. (Such laws have for some time been in effect in some European countries and in some Australian states.) Recently in the U.S., efforts have also been made to prevent local communities from so legislating, through referenda amending the state's constitution to forbid the passage of such a local law. The most famous example is that of Amendment 2 in the State of Colorado, which nullified anti-discrimination laws in three cities in the state, and prevented the passage of any new ones. I believe that there is no good argument for discrimination against gays and lesbians in housing and employment. (The repeated suggestion that such protection against discrimination would lead to quotas for this group and would therefore injure the prospects of other minorities was especially invidious and misleading; none of the local ordinances had even suggested quota policies.)

Along with the Supreme Court of Colorado (when it upheld a preliminary injunction against the law, laying the legal basis for the trial court judgment that found the law unconstitutional), I would make a further point. Such referenda, by depriving gays and lesbians of the right to organize at the local level to secure the passage of laws that protect them, thereby deprive them of equality with respect to the fundamental right of political participation. They, and they alone, have to amend the state constitution in order to pass a fair housing law in some town. Similar state laws have long been declared unconstitutional in the area of race. I believe that they are morally repugnant in this area as well.

The most serious issue that arises with regard to non-discrimination laws is that of religious freedom. Both institutions and individuals may sincerely believe that to be required to treat lesbians and gays as equal candidates for jobs (or as equal prospective tenants) is to be deprived of the freedom to exercise their religion. This argument seems more pertinent to some occupations than others. To hire someone as a teacher may plausibly be seen as conferring a certain role-model status on that person; to hire someone as an accountant can hardly be seen in this light. And it is not clear to me that a landlord's religious freedom is compromised by being forced to consider on an equal basis tenants he may deem immoral. (The U.S. Supreme Court recently refused to hear an appeal of an Alaska decision against a landlord who refused to rent on religious grounds to an unmarried heterosexual couple.)

Various responses are possible. The Denver statute exempted religious organizations from its non-discrimination provisions. The American Philosophical Association refused to exempt religious institutions from its (non-binding) non-discrimination policy for hiring and promotion, except in the case of discrimination on the basis of religious membership. I believe that we should combine these two approaches: religious organizations should in some cases be allowed greater latitude to follow their own beliefs; but in publicly funded and in large professional organizations, with sexuality as with race, freedom to discriminate should be limited by shared requirements of justice. I recognize, however, that many people of good faith with deep religious convictions are likely to disagree.

Even in the sensitive area of education, there is no evidence to show that the presence of gay and lesbian teachers harms children or adolescents. Gays are at least no more likely, and in some studies less likely to molest children than are heterosexual males; nor is there evidence to show that knowing or respecting a gay person has the power to convert children to homosexuality (any more than being taught by heterosexuals has converted gay youths to heterosexuality). The sexual harassment of students or colleagues should be dealt with firmly wherever it occurs. Beyond that, what one's colleagues do in bed should be irrelevant to their employment.

One further educational issue remains: this is the right to have opportunities to learn about lesbian and gay people. This right is of special interest to lesbian and gay students, but it is also, importantly, a right of all students, all of whom are citizens and need to learn something about their fellow citizens, especially as potential voters in referenda such as the one in Colorado. The study of homosexuality—historical, psychological, sociological, legal, literary—is now a burgeoning field of research. Do students of various ages have the right to learn about this work? In the U.S. the First Amendment makes a flat prohibition of such teaching unlikely (not impossible, since the First Amendment is not binding on private institutions), though teachers may be subtly penalized for introducing such material into their courses. In Britain, a 1986 law forbids local government to "intentionally promote homosexuality or publish material with the intention of promoting homosexuality" or to "promote the teaching in any maintained school of the acceptability of homosexuality as a pretended family relationship" (Local Government Act 1986, cited in *Symposium,* 1993, p. 7). This law would very likely be unconstitutional in the U.S. It is also, I think, morally repugnant for several reasons. First, it inhibits the freedom of inquiry. Second, it inhibits the freedom of political debate. Third, it creates just the sort of atmosphere of taboo and disgust that fosters discrimination and violence against gays and lesbians. Furthermore, I believe it to be counterproductive to the proponents' own ostensible goals of fostering morality as they understand it. For a moral doctrine to announce publicly that it needs to be backed up by informational restrictions of this sort is a clear confession of weakness. And Judge Richard Posner has cogently argued that such policies actually increase the likelihood that gay sex will be casual and promiscuous, presumably something the law's partisans wish to avoid. Deprived of the chance to learn about themselves in any way other than through action, Posner argues, young gay people will in all likelihood choose action earlier than they might have otherwise (Posner, 1992, p. 302). The atmosphere of concealment also makes courtship and dating difficult—so "they will tend to substitute the sex act, which can be performed in a very short time and in private, for courtship, which is public and protracted" (Posner, 1992, p. 302).

The Right to Military Service

It is clear enough that gays and lesbians can serve with distinction in the military, since many of them have done so (Shilts, 1992, *passim;* Posner, 1992, p. 317). Furthermore, the armies of quite a few nations have successfully integrated open homosexuals into the service: France, Germany, Israel, Switzerland, Sweden, Denmark, Norway, Finland, the Netherlands, Belgium, Australia, Spain and recently Canada. As Posner writes, "The idea that homosexuals will not or cannot fight seems a canard, on a par with the idea that Jews or blacks will not or cannot fight" (Posner, 1992, p. 317). Nor are they security risks, if they openly announce their homosexuality. Nor are they to be excluded because they might commit acts of sexual harassment. (If this were so, in the wake of recent sexual harassment scandals in the U.S. military we should first exclude all heterosexual males.) Sexual harassment should be dealt with firmly wherever it occurs; this has nothing to do with our issue.

The real issue that keeps coming up is that heterosexual males do not want to be forced to associate intimately with gay males, especially to be seen naked by them. The psychology of this intense fear of the gaze of the homosexual is interesting. (It has even been attempted as a legal defense in gay-bashing cases, under the description "homosexual panic.") This fear may have something to do with the idea expressed by Comstock's gay-basher, when he perceptively noted that his aggression assailed something within himself. It may also be connected with the thought that this man will look at me in the way I look at a woman—i.e. not in a respectful or personal way, but a way that says "I want to fuck you"—and that this gaze will somehow humiliate me. What should be noted, however, is that this fear goes away when it needs to, and quite quickly too. As a frequenter of health clubs, I note that in that setting both males and females undress all the time in front of other patrons, many of whom they can be sure are gay; frequently it is clear through conversation who the gays and lesbians are. Nonetheless, we do not observe an epidemic of muscular failure. Straight men do not leap off the treadmill or drop their barbells in panic. They know they cannot root out and eject these people, so they forget about the issue. Moving on, we note that openly gay officers have been included in the police forces of New York City, Chicago, San Francisco, Los Angeles and probably others by now, without incident. During wartime, moreover, when the need for solidarity and high morale is greatest, toleration of gay and lesbian soldiers has gone up, not down (see Shilts, 1992). It seems likely that gays could be integrated relatively painlessly into the U.S. Armed Forces, if firm leadership were given from the top. The unfortunate fact, however, is that, here as with the harassment of women, high-ranking officers do not give the requisite leadership. As Judge Posner writes, "it is terrible to tell people they are unfit to serve their country, unless they really are unfit, which is not the case here" (Posner, 1992, p. 321).

The Right to Marriage and/or the Legal and Social Benefits of Marriage

Gays and lesbians in Denmark, Sweden and Norway can form a registered partnership that gives all the tax, inheritance and other civic benefits of marriage; similar legislation is soon to be passed in Finland. Many businesses, universities and other organizations within other nations, including the U.S., have extended their marriage benefits to registered same-sex domestic partners. Gay marriage is currently a topic of intense debate in Judaism and in every major branch of Christianity.

Why are marriage rights important to gays? Legally, marriage is a source of many benefits, including favorable tax, inheritance and insurance status; immigration rights; custody rights; the right to collect unemployment benefits if one partner quits a job to move to be where his or her partner has found employment; the spousal privilege exception when giving testimony; the right to bring a wrongful death action upon the negligent death of a spouse; the right to the privileges of next-of-kin in hospital visitations, decisions about burial, etc. (Mohr, 1994, pp. 72–73, Nava and Dawidoff, 1994, p. 155, citing Hawaii Sup. Ct, *Baehr v. Lewin*). Many gays and lesbians have discovered in the most painful way that they lack these rights, although they may have lived together loyally for years.

Emotionally and morally, being able to enter a legally recognized form of marriage means the opportunity to declare publicly an intent to live in commitment and partnership. Although many lesbian and gay people consider themselves married and have frequently solemnized their commitment in ceremonies not recognized by the state, they still seek to do so in a recognized manner, because they attach importance to the public recognition of their union.

As the Norwegian Ministry of Children and Family Affairs writes, supporting Norway's 1993 law: "It can be detrimental for a person to have to suppress fundamental feelings concerning attachment and love for another person. Distancing oneself from these feelings or attempts to suppress them may destroy one's self-respect" (Norwegian Act on Registered Partnerships for Homosexual Couples, 1993). Noting that 92 percent of gays and lesbians polled in a comprehensive Swedish survey were either part of a registered couple or stated that they would like to be, the Ministry concluded that the primary obstacle to stable marital unions in the gay community is negative attitudes from the social environment.

These seem to be very plausible views. And yet gay marriage is widely opposed. On what grounds? On what account of marriage is it an institution that should remain closed to lesbians and gay men? The basis of marriage in the U.S. and Europe is generally taken to be a stated desire to live together in intimacy, love and partnership, and to support one another, materially and emotionally, in the conduct of daily life. Of course many people enter marriage unprepared, and many marriages fail; but the law cannot and should not undertake a stringent inquiry into the character and behavior of the parties before admitting them to the benefits of that status.

Many people do believe that a central purpose of marriage is to have and educate children. But (apart from the fact that many lesbian and gay people do have and raise children, whether their own from previous unions or conceived by artificial insemination within the relationship) nobody has seriously suggested denying marriage rights to post-menopausal women, to sterile individuals of any age or to people who simply know (and state) that they don't want children and won't have them. It therefore seems flatly inconsistent and unjust to deny these rights to other individuals who wish to form exactly this type of committed yet childless union.

No doubt the extension of marriage rights to gays and lesbians will change the way we think about "the family." On the other hand, "the family" has never been a single thing in western, far less in world, history, and its nuclear heterosexual form has been associated with grave problems of child abuse and gender inequality, so there is no reason to sentimentalize it as a morally perfect institution. Studies have shown that homosexual households have a more equal division of domestic labor than heterosexual ones (Blumstein and Schwartz, 1983). So they may even have valuable contributions to make to our understanding of what personal commitment and marital fairness are.

The Right to Retain Custody of Children and/or to Adopt

Gays and lesbians have and raise children. In a 1970s California survey, 20 percent of male homosexuals and more than a third of female homosexuals have been married (Posner, 1992, p. 417), and many of those have had children. Lesbian couples can have children through artificial insemination or sex with a male; a gay man can obtain a child through some sort of surrogacy arrangement. Should these things be (or remain) legal? Experience shows that children raised in homosexual households showed no differences from other groups, either in sexual orientation or in general mental health or social adjustment. Indeed, there was evidence that children raised by an unmarried heterosexual woman had more psychological problems than others (Posner, 1992, p. 418). We need more research on these issues, clearly; samples have been small and have covered a relatively short time-span. But so far there is no evidence to justify a court in removing a child from its parent's custody on the grounds that he or she is living in a homosexual union. If one were to argue that such a child will inevitably be the target of social prejudice, no matter how well its parent is doing, it seems plausible that the Constitution will intervene to block that argument. In a 1984 case, *Palmore v. Sidoti,* in which a child was removed from its (white) mother's custody because she had remarried to a black man—grounds for change of custody being that such a child will suffer from public racial prejudice—the U.S. Supreme Court returned custody to the child's mother, holding that the law may not give public legitimacy to private prejudices. This case was cited as a precedent in a 1985 Alaska decision granting custody to a gay parent (Mison, 1992, p. 175). In general, it seems especially important that children should not be removed from the custody of parents who love and care for them successfully, without compelling reason.

As for adoption and foster-parenting, I concur with Judge Posner that courts should take a case-by-case approach, rejecting a flat ban. Frequently, especially where foster-parenting is concerned, such a placement might be a child's best chance for a productive home life (Posner, 1992, p. 420). Once again, the reason for refusing a homosexual couple must not be the existence of public prejudice against homosexuality; and yet, no feature intrinsic to homosexuality as such has been demonstrated to have a detrimental effect on children.

Journal/Discussion Questions

✍ *Nussbaum's essay covers a wide range of issues relating to gay and lesbian life. Which of these areas did you find particularly interesting? Controversial? Discuss.*

1. What arguments does Nussbaum advance against anti-sodomy laws? Critically evaluate her claims.
2. What arguments does Nussbaum present for the right to marriage for gays and lesbians? What do you think is the strongest argument? Do you agree with her?
3. Discuss Nussbaum's analysis of the right to military service for homosexuals in light of the essay, "A Quiet Siege," at the beginning of this chapter.

James Q. Wilson
"Against Homosexual Marriage"

James Q. Wilson is Collins professor of management and public policy at UCLA. His books include The Moral Sense, On Character, Moral Judgment: Does the Abuse Excuse Threaten Our Legal System?, *and* Thinking about Crime.

Using Andrew Sullivan's Virtually Normal *as a counterpoint, Wilson develops his arguments against homosexual marriage.*

As You Read, Consider This:

1. What, according to Wilson, are the prohibitionist, conservative, and liberal positions on the issue of homosexual marriage? Which of these is closest to Wilson's position?

Our courts, which have mishandled abortion, may be on the verge of mishandling homosexuality. As a consequence of two pending decisions, we may be about to accept homosexual marriage.

In 1993 the supreme court of Hawaii ruled that, under the equal-protection clause of that state's constitution, any law based on distinctions of sex was suspect, and thus subject to strict judicial scrutiny. Accordingly, it reversed the denial of a marriage permit to a same-sex couple, unless the state could first demonstrate a "compelling state interest" that would justify limiting marriages to men and women. A new trial is set for early this summer. But in the meantime, the executive branch of Hawaii appointed a commission to examine the question of same-sex marriages; its report, by a vote of five to two, supports them. The legislature, for its part, holds a different view of the matter, having responded to the court's decision by passing a law unambiguously reaffirming the limitation of marriage to male-female couples.

No one knows what will happen in the coming trial, but the odds are that the Hawaiian version of the equal-rights amendment may control the outcome. If so, since the United States Constitution has a clause requiring that "full faith and credit shall be given to the public acts, records, and judicial proceedings of every other state," a homosexual couple in a state like Texas, where the population is overwhelmingly opposed to such unions, may soon be able to fly to Hawaii, get married, and then return to live in Texas as lawfully wedded. A few scholars believe that states may be able to impose public-policy objections to such; out-of-state marriages—Utah has already voted one in, and other states may follow—but only at the price of endless litigation.

That litigation may be powerfully affected by the second case. It concerns a Colorado statute, already struck down by that state's supreme court, that would prohibit giving to homosexuals "any claim of minority status, quota preferences, protected status, or claim of discrimination." The U.S. Supreme Court is now reviewing the appeals. If its decision upholds the Colorado Supreme Court and thus allows homosexuals to acquire a constitutionally protected status, the chances will decline of successful objections to homosexual marriage based on considerations of public policy.

Contemporaneous with these events, an important book has appeared under the title *Virtually Normal.* In it, Andrew Sullivan, the editor of the *New Republic,* makes a strong case for a new policy toward homosexuals. He argues that "all public (as opposed to private) discrimination against homosexuals be ended. . . . And that is all." The two key areas where this change is necessary are the military and marriage law. Lifting bans in those areas, while also disallowing anti-sodomy laws and providing information about homosexuality in publicly supported schools, would put an end to the harm that gays have endured. Beyond these changes, Sullivan writes, American society would need no "cures of homophobia or reeducations, no wrenching private litigation, no political imposition of tolerance."

It is hard to imagine how Sullivan's proposals would, in fact, end efforts to change private behavior toward homosexuals, or why the next, inevitable, step would not involve attempts to accomplish just that purpose by using cures and reeducations, private litigation, and the political imposition of tolerance. But apart from this, Sullivan—an English Catholic, a homosexual, and someone who has on occasion referred to himself as a conservative—has given us the most sensible and coherent view of a program to put homosexuals and heterosexuals on the same public footing. His analysis is based on a careful reading of serious opinions and his book is written quietly, clearly, and thoughtfully. In her review of it in *First Things* (January 1996), Elizabeth Kristol asks us to try to answer the following question: What would life be like if we were not allowed to marry? To most of us, the thought is unimaginable; to Sullivan, it is the daily existence of declared homosexuals. His response is to let homosexual couples marry.

Sullivan recounts three main arguments concerning homosexual marriage, two against and one for. He labels them prohibitionist, conservative, and liberal. (A fourth camp, the liberationist, which advocates abolishing all distinctions between heterosexuals and homosexuals, is also described—and scorched for its "strange confluence of political abdication and psychological violence.") I think it easier to grasp the origins of the three main arguments by referring to the principles on which they are based.

The prohibitionist argument is in fact a biblical one; the heart of it was stated by Dennis Prager in an essay in the *Public Interest* ("Homosexuality, the Bible, and Us," Summer 1993).

When the first books of the Bible were written, and for a long time thereafter, heterosexual love is what seemed at risk. In many cultures—not only in Egypt or among the Canaanite tribes surrounding ancient Israel but later in Greece, Rome, and the Arab world, to say nothing of large parts of China, Japan, and elsewhere—homosexual practices were common and widely tolerated or even exalted. The Torah reversed this, making the family the central unit of life, the obligation to marry one of the first responsibilities of man, and the linkage of sex to procreation the highest standard by which to judge sexual relations. Leviticus puts the matter sharply and apparently beyond quibble:

> Thou shalt not live with mankind as with womankind; it is an abomination. . . . If a man also lie with mankind, as he lieth with a woman, both of them have committed an abomination; they shall surely be put to death; their blood shall be upon them.

Sullivan acknowledges the power of Leviticus but deals with it by placing it in a relative context. What is the nature of this "abomination" Is it like killing your mother or stealing a neighbor's bread, or is it more like refusing to eat shellfish or having sex during menstruation? Sullivan suggests that all of these injunctions were written on the same moral level and hence can be accepted or ignored as a whole. He does not fully sustain this view, and in fact a refutation of it can be found in Prager's essay. In Prager's opinion and mine, people at the time of Moses, and for centuries before him, understood that there was a fundamental difference between whom you killed and what you ate, and in all likelihood people then and for centuries earlier linked whom you could marry closer to the principles that defined life than they did to the rules that defined diets.

The New Testament contains an equally vigorous attack on homosexuality by St. Paul. Sullivan partially deflects it by noting Paul's conviction that the earth was about to end and the Second Coming was near; under these conditions, all forms of sex were suspect. But Sullivan cannot deny that Paul singled out homosexuality as deserving of special criticism. He seems to pass over this obstacle without effective retort.

Instead, he takes up a different theme, namely, that on grounds of consistency many heterosexual practices—adultery, sodomy, premarital sex, and divorce, among others—should be outlawed equally with homosexual acts of the same character. The difficulty with this is that it mistakes the distinction alive in most people's minds between marriage as an institution and marriage as a practice. As an institution, it deserves unqualified support; as a practice, we recognize that married people are as imperfect as anyone else. Sullivan's understanding of the prohibitionist argument suffers from his unwillingness to acknowledge this distinction.

The second argument against homosexual marriage—Sullivan's conservative category—is based on natural law as originally set forth by Aristotle and Thomas Aquinas and more recently restated by Hadley Arkes, John Finnis, Robert George, Harry V Jaffa, and others. How it is phrased varies a bit, but in general its advocates support a position like the following: man cannot live without the care and support of other people; natural law is the distillation of what thoughtful people have learned about the conditions of that care. The first thing they have learned is the supreme importance of marriage, for without it the newborn infant is unlikely to survive or, if he survives, to prosper. The necessary conditions of a decent family life are the acknowledgment by its members that a man will not sleep with his daughter or a woman with her son and that neither will openly choose sex outside marriage.

Now, some of these conditions are violated, but there is a penalty in each case that is supported by the moral convictions of almost all who witness the violation. On simple utilitarian grounds it may be hard to object to incest or adultery; if both parties to such an act welcome it and if it is secret, what differences does it make? But very few people, and then only ones among the overeducated, seem to care much about mounting a utilitarian assault on the family. To this assault, natural-law theorists respond much as would the average citizen—never mind "utility," what counts is what is right. In particular, homosexual uses of the reproductive organs violate the condition that sex serve solely as the basis of heterosexual marriage.

To Sullivan, what is defective about the natural-law thesis is that it assumes different purposes in heterosexual and homosexual love: moral consummation in the first case and pure utility or pleasure alone in the second. But in fact, Sullivan suggests, homosexual love can be as consummatory as heterosexual. He notes that as the Roman Catholic Church has deepened its understanding of the involuntary—that is, in some sense genetic—basis of homosexuality, it has attempted to keep homosexuals in the church as objects of affection and nurture, while banning homosexual acts as perverse.

But this, though better than nothing, will not work, Sullivan writes. To show why, he adduces an analogy to a sterile person. Such a person is permitted to serve in the military or enter an unproductive marriage; why not homosexuals? If homosexuals marry without procreation, they are no different (he suggests) from a sterile man or woman who marries without hope of procreation. Yet people, I think, want the form observed even when the practice varies; a sterile marriage, whether from choice or necessity, remains a marriage of a man and a woman. To this Sullivan offers essentially an aesthetic response, just as albinos remind us of the brilliance of color and genius teaches us about moderation, homosexuals are a "natural foil" to the heterosexual union, "a variation that does not eclipse the theme." Moreover, the threat posed by the foil to the theme is slight as compared to the threats posed by adultery, divorce, and prostitution. To be consistent, Sullivan once again reminds us, society would have to ban adulterers from the military as it now bans confessed homosexuals.

But again this misses the point. It would make more sense to ask why an alternative to marriage should be invented and praised when we are having enough trouble maintaining the institution at all. Suppose that gay or lesbian marriage were authorized; rather than producing a "natural foil" that would "not eclipse the theme," I suspect such a move would call even more seriously into question the role of marriage at a time when the threats to it, ranging from single-parent families to common divorces, have hit record highs. Kenneth Minogue recently wrote of Sullivan's book that support for homosexual marriage would strike most people as "mere parody," one that could farther weaken an already strained institution.

To me, the chief limitation of Sullivan's view is that it presupposes that marriage would have the same, domesticating, effect on homosexual members as it has on heterosexuals, while leaving the latter largely unaffected. Those are very large assumptions that no modern society has ever tested.

Nor does it seem plausible to me that a modern society resists homosexual marriages entirely out of irrational prejudice. Marriage is a union, sacred to most, that unites a man and woman together for life. It is a sacrament of the Catholic Church and central to every other faith. Is it out of misinformation that every modern society has embraced this view and rejected the alternative? Societies differ greatly in their attitude toward the income people may have, the relations among their various races, and the distribution of political power. But they differ scarcely at all over the distinctions between heterosexual and homosexual couples. The former are overwhelmingly preferred over the latter. The reason, I believe, is that these distinctions involve the nature of marriage and thus the very meaning—even more, the very possibility—of society.

The final argument over homosexual marriage is the liberal one, based on civil rights.

As we have seen, the Hawaiian Supreme Court ruled that any state-imposed sexual distinction would have to meet the test of strict scrutiny, a term used by the U.S. Supreme Court only for racial and similar classifications. In doing this, the Hawaiian court distanced itself from every other state court decision—there are several—in this area so far. A variant of the suspect-class argument, though, has been suggested by some scholars who contend that denying access to a marriage license by two people of the same sex is no different from denying access to two people of different sexes but also different races. The Hawaiian Supreme Court embraced this argument as well, explicitly comparing its decision to that of the U.S. Supreme Court when it overturned state laws banning marriages involving miscegenation.

But the comparison with black-white marriages is itself suspect. Beginning around 1964, and no doubt powerfully affected by the passage of the Civil Rights Act of that year, public attitudes toward race began to change dramatically. Even allowing for exaggerated statements to pollsters, there is little doubt that people in fact acquired a new view of blacks. Not so with homosexuals. Though the campaign to aid them has been going on vigorously for about a quarter of a century, it has produced few, if any, gains in public acceptance, and the greatest resistance, I think, has been with respect to homosexual marriages.

Consider the difference. What has been at issue in race relations is not marriage among blacks (for over a century, that right has been universally granted) or even miscegenation (long before the civil-rights movement, many Southern states had repealed such laws). Rather, it has been the routine contact between the races in schools, jobs, and neighborhoods. Our own history, in other words, has long made it clear that marriage is a different issue from the issue of social integration.

There is another way, too, in which the comparison with race is less than helpful, as Sullivan himself points out. Thanks to the changes in public attitudes I mentioned a moment ago, gradually race was held to be not central to decisions about hiring, firing, promoting, and schooling, and blacks began to make extraordinary advances in society. But then, in an effort to enforce this new view, liberals came to embrace affirmative action, a policy that said that race was central to just such issues, in order to ensure that real mixing occurred. This move created a crisis, for liberalism had always been based on the proposition that a liberal political system should encourage, as John Stuart Mill put it, "experiments in living" free of religious or political direction. To contemporary liberals, however, being neutral about race was tantamount to being neutral about a set of human preferences that in such matters as neighborhood and schooling left groups largely (but not entirely) separate.

Sullivan, who wisely sees that hardly anybody is really prepared to ignore a political opportunity to change lives, is not disposed to have much of this either in the area of race or in that of sex. And he points out with great clarity that popular attitudes toward sexuality are anyway quite different from those about race, as is evident from the fact that wherever sexual orientation is subject to local regulations, such regulations are rarely invoked. Why? Because homosexuals can "pass" or not, as they wish; they can and do accumulate education and wealth; they exercise political power. The two things a homosexual cannot do are join the military as an avowed homosexual or marry another homosexual.

The result, Sullivan asserts, is a wrenching paradox. On the one hand, society has historically tolerated the brutalization inflicted on people because of the color of their skin, but freely allowed them to marry; on the other hand, it has given equal opportunity to homosexuals, while denying them the right to marry. This, indeed, is where Sullivan draws the line. A black or Hispanic child, if heterosexual, has many friends, he writes, but a gay child "generally has no one." And that is why the social stigma attached to homosexuality is different from that attached to race or ethnicity—"because it attacks the very heart of what makes a human being human: the ability to love and be loved." Here is the essence of Sullivan's case. It is a powerful one, even if (as I suspect) his pro-marriage sentiments are not shared by all homosexuals.

Let us assume for the moment that a chance to live openly and legally with another homosexual is desirable. To believe that, we must set aside biblical injunctions, a difficult matter in a profoundly religious nation. But suppose we manage the diversion, perhaps on the grounds that if most Americans skip church, they can as readily avoid other errors of (possibly) equal magnitude. Then we must ask on what terms the union shall be arranged. There are two alternatives—marriage or domestic partnership.

Sullivan acknowledges the choice, but disparages the domestic-partnership laws that have evolved in some foreign countries and in some American localities. His reasons, essentially conservative ones, are that domestic partnerships are too easily formed and too easily broken. Only real marriages matter. But—aside from the fact that marriage is in serious decline, and that only slightly more than half of all marriages performed in the United States this year will be between never-before-married heterosexuals—what is distinctive about marriage is that it is an institution created to sustain child-rearing. Whatever losses it has suffered in this respect, its function remains what it has always been.

The role of raising children is entrusted in principle to married heterosexual couples because after much experimentation—several thousand years, more or less—we have found nothing else that works as well. Neither a gay nor a lesbian couple can of its own resources produce a child; another party must be involved. What do we call this third party? A friend? A sperm or egg bank? An anonymous donor? There is no settled language for even describing, much less approving of, such persons.

Suppose we allowed homosexual couples to raise children who were created out of a prior heterosexual union or adopted from someone else's heterosexual contact. What would we think of this? There is very little research on the matter. Charlotte Patterson's famous essay, "Children of Gay and Lesbian Parents" (*Journal of Child Development,* 1992), begins by conceding that the existing studies focus on children born into a heterosexual union that ended in divorce or that was transformed when the mother or father "came out" as a homosexual. Hardly any research has been done on children acquired at the outset by a homosexual couple. We therefore have no way of knowing how they would behave. And even if we had such studies, they might tell us rather little unless they were conducted over a very long period of time.

But it is one thing to be born into an apparently heterosexual family and then many years later to learn that one of your parents is homosexual. It is quite another to be acquired as an infant from an adoption agency or a parent-for-hire and learn from the first years of life that you are, because of your family's position, radically different from almost all other children you will meet. No one can now say how grievous this would be. We know that young children tease one another unmercifully; adding this dimension does not seem to be a step in the right direction.

Of course, homosexual "families," with or without children, might be rather few in number. Just how few, it is hard to say. Perhaps Sullivan himself would marry, but, given the great tendency of homosexual males to be promiscuous, many more like him would not, or if they did, would not marry with as much seriousness.

That is problematic in itself. At one point, Sullivan suggests that most homosexuals would enter a marriage "with as much (if not more) commitment as heterosexuals." Toward the end of his book, however, he seems to withdraw from so optimistic a view. He admits that the label "virtually" in the title of his book is deliberately ambiguous, because homosexuals as a group are not "normal." At another point, he writes that the "openness of the contract" between two homosexual males means that such a union will in fact be more durable than a heterosexual marriage because the contract contains an "understanding of the need for *extramarital outlets*" (emphasis added). But no such "understanding" exists in heterosexual marriage; to suggest that it might in homosexual ones is tantamount to saying that we are now referring to two different kinds of arrangements. To justify this difference, perhaps, Sullivan adds that the very "lack of children" will give "gay couples greater freedom." Freedom for what? Freedom, I think, to do more of those things that heterosexual couples do less of because they might hurt the children.

The courts in Hawaii and in the nation's capital must struggle with all these issues under the added encumbrance of a contemporary outlook that makes law the search for rights, and responsibility the recognition of rights. Indeed, thinking of laws about marriage as documents that confer or withhold rights is itself an error of fundamental importance—one that the highest court in Hawaii has already committed. "Marriage," it wrote, "is a state-conferred legal-partnership status, the existence of which gives rise to a multiplicity of rights and benefits. . ." A state-conferred legal partnership? To lawyers, perhaps; to mankind, I think not. The Hawaiian court has thus set itself on the same course of action as the misguided Supreme Court in 1973 when it thought that laws about abortion were merely an assertion of the rights of a living mother and an unborn fetus.

I have few favorable things to say about the political systems of other modern nations, but on these fundamental matters—abortion, marriage, military service—they often do better by allowing legislatures to operate than we do by deferring to courts. Our challenge is to find a way of formulating a policy with respect to homosexual unions that is not the result of a reflexive act of judicial rights-conferring, but is instead a considered expression of the moral convictions of a people.

Journal/Discussion Questions

✍ *Wilson refers briefly to the experience of adolescents who are gay and the difficulties they encounter in coming of age in our society. Have your own experiences and observations confirmed Wilson's observations? What moral significance do those experiences have?*

1. At several points in his essay, Wilson discusses the relationship between issues of race and ethnicity and issues of sexual orientation. In what ways are they similar? In what ways are they different?
2. Some have offered "domestic parternship laws" as an alternative to legalizing homosexual marriages. What is Wilson's position on this alternative? Do you agree or disagree?

Concluding Discussion Questions

Where Do You Stand Now?

Instructions

You have already answered the following questions in your moral problems self-quiz at the beginning of this book. Now that you have studied the material in this section, take a moment to answer the same questions again.

	Strongly Agree	*Agree*	*Undecided*	*Disagree*	*Strongly Disagree*	*Chapter 7: Sexual Orientation*
31.	❑	❑	❑	❑	❑	Gays and lesbians should be allowed to serve openly in the military.
32.	❑	❑	❑	❑	❑	Gays and lesbians should not be discriminated against in hiring or housing.
33.	❑	❑	❑	❑	❑	Homosexuality is unnatural.
34.	❑	❑	❑	❑	❑	Same-sex marriages should be legal.
35.	❑	❑	❑	❑	❑	Homosexuality is a matter of personal choice.

Compare your answers to the present self-quiz with the answers to the initial self-quiz. How, if at all, have your answers changed? How have the *reasons* for your answers changed?

Journal/Discussion Questions

✍ *How well do you think the articles in this section have understood the* experience *of being gay? How well do you think they have understood the experience of being heterosexual? What do you think they have left out or misunderstood?*

1. Imagine that you have been hired by a congressional committee charged with the responsibility of drafting new legislation to articulate the place of gays and lesbians in society. How would you advise the committee? What laws, if any, would you propose to add? To delete?
2. Should prominent gays and lesbians publicly reveal their sexual orientation? If they refuse to do so, are others—either

gay or not—entitled to reveal it against their wishes?

3. Imagine a round table discussion of the issue of whether openly gay individuals should be allowed to serve in the military. The participants include you, Senator Goldwater, and Professors Nussbaum and Wilson. Recount the dialogue that would occur in such a discussion.

For Further Reading

Web Resources

For Web-based resources on sexual orientation, see the Sexual Orientation page of *Ethics Updates* (http://ethics.acusd.edu). This page includes court decisions relating to sexual orientation.

Review Articles and Bibliographies

For a short overview of some of the philosophical issues about homosexuality, see Richard D. Mohr, "Homosexuality," *Encyclopedia of Ethics,* edited by Lawrence C. Becker and Charlotte B. Becker (New York: Garland, 1992), Vol. I, pp. 552–554. For a bibliographical survey, see Robert B. Marks Ridinger, *The Homosexual and Society: An Annotated Bibliography* (New York: Greenwood Press, 1990).

General Books, Anthologies, and Articles

Perhaps the best sympathetic philosophical approach to these issues is to be found in Richard D. Mohr's *Gays/Justice: A Study of Ethics, Society, and Law* (New York: Columbia University Press, 1988) and his *A More Perfect Union: Why Straight America Must Stand Up for Gay Rights* (Boston: Beacon Press, 1995). For a much different perspective, see Roger Scruton, *Sexual Desire* (London: Weidenfeld and Nicolson, 1985). For the exchange between Scruton and Martha Nussbaum, see *The Liberation Debate: Rights at Issue,* edited by Michael Leahy and Dan Cohn-Sherbok (London: Routledge, 1996), pp. 89–133. Also see Michael Ruse, *Homosexuality: A Philosophical Inquiry* (New York: Basil Blackwell, 1968); *Homosexuality and Ethics,* edited by Edward Batchelor, Jr. (New York: Pilgrim Press, 1980); Roger J. Magnuson *Are Gay Rights Right? Making Sense of the Controversy,* Updated Edition (Portland, OR: Multnomah, 1990); *Homosexuality: Debating the Issues,* edited by Robert M. Baird and M. Katherine Baird (New York: Prometheus Books, 1995); and, for shorter and more popular readings, *Homosexuality: Opposing Viewpoints,* edited by William Dudley (San Diego: Greenhaven Press, 1993).

On the "social construction" of the concept of homosexuality, see Edward Stein, *Forms of Desire: Sexual Orientation and the Social Constructionist Controversy* (New York: Routledge, 1992); David Halperin's *One Hundred Years of Homosexuality* (London: Routledge, 1992); and John Thorp's "The Social Construction of Homosexuality," *Phoenix,* Vol. 46, No. 1 (Spring 1992), pp. 54–61.

Homosexual Marriage

On the issue of gay and lesbian marriages, see Susanne Sherman, *Lesbian and Gay Marriage* (Philadelphia: Temple University Press, 1992); John Stott, *Homosexual Partnerships? Why Same-Sex*

Relationships Are Not a Christian Option (Downers Grove, IL: InterVarsity Press, 1985); *Lesbian and Gay Marriage: Private Commitments, Public Ceremonies,* edited by Suzanne Sherman (Philadelphia: Temple University Press, 1992); *Fear of a Queer Planet: Queer Politics and Social Theory,* edited by Michael Warner (Minneapolis: University of Minnesota Press, 1993); *Is Gay Good? Ethics, Theology, and Homosexuality,* edited by W. Dwight Oberholtzer (Philadelphia: Westminster Press, 1971); John D'Emilio, *Making Trouble: Essays on Gay History, Politics and the University.* (New York: Routledge, 1992); Henry Abelove, et al., editors, *The Lesbian and Gay Studies Reader* (New York: Routledge, 1993); Michael Nava and Robert Dawidoff, *Created Equal: Why Gay Rights Matter to America* (New York: St. Martin's Press, 1994).

Sexual Orientation and the Law

For an excellent introduction to some of the legal issues surrounding homosexuality, see *Harvard Law Review,* editors, *Sexual Orientation and the Law* (Cambridge: Harvard University Press, 1989) and William B. Rubenstein, editor, *Lesbians, Gay Men, and the Law* (New York: The New Press, 1993).

Homosexuality and the Natural Law Tradition

For a discussion of *homosexuality and the natural law tradition,* see John M. Finnis, "Natural Law and Unnatural Acts," *Heythrop Journal,* Vol. 11 (1970), pp. 365–387; and Harry V. Jaffa, *Homosexuality and the Natural Law,* (Montclair, CA: Center for the Study of the Natural Law (Claremont Institute, 1990). For the positions of various churches on this issue, see G. Gordon Melton, *The Churches Speak On: Homosexuality* (Detroit: Gale Research, Inc., 1991). For an interesting exchange on the question of *whether homosexuality is unnatural* or not, see James A. Gould, "The 'Natural' and Homosexuality," *International Journal of Applied Philosophy,* Vol. 4 (Fall 1988), pp. 51–54 for a series of arguments about why homosexuality is not unnatural; the reply by Gerard J. Dalcourt, "Professor Gould and the 'Natural'," *International Journal of Applied Philosophy,* Vol. 5, No. 1 (Spring 1990), pp. 75–77; a rejoinder to Dalcourt by Joseph J. Sartorelli, "Professor Dalcourt on the 'Natural'," *International Journal of Applied Philosophy,* Vol. 8, No. 2 (Winter–Spring 1994), pp. 49–52; Delacourt's reply to Sartorelli, "Professor Sartorelli and the 'Natural'," *International Journal of Applied Philosophy,* Vol. 8, No. 2 (Winter–Spring 1994), pp. 53–56; and Gould's reply to everyone, "Is Homosexuality Natural?," *International Journal of Applied Philosophy,* Vol. 8, No. 2 (Winter–Spring 1994), pp. 57–58. On this issue, also see the exchange between Michael Level, "Why Homosexuality Is Abnormal," *The Monist,* Vol. 67 (April 1984), pp. 251–283 and the reply by Timothy F. Murphy, "Homosexuality and Nature: Happiness and the Law at Stake," *Journal of Applied Philosophy,* Vol. 4 (October 1987), pp. 195–204. On the implications of this discussion for the *family,* see *Sex, Preference, and Family: Essays on Law and Nature,* edited by Avid M. Estlund and Martha C. Nussbaum (New York: Oxford, 1997).

For a discussion of this issue within *Christianity,* see Charles E. Curran, "Homosexuality and Moral Theology: Methodological and Substantive Considerations," *The Thomist,* Vol. 35 (July 1971), pp. 447–481; Bruce A. Williams, "Homosexuality and Christianity: A Review Discussion," *The Thomist,* Vol. 46 (October 1982), pp. 609–625; Gerald D. Coleman, "The Vatican Statement on Homosexuality," *Theological Studies,* Vol. 48 (1987), pp. 727–734; and the reply by Anthony C.

Daly, "Aquinas on Disordered Pleasures and Conditions," *The Thomist,* Vol. 56, No. 4 (October 1992), pp. 583–612. For a Buddhist perspective, see several of the essays in *Buddhism, Sexuality, and Gender,* edited by Jose I. Cabezon (Albany: SUNY Press, 1992). For *multi-religious perspectives,* see *Sexual Orientation and Human Rights in American Religious Discourse,* edited by Saul M. Olyan and Martha C. Nussbaum (New York: Oxford, 1998).

Gays and the Military

For a "novelistic" account of the U.S. military's treatment of gays and lesbians, see Randy Shilts, *Conduct Unbecoming* (New York: St. Martin's Press, 1993); also see the articles in R.D. Ray, *Gays: In or Out? The U.S. Military and Homosexuals—A Source Book* (McLean, VA: Brassey's (US), 1993).

CHAPTER 8

Poverty and Welfare

Videotape:

Topic: Working for Welfare—Fair Deal or Slavery?
ABCNEWS *Source:* ABC *20/20* (March 8, 1998)
Anchor: Hugh Downs, John Stossel

Narrative Account

Rosemary L. Bray
"So How Did I Get Here?"

Rosemary L. Bray is a former editor of The New York Times Book Review. *She is the author of* Unafraid of the Dark, *(1998) about African-American attitudes and identity.*

Ms. Bray describes her experiences growing up on welfare in Chicago, and suggests ways in which the question of welfare is also one of race and women as well.

Growing up on welfare was a story I had planned to tell a long time from now, when I had children of my own. My childhood on Aid to Families with Dependent Children (A.F.D.C.) was going to be one of those stories I would tell my kids about the bad old days, an urban legend equivalent to Abe Lincoln studying by firelight. But I know now I cannot wait, because in spite of a wealth of evidence about the true nature of welfare and poverty in America, the debate has turned ugly, vicious and racist. The "welfare question" has become the race question and the woman question in disguise, and so far the answers bode well for no one.

In both blunt and coded terms, comfortable Americans more and more often bemoan the waste of their tax money on lazy black women with a love of copulation, a horror of birth control and a lack of interest in marriage. Were it not for the experiences of half my life, were I not black and female and of a certain age, perhaps I would be like so many people who blindly accept the lies and distortions, half-truths and wrongheaded notions about welfare. But for better or worse, I do know better. I know more than I want to know about being poor. I know that the welfare system is designed to be inadequate, to leave its constituents on the edge of survival. I know because I've been there.

And finally, I know that perhaps even more dependent on welfare than its recipients are the large number of Americans who would rather accept this patchwork of economic horrors than fully address the real needs of real people.

My mother came to Chicago in 1947 with a fourth-grade education, cut short by working in the Mississippi fields. She pressed shirts in a laundry for a while and later waited tables in a restaurant, where she met my father. Mercurial and independent, with a sixth-grade education, my Arkansas-born father worked at whatever came to hand. He owned a lunch wagon for a time and prepared food for hours in our kitchen on the nights before he took the wagon out. Sometimes he hauled junk and sold it in the open-air markets of Maxwell Street on Sunday mornings. Eight years after they met—seven years after they married—I was born. My father made her quit her job; her work, he told her, was taking care of me. By the time I was 4, I had a sister, a brother and another brother on the way. My parents, like most other American couples of the 1950s, had their own

American dream—a husband who worked, a wife who stayed home, a family of smiling children. But as was true for so many African-American couples, their American dream was an illusion.

The house on the corner of Berkeley Avenue and 45th Street is long gone. The other houses still stand, but today the neighborhood is an emptier, bleaker place. When we moved there, it was a street of old limestones with beveled glass windows, all falling into vague disrepair. Home was a four-room apartment on the first floor, in what must have been the public rooms of a formerly grand house. The rent was $110 a month. All of us kids slept in the big front room. Because I was the oldest, I had a bed of my own, near a big plate-glass window.

My mother and father had been married for several years before she realized he was a gambler who would never stay away from the track. By the time we moved to Berkeley Avenue, Daddy was spending more time gambling, and bringing home less and less money and more and more anger. Mama's simplest requests were met with rage. They fought once for hours when she asked for money to buy a tube of lipstick. It didn't help that I always seemed to need a doctor. I had allergies and bronchitis so severe that I nearly died one Sunday after church when I was about 3.

It was around this time that my mother decided to sign up for A.F.D.C. She explained to the caseworker that Daddy wasn't home much, and when he was he didn't have any money. Daddy was furious; Mama was adamant. "There were times when we hardly had a loaf of bread in here," she told me years later. "It was close. I wasn't going to let you all go hungry."

Going on welfare closed a door between my parents that never reopened. She joined the ranks of unskilled women who were forced to turn to the state for the security their men could not provide. In the sterile relationship between herself and the State of Illinois, Mama found an autonomy denied her by my father. It was she who could decide, at last, some part of her own fate and ours. A.F.D.C. relegated marginally productive men like my father to the ranks of failed patriarchs who no longer controlled the destiny of their families. Like so many of his peers, he could no longer afford the luxury of a woman who did as she was told because her economic life depended on it. Daddy became one of the shadow men who walked out back doors as caseworkers came in through the front. Why did he acquiesce? For all his anger, for all his frightening brutality, he loved us, so much that he swallowed his pride and periodically ceased to exist so that we might survive.

In 1960, the year my mother went on public aid, the poverty threshold for a family of five in the United States was $3,560 and the monthly payment to a family of five from the State of Illinois was $182.56, a total of $2,190.72 a year. Once the $110 rent was paid, Mama was left with $72.56 a month to take care of all the other expenses. By any standard, we were poor. All our lives were proscribed by the narrow line between not quite and just enough.

What did it take to live?

It took the kindness of friends as well as strangers, the charity of churches, low expectations, deprivation and patience. I can't begin to count the hours spent in long lines, long waits, long walks in pursuit of basic things. A visit to a local clinic (one housing doctors, a dentist and pharmacy in an incredibly crowded series of rooms) invariably took the better part of a day; I never saw the same doctor twice.

It took, as well, a turning of our collective backs on the letter of a law that required reporting even a small and important miracle like a present of $5.

All families have their secrets, but I remember the weight of an extra burden. In a world where caseworkers were empowered to probe into every nook and cranny of our lives, silence became defense. Even now, there are things I will not publicly discuss because I cannot shake the fear that we might be hounded by the state, eager to prosecute us for the crime of survival.

All my memories of our years on A.F.D.C. are seasoned with unease. It's painful to remember how much every penny counted, how even a gap of 25 cents could make a difference in any given week. Few people understand how precarious life is from welfare check to welfare check, how the word "extra" has no meaning. Late mail, a bureaucratic mix-up . . . and a carefully planned method of survival lies in tatters.

What made our lives work as well as they did was my mother's genius at making do—worn into her by a childhood of rural poverty—along with her vivid imagination. She worked at home endlessly, shopped ruthlessly, bargained, cajoled, charmed. Her food store of choice was the one that stocked pork and beans, creamed corn, sardines, Vienna sausages and potted meat all at 10 cents a can. Clothing was the stuff of rummage sales, trips to Goodwill and bargain basements, where thin cotton and polyester reigned supreme. Our shoes came from a discount store that sold two pairs for $5.

It was an uphill climb, but there was no time for reflection; we were too busy with our everyday lives. Yet I remember how much it pained me to know that Mama, who recruited a neighbor to help her teach me how to read when I was 3, found herself left behind by her eldest daughter, then by each of us in turn. Her biggest worry was that we would grow up uneducated, so Mama enrolled us in parochial school.

When one caseworker angrily questioned how she could afford to send four children to St. Ambrose School, my mother, who emphatically declared "My kids need an education," told her it was none of her business. (In fact, the school had a volume discount of sorts; the price of tuition dropped with each child you sent. I still don't know quite how she managed it.) She organized our lives around church and school, including Mass every morning at 7:45. My brother was an altar boy; I laid out the vestments each afternoon for the next day's Mass. She volunteered as a chaperone for every class trip, sat with us as we did homework she did not understand herself. She and my father reminded us again and again and again that every book, every test, every page of homework was in fact a ticket out and away from the life we lived.

My life on welfare ended on June 4, 1976—a month after my 21st birthday, two weeks after I graduated from Yale. My father, eaten up with cancer and rage, lived just long enough to know the oldest two of us had graduated from college and were on our own. Before the decade ended, all of us had left the welfare rolls. The eldest of my brothers worked at the post office, assumed support of my mother (who also went to work, as a companion to an elderly woman) and earned his master's degree at night. My sister married and got a job at a bank. My baby brother parked cars and found a wife. Mama's biggest job was done at last; the investment made in our lives by the State of Illinois had come to fruition. Five people on welfare for 18 years had become five working, taxpaying adults. Three of us went to college, two of us finished; one of us has an advanced degree; all of us can take care of ourselves.

Ours was a best-case phenomenon, based on the synergy of church and state, the government and the private sector and the thousand points of light that we called friends and neighbors. But there was something more: What fueled our dreams and fired our belief that our lives could change for the better was the promise of the civil rights movement and the war on poverty—for millions of African-Americans the defining events of the 1960s. Caught up in the heady atmosphere of imminent change, our world was filled not only with issues and ideas but with amazing images of black people engaged in the struggle for long-denied rights and freedoms. We knew other people lived differently than we did, we knew we didn't have much, but we didn't mind, because we knew it wouldn't be long. My mother borrowed a phrase I had read to her once from Dick Gregory's autobiography: Not poor, just broke. She would repeat it often, as often as she sang hymns in the kitchen. She loved to sing a spiritual Mahalia Jackson had made famous: "Move On Up a Little Higher." Like so many others, Mama was singing about earth as well as heaven.

These are the things I remember every time I read another article outlining America's welfare crisis. The rage I feel about the welfare debate comes from listening to a host of lies, distortions and exaggerations—and taking them personally.

I am no fool. I know of few women—on welfare or off—with my mother's grace and courage and stamina. I know not all women on welfare are cut from the same cloth. Some are lazy; some are ground down. Some are too young; many are without husbands. A few have made welfare fraud a lucrative career; a great many more have pushed the rules on outside income to their very limits.

I also know that none of these things justify our making welfare a test of character and worthiness, rather than an acknowledgment of need. Near-sainthood should not be a requirement for financial and medical assistance.

But all manner of sociologists and policy gurus continue to equate issues that simply aren't equivalent—welfare, race, rates of poverty, crime, marriage and childbirth—and to reach conclusions that serve to demonize the poor. More than one social arbiter would have us believe that we have all been mistaken for the last 30 years—that the efforts to relieve the most severe effects of poverty have not only failed but have served instead to increase and expand the ranks of the poor. In keeping women, children and men from starvation, we are told, we have also kept them from self-sufficiency. In our zeal to do good, we have undermined the work ethic, the family and thus, by association, the country itself.

So how did I get here?

Despite attempts to misconstrue and discredit the social programs and policies that changed—even saved—my life, certain facts remain. Poverty was reduced by 39 percent between 1960 and 1990, according to the Census Bureau, from 22.2 percent to 13.5 percent of the nation's population. That is far too many poor people, but the rate is considerably lower than it might have been if we had thrown up our hands and reminded ourselves that the poor will always be with us. Of black women considered "highly dependent," that is, on welfare for more than seven years, 81 percent of their daughters grow up to live productive lives off the welfare rolls, a 1992 Congressional report stated; the 19 percent who become second-generation welfare recipients can hardly be said to constitute an epidemic of welfare dependency. The vast majority of African-Americans are now working or middle class, an achievement that occurred in the past 30 years, most specifically between 1960 and 1973, the years of expansion in the very same social programs that it is so popular now to savage. Those were the same years in which I changed from girl to woman, learned to read and think, graduated from high school and college, came to be a working woman, a taxpayer, a citizen.

In spite of all the successes we know of, in spite of the reality that the typical welfare recipient is a white woman with young children, ideologues have continued to fashion from whole cloth the specter of the mythical black welfare mother, complete with a prodigious reproductive capacity and a galling laziness, accompanied by the uncaring and equally lazy black man in her life who will not work, will not marry her and will not support his family.

Why has this myth been promoted by some of the best (and the worst) people in government, academia, journalism and industry? One explanation may be that the constant presence of poverty frustrates even the best-intentioned among us. It may also be because the myth allows for denial about who the poor in America really are and for denial about the depth and intransigence of racism regardless of economic status. And because getting tough on welfare is for some a first-class career move; what better way to win a position in the next administration than to trash those people least able to respond? And, finally, because it serves to assure white Americans that lazy black people aren't getting away with anything.

Many of these prescriptions for saving America from the welfare plague not only reflect an insistent, if sometimes unconscious, racism but rest on the bedrock of patriarchy. They are rooted in the fantasy of a male presence as a path to social and economic salvation and in its corollary—the image of woman as passive chattel, constitutionally so afflicted by her condition that the only recourse is to transfer her care from the hands of the state to the hands of a man with a job. The largely ineffectual plans to create jobs for men in communities ravaged by disinvestment, the state-sponsored dragnets for men who cannot or will not support their children, the exhortations for women on welfare to find themselves a man and get married, all are the institutional expressions of the same worn cultural illusion—that women and children without a man are fundamentally damaged goods. Men are such a boon, the reasoning goes, because they make more money than women do.

Were we truly serious about an end to poverty among women and children, we would take the logical next step. We would figure out how to make sure women who did a dollar's worth of work got a dollar's worth of pay. We would make sure that women could go to work with their minds at ease, knowing their children were well cared for. What women on welfare need, in large measure, are the things key to the life of every adult woman: economic security and autonomy. Women need the skills and the legitimate opportunity to earn a living for ourselves as well as for people who may rely on us; we need the freedom to make choices to improve our own lives and the lives of those dear to us.

"The real problem is not welfare," says Kathryn Edin, a professor of sociology at Rutgers University and a scholar in residence at the Russell Sage Foundation. "The real problem is the nature of low-wage work and lack of support for these workers—most of whom happen to be women raising their children alone." Completing a five-year study of single mothers—some low-wage workers, some welfare recipients—Edin is quantifying what common sense and bitter experience have told millions of women who rotate off and on the welfare rolls: Women, particularly unskilled women with children, get the worst jobs available, with the least amount of health care, and are the most frequently laid off. "The workplace is not oriented toward people who have family responsibilities," she says. "Most jobs are set up assuming that someone else is minding the kids and doesn't need assistance."

But the writers and scholars and politicians who wax most rhapsodic about the need to replace welfare with work make their harsh judgments from the comfortable and supportive environs of offices and libraries and think tanks. If they need to go to the bathroom midsentence, there is no one timing their absence. If they take longer than a half-hour for lunch, there is no one waiting to dock their pay. If their baby sitter gets sick, there is no risk of someone having taken their place at work by the next morning. Yet these are conditions that low-wage women routinely face, which inevitably lead to the cyclical nature of their welfare histories. These are the realities that many of the most vocal and widely quoted critics of welfare routinely ignore. In his book *The End of Equality,* for example, Mickey Kaus discusses social and economic inequity, referring to David Ellwood's study on long-term welfare dependency without ever mentioning that it counts anyone who uses the services for at least one month as having been on welfare for the entire year.

In the heated atmosphere of the welfare debate, the larger society is encouraged to believe that women on welfare have so violated the social contract that they have forfeited all rights common to those of us lucky enough not to be poor. In no area is this attitude more clearly demonstrated than in issues of sexuality and childbearing. Consider the following: A *Philadelphia Inquirer* editorial of Dec. 12, 1990, urges the use of Norplant contraceptive inserts for welfare recipients—in spite of repeated warnings from women's health groups of its dangerous side effects—in the belief that the drug "could be invaluable in breaking the cycle of inner-city poverty." (The newspaper apologized for the editorial after it met widespread criticism, both within and outside the paper.) A California judge orders a woman on welfare, convicted of abusing two of her four children, to use Norplant; the judge's decision was appealed. The Washington state legislature considers approving cash payments of up to $10,000 for women on welfare who agree to be sterilized. These and other proposals, all centering on women's reproductive capacities, were advanced in spite of evidence that welfare recipients have fewer children than those not on welfare.

The punitive energy behind these and so many other Draconian actions and proposals goes beyond the desire to decrease welfare costs; it cuts to the heart of the nation's racial and sexual hysteria. Generated neither by law nor by fully informed public debate, these actions amount to social control over "those people on welfare"—a control many Americans feel they have bought and paid for every April 15. The question is obvious: If citizens were really aware of who receives welfare in America, however inadequate it is, if they acknowledged that white women and children were welfare's primary beneficiaries, would most of these things be happening?

Welfare has become a code word now. One that enables white Americans to mask their sometimes malignant, sometimes benign racism behind false concerns about the suffering ghetto poor and their negative impact on the rest of us. It has become the vehicle many so-called tough thinkers use to undermine compassionate policy and engineer the reduction of social programs.

So how did I get here?

I kept my drawers up and my dress down, to quote my mother. I didn't end up pregnant because I had better things to do. I knew I did because my uneducated, Southern-born parents told me so. Their faith, their focus on our futures are a far cry from the thesis of Nicholas Lemann, whose widely acclaimed book *The Promised Land* perpetuates the myth of black Southern sharecropping society as a primary source of black urban malaise. Most important, my family and I had every reason to believe that I had better things to do and that when I got older I would be able to do them. I had a mission, a calling, work to do that only I could do. And that is knowledge transmitted not just by parents, or school, or churches. It is a palpable thing, available by osmosis from the culture of the neighborhood and the world at large.

Add to this formula a whopping dose of dumb luck. It was my sixth-grade teacher, Sister Maria Sarto, who identified in me the first signs of a stifling boredom and told my mother that I needed a tougher, more challenging curriculum than her school could provide. It was she who then tracked down the private Francis W. Parker School, which agreed to give me a scholarship if I passed the admissions test.

Had I been born a few years earlier, or a decade later, I might now be living on welfare in the Robert Taylor Homes or working as a hospital nurse's aide for $6.67 an hour. People who think such things could never have happened to me haven't met enough poor people to know better. The avenue of escape can be very narrow indeed. The hope and energy of the 1960s—fueled not only by a growing economy but by all the passions of a great national quest—is long gone. The sense of possibility I knew has been replaced with the popular cultural currency that money and those who have it are everything and those without are nothing.

Much has been made of the culture of the underclass, the culture of poverty, as though they were the free-floating illnesses of the African-American poor, rendering them immune to other influences: the widespread American culture of greed, for example, or of cynicism. It is a thinly veiled continuation of the endless projection of "dis-ease" onto black life, a convenient way to sidestep a more painful debate about the loss of meaning in American life that has made our entire nation depressed and dispirited. The malaise that has overtaken our country is hardly confined to African-Americans or the poor, and if both groups should disappear tomorrow, our nation would still find itself in crisis. To talk of the black "underclass threat" to the public sphere, as Mickey Kaus does, to demonize the poor among us and thus by association all of us—ultimately this does more damage to the body politic than a dozen welfare queens.

When I walk down the streets of my Harlem neighborhood, I see women like my mother, hustling, struggling, walking their children to school and walking them back home. And I also see women who have lost both energy and faith, talking loud, hanging out. I see the shadow men of a new generation, floating by with a few dollars and a toy, then drifting away to the shelters they call home. And I see, a dozen times a day, the little girls my sister and I used to be, the little boys my brothers once were.

Even the grudging, inadequate public help I once had is fading fast for them. The time and patience they will need to re-create themselves is vanishing under pressure for the big, quick fix and the crushing load of blame being heaped upon them. In the big cities and the small towns of America, we have let theory, ideology and mythology about welfare and poverty overtake these children and their parents.

Journal/Discussion Questions

✍ *Discuss your own experiences with welfare. Have you ever experienced it directly? Have you ever been close to anyone on welfare? Have you talked to them about the experience? In what ways was it helpful? In what ways was it either not helpful or perhaps even harmful to them?*

1. In light of Bray's article, what typically happens to *men* in families that receive A.F.D.C.? How can that issue be best addressed?
2. Currently, there is much talk about—and even legislative action toward—reducing or eliminating A.F.D.C. Discuss these proposals in light of Bray's description of her family's experience.

An Introduction to the Moral Issues

We have only to walk down any major street in downtown New York—or any other major American city—to see the stark contrast between wealth and poverty in America. Gleaming limousines pull up next to homeless people seeking warmth from the heating grates of skyscrapers. Similarly, we have only to buy a cup of coffee to encounter the redistribution of some of that wealth in America—the tax on a cup of coffee, taken from the coffee drinker, is redistributed by the government. In these two experiences, we find the central questions about poverty and welfare in America today. *What,* first of all, *is the extent and nature of poverty in the United States?* Second, *what, if anything, should the government do about that poverty?*

The Nature of Poverty in the United States

What are the nature and causes of poverty in the United States?

There is little doubt that poverty exists in the United States—it does not take a skilled economist to prove that, although the precise measurement of poverty is a more difficult matter. Moreover, it is important to draw two initial distinctions as we approach the issue of poverty. First, we must realize that in most instances we are not talking as much about absolute poverty as we are about *relative impoverishment.* We are not concerned that the country as a whole is poor, but rather with the way in which some people in our country have less than others. Second, we must distinguish between *short-term poverty* and *long-term poverty.* Some people might be temporarily poor for a variety of reasons—they might just be beginning their careers, they might be temporarily between jobs, or the like. Yet our central concern is with those who experience long-term poverty—that is, are poor and have little prospect of changing their economic situation significantly.

The ways in which we explain the nature and causes of poverty have a profound influence on our moral understanding of poverty and the appropriate responses to it. Three competing models—none conclusively proven, but all psychologically powerful—dominate the contemporary popular discussion of poverty. Let's briefly consider each of these.

The Discrimination Model of Poverty

Many people see poverty as the result of discrimination—primarily racism, but also sexism. Indeed, the correlation is easy to establish between low income and groups—most notably African-Americans, Native Americans, and women—that have historically been objects of discrimination. Michael Harrington's *The Other America* was one of the most influential early articulations of this view.[1] *Causal* connections, of course, are more difficult to establish, but there is certainly an intuitive plausibility to the claim that the discrimination caused the poverty. However, other groups—

Jews, many European ethnic groups including the Irish and the Italians, and Asians—have been the objects of discrimination and yet have been more successful in overcoming poverty, and the discrimination model has difficulty in explaining these differences solely in terms of the forces of discrimination.

The Random Market Forces Model of Poverty

Some see poverty in the United States as the result of forces that are essentially unconnected with either discrimination or individual merit; rather, the impersonal forces of the market rob some of jobs and reward others with an abundance of employment opportunities. Employment opportunities diminish in steel factories and increase in electronics plants, but steel workers cannot easily shift to another area of manufacturing—sometimes because it requires new skills, sometimes because the jobs are located in another city. Such changes create hapless victims and fortunate recipients.

Is poverty sometimes just a matter of bad luck?

The Just Deserts Model of Poverty

Finally, some see poverty as the result of individual failings of character—that the poor are poor because on some level they have done something to deserve it. Advocates of this model see the poor as lazy, undisciplined, and wanting to be taken care of. In some versions of this position, the claim is made that a "culture of poverty"—to use the term coined by the sociologist Oscar Lewis—arises that undermines the motivation of the poor and encourages feelings of dependency, helplessness, and inferiority.

Are the poor ever poor because they lack good character?

The Case of the Children

One of the most troubling aspects of poverty is the plight of the children. We may argue about whether the parents deserve their fate, whether they should try harder to find employment, and the like, but there is little disagreement that children are the innocent victims in all this. Children don't decide where to be born, and there is no question of merit involved in their fate. A four-year-old child in a rich family is no more deserving of his or her fate than one in a poor family. If anything seems unfair, it is this.

Does the fact that some of the poor are children affect our response to poverty?

Compassion. Two aspects about the issue of children stand out. First, our response to the fate of impoverished children is, first and foremost, an emotional one: *compassion.* We see their suffering, and on some fundamental level we identify with that suffering, realizing that it is just as valuable as ours. (In this respect, compassion is fundamentally different from pity. Whereas pity looks down on its object, compassion sees the one who is suffering as a moral equal. Although there may be moments when we appreciate the compassion of other people, none of us wants to be an object of pity, for pity always puts us down in relation to that pitier.) The strength of compassion as a motive for change is that it moves the whole person, not just the intellect.

The circle of poverty. There is a less visceral, but equally compelling, dimension to the problem of children and poverty. The danger that many people see is that a circle of poverty arises, and poverty is passed on from one generation to another with little hope that individuals can break free from the cycle. Children who lack basic nutrition, children who do not receive regular medical care, children with little support for either their homes or their homework at home, children who are more afraid of being shot in school than receiving an "F"—these children can hardly be expected to fight against the odds and break out of the cycle of poverty they have known since birth. The focus of many welfare programs has been precisely here: to break the circle of poverty by intervening with the children, giving them the skills and opportunities denied to their parents.

Visions of the Ideal Role of Government in the Economy

The second major factor shaping our response to poverty is our vision of the ideal role of government in the operation of the economy. Some—conservative and libertarian thinkers occupy this camp—think that the economy will simply regulate itself; others—in the middle of the political spectrum—believe that some government intervention is necessary; and the remaining few—those on the far left of the political spectrum—believe that the government should actively and strongly intervene to guide the development of the economy.

The Self-Regulating Model: Conservativism and Libertarianism

Ever since Adam Smith described the "invisible hand" of the market as guiding society's development, some theorists have maintained that the economy possesses a natural equilibrium which it finds without any external guidance. Indeed, those in this tradition generally feel that attempts to guide the economy will be more likely to produce greater problems than they solve.

Proponents of this model are divided about what kind of society this produces. Some see the invisible hand of the market as producing significant suffering and hardship, but maintain that this is simply and unavoidably the way things are. Others claim that, at least in the long run, such a society is in everybody's best interest. Certainly if such claims were true, many people's concern about the suffering of the poor would be greatly reduced.

The Strong Interventionist Model: Communism and Socialism

At the other end of the political spectrum are those who maintain that a high degree of government intervention in the economy is justified, usually in order to produce a good society—one in which everyone is (roughly) economically equal, a society without rich or poor. This is the vision of society that inspired communism, and, to a large extent, socialism. In contrast to advocates of giving the market a free hand, egalitarians espouse a highly controlled market. Many maintain that the breakup of the Soviet Union marked the end of this kind of market.

The Moderate Interventionist Model: Liberalism

Classical liberals have sought to stake out a middle ground between these two visions of the role of government in the economy, one which required the government to establish a minimum level—or floor—below which people would not be allow to sink, but which imposed no maximum limits—or ceiling—on how high they could go. The intent of this model is to permit government intervention in the economy to eliminate extreme poverty but otherwise to restrict such intervention to preserve the incentives for individual initiative and hard work.

Moral Frameworks for Responding to Poverty

Responses to poverty arise out of a combination of at least three factors: (1) one's views on the nature of poverty, (2) one's vision of the role of government in the economy, and (3) one's views on the moral frameworks—human rights, consequences, and compassion are the most important of these—that shape the way in which we move from the actual situation to the ideal. Let's now turn to a consideration of each of these three types of moral frameworks.

Rights-Based Approaches to Poverty and Welfare

Those who see poverty in terms of the issue of rights fall along a predictable spectrum. At the one extreme—these are the *conservatives* and *libertarians*—are those who maintain (1) that poverty is a matter of individual desert and (2) that the government ought not to intervene in order to adjust the balance of wealth. At the other extreme—these are *socialists* and *communists*—are those who maintain (1) that poverty is not a matter of desert but a combination of bad luck and discrimination and (2) that the government ought to adjust the balance of wealth in such a way that all persons are approximately financially equal. In the middle are those—usually called *liberals*—who maintain that (1) at least some poverty is the result of factors beyond the impoverished individual's control and that (2) the government ought to intervene at least to ameliorate the more egregious effects of poverty, especially in those instances where poverty is clearly not deserved. Notice that in each of these cases, the position is actually composed on two components, one dealing with the origins of poverty and the other dealing with the issue of government intervention.

Negative and positive rights. Philosophers typically distinguish between negative and positive rights. Negative rights, sometimes called liberties, are simply rights not to be interfered with in some particular way. Positive rights, sometimes called *welfare rights* or *entitlements,* go further, claiming that others are obligated to provide me with something so that I may successfully exercise my right. If I have a negative right to free speech, no one is allowed to prevent me from expressing my thoughts—they cannot confiscate my printing press, take away my microphone, or the like. If, however, I have a positive right to free speech, then I am entitled to more than just noninterference:

others (society, the government) are obligated to provide me with the means for expressing my thoughts—they must give me access to printing press, microphone, and so on.

Of course, no right—despite the impression created by much of contemporary rhetoric—is absolute. At the very least, most advocates of negative rights draw the line at respecting a right when it infringes on someone else's similar right. I may have the right to free speech, but that does not mean I have the right to speak in such a way as to prevent others from speaking. Similarly, although this is seldom done, we must always recognize that rights are rarely absolute. Even something like the right to property presupposes a context, and it would seem odd to claim that individuals in a society which did not recognize private property would have a right to property.

The liberal approach to welfare rights during the past several decades in the United States has developed along an interesting path. The principal argument has not been in favor of adding new positive rights out of thin air, as it were. Rather, the argument has been that the effective exercise of certain already—recognized rights mandates certain welfare rights as necessary conditions for exercising other, more basic rights. Consider the right to equal treatment when applying to, say, medical school. Such equality of opportunity is of little practical benefit if it is not accompanied by a wider range of equal opportunities earlier in the student's life. If I did not have adequate nutrition to pay attention in elementary and secondary school, if I did not have access to educational benefits (such as computers) available to other students, if my teachers never believed in me because they thought no one of my race (or sex) was academically gifted, if I had to work full-time while going to school because my siblings and mother needed the income in order to just get by, then by the time I am twenty-two years old, it will make little difference to me that no one will arbitrarily bar me from medical school. To have genuine equality of opportunity at this stage, it would have been necessary to have equality of opportunity at many earlier stages—and such equality can only be insured through aggressive intervention by the government.

Consequentialist Approaches to Poverty

Some advocates of government intervention to reduce the problem of poverty sidestep the entire issue of whether individuals have a right to welfare and turn their attention instead to an examination of the (likely) consequences of either extending or withdrawing such support.

The main outline of consequentialist arguments on both sides of this issue is clear, even though there is significant disagreement about both facts and predictions. Consequentialist supporters of government intervention to reduce poverty maintain that, although money and services are ostensibly given only to the poor, in the long run everyone benefits from such actions. These benefits may be in the form of a more capable workforce, a physically healthier population (with less cost to the economy as a whole for sickness), less crime due to increased economic prosperity, and the like—all factors which would enhance the lives of everyone in society, not just the few who receive welfare benefits directly.

Consequentialist opponents of such intervention question the reliability of such claims in two ways. First, they ask whether present programs—perhaps, *any* programs—will produce the consequences that supporters claim. Will welfare programs, for example, produce a more capable workforce? Second, they ask whether such programs will not produce other, unwanted and undesirable consequences that their supporters ignore. For example, do such programs unintentionally foster dependency? Do programs such as Aid to Families with Dependent Children unintentionally undermine family structure? In *"The Coming White Underclass," Charles Murray* argues precisely this point, maintaining that AFDC is unintentionally producing an underclass, among both blacks and whites, by rewarding illegitimacy.

In response to such criticisms, defenders of consequentialist approaches to poverty are focusing more on programs that see welfare as a temporary measure intended to bring people into the workforce. The rise of interest in workfare has been symptomatic of this shift.

Compassion-Based Approaches to Poverty

What role should compassion have in our response to poverty in America?

Finally, some approaches to the issue of poverty in our society appeal, first and foremost, to some central moral emotion—usually compassion—as the foundation of our response to poverty. Instead of seeing the reduction of poverty as an issue of rights or of consequences, advocates of this view see it simply as the humane and decent thing to do. We help the poor, they say, simply because we care about their suffering. To do anything less would be inhumane, and it would diminish our humanity as well as perpetuate the suffering of the poor.

Critics of this position are obviously in a difficult position, for they would seem to be forced into defending moral callousness, if not outright cruelty. Although some have been willing to bite the bullet, as it were, on this issue and simply accept the label of moral callousness, others have refused that characterization of their position. We must distinguish, conservatives such as Marvin Olasky—the author of *The Tragedy of American Compassion*—argue, between *feeling compassion* and *acting* on the basis of such feelings.[2] They endorse the feeling, but then argue that the proposed actions in fact fail (at least in the long run) to alleviate the suffering to which they are a response. Imagine someone snatching a crying baby from the hands of a physician who was performing a painful medical procedure intended to save the baby's life. Snatching the baby away might be well-motivated by compassion for the baby's suffering, but it may still be the wrong thing to do, ultimately probably causing more harm than good.

Private charity. Whereas right-based approaches to poverty see basic subsistence as a right that the poor can claim, compassion-based approaches do not necessarily see the poor as having a *right* to welfare. Consequently, compassion-based approaches will be more likely to emphasize the importance of charity—and, especially, of private charity and individual acts of compassion.

Diversity and Consensus

Despite the deep divisions in our society over the issue of poverty and the ways in which we are to respond to it, there seems to be a reasonable prospect for achieving a common ground *if* certain empirical questions can be answered. The disagreements, at least between conservatives and liberals, seem to be more about empirical issues than value issues.

No one, for example, advocates creating dependency, just as no one—at least, neither conservatives nor liberals—is in favor of undermining the traditional family and its underlying values.

The central issue, at least among both conservatives and liberals, is whether welfare works or not. This is primarily an empirical question, not a moral one.

Yet what happens if we find out that welfare does not work? We are still left with the problem of poverty in our society and with the task of finding other, more effective ways of responding to it.

Endnotes

1. Michael Harrington, *The Other America* (New York: Penguin Books, 1992).
2. Marvin Olasky, *The Tragedy of American Compassion* (Wheaton, IL: Crossway Books, 1992).

The Arguments

James Sterba
"A Libertarian Justification for a Welfare State"

James Sterba, professor of philosophy at the University of Notre Dame, has published widely in the area of ethics, most recently, How to Make People Just *and* Justice for Here and Now.

Libertarians typically oppose welfare rights and the welfare state, in part because they represent an unwelcome intrusion of government into the private sphere. Sterba argues that such rights are justifiable even on libertarian grounds.

As You Read, Consider This:

1. What is the difference between Spencerian and Lockian libertarianism? How are the two conceptually related to one another? Why is this distinction important for Sterba's argument?
2. Throughout his article, Sterba presents his position and then considers a number of possible objections to his position and offers replies to those objections. As you read, make a note in the margin for each of these objections and for Sterba's replies.

Libertarians today are deeply divided over whether a night watchman state can be morally justified. Some, like Robert Nozick, hold that a night watchman state would tend to arise by an invisible-hand process if people generally respected each other's Lockean rights.[1] Others, like Murray Rothbard, hold that even the free and informed consent of all the members of a society would not justify such a state.[2] Despite this disagreement, libertarians are strongly united in opposition to welfare rights and the welfare state. According to Nozick, "the state may not use its coercive apparatus for the purpose of getting some citizens to aid others."[3] For Rothbard, "the libertarian position calls for the complete abolition of governmental welfare and reliance on private charitable aid."[4] Here I argue that this libertarian opposition to welfare rights and a welfare state is ill-founded. Welfare rights can be given a libertarian justification, and once this is recognized, a libertarian argument for a welfare state, unlike libertarian arguments for the night watchman state, is both straightforward and compelling. . . .

Libertarians have defended their view in basically two different ways. Some libertarians, following Herbert Spencer, have (1) defined liberty as the absence of constraints, (2) taken a right to liberty to be the ultimate political ideal, and (3) derived all other rights from this right to liberty. Other libertarians, following John Locke, have (1) taken a set of rights, including, typically, a right to life or self-ownership and a right to property, to be the ultimate political ideal, (2) defined liberty as the absence of constraints in the exercise of these fundamental rights, and (3) derived all other rights, including a right to liberty, from these fundamental rights.

Each of these approaches has its difficulties. The principal difficulty with the first approach is that unless one arbitrarily restricts what is to count as an interference, conflicting liberties will abound, particularly in all areas of social life.[5] The principal difficulty with the second approach is that as long as a person's rights have not been violated, her liberty would not have been restricted either, even if she were kept in prison for the rest of her days.[6] I don't propose to try to decide between these two approaches. What I do want to show, however, is that on either approach welfare rights and a welfare state are morally required.

Spencerian Libertarianism

Thus suppose we were to adopt the view of those libertarians who take a right to liberty to be the ultimate political ideal. According to this view, liberty is usually defined as follows:

> *The Want Conception of Liberty:* Liberty is being unconstrained by other persons from doing what one wants.

This conception limits the scope of liberty in two ways. First, not all constraints whatever their source count as a restriction of liberty; the constraints must come from other persons. For example, people who are constrained by natural forces from getting to the top of Mount Everest do not lack liberty in this regard. Second, constraints that have their source in other persons, but that do not run counter to an individual's wants, constrain without restricting that individual's liberty. Thus, for people who do not want to hear Beethoven's Fifth Symphony, the fact that others have effectively proscribed its performance does not restrict their liberty, even though it does constrain what they are able to do.

Of course, libertarians may wish to argue that even such constraints can be seen to restrict a person's liberty once we take into account the fact that people normally want, or have a general desire, to be unconstrained by others. But other philosophers have thought that the possibility of such constraints points to a serious defect in this conception of liberty,[7] which can only be remedied by adopting the following broader conception of liberty:

> *The Ability Conception of Liberty:* Liberty is being unconstrained by other persons from doing what one is able to do.

Applying this conception to the above example, we find that people's liberty to hear Beethoven's Fifth Symphony would be restricted even if they did not want to hear it (and even if, perchance, they did not want to be unconstrained by others) since other people would still be constraining them from doing what they are able to do. . . .

Of course, there will be numerous liberties determined by the Ability Conception that are not liberties according to the Want Conception. For example, there will be highly talented students who do not want to pursue careers in philosophy, even though no one constrains them from doing so. Accordingly, the Ability Conception but not the Want Conception would view them as possessing a liberty. And even though such liberties are generally not as valuable as those liberties that are common to both conceptions, they still are of some value, even when the manipulation of people's wants is not at issue.

Yet even if we accept all the liberties specified by the Ability Conception, problems of interpretation still remain. The major problem in this regard concerns what is to count as a constraint. On the one hand, libertarians would like to limit constraints to positive acts (that is, acts of commission) that prevent people from doing what they are otherwise able to do. On the other hand, welfare liberals and socialists interpret constraints to include, in addition, negative acts (that is, of omission) that prevent people from doing what they are otherwise able to do. In fact, this is one way to understand the debate between defenders of "negative liberty" and defenders of "positive liberty." For defenders of negative liberty would seem to interpret constraints to include only positive acts of others that prevent people from doing what they otherwise are able to do, while defenders of positive liberty would seem to interpret constraints to include both positive and negative acts of others that prevent people from doing what they are otherwise able to do.[8]

Suppose we interpret constraints in the manner favored by libertarians to include only positive acts by others that prevent people from doing what they are otherwise able to do, and let us consider a typical conflict situation between the rich and the poor.

In this conflict situation, the rich, of course, have more than enough resources to satisfy their basic needs. By contrast, the poor lack the resources to meet their most basic nutritional needs even though they have tried all the means available to them that libertarians regard as legitimate for acquiring such resources. Under circumstances like these, libertarians usually maintain that the rich should have the liberty to use their resources to satisfy their luxury needs if they so wish. Libertarians recognize that this liberty might well be enjoyed at the expense of the satisfaction of the most basic nutritional needs of the poor. Libertarians just think that a right to liberty always has priority over other political ideals, and since they assume that the liberty of the poor is not at stake in such conflict situations, it is easy for them to conclude that the rich should not be required to sacrifice their liberty so that the basic nutritional needs of the poor may be met.

From a consideration of the liberties involved, libertarians claim to derive a number of more specific requirements, in particular, a right to life, a right to freedom of speech, press and assembly, and a right to property.

Here it is important to observe that the libertarian's right to life is not a right to receive from others the goods and resources necessary for preserving one's life; it is simply a right not to be killed unjustly. Correspondingly, the libertarian's right to property is not a right to receive from others the goods and resources necessary for one's welfare, but rather a right to acquire goods and resources either by initial acquisition or by voluntary agreement.

Rights such as these, libertarians claim, can at best support only a limited role for government. That role is simply to prevent and punish initial acts of coercion—the only wrongful actions for libertarians. And, as we noted before, libertarians are deeply divided over whether a government with even such a limited role, that is, a night watchman state, can be morally justified.

Of course, libertarians would allow that it would be nice of the rich to share their surplus resources with the poor. Nevertheless, according to libertarians, such acts of charity should not be coercively required, because the liberty of the poor is not thought to be at stake in such conflict situations.

In fact, however, the liberty of the poor is at stake in such conflict situations. What is at stake is the liberty of the poor to take from the surplus possessions of the rich what is necessary to satisfy their basic nutritional needs. When libertarians are brought to see that this is the case, they are often genuinely surprised, for they had not previously seen the conflict between the rich and the poor as a conflict of liberties.[9]

When the conflict between the rich and the poor is viewed as a conflict of liberties, we can either say that the rich should have the liberty to use their surplus resources for luxury purposes, or we can say that the poor should have the liberty to take from the rich what they require to meet their basic nutritional needs. If we choose one liberty, we must reject the other. What needs to be determined, therefore, is which liberty is morally preferable: the liberty of the rich or the liberty of the poor.

I submit that the liberty of the poor, which is the liberty to take from the surplus resources of others what is required to meet one's basic nutritional needs, is morally preferable to the liberty of the rich, which is the liberty to use one's surplus resources for luxury purposes. To see that this is the case we need only appeal to one of the most fundamental principles of morality, one that is common to all political perspectives, namely the "ought" implies "can" principle. According to this principle, people are not morally required to do what they lack the power to do or what would involve so great a sacrifice that it would be unreasonable to ask them to perform such an action.[10] For example, suppose I promised to attend a meeting on Friday, but on Thursday I am involved in a serious car accident which puts me into a coma. Surely it is no longer the case that I ought to attend the meeting now that I lack the power to do so. Or suppose instead that on Thursday I develop a severe case of pneumonia for which I am hospitalized. Surely I could legitimately claim that I no longer ought to attend the meeting on the grounds that the risk to my health involved in attending is a sacrifice that it would be unreasonable to ask me to bear.

Now applying the "ought" implies "can" principle to the case at hand, it seems clear that the poor have it within their power to willingly relinquish such an important liberty as the liberty to take from the rich what they require to meet their basic nutritional needs. Nevertheless, it would be unreasonable to require them to make so great a sacrifice. In the extreme case, it would involve requiring the poor to sit back and starve to death. Of course, the poor may have no real alternative to relinquishing this liberty. To do anything else may involve worse consequences for themselves and their loved ones and may invite a painful death. Accordingly, we may expect that the poor would acquiesce, albeit unwillingly, to a political system that denied them the welfare rights supported by such a liberty, at the same time that we recognize that such a system imposed an unreasonable sacrifice upon the poor—a sacrifice that we could not morally blame the poor for trying to evade.[11] Analogously, we might expect that a woman whose life was threatened would submit to a rapist's demands, at the same time that we recognize the utter unreasonableness of those demands.

By contrast, it would not be unreasonable to require the rich to sacrifice the liberty to meet some of their luxury needs so that the poor can have the liberty to meet their basic nutritional needs. Naturally, we might expect that the rich for reasons of self-interest and past contribution might be disinclined to make such a sacrifice. We might even suppose that the past contribution of the rich provides a good reason for not sacrificing their liberty to use their surplus for luxury purposes. Yet, unlike the poor, the rich could not claim that relinquishing such a liberty involved so great a sacrifice that it would be unreasonable to require them to make it; unlike the poor, the rich could be morally blameworthy for failing to make such a sacrifice.

Consequently, if we assume that however else we specify the requirements of morality, they cannot violate the "ought" implies "can" principle, it follows that, despite what libertarians claim, the right to liberty endorsed by libertarians actually favors the liberty of the poor over the liberty of the rich.

Yet, couldn't libertarians object to this conclusion, claiming that it would be unreasonable to require the rich to sacrifice the liberty to meet some of their luxury needs so that the poor could have the liberty to meet their basic nutritional needs? As I have pointed out, libertarians don't usually see the situation as a conflict of liberties, but suppose they did. How plausible would such an objection be? Not very plausible at all, I think.

Consider this: what are libertarians going to say about the poor? Isn't it clearly unreasonable to require the poor to sacrifice the liberty to meet their basic nutritional needs so that the rich can have the liberty to meet their luxury needs? Isn't it clearly unreasonable to require the poor to sit back and starve to death? If it is, then there is no resolution of this conflict that would be reasonable to require both the rich and the poor to accept. But that would mean that the libertarian ideal of liberty cannot be a moral ideal that resolves conflicts of interest in ways that it would be reasonable to require everyone affected to accept. Therefore, as long as libertarians think of themselves as putting forth such a moral ideal, they cannot allow that it would be unreasonable both to require the rich to sacrifice the liberty to meet some of their luxury needs in order to benefit the poor and to require the poor to sacrifice the liberty to meet their basic nutritional needs in order to benefit the rich. But I submit that if one of these requests is to be judged reasonable, then, by any neutral assessment, it must be the requirement that the rich sacrifice the liberty to meet some of their luxury needs so that the poor can have the liberty to meet their basic nutritional needs; there is no other plausible resolution, if libertarians intend to be putting forth a moral ideal that reasonably resolves conflicts of interest.

But might not libertarians hold that putting forth a moral ideal means no more than being willing to universalize one's fundamental commitments? Surely we have no difficulty imagining the rich willing to universalize their commitments to relatively strong property rights. Yet, at the same time, we have no difficulty imagining the poor and their advocates willing to universalize their commitments to relatively weak property rights. Consequently, if the libertarian's moral ideal is interpreted in this fashion, it would not be able to provide a basis for reasonably resolving conflicts of interest between the rich and the poor. But without such a basis for conflict resolution, how could societies flourish, as libertarians claim they would, under a minimal state or with no state at all?[12] Surely, in order for societies to flourish in this fashion, the libertarian ideal must resolve conflicts of interest in ways that it would be reasonable to require everyone affected to accept. But, as we have seen, that requirement can only be satisfied if the rich sacrifice the liberty to meet some of their luxury needs so that the poor can have the liberty to meet their basic nutritional needs.

It should also be noted that this case for restricting the liberty of the rich depends upon the willingness of the poor to take advantage of whatever opportunities are available to them for satisfying their basic needs by engaging in mutually beneficial work, so that failure of the poor to take advantage of such opportunities would normally either cancel or at least significantly reduce the obligation of the rich to restrict their own liberty for the benefit of the poor.[13] In addition, the poor would be required to return the equivalent of any surplus possessions they have taken from the rich once they are able to do so and still satisfy their basic needs. Nor would the poor be required to keep the liberty to which they are entitled. They could give up part of it, or all of it, or risk losing it on the chance of gaining a greater share of liberties or other social goods.[14] Consequently, the case for restricting the liberty of the rich for the benefit of the poor is neither unconditional nor inalienable.

Even so, libertarians would have to be disconcerted about what turns out to be the practical upshot of taking a right to liberty to be the ultimate political ideal. For libertarians contend that their political ideal would support welfare rights only when constraints are "illegitimately" interpreted to induce both positive and negative acts by others that prevent people from doing what they are otherwise able to do. By contrast, when constraints are interpreted to include only positive acts, libertarians contend, no such welfare rights can be justified.

Nevertheless, what the foregoing argument demonstrates is that this view is mistaken. For even when the interpretation of constraints favored by libertarians is employed, a moral assessment of the competing liberties still requires an allocation of liberties to the poor that will be generally sufficient to provide them with the goods and resources necessary for satisfying their basic nutritional needs.

One might think that once the rich realize that the poor should have the liberty not to be interfered with when taking from the surplus possessions of the rich what they require to satisfy their basic needs, it would be in the interest of the rich to stop producing any surplus whatsoever. Yet that would only be the case if first, the recognition of the rightful claims of the poor would exhaust the surplus of the rich and second, the poor would never be in a position to be obligated to repay what they appropriated from the rich. Fortunately for the poor, both of these conditions are unlikely to be obtained.

Of course, there will be cases where the poor fail to satisfy their basic nutritional needs, not because of any direct restriction of liberty on the part of the rich, but because the poor are in such dire need that they are unable even to attempt to take from the rich what they require to meet their basic nutritional needs. Accordingly, in such cases, the rich would not be performing any act of commission that prevents the poor from taking what they require. Yet, even in such cases, the rich would normally be performing acts of commission that prevent other persons from aiding the poor by taking from the surplus possessions of the rich. And when assessed from a moral point of view, restricting the liberty of these other persons would not be morally justified for the very same reason that restricting the liberty of the poor to meet their own basic nutritional needs would not be morally justified: it would not be reasonable to ask all of those affected to accept such a restriction of liberty. . . .

In brief, what this shows is that if a right to liberty is taken to be the ultimate political ideal, then, contrary to what libertarians claim, not only would a system of welfare rights be morally required, but also such a system would clearly benefit the poor.

Lockean Libertarianism

Yet suppose we were to adopt the view of those libertarians who do not take a right to liberty to be the ultimate political ideal. According to this view, liberty is defined as follows:

> *The Rights Conception of Liberty:* Liberty is being unconstrained by other persons from doing what one has a right to do.

The most important ultimate rights in terms of which liberty is specified are, according to this view, a right to life understood as a right not to be killed unjustly and a right to property understood as a right to acquire goods and resources either by initial acquisition or voluntary agreement. In order to evaluate this view, we must determine what are the practical implications of these rights.

Presumably, a right to life understood as a right not to be killed unjustly would not be violated by defensive measures designed to protect one's person from life-threatening attacks. Yet would this right be violated when the rich prevent the poor from taking what they require to satisfy their basic nutritional needs? Obviously, as a consequence of such preventive actions poor people sometimes do starve to death. Have the rich, then, in contributing to this result, killed the poor, or simply let them die; and, if they have killed the poor, have they done so unjustly?

Sometimes the rich, in preventing the poor from taking what they require to meet their basic nutritional needs, would not in fact be killing the poor, but only causing them to be physically or mentally debilitated. Yet since such preventive acts involve resisting the life-preserving activities of the poor, when the poor do die as a consequence of such acts, it seems clear that the rich would be killing the poor, whether intentionally or unintentionally.

Of course, libertarians would want to argue that such killing is simply a consequence of the legitimate exercise of property rights, and hence, not unjust. But to understand why libertarians are mistaken in this regard, let us appeal again to that fundamental principle of morality, the "ought" implies "can" principle. In this context, the principle can be used to assess two opposing accounts of property rights. According to the first account, a right to property is not conditional upon whether other persons have sufficient opportunities and resources to satisfy their basic needs. This view holds that the initial acquisition and voluntary agreement of some can leave others, through no fault of their own, dependent upon charity for the satisfaction of their most basic needs. By contrast, according to the second account, initial acquisition and voluntary agreement can confer title of property on all goods and resources except those surplus goods and resources of the rich that are required to satisfy the basic needs of those poor who through no fault of their own lack opportunities and resources to satisfy their own basic needs.

Clearly, only the first of these two accounts of property rights would generally justify the killing of the poor as a legitimate exercise of the property rights of the rich. Yet it would be unreasonable to require the poor to accept anything other than some version of the second account of property rights. Moreover, according to the second account, it does not matter whether the poor would actually die or are only physically or mentally debilitated as a result of such acts of prevention. Either result would preclude property rights from arising. Of course, the poor may have no real alternative to acquiescing to a political system modeled after the first account of property rights, even though such a system imposes an unreasonable sacrifice upon them—a sacrifice that we could not blame them for trying to evade. At the same time, although the rich would be disinclined to do so, it would not be unreasonable to require them to accept a political system modeled after the second account of property rights—the account favored by the poor.

Consequently, if we assume that however else we specify the requirements of morality, they cannot violate the "ought" implies "can" principle, it follows that, despite what libertarians claim, the right to life and the right to property endorsed by libertarians actually support a system of welfare rights. . . .

Nevertheless, it might be objected that the welfare rights that have been established against the libertarian are not the same as the welfare rights endorsed by welfare liberals. We could mark this difference by referring to the welfare rights that have been established against the libertarian as "action welfare rights" and referring to the welfare rights endorsed by welfare liberals as both "action and recipient welfare rights." The significance of this difference is that a person's action welfare right can be violated only when other people through acts of commission interfere with a person's exercise of that right, whereas a person's action and recipient welfare right can be violated by such acts of commission and by acts of omission as well. However, this difference will have little practical import. For once libertarians come to recognize the legitimacy of action welfare rights, then in order not to be subject to the poor person's discretion in choosing when and how to exercise her action welfare right, libertarians will tend to favor two morally legitimate ways of preventing the exercise of such rights. First, libertarians can provide the poor with mutually beneficial job opportunities. Second, libertarians can institute adequate recipient welfare rights that would take precedence over the poor's action welfare rights. Accordingly, if libertarians adopt either or both of these ways of legitimately preventing the poor from exercising their action welfare rights, libertarians will end up endorsing the same sort of welfare institutions favored by welfare liberals.

Finally, once a system of welfare rights is seen to follow irrespective of whether one takes a right to liberty or rights to life and property as the ultimate political ideal, the justification for a welfare state becomes straightforward and compelling. For while it is at least conceivable that rights other than welfare rights could be adequately secured in a society without the enforcement agencies of a state, it is inconceivable that welfare rights themselves could be adequately secured without such enforcement agencies. Only a welfare state would be able to effectively solve the large-scale coordination problem necessitated by the provision of welfare. Consequently, once a system of welfare rights can be seen to have a libertarian justification, the argument for a welfare state hardly seems to need stating.[15]

Endnotes

1. Robert Nozick, *Anarchy, State and Utopia* (New York: Basic Books, 1974), Part I.
2. Murray Rothbard, *The Ethics of Liberty* (Atlantic Highlands: Humanities Press, 1982), p. 230.
3. Nozick, *Anarchy, State and Utopia,* p. ix.
4. Murray Rothbard, *For a New Liberty* (New York: Collier Books, 1978), p. 148.
5. See, for example, James P. Sterba, "Neo-Libertarianism," *American Philosophical Quarterly* 15 (1978): 17–19; Ernest Loevinsohn, "Liberty and the Redistribution of Property," *Philosophy and Public Affairs* 6 (1977): 226–239; David Zimmerman, "Coercive Wage Offers," *Philosophy and Public Affairs* 10 (1981): 121–145. To limit what is to count as coercive, Zimmerman claims that in order for P's offer to be coercive:

   > [I]t must be the case that P does more than merely prevent Q *from taking from* P resources necessary for securing Q's strongly preferred preproposal situation; P must prevent Q *from acting on his own* (or with the help of others) *to produce or procure* the strongly preferred preposal situation.

   But this restriction seems arbitrary, and Zimmerman provides little justification for it. See David Zimmerman, "More on Coercive Wage Offers," *Philosophy and Public Affairs* 12 (1983): 67–68.

6. It might seem that this second approach could avoid this difficulty if a restriction of liberty is understood as the curtailment of one's prima facie rights. But in order to avoid the problem of a multitude of conflicting liberties, which plagues the first approach, the specification of prima facie rights must be such that they only can be overridden when one or more of them is violated. And this may involve too much precision for our notion of prima facie rights.
7. Isaiah Berlin, *Four Essays on Liberty* (New York: Oxford University Press, 1969), pp. XXXVIII–XL.
8. On this point, see Maurice Cranston, *Freedom* (New York: Basic Books, 1953), pp. 52–53; C.B. Macpherson, *Democratic Theory* (Oxford: Oxford University Press, 1973), p. 95; Joel Feinberg, *Rights, Justice and the Bounds of Liberty* (Princeton, NJ: Princeton University Press, 1980), Chapter 1.
9. See John Hospers, *Libertarianism* (Los Angeles: Nash, 1971), Chapter 7.
10. Alvin Goldman, *A Theory of Human Action* (Englewood Cliffs, NJ: Prentice-Hall, 1970), pp. 208–215; William Frankena, "Obligation and Ability," in *Philosophical Analysis,* edited by Max Black (Ithaca, NY: Cornell University Press, 1950), pp. 157–175.

    Judging from some recent discussions of moral dilemmas by Bernard Williams and Ruth Marcus, one might think that the "ought" implies "can" principle would only be useful for illustrating moral conflicts rather than resolving them.

    See Bernard Williams, *Problems of the Self* (Cambridge: Cambridge University Press, 1977), Chapters 11 and 12; Ruth Marcus, "Moral Dilemmas and Consistency," *The Journal of Philosophy* 80 (1980): 121–136. See also Terrance C. McConnell, "Moral Dilemmas and Consistency in Ethics," *Canadian Journal of Philosophy* 18 (1978): 269–287. But this is only true if one interprets the "can" in the principle to exclude only "what a person lacks the power to do." If one interprets the "can" to exclude in addition "what would involve so great a sacrifice that it would be unreasonable to ask the person to do it" then the principle can be used to resolve moral conflicts as well as state them. Nor would libertarians object to this broader interpretation of the "ought" implies "can" principle since they do not ground their claim to liberty on the existence of irresolvable moral conflicts.
11. See James P. Sterba, "Is there a Rationale for Punishment?" *The American Journal of Jurisprudence* 29 (1984): 29–44.
12. As further evidence, notice that those libertarians who justify a minimal state do so on the grounds that such a state would arise from reasonable disagreements concerning the application of libertarian rights. They do not justify the minimal state on the grounds that it would be needed to keep in submission large numbers of people who could not come to see the reasonableness of libertarian rights.
13. Obviously, the employment opportunities offered to the poor must be honorable and supportive of self-respect. To do otherwise would be to offer the poor the opportunity to meet some of their basic needs at the cost of denying some of their other basic needs.
14. The poor cannot, however, give up the liberty to which their children are entitled.
15. Of course, someone might still want to object to welfare states on the grounds that they "force workers to sell their labor" (see G.A. Cohen, "The Structure of Proletarian Unfreedom," *Philosophy and Public Affairs* 12 (1982): 3–33) and subject workers to "coercive wage offers."

(See Zimmerman, "Coercive Wage Offers.") But for a defense of at least one form of welfare state against such an objection, see James P. Sterba, "A Marxist Dilemma for Social Contract Theory," *American Philosophical Quarterly* 21 (1981): 51–59.

Journal/Discussion Questions

✍ *Imagine walking down the street and being approached for money by a homeless person. How would Sterba perceive that situation? Is this the same way that you would see it? Discuss.*

1. Sterba argues that "the liberty of the poor . . . is morally preferable to the liberty of the rich." Explain what he means by this. What conclusions does he draw from this? In what ways do you agree with him? Disagree?
2. Sterba sees the conflict between rich and poor in terms of a conflict of *liberties*. How does this affect his argument? In what other ways could that conflict be seen?
3. The rich, Sterba argues, would be morally blameworthy if they refused to sacrifice "their liberty to meet their luxury needs so that the poor can have the liberty to meet their basic nutritional needs." Do you agree with Sterba? Disagree? Discuss your reasons.

Tibor Machan
"The Nonexistence of Basic Welfare Rights"

Born in Hungary at the beginning of World War II, Tibor Machan is a professor of philosophy at Chapman University and the author of numerous articles and books in social and moral philosophy, including Generosity: Virtue in Civil Society, Human Rights and Human Liberties, *and* Individuals and Their Rights, *from which the present selection is drawn.*

Arguing specifically against James Sterba's "From Liberty to Welfare" and in general against liberalism, Machan presents and defends a libertarian analysis of the issue of welfare rights.

As You Read, Consider This:

1. The word "liberty" may have several different meanings. Note the different senses of this term in the following essay.
2. What does Machan mean by "ought implies can"? What role does this distinction play in his argument?

James Sterba and others maintain that we all have the right to "receive the goods and resources necessary for preserving" ourselves. This is not what I have argued human beings have a right to. They have the right, rather, not to be killed, attacked, and deprived of their property—by persons in or outside of government. As Abraham Lincoln put it, "no man is good enough to govern another man, without that other's consent."[1]

Sterba claims that various political outlooks would have to endorse these "rights." He sets out to show, in particular, that welfare rights follow from libertarian theory itself.[2] Sterba wishes to show that *if* Lockean libertarianism is correct, then we all have rights to welfare and equal (economic) opportunity. What I wish to show is that since Lockean libertarianism—as developed in this work—is true, and since the rights to welfare and equal opportunity require their violation, no one has these latter rights. The reason some people, including Sterba, believe otherwise is that they have found some very rare instances in which some citizens could find themselves in circumstances that would require disregarding rights altogether. This would be in situations that cannot be characterized to be "where peace is possible."[3] And every major libertarian thinker from Locke to the present has treated these kinds of cases.[4]

Let us be clear about what Sterba sets out to show. It is that libertarians are philosophically unable to escape the welfare-statist implication of their commitment to negative liberty. This means that despite their belief that they are only supporting the enforceable right of every person not to be coerced by other persons, libertarians must accept, by the logic of their own position, that individuals also possess basic enforceable rights to being provided with various services from others. He holds, then, that basic negative rights imply basic positive rights.

To Lockean libertarians the ideal of liberty means that we all, individually, have the right not to be constrained against our consent within our realm of authority—ourselves and our belongings. Sterba states that for such libertarians "Liberty is being unconstrained by persons from doing what one has a right to do."[5] Sterba adds, somewhat misleadingly, that for Lockean libertarians "a right to life [is] a right not to be killed unjustly and a right to property [is] a right to acquire goods and resources either by initial acquisition or voluntary agreement."[6] Sterba does realize that these rights do not entitle one to receive from others the goods and resources necessary for preserving one's life.

A problem with this foundation of the Lockean libertarian view is that political justice—not the justice of Plato, which is best designated in our time as "perfect virtue"—for natural-rights theorists presupposes individual rights. One cannot then explain rights in terms of justice but must explain justice in terms of rights.

For a Lockean libertarian, to possess any basic right to receive the goods and resources necessary for preserving one's life conflicts with possessing the right not to be killed, assaulted, or stolen from. The latter are rights Lockean libertarians consider to be held by all individual human beings. Regularly to protect and maintain—that is, enforce—the former right would often require the violation of the latter. A's right to the food she has is incompatible with B's right to take this same food. Both the rights could not be fundamental in an integrated legal system. The situation of one's having rights to welfare, and so forth, and another's having rights to life, liberty, and property is thus theoretically intolerable and practically unfeasible. The point of a system of rights is the securing of mutually peaceful and consistent moral conduct on the part of human beings. As Rand observes,

> "Rights" are . . . the link between the moral code of a man and the legal code of a society, between ethics and politics. *Individual rights are the means of subordinating society to moral law.*[7]

Sterba asks us—in another discussion of his views—to consider what he calls "a *typical* conflict situation between the rich and the poor." He says that in his situation "the rich, of course, have more than enough resources to satisfy their basic needs. By contrast, the poor lack the resources to meet their most basic needs even though *they have tried all the means available to them that libertarians regard as legitimate for acquiring such resources*"[8] (my emphasis).

The goal of a theory of rights would be defeated if rights were typically in conflict. Some bureaucratic group would have to keep applying its moral intuitions on numerous occasions when rights claims would *typically* conflict. A constitution is workable if it helps remove at least the largest proportion of such decisions from the realm of arbitrary (intuitive) choice and avail a society of men and women of objective guidelines that are reasonably integrated, not in relentless discord.

Most critics of libertarianism assume some doctrine of basic needs which they invoke to show that whenever basic needs are not satisfied for some people, while others have "resources" which are not basic needs for them, the former have just claims against the latter. (The language of resources of course loads the argument in the critic's favor since it suggests that these goods simply come into being and happen to be in the possession of some people, quite without rhyme or reason, arbitrarily [as John Rawls claims].)[9]

This doctrine is full of difficulties. It lacks any foundation for why the needs of some persons must be claims upon the lives of others. And why are there such needs anyway—to what end are they needs, and whose ends are these and why are not the persons whose needs they are held responsible for supplying the needs? (Needs, as I have already observed, lack any force in moral argument without the prior justification of the purposes they serve or the goals they help to fulfill. A thief has a basic need of skills and powers that are clearly not justified if theft is morally unjustified. If, however, the justification of basic needs, such as food and other resources, presupposes the value of human life, and if the value of human life justifies, as I have argued earlier, the principle of the natural rights to life, liberty and property, then the attainment or fulfillment of the basic need for food may not involve the violation of these rights.)

Sterba claims that without guaranteeing welfare and equal-opportunity rights, Lockean libertarianism violates the most basic tenets of any morality, namely, that "ought" implies "can." The thrust of "'ought' implies 'can'" is that one ought to do that which one is free to do, that one is morally responsible only for those acts that one had the power either to choose to engage in or to choose not to engage in. (There is debate on just how this point must be phrased—in terms of the will being free or the person being free to will something. For our purposes, however, all that counts is that the person must have [had] a genuine option to do X or not to do X before it can be true that he or she ought to do X or ought to have done X.) If an innocent person is forced by the actions of another to forgo significant moral choices, then that innocent person is not free to act morally and thus his or her human dignity is violated.

This is not so different from the commonsense legal precept that if one is not sound of mind one cannot be criminally culpable. Only free agents, capable of choosing between right and wrong, are open to moral evaluation. This indeed is the reason that many so-called moral theories fail to be anything more than value theories. They omit from consideration the issue of self-determination. If either hard or soft determinism is true, morality is impossible, although values need not disappear.[10]

If Sterba were correct about Lockean libertarianism typically contradicting "'ought' implies 'can,'" his argument would be decisive. (There are few arguments against this principle that I know of and they have not convinced me. They trade on rare circumstances when persons feel guilt for taking actions that had bad consequences even though they could not have avoided them.)[11] It is because Karl Marx's and Herbert Spencer's systems typically, normally, indeed in every case, violate this principle that they are not bona fide moral systems. And quite a few others may be open to a similar charge.[12]

Sterba offers his strongest argument when he observes that "'ought' implies 'can'" is violated "when the rich prevent the poor from taking what they require to satisfy their basic needs even though they have tried all the means available to them that libertarians regard as legitimate for acquiring such resources."[13]

Is Sterba right that such are—indeed, must be—typical conflict cases in a libertarian society? Are the rich and poor, even admitting that there is some simple division of people into such economic groups, in such hopeless conflict all the time? Even in the case of homeless people, many find help without having to resort to theft. The political factors contributing to the presence of helpless people in the United States and other Western liberal democracies are a hotly debated issue, even among utilitarians and welfare-state supporters. Sterba cannot make his argument for the typicality of such cases by reference to history alone. (Arguably, there are fewer helpless poor in near-libertarian, capitalist systems than anywhere else—why else would virtually everyone wish to live in these societies rather than those where welfare is guaranteed, indeed enforced? Not, at least originally, for their welfare-statist features. Arguably, too, the disturbing numbers of such people in these societies could be due, in part, to the lack of consistent protection of all the libertarian natural rights.)

Nonetheless, in a system that legally protects and preserves property rights there will be cases where a rich person prevents a poor person from taking what belongs to her (the rich person)—for example, a chicken that the poor person might use to feed herself. Since after such prevention the poor person might starve, Sterba asks the rhetorical question "Have the rich, then, in contributing to this result, killed the poor, or simply let them die; and if they have killed the poor, have they done so unjustly?"[14] His answer is that they have. Sterba holds that a system that accords with the Lockean libertarian's idea that the rich person's preventive action is just "imposes an unreasonable sacrifice upon" the poor, one "that we could not blame them for trying to evade." Not permitting the poor to act to satisfy their basic needs is to undermine the precept that "'ought' implies 'can'" since, as Sterba claims, that precept means, for the poor, that they ought to satisfy their basic needs. This they must have the option to do if they ought to do it. . . .

When people defend their property, what are they doing? They are protecting themselves against the intrusive acts of some other person, acts that would normally deprive them of something to which they have a right, and the other has no right. As such, these acts of protectiveness make it possible for men and women in society to retain their own sphere of jurisdiction intact, protect their own "moral space."[15] They refuse to have their human dignity violated. They want to be sovereigns and govern their own lives, including their own productive decisions and actions. Those who mount the attack, in turn, fail or refuse to refrain from encroaching upon the moral space of their victims. They are treating the victim's life and its productive results as though these were unowned resources for them to do with as they choose.

Now the argument that cuts against the above account is that on some occasions there can be people who, with no responsibility for their situation, are highly unlikely to survive without disregarding the rights of others and taking from them what they need. This is indeed possible. It is no less possible that there be cases in which someone is highly unlikely to survive without obtaining the services of a doctor who is at that moment spending time healing someone else, or in which there is a person who is highly unlikely to survive without obtaining one of the lungs of another person, who wants to keep both lungs so as to be able to run the New York City marathon effectively. And such cases could be multiplied indefinitely.

But are such cases typical? The argument that starts with this assumption about a society is already not comparable to the libertarianism that has emerged in the footsteps of Lockean natural-rights doctrine, including the version advanced in this book. That system is developed for a human community in which "peace is possible." Libertarian individual rights, which guide men and women in such an adequately hospitable environment to act without thwarting the flourishing of others, are thus suitable bases for the legal foundations for a human society. It is possible for people in the world to pursue their proper goals without thwarting a similar pursuit by others.

The underlying notion of society in such a theory rejects the description of human communities implicit in Sterba's picture. Sterba sees conflict as typically arising from some people producing and owning goods, while others having no alternative but to take these goods from the former in order to survive. But these are not the typical conflict situations even in what we today consider reasonably free human communities—most thieves and robbers are not destitute, nor are they incapable of doing something aside from taking other people's property in order to obtain their livelihood.

The typical conflict situation in society involves people who wish to take shortcuts to earning their living (and a lot more) by attacking others, not those who lack any other alternative to attacking others so as to reach that same goal. This may not be evident from all societies that team with human conflict—in the Middle East, or Central and South America, for example. But it must be remembered that these societies are far from being even near-libertarian. Even if the typical conflicts there involved the kind Sterba describes, that would not suffice to make his point. Only if it were true that in comparatively free countries the typical conflict involved the utterly destitute and helpless arrayed against the well-to-do, could his argument carry any conviction.

The Lockean libertarian has confidence in the willingness and capacity of virtually all persons to make headway in life in a free society. The very small minority of exceptional cases must be taken care of by voluntary social institutions, not by the government, which guards self-consistent individual rights.

The integrity of law would be seriously endangered if the government entered areas that required it to make very particular judgments and depart from serving the interest of the public as such. We have already noted that the idea of "satisfying basic needs" can involve the difficulty of distinguishing those whose actions are properly to be so characterized. Rich persons are indeed satisfying their basic needs as they protect and preserve their property rights. . . . Private property rights are necessary for a morally decent society.

The Lockean libertarian argues that private property rights are morally justified in part because they are the concrete requirement for delineating the sphere of jurisdiction of each person's moral authority, where her own judgment is decisive.[16] This is a crucial basis for the right to property. And so is the contention that we live in a metaphysically hospitable universe wherein people normally need not suffer innocent misery and deprivation—so that such a condition is usually the result of negligence or the violation of Lockean rights, a violation that has made self-development and commerce impossible. If exceptional emergencies set the agenda for the law, the law itself will disintegrate. (A just legal system makes provision for coping with emergencies that are brought to the attention of the authorities, for example, by way of judicial discretion, without allowing such cases to determine the direction of the system. If legislators and judges don't uphold the integrity of the system, disintegration ensues. This can itself encourage the emergence of strong leaders, demagogues, who promise to do what the law has not been permitted to do, namely, satisfy people's sense of justice. Experience with them bodes ill for such a prospect.)

Normally persons do not "lack the opportunities and resources to satisfy their own basic needs." Even if we grant that some helpless, crippled, retarded, or destitute persons could offer nothing to anyone that would merit wages enabling them to carry on with their lives and perhaps even flourish, there is still the other possibility for most actual, known hard cases, that is, seeking help. I am not speaking here of the cases we know: people who drop out of school, get an unskilled job, marry and have kids, only to find that their personal choice of inadequate preparation for life leaves them relatively poorly off. "'Ought' implies 'can'" must not be treated ahistorically—some people's lack of current options results from their failure to exercise previous options prudently. I refer here to the "truly needy," to use a shop-worn but still useful phrase—those who have never been able to help themselves and are not now helpless from their own neglect. Are such people being treated *unjustly,* rather than at most uncharitably, ungenerously, indecently, pitilessly, or in some other respect immorally—by those who, knowing of the plight of such persons, resist forcible efforts to take from them enough to provide the ill-fated with what they truly need? Actually, if we tried to pry the needed goods or money from the well-to-do, we would not even learn if they would act generously. Charity, generosity, kindness, and acts of compassion presuppose that those well enough off are not coerced to provide help. These virtues cannot flourish, nor can the corresponding vices, of course, without a clearly identified and well-protected right to private property for all.

If we consider the situation as we are more likely to find it, namely, that desperate cases not caused by previous injustices (in the libertarian sense) are rare, then, contrary to what Sterba suggests, there is much that unfortunate persons can and should do in those plausible, non-emergency situations that can be considered typical. They need not resort to violating the private-property rights of those who are better off. The destitute can appeal for assistance both from the rich and from the many voluntary social service agencies which emerge from the widespread compassion of people who know about the mishaps that can at times strike perfectly decent people.

Consider, as a prototype of this situation on which we might model what concerns Sterba, that if one's car breaks down on a remote road, it would be unreasonable to expect one not to seek a phone or some other way of escaping one's unfortunate situation. So one ought to at least try to obtain the use of a phone.

But should one break into the home of a perfect stranger living nearby? Or ought one instead to request the use of the phone as a favor? "'Ought' implies 'can'" is surely fully satisfied here. Actual practice makes this quite evident. When someone is suffering from misfortune and there are plenty of others who are not, and the unfortunate person has no other avenue for obtaining help than to obtain it from others, it would not be unreasonable to expect, morally, that the poor seek such help as surely might be forthcoming. We have no justification for assuming that the rich are all callous, though this caricature is regularly painted by communists and by folklore. Supporting and gaining advantage from the institution of private property by no means implies that one lacks the virtue of generosity. The rich are no more immune to virtue than the poor are to vice. The contrary view is probably a legacy of the idea that only those concerned with spiritual or intellectual matters can be trusted to know virtue—those concerned with seeking material prosperity are too base.

The destitute typically have options other than to violate the rights of the well-off. "'Ought' implies 'can'" is satisfiable by the moral imperative that the poor ought to seek help, not loot. There is then no injustice in the rich preventing the poor from seeking such loot by violating the right to private property. "'Ought' implies 'can'" is fully satisfied if the poor can take the kind of action that could gain them the satisfaction of their basic needs, and this action could well be asking for help.

All along here I have been considering only the helplessly poor, who through no fault of their own, nor again through any rights violation by others, are destitute. I am taking the hard cases seriously, where violation of "'ought' implies 'can'" would appear to be most probable. But such cases are by no means typical. They are extremely rare. And even rarer are those cases in which all avenues regarded as legitimate from the libertarian point of view have been exhausted, including appealing for help.

The bulk of poverty in the world is not the result of natural disaster or disease. Rather it is political oppression, whereby people throughout many of the world's countries are not legally permitted to look out for themselves in production and trade. The famines in Africa and India, the poverty in the same countries and in Central and Latin America, as well as in China, the Soviet Union, Poland, Rumania, and so forth, are not the result of lack of charity but of oppression. It is the kind that those who have the protection of even a seriously compromised document and system protecting individual negative human rights, such as the U.S. Constitution, do not experience. The first requirement for men and women to ameliorate their hardship is to be free of other people's oppression, not to be free to take other people's belongings.

Of course, it would be immoral if people failed to help out when this was clearly no sacrifice for them. But charity or generosity is not a categorical imperative, even for the rich. There are more basic moral principles that might require the rich to refuse to be charitable—for example, if they are using most of their wealth for the protection of freedom or a just society. Courage can be more important than charity or benevolence or compassion. But a discussion of the ranking of moral virtues would take us far afield. One reason that many critics of libertarianism find their own cases persuasive is that they think the libertarian can only subscribe to *political* principles or values. But this is mistaken.[17]

There can be emergency cases in which there is no alternative available to disregarding the rights of others. But these are extremely rare, and not at all the sort invoked by critics such as Sterba. I have in mind the desert-island case found in ethics books where instantaneous action, with only one violent alternative, faces persons—the sort we know from the law books in which the issue is one of immediate life and death. These are not cases, to repeat the phrase quoted from Locke by H.L.A. Hart, "where peace is possible." They are discussed in the libertarian literature and considerable progress has been made in integrating them with the concerns of law and politics.

Since we are here discussing law and politics, which are general systematic approaches to how we normally ought to live with one another in human communities, these emergency situations do not help us except as limiting cases. And not surprisingly many famous court cases illustrate just this point as they now and then confront these kinds of instances after they have come to light within the framework of civilized society. . . .

Endnotes

1. Quoted in Harry V. Jaffa, *How to Think about the American Revolution* (Durham, NC: Carolina Academic Press, 1978), p. 41 (from *The Collected Works of Abraham Lincoln* [R. Basler (ed.), 1953], pp. 108–115).

2. See, in particular, James Sterba, "A Libertarian Justification for a Welfare State," *Social Theory and Practice,* vol. 11 (Fall 1985), 285–306 [reprinted in this volume]. I will be referring to this essay as well as a more developed version, titled "The U.S. Constitution: A Fundamentally Flawed Document" in *Philosophical Reflections on the United States Constitution,* edited by Christopher Gray (1989).
3. H.L.A. Hart, "Are There Any Natural Rights?" *Philosophical Review,* vol. 64 (1955), 175.
4. See, for my own discussions, Tibor R. Machan, *Human Rights and Human Liberties* (Chicago: Nelson-Hall, 1975), pp. 213–222; "Prima Facie versus Natural (Human) Rights," *Journal of Value Inquiry,* vol. 10 (1976), 119–131; "Human Rights: Some Points of Clarification," *Journal of Critical Analysis,* vol. 5 (1973), 30–39.
5. Sterba, *op. cit.,* "A Libertarian Justification," p. 295.
6. Ibid.
7. Ayn Rand, "Value and Rights," in J. Hospers (ed.), *Readings in Introductory Philosophical Analysis* (Englewood Cliffs, NJ: Prentice-Hall, 1968), p. 382.
8. Sterba, "The U.S. Constitution: A Fundamentally Flawed Document."
9. John Rawls, *A Theory of Justice* (Cambridge, MA: Harvard University Press, 1971), pp. 101–102. For a discussion of the complexities in the differential attainments of members of various ethnic groups—often invoked as evidence for the injustice of a capitalist system, see Thomas Sowell, *Ethnic America: A History* (New York: Basic Books, 1981). There is pervasive prejudice in welfare-state proponents' writings against crediting people with the ability to extricate themselves from poverty without special political assistance. The idea behind the right to negative liberty is to set people free from others so as to pursue their progressive goals. This is the ultimate teleological justification of Lockean libertarian natural rights. See Tibor R. Machan, *Human Rights and Human Liberties: A Radical Reconsideration of the American Political Tradition* (Chicago: Nelson-Hall, 1975). Consider also this thought from Herbert Spencer:

   > The feeling which vents itself in "poor fellow!" on seeing one in agony, excludes the thought of "bad fellow," which might at another time arise. Naturally, then, if the wretched are unknown or but vaguely known, all the demerits they may have are ignored: and thus it happens that when the miseries of the poor are dilated upon, they are thought of as the miseries of the deserving poor, instead of being thought of as the miseries of undeserving poor, which in large measure they should be. Those whose hardships are set forth in pamphlets and proclaimed in sermons and speeches which echo throughout society, are assumed to be all worthy souls, grievously wronged; and none of them are thought of as bearing the penalties of their own misdeeds. (*Man versus the State* [Caldwell, ID: Caxton Printers, 1940], p. 22)

10. Tibor R. Machan, "Ethics vs. Coercion: Morality of Just Values?" in L.H. Rockwell, Jr. et al., (ed.), *Man, Economy and Liberty: Essays in Honor of Murray N. Rothbard* (Auburn, AL: Ludwig von Mises Institute, 1988), pp. 236–246.
11. John Kekes, "'Ought' Implies 'Can' and Two Kinds of Morality," *The Philosophical Quarterly,* vol. 34 (1984), 459–467.

12. Tibor R. Machan, "Ethics vs. Coercion." In a vegetable garden or even in a forest, there can be good things and bad, but no morally good things and morally evil things (apart from people who might be there).
13. Sterba, "The U.S. Constitution: A Fundamentally Flawed Document."
14. Sterba, "A Libertarian Justification," pp. 295–296.
15. Robert Nozick, *Anarchy, State, and Utopia* (New York: Basic Books, 1974), p. 57. See, also, Tibor R. Machan, "Conditions for Rights, Sphere of Authority," *Journal of Human Relations,* vol. 19 (1971), 184–187, where I argue that "within the context of a legal system where the *sphere of authority* of individuals and groups of individuals cannot be delineated independently of the sphere of authority of the public as a whole, there is an inescapable conflict of rights specified by the same legal system" (186). See, also, Tibor R. Machan, "The Virtue of Freedom in Capitalism," *Journal of Applied Philosophy,* vol. 3 (1986), 49–58, and Douglas J. Den Uyl, "Freedom and Virtue," in Tibor R. Machan (ed.), *The Main Debate: Communism versus Capitalism* (New York: Random House, 1987), pp. 200–216. This last essay is especially pertinent to the understanding of the ethical or moral merits of coercion and coerced conduct. Thus it is argued here that "coercive charity" amounts to an oxymoron.
16. See, Machan, *op. cit.,* "The Virtue of Freedom in Capitalism" and "Private Property and the Decent Society," in J.K. Roth and R.C. Whittemore (eds.), *Ideology and American Experience* (Washington, DC: Washington Institute Press, 1986).
17. E.g., James Fishkin, *Tyranny and Legitimacy* (Baltimore, MD: Johns Hopkins University Press, 1979). Cf., Tibor R. Machan, "Fishkin on Nozick's Absolute Rights," *Journal of Libertarian Studies.* vol. 6 (1982), 317–320.

Journal/Discussion Questions

✍ *Machan and Sterba differ on the question of whether "desperate cases" are usually caused by previous injustices or not. Discuss this issue in terms of your own experience.*

1. What is the difference between negative and positive liberty. Does negative liberty ultimately entail at least some positive liberties?
2. What role does a doctrine of basic human needs play for critics of libertarianism? For libertarians?
3. Why, according to Lockean libertarianism, are property rights fundamental? In what ways do you agree with this claim? Disagree?

Charles Murray
"The Coming White Underclass"

Charles Murray, the author of Losing Ground *and co-author of* The Bell Curve, *is the Bradley Fellow at the American Enterprise Institute.*

In this article, which first appeared in The Wall Street Journal *and was quickly and widely reprinted, Murray argues that the continuing rise in illegitimate birth constitutes a major problem for American society, both black and white. He advocates ending Aid to Families with Dependent Children because it encourages such illegitimacy.*

As You Read, Consider This:

1. Murray draws a distinction between illegitimate children and their parents. What role does this distinction play in his argument?

Every once in a while the sky really is falling, and this seems to be the case with the latest national figures on illegitimacy.

The unadorned statistic is that, in 1991, 1.2 million children were born to unmarried mothers, within a hair of 30 percent of all live births. How high is 30 percent? About four percentage points higher than the black illegitimacy rate in the early 1960s that motivated Daniel Patrick Moynihan to write his famous memorandum on the breakdown of the black family.

The 1991 story for blacks is that illegitimacy has now reached 68 percent of births to black women. In inner cities, the figure is typically in excess of 80 percent. But the black story, however dismaying, is old news. The new trend that threatens the United States is white illegitimacy.

In 1991, 707,502 babies were born to single white women, 22 percent of white births. A few months ago, a Census Bureau study showed that births to single women with college degrees doubled in the last decade to 6 percent from 3 percent. This is an interesting trend, but of minor social importance. The real news is that the proportion of single mothers with less than a high school education jumped to 48 percent from 35 percent in a single decade.

Women with college degrees contribute only 4 percent of white illegitimate babies, while women with high school educations or less contribute 82 percent. Women with family incomes of $75,000 or more contribute 1 percent of white illegitimate babies, while women with family incomes under $20,000 contribute 69 percent.

A Labor Department study that has tracked more than 10,000 youths since 1979 shows an even more dramatic picture. For white women below the poverty line in the year prior to giving birth, 44 percent of births have been illegitimate, compared with only 6 percent for women above the poverty line. White illegitimacy is overwhelmingly a lower-class phenomenon.

This brings us to the emergence of a white underclass. Now the overall white illegitimacy rate is 22 percent. The figure in low-income, working-class communities may be twice that. How much illegitimacy can a community tolerate? Nobody knows, but the historical fact is that the trend lines on black crime, dropout from the labor force and illegitimacy all shifted sharply upward as the overall black illegitimacy rate passed 25 percent.

I blame the revolution in social policy during that period, while others blame the sexual revolution, broad shifts in cultural norms, or structural changes in the economy. But the white illegitimacy rate is approaching that same problematic 25 percent region at a time when social policy is more comprehensively wrongheaded than it was in the mid-1960s, and the cultural and sexual norms are still more degraded.

The white underclass will begin to show its face in isolated ways. Look for certain schools in white neighborhoods to get a reputation as being unteachable, with large numbers of disruptive students and indifferent parents. Talk to the police; listen for stories about white neighborhoods where the incidence of domestic disputes and casual violence has been shooting up. Look for white neighborhoods with high concentrations of drug activity and large numbers of men who have dropped out of the labor force. As the spatial concentration of illegitimacy reaches critical mass, we should expect the deterioration to be as fast among low-income whites in the 1990s as it was among low-income blacks in the 1960s.

My proposition is that illegitimacy is the single most important social problem of our time—more important than crime, drugs, poverty, illiteracy, welfare or homelessness—because it drives everything else. Doing something about it is not just one more item on the American policy agenda, but should be at the top.

The constants are that boys like to sleep with girls and that girls think babies are endearing. Human societies have historically channeled these elemental forces of human behavior via thick walls of rewards and penalties that constrained the overwhelming majority of births to take place within marriage. The past 30 years have seen those walls cave in. It is time to rebuild them.

Bringing a child into the world when one is not emotionally or financially prepared to be a parent is wrong. The child deserves society's support. The parent does not.

To restore the rewards and penalties of marriage does not require social engineering. Rather, it requires that the state stop interfering with the natural forces that have done the job quite effectively for millennia.

I begin with the penalties, of which the most obvious are economic. Throughout human history, a single woman with a small child has not been a viable economic unit. Neither have the single woman and child been a legitimate social unit. In small numbers, they must be a net drain on the community's resources. In large numbers, they must destroy the community's capacity to sustain itself. Communities everywhere have augmented the economic penalties of single parenthood with severe social stigma.

Restoring economic penalties translates into the first and central policy prescription: to end all economic support for single mothers. The Aid to Families with Dependent Children payment goes to zero. Single mothers are not eligible for subsidized housing or for food stamps. An assortment of other subsidies and in-kind benefits disappear. Since universal medical coverage appears to be an idea whose time has come, I will stipulate that all children have medical coverage. But with that exception, the signal is loud and unmistakable: From society's perspective, to have a baby that you cannot care for yourself is profoundly irresponsible, and the government will no longer subsidize it.

How does a poor young mother survive without government support? The same way she has since time immemorial. If she wants to keep a child, she must enlist support from her parents, boyfriend, siblings, neighbors, church or philanthropies. She must get support from somewhere, anywhere, other than the government.

The objectives are threefold.

First, enlisting the support of others raises the probability that other mature adults are going to be involved with the upbringing of the child.

Second, the need to find support forces a self-selection process. One of the most shortsighted excuses made for current behavior is that an adolescent who is utterly unprepared to be a mother "needs someone to love." Childish yearning isn't a good enough selection device. We need to raise the probability that a young single woman who keeps her child is doing so volitionally and thoughtfully. Forcing her to find a way of supporting the child does this. It will lead many young women who shouldn't be mothers to place their babies for adoption. This is good. It will lead others, watching what happens to their sisters, to take steps not to get pregnant.

Third, stigma will regenerate. The pressure on relatives and communities to pay for the folly of their children will make an illegitimate birth the socially horrific act it used to be, and getting a girl pregnant something boys do at the risk of facing a shotgun. Stigma and shotgun marriages may or may not be good for those on the receiving end, but their deterrent effect on others is wonderful and indispensable. What about women who can find no support but keep the baby anyway? There are laws already on the books about the right of the state to take a child from a neglectful parent. Society's main response, however, should be to make it as easy as possible for those mothers to place their children for adoption at infancy.

The first step is to make adoption easy for any married couple who can show reasonable evidence of having the resources and stability to raise a child. Lift all restrictions on interracial adoption. Ease age limitations for adoptive parents.

The second step is to restore the traditional legal principle that placing a child for adoption means irrevocably relinquishing all legal rights to the child. The adoptive parents are parents without qualification. Records are sealed until the child reaches adulthood, at which time they may be unsealed only with the consent of biological child and parent.

Some small proportion of infants and larger proportion of older children will not be adopted. For them, the government should spend lavishly on orphanages. In 1993, we know a lot about how to provide a warm, nurturing environment for children, and getting rid of the welfare system frees up lots of money to do it. Those who prattle about the importance of keeping children with their biological mothers may wish to spend some time in a patrol car or with a social worker seeing what the reality of life with welfare-dependent biological mothers can be like.

One of the few concrete things that the government can do to increase the rewards of marriage is make the tax code favor marriage and children. Those of us who are nervous about using the tax code for social purposes can advocate making the tax code at least neutral.

A more abstract but ultimately crucial step in raising the rewards of marriage is to make marriage once again the sole legal institution through which parental rights and responsibilities are defined and exercised.

Little boys should grow up knowing from their earliest memories that if they want to have any rights whatsoever regarding a child that they sire; more vividly, if they want to grow up to be a daddy they must marry. Little girls should grow up knowing from their earliest memories that if they want to have any legal claims whatsoever on the father of their children, they must marry. A marriage certificate should establish that a man and a woman have entered into a unique legal relationship. The changes in recent years that have blurred the distinctiveness of marriage are subtly but importantly destructive.

Together, these measures add up to a set of signals, some with immediate and tangible consequences, others with long-term consequences. They should be supplemented by others based on a re-examination of divorce law and its consequences.

That these policy changes seem drastic and unrealistic is a peculiarity of our age, not of the policies themselves. With embellishments, I have endorsed the policies that were the uncontroversial law of the land as recently as John Kennedy's presidency. Then, America's elites accepted as a matter of course that a free society such as America's can sustain itself only through virtue and temperance in the people.

Three decades after that consensus disappeared, we face an emerging crisis. The long, steep climb in black illegitimacy has been calamitous for black communities and painful for the nation.

The reforms I have described will work for blacks as for whites, and have been needed for years. But the brutal truth is that American society as a whole could survive when illegitimacy became epidemic within a comparatively small ethnic minority. It cannot survive the same epidemic among whites.

Journal/Discussion Questions

✍ *In your own experience, is illegitimacy common in the United States? Do you think there is anything wrong with it?*

1. "Illegitimacy," Murray maintains, "is the single most important social problem of our time—more important than crime, drugs, poverty, illiteracy, welfare or homelessness—because it drives everything else." What support does he offer for this claim? Do you agree with him? Why or why not?
2. What role should the government have in regard to the issue of illegitimacy?

Concluding Discussion Questions

Where Do You Stand Now?

Instructions

You have already answered the following questions in your moral problems self-quiz at the beginning of this book. Now that you have studied the material in this section, take a moment to answer the same questions again.

	Strongly Agree	Agree	Undecided	Disagree	Strongly Disagree	*Chapter 8: Poverty and Welfare*
36.	❑	❑	❑	❑	❑	People are poor mainly because they do not have the proper ability, training, motivation, or interest in working hard.
37.	❑	❑	❑	❑	❑	Everyone has a right to a minimum income, whether they work or not.
38.	❑	❑	❑	❑	❑	Everyone has a right to a minimum income, if they want to work but cannot find a job.
39.	❑	❑	❑	❑	❑	Society ought to continue welfare support for women with illegitimate children.
40.	❑	❑	❑	❑	❑	Society ought to provide welfare support to elderly people who are no longer able to work.

Compare your answers to the present self-quiz with the answers to the initial self-quiz. How, if at all, have your answers changed? How have the *reasons* for your answers changed?

Journal/Discussion Questions

✍ *Welfare reform remains a controversial issue in the United States today, one which elicits a tremendous amount of emotion. On the level of emotions, what responses do you feel to the welfare debate? What responses do you think other people experience?*

1. Imagine that you have just been hired by a new think-tank called BOBS, the Best of Both Sides. Knowing that you have read the selections in this chapter, they believe that you have an excellent grasp of the issues involved in welfare reform. They

want you to write a policy recommendation on the issue of welfare reform that incorporates the strengths of proposals by both advocates and critics of welfare without the accompanying liabilities—in other words, the best of both sides.

2. To what extent do you think the *government* should play a role in attempting to eliminate poverty? To what extent do *private individuals,* especially comparatively affluent ones, have an obligation to attempt to eliminate (or at least reduce) poverty?

For Further Reading

The Nature of Poverty

William Julius Wilson, *The Truly Disadvantaged* (Chicago: University of Chicago Press, 1988); also see the symposium in *Ethics,* Vol. 101, No. 3 (April 1991), pp. 560–609, devoted to this work, with articles by Jennifer Hochschild, "The Politics of the Estranged Poor," and Bernard Boxill, "Wilson on the Truly Disadvantaged," and the response by Wilson.

Poverty and Welfare

Among recent works on poverty and welfare in the United States, see Phoebe H. Cottingham and David T. Ellwood, eds., *Welfare Policy for the 1990s* (Cambridge, MA: Harvard University Press, 1989); William P. O'Hare, *Real Life Poverty in America: Where the American Public Would Set the Poverty Line* (Washington, DC: Center on Budget and Policy Priorities, 1990); Joel F. Handler and Yeheskel Hasenfield, *The Moral Construction of Poverty: Welfare Reform in America* (Newbury Park, CA: Sage, 1991); Christopher Jencks and Paul E. Peterson, *The Urban Underclass* (Washington: DC: Brookings Institution, 1991); Marvin Olasky, *The Tragedy of American Compassion* (Washington, DC: Regnery Gateway, 1992); and, for a conservative review of how the issue of single mothers with dependent children was handled in the nineteenth century, also see Olasky's "History's Solutions: Problems of Single Mother and Child Poverty," *National Review,* Vol. 46, No. 2 (February 7, 1994), p. 45 ff.; Jacqueline Jones, *The Dispossessed: America's Underclasses from the Civil War to the Present* (New York: Basic Books, 1992); for a more liberal view of these issues, see Mickey Kaus, *The End of Equality* (New York: Basic Books, 1992); Michael B. Katz, ed., *The "Underclass" Debate* (Princeton: Princeton University Press, 1993); R. Shep Melnick, *Between the Lines: Interpreting Welfare Rights* (Washington, DC: Brookings Institution, 1994). Theresa Funiciello's *Tyranny of Kindness: Dismantling the Welfare System to End Poverty in America* (New York: Atlantic Monthly Press, 1993) argues against the bureaucracy of the welfare system and in favor of a guaranteed minimal income. William J. Bennett and Peter Wehner, "Root Causes of Social Ills Lie in Welfare; Public Welfare Reform," *Insight on the News,* Vol. 10; No. 9 (February 28, 1994), p. 32 f.; Robert Rector, "Try the Difference Values Can Make; How Public Welfare Assistance Has Contributed to the Demise of Social, Moral, and Family Values," *Insight on the News,* Vol. 9, No. 50 (December 13, 1993), p. 22 ff.; for a good overview of the various—primarily conservative—participants in the welfare discussion and their ideas, see Tom Bethell, "They Had a Dream; the Challenge of Welfare Reform," *National Review,* Vol. 45; No. 16 (August 23, 1993), p. 31 ff.

Narrative Accounts

For some extended narrative accounts of poverty, see Irene Glasser, *More Than Bread: Ethnography of a Soup Kitchen* (Tuscaloosa: University of Alabama Press, 1988); Elliot Liebow, *Tell*

Them Who I Am: The Lives of Homeless Women (New York: Free Press, 1993); Valeria Polakow, *Lives on the Edge: Single Mothers and Their Children in the Other America* (Chicago: University of Chicago Press, 1993); Robert D. Bullard, ed., *Confronting Environmental Racism: Voices from the Grassroots* (Boston: South End Press, 1993). For some narrative accounts in newspapers, see Jeanie Russell Kasindorf, "Are They the Problem? Welfare Mothers; Interview," *New York Magazine,* Vol. 28; No. 6 (February 6, 1995), p. 28 ff.; Barbara Vobejda, "Welfare an Afterthought, Teen Mothers Say," *The Washington Post,* (February 14, 1995), A Section; p. A 01 ff.; Isabel Wilkerson, "An Intimate Look at Welfare: Women Who've Been There," *The New York Times* (February 17, 1995), Section A, p. 1 ff.; and "Benefits and Doubts," *The Washington Post* (February 26, 1995), Magazine, p. W12 ff. For a good overview of some of the social issues and the available data, see David Whitman, Dorian Friedman, Mike Tharp, and Kate Griffin, "Welfare: The Myth of Reform," *U.S. News & World Report,* Vol. 118, No. 2 (January 16, 1995), p. 30 ff., and the accompanying editorial, Mortimer B. Zuckerman, "Fixing the Welfare Mess," *U.S. News & World Report,* Vol. 118; No. 2 (January 16, 1995), p. 68 ff.

Women and Poverty

The issue of poverty has a special impact on women. For some narrative accounts, see the Lievow and Polakow volumes cited above. Among the excellent recent studies of this issue are Paul E. Zoph, Jr., *American Women in Poverty* (Westport, CT: Greenwood Press, 1989); Lourdes Beneria and Shelley Feldman, eds., *Unequal Burden: Economic Crises, Persistent Poverty, and Women's Work* (Boulder, CO: Westview Press, 1992); Pamela D. Couture, *Blessed Are the Poor? Women's Poverty, Family Policy, and Practical Theology* (Nashville: Abingdon Press, 1991); Harrell R. Rodgers, Jr., *Poor Women, Poor Families: Single Mothers and Their Children in the Other America* (Chicago: University of Chicago Press, 1993).

Race and Poverty

For contrasting views of *Latinos and poverty* in the United States, see Linda Chavez, *Out of the Barrio: Toward New Politics of Hispanic Assimilation* (New York: Basic Books, 1991) and Rebecca Morales and Frank Bonilla, eds., *Latinos in a Changing U.S. Economy: Comparative Perspectives on Growing Inequality* (Newbury Park: Sage, 1993).

Among the works on *African-Americans and poverty* (in addition to those already cited), see Laurence E. Lynn, Jr., and Michael G.H. McGeary, eds., *Inner-City Poverty in the United States* (Washington, DC: National Academy Press, 1990); Nicholas Lemann, *The Promised Land: The Great Black Migration and How It Changed America* (New York: Knopf, 1991); Gary Orfield and Carol Ashkinaze, The Closing Door: Conservative Policy and Black Opportunity (Chicago: University of Chicago Press, 1991); Christopher Jencks, *Rethinking Social Policy: Race, Poverty, and the Underclass* (Cambridge: Harvard University Press, 1992); Andrew Hacker, *Two Nations: Black and White, Separate, Hostile, Unequal* (New York: Scribner's, 1992); James Jennings, ed., *Race, Politics, and Economic Development: Community Perspectives* (New York: Verso, 1992); Douglas S. Massey and Nancy A. Denton, *American Apartheid: Segregation and the Making of the Underclass* (Cambridge: Harvard University Press, 1993).

Distributive Justice

One of the central moral issues raised in this chapter has been the nature of distributive justice. Among the excellent anthologies in this area, see John Arthur and William Shaw, eds., *Justice and Economic Distribution* (Englewood Cliffs, NJ: Prentice-Hall, 1978) and Virginia Held, ed., *Property, Profits, and Economic Justice* (Belmont, CA: Wadsworth, 1980). For a collection of libertarian pieces on this issue, see Tibor Machan, ed., *The Libertarian Alternative: Essays in Social and Political Philosophy* (Chicago: Nelson-Hall Co., 1977).

For a strong statement of the *liberal conception of justice,* see John Rawls, *A Theory of Justice* (Cambridge: Harvard, 1974) and, more recently, *Political Liberalism* (New York: Columbia, 1993); also see Brian Barry's *Theories of Justice* (Berkeley: University of California Press, 1989). For a strongly contrasting *libertarian conception of justice,* see: Robert Nozick's *Anarchy, State, and Utopia* (New York: Basic Books, 1974); the work of F.A. Hayek, especially *The Mirage of Social Justice,* which is volume 2 of his *Law, Legislation, and Liberty* (Chicago: University of Chicago Press, 1976); and Tibor Machan's *Individuals and Their Rights* (LaSalle, IL: Open Court, 1989). For an excellent attempt to *reconcile these and other widely divergent views of justice,* see James P. Sterba, *How to Make People Just: A Practical Reconciliation of Alternative Concepts of Justice* (Totowa, NJ: Rowman and Littlefield, 1988); for his most recent reply to Machan and others, see James P. Sterba, "From Liberty to Welfare," *Ethics,* 105, 1 (October 1994), pp. 64–98. For an excellent short survey of distributive conceptions of justice, see Allen Buchanan, "Justice, Distributive," in *Encyclopedia of Ethics,* edited by Lawrence C. Becker and Charlotte B. Becker (New York: Garland, 1992), Vol. I, pp. 655–661.

P A R T   T H R E E

Expanding the Circle

In the final section of this book, we turn to a consideration of the scope of our moral duties. Although both classical deontological and utilitarian thought seem in principle largely neutral in regard to things such as national borders, in fact the boundaries of our nation often mark the boundaries of our moral obligation for many people. Egoistic theories seem to make the boundaries of our obligation much narrower yet.

In Part Three, we are asking the question of how far beyond our border our obligations extend. Chapter 9 deals with issues of world hunger, and whether we have obligations to impoverished nations often far distant from our own. Chapter 10 asks whether our obligations extend yet further, to include nonhuman animals, the sentient world as a whole. Chapter 11 pursues the question of our obligations to the earth itself and the environment on which we constantly depend.

The following diagram illustrates the various ways of expanding the circle of morality that philosophers have proposed:

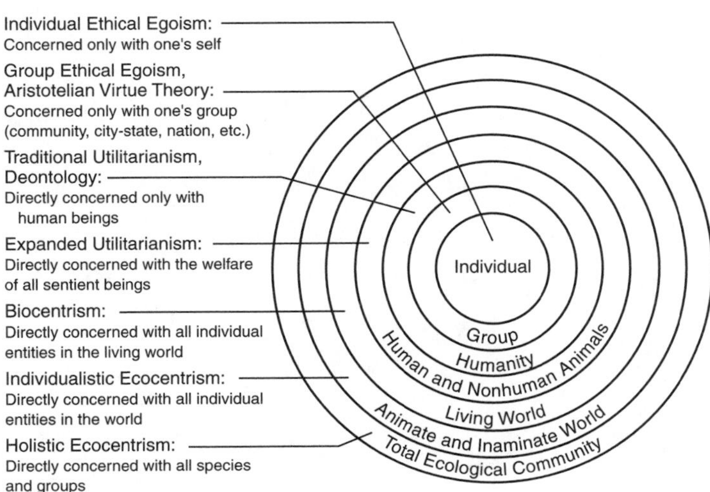

Individual Ethical Egoism:
Concerned only with one's self
Group Ethical Egoism,
Aristotelian Virtue Theory:
Concerned only with one's group
(community, city-state, nation, etc.)
Traditional Utilitarianism,
Deontology:
Directly concerned only with
human beings
Expanded Utilitarianism:
Directly concerned with the welfare
of all sentient beings
Biocentrism:
Directly concerned with all individual
entities in the living world
Individualistic Ecocentrism:
Directly concerned with all individual
entities in the world
Holistic Ecocentrism:
Directly concerned with all species
and groups
Individual
Group
Humanity
Human and Nonhuman Animals
Living World
Animate and Inaminate World
Total Ecological Community

As you consider each of the topics in the next three chapters, try to situate yourself within this map and see where you think the boundaries of our moral obligation should be drawn.

CHAPTER 9

World Hunger and Poverty

Videotape:

Topic: Millions of People at Risk of Starving in the Sudan
ABCNEWS *Source:* ABC *Nightline* (August 12, 1998)
Anchors: Dave Marash, Ted Koppel

Narrative Account

Lawrence B. Salander
"The Hunger"

The author is president of Salander-O'Reilly Galleries in New York. He is also a painter with many solo and group exhibitions to his credit. He lives in New York.

In this article, Salander describes his experiences accompanying a CARE relief team to a famine-ridden town west of Mogadishu.

Baidoa is a provincial town approximately 120 miles west of Mogadishu. The pre-famine population of this godforsaken place is anyone's guess. I've read figures that range from 40,000 to 60,000. There are more people than that here now. The place is teeming with refugees who have made their way here because they have heard that it is better. Better than what?

You don't see many young children in Baidoa, because most of them are dead. One report commissioned by the United Nations estimates that 71 percent of the children of Baidoa under 5 years old have died. The accuracy of the figure is debatable, but whatever the true number, it is clearly horrific. And it's not as though these kids are dying from anything exotic. The two biggest killers are diarrhea and the measles. The medicine and food they need sits in storage in Mogadishu.

Rancid, disease-carrying water. Life in a six-foot-square grass-covered hut, home to eight people. Mothers and fathers driven mad by the hopelessness of their situation, watching their children die. Many of them seem to refuse to believe it, and carry on as if everything were normal. Human feces are everywhere, and swarms of flies surround the children not yet sick enough to be out of pain, their hair turned orange by malnutrition before falling out in clumps. Many have silver-dollar-size oozing sores caused by a lice-like animal that bores through their skin to the bone. These children with their distended stomachs, half-naked and filthy. Each one coughing a death cough.

I traveled here under the auspices of CARE. With machine-gun fire as background music, one of the organization's employees, Mary Jane Hammond, who for the last several months has been a resident of Baidoa, began what seemed to be a daily exercise with these kids. Surrounded by thirty or forty of them, she started to count to ten, out loud in English. The children picked up the count. When they reached ten they all gave themselves a round of applause, and then all of them broke into the most wonderful smiles—made larger, it seemed, by their emaciated faces. The few optimistic moments in Baidoa clearly defined the almost unbearable misery. Death was not the worst of it.

I went to the "hospital" to visit the dying. As terrible as it was, it was almost a relief to see these kids out of pain. It's their parents who need our compassion. Two dark and damp ten-by-twenty-foot adjoining rooms serve as the "pediatric ward." Each room contains seven or eight beds—wooden platforms that two children often share. One mother pointed out her dying infant, who was too small to see at first. She searched my eyes for the hope I could not give her. A father took my arm and led me to the bed where his 5-year-old boy lay moments from death. He pulled back the cover to show me the boy's dissipated body, and then took my hand and placed it on what was left of his son's stomach.

We climbed back into our Jeep-like vehicle, with a crew of "security men" hired for the day by CARE. A 15-year-old manned the machine gun on the roof while two other riflemen rode shotgun. The driver was the boss, the oldest and the biggest. They were high from chewing khat all day. The next stop was the airstrip, and the man was in a hurry to get there. Moving targets must be harder to hit. The dust was flying as people scattered to avoid us. A young boy made a run for it, to join his friends across the street. The driver hit the brakes, and the kid froze. We missed him by inches.

This thug, the driver, got out of the car with a bamboo stick and chased the boy down. He hit him twice. I turned away in rage and disgust. But then I realized that this single, barbaric act was the most hopeful thing I'd seen all day. This guy was beating the child to teach him to be more careful. And that implies a belief in tomorrow, which in Baidoa is no small thing.

Journal/Discussion Questions

✍ *Have you had any direct experience with relief efforts in counties with famines? If so, discuss those experiences in light of Salander's description of his own.*

1. Why did Salander describe the beating on the child as "hopeful"? Discuss your reactions to this description.

An Introduction to the Moral Issues

The Problem

We cannot help but be struck by the vast differences in standards of living between the United States (and other comparable industrialized nations) and developing countries. We have only to turn on the evening news to see clips of famine and starvation, natural disasters, and other political turmoil throughout the world. We may believe the political disagreements are best resolved among the disputants themselves. The natural disasters are transitory, but perhaps more evenly distributed among all the countries of the world. The hunger and starvation, however, are more disturbing, especially when we look around at our own affluence as a nation.

Should we help other nations, especially those in great poverty whose population is starving? Let's look more closely at these issues, beginning with the arguments in favor of helping other countries that are impoverished and whose population is starving.

The Case for Helping Other Countries

There are a number of strong reasons for helping countries that are impoverished and starving. The first of these centers on our character, and in particular on the virtue of compassion. Others center on consequences, rights, and the duty to beneficence.

The Argument from Virtue

How can we ignore the terrible suffering of starving nations?

The moral force of suffering. The mere sight of the deep suffering associated with poverty and starvation has a moral force all its own: It touches the deepest roots of human compassion to see such suffering. Anyone who possesses the virtue of compassion cannot help but respond to such suffering. To turn our backs in the face of such human misery would be cold-hearted indeed. Such a response would not only fail to relieve the suffering of others, but it would also diminish us, revealing a disturbing moral indifference. A virtuous person *must* respond to such suffering.

The issue of luck. Our moral disquiet about this poverty and hunger is intensified by the fact that we know we as individuals do not deserve this affluence any more or less than those in famine-ridden countries deserve their destitution and hunger. This is not to deny that we work hard. But if we had been born in Rwanda or Somalia, we could be working just as hard and starving to death.

The overall affluence of our society is not something we have because of our merit; it is largely a matter of luck.

The place of the children. The children have a special place in all of this, but if there are any innocents left in the world, it is the children. Whatever we may say about the political and economic leaders of a country, we cannot help but feel that the children deserve better. In a sea of suffering, their suffering stands out as having a special and undeniable moral force. It pulls us out of our moral complacency and demands a response from us.

Are we under a greater obligation to the starving when they are children?

The statistics. When we begin to look at the statistics, we realize that our impressionistic view of global inequalities and suffering is born out by the facts. The United States possesses a startling share of the world's wealth, consumes a highly disproportionate amount of its resources, and even produces an excessive percentage of its waste.

The Issue of Complicity

We don't deserve to be born into an affluent society any more than we deserve to be born into an impoverished one. It is simply a matter of luck. But is it purely a matter of luck that some societies are rich and others are poor? Here the issue becomes more complex. The argument, put forth by many, is that the affluence of countries like the United States is built in part on the impoverishment of developing nations. The natural resources and labor of such nations are often exploited by major industrial nations in ways that are profoundly destructive to the social, economic, and political well-being of developing nations.

If this is the case, then the poverty and starvation of developing nations has an added moral force: we, the affluent, may be partly responsible for it. If this is the case, then we would seem to have some added duty to help relieve that suffering. We can understand the difference in terms of an analogy. Consider the different obligations in the following two situations. First, we see the victim of an automobile accident on the side of the road as we are driving by. Presumably we have some, although perhaps not always overriding, obligation to stop and try to help. Second, we cause an automobile accident that injures someone else. Presumably in this situation, we have a much greater obligation to render assistance, for we are responsible for the accident in the first place. The situation would seem to be similar with world poverty and starvation. If we are partly responsible for causing it, then we have a greater obligation to do something about it.

The complicity argument would seem to be most effective in creating obligations on the country-to-country level rather than the individual-to-individual level. For example, if the United States has systematically exploited Rouratania, then it seems that the United States has an obligation (all other things being equal) to Rouratania to make up for the harm that it has caused. It is less clear that individual citizens of the United States, some of whom might not have even agreed to the exploitive policies if they had been asked, would be obligated to the individual citizens of Rouratania. Moreover, even the country-to-country level has difficulties, since in many cases we are dealing with exploitation by corporations rather than by governments directly.

The Group Egoist Argument

The compassionate response demands that we set aside self-interest and respond directly to relieve the suffering of others, even when we must make sacrifices to do so. This is a morally demanding response, and some have argued that we may not always be able or willing to respond so selflessly. Some in this tradition have argued that there are still good, self-centered moral reasons for trying to relieve the suffering of other countries.

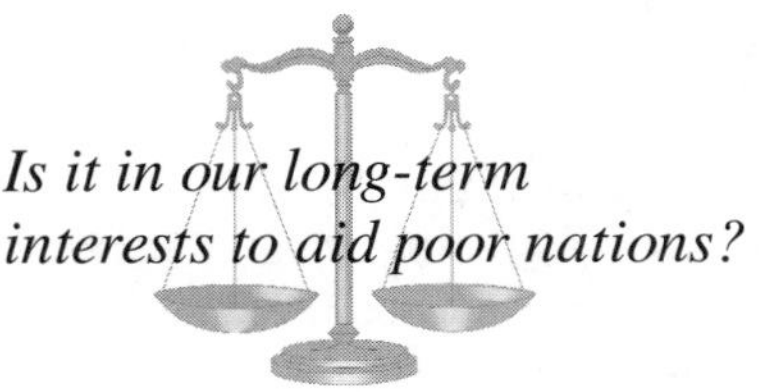

Is it in our long-term interests to aid poor nations?

The basic *moral premise* of this argument is what we may call group egoism, the belief that we ought to act in ways that further the interests of our group. In this case, we can take our group as being equivalent to the nation. The claim here is that it is in our best interests as a nation to help other, less affluent nations, even if there is a short-term cost to ourselves.

This moral premise must then be followed by an *empirical premise* stating that helping impoverished and starving countries contributes to our national welfare in the long run. Often such a premise is economic in character, and seems to be most plausible when discussing either a neighboring country or a country in a region where we have important economic interests. In both types of cases, our economic well-being is closely tied with the economic well-being of those other countries. If they fall upon hard times, we will also suffer. Thus, their prosperity is directly tied to ours.

Critics of this argument often attack the empirical premise in several ways. First, it is extremely difficult to prove such connections between countries conclusively, simply because of the complexity of the economic interactions and the fallibility of our predictive powers in this area. Second, some would argue that, far from benefiting from the well-being of other nations, we often benefit much more from their exploitability. Many actions intended to enhance another country's well-being might diminish its exploitability. Finally, critics point out that this argument, even if sound, really only obligates us to assist those countries in our direct economic sphere. We would seemingly be under no obligation to countries with which we have little economic contract.

The Strict Utilitarian Argument

Utilitarianism, as we have said before, is a very demanding moral doctrine, for it asserts (1) that we should give our own happiness and pain no special weight, and (2) that we should always do what produces the *greatest* overall amount of utility. When we combine these principles, we begin to get a strong argument that morally requires rich nations to reduce the gap between themselves and poor nations until they are relatively equal. Once one accepts the strongly impartialist premise that anyone else's suffering counts just as much as your own in the moral calculus, then it is a comparatively short step to concluding that we should reduce everyone else's suffering to the same level as our own.

In order to take this short step to such a conclusion, however, one more premise is necessary, a premise about the moral difference between action and inaction. Critics of the argument outlined in the previous paragraph could maintain that, while we are obliged to *refrain* from actively doing anything to increase or perpetuate the suffering of those in impoverished countries, that alone does not entail that we are obliged to actively *do* something to reduce their suffering. In *"Rich and Poor,"*

Peter Singer supplies just such a premise, arguing that it is morally just as bad to let someone die (when you could save them without great cost to yourself) as to actively kill them.

Needless to say, this argument has many critics. Many simply reject utilitarianism as a whole, not just this particular application of it. Others try to retard the movement from a negative obligation to avoid harming others to a positive obligation to assist them. Some maintain that relief efforts do not in fact have the consequences that utilitarians intend them to have. Yet even if these objections could be met, there seems to be another, even more formidable problem about moral motivation. What would motivate the affluent to radically diminish their own lifestyles in order to help the poor and the hungry? Even more specifically, what would motivate the affluent to radically diminish the lifestyles of those they love in order to help complete strangers in distant lands? We shall return to this issue below in our discussion of moral particularity.

The Basic Rights Argument

Some authors, including Henry Shue in *Basic Rights,* have argued that everyone has a right to minimal subsistence, and that this is a positive right. Recall the difference between a negative right and a positive one. If I have a negative right, that simply prohibits others from interfering with me in the exercise of that right. A negative right to free speech prevents others from silencing me, but it does not require them to give me a microphone, even if they have an extra one. A positive right, in contrast, obligates other people to assist me in the exercise of my right. If I have a positive right to free speech, others (usually the state) must provide me with the opportunity and means for exercising that right. The right to subsistence, Shue argues, is a positive right that obligates others (particularly those with an overabundance of food) to assist me in continuing to subsist.

Do all people have a right to basic subsistence?

The Kantian Imperfect Duty Argument

In his discussion of moral duties, Immanuel Kant distinguished between two types of duties. *Perfect duties* are those that require specific actions and that must be met all the time. The duty to tell the truth, for example, is a perfect duty. We must always tell the truth. *Imperfect duties,* in contrast, require that we perform some among a group of actions but do not mandate each and every action. The duty to benevolence is an imperfect duty. We are morally required, Kant says, to perform acts of benevolence toward those in need, but this does not mean that we are required to act benevolently toward each and every person in need and on each and every occasion of such need. We are morally obligated to act benevolently, but we have a considerable amount of moral freedom to decide about the particular occasions of such benevolence.

One of the strengths of Kant's position is that it allows us to find a middle ground between those who maintain that we have no duties to other countries and those who claim that we have seemingly overwhelming obligations to them. We have a duty to some benevolence, but we do not have a duty to reduce our standard of living to the point of equality with the poor of the world. In this respect, Kant's position seems to correspond with the moral intuitions of many people today.

The Case against Helping Other Countries

Several different types of arguments have been advanced against claims that we should provide aid to impoverished and starving peoples.

The Lifeboat Argument

In one of the most controversial articles ever written on this subject, Garrett Hardin in "Lifeboat Ethics" argues that we have a duty *not* to help the poor and starving of other countries. This is a strong and startling claim. Hardin is not simply saying that it was acceptable not to aid the poor—he was saying that it was *wrong* to help them.

The lifeboat metaphor. Hardin suggests that rich nations are like lifeboats, and swimming around them are the poor of the world, who are clambering to get into the lifeboat. If we let them into the lifeboat—that is, if we provide aid or permit immigration in significant degrees—then we will surely swamp the lifeboat and everyone, not just the poor already in the water, will be adrift. The answer—at least from the standpoint of those in the lifeboat—is not to take as many people in as possible until it is on the verge of sinking, but rather to preserve the integrity and long-term survivability of the boat itself. Hardin admits that it is purely a matter of luck that one is born in the lifeboat rather than in the water, but he does not see this as changing his position. Those who really feel it is unfair can give up their places in the lifeboat to people in the water.

Evaluating the metaphor. This has proved to be a powerful metaphor, but certainly not one without its misleading aspects. First, it presupposes that rich nations are like boats, and that the poor of the world are like individuals floundering in the water. This metaphor would seem to fit best when describing the relationship between a wealthy nation and a poor one whose government had collapsed. In most cases, however, the more accurate metaphor—if one wants to stay within this nautical range—would be numerous ships on the sea, some more seaworthy than others and some with a better store of provisions than other. (Other countries generally do not want to get into our boat; they simply do not want their own boat to sink.) Yet even this is misleading, since the notion of a "store of provisions" is a static one that fails to do justice to the dynamic ways in which food can be *produced* in countries. Second, this metaphor presupposes that the continuing existence and ultimate fate of those in the lifeboat is independent of the lives of those in the water. Yet this hardly seems to be the case. Countries are in constant and complex interactions with one another, interactions not captured by this metaphor. Certainly rich nations historically have exploited poor nations. Here the more adequate metaphor might be people swimming in the water after we have helped to sink their boat. Moreover, the continued existence of wealthy nations may well depend—in terms of politics and markets as well as labor and resources—on continuing interactions with poor nations. One philosopher, Onora O'Neill, has suggested that the more appropriate metaphor would be that *the earth* is a lifeboat.

Immigration. Relief programs, Hardin points out, bring food to the starving; open immigration policies make it possible to bring people to the food. Hardin is equally opposed to open immigration policies, and for the same reason: such policies threaten to swamp the lifeboat.

The Effectiveness Argument

Is economic aid to poor countries really effective in the long run?

Arguments that wealthy nations are obligated to aid poor nations contain not only a moral premise about obligation but also an implicit pragmatic premise that such aid can be effective. Some critics of aid have maintained that this issue can be settled on pragmatic grounds: aid, they argue, just doesn't *work*. And since it doesn't, we are under no moral obligation to do it. Here are some of the arguments they have advanced along these lines.

Administration. Bureaucracies tend to perpetuate themselves, and often—in order to continue to exist—they need to perpetuate the problems they were originally created to eliminate. Overhead is tremendously high is many such relief efforts, both governmental and private. For these reasons, many have argued that relief efforts are inevitably about supporting relief agencies rather than eradicating hunger.

Local economy. Some critics of relief projects to help the impoverished and the hungry in developing countries have argued that such assistance has significant negative consequences. A sudden influx of food from relief agencies into a local economy can, for example, depress the prices of existing crops, resulting in farmers' being unable to sell their crops at a profit. This, in turn, can mean that they will not have the money to buy seed for the next planting, and that will mean that they will soon be destitute and the country will find that the problem of starvation is even more severe next season.

Dependency. It is easy to see, from the preceding paragraph, the way in which well-intentioned aid could inadvertently create dependency among the recipients. Critics of aid programs often espouse a kind of social Darwinism, claiming that we should avoid aid simply because it reduces people's ability to survive and promotes the survival of the weakest instead of the strongest.

Futility. Moreover, some critics of aid advocate ceasing all aid right now because *eventually* it will prove futile. Aid, they argue, postpones problems but never ultimately solves them. Thus it might be possible, through massive relief efforts, to save the lives of 100,000 starving people this year, but that simply means that a decade from now we will be faced with the *impossible* task of saving 500,000 lives. Since that it impossible, what is the point—such critics ask—of saving some lives now? It only means that more will perish later. Given the ultimate futility of such relief efforts, these critics maintain that we should cease them now.

The local corruption. Finally, some critics have pointed out that in some cases hunger is as much the result of political disagreements as of anything else. Indeed, in some cases starvation is used as a weapon for subjugating either opposing nations or groups within one's own nation. Similarly, food relief efforts are often hampered by local political opposition to the relief. In cases such as these, critics often conclude that those involved should be left to settle their own problems.

The Libertarian Argument

Some claim that we have only negative rights and thus only negative duties. Libertarianism is the clearest political expression of this doctrine, and the work of Ayn Rand is the most popular literary expression of it. For a libertarian, the right to life is purely a negative one. No one is entitled to take my life away from me, but certainly no one is obligated to support my existence. Each person is solely responsible for his or her own existence, and society as a whole owes me nothing positive.

Furthermore, many in this tradition hold the right to property to be practically as strong as the right to life. This has important implications for any analysis of the unequal distribution of wealth. The libertarians maintain that the government has very few, if any, rights to deprive individuals of their property. (Many, for this reason, are strongly opposed to most taxes.) Thus libertarians see this issue as a conflict between an extremely weak or nonexistent claim (the right of the poor to aid) against a very strong claim (the right of individuals to acquire and retain their own property). For them, the choice is easy.

Critics of this position usually challenged the very foundations of ethical egoism. They maintain that it is simply moral callousness dressed up as moral theory. The moral life, they maintain, is not about selfishness, but about overcoming selfishness. Ethical egoism, they maintain, simply makes a virtue of what all other moral standpoints consider to be a vice.

The Particularity Argument

Special moral obligation to take care of our own. As we indicated above, there is something suspicious about a moral theory that requires us to care so much about strangers that we diminish the quality of life for those nearest and dearest to us. Consider this in relation to children. I love my daughter dearly, and I work hard to try to insure that she has the opportunities for a good life. If I am a utilitarian, am I obligated to give up money I would spend on my daughter to relieve the (admittedly, quite worse) suffering of complete strangers on the other side of the globe?

To raise this question is to call into doubt one of the most fundamental premises of most ethical theories: impartiality. Both Kantians and utilitarians would agree that the moral point of view is one of strict impartiality. I should not give more weight to the suffering of those I love than I do to the suffering of strangers. Yet in recent years this premise has come under increasing challenge, and some have argued that particularity may have more positive significance in the moral life than previously thought. In fact, some in this tradition would argue that there is something morally alienating about individuals who do not put the interests of those they love above the interests of strangers. This continues to be a point of great controversy among philosophers.

The efficiency argument. Seeking a compromise between the impartialists and the particularists, some have argued that we can retain both. Impartiality, they agree, is the hallmark of the moral point of view. However, even while we admit that everyone's interests count equally in principle, it may be more *efficient* for us to allow individuals to protect the interests of those they care about. This moral division of labor would allow us to care for those we care about, and yet not completely surrender the notion that everyone's suffering has an equal moral weight. The difficulty with such an argument, of course, is that it presumes that everyone has people who care about them and who are able to do so effectively. Unfortunately, this is far from true.

Epistemological considerations. There is a final dimension to the case for particularity. Some have argued that we know best what's good for our own citizens, other countries know best what's good for their own citizens. Here the claim is that we should "take care of our own" because we know best what they need and want in order to feel taken care of. Thus this is primarily an epistemological consideration, that is, a concern about what we can *know* about ourselves and other people.

The obvious reply to this argument is that, if people are starving to death, it is not difficult to know what they need. It is easy to see that people need water, food, medicine, and the like. Yet even here the matter proves to be more subtle, for that response is a very Western one, the response of a technocrat. To be sure, people may need these things, but those needs may be part of a larger, more complex set of physical, psychological, and spiritual needs that escape the notice of relief officials.

The Liberal State Argument

The final argument that has been advanced against claims of obligations to impoverished and starving nations could be considered a political version of the particularity argument or a type of group egoism argument. The argument is a simple one. The liberal state can only function well—that is, provide the services to its citizens that it promises—if it rests on a solid economic foundation. If that foundation is threatened either through massive foreign aid or through massive immigration, then the state may no longer be able to provide any of its members with the traditional benefits of a liberal state. Education, defense, health care, construction and maintenance of infrastructure—all of these things would be drastically reduced if the liberal state were suddenly paying out huge sums for foreign aid or trying to meet the needs of a vast influx of immigrants.

Once again, this is an argument that contains both empirical and normative claims. On the empirical side is a claim that the minimal economic foundation of the liberal state will be eroded through massive aid or immigration. Social scientists and economists must determine whether this is true. The normative claim is less explicit, but it must be something to the effect that the continued existence of the liberal state is morally worth the suffering and death that could be averted in starving nations through massive aid. This is a much more difficult claim to support. Although it is presumably true that the continued existence of the liberal state is valuable to those who live in it, it is far from clear that it is of value to everyone, especially those who will die.

Diversity and Consensus

Short-Term Relief

Many of the issues surrounding relief, both short-term and long-term, are empirical issues concerning effectiveness. As we have already seen in our earlier discussion of efficiency, critics of even short-term relief often express their greatest doubts about the *efficacy* of such relief. One of the principal challenges to supporters of such aid is to show that such aid does more good than harm in the long run.

Despite these criticisms, the moral bottom line about short-term relief centers around the issue of compassion. How can we, in the face of such suffering and in the midst of our relative affluence, turn away in indifference? To fail to respond seems inhumane. The moral challenge is to discern how to respond wisely and effectively.

Long-Term Assistance

Assistance programs are generally oriented toward helping recipient countries to become self-sustaining, rather than at establishing a long-term relationship of aid and dependency. How we can do this with skill and efficiency is an extremely complex question, but one that must be answered. In the process of answering it, we must also deal with questions about exploitation, population control, human rights, and respect for diverse cultural traditions. Moreover, we must figure out a way of determining how far we should go in offering assistance and support. The two extremes—Hardin, who advocates not helping at all, and Singer, who says we should help to the point of relative equality—leave a vast middle ground. Presumably the truth is somewhere in the middle here.

A Common World

What kind of world do we envision for our future? Is it a world of vast inequities, the superfluously rich and the starving poor? Or is it a world in which all human beings have the minimal conditions of a good life? And if it is the latter type of world that we hope for, then we must ask ourselves how we shall achieve it.

THE ARGUMENTS

Garrett Hardin
"Lifeboat Ethics: The Case against Helping the Poor"

Garrett Hardin is professor emeritus of biology at the University of California, Santa Barbara. A collection of his essays, Naked Emperors, *appeared in 1983.*

This is one of the most controversial articles published about the problem of world hunger, for in it Hardin argues that rich nations should not try to help poor, starving ones. Rich nations, Hardin suggests, are like lifeboats, sailing in a sea amidst drowning poor people who want to get into their boats. If the poor get in the boats, they will only sink them and everyone will perish.

As You Read, Consider This:

1. Much of what Hardin says depends on acceptance of the lifeboat metaphor. What are the strengths of this metaphor? In what ways is it misleading? In what ways is it different from the spaceship metaphor?
2. What does Hardin mean by "the tragedy of the commons"? What support is there for his claim that those who own property will care for it responsibly? What evidence is there against that claim?

Environmentalists use the metaphor of the earth as a "spaceship" in trying to persuade countries, industries and people to stop wasting and polluting our natural resources. Since we all share life on this planet, they argue, no single person or institution has the right to destroy, waste, or use more than a fair share of its resources.

But does everyone on earth have an equal right to an equal share of its resources? The spaceship metaphor can be dangerous when used by misguided idealists to justify suicidal policies for sharing our resources through uncontrolled immigration and foreign aid. In their enthusiastic but unrealistic generosity, they confuse the ethics of a spaceship with those of a lifeboat.

A true spaceship would have to be under the control of a captain, since no ship could possibly survive if its course were determined by committee. Spaceship Earth certainly has no captain; the United Nations is merely a toothless tiger, with little power to enforce any policy upon its bickering members.

If we divide the world crudely into rich nations and poor nations, two thirds of them are desperately poor, and only one third comparatively rich, with the United States the wealthiest of all. Metaphorically each rich nation can be seen as a lifeboat full of comparatively rich people. In the ocean outside each lifeboat swim the poor of the world, who would like to get in, or at least to share some of the wealth. What should the lifeboat passengers do?

First, we must recognize the limited capacity of any lifeboat. For example, a nation's land has a limited capacity to support a population and as the current energy crisis has shown us, in some ways we have already exceeded the carrying capacity of our land.

Adrift in a Moral Sea

So here we sit, say fifty people in our lifeboat. To be generous, let us assume it has room for ten more, making a total capacity of sixty. Suppose the fifty of us in the lifeboat see 100 others swimming in the water outside, begging for admission to our boat or for handouts. We have several options: we may be tempted to try to live by the Christian ideal of being "our brother's keeper," or by the Marxist ideal of "to each according to his needs." Since the needs of all in the water are the same, and since they can all be seen as "our brothers," we could take them all into our boat, making a total of 150 in a boat designed for sixty. The boat swamps, everyone drowns. Complete justice, complete catastrophe.

Since the boat has an unused excess capacity of ten more passengers, we could admit just ten more to it. But which ten do we let in? How do we choose? Do we pick the best ten, the neediest ten, "first come, first served"? And what do we say to the ninety we exclude? If we do let an extra ten into our lifeboat, we will have lost our "safety factor," an engineering principle of critical importance. For example, if we don't leave room for excess capacity as a safety factor in our country's agriculture, a new plant disease or a bad change in the weather could have disastrous consequences.

Suppose we decide to preserve our small safety factor and admit no more to the lifeboat. Our survival is then possible, although we shall have to be constantly on guard against boarding parties.

While this last solution clearly offers the only means of our survival, it is morally abhorrent to many people. Some say they feel guilty about their good luck. My reply is simple: "Get out and yield your place to others." This may solve the problem of the guilt-ridden person's conscience, but it does not change the ethics of the lifeboat. The needy person to whom the guilt-ridden person yields his place will not himself feel guilty about his good luck. If he did, he would not climb aboard. The net result of conscience-stricken people giving up their unjustly held seats is the elimination of that sort of conscience from the lifeboat.

This is the basic metaphor within which we must work out our solutions. Let us now enrich the image, step by step, with substantive additions from the real world, a world that must solve real and pressing problems of overpopulation and hunger.

The harsh ethics of the lifeboat become even harsher when we consider the reproductive differences between the rich nations and the poor nations. The people inside the lifeboats are doubling in numbers every eighty-seven years; those swimming around outside are doubling, on the average, every thirty-five years, more than twice as fast as the rich. And since the world's resources are dwindling, the difference in prosperity between the rich and the poor can only increase.

As of 1973, the U.S. had a population of 210 million people, who were increasing by 0.8 percent per year. Outside our lifeboat, let us imagine another 210 million people (say the combined populations of Colombia, Ecuador, Venezuela, Morocco, Pakistan, Thailand and the Philippines), who are increasing at a rate of 3.3 percent per year. Put differently, the doubling time for this aggregate population is twenty-one years, compared to eighty-seven years for the U.S.

Multiplying the Rich and the Poor

Now suppose the U.S. agreed to pool its resources with those seven countries, with everyone receiving an equal share. Initially the ratio of Americans to non-Americans in this model would be one-to-one. But consider what the ratio would be after eighty-seven years, by which time the Americans would have doubled to a population of 420 million. By then, doubling every twenty-one years, the other group would have swollen to 354 billion. Each American would have to share the available resources with more than eight people.

But, one could argue, this discussion assumes that current population trends will continue, and they may not. Quite so. Most likely the rate of population increase will decline much faster in the U.S. than it will in the other countries, and there does not seem to be much we can do about it. In sharing with "each according to his needs," we must recognize that needs are determined by population size, which is determined by the rate of reproduction, which at present is regarded as a sovereign right of every nation, poor or not. This being so, the philanthropic load created by the sharing ethic of the spaceship can only increase.

The Tragedy of the Commons

The fundamental error of spaceship ethics, and the sharing it requires, is that it leads to what I call "the tragedy of the commons." Under a system of private property, the men who own property recognize their responsibility to care for it, for if they don't they will eventually suffer. A farmer, for instance, will allow no more cattle in a pasture than its carrying capacity justifies. If he overloads it, erosion sets in, weeds take over, and he loses the use of the pasture.

If a pasture becomes a commons open to all, the right of each to use it may not be matched by a corresponding responsibility to protect it. Asking everyone to use it with discretion will hardly do, for the considerate herdsman who refrains from overloading the commons suffers more than a selfish one who says his needs are greater. If everyone would restrain himself, all would be well; but it takes only one less than everyone to ruin a system of voluntary restraint. In a crowded world of less than perfect human beings, mutual ruin is inevitable if there are no controls. This is the tragedy of the commons.

One of the major tasks of education today should be the creation of such an acute awareness of the dangers of the commons that people will recognize its many varieties. For example, the air and water have become polluted because they are treated as commons. Further growth in the population or per-capita conversion of natural resources into pollutants will only make the problem worse. The same holds true for the fish of the oceans. Fishing fleets have nearly disappeared in many parts of the world, technological improvements in the art of fishing are hastening the day of complete ruin. Only the replacement of the system of the commons with a responsible system of control will save the land, air, water and oceanic fisheries.

In recent years there has been a push to create a new commons called a World Food Bank, an international depository of food reserves to which nations would contribute according to their abilities and from which they would draw according to their needs. This humanitarian proposal has received support from many liberal international groups, and from such prominent citizens as Margaret Mead, U.N. Secretary General Kurt Waldheim, and Senators Edward Kennedy and George McGovern.

A world food bank appeals powerfully to our humanitarian impulses. But before we rush ahead with such a plan, let us recognize where the greatest political push comes from, lest we be disillusioned later. Our experience with the "Food for Peace program," or Public Law 480, gives us the answer. This program moved billions of dollars worth of U.S. surplus grain to food-short, population-long countries during the past two decades. But when P.L. 480 first became law, a headline in the business magazine *Forbes* revealed the real power behind it: "Feeding the World's Hungry Millions: How It Will Mean Billions for U.S. Business."

And indeed it did. In the years 1960 to 1970, U.S. taxpayers spent a total of $7.9 billion on the Food for Peace program. Between 1948 and 1970, they also paid an additional $50 billion for other economic-aid programs, some of which went for food and food-producing machinery and technology. Though all U.S. taxpayers were forced to contribute to the cost of P.L. 480, certain special interest groups gained handsomely under the program. Farmers did not have to contribute the grain; the government, or rather the taxpayers, bought it from them at full market prices. The increased demand raised prices of farm products generally. The manufacturers of farm machinery, fertilizers and pesticides benefited by the farmers' extra efforts to grow more food. Grain elevators profited from storing the surplus until it could be shipped. Railroads made money hauling it to ports, and shipping lines profited from carrying it overseas. The implementation of P.L. 480 required the creation of a vast government bureaucracy, which then acquired its own vested interest in continuing the program regardless of its merits.

Extracting Dollars

Those who proposed and defended the Food for Peace program in public rarely mentioned its importance to any of these special interests. The public emphasis was always on its humanitarian effects. The combination of silent selfish interests and highly vocal humanitarian apologists made a powerful and successful lobby for extracting money from taxpayers. We can expect the same lobby to push now for the creation of a World Food Bank.

However great the potential benefit to selfish interests, it should not be a decisive argument against a truly humanitarian program. We must ask if such a program would actually do more good than harm, not only momentarily but also in the long run. Those who propose the food bank usually refer to a current "emergency" or "crisis" in terms of world food supply. But what is an emergency? Although they may be infrequent and sudden, everyone knows that emergencies will occur from time to time. A well-run family, company, organization or country prepares for the likelihood of accidents and emergencies. It expects them, it budgets for them, it saves for them.

Learning the Hard Way

What happens if some organizations or countries budget for accidents and others do not? If each country is solely responsible for its own well-being, poorly managed ones will suffer. But they can learn from experience. They may mend their ways, and learn to budget for infrequent but certain emergencies. For example, the weather varies from year to year, and periodic crop failures are certain. A wise and competent government saves out of the production of the good years in anticipation of bad years to come. Joseph taught this policy to Pharaoh in Egypt more than 2,000 years ago. Yet the great majority of the governments in the world today do not follow such a policy. They lack either the wisdom or the competence, or both. Should those nations that do manage to put something aside be forced to come to the rescue each time an emergency occurs among the poor nations?

"But it isn't their fault!" some kindhearted liberals argue. "How can we blame the poor people who are caught in an emergency? Why must they suffer for the sins of their governments?" The concept of blame is simply not relevant here. The real question is, what are the operational consequences of establishing a world food bank? If it is open to every country every time a need develops, slovenly rulers will not be motivated to take Joseph's advice. Someone will always come to their aid. Some countries will deposit food in the world food bank, and others will withdraw it. There will be almost no overlap. As a result of such solutions to food shortage emergencies, the poor countries will not learn to mend their ways, and will suffer progressively greater emergencies as their populations grow.

Population Control the Crude Way

On the average, poor countries undergo a 2.5 percent increase in population each year; rich countries, about 0.8 percent. Only rich countries have anything in the way of food reserves set aside, and even they do not have as much as they should. Poor countries have none. If poor countries received no food from the outside, the rate of their population growth would be periodically checked by crop failures and famines. But if they can always draw on a world food bank in time of need, their population can continue to grow unchecked, and so will their "need" for aid. In the short run, a world food bank may diminish that need, but in the long run it actually increases the need without limit.

Without some system of worldwide food sharing, the proportion of people in the rich and poor nations might eventually stabilize. The overpopulated poor countries would decrease in numbers, while the rich countries that had room for more people would increase. But with a well-meaning system of sharing, such as a world food bank, the growth differential between the rich and the poor countries will not only persist, it will increase. Because of the higher rate of population growth in the poor countries of the world, 88 percent of today's children are born poor, and only 12 percent rich. Year by year the ratio becomes worse, as the fast-reproducing poor outnumber the slow-reproducing rich.

A world food bank is thus a commons in disguise. People will have more motivation to draw from it than to add to any common store. The less provident and less able will multiply at the expense of the abler and more provident, bringing eventual ruin upon all who share in the commons. Besides, any system of "sharing" that amounts to foreign aid from the rich nations to the poor nations will carry the taint of charity, which will contribute little to the world peace so devoutly desired by those who support the idea of a world food bank.

As past U.S. foreign-aid programs have amply and depressingly demonstrated, international charity frequently inspires mistrust and antagonism rather than gratitude on the part of the recipient nation.

Chinese Fish and Miracle Rice

The modern approach to foreign aid stresses the export of technology and advice, rather than money and food. As an ancient Chinese proverb goes: "Give a man a fish and he will eat for a day; teach him how to fish and he will eat for the rest of his days." Acting on this advice, the Rockefeller and Ford Foundations have financed a number of programs for improving agriculture in the hungry nations. Known as the "Green Revolution," these programs have led to the development of "miracle rice" and "miracle wheat," new strains that offer bigger harvests and greater resistance to crop damage. Norman Borlaug, the Nobel Prize winning agronomist who, supported by the Rockefeller Foundation, developed miracle wheat, is one of the most prominent advocates of a world food bank.

Whether or not the Green Revolution can increase food production as much as its champions claim is a debatable but possibly irrelevant point. Those who support this well-intended humanitarian effort should first consider some of the fundamentals of human ecology. Ironically, one man who did was the late Alan Gregg, a vice president of the Rockefeller Foundation. Two decades ago he expressed strong doubts about the wisdom of such attempts to increase food production. He likened the growth and spread of humanity over the surface of the earth to the spread of cancer in the human body, remarking that "cancerous growths demand food; but, as far as I know, they have never been cured by getting it."

Overloading the Environment

Every human born constitutes a draft on all aspects of the environment: food, air, water, forests, beaches, wildlife, scenery and solitude. Food can, perhaps, be significantly increased to meet a growing demand. But what about clean beaches, unspoiled forests, and solitude? If we satisfy a growing population's need for food, we necessarily decrease its per capita supply of the other resources needed by men.

India, for example, now has a population of 600 million, which increases by 15 million each year. This population already puts a huge load on a relatively impoverished environment. The country's forests are now only a small fraction of what they were three centuries ago, and floods and erosion continually destroy the insufficient farmland that remains. Every one of the 15 million new lives added to India's population puts an additional burden on the environment, and increases the economic and social costs of crowding. However humanitarian our intent, every Indian life saved through medical or nutritional assistance from abroad diminishes the quality of life for those who remain, and for subsequent generations. If rich countries make it possible, through foreign aid, for 600 million Indians to swell to 1.2 billion in a mere twenty-eight years, as their current growth rate threatens, will future generations of Indians thank us for hastening the destruction of their environment? Will our good intentions be sufficient excuse for the consequences of our actions?

My final example of a commons in action is one for which the public has the least desire for rational discussion—immigration. Anyone who publicly questions the wisdom of current U.S. immigration policy is promptly charged with bigotry, prejudice, ethnocentrism, chauvinism, isolationism or selfishness. Rather than encounter such accusations, one would rather talk about other matters, leaving immigration policy to wallow in the crosscurrents of special interests that take no account of the good of the whole, or the interests of posterity.

Perhaps we still feel guilty about things we said in the past. Two generations ago the popular press frequently referred to Dagos, Wops, Polacks, Chinks and Krauts, in articles about how America was being "overrun" by foreigners of supposedly inferior genetic stock. But because the implied inferiority of foreigners was used then as justification for keeping them out, people now assume that restrictive policies could only be based on such misguided notions. There are other grounds.

A Nation of Immigrants

Just consider the numbers involved. Our government acknowledges a net inflow of 400,000 immigrants a year. While we have no hard data on the extent of illegal entries, educated guesses put the figure at about 600,000 a year. Since the natural increase (excess of births over deaths) of the resident population now runs about 1.7 million per year, the yearly gain from immigration amounts to at least 19 percent of the total annual increase, and may be as much as 37 percent if we include the estimate for illegal immigrants. Considering the growing use of birth-control devices, the potential effect of educational campaigns by such organizations as Planned Parenthood Federation of America and Zero Population Growth, and the influence of inflation and the housing shortage, the fertility rate of American women may decline so much that immigration could account for all the yearly increase in population. Should we not at least ask if that is what we want?

For the sake of those who worry about whether the "quality" of the average immigrant compares favorably with the quality of the average resident, let us assume that immigrants and native-born citizens are of exactly equal quality, however one defines that term. We will focus here only on quantity; and since our conclusions will depend on nothing else, all charges of bigotry and chauvinism become irrelevant.

Immigration vs. Food Supply

World food banks *move food to the people,* hastening the exhaustion of the environment of the poor countries. Unrestricted immigration, on the other hand, *moves people to the food,* thus speeding up the destruction of the environment of the rich countries. We can easily understand why poor people should want to make this latter transfer, but why should rich hosts encourage it?

As in the case of foreign-aid programs, immigration receives support from selfish interests and humanitarian impulses. The primary selfish interest in unimpeded immigration is the desire of employers for cheap labor, particularly in industries and trades that offer degrading work. In the past, one wave of foreigners after another was brought into the U.S. to work at wretched jobs for wretched wages. In recent years the Cubans, Puerto Ricans and Mexicans have had this dubious honor. The interests of the employers of cheap labor mesh well with the guilty silence of the country's liberal intelligentsia. White Anglo-Saxon Protestants are particularly reluctant to call for a closing of the doors to immigration for fear of being called bigots.

But not all countries have such reluctant leadership. Most educated Hawaiians, for example, are keenly aware of the limits of their environment, particularly in terms of population growth. There is only so much room on the islands, and the islanders know it. To Hawaiians, immigrants from the other forty-nine states present as great a threat as those from other nations. At a recent meeting of Hawaiian government officials in Honolulu, I had the ironic delight of hearing a speaker, who like most of his audience was of Japanese ancestry, ask how the country might practically and constitutionally close its doors to further immigration. One member of the audience countered: "How can we shut the doors now? We have many friends and relatives in Japan that we'd like to bring here some day so that they can enjoy Hawaii too." The Japanese-American speaker smiled sympathetically and answered: "Yes, but we have children now, and someday we'll have grandchildren too. We can bring more people here from Japan only by giving away some of the land that we hope to pass on to our grandchildren some day. What right do we have to do that?"

At this point, I can hear U.S. liberals asking: "How can you justify slamming the door once you're inside? You say that immigrants should be kept out. But aren't we all immigrants, or the descendants of immigrants? If we insist on staying, must we not admit all others?" Our craving for intellectual order leads us to seek and prefer symmetrical rules and morals: a single rule for me and everybody else; the same rule yesterday, today, and tomorrow. Justice, we feel, should not change with time and place.

We Americans of non-Indian ancestry can look upon ourselves as the descendants of thieves who are guilty morally, if not legally, of stealing this land from its Indian owners. Should we then give back the land to the now living American descendants of those Indians? However morally or logically sound this proposal may be, I, for one, am unwilling to live by it and I know no one else who is. Besides, the logical consequence would be absurd. Suppose that, intoxicated with a sense of pure justice, we should decide to turn our land over to the Indians. Since all our wealth has also been derived from the land, wouldn't we be morally obliged to give that back to the Indians too?

Pure Justice vs. Reality

Clearly, the concept of pure justice produces an infinite regression to absurdity. Centuries ago, wise men invented statutes of limitations to justify the rejection of such pure justice, in the interest of preventing continual disorder. The law zealously defends property rights, but only relatively recent property rights. Drawing a line after an arbitrary time has elapsed may be unjust, but the alternatives are worse.

We are all the descendants of thieves, and the world's resources are inequitably distributed. But we must begin the journey to tomorrow from the point where we are today. We cannot remake the past. We cannot safely divide the wealth equitably among all peoples so long as people reproduce at different rates. To do so would guarantee that our grandchildren, and everyone else's grandchildren, would have only a ruined world to inhabit.

To be generous with one's own possessions is quite different from being generous with those of posterity. We should call this point to the attention of those who, from a commendable love of justice and equality, would institute a system of the commons, either in the form of a world food bank, or of unrestricted immigration. We must convince them if we wish to save at least some parts of the world from environmental ruin.

Without a true world government to control reproduction and the use of available resources, the sharing ethic of the spaceship is impossible. For the foreseeable future, our survival demands that we govern our actions by the ethics of a lifeboat, harsh though they may be. Posterity will be satisfied with nothing less.

Journal/Discussion Questions

✍ *Hardin's article is one that usually elicits strong emotional reactions. What did you feel when you read his article? To what extent are your feelings supported by your arguments?*

1. Hardin argues that programs such as the World Food Bank appear humanitarian in motivation, but in fact are highly beneficial to many commercial interests. What is the force of this kind of objection?

Does it undermine the value of such programs? Why? Why not?

2. Hardin cites Alan Gregg as saying that the spread of humanity is like a cancer. Discuss the strengths and weaknesses of this metaphor. What conclusions does acceptance of this metaphor lead to? Do you agree with those conclusions? Why or why not?
3. On what basis does Hardin object to current U.S. immigration policies? Critically evaluate his position on this issue?
4. Hardin concludes that "the concept of pure justice produces an infinite regression to absurdity." Explain what he means by this conclusion. Discuss the reasons why you agree with him and why you disagree with him. Is his concept of "pure justice" a straw man?

Peter Singer
"Rich and Poor"

Peter Singer, DeCamp Professor in Princeton University's Center for Human Values, is the author of numerous works in ethics, especially in applied ethics. His books include The Expanding Circle, Animal Liberation, Practical Ethics, *and, most recently,* Rethinking Life and Death *and* How Are We to Live? *He has also edited a number of books, including* A Companion to Ethics. *In his work, Singer sees himself as holding our conventional moral beliefs to a standard of consistency, coherence, and the avoidance of arbitrary distinctions. He finds that many of these traditional beliefs are remnants of earlier, religiously inspired doctrines that he believes many people no longer accept, while other beliefs survive only because they promote some form of group selfishness.*

Writing from a strict utilitarian standpoint, Singer argues that rich nations have an obligation to aid poor and starving ones up to the point of relative equality between rich and poor. Letting people starve to death when we could prevent it without giving up our own lives, Singer argues, is the moral equivalent of actively killing them—and since killing them is clearly wrong, so too is letting them starve to death under the present conditions. Singer considers various objections to his position, but finds none of them sufficiently strong to undermine his position.

As You Read, Consider This:

1. Singer maintains that "If we stopped feeding animals on grains and soybeans, the amount of food saved would—if distributed to those who need it—be more than enough to end hunger throughout the world." How do you think the issue of vegetarianism is related to world hunger? If people are asked to give up eating meat, are they being asked to give up something morally signficant, something to which they have a strong right?
2. Singer maintains that if "allowing someone to die is not intrinsically different from killing someone, it would seem that we are all murderers." What is the moral difference between actively killing someone and passively letting someone die whom you could save? How does this issue play a role in the development of Singer's position? Do you agree with his principle, "if

it is in our power to prevent something very bad from happening, without thereby sacrificing anything of comparable moral significance, we ought to do it"?

Some Facts about Poverty

Consider these facts: by the most cautious estimates, 400 million people lack the calories, protein, vitamins and minerals needed to sustain their bodies and minds in a healthy state. Millions are constantly hungry; others suffer from deficiency diseases and from infections they would be able to resist on a better diet. Children are the worst affected. According to one study, 14 million children under five die every year from the combined effects of malnutrition and infection. In some districts half the children born can be expected to die before their fifth birthday.

Nor is lack of food the only hardship of the poor. To give a broader picture, Robert McNamara, when president of the World Bank, suggested the term "absolute poverty." The poverty we are familiar with in industrialized nations is relative poverty—meaning that some citizens are poor, relative to the wealth enjoyed by their neighbors. People living in relative poverty in Australia might be quite comfortably off by comparison with pensioners in Britain, and British pensioners are not poor in comparison with the poverty that exists in Mali or Ethiopia. Absolute poverty, on the other hand, is poverty by any standard. In McNamara's words:

> Poverty at the absolute level . . . is life at the very margin of existence. The absolute poor are severely deprived human beings struggling to survive in a set of squalid and degraded circumstances almost beyond the power of our sophisticated imaginations and privileged circumstances to conceive.
>
> Compared to those fortunate enough to live in developed countries, individuals in the poorest nations have:
>
> An infant mortality rate eight times higher;
>
> A life expectancy one-third lower;
>
> An adult literacy rate 60 percent less;
>
> A nutritional level, for one out of every two in the population, below acceptable standards;
>
> And for millions of infants, less protein than is sufficient to permit optimum development of the brain.

McNamara has summed up absolute poverty as "a condition of life so characterized by malnutrition, illiteracy, disease, squalid surroundings, high infant mortality and low life expectancy as to be beneath any reasonable definition of human decency."

Absolute poverty is, as McNamara has said, responsible for the loss of countless lives, especially among infants and young children. When absolute poverty does not cause death, it still causes misery of a kind not often seen in the affluent nations. Malnutrition in young children stunts both physical and mental development. According to the United Nations Development Programme, 180 million children under the age of five suffer from serious malnutrition. Millions of people on poor diets suffer from deficiency diseases, like goitre, or blindness caused by a lack of vitamin A. The food value of what the poor eat is further reduced by parasites such as hookworm and ringworm, which are endemic in conditions of poor sanitation and health education.

Death and disease apart, absolute poverty remains a miserable condition of life, with inadequate food, shelter, clothing, sanitation, health services and education. The Worldwatch Institute estimates that as many as 1.2 billion people—or 23 percent of the world's population—live in absolute poverty. For the purposes of this estimate, absolute poverty is defined as "the lack of sufficient income in cash or kind to meet the most basic biological needs for food, clothing, and shelter." Absolute poverty is probably the principal cause of human misery today.

Some Facts about Wealth

This is the background situation, the situation that prevails on our planet all the time. It does not make headlines. People died from malnutrition and related diseases yesterday, and more will die tomorrow. The occasional droughts, cyclones, earthquakes, and floods that take the lives of tens of thousands in one place and at one time are more newsworthy. They add greatly to the total amount of human suffering; but it is wrong to assume that when there are no major calamities reported, all is well.

The problem is not that the world cannot produce enough to feed and shelter its people. People in the poor countries consume, on average, 180 kilos of grain a year, while North Americans average around 900 kilos. The difference is caused by the fact that in the rich countries we feed most of our grain to animals, converting it into meat, milk, and eggs. Because this is a highly inefficient process, people in rich countries are responsible for the consumption of far more food than those in poor countries who eat few animal products. If we stopped feeding animals on grains and soybeans, the amount of food saved would—if distributed to those who need it—be more than enough to end hunger throughout the world.

These facts about animal food do not mean that we can easily solve the world food problem by cutting down on animal products, but they show that the problem is essentially one of distribution rather than production. The world does produce enough food. Moreover, the poorer nations themselves could produce far more if they made more use of improved agricultural techniques.

So why are people hungry? Poor people cannot afford to buy grain grown by farmers in the richer nations. Poor farmers cannot afford to buy improved seeds, or fertilizers, or the machinery needed for drilling wells and pumping water. Only by transferring some of the wealth of the rich nations to the poor can the situation be changed.

That this wealth exists is clear. Against the picture of absolute poverty that McNamara has painted, one might pose a picture of "absolute affluence." Those who are absolutely affluent are not necessarily affluent by comparison with their neighbors, but they are affluent by any reasonable definition of human needs. This means that they have more income than they need to provide themselves adequately with all the basic necessities of life. After buying (either directly or through their taxes) food, shelter, clothing, basic health services, and education, the absolutely affluent are still able to spend money on luxuries. The absolutely affluent choose their food for the pleasures of the palate, not to stop hunger; they buy new clothes to look good, not to keep warm; they move house to be in a better neighborhood or have a playroom for the children, not to keep out the rain; and after all this there is still money to spend on stereo systems, video-cameras, and overseas holidays.

At this stage I am making no ethical judgments about absolute affluence, merely pointing out that it exists. Its defining characteristic is a significant amount of income above the level necessary to provide for the basic human needs of oneself and one's dependents. By this standard, the majority of citizens of Western Europe, North America, Japan, Australia, New Zealand, and the oil-rich Middle Eastern states are all absolutely affluent. To quote McNamara once more:

> The average citizen of a developed country enjoys wealth beyond the wildest dreams of the one billion Deonle in countries with per capita incomes under $200. These, therefore, are the countries—and individuals—who have wealth that they could, without threatening their own basic welfare, transfer to the absolutely poor.

At present, very little is being transferred. Only Sweden, the Netherlands, Norway, and some of the oil-exporting Arab states have reached the modest target, set by the United Nations, of 0.7 percent of gross national product (GNP). Britain gives 0.31 percent of its GNP in official development assistance and a small additional amount in unofficial aid from voluntary organizations. The total comes to about £2 per month per person, and compares with 5.5 percent of GNP spent on alcohol, and 3 percent on tobacco. Other, even wealthier nations, give little more: Germany gives 0.41 percent and Japan 0.32 percent. The United States gives a mere 0.15 percent of its GNP.

The Moral Equivalent of Murder?

If these are the facts, we cannot avoid concluding that by not giving more than we do, people in rich countries are allowing those in poor countries to suffer from absolute poverty, with consequent malnutrition, ill health, and death. This is not a conclusion that applies only to governments. It applies to each absolutely affluent individual, for each of us has the opportunity to do something about the situation; for instance, to give our time or money to voluntary organizations like Oxfam, Care, War on Want, Freedom from Hunger, Community Aid Abroad, and so on. If, then, allowing someone to die is not intrinsically different from killing someone, it would seem that we are all murderers.

Is this verdict too harsh? Many will reject it as self-evidently absurd. They would sooner take it as showing that allowing to die cannot be equivalent to killing than as showing that living in an affluent style without contributing to an overseas aid agency is ethically equivalent to going over to Ethiopia and shooting a few peasants. And no doubt, put as bluntly as that, the verdict is too harsh.

There are several significant differences between spending money on luxuries instead of using it to save lives, and deliberately shooting people.

First, the motivation will normally be different. Those who deliberately shoot others go out of their way to kill; they presumably want their victims dead, from malice, sadism, or some equally unpleasant motive. A person who buys a new stereo system presumably wants to enhance her enjoyment of music—not in itself a terrible thing. At worst, spending money on luxuries instead of giving it away indicates selfishness and indifference to the sufferings of others, characteristics that may be undesirable but are not comparable with actual malice or similar motives. Second, it is not difficult for most of us to act in accordance with a rule against killing people: it is, on the other hand, very difficult to obey a rule that commands us to save all the lives we can. To live a comfortable, or even luxurious life it is not necessary to kill anyone; but it is necessary to allow some to die whom we might have saved, for the money that we need to live comfortably could have been given away. Thus the duty to avoid killing is much easier to discharge completely than the duty to save. Saving every life we could would mean cutting our standard of living down to the bare essentials needed to keep us alive.[1] To discharge this duty completely would require a degree of moral heroism utterly different from that required by mere avoidance of killing.

A third difference is the greater certainty of the outcome of shooting when compared with not giving aid. If I point a loaded gun at someone at close range and pull the trigger, it is virtually certain that the person will be killed; whereas the money that I could give might be spent on a project that turns out to be unsuccessful and helps no one.

Fourth, when people are shot there are identifiable individuals who have been harmed. We can point to them and to their grieving families. When I buy my stereo system, I cannot know who my money would have saved if I had given it away. In a time of famine I may see dead bodies and grieving families on television reports, and I might not doubt that my money would have saved some of them; even then it is impossible to point to a body and say that had I not bought the stereo, that person would have survived.

Fifth, it might be said that the plight of the hungry is not my doing, and so I cannot be held responsible for it. The starving would have been starving if I had never existed. If I kill, however, I am responsible for my victims' deaths, for those people would not have died if I had not killed them.

These differences need not shake our previous conclusion that there is no intrinsic difference between killing and allowing to die. They are extrinsic differences, that is, differences normally but not necessarily associated with the distinction between killing and allowing to die. We can imagine cases in which someone allows another to die for malicious or sadistic reasons; we can imagine a world in which there are so few people needing assistance, and they are so easy to assist, that our duty not to allow people to die is as easily discharged as our duty not to kill; we can imagine situations in which the outcome of not helping is as sure as shooting; we can imagine cases in which we can identify the person we allow to die. We can even imagine a case of allowing to die in which, if I had not existed, the person would not have died—for instance, a case in which if I had not been in a position to help (though I don't help) someone else would have been in my position and would have helped.

Our previous discussion of euthanasia illustrates the extrinsic nature of these differences, for they do not provide a basis for distinguishing active from passive euthanasia. If a doctor decides, in consultation with the parents, not to operate on—and thus to allow to die—a Down's syndrome infant with an intestinal blockage, her motivation will be similar to that of a doctor who gives a lethal injection rather than allow the infant to die. No extraordinary sacrifice or moral heroism will be required in either case. Not operating will just as certainly end in death as administering the injection. Allowing to die does have an identifiable victim. Finally, it may well be that the doctor is personally responsible for the death of the infant she decides not to operate upon, since she may know that if she had not taken this case, other doctors in the hospital would have operated.

Nevertheless, euthanasia is a special case, and very different from allowing people to starve to death. (The major difference being that when euthanasia is justifiable, death is a good thing.) The extrinsic differences that *normally* mark off killing and allowing to die do explain why we *normally* regard killing as much worse than allowing to die.

To explain our conventional ethical attitudes is not to justify them. Do the five differences not only explain, but also justify, our attitudes? Let us consider them one by one:

1. Take the lack of an identifiable victim first. Suppose that I am a traveling salesperson, selling tinned food, and I learn that a batch of tins contains a contaminant, the known effect of which, when consumed, is to double the risk that the consumer will die from stomach cancer.

Suppose I continue to sell the tins. My decision may have no identifiable victims. Some of those who eat the food will die from cancer. The proportion of consumers dying in this way will be twice that of the community at large, but who among the consumers died because they ate what I sold, and who would have contracted the disease anyway? It is impossible to tell; but surely this impossibility makes my decision no less reprehensible than it would have been had the contaminant had more readily detectable, though equally fatal, effects.

2. The lack of certainty that by giving money I could save a life does reduce the wrongness of not giving, by comparison with deliberate killing; but it is insufficient to show that not giving is acceptable conduct. The motorist who speeds through pedestrian crossings, heedless of anyone who might be on them, is not a murderer. She may never actually hit a pedestrian; yet what she does is very wrong indeed.
3. The notion of responsibility for acts rather than omissions is more puzzling. On the one hand, we feel ourselves to be under a greater obligation to help those whose misfortunes we have caused. (It is for this reason that advocates of overseas aid often argue that Western nations have created the poverty of third world nations, through forms of economic exploitation that go back to the colonial system.) On the other hand, any consequentialist would insist that we are responsible for all the consequences of our actions, and if a consequence of my spending money on a luxury item is that someone dies, I am responsible for that death. It is true that the person would have died even if I had never existed, but what is the relevance of that? The fact is that I do exist, and the consequentialist will say that our responsibilities derive from the world as it is, not as it might have been.

One way of making sense of the non-consequentialist view of responsibility is by basing it on a theory of rights of the kind proposed by John Locke or, more recently, Robert Nozick. If everyone has a right to life, and this right is a right *against* others who might threaten my life, but not a right to assistance from others when my life is in danger, then we can understand the feeling that we are responsible for acting to kill but not for omitting to save. The former violates the rights of others, the latter does not. Should we accept such a theory of rights? If we build up our theory of rights by imagining, as Locke and Nozick do, individuals living independently from each other in a "state of nature," it may seem natural to adopt a conception of rights in which as long as each leaves the other alone, no rights are violated. I might, on this view, quite properly have maintained my independent existence if I had wished to do so. So if I do not make you any worse off than you would have been if I had had nothing at all to do with you, how can I have violated your rights? But why start from such an unhistorical, abstract and ultimately inexplicable idea as an independent individual? Our ancestors were—like other primates—social beings long before they were human beings, and could not have developed the abilities and capacities of human beings if they had not been social beings first. In any case, we are not, now, isolated individuals. So why should we assume that rights must be restricted to rights against interference? We might, instead, adopt the view that taking rights to life seriously is incompatible with standing by and watching people die when one could easily save them.

4. What of the difference in motivation? That a person does not positively wish for the death of another lessens the severity of the blame she deserves; but not by as much as our present attitudes to giving aid suggest. The behavior of the speeding motorist is again comparable, for

such motorists usually have no desire at all to kill anyone. They merely enjoy speeding and are indifferent to the consequences. Despite their lack of malice, those who kill with cars deserve not only blame but also severe punishment.

5. Finally, the fact that to avoid killing people is normally not difficult, whereas to save all one possibly could save is heroic, must make an important difference to our attitude to failure to do what the respective principles demand. Not to kill is a minimum standard of acceptable conduct we can require of everyone; to save all one possibly could is not something that can realistically be required, especially not in societies accustomed to giving as little as ours do. Given the generally accepted standards, people who give, say, $1,000 a year to an overseas aid organization are more aptly praised for above average generosity than blamed for giving less than they might. The appropriateness of praise and blame is, however, a separate issue from the rightness or wrongness of actions. The former evaluates the agent: the latter evaluates the action. Perhaps many people who give $1,000 really ought to give at least $5,000, but to blame them for not giving more could be counterproductive. It might make them feel that what is required is too demanding, and if one is going to be blamed anyway, one might as well not give anything at all.

(That an ethic that put saving all one possibly can on the same footing as not killing would be an ethic for saints or heroes should not lead us to assume that the alternative must be an ethic that makes it obligatory not to kill, but puts us under no obligation to save anyone. There are positions in between these extremes, as we shall soon see.)

Here is a summary of the five differences that normally exist between killing and allowing to die, in the context of absolute poverty and overseas aid. The lack of an identifiable victim is of no moral significance, though it may play an important role in explaining our attitudes. The idea that we are directly responsible for those we kill, but not for those we do not help, depends on a questionable notion of responsibility and may need to be based on a controversial theory of rights. Differences in certainty and motivation are ethically significant, and show that not aiding the poor is not to be condemned as murdering them; it could, however, be on a par with killing someone as a result of reckless driving, which is serious enough. Finally, the difficulty of completely discharging the duty of saving all one possibly can makes it inappropriate to blame those who fall short of this target as we blame those who kill; but this does not show that the act itself is less serious. Nor does it indicate anything about those who, far from saving all they possibly can, make no effort to save anyone.

These conclusions suggest a new approach. Instead of attempting to deal with the contrast between affluence and poverty by comparing not saving with deliberate killing, let us consider afresh whether we have an obligation to assist those whose lives are in danger, and if so, how this obligation applies to the present world situation.

The Obligation to Assist

The Argument for an Obligation to Assist

The path from the library at my university to the humanities lecture theater passes a shallow ornamental pond. Suppose that on my way to give a lecture I notice that a small child has fallen in and is in danger of drowning. Would anyone deny that I ought to wade in and pull the child out? This will mean getting my clothes muddy and either canceling my lecture or delaying it until I can find something dry to change into; but compared with the avoidable death of a child this is insignificant.

A plausible principle that would support the judgment that I ought to pull the child out is this: if it is in our power to prevent something very bad from happening, without thereby sacrificing anything of comparable moral significance, we ought to do it. This principle seems uncontroversial. It will obviously win the assent of consequentialists; but non-consequentialists should accept it too, because the injunction to prevent what is bad applies only when nothing comparably significant is at stake. Thus the principle cannot lead to the kinds of actions of which non-consequentialists strongly disapprove—serious violations of individual rights, injustice, broken promises, and so on. If non-consequentialists regard any of these as comparable in moral significance to the bad thing that is to be prevented, they will automatically regard the principle as not applying in those cases in which the bad thing can only be prevented by violating rights, doing injustice, breaking promises, or whatever else is at stake. Most non-consequentialists hold that we ought to prevent what is bad and promote what is good. Their dispute with consequentialists lies in their insistence that this is not the sole ultimate ethical principle: that it is an ethical principle is not denied by any plausible ethical theory.

Nevertheless the uncontroversial appearance of the principle that we ought to prevent what is bad when we can do so without sacrificing anything of comparable moral significance is deceptive. If it were taken seriously and acted upon, our lives and our world would be fundamentally changed. For the principle applies, not just to rare situations in which one can save a child from a pond, but to the everyday situation in which we can assist those living in absolute poverty. In saying this I assume that absolute poverty, with its hunger and malnutrition, lack of shelter, illiteracy, disease, high infant mortality, and low life expectancy, is a bad thing. And I assume that it is within the power of the affluent to reduce absolute poverty, without sacrificing anything of comparable moral significance. If these two assumptions and the principle we have been discussing are correct, we have an obligation to help those in absolute poverty that is no less strong than our obligation to rescue a drowning child from a pond. Not to help would be wrong, whether or not it is intrinsically equivalent to killing. Helping is not, as conventionally thought, a charitable act that it is praiseworthy to do, but not wrong to omit; it is something that everyone ought to do.

This is the argument for an obligation to assist. Set out more formally, it would look like this.

First premise: If we can prevent something bad without sacrificing anything of comparable significance, we ought to do it.

Second premise: Absolute poverty is bad.

Third premise: There is some absolute poverty we can prevent without sacrificing anything of comparable moral significance.

Conclusion: We ought to prevent some absolute poverty.

The first premise is the substantive moral premise on which the argument rests, and I have tried to show that it can be accepted by people who hold a variety of ethical positions.

The second premise is unlikely to be challenged. Absolute poverty is, as McNamara put it, "beneath any reasonable definition of human decency" and it would be hard to find a plausible ethical view that did not regard it as a bad thing.

The third premise is more controversial, even though it is cautiously framed. It claims only that some absolute poverty can be prevented without the sacrifice of anything of comparable moral significance. It thus avoids the objection that any aid I can give is just "drops in the ocean" for the point is not whether my personal contribution will make any noticeable impression on world poverty as a whole (of course it won't) but whether it will prevent some poverty. This is all the argument needs to sustain its conclusion, since the second premise says that any absolute poverty is bad, and not merely the total amount of absolute poverty. If without sacrificing anything of comparable moral significance we can provide just one family with the means to raise itself out of absolute poverty, the third premise is vindicated.

I have left the notion of moral significance unexamined in order to show that the argument does not depend on any specific values or ethical principles. I think the third premise is true for most people living in industrialized nations, on any defensible view of what is morally significant. Our affluence means that we have income we can dispose of without giving up the basic necessities of life, and we can use this income to reduce absolute poverty. Just how much we will think ourselves obliged to give up will depend on what we consider to be of comparable moral significance to the poverty we could prevent: stylish clothes, expensive dinners, a sophisticated stereo system, overseas holidays, a (second?) car, a larger house, private schools for our children, and so on. For a utilitarian, none of these is likely to be of comparable significance to the reduction of absolute poverty; and those who are not utilitarians surely must, if they subscribe to the principle of universalisability, accept that at least some of these things are of far less moral significance than the absolute poverty that could be prevented by the money they cost. So the third premise seems to be true on any plausible ethical view—although the precise amount of absolute poverty that can be prevented before anything of moral significance is sacrificed will vary according to the ethical view one accepts.

Objections to the Argument

Taking care of our own. Anyone who has worked to increase overseas aid will have come across the argument that we should look after those near us, our families, and then the poor in our own country, before we think about poverty in distant places.

No doubt we do instinctively prefer to help those who are close to us. Few could stand by and watch a child drown; many can ignore a famine in Africa. But the question is not what we usually do, but what we ought to do, and it is difficult to see any sound moral justification for the view that distance, or community membership, makes a crucial difference to our obligations.

Consider, for instance, racial affinities. Should people of European origin help poor Europeans before helping poor Africans? Most of us would reject such a suggestion out of hand, and our discussion of the principle of equal consideration of interests in Chapter 2 [of *Practical Ethics*] has shown why we should reject it: people's need for food has nothing to do with their race, and if Africans need food more than Europeans, it would be a violation of the principle of equal consideration to give preference to Europeans.

The same point applies to citizenship or nationhood. Every affluent nation has some relatively poor citizens, but absolute poverty is limited largely to the poor nations. Those living on the streets of Calcutta, or in the drought-prone Sahel region of Africa, are experiencing poverty unknown in the West. Under these circumstances it would be wrong to decide that only those fortunate enough to be citizens of our own community will share our abundance. We feel obligations of kinship more strongly than those of citizenship. Which parents could give away their last bowl of rice if their own children were starving? To do so would seem unnatural, contrary to our nature as biologically evolved beings—although whether it would be wrong is another question altogether. In any case, we are not faced with that situation, but with one in which our own children are well-fed, well-clothed, well-educated, and would now like new bikes, a stereo set, or their own car. In these circumstances any special obligations we might have to our children have been fulfilled, and the needs of strangers make a stronger claim upon us.

The element of truth in the view that we should first take care of our own, lies in the advantage of a recognized system of responsibilities. When families and local communities look after their own poorer members, ties of affection and personal relationships achieve ends that would otherwise require a large, impersonal bureaucracy. Hence it would be absurd to propose that from now on we all regard ourselves as equally responsible for the welfare of everyone in the world; but the argument for an obligation to assist does not propose that. It applies only when some are in absolute poverty, and others can help without sacrificing anything of comparable moral significance. To allow one's own kin to sink into absolute poverty would be to sacrifice something of comparable significance; and before that point had been reached, the breakdown of the system of family and community responsibility would be a factor to weigh the balance in favor of a small degree of preference for family and community. This small degree of preference is, however, decisively outweighed by existing discrepancies in wealth and property.

Property myths. Do people have a right to private property, a right that contradicts the view that they are under an obligation to give some of their wealth away to those in absolute poverty? According to some theories of rights (for instance, Robert Nozick's), provided one has acquired one's property without the use of unjust means like force and fraud, one may be entitled to enormous wealth while others starve. This individualistic conception of rights is in contrast to other views, like the early Christian doctrine to be found in the works of Thomas Aquinas, which holds that since property exists for the satisfaction of human needs, "whatever a man has in superabundance is owed, of natural right, to the poor for their sustenance." A socialist would also, of course, see wealth as belonging to the community rather than the individual, while utilitarians, whether socialist or not, would be prepared to override property rights to prevent great evils.

Does the argument for an obligation to assist others therefore presuppose one of these other theories of property rights, and not an individualistic theory like Nozick's? Not necessarily. A theory of property rights can insist on our *right* to retain wealth without pronouncing on whether the rich *ought* to give to the poor. Nozick, for example, rejects the use of compulsory means like taxation to redistribute income, but suggests that we can achieve the ends we deem morally desirable by voluntary means. So Nozick would reject the claim that rich people have an "obligation" to give to the poor, in so far as this implies that the poor have a right to our aid, but might accept that giving is something we ought to do and failing to give, though within one's rights, is wrong—for there is more to an ethical life than respecting the rights of others.

The argument for an obligation to assist can survive, with only minor modifications, even if we accept an individualistic theory of property rights. In any case, however, I do not think we should accept such a theory. It leaves too much to chance to be an acceptable ethical view. For instance, those whose forefathers happened to inhabit some sandy wastes around the Persian Gulf are now fabulously wealthy, because oil lay under those sands; while those whose forefathers settled on better land south of the Sahara live in absolute poverty, because of drought and bad harvests. Can this distribution be acceptable from an impartial point of view? If we imagine ourselves about to begin life as a citizen of either Bahrein or Chad—but we do not know which—would we accept the principle that citizens of Bahrein are under no obligation to assist people living in Chad?

Population and the ethics of triage. Perhaps the most serious objection to the argument that we have an obligation to assist is that since the major cause of absolute poverty is overpopulation, helping those now in poverty will only ensure that yet more people are born to live in poverty in the future.

In its most extreme form, this objection is taken to show that we should adopt a policy of "triage." The term comes from medical policies adopted in wartime. With too few doctors to cope with all the casualties, the wounded were divided into three categories: those who would probably survive without medical assistance, those who might survive if they received assistance, but otherwise probably would not, and those who even with medical assistance probably would not survive. Only those in the middle category were given medical assistance. The idea, of course, was to use limited medical resources as effectively as possible. For those in the first category, medical treatment was not strictly necessary; for those in the third category, it was likely to be useless. It has been suggested that we should apply the same policies to countries, according to their prospects of becoming self-sustaining. We would not aid countries that even without our help will soon be able to feed their populations. We would not aid countries that, even with our help, will not be able to limit their population to a level they can feed. We would aid those countries where our help might make the difference between success and failure in bringing food and population into balance. Advocates of this theory are understandably reluctant to give a complete list of the countries they would place into the "hopeless" category; Bangladesh has been cited as an example, and so have some of the countries of the Sahel region of Africa. Adopting the policy of triage would, then, mean cutting off assistance to these countries and allowing famine, disease, and natural disasters to reduce the population of those countries to the level at which they can provide adequately for all. In support of this view Garrett Hardin has offered a metaphor: we in the rich nations are like the occupants of a crowded lifeboat adrift in a sea full of drowning people. If we try to save the drowning by bringing them aboard, our boat will be overloaded and we shall all drown. Since it is better that some survive than none, we should leave the others to drown. In the world today, according to Hardin, "lifeboat ethics" apply. The rich should leave the poor to starve, for otherwise the poor will drag the rich down with them.

Against this view, some writers have argued that overpopulation is a myth. The world produces ample food to feed its population, and could, according to some estimates, feed ten times as many. People are hungry not because there are too many but because of inequitable land distribution, the manipulation of third world economies by the developed nations, wastage of food in the West, and so on. Putting aside the controversial issue of the extent to which food production might one day be increased, it is true, as we have already seen, that the world now produces enough to feed its inhabitants—the amount lost by being fed to animals itself being enough to meet existing grain shortages. Nevertheless population growth cannot be ignored. Bangladesh could, with land reform and using better techniques, feed its present population of 115 million; but by the year 2000, according to United Nations Population Division estimates, its population will be 150 million. The enormous effort that will have to go into feeding an extra 35 million people, all added to the population within a decade, means that Bangladesh must develop at full speed to stay where it is. Other low-income countries are in similar situations. By the end of the century, Ethiopia's population is expected to rise from 49 to 66 million; Somalia's from 7 to 9 million, India's from 853 to 1041 million, Zaire's from 35 to 49 million.[2]

What will happen if the world population continues to grow? It cannot do so indefinitely. It will be checked by a decline in birth rates or a rise in death rates. Those who advocate triage are proposing that we allow the population growth of some countries to be checked by a rise in death rates—that is, by increased malnutrition, and related diseases; by widespread famines; by increased infant mortality; and by epidemics of infectious diseases.

The consequences of triage on this scale are so horrible that we are inclined to reject it without further argument. How could we sit by our television sets, watching millions starve while we do nothing? Would not that be the end of all notions of human equality and respect for human life? (Those who attack the proposals for legalizing euthanasia discussed in Chapter 7 [of *Practical Ethics*], saying that these proposals will weaken respect for human life, would surely do better to object to the idea that we should reduce or end our overseas aid programs, for that proposal, if implemented, would be responsible for a far greater loss of human life.) Don't people have a right to our assistance, irrespective of the consequences? Anyone whose initial reaction to triage was not one of repugnance would be an unpleasant sort of person. Yet initial reactions based on strong feelings are not always reliable guides. Advocates of triage are rightly concerned with the long-term consequences of our actions. They say that helping the poor and starving now merely ensures more poor and starving in the future. When our capacity to help is finally unable to cope—as one day it must be—the suffering will be greater than it would be if we stopped helping now. If this is correct, there is nothing we can do to prevent absolute starvation and poverty, in the long run, and so we have no obligation to assist. Nor does it seem reasonable to hold that under these circumstances people have a right to our assistance. If we do accept such a right, irrespective of the consequences, we are saying that, in Hardin's metaphor, we should continue to haul the drowning into our lifeboat until the boat sinks and we all drown. If triage is to be rejected it must be tackled on its own ground, within the framework of consequentialist ethics. Here it is vulnerable. Any consequentialist ethics must take probability of outcome into account. A course of action that will certainly produce some benefit is to be preferred to an alternative course that may lead to a slightly larger benefit, but is equally likely to result in no benefit at all. Only if the greater magnitude of the uncertain benefit outweighs its uncertainty should we choose it. Better one certain unit of benefit than a 10 percent chance of five units; but better a 50 pecent chance of three units than a single certain unit. The same principle applies when we are trying to avoid evils.

The policy of triage involves a certain, very great evil: population control by famine and disease. Tens of millions would die slowly. Hundreds of millions would continue to live in absolute poverty, at the very margin of existence. Against this prospect, advocates of the policy place a possible evil that is greater still: the same process of famine and disease, taking place in, say, fifty years' time, when the world's population may be three times its present level, and the number who will die from famine, or struggle on in absolute poverty, will be that much greater. The question is: how probable is this forecast that continued assistance now will lead to greater disasters in the future?

Forecasts of population growth are notoriously fallible, and theories about the factors that affect it remain speculative. One theory, at least as plausible as any other, is that countries pass through a "demographic transition" as their standard of living rises. When people are very poor and have no access to modern medicine their fertility is high, but population is kept in check by high death rates. The introduction of sanitation, modern medical techniques, and other improvements reduces the death rate, but initially has little effect on the birth rate. Then population grows rapidly. Some poor countries, especially in sub-Saharan Africa, are now in this phase. If standards of living continue to rise, however, couples begin to realize that to have the same number of children surviving to maturity as in the past, they do not need to give birth to as many children as their parents did. The need for children to provide economic support in old age diminishes. Improved education and the emancipation and employment of women also reduce the birthrate, and so population growth begins to level off. Most rich nations have reached this stage, and their populations are growing only very slowly, if at all. If this theory is right, there is an alternative to the disasters accepted as inevitable by supporters of triage. We can assist poor countries to raise the living standards of the poorest members of their population. We can encourage the governments of these countries to enact land reform measures, improve education, and liberate women from a purely child-bearing role. We can also help other countries to make contraception and sterilization widely available. There is a fair chance that these measures will hasten the onset of the demographic transition and bring population growth down to a manageable level. According to United Nations estimates, in 1965 the average woman in the third world gave birth to six children, and only 8 percent were using some form of contraception; by 1991 the average number of children had dropped to just below four, and more than half the women in the third world were taking contraceptive measures. Notable successes in encouraging the use of contraception had occurred in Thailand, Indonesia, Mexico, Colombia, Brazil, and Bangladesh. This achievement reflected a relatively low expenditure in developing countries—considering the size and significance of the problem—of $3 billion annually, with only 20 percent of this sum coming from developed nations. So expenditure in this area seems likely to be highly cost-effective. Success cannot be guaranteed; but the evidence suggests that we can reduce population growth by improving economic security and education, and making contraceptives more widely available. This prospect makes triage ethically unacceptable. We cannot allow millions to die from starvation and disease when there is a reasonable probability that population can be brought under control without such horrors.

Population growth is therefore not a reason against giving overseas aid, although it should make us think about the kind of aid to give. Instead of food handouts, it may be better to give aid that leads to a slowing of population growth. This may mean agricultural assistance for the rural poor, or assistance with education, or the provision of contraceptive services. Whatever kind of aid proves most effective in specific circumstances, the obligation to assist is not reduced. One awkward question remains. What should we do about a poor and already overpopulated country that, for religious or nationalistic reasons, restricts the use of contraceptives and refuses to slow its population growth? Should we nevertheless offer development assistance? Or should we make our offer conditional on effective steps being taken to reduce the birthrate? To the latter course, some would object that putting conditions on aid is an attempt to impose our own ideas on independent sovereign nations. So it is—but is this imposition unjustifiable? If the argument for an obligation to assist is sound, we have an obligation to reduce absolute poverty; but we have no obligation to make sacrifices that, to the best of our knowledge, have no prospect of reducing poverty in the long run. Hence we have no obligation to assist countries whose governments have policies that will make our aid ineffective. This could be very harsh on poor citizens of these countries—for they may have no say in the government's policies—but we will help more people in the long run by using our resources where they are most effective. (The same principles may apply, incidentally, to countries that refuse to take other steps that could make assistance effective—like refusing to reform systems of land holding that impose intolerable burdens on poor tenant farmers.)

Leaving it to the government. We often hear that overseas aid should be a government responsibility, not left to privately run charities. Giving privately, it is said, allows the government to escape its responsibilities. Since increasing government aid is the surest way of making a significant increase to the total amount of aid given, I would agree that the governments of affluent nations should give much more genuine, no-strings-attached, aid than they give now. Less than one-sixth of one per cent of GNP is a scandalously small amount for a nation as wealthy as the United States to give. Even the official UN target of 0.7 percent seems much less than affluent nations can and should give—though it is a target few have reached. But is this a reason against each of us giving what we can privately, through voluntary agencies? To believe that it is seems to assume that the more people there are who give through voluntary agencies, the less likely it is that the government will do its part. Is this plausible? The opposite view—that if no one gives voluntarily the government will assume that its citizens are not in favor of overseas aid, and will cut its programme accordingly—is more reasonable. In any case, unless there is a definite probability that by refusing to give we would be helping to bring about an increase in government assistance, refusing to give privately is wrong for the same reason that triage is wrong: it is a refusal to prevent a definite evil for the sake of a very uncertain gain. The onus of showing how a refusal to give privately will make the government give more is on those who refuse to give.

This is not to say that giving privately is enough. Certainly we should campaign for entirely new standards for both public and private overseas aid. We should also work for fairer trading arrangements between rich and poor countries, and less domination of the economies of poor countries by multinational corporations more concerned about producing profits for shareholders back home than food for the local poor. Perhaps it is more important to be politically active in the interests of the poor than to give to them oneself—but why not do both? Unfortunately, many use the view that overseas aid is the government's responsibility as a reason against giving, but not as a reason for being politically active.

Too high a standard? The final objection to the argument for an obligation to assist is that it sets a standard so high that none but a saint could attain it. This objection comes in at least three versions. The first maintains that, human nature being what it is, we cannot achieve so high a standard, and since it is absurd to say that we ought to do what we cannot do, we must reject the claim that we ought to give so much. The second version asserts that even if we could achieve so high a standard, to do so would be undesirable. The third version of the objection is that to set so high a standard is undesirable because it will be perceived as too difficult to reach, and will discourage many from even attempting to do so.

Those who put forward the first version of the objection are often influenced by the fact that we have evolved from a natural process in which those with a high degree of concern for their own interests, or the interests of their offspring and kin, can be expected to leave more descendants in future generations, and eventually to completely replace any who are entirely altruistic. Thus the biologist Garrett Hardin has argued, in support of his "lifeboat ethics," that altruism can only exist "on a small scale, over the short term, and within small, intimate groups"; while Richard Dawkins has written, in his provocative book *The Selfish Gene:* "Much as we might wish to believe otherwise, universal love and the welfare of the species as a whole are concepts which simply do not make evolutionary sense." I have already noted, in discussing the objection that we should first take care of our own, the very strong tendency for partiality in human beings. We naturally have a stronger desire to further our own interests, and those of our close kin, than we have to further the interests of strangers. What this means is that we would be foolish to expect widespread conformity to a standard that demands impartial concern, and for that reason it would scarcely be appropriate or feasible to condemn all those who fail to reach such a standard. Yet to act impartially, though it might be very difficult, is not impossible. The commonly quoted assertion that "ought" implies "can" is a reason for rejecting such moral judgments as "You ought to have saved all the people from the sinking ship," when in fact if you had taken one more person into the lifeboat, it would have sunk and you would not have saved any. In that situation, it is absurd to say that you ought to have done what you could not possibly do. When we have money to spend on luxuries and others are starving, however, it is clear that we can all give much more than we do give, and we can therefore all come closer to the impartial standard proposed in this chapter. Nor is there, as we approach closer to this standard, any barrier beyond which we cannot go. For that reason there is no basis for saying that the impartial standard is mistaken because "ought" implies "can" and we cannot be impartial.

The second version of the objection has been put by several philosophers during the past decade, among them Susan Wolf in a forceful article entitled "Moral Saints." Wolf argues that if we all took the kind of moral stance defended in this chapter, we would have to do without a great deal that makes life interesting: opera, gourmet cooking, elegant clothes, and professional sport, for a start. The kind of life we come to see as ethically required of us would be a single-minded pursuit of the overall good, lacking that broad diversity of interests and activities that, on a less demanding view, can be part of our ideal of a good life for a human being. To this, however, one can respond that while the rich and varied life that Wolf upholds as an ideal may be the most desirable form of life for a human being in a world of plenty, it is wrong to assume that it remains a good life in a world in which buying luxuries for oneself means accepting the continued avoidable suffering of others. A doctor faced with hundreds of injured victims of a train crash can scarcely think it defensible to treat fifty of them and then go to the opera, on the grounds that going to the opera is part of a well-rounded human life. The life-or-death needs of others must take priority. Perhaps we are like the doctor in that we live in a time when we all have an opportunity to help to mitigate a disaster. Associated with this second version of the objection is the claim that an impartial ethic of the kind advocated here makes it impossible to have serious personal relationships based on love and friendship; these relationships are, of their nature, partial. We put the interests of our loved ones, our family, and our friends ahead of those of strangers; if we did not do so, would these relationships survive? I have already indicated, in the response I gave when considering the objection that we should first take care of our own, that there is a place, within an impartially grounded moral framework, for recognizing some degree of partiality for kin, and the same can be said for other close personal relationships. Clearly, for most people, personal relationships are among the necessities of a flourishing life, and to give them up would be to sacrifice something of great moral significance. Hence no such sacrifice is required by the principle for which I am here arguing.

The third version of the objection asks: might it not be counterproductive to demand that people give up so much? Might not people say: "As I can't do what is morally required anyway, I won't bother to give at all." If, however, we were to set a more realistic standard, people might make a genuine effort to reach it. Thus setting a lower standard might actually result in more aid being given.

It is important to get the status of this third version of the objection clear. Its accuracy as a prediction of human behavior is quite compatible with the argument that we are obliged to give to the point at which by giving more we sacrifice something of comparable moral significance. What would follow from the objection is that public advocacy of this standard of giving is undesirable. It would mean that in order to do the maximum to reduce absolute poverty, we should advocate a standard lower than the amount we think people really ought to give. Of course we ourselves—those of us who accept the original argument, with its higher standard—would know that we ought to do more than we publicly propose people ought to do, and we might actually give more than we urge others to give. There is no inconsistency here, since in both our private and our public behavior we are trying to do what will most reduce absolute poverty.

For a consequentialist, this apparent conflict between public and private morality is always a possibility, and not in itself an indication that the underlying principle is wrong. The consequences of a principle are one thing, the consequences of publicly advocating it another. A variant of this idea is already acknowledged by the distinction between the intuitive and critical levels of morality, of which I have made use in previous chapters. If we think of principles that are suitable for the intuitive level of morality as those that should be generally advocated, these are the principles that, when advocated, will give rise to the best consequences. Where overseas aid is concerned, those will be the principles that lead to the largest amount being given by the affluent to the poor.

Is it true that the standard set by our argument is so high as to be counterproductive? There is not much evidence to go by, but discussions of the argument, with students and others have led me to think it might be. Yet, the conventionally accepted standard—a few coins in a collection tin when one is waved under your nose—is obviously far too low. What level should we advocate? Any figure will be arbitrary, but there may be something to be said for a round percentage of one's income like, say, 10 percent—more than a token donation, yet not so high as to be beyond all but saints. (This figure has the additional advantage of being reminiscent of the ancient tithe, or tenth, that was traditionally given to the church, whose responsibilities included care of the poor in one's local community. Perhaps the idea can be revived and applied to the global community.) Some families, of course, will find 10 percent a considerable strain on their finances. Others may be able to give more without difficulty. No figure should be advocated as a rigid minimum or maximum; but it seems safe to advocate that those earning average or above average incomes in affluent societies, unless they have an unusually large number of dependents or other special needs, ought to give a tenth of their income to reducing absolute poverty. By any reasonable ethical standards this is the minimum we ought to do, and we do wrong if we do less.

Endnotes

1. Strictly, we would need to cut down to the minimum level compatible with earning the income which, after providing for our needs, left us most to give away. Thus if my present position earns me, say, $40,000 a year, but requires me to spend $5,000 a year on dressing respectably and maintaining a car, I cannot save more people by giving away the car and clothes if that will mean taking a job that, although it does not involve me in these expenses, earns me only $20,000.

2. Ominously, in the twelve years that have passed between editions of this book, the signs are that the situation is becoming even worse than was then predicted. In 1979, Bangladesh had a population of 80 million and it was predicted that by 2000 its population would reach 146 million; Ethiopia's was only 29 million, and was predicted to reach 54 million; and India's was 620 million and predicted to reach 958 million.

Journal/Discussion Questions

✍ *In the concluding pages of his essay, Singer deals with the issue of whether his position is too demanding. On a personal level, do you feel that Singer's position places too high a set of expectation on you? Discuss this issue in light of his comments.*

1. Singer maintains that affluent *individuals* as well as affluent societies are obligated to help poor nations. What is the relationship between individual responsibility and collective responsibility? If we *as a nation* have an obligation to poorer nations, does it follow that each of us *as individuals* also has such an obligation? Discuss.
2. Singer considers five possible ways in which killing is morally different from letting die. What are these five possible differences? What reasons does Singer give for claiming that they do not undermine his claim that letting die is the moral equivalent of killing?
3. Singer maintains that "any consequentialist would insist that we are responsible for all the consequences of our actions." Do you think this is true? Can you imagine a situation in which you might not be responsible for all the consequences of your acts, even if those consequences are foreseeable?
4. How does Singer explain that "taking care of our own" argument? Do you think his presentation of the argument puts that argument in its best light? What objections does Singer offer to this argument? Critically assess his objections.
5. What objections does Singer offer to the triage argument—and the related argument about population expansion—advanced by Hardin and others? Critically evaluate his objections.

Henry Shue
"Solidarity Among Strangers and the Right to Food"

Henry Shue, a founding member of the Institute for Philosophy and Public Policy at the University of Maryland, is the Wyn and William Y. Hutchinson Professor of Ethics and Public Life at Cornell University. He is the author of Basic Rights: Subsistence, Affluence, and U.S. Foreign Policy.

In this article, Henry Shue explores the philosophical foundation of basic rights to subsistence, especially the right to food. He focuses on the question of what duties the right to food imposes on those in affluent nations.

As You Read, Consider This:

1. What, according to Shue, is the foundation of a person's claim to a right to food?
2. What does Shue mean by "solidarity among strangers"?
3. What is the difference between a negative and a positive right? How does this distinction affect Shue's argument?

> It is this solidarity among strangers, this transformation through the division of labor of into rights and rights into care that gives us whatever fragile basis we have for saying that we live in a moral community.[1]

Rights are for the bad days. It is difficult for those of us who are among the best-off members of the best-off societies in human history to appreciate fully that, for a billion or so of our contemporaries, every day is a bad day, although some days are still worse than others and, for many young people, the days are few.[2]

People decide which rights to grant to each other. A human does not come into life accompanied by a printed list of his or her rights, like a new toaster with its limited warranty, set of instructions ("Do not submerge in water"), and list of addresses of authorized repair stations. But decisions about which rights are to be granted need not be made arbitrarily and cannot be made individualistically. Judgments about rights are made for reasons, which embody our best understanding of the realities of human life. Sifting through the various considerations advanced as reasons for acknowledging or not acknowledging specific rights is a deeply social, and gradually evolving, process. Or so I will now argue.

Justifying Rights and Duties

Much paper has been consumed by debates about whether rights are natural. The answer is: yes and no. If "natural" means given—"just there" to be seen by any clear-eyed observer—then rights are not natural. For individual persons, there are no instructions from the manufacturer (and no manufacturer). Not much is natural in the sense of given independent of human judgment, of course, since social choices about the boundaries of any concept contribute to the determination of what does and does not fall within the concept. If, on the other hand, "natural" means based on what individual humans and human societies are actually like—what persons need and what enables them to thrive as humans—then rights are natural. The concept of human thriving or flourishing—like all concepts—becomes highly debatable on its outer edges, with increasing scope for judgment and ultimately perhaps for bare preference, but the concept's core of needs is as firm and well established as any.

Vital. We have a reason to make something the content of a fundamental right only if it is vital to human life, but different things are vitally important in radically different, almost opposite ways. Some liberties, on the one hand, are vital because they are preconditions for the crowning glories of human life: the creativity and refinement that seem to be possible only for humans, among this planet's species. Food, clean water, and clean air (and some other liberties), on the other hand, are vital because they are preconditions for the bare maintenance of human life. Ingesting basic nutrition and exercising artistic freedom are about as different as activities can be, but each is essential to a flourishing human life. The first step in showing that something ought to be the content of a right is showing that it is vital—either literally necessary to, or highly valuable to, living as a human.

Vulnerable. The second step in justifying a right is showing that, besides being vital, the thing in question is generally vulnerable: subject to widespread threats that individuals on their own often could not ward off. Besides taking in nutrition regularly, we also need, for example, for our hearts to beat regularly. But we face no general threat to regular heartbeat that is analogous to the general threat to regular nutrition constituted by fragile food-systems. If we were born with hearts that depended on rechargeable batteries—everyone in effect had an inborn pacemaker from the start—and there were millions of people who could not reach recharging equipment, just as there now are (hundreds of) millions who cannot grow or otherwise obtain adequate food under our current arrangements, it might make sense to propose "access to recharging equipment" as a human right. Although in the end many of us will die of failing hearts, ordinarily a person can lead a long and vigorous life without needing to rely on special social arrangements to keep her heart beating. Normally, heartbeat itself is not subject to chronic direct threats that individuals cannot handle on their own, so it needs no special protection. It is vital but not generally vulnerable. Food is vital, and food supplies are highly vulnerable.

I noted already that "we have a reason to make something the content of a right only if it is vital to human life, but different things are vitally important in radically different, almost opposite ways." Jeremy Waldron sums up Joseph Raz's widely accepted definition of a right as follows: "to have a right is for it to be the case that one's interest justifies holding someone else to have a duty."[3] One's interest must, in my terms, be "vitally important" in order for it to deserve to be the subject of a right—so important that, as Raz emphasizes, other people (who may not even know me, or may know me but not like me) can justifiably be expected to conduct their lives so that this interest of mine is protected or promoted.

There is a reason why starving children are usually dressed in rags, and wandering far from home. The reason is that the distributions of different material commodities like food, clothing, and shelter are not so discrete, or distinct from each other, that a person is likely to be missing out on just one commodity while being well supplied with the others.[4] The fact that things tend to come in bundles is one reason why rights should come in bundles as well. Nevertheless, since this book is about hunger and food, I will focus on reasons for the right to food, but with frequent comparisons with other equally fundamental rights.[5]

People often say something like the following: "A right to food? Sure. Without food you die; and if you are dead, you can't exercise any rights. If there were no right to food, no other right would mean much." Unfortunately—since I welcome its conclusion that there is a right to food—this is not a convincing argument. This argument is too quick and too simple, but we can note some important features of better arguments by seeing why. The observation that "without food you die" functions as an appeal to some such tacit premise as: a person has a right to whatever she needs in order to stay alive.[6] But this premise is much too strong. Few of us believe that a person has a right to whatever she needs in order to stay alive, and we could not afford to act on this premise for long if we did believe it. The premise would commit us, for example, to the judgment that if a 75-year-old person would die without a mechanical heart, she has a right to a mechanical heart.[7]

The most important reason why we do not make this judgment is the extraordinary nature of the medical care currently constituted by implantation of a mechanical heart and its resultant extraordinary expense. This, of course, could change. Surgery, antibiotics, and all kinds of care now taken for granted (in rich societies) were extraordinary even during the lifetimes of current 75-year olds. Maybe someday mechanical hearts will be mass produced and as readily provided as, say, contact lenses are now; if so, they will have then become routine and be part of ordinary care at that time. In those circumstances it might well be plausible to argue that everyone who needs one has a right to be provided one if he or she cannot afford it on one's own, just as one can argue now that every child has a right to, say, polio vaccine as part of any elementary package of preventive medicine in spite of the fact that polio vaccine did not even exist in 1950. How can it be that there was no right to polio vaccine in 1950, but there is in 1995?

The short answer is that there is an enduring general right to protection against common, easily and cheaply preventable threats to life and that a cheap protection against a severe threat to life became available between 1950 and now. The basic right to life always entailed a package of protections; it became affordable to add an item—polio vaccine—to the package. Today it is outrageous to deny a child a dose of polio vaccine because he or she cannot pay for it, because we are refusing to implement one's right to life for the sake of a trivial amount of money. If a dose of polio vaccine still cost as much as a mechanical heart now does, we would have to refuse to guarantee it to all children. As with police protection and all other protections for our lives entailed by rights, the measures we judge appropriate do depend partly on cost. Costs of technologies often decline as they are mass produced, the extraordinary becomes the ordinary, and it becomes reasonable to insist that everyone have it. This is one way that rights change. How much it would take to keep someone going—hundreds of thousands of dollars of high-tech medical care or a few dollars a day of ordinary food—cannot be ignored. Expense is an issue, as we will see more fully, because it affects the reasonableness of the duties that the recognition of the right would impose on the duty-bearers.

So what can we see generally about what it takes for an interest to justify holding someone else to have a duty? As indicated in the beginning, there is no one feature of an interest that qualifies it to be the content of a right. This can now be seen to be true for two different reasons. On the one hand, the interest must be important or vital, but "important" and "vital" are general categories and can be specified in multiple ways. On the other hand, importance to potential right-bearers—however exactly it is spelled out—is not definitive by itself. A mechanical heart may be supremely important to an aged person with a failing heart, but that by itself is not a sufficient ground for concluding that (all or some of) the rest of us have a duty to provide it. We must in addition consider which measures are normal and which are extraordinary, because we must consider cost. It is possible for what can satisfy a vital need inexpensively to be the content of a right, while what could satisfy another equally vital need, but only at great expense, not to be.

What it is reasonable to demand of others depends partly on what it would cost them to fulfill the demand. What I have so far called "vital" is what the content of a right means to the bearer of the right. But one must also inquire what fulfillment of a possible right would mean to those who would fulfill it, the duty-bearers. If fulfillment of a duty integral to a right would cost the duty-bearer something vital, that is a weighty reason against imposing the duty.[8]

Solidarity with Strangers

Rights are profoundly social.[9] The social solidarity involved in rights may be less readily apparent than their individualistic aspects, but it comes through when, and if, consideration of possible rights turns to their costs to duty-bearers, as I have just been advocating. Some proponents of rights appear to find such consideration of costs at best undignified, even ignoble, or mean-spirited.[10] Rights seem to them to be too elevated a matter for discussions of expenses to be dragged in. I am suggesting, on the contrary, that the refusal to enter into serious examination of the duties entailed by any proposed right not only is intellectually irresponsible, leaving the right largely unspecified and blowing in the wind, but fails to appreciate the full social basis of the right, which rests on the responses of other people. To ignore the point of view of duty-bearers, while considering only the point of view of right-bearers, is to construct an extremely truncated picture of how rights actually work.

It is not enough simply to declare that everyone has a right to, say, security and privacy in his or her own home, even if one adds: "So the rest of us must not interfere—we must leave them alone." Of course this right involves such a negative duty not to invade the security and privacy justifies the imposition of a duty on everyone else not to interfere with us. While this duty is at the heart of rights to security and privacy, it is far from the whole story because in fact many people will choose to violate their negative duty to leave others alone and will, for example, break into houses in order to steal money or easily saleable electronic equipment in order, for instance, to maintain their drug habits. It is utterly fatuous to say: "Oh, now you are bringing up the problem of drugs—I was talking about human rights." Talk about rights to privacy and security in the home is at least half empty if one does not ask at least the questions: "What are the most serious threats to this right, and what would it cost to protect the enjoyment of the right against those main threats?"

Every night in this country homes are broken into, and pedestrians are mugged, by people who are addicted to hard drugs and consequently desperately want money. Drug addiction is one of the most serious threats to genuine enjoyment of security in one's home. Everyone, including people with addictions, certainly has a negative duty not to mug or burglarize. To think, however, that one was doing something significant to implement the right to security if one simply reminded or admonished the people with the addictions not to violate their duties would be a joke. In order to protect security we need to do something about the political conditions that allow drug dealing to thrive. That would be dangerous and expensive. Consequently, any analysis of the duties correlative to this right has to ask, who will bear the danger and who will bear the expense, that is, how are the positive duties to be allocated?

Ignoring the positive duties correlative to a right, and their costs, is like saying: "we believe people have a 'right not to be flooded,' but we don't want to talk about dams, which are expensive economic projects"—what would a "right not to be flooded" mean if nothing were done to block the flow of water? The positive protections for a right are the dams against the threats to the right. Environmentally well-informed people know, of course, that dams are often not the best, and sometimes are not even a good, measure for preventing flooding. One often must, for example, also prevent deforestation in the watershed of the stream in question or dams will merely redistribute the flooding to different locations. A serious flood prevention program is not merely a dam-building program. This too has its analogue in the case of the right to security in the home. An approach to implementation that is not politically cynical must involve measures that go deeper than more police and more jails and must move aggressively to stop drug-dealing from consistently having one of the highest profit margins of any business in the world.

Two different points are intertwined here. One is that seriousness about rights leads to seriousness about duties. It is irresponsibly dreamy simply to muse wishfully about rights that it might be nice for people to have without moving to the next step of considering what arrangements, formal or informal, local or global, governmental or nongovernmental, are necessary for the rights imagined to be implemented. The other point is that seriousness about duties opens up the underlying social character of rights, the respects in which, while the rights belong to individuals, their protection is an expression of solidarity across a community. In order for that solidarity to be forthcoming, in many cases, and certainly in order for the cooperation required by the implementation of rights to be fair to all concerned, consideration must be given not only to the importance of the interests at stake for potential right-bearers in whether a particular right is recognized but also to the importance of the interests at stake for potential duty-bearers. For just as certain interests will be made secure if a particular right is recognized and implemented, that very implementation will involve costs and/or burdens to be borne by those who are assigned the correlative duties. The reasonableness of those duties is part of the reasonableness of the rights they implement. If it would not be reasonable to expect those who would bear the necessary duties to perform them, it cannot be reasonable to acknowledge the right.[12]

One common response to questions about the allocation of the burdens of implementing rights is to point out that right-bearers and duty-bearers are not two separate classes such that some people are exclusively right-bearers and receive only the benefits of whatever rights there are, while other people are exclusively duty-bearers and simply carry burdens. If a right is a universal human right, it belongs to everyone, and anyone can invoke its protections when the interest that it protects is threatened. So the very right whose implementation may sometimes impose burdens of duty on me may also protect the same interest in my own case on the day that my own crisis comes.

Now this is correct, and it is important, but its practical significance can easily be misconstrued. I am certainly not immune to disaster, and I might very well someday find myself hungry and homeless, especially in a country like the United States where even the basic entitlements in the social safety net are under sustained assault by political reactionaries. So institutional arrangements to implement a right to food will not necessarily always find even people as well-off as I am now on the giving, rather than the receiving, end. Nevertheless, in practice the probability of my actually needing to invoke the right to food is orders of magnitude smaller than the probability that, say, many children in Burundi or Harlem will need to invoke it. Hunger is the least of my current worries about myself. Odds definitely are that, with regard to the right to food, I will always find myself in the status of a duty-bearer and never function actively as a right-bearer, a fact that of course it is only sane to welcome, not to regret. (Should I instead hope to have the problems of Burundian children so that I can receive "my share" of the material benefits from the social acknowledgment of the right to food?) The point is only that it would be implausible to maintain that the right to food is going to be equally advantageous materially to everyone just because it does indeed belong to everyone.[13] Anatole France's famous observation, "The law in its majestic equality forbids the rich as well as the poor to sleep under the bridges," poignantly captures the importance of differences in circumstances.[14] The same prohibition, or the same right, will have very different material benefits for people in different situations.

This discussion of benefits from rights is so far extremely simplistic, especially in two respects. First, one must distinguish what might be called insurance benefits from direct material benefits. Rights are in important respects like insurance policies, providing protection against eventualities that one hopes will not occur, like early death. Suppose there are two young couples, the Roses and the Thorns, each with a young child. Each couple decides to buy life insurance for the breadwinner(s) of the family in order that their child will have enough money to pay for college even if the breadwinner(s) should die young. The breadwinner for the Rose family does in fact meet an early death, and the survivor and their child collect the insurance. The Thorns on the other hand, enjoy a long and happy life, living to see their grandchildren while still paying annual premiums on the life insurance policies, until finally they just cancel the life insurance policies, without ever collecting any "death benefits." Do we judge, then, that while the Roses benefited from one of their life insurance policies, because one of them died young and the spouse and child collected money that they needed, the Thorns failed to benefit? No. None of the Thorns benefited materially by receiving a check for a death benefit from the insurance company, but they did benefit from the security provided for their child's education. The insurance policy guaranteed the Thorns that, whether they lived or died, their child would have its education paid for. That security is itself a benefit—and an objective one. That is, it is not merely that they felt secure subjectively about their child's education—that could have resulted from their mistakenly believing they were covered by a policy that did not in fact cover them. Their child's education was objectively secure: it was in reality going to be paid for, one way or another. Their life insurance did them a lot of good. It provided them what I am calling insurance benefits.

Rights also provide insurance benefits, as well as material benefits. I do not benefit from a right to food only when I am too weak to secure my own meals. I benefit from the fact—or would benefit if in this country it were the fact—that arrangements are in place for the day, should it come, when I become so weak. Since this is not one of the problems I worry about, I would not benefit subjectively—not be relieved of any anxiety on this score. Nevertheless, I would be objectively better-off, specifically more secure, than I am without institutions guaranteeing food to those unable to get it for themselves.

The second respect in which the initial discussion above of rights and benefits is simplistic is in attempting to look at only one right at a time. Specific rights protect against specific threats to specific interests. At any one time some people will be subject to any given threat, other people will definitely not be the subject, and others still will be more or less likely to be subject to it. Every right does have insurance benefits even if it protects against threats that are, at any given time, distant or irrelevant, as we noticed just above. It is also important, however, that any one right normally comes in a system of rights. For any given person, while certain rights protect against threats that are not immediate, other rights protect against other threats that are. A particular person is likely to be receiving material benefits from a few rights and insurance benefits from many others, if she is lucky, or, if she is not as lucky, material benefits from many rights. The more threats from which one would actually suffer but for one's rights, the more material benefits one receives from the system of rights.

Often a kind of mirror effect occurs between different rights. I am not worried about running out of food because I have more than enough wealth to buy food for myself. That, in turn, may mean that what I have to worry about protecting is my wealth. If I have enough wealth not to need to invoke any arrangements for implementing the right to food, I may well benefit instead from the arrangements for the right to physical security that protect me against any assault that would be involved in taking some of my wealth from me by force. This is a certain sort of reciprocity among rights.

Reciprocity among Right-bearers

A far more important reciprocity holds among persons, if they are the bearers of rights. This reciprocity is the specific form that systems of rights give to solidarity with strangers. I might, for instance, reasonably expect a hungry child—let us call her Wanda[15]—not to attack me physically in order to take some of my money for food, just as she might reasonably expect that I will not merely turn away clutching my money and let her starve. The interest protected in the case of each of us would be physical survival. A well-designed system of rights could protect the vital interest of us both equally well, if we each performed our duties.

Her duty may be far more onerous than mine in spite of the fact that, in the encounter I have just sketched, mine is positive and hers is negative. My duty might be, say, to provide her with enough money for food for a month while she looks for a job. If I were her last hope—as I might or might not be—my failure to do my duty in implementing her right to food would have as its effect her death within the next month from starvation. The cost to me of fulfilling my duty to her might be, assuming she lives in a poor Third World country and could eat for a little more than $1 a day, say $50. My duty is positive, but in this one case taken by itself, trivial in amount for a member of the U.S. middle class; I might just get inside the door of a Broadway show for this amount (leaving aside what it would cost me to get to New York City and to have a comfortable bed for the night).[16]

Her duty in implementing my right to physical security, on the other hand, is the purely negative one of not attacking and attempting to rob me, irrespective of whether I turn and start walking away from her. The effect on me of her failure to do her duty toward me might be, assuming that she is weak from malnutrition and not armed, that I fight her off with only cuts and bruises or that I buy her off at the last minute, under direct threat of attack, with the contents of my wallet, which—let us assume for the sake of neatness—is $50. The effect upon her of her doing her purely negative duty of leaving me alone, if I am in fact walking away from her, is death within the next month from starvation, assuming that I am the only rich-country tourist passing through the village and there is no one else available over the short-term either to help her voluntarily, to employ her, or to be robbed by her. In short, my performance of my positive duty would cost me $50; her performance of her negative duty would cost her her life. Contrary to common assumption, the fulfillment of a positive duty need not be more costly or more difficult than the fulfillment of a negative duty. No such generalizations are available at the high level of abstraction represented by the concepts of positive and negative duties; one must look at specific duties and at features other than whether they are positive or negative, which is a feature of little real significance in spite of its popularity in abstract theories.[17]

On the other hand, while avoiding for a month the death of one malnourished youth in the Third World may cost only a trivial amount like $50 (less than the cost of most new books), tens of millions of other young people fit Wanda's general description. Reiterating fulfillment of the same modest duty endlessly could exhaust any one person's resources. If that were the implication of acknowledging a right for Wanda, the apparent unreasonableness of the implication might be taken to show the unreasonableness of the premise from which it follows. A supposed right that implied such unreasonable duties would be an unreasonable right. However, it is usually thought that, if Wanda has a general right to help from someone, it can only be from someone who has not yet done his or her share to fulfill such general rights.[18] Do we each have a share, the performance of which is the limit on our general duties?

Now it is obvious that a person's general duties—that is, duties in response to general rights (rights belonging to everyone)—either are limited or are not limited. If they are not limited, then one is never finished with one's general duties; however much one has done or given, more—endlessly more—remains. This is not an obviously incoherent view. It is only an overwhelming view. If it is correct, one's duty is simply never done until one's last breath is gone, precisely as many martyrs, saints, and other passionate servants of humanity have believed. In this age, this view would be a hard sell, but that may tell us more about the age than about the view.

If, on the other hand, a person's general duties are limited, there is such a thing as having done all that one has any duty to do. One can be finished doing everything that one ought to do for the sake of human rights. Since the planet contains at least a billion people whose rights are not being protected or respected, one is very likely—more likely in some places than others—to encounter people who are desperate because interests important enough to deserve the protection of rights are, in their cases, going unprotected and unfulfilled. Still, if the notion of a limit to duty is to mean anything at all, one must be entitled at some point to walk by on the other side of the road. One is entitled to look the Wandas of the world in the eye, sadly but not guiltily, and walk calmly away.

Or maybe not so calmly. It may be—unless I am an insensitive brute—it will be uncomfortable for me to walk away from Wanda's desperate need. I will be greatly tempted to deceive myself into believing that she will, if I leave her, somehow be taken care of, even if I have absolutely no good reason for this optimism. I am free of course to be generous in excess of my fair share of general duty—nothing prohibits me from helping people I am under no duty to help. If, however, my "generosity" is a salve for feelings of guilt at the thought of walking away, my guilt is irrational if my limited duty had already been done. It is, in a way, just bad luck for me that I have encountered Wanda—and of course bad luck for her that it was me, not someone with unfulfilled general duties, that encountered her. If I were in my home, not hers, I wouldn't see her; and I would not have to avoid her plaintive eyes as I turn to leave her.

If I were at home, she would of course still be where she is, just as desperate. But I know that wherever I happen to be, there or at home, hundreds of thousands of other desperately hungry youths stand on hundreds of thousands of other dirty street corners. They cannot all be my responsibility—that would make my duty absurdly great and thereby demonstrate the supposed right to be unreasonable. The others do not threaten to haunt me the way that Wanda does, but that is only because I can see her face—must see her face. That I see her face is perhaps merely an arbitrary contingency, an unfortunate coincidence, like seeing a terrible accident on the highway that occurs just before one happens to pass. If her face is otherwise going to haunt me, perhaps I should give her the $50 to buy myself the peace of mind (and stay out of the Third World in the future). But if I do give it to her, I should admit to myself that this is irrational guilt-money, more weakness than generosity.

And yet I believe that it is right that we should hesitate to become the kind of people who are really good at walking away. The reluctance that decent people feel seems to me to be healthfully human and even morally admirable. That the reluctance is felt shows that the sense of solidarity undergirding systems of rights is in fact deeply felt. The implication cannot, however, simply be not to walk away. That would be to deny, after all, that duty has a limit. And that would just be to go around the circle one more time: either a person's general duties are limited or they are not. . . . At this level the logic is inescapable. We need a fresh perspective.

Individual Rights and Social Forces

The greatest failing of rights theories, I believe, has been their tendency to rest content with an asocial individualistic level of descriptive analysis.[19] The right to food is an individual right, that is, a right of each individual person. It thus has, if you like, an individualistic grounding: it is the importance to each individual of her interest in adequate food that makes food an appropriate subject for recognition as a right. The right to food has, then, its individualistic aspect. But this is no excuse for settling for simplistic pictures of social reality that implicitly portray human societies as if they were piles of undifferentiated grains of sand. Normative individualism does not entail or presuppose descriptive individualism. And descriptive individualism is clearly inadequate.

Currently in the neighborhood of a billion people on this planet are malnourished, and hundreds are starving to death at any given moment. It would be deeply silly to think that an adequate analysis of what to do about a problem this engrained and persistent could possibly take the form of random individuals relating directly to other random individuals, for example, my giving or not giving $50 to Wanda. This would be analogous to thinking about how, in the early 1940s, to recapture the European continent from the Nazis by saying: "Well, you could get a rowboat and cross the English Channel; and I'll get another rowboat, and we'll rendezvous at Normandy—be sure to bring a rifle and plenty of ammunition." Or thinking that, since putting a man on the moon was about an individual, the first question should be: which man? Ultimately in all these cases—invading Normandy, putting a man on the moon, and eliminating widespread human hunger—duties for individuals must be specified, and individuals must then act as they ought. But only hopeless ignorance of the functioning of social institutions could allow us to think that the form of analysis by means of which we should arrive at the responsibilities of individuals is to imagine isolated human atoms each trying to do her duty: "I will give $50 to Wanda and five relevantly similar individuals, and you provide seeds and a plow to Abdul and five relevantly similar individuals." This is as fatuous as thinking that a plan for the Normandy invasion would have the form: "You shoot every Nazi you see, and meanwhile I will fix us some lunch." In order to arrive at a sane allocation of responsibilities to individuals, one needs an adequate analysis of the critical social forces and institutions: a reasonably accurate account of the political economy of why so many people on a planet this wealthy lack adequate food and how that can be changed.

That I can say that what we need is an adequate analysis of the social dynamics and how to change them does not, unfortunately, mean that I myself have the analysis ready to give.[20] But it is possible to indicate directions for reorientation of our thinking. Negatively, but importantly, it is no good just anguishing about terrible choices for individuals acting in isolation, like whether I should hand $50 to Wanda or let her starve during the subsequent few weeks. Hard choices will doubtless always be with us no matter how creative we are about our institutional innovation, but to think that they are the heart of the matter would be to accept a hopelessly atomistic, individualistic picture of the problem: the world's population consists of individuals with unfulfilled rights, like Wanda, wandering around their villages and of other individuals, like me, who blunder in with $50 in their pocket and wonder what to do with it. It is no surprise that it seems impossible to decide what an individual should do, since such uncoordinated individual actions are virtually certain not to solve the underlying problems. Actions must be coordinated, and effective institutions must be built just as they are in any other serious undertaking.

Also negatively but importantly, we can begin by admitting that so far things have not gone well. What our normative individualism—that is, our commitment to arranging to protect the interests vital to individual persons—tells us is that the world is extremely badly run when in some parts of it children die like flies while in other parts of it resources abound. It may seem perverse to insist on such a negative judgment, but in the wake of the end of the Cold War we in this part of the world are suffering an orgy of self-congratulation about the splendors of our political economy. Ours is certainly superior to the former Soviet one, but that is not saying much. And everything is going beautifully for us only if "us" excludes the billion or so human beings mired in desperate poverty. Being more constructive is difficult. But the need to be constructive—and imaginative and innovative—can be clear only if we are not smothered in smugness about how well the economy of the "Free World" already works.

The one thing that can be said in favor of examples like "Wanda" is that they try to put names and faces on human beings. That is important. It helps to keep the normative individualism, the sense that no individual person is expendable, alive. But it is not enough—we must also harness whatever real understanding we can put together from political science, economics, anthropology, and the other social sciences, granted that much of them too, like much of ethics, is devoted to simplistic and useless abstractions.

More positively, we can be sure that we must think in terms of divisions of moral labor, because the duties involved in implementing the right to food must be assigned in a manner that satisfies at least two criteria: (1) the interest of right-bearers in a secure food supply is actually guaranteed as well as is humanly possible and (2) at the same time the same and other vital interests of duty-bearers are similarly guaranteed. In short, the right to food cannot be guaranteed by an assignment of duties that ignores equally vital interests on the part of duty-bearers.[21]

One of the misleading clichés within what is supposed to be common sense about rights is: if a right is universal, the correlative duties must be universal too. This is false, however often it is repeated, as I hope I have shown. It is not the case that everyone's duties are the same, even if everyone's rights are the same. The cliché arises from ignoring all the duties necessary to the implementation of a right except the purely negative ones, which indeed must be universal. For example, if everyone has a right to physical security, everyone else—literally, everyone—has toward everyone else—literally, everyone else—a duty not to torture, a duty not to execute arbitrarily, a duty not to rape, a duty not to assault, and so on. It is impossible for anyone to be exempt from these negative duties toward anyone else because a person who was exempt even with regard to a few other people—call him Mr. Special—would be free to, say, assault those people as he wished. In the *ante bellum* South, for example, a slave-owner was Mr. Special. A slave had the duty not to assault toward everyone else, slave and free: he or she was not to assault anyone, although the punishment was certainly incomparably more severe if the person assaulted was free, that is, "white." Mr. Special probably was understood to have the duty not to assault generally toward other adult free people—there, of course, was some "disciplining" of wives as well as of slaves—but was certainly understood not to have any such duty toward slaves. Slaves could be struck, beaten, whipped, and raped. It was not in one's interest to damage one's property, so there were in fact fewer severe beatings than there could have been, but not out of any sense of a duty owed to the slave. This is a system in which negative duties are not universal, and it is repulsive.

Another crucial element in the implementation of any right, as we saw earlier, is fulfillment of the duty to protect right-bearers against the people who do not honor, or mistakenly think they do not have, negative duties. If the only actions taken to fulfill rights were efforts to convince people of their negative duties, many rights would be violated. Even if we do not fully understand the source of human violence against humans, we know perfectly well that preventing it involves more than promulgating negative duties and attempting to persuade people that they all have them all. In order for people to be reasonably physically secure they must be protected against those who violate their negative duties. To some extent people need to be guarded by, for example, police on the beat.

What I am calling "the duty to protect" is whatever set of institutional arrangements would most effectively provide for persons' physical security, while also respecting their other crucial interests. It is possible to debate whether these arrangements should include a Uzzi in every home and dozens of new prisons, or what I would take to be saner programs. What is abundantly clear either way is that positive duties will have to be performed. Police will have to be on the streets, judges will have to be in the criminal courts, at least guards—possibly teachers and counselors—will have to be in the prisons, and so on. On the other hand, not everyone needs to join the police force, the criminal justice system, or the prison system. There is a division of labor in the fulfillment of the duty to protect physical security.

Now it would be difficult to say whether the causes of violence or the causes of hunger are less well understood.[22] Concerning hunger too, we have serious disputes. Is the World Bank part of the solution, or part of the problem? Will U.S.A.I.D. ever stop spending huge portions of its budget on U.S. academics (as consultants)? Can weak national governments in poor countries, desperate for foreign exchange to service crushing debts, ever protect their agricultural sectors against distortions by multinational agribusinesses with no interest in local diets but interest only in exports to rich countries? And so on. What we do know, however, is that agricultural systems do need protection from all sorts of market-driven predators, including wolves in sheep's clothing, since feeding poor people is rarely the most profitable use of valuable resources. If there were lots of profit to be made in solving the world's hunger problem, market forces would presumably have sent people rushing in to solve it long ago.

Individual donations by individual donors—I give $50 to Wanda, who is already malnourished—are at best too little, too late, too uncoordinated. They may also be myopically off-target by focusing too directly on food itself; for many Third World countries, more or less food assistance, or even agricultural development aid, is far less important than some solution to their staggering burdens of debt to foreign, rich-country banks, which is one of the main forces driving the diversion of land and other resources out of the production of food. The philosophical point is that the duties necessary to implement the right to food depend on the design of effective institutions for food security. The design of effective institutions for food security depends on sources other than philosophy, namely our best understanding of political economy and of social dynamics generally.

Serious efforts at social analysis provide more assistance with the question of what kind of action to take than with the question of how much sacrifice of one's own material interests to make in taking the action. I understand one's duty is to play a role in operating an existing, effective institution, or in creating an effective institution where none exists. Different persons will play different roles. Most roles will probably require intelligence, imagination, and other human virtues, besides a willingness to share the resources that one commands, because whatever resources one sacrifices should be invested in changing fundamental dynamics, not merely consumed in smoothing over some bad effects of existing dynamics. Blocking further deprivations of food by others who are ignoring their own duties and creating mechanisms that will multiply the effectiveness of attempts to help the deprived is much more valuable than merely patching up bad effects while leaving their causes to continue doing harm.[23]

The question, how much one should sacrifice in these efforts? remains, however. The superficial answer is that one's duty is at least to do one's fair share in the overall task of guaranteeing this, and other equally basic, rights. The specification of a fair share raises further questions that I cannot take up here. First, if the right to food is one of a bundle of equally basic rights, as I believe, it may be a discretionary matter whether one does more to guarantee this right and less to guarantee others, or vice versa. Especially if a right cannot be guaranteed in isolation from other equally basic rights, arranging for the whole bundle of rights is the only available option in any case. Consequently, it may be a good thing if different people work on different rights.

Second, and much more troubling, is the question whether one's fair share is to be calculated on the ideal assumption that everyone else will do his or her fair share, which it is perfectly obvious is not in fact happening, or is to be calculated on the realistic basis of the way things actually are, namely that many people are by no stretch of the imagination doing their share of the positive duties and quite a few are in addition violating their negative duties. If one's share is calculated on the realistic basis, one's share will be considerably greater than otherwise, and one will in fact be picking up balls dropped by others; on the other hand, the job of guaranteeing the right for everyone may be accomplished. If one's share is calculated on the ideal assumption that everyone who should carry out duties will do so, one's share will be much less; on the other hand, the job of guaranteeing the right for everyone will surely not be accomplished. While we think about whether we are bound to do our share according to the more demanding calculation, we might get started doing our share on the less demanding one.

Endnotes

1. Michael Ignatieff, *The Needs of Strangers* (London: Chatto and Windus, 1984), pp. 9–10. Quoted in Jeremy Waldron, *Liberal Rights: Collected Papers, 1981–1991* (New York: Cambridge University Press, 1993), p. 382.
2. One good source of general information is: *Causes of Hunger, Hunger 1995,* Fifth Annual Report on the State of World Hunger (Silver Spring, MD: Bread for the World Institute, 1994.)
3. Jeremy Waldron, *Liberal Rights: Collected Papers, 1981–1991* (New York: Cambridge University Press, 1993), p. 353. For Raz's own account, see Joseph Raz, "Right-based Moralities," *Theories of Rights,* Waldron, Jeremy, ed. (Oxford: Oxford University Press, 1984), p. 183.
4. That was much more likely before the commodification of almost everything. When people made their own clothes and grew their own food, rather than purchasing them from others, it was quite possible to have enough food but no coat because the sheep had died, leaving no wool for a coat, and no one made coats in order to sell them. Now, if you have the money, you can buy anything; and if you don't, you are likely not to have it unless you are entitled to it by right. I am not suggesting that we should, or even could, "go back," but it is important to understand that not every feature of the modern is good—see Karl Polanyi, *The Great Transformation: The Political and Economic Origins of Our Time* (Boston: Beacon Press, 1957).
5. I mean a moral right to food, even if the moral right is not embodied in legal rights. Legal rights to food have, however, come to be fairly well entrenched—see Philip Alston, "International

Law and the Human Right to Food," *The Right to Food,* Alston, P. and Tomasevski, K. eds. (Dordrecht: Martinus Nijhoff for the Netherlands Institute for Human Rights, 1984), pp. 9–68.

6. The argument, then, is something like this: a person has a meaningful right only if she will be alive to exercise it; she will be alive to exercise it only if she has whatever she needs to stay alive; she needs food; so if a person is to have any meaningful right, she needs food. If we want people to have meaningful rights, then we must, as a means to that end, guarantee them food.
7. On this kind of case more generally, see Daniel Callahan, *The Troubled Dream of Life: Living with Mortality* (New York: Simon and Schuster, 1993).
8. Not necessarily a decisive reason: most people seem to think that a young person can have a duty to sacrifice his or her life, if need be, in defense of a state or nation (leaving aside here exactly what we refer to by "state" and "nation") in spite of the fact that fulfillment of that duty may cost something utterly vital.
9. The significance of this has been missed by some contemporary critics of rights like Mary Ann Glendon in *Rights Talk: The Impoverishment of Political Discourse* (New York: Free Press, 1991).
10. James W. Nickel deserves credit for having persisted in working out this unpopular side of the theory of rights. See, for example, James W. Nickel, *Making Sense of Human Rights: Philosophical Reflections on the Universal Declaration of Human Rights* (Berkeley: University of California Press, 1987), Chapter 7, "Resources and Rights."
11. A negative duty is a duty to refrain from acting; a positive duty is a duty to act. In the course of this essay I will note various respects in which this simple negative/positive distinction, which is often invoked in the literature about rights as if it is momentous, is largely inconsequential even where it is worth noticing for a little additional clarity.
12. The issue consequently is not only whether the duties are reasonable in themselves (whatever exactly that would mean) but whether they are reasonable demands specifically upon the [kinds of] people upon whom they would fall.
13. Nor is there, of course, any reason why arrangements about rights need to be mutually advantageous for all participants in order for the arrangements to be justified. The justification of morality does not depend upon mutual advantage.
14. Anatole France, *Le Lys Rouge,* rev. ed. (Paris: 1923), pp. 117–118: quoted and translated in Waldron, *Liberal Rights,* p. 460.
15. Yes, if you like, you may call her Rwanda.
16. I realize that there may be other cases—I am coming to that. This problem of numbers has been emphasized by James S. Fishkin, *The Limits of Obligation* (New Haven, CT: Yale University Press, 1982). Compare Henry Shue, "Fishkin, the Limits of Obligation," *Political Theory,* vol. 11 (1983), pp. 269–272.
17. This is argued more fully in Shue, *Basic Rights,* Chapter 2, "Correlative Duties."
18. General rights are rights that belong to every person and are not contingent on any special relationships between right-bearer and duty-bearer or any particular histories involving them with each other.

19. I will not take up here the vexed question of whether, in addition to rights of individuals, there are also rights of groups of some kind. Valuable discussions include Philip Alston, "Making Space for New Human Rights: The Case of the Right to Development," *Human Rights Yearbook,* vol. 1 (1988), pp. 3–40; and Waldron, *Liberal Rights,* Chapter 14, "Can Communal Goods be Human Rights?"
20. An excellent example of the kind of analysis I mean is: Jean Drèze and Amartya Sen. *Hunger and Public Action,* WIDER Studies in Development Economics (Oxford: Clarendon Press, 1989).
21. It may be that the assignment of duties must respect as well *some* less important, but nevertheless genuinely important, interests on the part of duty-bearers. This is a complex but critical issue, at least partly about the interpretation of human equality, at which I took a fairly simple crack in Shue, *Basic Rights,* Chapter 5. "Affluence and Responsibility" (summarized in the table on p. 115). For a different view, see Samuel Scheffler, *Human Morality* (New York: Oxford University Press, 1992).
22. My bet, for what it is worth, is that we understand the dynamics of hunger better. I am not sure that the eradication of violence is possible, but I do not see why widespread malnutrition could not be eliminated.
23. See the chapter by James W. Nickel.

Journal/Discussion Questions

✍ *As a resident of one of the most affluent nations on earth, what do you think your own personal obligations are in regard to world hunger? How much should you sacrifice for the sake of those who are starving and malnourished?*

1. What, according to Shue, is the greatest shortcoming of most accounts of rights? How does his approach to rights rectify this shortcoming?
2. According to Shue, if rights are universal, does it follow that duties are universal as well? Explain.

Hugh LaFollette and Larry May
"Suffer the Little Children"

Hugh LaFollete is a professor of philosophy at East Tennessee State University. He has published widely in the area of ethics, including Personal Relationships: Love, Friendship and Morality *and (with Niall Shanks)* Brute Science: The Dilemmas of Animal Experimentation. *Larry May is a professor of philosophy at Washington University, and his books include* The Morality of Groups, Sharing Responsibility, *and* The Socially Responsible Self.

When we see pictures of starving children, we want to help. LaFollette and May explore the philosophical foundations of this immediate reaction and argue that "those of us who are in a position to help are responsible to the malnourished and starving children of the world." They consider several counterarguments to their position.

As You Read, Consider This:

1. What are the two characteristics of starving children that account for our initial sense of responsbility toward them?
2. What, according to LaFollette and May, is the purpose of morality?
3. What is the difference between acute need and chronic need? What role does this distinction play in LaFollette and May's argument?

Children are the real victims of world hunger: at least 70 percent of the malnourished people of the world are children. By best estimates forty thousand children a day die of starvation (FAO 1989: 5). Children do not have the ability to forage for themselves, and their nutritional needs are exceptionally high. Hence, they are unable to survive for long on their own, especially in lean times. Moreover, they are especially susceptible to diseases and conditions which are the staple of undernourished people: simple infections and simple diarrhea (UNICEF 1993: 22). Unless others provide adequate food, water, and care, children will suffer and die (WHO 1974: 677, 679). This fact must frame any moral discussions of the problem.

And so it does—at least pre-philosophically. When most of us first see pictures of seriously undernourished children, we want to help them, we have a sense of responsibility to them, we feel sympathy toward them (Hume 1978: 368–71). Even those who think we needn't or shouldn't help the starving take this initial response seriously: they go to great pains to show that this sympathetic response should be constrained. They typically claim that assisting the hungry will demand too much of us, or that assistance would be useless and probably detrimental. The efforts of objectors to undermine this natural sympathetic reaction would be pointless unless they saw its psychological force.

We want to explain and bolster this sympathetic reaction—this conviction that those of us in a position to help are responsible to the malnourished and starving children of the world. We contend that we have this responsibility to starving children unless there are compelling reasons which show that this sympathetic reaction is morally inappropriate (Ibid.: 582). This requires, among other things, that we seek some "steady and general point of view" from which to rebut standard attempts to explain away this instinctive sympathetic response. By showing that assistance is neither too demanding nor futile, we think more people will be more inclined to act upon that pre-philosophical sense of responsibility. And, by philosophically championing that sense of responsibility, we will make most people feel more justified in so acting.

Vulnerability and Innocence

Our initial sense of responsibility to the starving and malnourished children of the world is intricately tied to their being paradigmatically vulnerable and innocent. They are paradigmatically vulnerable because they do not have the wherewithal to care for themselves; they must rely on others to care for them. All children are directly dependent on their parents or guardians, while children whose parents cannot provide them food—either because of famine or economic arrangements—are also indirectly dependent on others: relief agencies or (their own or foreign) governments. Children are paradigmatically innocent since they are neither causally nor morally responsible for their plight. They did not cause drought, parched land, soil erosion, and over-population; nor are they responsible for social, political, and economic arrangements which make it more difficult for their parents to obtain food. If anyone were ever an innocent victim, the children who suffer and die from hunger are.

Infants are especially vulnerable. They temporarily lack the capacities which would empower them to acquire the necessities of life. Thus, they are completely dependent on others for sustenance. This partly explains our urge to help infants in need. James Q. Wilson claims that our instinctive reaction to the cry of a newborn child is demonstrated quite early in life.

> As early as ten months of age, toddlers react visibly to signs of distress in others, often becoming agitated; when they are one and a half years old they seek to do something to alleviate the other's distress; by the time they are two years old they verbally sympathize . . . and look for help (Wilson 1993: 139–140).

Although this response may be partly explained by early training, available evidence suggests that humans have an "innate sensitivity to the feelings of others" (Wilson 1993: 140). Indeed, Hans Jonas claims the parent-child relationship is the "archetype of responsibility," where the cry of the newborn baby is an ontic imperative "in which the plain factual 'is' evidently coincides with an 'ought' " (1983: 30).

This urge to respond to the infant in need is, we think, the appropriate starting point for discussion. But we should also explain how this natural response generates or is somehow connected to moral responsibility.

The Purpose of Morality

The focus of everyday moral discussion about world hunger is on the children who are its victims. Yet the centrality of children is often lost in more abstract debates about rights, obligations, duties, development, and governmental sovereignty. We do not want to belittle either the cogency or the conclusions of those arguments. Rather, we propose a different way of conceptualizing this problem. Although it may be intellectually satisfying to determine whether children have a right to be fed or whether we have an obligation to assist them, if those arguments do not move us to action, then it is of little use—at least to the children in need. So we are especially interested in philosophical arguments which are more likely to motivate people to act. We think arguments which keep the spotlight on starving children are more likely to have that effect.

Moreover, by thinking about hunger in these ways we can better understand and respond to those who claim we have no obligation to assist the starving. For we suspect that when all the rhetoric of rights, obligations, and population control are swept away, what most objectors fear is that asking people to assist the starving and undernourished is to ask too much. Morality or no, people are unlikely to act in ways they think require them to substantially sacrifice their personal interests. Thus, as long as most people think helping others demands too much, they are unlikely to provide help.

John Arthur's critique of Peter Singer highlights just this concern. Arthur objects to moral rules which require people to abandon important things to which they have a right.

Rights or entitlements to things that are our own reflect important facts about people. Each of us has only one life and it is uniquely valuable to each of us. Your choices do not constitute my life, nor do mine yours. . . . It seems, then, that in determining whether to give aid to starving persons . . . [agents must assign] special weight to their own interests (1977: 43).

Thus, people need not assist others if it requires abandoning something of substantial moral significance. Since what we mean by "substantial moral significance" has an ineliminable subjective element (Ibid.: 47), some individuals may conclude that sending *any* money to feed the starving children would be to ask too much of them. Arthur thereby captures a significant element of most people's worries about assisting the needy. The concern for our own projects and interests is thought to justify completely repressing, or at least constraining, our natural sympathies for children in need.

At bottom, we suspect that what is at issue is the proper conception and scope of morality. Some philosophers have argued that morality should not be exceedingly demanding; indeed, one of the stock criticisms of utilitarianism is that it is far too demanding. On the other hand, some theorists, including more than a few utilitarians, have bitten the proverbial bullet and claimed that morality is indeed demanding, and that its demandingness in no way counts against its cogency (Parfit, 1984; Kegan, 1988). On the former view, morality should set expectations which all but the most weak-willed and self-centered person can satisfy; on the latter view, morality makes demands which are beyond the reach of most, if not all, of us.

We wish to take the middle ground and suggest that morality is a delicate balancing act between Milquetoast expectations which merely sanctify what people already do, and expectations which are *excessively* demanding and, thus, are psychologically impossible—or at least highly improbable. Our view is that the purpose of morality is not to establish an edifice which people fear, but to set expectations which are likely to improve us, and—more relevant to the current issue—to improve the lot of those we might assist. Morality would thus be like any goals which enable us to grow and mature: they must be within reach, yet not easily reachable (LaFollette 1989: 503–6). Of course, what is within reach changes over time; and what is psychologically probable depends, in no small measure, on our beliefs about what is morally expected of us. So by expecting ourselves to do more and to be more than we currently do and are, we effectively stimulate ourselves to grow and improve. But all that is part of the balancing act of which we speak.

Thus, we frame the moral question in the following way: what should responsible people do? Our initial sympathetic response is to help the starving children. Are there any compelling reasons to think our compassion should, from some "steady and general point of view," be squelched? We think the answer is "No." Are there additional reasons which bolster this initial reaction? We think the answer is "Yes." In short, we think our initial conviction that we are responsible to malnourished children is not only undefeated, it is also rationally justified.

Moral Responsibility

We "instinctively" respond to the needs of starving and malnourished children. But are we, in fact, morally responsible for their plight? There are, of course, two different questions intermingled here: (1) Are we *causally* responsible *for* their condition—did we, individually or collectively, cause their hunger or create the environment which made their hunger and malnourishment more likely? (2) Are we *morally* responsible *to* these children, whether or not we are causally responsible for the conditions which make them hungry?

It is a commonplace of moral argument that people are morally responsible to those to whom they cause harm. If I run a stoplight and hit your auto, then I must pay any medical bills and either repair or replace your auto. If I trip you, causing you to break your arm, then I am expected to carry any resulting financial burden. The principle here is that we should respond to those whose cry for help results from our actions. If others are contributing causes to the harm, we may be jointly responsible to you (Hart and Honore 1959: 188–229). Or, if my action was itself caused by the actions of some other agent—e.g., if someone shoved me into you—then this other person is both causally and morally responsible for the harm. But, barring such conditions, a person is morally responsible for harms he or she causes.

Some commentators have argued that the affluent nations, especially colonial powers, are morally responsible to the starving because they created the conditions which make world-wide starvation possible, and perhaps inevitable (O'Neill 1993: 263–4). We find such claims plausible. But, such claims, although plausible, are contentious. Hence, for purposes of argument, we will assume that we in affluent nations are in no way causally responsible for the plight of the starving. If we can show we are (morally) responsible to the children, even if we are not (causally) responsible for their plight, then our responsibility to them will be all the stronger if, as we suspect, these causal claims are true.

Shared Responsibility

If we are the cause of harm, then we are responsible *to* the "victim" because we are responsible *for* their condition. For instance, we assume biological parents have *some* responsibility *to* children because they were responsible *for* bringing them into the world. However, being the cause of harm is not the only condition which creates a responsibility *to* someone. We are also responsible to those whom we have explicitly agreed or promised to help. For instance, by assuming a job as a lifeguard, I have agreed to care for those who swim at my beach or pool, even if they, through lack of care or foresight, put themselves into jeopardy.

More important for the current argument, responsibilities also arise from actions which, although not explicit agreements, nonetheless create reasonable expectations of care. For example, although *some* of the parents responsibilities to their children is explained by their being the cause of the children's existence, this clearly does explain the full *range* of parental responsibilities. For even when an agent is indisputably responsible *for* the harm to another, we would *never* think the agent is obliged to change the "victim's" soiled pants, to hold her at night when she is sick, or to listen patiently as she recounts her afternoon's activities. Yet we *do* expect this—and much more—of parents.

Our ordinary understanding of parental responsibilities makes no attempt to ground specific responsibilities *to* the child on any causal claims about the parents' responsibility *for* the child's condition. Rather, this understanding focuses on the needs of the child, and the fact that the parents are in the best position to respond to those needs. This is exactly where the focus should be.

Although for any number of reasons these responsibilities typically fall to the child's biological parents, the responsibilities are not limited to the parents. Others of us (individually or collectively) have a responsibility to care for children whose parents die or abandon them. It matters not that we neither brought these children into the world nor did we voluntarily agree to care for them. Rather, as responsible people we should care for children in need, especially since they are paradigmatically vulnerable and innocent. This is our natural sympathetic reaction. "No quality of human nature is more remarkable, both in itself and in its consequences, than the propensity we have to sympathize with others" (Hume 1978: 316).

This helps explain our shared moral responsibility to care for children who are not being cared for by their parents. Since the range of parental responsibilities cannot be explained either by the parents' being the cause of the child's existence or by their explicitly agreeing to care for the child, it should not be surprising that our shared responsibility likewise does not depend on an explicit agreement or an implicit assumption of responsibility. We assume responsible people will, in fact, care for abandoned children. This shared responsibility springs from our common vulnerability, and from our ability to respond to others who are similarly situated.

Acute Need

Until now we have spoken as if all starvation and malnutrition were created equal. They are not. The hunger with which we are most familiar—the hunger whose images often appear on our television sets—is hunger caused by famine. And famines tend to be episodic; often they are unpredictable. An extended drought or a devastating flood may destroy crops in a region, so that the people of that region can no longer feed themselves. (Or, as is more often the case, these environmental catastrophes may not destroy all crops, but primarily that portion of the crop which is used to feed the local population; crops used for export may be protected in some way.) In these cases the problem may emerge quickly and, with some assistance, may disappear quickly. Such need is acute.

The nature of our responsibility to the starving arguably depends on the nature of their need. Peter Singer offers a vivid example of acute need and claims his example shows we have a serious moral obligation to relieve world starvation.

> If I am walking past a shallow pond and see a child drowning in it, I ought to wade in and pull the child out. That will mean getting my clothes muddy, but this is insignificant when the death of the child would presumably be a very bad thing. (1971: 231)

This case, Singer claims, illustrates the intuitive appeal of the following moral principle: "if it is in our power to prevent something bad from happening, without thereby sacrificing something of comparable moral importance, we ought, morally, to do it." In the case in question, this is sage moral advice. If muddying my clothes saves the life of an innocent child, then it is time for me to send the cleaners some additional business.

Singer's example vividly illustrates our fundamental moral responsibility to meet acute need, especially the acute need of children—those who are paradigmatically vulnerable and innocent. In Singer's example, the child is in immediate danger; with relatively little effort we can remove her from danger. As we argued earlier, we have a shared moral responsibility which arises from our common vulnerability. None of us has complete control over our lives. All of us are vulnerable to circumstances beyond our control: floods, hurricanes, droughts, etc. Through no fault of our own, our lives and welfare may be jeopardized. Admittedly some acute need results from our ignorance or stupidity. Even so, others should assist us when feasible, at least if the cost to them is slight. After all, even the most careful person occasionally makes mistakes. When need is caused by natural disaster or personal error, we each want others to come to our aid. Indeed, we think they *should* come to our aid. If, upon reflection, our desire for assistance is reasonable when *we* are in need, then, by extension, we should acknowledge that we should help others in similar need. Shared responsibility and sympathy conspire to create the sense that we should go to the aid of those who cannot alleviate their own acute needs.

Although we are here emphasizing responsibility rather than justice (narrowly defined), it is noteworthy that the conditions which generate responsibility to help others in acute need resemble the conditions Hume cites as generating our sense of justice: "*. . . 'tis only from selfishness and confin'd generosity of man, along with the scanty provision nature has made for his wants, that justice derives its origin*" (1978: 495; emphasis his). Our common vulnerability to circumstances and to the "scanty provision nature has made" leads us to seek ways to protect ourselves against misfortune and error. Natural disasters occur. They may occur where I live; they may not. Prudent people will recognize that we are all more secure, and thus, better off, if we recognize a shared responsibility to assist others in acute need.

As we have suggested throughout this essay, this responsibility is all the more apparent when those in need cannot care for themselves and are in no way responsible for their plight. In short, the responsibility is greatest (and less contentious) when children are the victims. In fact, when children are in acute need, especially when many are in a position to help, there's little moral difference between the responsibility of biological parents and others. If a child is drowning, then even if the parents (or some third party) tossed the child into the pond (and are thus singularly responsible for the child's plight), we should still rescue her if we can. Likewise, if a child is starving, and her need is acute, then even if the child's parents and its government have acted irresponsibly, we should still feed the child if we can.

Arguably the problem is different if the acute need is so substantial and so widespread as to require us to make considerable sacrifices to help those in need. In this case our responsibilities to the children in acute need may resemble our responsibilities to children in chronic need.

Chronic Need

Acute need arises once (or at least relatively infrequently). It requires immediate action, which, if successful, often alleviates the need. But most hunger is not acute, it is chronic. Chronic hunger is the hunger of persistently malnourished children, where the causes of hunger are neither episodic nor easily removed. If the need can be met at all, it can be met only through more substantial, sustained effort, and often only by making numerous (and perhaps fundamental) institutional changes, both within our countries, and the other countries in need of aid.

That is why Singer's case is disanalogous with most world hunger. The drowning child is in acute need. Suppose, however, that Singer's fictional child lives on the edge of a pond where she is relatively unsupervised. We cannot protect this child by simply dirtying our clothes once. Rather, we must camp on the pond's edge, poised to rescue her whenever she falls or slips into the water. However, can we reasonably expect anyone to devote her entire life (or even the next six years) as this child's lifeguard? It is difficult to see how. The expectation seems even less appropriate if there are many children living beside the pond.

Likely the only sensible way to protect the child from harm is to relocate her away from the pond. Or perhaps we could teach her to swim. But are we responsible to make these efforts? Do we have the authority to forcibly relocate the child or to erect an impregnable fence around the pond? Can we *require* her to take swimming lessons? Can we *force* her government to make substantial internal economic and political changes? In short, even though we are morally responsible to assist those in acute need (and especially children), we cannot straightforwardly infer that we must assist those (even children) in chronic need.

For instance, if we try to save a child from famine, we may have reason to think that quick action will yield substantial results. Not so with chronic hunger. Since we are less likely to see the fruits of our efforts, we may be less motivated to assist. Moreover, some have argued that we can alleviate chronic need only if we exert enormous effort, over a long period of time. If so, expecting someone to respond to chronic need arguably burdens her unduly. Responsible people need not spend all their time and resources helping those in chronic need, especially if there is only a small chance of success. This is surely the insight in Arthur's view.

Consider the following analogy which illuminates that insight. Suppose an adult builds a house by the side of a river that floods every few years. After the first flood we may help them, thinking we should respond to someone who appears to be in acute need. However, after the second or third flood, we will feel it is asking too much of us to continue to help. We would probably conclude that this adult has intentionally chosen a risky lifestyle. They have made their own bed; now they must sleep in it. Although this case may well be disanalogous to the plight of starving adults—since most have little control over the weather, soil erosion, or governmental policy—nonetheless, many people in affluent nations think it is analogous.

What is indisputable, however, is the case is totally disanalogous to the plight of children. Children did not choose to live in an economically deprived country or in a country with a corrupt government. Nor can they abandon their parents and relocate in a land of plenty, or in a democratic regime. Hence, they are completely innocent—in no sense did they cause their own predicament. Moreover, they are paradigms of vulnerability.

Since they are the principal victims of chronic malnutrition, it is inappropriate to refuse to help them unless someone can show that assisting them would require an unacceptable sacrifice. That, of course, demands that we draw a line between reasonable and unreasonable sacrifice. We do not know how to draw that line. Perhaps, though, before drawing the line we should ask: if it were our child who was starving, where would we want the line to be drawn?

A Dose of Reality

Evidence suggests, however, that this whole line of inquiry is beside the point. Although it would be theoretically interesting to determine how to draw the line between reasonable and unreasonable sacrifices, this is not a determination we need make when discussing world hunger. Doomsayers like Garrett Hardin claim we have long-since crossed that line: that feeding starving children requires more than we can reasonably expect even highly responsible people to do; indeed, Hardin claims such assistance is effectively suicide (1974; reprinted here). However, the doomsayers are mistaken. Current efforts to alleviate hunger have been far short of efforts which would require a substantial sacrifice from any of us. Nonetheless, even these relatively measly efforts have made a noticeable dent in the problem of world hunger. And these successes have been achieved with smaller than anticipated growth in population. According to the FAO:

> The number of chronically undernourished people in developing countries with populations exceeding 1 million is estimated at 786 million for 1988–90, reflecting a decline from 941 million in 1969–71 and a lowering of their proportion of the population from 36 to 20 percent . . ." (FAO 1992b: 1)
>
> During the same period, the average number of calories consumed per person per day went from 2430 to 2700—more than a 10 percent increase. (FAO 1992b: 3)

Since the relatively meager efforts to assist the starving has made a noticeable dent in the incidence of world hunger, then, although enormous problems clearly remain, we have good reason to think that heightened efforts—efforts still *far* short of those requiring substantial sacrifices from the affluent—could seriously curtail, if not completely eliminate, world starvation. If so, we do not need to decide where the line should be drawn. We are still some distance from that line. Put differently, many of the world's poor are not like the unsupervised child who lives on the side of the lake. Even though their need may be chromic, their needs can be met short of the enormous efforts that would require us to camp next to the pond for the remainder of our days. To that extent, our responsibility to chronically starving children is, despite first appearances, similar to our responsibility to children in acute need.

How to Act Responsibly

Many people are already motivated to help others (and especially children) in need. Indeed, this helps explain the influence and appeal of Singer's essay more than two decades after its publication. Thus, the claim that we have a shared responsibility to meet the needs of others in acute need is psychologically plausible. Even so, it is often difficult to motivate people to respond to others in chronic need. Many in affluent nations feel or fear that aid just won't do anything more than line the pockets of charitable organizations or corrupt governments. Doubtless some money sent for aid does not reach its intended source. But that may simply reflect our inability to determine which relief agencies are most effective. Moreover, even if some aid does not reach those in need, it is even more obvious that most relief aid *does* reach its desired target. That is what the statistics cited in the last section demonstrate.

We suspect that the strongest barrier to helping those in chronic need is more psychological than philosophical: most people just don't feel any connection with someone starving half-way around the world (or, for that matter, in the ghetto across town). As Hume noted, most of us do tend to feel more sympathy for what we see than for what we do not see. This at least partly explains why many of us are less willing to help starving children in foreign lands—we don't see them, and thus, don't feel a tie or connection to them. As we have argued through the paper, this is the core insight in Arthur's view: moral obligations which require us to abandon what is important to us, especially in the absence of some connection with those in need, will rarely be met by many people—and thus, will make no moral difference. Someone might argue, on more abstract philosophical grounds, that we should not need that link. Perhaps that is true. But, whether we should need to feel this connection, the fact is, most people do need it. And our concern in this paper is how to help meet the needs of the children. Thus, we want to know what will *actually* motivate people to act.

Of course, just as we should not take our initial sense of responsibility *to* children as *determining* our moral obligations, neither should we put too much weight on the unanalyzed notion of "normal ties." Doing so ignores ways in which our moral feelings can be shaped for good and for ill. So perhaps the better question is not whether we have such feelings, but whether we could cultivate them in ourselves and perhaps all humanity, and, if so, whether that would be appropriate. We suspect, though, that many of us cannot develop a sense of shared responsibility for *every* person in need. More likely we must rely on a more limited sense of shared responsibility; certainly that is not beyond the psychological reach of most of us. Indeed, it is already present in many of us. Thus, working to cultivate this sense of responsibility in ourselves and others would increase the likelihood that we could curtail starvation.

Since people have a natural sympathetic response to the cry of children, the best way to cultivate this connection is to keep people focused on children as the real victims of starvation and malnutrition. If we keep this fact firmly in the fore of our minds, we are more likely, individually and collectively to feel and act upon this sense of shared responsibility.

But even if we acknowledge this responsibility, how should we meet it? Should we provide food directly? Perhaps sometimes. But this direct approach will not solve chronic starvation. More likely we should empower the children's primary caretakers so they can feed and care for their children. To this extent our shared responsibility to hungry children is mediated by the choices and actions of others. Thus, it might be best conceptualized as akin to (although obviously not exactly like) our responsibility to provide education. Our responsibility is not to ensure that each child receives an education (although we will be bothered if a child "slips through the cracks"). Rather, our responsibility is to establish institutions which make it more likely that all will be educated. By analogy, since it is virtually impossible to feed children directly, our responsibility is not to particular children, but a responsibility to change the circumstances which make starvation likely.

Changing those circumstances might occasionally require that we be a bit heavy-handed. Perhaps such heavy-handedness is unavoidable if we wish to achieve the desired results. OXFAM, for example, provides aid to empower people in lands prone to famine and malnutrition to feed themselves and their children. If the recipients do not use the aid wisely, then OXFAM will be less likely to provide aid again. This is only a bit Draconian, but perhaps not so much as to be morally objectionable.

Conclusion

In both cases of chronic and acute need, we must remember the children who are the real victims of world hunger. The suffering child is paradigmatically vulnerable and innocent. Since we can, without serious damage to our relatively affluent lifestyles, aid these children, we should help. We share a responsibility *to* them because we are well-placed to help them, and because we can do so without substantially sacrificing our own interests. This is so even if we in *no way* caused or sustained the conditions which make their hunger likely.

However, if the stronger claim that we *caused* their starvation (or created the conditions which made their starvation more likely) can be defended—as we think it probably can—this responsibility becomes a stronger imperative. Thus, if the views of Sen, Crocker, and others are correct—and we suspect they are—then most of our responsibility is to cease supporting national and international institutions which cause and sustain conditions which make hunger likely. And *this* responsibility could be explained much more simply as a responsibility to not harm others.[1]

Endnote

1. We wish to thank William Aiken, John Hardwig, and Carl Wellman for helpful comments on earlier drafts of this paper.

References

Aiken and LaFollette, 1996: Aiken, William and LaFollette, Hugh. *World Hunger and Morality.* 2nd ed. (Englewood Cliffs, NJ: Prentice-Hall, 1996).

Arthur, J. "Rights and the Duty to Bring Aid." In W. Aiken and H. LaFollette, *World Hunger and Moral Obligation* (Englewood Cliffs, NJ: Prentice-Hall, 1977).

Brown, L. *The State of the World 1994: A World Watch Institute Report on Progress Toward a Sustainable Society* (New York: W.W. Norton, 1994).

______. *In the Human Interest* (New York: W.W. Norton, 1974).

Food and Agricultural Organization (FAO) *World Food Supplies and Prevalence of Chronic Undernutrition in Developing Regions as Assessed in 1992.* (Rome: FAO Press, 1992).

______. FAO News Release. (Rome: FAO Press, 1992).

______. *World Hunger* (Rome: FAO Press, 1989).

Hardin, G. *Exploring a New Ethics for Survival* (New York: Penguin, 1975).

______. "Lifeboat Ethics: The Case Against Helping the Poor." *Psychology Today,* 8: 38–43, 123–6.

Hart, H. and Honore, A. *Causation in the Law* (Oxford: Oxford University Press, 1959).

Hume, D. *A Treatise of Human Nature,* L.A. Selby-Bigge (ed.) (Oxford: Oxford University Press, 1976).

Jonas, H. *The Imperative of Responsibility* (Chicago: University of Chicago Press, 1984).

Kegan, S. *The Limits of Morality* (Oxford: Oxford University Press, 1988).

LaFollette, H. "The Truth in Psychological Egoism." In J. Feinberg (ed.), *Reason and Responsibility* (Belmont, CA: Wadsworth, 1989).

May, L. 1996: *Socially Responsible Self,* forthcoming.

______. *Sharing Responsibility* (Chicago: University of Chicago Press, 1992).

Mesarovic, M. and Pestel, E. *Mankind at the Turning Point* (New York: Signet Books, 1974).

O'Neill, O. "Ending World Hunger." In T. Regan (ed.), *Matters of Life and Death* (New York: McGraw Hill, 1993).

Parfit, D. *Reasons and Persons* (Oxford: Oxford University Press, 1984).

Singer, P. "Famine, Affluence, and Morality." *Philosophy and Public Affairs,* 1: 229–43.

United Nations Children's Fund (UNICEF) *The State of the World's Children 1993* (Oxford: Oxford University Press, 1993).

Wilson, J. *The Moral Sense* (New York: The Free Press, 1993).

World Health Organization (WHO) *Health Statistics Report* (Geneva: World Health Organization, 1974).

Journal/Discussion Questions

✍ *All of us have seen posters of starving children? How do you react to these pictures? What moral significance do they have? Do you agree with LaFollette and May's analysis?*

1. Peter Singer introduces the example of the drowning child. What criticisms do LaFollette and May offer of this example? Do you agree with their critique of Singer?
2. How do chronic need and acute need differ from one another? Which is more common in world hunger? What moral implications do LaFollette and May draw from this distinction?
3. What criticisms do LaFollette and May offer of Hardin's lifeboat ethics? Do you agree with their assessment of Hardin's position? Discuss.

CONCLUDING DISCUSSION QUESTIONS

Where Do You Stand Now?

Instructions

You have already answered the following questions in your moral problems self-quiz at the beginning of this book. Now that you have studied the material in this section, take a moment to answer the same questions again.

Chapter 9: World Hunger and Poverty

	Strongly Agree	*Agree*	*Undecided*	*Disagree*	*Strongly Disagree*	
41.	❑	❑	❑	❑	❑	Only the morally heartless would refuse to help the starving.
42.	❑	❑	❑	❑	❑	We should help starving nations until we are as poor as they are.
43.	❑	❑	❑	❑	❑	In the long run, relief aid to starving nations does not help them.
44.	❑	❑	❑	❑	❑	Overpopulation is the main cause of world hunger and poverty.
45.	❑	❑	❑	❑	❑	The world is gradually becoming a better place.

Compare your answers to the present self-quiz with the answers to the initial self-quiz. How, if at all, have your answers changed? How have the *reasons* for your answers changed?

Journal/Discussion Questions

✍ *Let's return to rock-bottom experiences. We are left with the fact that there are people throughout the world who are starving to death, slowly and painfully. We are—at least as a nation, and at least comparatively as individuals—affluent. How do you respond as a compassionate human being to the fact of such suffering?*

1. Imagine that you have been asked to address the annual convention of ethical egoists (ACEE) on the issue of world hunger. What could you say about world hunger to those who believe that their only moral duty is to promote their own welfare?
2. Imagine that you have been asked to address the annual convention of compassionate persons on the issue of world hunger and the *dangers* of compassion. What would you have to say to this audience of compassionate people about the dangers and pitfalls of compassionate responses to world hunger?
3. Imagine that you have been asked by the president of the United States to draft a policy statement on the question of how the United States should respond to world hunger. What main elements would it contain?

For Further Reading

Web Resources

The World Hunger and Poverty page of *Ethics Updates* (http://ethics.acusd.edu) contains numerous on-line resources relating to poverty and world hunger. In addition to extensive statistical information and a PowerPoint presentation on World Hunger, this page includes links to on-line texts by Amaryta Sen, Peter Unger, and others, as well as RealVideo lectures by Amaryta Sen and by Oscar Arias.

Journals

In addition to the standard ethics journals mentioned in the bibliographical essay at the end of Chapter 1, also see the journals *Ethics and International Affairs* and *World Development.*

Review Articles

Nigel Dower's "World Poverty" in *A Companion to Ethics,* edited by Peter Singer (Cambridge: Blackwell, 1991) surveys the literature and argues "for a moderate but significant duty of caring in response to the evils of extreme poverty." Onora O'Neill, "International Justice: Distribution," *Encyclopedia of Ethics,* edited by Lawrence C. Becker and Charlotte B. Becker (New York: Garland, 1992), Vol. I, pp. 624–628 provides an insightful and nuanced discussion of the issues of distributive justice, especially insofar as they relate to world hunger.

Reports

Several reports on the state of the world have helped to share the international discussion of these issues. In the United States, the Presidential Commission on World Hunger, established by Jimmy Carter, issued *Overcoming World Hunger: The Challenge Ahead* (Washington, DC: Government Printing Office, 1980). For a more global perspective, see the *Brandt Report,* formally known as the Report of the Independent Commission on International Development Issues, *North-South: A Program for Survival* (Cambridge: M.I.T. Press, 1980). For replies to this, see Teresa Hayter, *The Creation of World Poverty: An Alternative View to the Brandt Report* (London: Pluto Press, 1981); Denis Goulet and Michael Hudson, *The Myth of Aid: The Hidden Agenda of the Development Reports* (New York: IDOC/Maryknoll Press, 1971); and Frances Moore Lappe, Joseph Collins, and David Kinley, *Aid as Obstacle: Twenty Questions about our Foreign Aid and the Hungry* (San Francisco: Institute for Food and Development Policy, 1980/1981). Also see the *Brundtland Report,* formally known as the World Commission on Environment and Development, *Our Common Future* (New York: Oxford University Press, 1987). On the *Rio report,* see *Agenda 21: The Earth Summit Strategy to Save Our Planet,* edited by Daniel Sitarz (Boulder: Earthpress, 1993). Also see the excellent Worldwatch Institute Report on Progress Toward a Sustainable Society, *State of the World 1994,* by Lester R. Brown et al. (New York: W.W. Norton, 1994).

Among the popular books that have been influential in this discussion, see Albert Gore, *Earth in the Balance: Ecology and the Human Spirit* (Boston: Houghton Mifflin: 1992). Frances Moore Lappe and Joseph Collins, *Food First: Beyond the Myth of Scarcity,* revised and updated (New York: Ballantine Books, 1978) and also their *World Hunger: Twelve Myths* (San Francisco: Institute for Food and Development Policy, 1982). For a much more optimistic view, see Julian Simon, *The Ultimate Resource* (Princeton: Princeton University Press, 1981) and Julian Simon and Herman Kahn, *The Resourceful Earth* (Oxford: Blackwell, 1984).

Anthologies

Several valuable anthologies are available. William Aiken and Hugh LaFollette's *World Hunger and Moral Obligation,* 2nd ed. (Englewood Cliffs, NJ: Prentice-Hall, 1996) contains all the classic papers and a number of excellent recent articles; see especially the pieces by Hardin, Singer, Arthur, Narveson, Slote, and O'Neill. *International Justice and the Third World,* edited by Robin Attfield and Barry Wilkins (New York: Routledge, 1992) contains eight papers discussing notions of global justice and its implications for the Third World; the papers also relate Third World development to sustainability, issues of gender, environmentalism, and Third World debt. *Poverty, Justice, and the Law: New Essays on Needs, Rights, and Obligations,* edited by George R. Lucas, (Lantham: University Press of America, 1986) contains several excellent papers in this area. *Problems of International Justice,* edited by Stephen Luper-Foy (Boulder: Westview Press, 1988) deals with more international issues than just world hunger, but the essays are uniformly excellent. Two volumes in the Opposing Viewpoints contain relevant material: *The Third World: Opposing Viewpoints,* edited by Janelle Rohr (San Diego: Greenhaven Press, 1989) and *Immigration: Opposing Viewpoints,* edited by William Dudley (San Diego: Greenhaven Press, 1990). Also see the essays in G.E. McCuen, ed., *World Hunger and Social Justice* (Ideas in Conflict Series: Wisconsin: G.E. McCuen, 1986).

These issues also arise within the context of environmental ethics. Among the excellent anthologies in this area, see Donald VanDeVeer and Christine Pierce, eds., *The Environmental Ethics and Policy Book* (Belmont, CA: Wadsworth, 1994) and Susan J. Armstrong and Richard G. Botzler, eds., *Environmental Ethics: Divergence and Convergence* (New York: McGraw-Hill, 1993).

Responses to Hardin

Garrett Hardin's "Lifeboat Ethics" (and relate versions of the same piece) stirred extensive discussion. A number of the articles in Aiken and LaFollette, *World Hunger and Moral Obligation,* respond to Hardin; see especially Onora O'Neill's "Lifeboat Earth" in this collection. Also see some of the articles in *Problems of International Justice,* especially Onora O'Neill's "Hunger, Needs, and Rights" and William Aiken's "World Hunger, Benevolence, and Justice." Robert Coburn's "On Feeding the Hungry," *Journal of Social Philosophy,* 7 (Spring 1976), pp. 11–16, and Daniel Callahan's "Garrett Hardin's 'Lifeboat Ethic.'" *Hastings Center Report,* 4 (December 1974), pp. 1–4, both strongly criticize Hardin's position. Jesse A. Mann, "Ethics and the Problem of World Hunger," *Listening,* 16 (Winter 1982) pp. 67–76 attempts to sketch out a middle ground between Singer and Hardin. Nick Eberstadt's "Myths of the Food Crisis," *New York Review of Books* (February 19, 1976), pp. 32–37 challenges some of the assumptions that lead to Hardin's pessimism, while "Population and Food: Metaphors and the Reality," by William W. Murdoch and Allan Oaten, *Bioscience* (September 9, 1975), pp. 561–567, offers a perceptive discussion of the underlying metaphors in Hardin's work. On the utilitarian dimensions of this issue, see Thomas L. Carson, "Utilitarianism and World Poverty" in *The Limits of Utilitarianism,* edited by Harlan B. Miller (Minneapolis: University Minnesota Press, 1982), pp. 242–251.

General Defenses of the Duty to Aid Poor and Starving Nations

Henry Shue, Basic Rights: *Subsistence, Affluence, and U.S. Foreign Policy,* 2nd ed. (Princeton: Princeton University Press, 1996), offers a strong conceptual foundation for positive basic rights; also see his anthology (co-edited with Peter G. Brown), *Food Policy* (New York: The Free Press, 1977). Peter Unger's *Living High and Letting Die: Our Illusion of Innocence* (New York: Oxford, 1996) offers a strong case for much greater responsibility toward impoverished peoples. Robert Goodin's *Protecting the Vulnerable* (Chicago: University of Chicago Press, 1986) is very carefully argued. Nicholas Dower, in *What Is Development? A Philosopher's Answer* (Glasgow University Centre for Development Studies: Occasional Paper Series No. 3, 1988) argues for significant but not overpowering obligation to aid poor nations. Onora O'Neill's *Faces of Hunger* (London: Allen & Unwin, 1986) derives the obligation to aid from people's right not to be killed. Amartya Sen, *Poverty and Famines: An Essay on Entitlement and Deprivation* (New York: Oxford University Press, 1981) stresses the way in which famines are rarely due to natural causes alone; also see Jean Drèze and Amartya Sen, *Hunger and Public Action* (Oxford: Clarendon Press, 1989). John Howie, in "World Hunger and a Moral Right to Subsistence," *Journal of Social Philosophy,* Vol. 18 (Fall 1987), pp. 27–31, argues in favor of a moral right to subsistence and the obligation of affluent nations to starving ones. Robert N. Van Wyk, "Perspectives on World Hunger and the Extent of Our Positive Duties," *Public Affairs Quarterly,* Vol. 2 (April 1988), pp. 75–90 seeks to find a middle way between Peter Singer's utilitarianism, which implies that we have a duty to do everything we can for the sake of the hungry, and Nozick's libertarianism, which says we have no positive duties at all. James P. Sterba's "The Welfare Rights of Distant Peoples and Future Generations: Moral Side-Constraints on Social Policy." *Social Theory and Practice,* 7 (Spring 1981), pp. 99–119 discusses the ways in which welfare rights of distant peoples "can be grounded on fundamental moral requirements to which many of us are already committed." Michael McKinsey's "Obligations to the Starving," *Nous,* 15, (Spring 1981), pp. 309–324, argues that the principles of benevolence that are most often appealed to as a source of individuals' obligations to the starving are all either false or do not in fact yield such obligations on the part of individuals, but there are obligations on the part of groups. In "Killing and Starving to Death," *Philosophy,* Vol. 54 (April 1979), pp. 159–171, James Rachels argues that it is morally just as bad to let someone starve as it is to kill them. Rodney G. Peffer argues for obligations of the rich nations to the poor in "World Justice, Population, and the Environment: A Programmatic and Philosophical Approach," *World Political Ecology,* edited by David Bell (York: York University Press, 1995). Chapter Four of Stanley Hoffmann's *Duties Beyond Borders: On the Limits and Possibilities of Ethical International Politics* (Syracuse: Syracuse University Press, 1981) offers a nuanced account of the political dimensions of these issues.

Arguments against the Duty to Aid

Jennifer Trusted, "The Problem of Absolute Poverty" in *The Environment in Question: Ethics and Global Issues,* edited by David E. Cooper (New York: Routledge, 1992), pp. 13–27, discusses the obligations of individuals in affluent countries to the Third World, arguing that there can be no duty of general beneficence and that it is not wrong to favor those who are near and dear to us. James S. Fishkin, *The Limits of Obligation* (New Haven: Yale University Press, 1982), especially Chapter 9: The Famine Review Argument, on the limits of the obligations of rich nations to poor ones. Ruth Lucier, "Policies For Hunger Relief: Moral Considerations" in *Inquiries into Values,* edited by Sander H. Lee (Lewiston: Mellen Press), pp. 477–493 suggests that food aid has moral ramifications stemming from present limitations on the aid available for distribution.

Other Perspectives

Bhikkhu Sunanda Putuwar, "The Buddhist Outlook on Poverty and Human Rights" in *The Wisdom of Faith: Essays in Honor of Dr. Sebastian Alexander Matczak* (Lanham: University Press of America, 1989).

CHAPTER 10

Living Together with Animals

Videotape:

Topic: Where Have All the Tigers Gone?
ABCNEWS *Source:* ABC *World News Tonight* (November 30, 1998)
Anchor: Peter Jennings

NARRATIVE ACCOUNT

Peter Singer
"Down on the Factory Farm"

Peter Singer, presently professor of philosophy and deputy director of the Center for Human Bioethics at Monash University (Melbourne), is the author of numerous works in ethics, especially in applied ethics. His books include The Expanding Circle, Animal Liberation, Practical Ethics, *and most recently,* Rethinking Life and Death *and* How Are We to Live? *He has also edited a number of books, including* A Companion to Ethics. *In his work, Singer sees himself as holding our conventional moral beliefs to a standard of consistency, coherence, and the avoidance of arbitrary distinctions. He finds that many of these traditional beliefs are remnants of earlier, religiously inspired doctrines that he believes many people no longer accept; while other beliefs survive only because they promote some form of group selfishness.*

One of the ways in which we avoid dealing with the issue of animal suffering is simply and literally by not seeing it. In this article, Peter Singer describes a number of the practices that are common in contemporary animal farming, concentrating on the treatment of chickens and veal calves.

As Your Read, Consider This:

1. How much of the animal suffering that Singer describes were you aware of? Do you think your views on eating meat and factroy farming would be changed if you had more direct contact with the reality of such situations?
2. How much does animal suffering count in your life? What moral weight does it have? Are your views on this changing as you read this article?

For most humans, especially those in modern urban and suburban communities, the most direct form of contact with non-human animals is at meal time: we eat them. This simple fact is the key to our attitudes to other animals, and also the key to what each one of us can do about changing these attitudes. The use and abuse of animals raised for food far exceeds, in sheer numbers of animals affected, any other kind of mistreatment. Hundreds of millions of cattle, pigs, and sheep are raised and slaughtered in the United States alone each year; and for poultry the figure is a staggering 3 billion. (That means that about 5,000 birds—mostly chickens—will have been slaughtered in the time it takes you to read this page.) It is here, on our dinner table and in our neighborhood supermarket or butcher's shop, that we are brought into direct touch with the most extensive exploitation of other species that has ever existed.

In general, we are ignorant of the abuse of living creatures that lies behind the food we eat. Consider the images conjured up by the word "farm": a house, a barn, a flock of hens, overseen by a strutting rooster, scratching around the farmyard, a herd of cows being brought in from the fields for milking, and perhaps a sow rooting around in the orchard with a litter of squealing piglets running excitedly behind her.

Very few farms were ever as idyllic as that traditional image would have us believe. Yet we still think of a farm as a pleasant place, far removed from our own industrial, profit-conscious city life. Of those few who think about the lives of animals on farms, not many know much of modern methods of animal raising. Some people wonder whether animals are slaughtered painlessly, and anyone who has followed a truckload of cattle must know that farm animals are transported in very crowded conditions; but few suspect that transportation and slaughter are anything more than the brief and inevitable conclusion of a life of ease and contentment, a life that contains the natural pleasures of animal existence without the hardships that wild animals must endure in the struggle for survival.

These comfortable assumptions bear little relation to the realities of modern farming. For a start, farming is no longer controlled by simple country folk. It is a business, and big business at that. In the last thirty years the entry of large corporations and assembly-line methods of production have turned farming into "agribusiness." . . .

The first animal to be removed from the relatively natural conditions of the traditional farms and subjected to the full stress of modern intensive farming was the chicken. Chickens have the misfortune of being useful to humans in two ways: for their flesh and for their eggs. There are now standard mass-production techniques for obtaining both these products.

Agribusiness enthusiasts consider the rise of the chicken industry to be one of the great success stories of farming. At the end of World War II chicken for the table was still relatively rare. It came mainly from small independent farmers or from the unwanted males produced by egg-laying flocks. Today "broilers"—as table chickens are now usually called—are produced literally by the million from the highly automated factory-like plants of the large corporations that own or control 98 percent of all broiler production in the United States.[1]

The essential step in turning the chicken from a farmyard bird into a manufactured item was confining them indoors. A broiler producer today gets a load of 10,000, 50,000, or even more day-old chicks from the hatcheries, and puts them straight into a long, windowless shed—usually on the floor, although some producers use tiers of cages in order to get more birds into the same size shed. Inside the shed, every aspect of the birds' environment is controlled to make them grow faster on less feed. Food and water are fed automatically from hoppers suspended from the roof. The lighting is adjusted according to advice from agricultural researchers: for instance, there may be bright light 24 hours a day for the first week or two, to encourage the chicks to gain quickly; then the lights may be dimmed slightly and made to go off and on every two hours, in the belief that the chickens are readier to eat after a period of sleep; finally there comes a point, around six weeks of age, when the birds have grown so much that they are becoming crowded, and the lights will then be made very dim at all times. The point of this dim lighting is to reduce the effects of crowding. Toward the end of the eight- or nine-week life of the chicken, there may be as little as half a square foot of space per chicken—or less than the area of a sheet of quarto paper for a 3½ lb. bird. Under these conditions with normal lighting the stress of crowding and the absence of natural outlets for the bird's energies lead to outbreaks of fighting, with birds pecking at each other's feathers and sometimes killing and eating one another. Very dim lighting has been found to reduce this and so the birds are likely to live out their last weeks in near-darkness.

Feather-pecking and cannibalism are, in the broiler producer's language, "vices." They are not natural vices, however—they are the result of the stress and crowding to which the modern broilerman subjects his birds. Chickens are highly social animals, and in the farmyard they develop a hierarchy, sometimes called a "pecking order." Every bird yields, at the food trough or elsewhere, to those above it in rank, and takes precedence over those below. There may be a few confrontations before the order is firmly established but more often than not a show of force, rather than actual physical contact, is enough to put a chicken in its place. As Konrad Lorenz, a renowned figure in the field of animal behavior, wrote in the days when flocks were still small:

> Do animals thus know each other among themselves? They certainly do. . . . Every poultry farmer knows that . . . there exists a very definite order, in which each bird is afraid of those that are above her in rank. After some few disputes, which need not necessarily come to blows, each bird knows which of the others she has to fear and which must show respect to her. Not only physical strength, but also personal courage, energy, and even the self-assurance of every individual bird are decisive in the maintenance of the pecking order.[2]

Other studies have shown that a flock of up to 90 chickens can maintain a stable social order, each bird knowing its place; but 10,000 birds crowded together in a single shed is obviously a different matter.[3] The birds cannot establish a social order, and as a result they fight frequently with each other. Quite apart from the inability of the individual bird to recognize so many other birds, the mere fact of extreme crowding probably contributes to irritability and excitability in chickens, as it does in humans and other animals. This is something farming magazines are aware of, and they frequently warn their readers:

> Feather-pecking and cannibalism have increased to a formidable extent of late years, due, no doubt, to the changes in technique and the swing towards completely intensive management of laying flocks and table poultry. . . . The most common faults in management which may lead to vice are boredom, overcrowding in badly ventilated houses. . . . Lack of feeding space, unbalanced food or shortage of water, and heavy infestation with insect pests.[4]

Clearly the farmer must stop "vices," because they cost him money; but although he may know that overcrowding is the root cause, he cannot do anything about this, since in the competitive state of the industry, eliminating overcrowding could mean eliminating his profit margin at the same time. He would have fewer birds to sell, but would have had to pay the same outlay for his building, for the automatic feeding equipment, for the fuel used to heat and ventilate the building, and for labor. So the farmer limits his efforts to reducing the consequences of the stress that costs him money. The unnatural way in which he keeps his birds causes the vices; but to control them the poultryman must make the conditions still more unnatural. Very dim lighting is one way of doing this. A more drastic step, though one now almost universally used in the industry, is "de-beaking." This involves inserting the chick's head in a guillotine-like device which cuts off part of its beak. Alternatively the operation may be done with a hot knife. Some poultrymen claim that this operation is painless, but an expert British Government committee under zoologist Professor F.W. Rogers Brambell appointed to look into aspects of intensive farming found otherwise:

> . . . between the horn and the bone is a thin layer of highly sensitive soft tissue, resembling the "quick" of the human nail. The hot knife used in de-beaking cuts through this complex of horn, bone and sensitive tissue, causing severe pain.[5]

De-beaking, which is routinely performed in anticipation of cannibalism by most poultrymen, does greatly reduce the amount of damage a chicken can do to other chickens. It also, in the words of the Brambell Committee, "deprives the bird of what is in effect its most versatile member" while it obviously does nothing to reduce the stress and overcrowding that lead to this unnatural cannibalism in the first place. . . .

"A hen," Samuel Butler once wrote, "is only an egg's way of making another egg." Butler, no doubt, was being humorous; but when Fred C. Haley, president of a Georgia poultry firm that controls the lives of 225,000 laying hens, describes the hen as "an egg producing machine" his words have more serious implications. To emphasize his businesslike attitude Haley adds: "The object of producing eggs is to make money. When we forget this objective, we have forgotten what it is all about."[6]

Nor is this only an American attitude. A British farming magazine has told its readers:

> The modern layer is, after all, only a very efficient converting machine, changing the raw material—feedingstuffs—into the finished product—the egg—less, of course, maintenance requirements.[7]

Remarks of this kind can regularly be found in the egg industry trade journals throughout the United States and Europe, and they express an attitude that is common in the industry. As may be anticipated, their consequences for the laying hens are not good.

Laying hens go through many of the same procedures as broilers, but there are some differences. Like broilers, layers have to be de-beaked, to prevent the cannibalism that would otherwise occur in their crowded conditions; but because they live much longer than broilers, they often go through this operation twice. So we find a poultry specialist at the New Jersey College of Agriculture advising poultrymen to de-beak their chicks when they are between one and two weeks old because there is, he says, less stress on the chicks at this time than if the operation is done earlier, and in addition "there are fewer culls in the laying flock as a result of improper de-beaking." In either case, the article continues, the birds must be de-beaked again when they are ready to begin laying, at around twenty weeks of age.[8]

Laying hens get no more individual attention than broilers. Alan Hainsworth, owner of a poultry farm in upstate New York, told an inquiring local reporter that four hours a day is all he needs for the care of his 36,000 laying hens, while his wife looks after the 20,000 pullets (as the younger birds not yet ready to lay are called): "It takes her about 15 minutes a day. All she checks is their automatic feeders, water cups and any deaths during the night."

This kind of care does not make for a happy flock as the reporter's description shows:

> Walk into the pullet house and the reaction is immediate—complete pandemonium. The squawking is loud and intense as some 20,000 birds shove to the farthest side of their cages in fear of the human intruders. [9]

Julius Goldman's Egg City, 50 miles northwest of Los Angeles, is one of the world's largest egg producing units, consisting of 2 million hens divided into block long buildings containing 90,000 hens each, five birds to a 16 by 18 inch cage. When the *National Geographic* magazine did an enthusiastic survey of new farming methods, Ben Shames, Egg City's executive vice-president, explained to its reporter the methods used to look after so many birds:

> We keep track of the food eaten and the eggs collected in 2 rows of cages among the 110 rows in each building. When production drops to the uneconomic point, all 90,000 birds are sold to processors for potpies or chicken soup. It doesn't pay to keep track of every row in the house, let alone indivdual hens; with 2 million birds on hand you have to rely on statistical samplings.[10]

Nearly all the big egg producers now keep their laying hens in cages. Originally there was only one bird to a cage; and the idea was that the farmer could then tell which birds were not laying enough eggs to give an economic return on their food. Those birds were then killed. Then it was found that more birds could be housed and costs per bird reduced if two birds were put in each cage. That was only the first step, and as we have seen, there is no longer any question of keeping a tally of each bird's eggs. The advantages of cages for the egg producer now consist in the greater number of birds that can be housed, warmed, fed, and watered in one building, and in the greater use that can be made of labor-saving automatic equipment.

The cages are stacked in tiers, with food and water troughs running along the rows, filled automatically from a central supply. They have sloping wire floors. The slope—usually a gradient of 1 in 5—makes it more difficult for the birds to stand comfortably, but it causes the eggs to roll to the front of the cage where they can easily be collected by hand or, in the more modern plants, carried by conveyor belt to a packing plant.

When a reporter from the *New York Daily News* wanted to see a typical modern egg farm, he visited Frenchtown Poultry Farm, in New Jersey, where he found that

> Each 18 by 24 inch cage on the Frenchtown farm contains nine hens who seemed jammed into them by some unseen hand. They barely have enough room to turn around in the cages.
>
> "Really, you should have no more than eight birds in a cage that size," conceded Oscar Grossman, the farm's lessor. "But sometimes you have to do things to get the most out of your stock."[11]

Actually, if Mr. Grossman had put only eight birds in his cages they would still have been grossly overcrowded; at nine to a cage they have only 1/3 square foot per bird.

In 1968 the farm magazine *American Agriculturalist* advised its readers in an article headed "Bird Squeezing" that it had been found possible to stock at ⅓ square foot per bird by putting four birds in a 12 by 16 inch cage. This was apparently a novel step at the time; the steady increase in densities over the years is indicated by the fact that a 1974 issue of the same magazine describing the Lannsdale Poultry Farm, near Rochester, New York, mentions the same housing density without any suggestion that it is unusual.[12] In reading egg industry magazines I have found numerous reports of similar high densities, and scarcely any that are substantially lower. My own visits to poultry farms in the United States have shown the same pattern. The highest reported density that I have read about is at the Hainsworth farm in Mt. Morris, New York, where four hens are squeezed into cages 12 inches by 12 inches, or just one square foot—and the reporter adds: "Some hold five birds when Hainsworth has more birds than room."[13] This means ¼, and sometimes ⅕, square foot per bird. At this stocking rate a *single sheet of quarto paper represents the living area of two to three hens.*

Under the conditions standard on modern egg farms in the United States and other "developed nations" every natural instinct the birds have is frustrated. They cannot walk around, scratch the ground, dustbathe, build a nest, or stretch their wings. They are not part of a flock. They cannot keep out of each other's way and weaker birds have no escape from the attacks of stronger ones, already maddened by the unnatural conditions. . . .

Intensive production of pigs and cattle is now also common; but of all the forms of intensive farming now practiced, the quality veal industry ranks as the most morally repugnant, comparable only with barbarities like the force-feeding of geese through a funnel that produces the deformed livers made into pate de foie gras. The essence of veal raising is the feeding of a high-protein food (that should be used to reduce malnutrition in poorer parts of the world) to confined, anemic calves in a manner that will produce a tender, pale-colored flesh that will be served to gourmets in expensive restaurants. Fortunately this industry does not compare in size with poultry, beef, or pig production; nevertheless it is worth our attention because it represents an extreme, both in the degree of exploitation to which it subjects its animals and in its absurd inefficiency as a method of providing people with nourishment.

Veal is the flesh of a young calf, and the term was originally reserved for calves killed before they had been weaned from their mothers. The flesh of these very young animals was paler and more tender than that of a calf that had begun to eat grass; but there was not much of it, since calves begin to eat grass when they are a few weeks old and still very small. So there was little money in veal, and the small amount available came from the unwanted male calves produced by the dairy industry. These males were a nuisance to the dairy farmers, since the dairy breeds do not make good beef cattle. Therefore they were sold as quickly as possible. A day or two after being born they were trucked to market where, hungry and frightened by the strange surroundings and the absence of their mothers, they were sold for immediate delivery to the slaughterhouse.

Once this was the main source of veal in the United States. Now, using methods first developed in Holland, farmers have found a way to keep the calf longer without the flesh becoming darker in color or less tender. This means that the veal calf, when sold, may weigh as much as 325 lbs., instead of the 90-odd lbs. that newborn calves weigh. Because veal fetches a premium price, this has made rearing veal calves a profitable occupation.

The trick depends on keeping the calf in highly unnatural conditions. If the calf were left to grow up outside, its playful nature would lead it to romp around the fields. Soon it would begin to develop muscles, which would make its flesh tough. At the same time it would eat grass and its flesh would lose the pale color that the flesh of newborn calves has. So the specialist veal producer takes his calves straight from the auction ring to a confinement unit. Here, in a converted barn or purpose-built shed, he will have rows of wooden stalls. Each stall will be 1 foot 10 inches wide and 4 feet 6 inches long. It will have a slatted wooden floor, raised above the concrete floor of the shed. The calves will be tethered by a chain around the neck to prevent them from turning around in their stalls. (The chain may be removed when the calves grow too big to turn around in such narrow stalls.) The stall will have no straw or other bedding, since the calf might eat it, spoiling the paleness of his flesh.

Here the calves will live for the next thirteen to fifteen weeks. They will leave their stalls only to be taken out to slaughter. They are fed a totally liquid diet, based on non-fat milk powder with added vitamins, minerals, and growth-promoting drugs. . . .

The narrow stalls and their slatted wooden floors are a serious source of discomfort for the calves. The inability to turn around is frustrating. When he lies down, the calf must lie hunched up, sitting almost on top of his legs rather than having them out to one side as he would do if he had more room. A stall too narrow to turn around in is also too narrow to groom comfortably in; and calves have an innate desire to twist their heads around and groom themselves with their tongues. A wooden floor without any bedding is hard and uncomfortable; it is rough on the calves' knees as they get up and lie down. In addition, animals with hooves are uncomfortable on slatted floors. A slatted floor is like a cattle grid, which cattle will always avoid, except that the slats are closer together. The spaces, however, must still be large enough to allow manure to fall or be washed through, and this means that they are large enough to make the calves uncomfortable.[14]

The special nature of the veal calf has other implications that show the industry's lack of genuine concern for the animals' welfare. Obviously the calves sorely miss their mothers. They also miss something to suck on. The urge to suck is strong in a baby calf, as it is in a baby human. These calves have no teat to suck on, nor do they have any substitute. From their first day in confinement—which may well be only the third or fourth day of their lives—they drink from a plastic bucket. Attempts have been made to feed calves through artificial teats, but the problems of keeping the teats clean and sterile are apparently too great for the farmer to try to overcome. It is common to see calves frantically trying to suck some part of their stalls, although there is usually nothing suitable; and if you offer a veal calf your finger he will immediately begin to suck on it, as a human baby sucks its thumb.

Later on the calf develops a desire to ruminate—that is, to take in roughage and chew the cud. But roughage is strictly forbidden and so, again, the calf may resort to vain attempts to chew the sides of its stall. Digestive disorders, including stomach ulcers, are common in veal calves, as are chronically loose bowel movements.

As if this were not enough, there is the fact that the calf is deliberately kept anemic. As one veal producers' journal has said,

> Color of veal is one of the primary factors involved in obtaining "topdollar" returns from the fancy veal market . . . "light color" veal is a premium item much in demand at better clubs, hotels and restaurants. "Light color" or pink veal is partly associated with the amount of iron in the muscle of the calves.[15]

So veal feeds are deliberately kept low in iron. A normal calf would obtain iron from grass or other forms of roughage, but since a veal calf is not allowed this he becomes anemic. Pale pink flesh is in fact anemic flesh. The demand for flesh of this color is a matter of snob appeal. The color does not affect the taste and it certainly does not make the flesh more nourishing—rather the opposite.

Calves kept in this manner are unhappy and unhealthy animals. Despite the fact that the veal producer selects only the strongest, healthiest calves to begin with, uses a medicated feed as a routine measure, and gives additional injections at the slightest sign of illness, digestive, respiratory and infectious diseases are widespread. It is common for a veal producer to find that one in ten of a batch of calves do not survive the fifteen weeks of confinement. Ten percent mortality over such a short period would be disastrous for anyone raising calves for beef, but the veal producer can tolerate this loss because of the high price restaurants are prepared to pay for his product. If the reader will recall that this whole laborious, wasteful, and painful process exists for the sole purpose of pandering to would-be gourmets who insist on pale, soft veal, no further comment should be needed.

Endnotes

1. Harrison Wellford, *Sowing the Wind: The Politics of Food, Safety and Agribusiness* (New York: Grossman Press, 1971), p. 104.
2. K. Lorenz, *King Solomon's Ring* (London: Methuen, 1964), p. 147.
3. Ian Duncan, "Can the Psychologist Measure Stress?" *New Scientist,* October 18, 1973.
4. *The Smallholder,* January 6, 1962; quoted by Ruth Harrison, *Animal Machines* (London: Vincent Stuart, 1964), p. 18.
5. *Report of the Technical Committee to Enquire into the Welfare of Animals Kept under Intensive Livestock Husbandry Systems* (London: Her Majesty's stationery Office, 1965), para. 97.
6. *Poultry Tribune,* January 1974.
7. *Farmer and Stockbreeder,* January 30, 1962; quoted by Ruth Harrison, *Animal Machines,* p. 50.
8. *American Agriculturist,* July 1966.
9. *Upstate,* August 5, 1973, report by Mary Rita Kiereck.
10. *National Geographic,* February 1970.
11. *New York Daily News,* September 1, 1971.
12. *American Agriculturist,* August 1968, April 1974.
13. *Upstate,* August 5, 1973.
14. Ruth Harrison, *Animal Machines,* p. 72.
15. *The Wall Street Journal,* published by Provimi, Inc., Watertown, Wisconsin, November 1973.

Journal/Discussion Questions

✍ *Do you have any direct experience with the raising and slaughtering of animals for food? (Did you grow up on a farm, or have you ever visited an animal farm or a slaughterhouse?) How have these experiences affected your views on animal rights? If you have not had any of these experiences, do you think this lack has affected your views? Discuss.*

1. If chickens are raised under the conditions that Singer describes, what implications—if any—does that have for eating eggs and meat from chickens under those conditions?
2. Singer stresses that modern animal agriculture is "big business," not the product of many small farmers. What moral implications, if any, does this have?
3. Why does Singer single out the "quality veal industry as the most morally repugnant" form of animal farming? Do you agree with his assessment? Discuss.

AN INTRODUCTION TO THE MORAL ISSUES

The Scope of the Moral Circle

To what extent do animals have a moral standing in their own right?

In this chapter, we shall examine whether the circle of morality ought to be extended to include animals—and, if so, how this would transform our world. Certainly there are many areas of our daily lives which involve animals either directly or indirectly. Many of us have pets, ride horses, visit zoos and places like Sea World, perhaps even go hunting or fishing. All of these involve animals directly. Many of us eat meat or fish, wear leather belts and shoes, use prescription medications, ride in cars with seat belts. Many of these involve animals indirectly as sources of food, as subjects of medical and safety research, and the like. Our relationship with animals pervades our daily lives in numerous, often unnoticed, ways.

Many of these relationships with animals must be revised if we discover that animals are persons, or even that they have a moral status beyond the little that has traditionally been accorded to them. A variety of different types of concern—religious, rights, consequentialist, and character-based—have been offered as reasons for either modifying or retaining our present view of the moral status of animals. Let's consider each of these issues.

Religious Concerns

Many advocates of animal rights and animal liberation maintain that religions, especially Christianity, has contributed strongly to the subjection and mistreatment of animals. Upon closer examination, however, we see that the picture is somewhat more complex than this, not only in Christianity, but in other religious traditions as well.

Christianity

Many Western philosophers have criticized religion in general, and Christianity in particular, for fostering a morally insensitive attitude toward nonhuman animals. The critique is partly theological, partly political.

The theologically oriented critique is three-pronged, relating to the message of the book of Genesis in the Bible, to the incarnation, and to the notion of a human soul. *First,* in the opening chapters of Genesis, animals and the natural environment are depicted as existing solely for the sake of human beings and their salvation. Such a view gives animals only an instrumental value, denying that they may have any moral significance in themselves. *Second,* by seeing Jesus as the incarnation of God in a human being, critics maintain, Christianity sets human beings apart from all other beings. There is an ontological chasm between human beings and all other types of beings because God became a human being in order to save human beings. Animals simply did not figure into the picture. *Third,* and finally, Christian theology sees human beings as having an immortal soul, but animals do not have such a soul. This reinforces the ontological gap initiated by the incarnation, and further demotes animals when seen in relation to human beings. It is easy to see how C.S. Lewis, a Christian theologian, could conclude in "Pain and Animal Suffering," that "The beasts are to be understood only in their relation to man and, through man, to God. . . . Everything a man does to an animal is either a lawful exercise, or a sacrilegious abuse, of an authority by divine right."[1]

The politically oriented critique is more scathing, although it does not necessarily indicate anything as intrinsic to Christianity as its theological commitments. Here the structure of the critique is simply to point out the Christian churches, both implicitly and by default, have acted in ways that undermine the rights of animals. There is no shortage of examples, whether it be a nineteenth-century Pope forbidding the establishment of an anti-cruelty-to-animals office in Rome (allegedly because humans do not have duties to animals) or simply the long history of Christianity's endorsement of eating meat. As Tom Regan put it so succinctly in the title of one of his essays, "Christians Are What Christians Eat."[2]

Defenders of the Christian tradition often acknowledge its shortcomings, but reply to these criticisms by pointing out that there is another, albeit secondary, tradition in Christianity that does acknowledge the moral standing of animals. Genesis not only contains a model of domination, but also a model of stewardship which emphasizes the ways in which the entirety of creation is to be respected and taken care of. Some defenders of Christianity, such as Andrew Linzey,[3] even see Genesis as offering a religious foundation for vegetarianism: "I give you all plants that bear seed everywhere on earth, and every tree bearing fruit which yields seed: They shall be yours for food" (Genesis 1:29). Moreover, saints such as St. Francis of Assisi have kept this tradition alive with their devotion to animals.

Buddhism

Compassion and respect for life. The teachings of the Buddha explicitly urge respect for all life, not just human life, and this has had a profound impact on shaping the attitudes of Buddhists toward animals. The central moral stance of a Buddhist toward the world is one of compassion for suffering, and that compassion is directed as much toward animal suffering as human suffering.

Reincarnation. Within the Buddhist tradition, as souls move through their journey of self-purification, they are reincarnated successively in different living beings, animals as well as human beings. Reincarnation in animals has a potentially profound impact on one's treatment of animals, since it opens up the possibility that the soul inhabiting an animal could—either in the past or the future—be the soul of a human being. This is in stark contrast with the Christian tradition, where the incarnation of God in Jesus separates human beings from all other animals.

Native American Religious Traditions

Harmony. Although Native American religions present a wide range of diverse beliefs and practices, it is certainly characteristic of most Native American religions that they emphasize the importance of a harmonious relationship with the natural world, that they see animals as often embodying both human and divine spirits, that the dividing line between human and animal is much less clearly marked than in Christian tradition, and that all animals are deserving of respect. Interestingly, this respect does not usually lead to absolute prohibitions on killing animals. Instead, it leads to prohibitions on unnecessary killing; moreover, it demands a respectful attitude toward even those animals that one kills. It is not inconsistent, in most Native American traditions, to kill an animal and to pray *to* (not just *for*) its spirit. Nor is it necessary to leave animals alone, as many strong supporters of animal rights seem to advocate. In the Native American tradition, human beings and animals interact with one another constantly, and harmony is to be achieved through rightly ordering those interactions.

A proper space. One of the ways in which our relationships with animals can be rightly ordered is through proper spatial relationships. Many Native American traditions are highly spatial. Animals, human beings, and even the gods are seen as having particular places. (This, incidentally, is one reason why relocation was often so traumatic for Native Americans: their particular gods resides in a specific space, and to move to a new location was to move to a place where the gods would not know you.) Part of the harmonious relationship between humans and animals in the Native American tradition stemmed from a recognition of proper place, and often disastrous interactions between human beings and animals (for example, being bitten by a snake) are seen as an encroachment by human beings on the animal's space. Consequently, the way to avoid such problems is to be more respectful of the animal's space. This is in marked contrast with mainstream American attitudes, which are puzzled and outraged when, after building huge subdivisions that destroy the native habitat of wolves and other animals, wolves and other animals appear in residential areas. The Native American traditions emphasize a harmonious, respectful, and yet at the same time highly interactive view of the relationship between human beings and animals.

Consequentialist Concerns

For many people, morality is primarily about consequences, about doing the thing that creates the most happiness and the least unhappiness. Yet the crucial question, at least in this context, is happiness *for whom?* Is it only happiness for human beings, or does the circle extend beyond this?

Utilitarian Concerns

From its origins in the work of Jeremy Bentham, utilitarianism has shown a sensitivity to the suffering of animals not found in, for example, the Kantian tradition. For Bentham, the notable moral fact is suffering, whether that be the suffering of animals or of human beings.

Not all versions of utilitarianism share the sensitivity to animal suffering that Bentham had. But even when utilitarianism is concerned only with the happiness or pleasure of human beings and such, it does not consign animals to moral oblivion. When we consider consequences solely for human beings, we notice that this by no means justifies all of our harmful treatment of animals in the past. Consider two examples: eating meat and cruelty to animals.

First, consider eating meat. Although vegetarianism is often espoused for the sake of animals, there may well be a strong, human-centered case for vegetarianism. What are the consequences of a diet rich in meat, especially red meat, for human beings? This is an empirical question, but it may well be the case that the overall effects of vegetarianism are significantly more healthful than the effects of a diet that contains meat. *Second,* consider cruelty to animals. Even if we leave aside for the moment the harmful effects on the animals themselves, it may well be the case that treating animals cruelly has harmful effects on human beings. Immanuel Kant, for example, argued that such cruelty makes us less morally sensitive beings and less likely to respond appropriately to the suffering of human beings. Cruelty to animals may well lead to cruelty to human beings, and is therefore to be avoided.

Thus, even when we assume a purely human-centered consequentialist approach to moral matters, we do not have to conclude that "anything goes" in regard to our treatment of animals. There may be important, human-centered constraints on our treatment of animals that have nothing to do with the moral status of the animals themselves.

Speciesism

The fundamental moral question which was raised in the 1970s by Peter Singer in his book *Animal Liberation* was whether utilitarianism was being arbitrary when it considered the pleasure and pain of only human beings. If utilitarianism is fundamentally a doctrine about increasing pleasure and reducing pain and suffering, then shouldn't *all* pleasure and *all* pain and suffering count, not just the pleasure and pain of one species?

The argument for this position is simple and elegant. On what basis do we say that the suffering of one species counts and the suffering of another species doesn't? Presumably, for this line to be drawn justifiably, there must be some nonarbitrary criterion. It's not enough to say about some beings, "they're one of us," and about others, "they're not one of us." Yet what can this nonarbitrary criterion be? The only reasonable candidate, Singer and others argue, is the ability to suffer. Any other criterion, such as language or rationality, would in fact exclude some human beings, such as the severely mentally disabled or those in comas. The only acceptable nonarbitrary criterion is the ability to suffer.

The tendency to ignore the suffering of animals and the view that only human beings count is *speciesism.* Animal liberationists liken speciesism to racism and sexism, all of which draw arbitrary moral lines that undermine the moral standing of the other sex, of other races, or of other species. A truly consistent utilitarianism will recognize that the suffering of all living beings, not just human beings, counts from a moral point of view.

Expanding the Circle of Utilitarianism: Animal Liberation

Once the suffering of animals has been acknowledged as having moral significance, the moral landscape changes dramatically. It is now populated by a myriad of different kinds of beings, not just human beings, and the moral calculation of consequences becomes much more complex. Moreover, they become more complex not just because more individual beings must be considered, but also because it is presumably more difficult to measure the extent to which animals are experiencing happiness, pleasure, pain, and suffering, since we cannot ask them directly in the same way that we

To what extent should the pain of animals count in weighing consequences?

can ask human beings. While some utilitarians—usually called *hedonistic* utilitarians—take pleasure and pain as the standard of utility, they are often criticized as having too base a standard. Other utilitarians—*eudaimonistic* utilitarians—take happiness and unhappiness as the standard. Although this seems to many to be a more appropriate standard, it is more difficult to quantify and apply, especially in the case of animals.

The utilitarian approach to the moral status of animals is subject to other difficulties as well, not the least of which is that it may not justify enough protection for animals. These are typical quandaries for utilitarians, irrespective of the issue of animals. Can one cow be killed if doing so will bring great pleasure to a dozen dogs? How do we treat the painless killing of animals? If a cow is killed instantaneously, painlessly, and without the cow's foreknowledge (so there is no anticipatory fear), does its death create any suffering to be considered in the utilitarian calculus?

Finally, if we grant that animals count in the moral world, *how much* do they count? Within the non-human animal world, is all animal suffering equal? Is the suffering of nonhuman animals of equal value to the suffering of humans? Is the suffering of a cow equal to the suffering of a worm? Of a human being?

Considerations about Rights

Concerns about the strength of Singer's proposed utilitarian foundation for our attitude toward animals has led some philosophers, most notably Tom Regan, to shift the focus from the *liberation* of animals to animal *rights.* Nonhuman animals, Regan argues in our selection "The Case for Animal Rights" and in his book of the same name, have rights, just as human animals do. The crucial factor about rights is that they are, as Ronald Dworkin once suggested, like "trump cards." In other words, they take precedence over anything else, including considerations of utility. Thus, even if from a utilitarian point of view the killing of animals was sometimes justified, they still may be protected because they have a right to life.

Who Has Rights?

Imagine that you were on a Star Trek mission to an unexplored planet, and that through a fluke accident you find yourself marooned on a planet that you know nothing about. Able to breathe the atmosphere, but lacking food and water, you are immediately faced with the question of what in your environment you may—both safely and morally—consume. Let's imagine that there is little plant matter, and the little that is available lacks nutritional content. You turn toward the living beings on the planet that are crawling, walking, hopping, running, and flying around the planet. Leaving aside the question of safety, how would you decide which creatures had a right to be respected and which creatures—if any—you were morally justified in eating?

As we tried to answer this question, presumably we would look for certain things—such as intelligence, language, culture, and the like—which would indicate that these beings are deserving of respect, are not to be used as a mere means to our nutritional goals. Similarly, when we look on earth at the nonhuman animal world around us, we must ask which animals have rights. The answer that animal rights advocates give is simple: the ability to feel pain (sentience) is what confers rights. What if the criterion is the ability to think and use language? Then certain kinds of animals—dolphins, chimps, and others—may qualify for rights, while other kinds of animals—

slugs, worms, and so on—would not qualify, nor would certain human beings—most notably, those with severe mental disabilities and those in deep comas. The extent of animal rights depends directly on the criterion for conferring rights.

How Do We Resolve Conflicts of Rights?

Authors such as Alasdair MacIntyre and Mary Ann Glendon have criticized the growing philosophical and political preoccupation with rights, and they have argued that the language of rights is only a fiction and that it leads to polarization and increased conflict. Certainly one of the difficulties is that rights are often presented as absolute, although the philosophically more defensible situation is to see virtually all rights as less than absolute. Otherwise we are left with the irresolvable situation of what to do when one absolute right conflicts with another absolute right. Obviously, we need some kind of hierarchy, some ordering of rights.

These considerations have a particular relevance in the area of animal rights. Advocates of animal rights have to answer three questions. *First,* what particular rights do all animals have? Do all animals have the right to life? The right not to suffer needlessly? The right to liberty? *Second,* do rights vary by species, or do all types of animals have equal rights? Does a worm have the same rights as a chimp and as a baby human being? *Third,* how do we resolve interspecies conflicts of rights? Is the right to life of a worm equal in moral standing to the right to life of a chimp and the right to life of a human infant? These are difficult questions, although not necessarily unanswerable. A strong defense of animal rights must, however, provide a plausible answer to these questions. In "The Case for Animal Rights," Tom Regan addresses each of these questions.

Animal Rights and Abortion

There is an interesting corollary of one's position on animal rights. When a very broad right-conferring property such as the ability to feel pain is used as the principal basis for recognizing rights, then it would appear that fetuses have rights too. Often the arguments used against fetal rights—namely, that fetuses lack certain human characteristics such as self-consciousness or rationality—would not be sound if the broader, more inclusive definitions of right-conferring properties were in force.

Concerns About Character

In addition to concerns about religion, consequences, and rights, defenders of animals have often pointed to the issue of *moral character* as providing a foundation for changing our attitudes toward animals. The argument has been that compassionate people will be more responsive to the suffering of animals, and that continuing mistreatment of animals in our society dulls our capacity for compassion in regard to all beings.

Compassion

Almost everyone has had the experience of seeing an animal in pain, and for most of us our immediate response is to want to relieve the animal's suffering. We may nurse an injured bird back to health, wash the wounds of a dog that has been in a fight, even try to set the broken leg of a kitten. Sometimes, whether rightly or wrongly, we may conclude that the animal cannot recover, and kill it in order to end its suffering. (Issues of animal rights prompt a reconsideration of euthanasia, not just abortion.)

Yet compassion initially seems to be a shaky foundation for our moral attitude toward animals. Sometimes, sympathy and compassion can turn into mere sentimentality—and some have criticized the animal rights movement for falling into the trap of sentimentality.

Proximity

Most people who eat meat in modern industrialized societies don't slaughter their own animals in order to do so, and this simple fact has important implications for the issue of character. If the cruelty of animal agriculture is kept from view, then sensitive and compassionate people may participate in such cruelty through ignorance. Of course, some would maintain that such ignorance is itself morally blameworthy, and some of the more visible protests by animal rights activists have been aimed at making cruelty to animals inescapably visible.

Common Ground

The various moral concerns outlined in the preceding pages come directly into play when we seek a common ground on a number of pressing issues in regard to our moral attitude toward animals. Let's briefly consider several of these areas: medical experimentation on animals, commercial agriculture, the keeping of pets, and our interactions with wild animals.

Medical Experimentation: Balancing Competing Concerns

To what extent ought we to use animals in biomedical research?

One of the most difficult areas in which to assert animal rights is medical experimentation. When the choice is simply between preserving the lives of animals *versus* being able to save the lives of human beings, for most people the choice is easy: the human takes priority over the animal. Few would agree with Ingrid Newkirk, the national director of PETA (People for the Ethical Treatment of Animals), who claims that "Animal liberationists do not separate out the human animal, so there is no rational basis for saying that a human being has special rights. A rat is a pig is a dog is a boy. They're all mammals."[4]

The difficulty is that we are rarely, if ever, presented with such a stark choice between the life of one human being and the life of one animal. The choices are more likely to be between the lives of hundreds of animals and the *possible* beneficial effects of some new drug for human beings. Often the issue of animal experimentation is about further confirmation of experimental results that are already available, or about determining what changes would occur if some small variable is altered. Sometimes the issue is simply training students and laboratory workers in experimental techniques.

The middle ground. *How much* should animal suffering count? If we are discontent with the wholesale endorsement of the use of animals in research, and if we have rejected the claim that there is no morally significant difference between human suffering and animal suffering, then where do we stand? The middle ground here would seem to be that animal suffering should be reduced whenever possible. Questions should be raised about whether the research is really necessary, whether it absolutely has to include animals, whether it can involve fewer animals, whether the suffering of the animals can be reduced in any way.

Commercial Animal Agriculture and Eating Meat

The cruelty of animal farming. In his selection "Down on the Factory Farm," Peter Singer gives us a glimpse of what commercial animal agriculture is like, and it is a disturbing picture indeed. Animals are raised under extremely harsh and unnatural conditions that deprive them of many of the natural consolations of their lives, such as sucking, grooming, pecking, and the like. Even if we leave aside the fact that their lives eventually end in slaughter, many of us would find much to object to in the way in which such animals are treated.

The vegetarian option. Many supporters of animal rights respond to this situation by espousing vegetarianism, since this is clearly the option that eliminates the need to raise and kill animals under these conditions. As we indicated earlier, vegetarianism has much to recommend in addition to the issue of animal suffering. However, if vegetarianism for the entire world is not a realistic option at this time, it is important to ask whether there would be any conditions under which the raising of animals for food would be morally acceptable.

Common ground. Two distinct issues arise in regard to raising animals for food: their deaths and their lives. Presumably it is morally better to kill animals painlessly (including a minimum of anticipatory fear as well as a minimum of physical pain) than painfully. If animals are slaughtered, it should be done in a way that minimizes their pain. Second, their lives should be (a) as free as possible from pain inflicted by human beings and (b) as natural as possible. The first requirement is clearly utilitarian in character, while the second relates to what we might call "quality of life." Part of respecting a being is that we recognize the natural rhythms and contours of that being's life, and we try to avoid unnecessarily disturbing them. For example, many animals groom themselves, and such grooming activity provides them with comfort on a variety of levels, psychological as well as physical. Whenever possible, we should raise animals in ways that allow them to follow their own natural inclinations.

Pets

How do you envision the ideal relationship between human beings and animals?

The issue of pets raises important questions about the moral status of animals, especially in regard to what we envision as the ideal relationship among the species. It's particularly interesting because we are not dealing with questions of cruelty and suffering—indeed, in many cases it is just the opposite. Pet owners love their pets, care for them deeply and attentively, and are often devastated when they die. Indeed, on the surface everyone—pets as well as people—seems to benefit from this relationship.

Yet many supporters of animal rights/liberation argue strongly against the keeping of pets. For opponents of pets and domestication of animals in general, one of the mainstays of their position is the claim that, on the whole, pets are often mistreated. But even putting such mistreatment aside, they argue that the relationship between owner and pet is misconstrued. People see themselves as *owning* their pets as pieces of property, and the standard view of ownership is that people may do whatever they want to their property. Yet, if animals have rights, then they are not the proper objects of ownership anymore than people are proper objects of ownership.

What, then, is the ideal relationship between human beings and other species? Some advocates of animal liberation seem to envision a largely separatist future in which human beings live with only minimal interactions with other species. In contrast to this view, Vicki Hearne has presented an interesting and provocative view based in part on her experience as an animal trainer.[5] She sets aside the issue of animal rights and concentrates instead on the question of animal happiness. Animals, she maintains, often achieve their greatest happiness in relationships with human beings. It often seems, she implies, that animal rights advocates, although deeply concerned with reducing animal suffering, neither know animals intimately nor love them directly and immediately.

Wild Animals: Zoos and Animal Preservation

How are we to interact with the wild animals of the world? Clearly we can't pretend that we don't interact with such animals and assume a "hands off" policy. Isolationism may have been a viable political option in the nineteenth century, but as we anticipate the coming of the twenty-first century, we can no longer reasonably expect to live in complete isolation from wild animals. Our paths increasingly cross, mainly because human beings intrude on their territory. Two issues relate immediately to this: zoos and hunting.

Zoos. At one time, zoos were little more than a carnival side-show exhibiting the exotic and the bizarre. In recent years, in part because of pressure from animal liberation/rights groups, zoos are rethinking their goals and their place both in human society and in the course of natural evolution. Instead of seeing themselves as just providing people with an opportunity to see unusual animals, they see their mission to be educating the public about the importance of the animal world and the subtlety of its structures and interactions. They often are highly effective spokepersons for preserving the natural habitat of animals and protecting them from the encroachments of human civilization. Similarly, their role vis-à-vis the natural environment is changing. Whereas they previously existed in a largely parasitic relationship with the natural world, plucking out choice specimens at their pleasure, they now see themselves as supporting and preserving nature. Endangered species are protected and bred in zoos, and then returned whenever possible to the wild. The zoo then becomes part of the evolutionary chain.

Animal rights-based critics of zoos remain skeptical and dissatisfied. They feel that interventions in the natural chain of evolution are seldom successful since they are usually based on a weak gene pool. Moreover, zoos are still based on the assumption that human beings are entitled to capture other beings and put them on display for their own (i.e., the human beings') pleasure.

Animal preservation. The larger issue raised by this critique of zoos is whether human beings should be involved at all in the project of animal preservation. The larger issue raised by this controversy is the ideal relationship between human beings and other species. At one extreme are those who see it in purely exploitative terms, the natural world being completely at the disposal of human beings. At the other extreme are those who see human beings as agents of harm and who thus maintain that human beings should simply assume a "hands off" policy toward the natural world as far as possible. In the middle are those who seek to develop a model of how human beings and animals can live together in ways that are mutually enhancing. The first challenge is to clearly articulate such a model; the second, even greater challenge, will be to realize it.

Endnotes

1. Cited in Matthew Scully, "Creature Teachers," *National Review,* Vol. 45, No. 9 (May 10, 1993), p. 56 ff.
2. Reprinted in Tom Regan, *The Thee Generation* (Philadelphia: Temple University Press, 1991), pp. 143–157.
3. See Andrew Linzey, *Animal Rights: A Christian Assessment* (London: SCM Press, 1976) and *Christianity and the Rights of Animals* (New York: Crossroad, 1988).
4. K. McCabe, "Who Will Live, Who Will Die?" *Washingtonian Magazine,* August 1986, 115.
5. Vicki Hearne, "What's Wrong with Animal Rights?" *Harper's Magazine.* September 1991, p. 59 ff.

THE ARGUMENTS

Tom Regan
"The Case for Animal Rights"

Tom Regan is one of the most articulate and powerful spokepersons for animal rights. He has published widely on a range of different topics, but his most influential work has been in the area of animal rights. His book, Animal Rights, *is one of the foundational works in that area.*

In this article, Regan argues that case for animal rights, maintaining that those who take animal rights seriously must be committed to abolishing the use of animals in science, animal agriculture, and commercial hunting and trapping. "The fundamental wrong," he writes, "is the system that allows us to view animals as our resources, here for us—to be eaten, or surgically manipulated, or exploited for sport or money." Regan considers and rejects several approaches to understanding our relationship to animals: indirect duty, contractarianism, and utilitarianism. Only a rights approach is able to recognize the inherent value of the individual, including the individual animal.

As You Read, Consider This:

1. Regan distinguishes between things that "make things worse" and the "fundamental wrong." If we could eliminate the factors that "make things worse" for animals, do you think that would be enough? What of Regan's arguments supports the claim that there is a "fundamental wrong" here?
2. Regan sees the animal rights movement as "cut from the same cloth" as human rights movements that oppose racism and sexism. Are the kinds of arguments that Regan advances for animal rights the same kinds of arguments that were advanced for human rights?

I regard myself as an advocate of animal rights—as a part of the animal rights movement. That movement, as I conceive it, is committed to a number of goals, including:

- the total abolition of the use of animals in science;
- the total dissolution of commercial animal agriculture;
- the total elimination of commercial and sport hunting and trapping.

There are, I know, people who profess to believe in animal rights but do not avow these goals. Factory farming, they say, is wrong—it violates animals' rights—but traditional animal agriculture is all right. Toxicity tests of cosmetics on animals violates their rights, but important medical research—cancer research, for example—does not. The clubbing of baby seals is abhorrent, but not the harvesting of adult seals. I used to think I understood this reasoning. Not any more. You don't change unjust institutions by tidying them up.

What's wrong—fundamentally wrong—with the way animals are treated isn't the details that vary from case to case. It's the whole system. The forlornness of the veal calf is pathetic, heart wrenching; the pulsing pain of the chimp with electrodes planted deep in her brain is repulsive; the slow, torturous death of the raccoon caught in the leg-hold trap is agonizing. But what is wrong isn't the pain, isn't the suffering, isn't the deprivation. These compound what's wrong. Sometimes—often—they make it much, much worse. But they are not the fundamental wrong.

The fundamental wrong is the system that allows us to view animals as our resources, here for us—to be eaten, or surgically manipulated, or exploited for sport or money. Once we accept this view of animals—as our resources—the rest is as predictable as it is regrettable. Why worry about their loneliness, their pain, their death? Since animals exist for us, to benefit us in one way or another, what harms them really doesn't matter—or matters only if it starts to bother us, makes us feel a trifle uneasy. . . .

In the case of animals in science, whether and how we abolish their use . . . are to a large extent political questions. People must change their beliefs before they change their habits. Enough people, especially those elected to public office, must believe in change—must want it—before we will have laws that protect the rights of animals. This process of change is very complicated, very demanding, very exhausting, calling for the efforts of many hands in education, publicity, political organization and activity, down to the licking of envelopes and stamps. As a trained and practicing philosopher, the sort of contribution I can make is limited but, I like to think, important. The currency of philosophy is ideas—their meaning and rational foundation—not the nuts and bolts of the legislative process, say, or the mechanics of community organization. That's what I have been exploring over the past ten years or so in my essays and talks and, most recently, in my book, *The Case for Animal Rights*. I believe the major conclusions I reach in the book are true because they are supported by the weight of the best arguments. I believe the idea of animal rights has reason, not just emotion, on its side.

In the space I have at my disposal here I can only sketch, in the barest outline, some of the main features of the book. Its main themes—and we should not be surprised by this—involve asking and answering deep, foundational moral questions about what morality is, how it should be understood and what is the best moral theory, all considered. I hope I can convey something of the shape I think this theory takes. The attempt to do this will be (to use a word a friendly critic once used to describe my work) cerebral, perhaps too cerebral. But this is misleading. My feelings about how animals are sometimes treated run just as deep and just as strong as those of my more volatile compatriots. Philosophers do—to use the jargon of the day—have a right side to their brains. If it's the left side we contribute (or mainly should), that's because what talents we have reside there.

How to proceed? We begin by asking how the moral status of animals has been understood by thinkers who deny that animals have rights. Then we test the mettle of their ideas by seeing how well they stand up under the heat of fair criticism. If we start our thinking in this way, we soon find that some people believe that we have no duties directly to animals, that we owe nothing to them, that we can do nothing that wrongs them. Rather, we can do wrong acts that involve animals, and so we have duties regarding them, though none to them. Such views may be called indirect duty views. By way of illustration: suppose your neighbor kicks your dog. Then your neighbor has done something wrong. But not to your dog. The wrong that has been done is a wrong to you. After all, it is wrong to upset people, and your neighbor's kicking your dog upsets you. So you are the one who is wronged, not your dog. Or again: by kicking your dog your neighbor damages your property. And since it is wrong to damage another person's property, your neighbor has done something wrong—to you, of course, not to your dog. Your neighbor no more wrongs your dog than your car would be wronged if the windshield were smashed. Your neighbor's duties involving your dog are indirect duties to you. More generally, all of our duties regarding animals are indirect duties to one another—to humanity.

How could someone try to justify such a view? Someone might say that your dog doesn't feel anything and so isn't hurt by your neighbor's kick, doesn't care about the pain since none is felt, is as unaware of anything as is your windshield. Someone might say this, but no rational person will, since, among other considerations, such a view will commit anyone who holds it to the position that no human being feels pain either—that human beings also don't care about what happens to them. A second possibility is that though both humans and your dog are hurt when kicked, it is only human pain that matters. But, again, no rational person can believe this. Pain is pain wherever it occurs. If your neighbor's causing you pain is wrong because of the pain that is caused, we cannot rationally ignore or dismiss the moral relevance of the pain that your dog feels.

Philosophers who hold indirect duty views—and many still do—have come to understand that they must avoid the two defects just noted: that is, both the view that animals don't feel anything as well as the idea that only human pain can be morally relevant. Among such thinkers the sort of view now favored is one or other form of what is called contractarianism.

Here, very crudely, is the root idea: morality consists of a set of rules that individuals voluntarily agree to abide by, as we do when we sign a contract (hence the name contractarianism). Those who understand and accept the terms of the contract are covered directly; they have rights created and recognized by, and protected in, the contract. And these contractors can also have protection spelled out for others who, though they lack the ability to understand morality and so cannot sign the contract themselves, are loved or cherished by those who can. Thus young children, for example, are unable to sign contracts and lack rights. But they are protected by the contract nonetheless because of the sentimental interests of others, most notably their parents. So we have, then, duties involving these children, duties regarding them, but no duties to them. Our duties in their case are indirect duties to other human beings, usually their parents.

As for animals, since they cannot understand contracts, they obviously cannot sign; and since they cannot sign, they have no rights. Like children, however, some animals are the objects of the sentimental interest of others. You, for example, love your dog or cat. So those animals that enough people care about (companion animals, whales, baby seals, the American bald eagle), though they lack rights themselves, will be protected because of the sentimental interests of people. I have, then, according to contractarianism, no duty directly to your dog or any other animal, not even the duty not to cause them pain or suffering; my duty not to hurt them is a duty I have to those people who care about what happens to them. As for other animals, where no or little sentimental interest is present—in the case of farm animals, for example, or laboratory rats—what duties we have grow weaker and weaker, perhaps to a vanishing point. The pain and death they endure, though real, are not wrong if no one cares about them.

When it comes to the moral status of animals, contractarianism could be a hard view to refute if it were an adequate theoretical approach to the moral status of human beings. It is not adequate in this latter respect, however, which makes the question of its adequacy in the former case, regarding animals, utterly moot. For consider: morality, according to the (crude) contractarian position before us, consists of rules that people agree to abide by. What people? Well, enough to make a difference—enough, that is, collectively to have the power to enforce the rules that are drawn up in the contract. That is very well and good for the signatories but not so good for anyone who is not asked to sign. And there is nothing in contractarianism of the sort we are discussing that guarantees or requires that everyone will have a chance to participate equally in framing the rules of morality. The result is that this approach to ethics could sanction the most blatant forms of social, economic, moral and political injustice, ranging from a repressive caste system to systematic racial or sexual discrimination. Might, according to this theory, does make right. Let those who are the victims of injustice suffer as they will. It matters not so long as no one else—no contractor, or too few of them—cares about it. Such a theory takes one's moral breath away . . . as if, for example, there would be nothing wrong with apartheid in South Africa if few white South Africans were upset by it. A theory with so little to recommend it at the level of the ethics of our treatment of our fellow humans cannot have anything more to recommend it when it comes to the ethics of how we treat our fellow animals.

The version of contractarianism just examined is, as I have noted, a crude variety, and in fairness to those of a contractarian persuasion it must be noted that much more refined, subtle and ingenious varieties are possible. For example, John Rawls, in his *A Theory of Justice,* sets forth a version of contractarianism that forces contractors to ignore the accidental features of being a human being—for example, whether one is white or black, male or female, a genius or of modest intellect. Only by ignoring such features, Rawls believes, can we ensure that the principles of justice that contractors would agree upon are not based on bias or prejudice. Despite the improvement a view such as Rawls's represents over the cruder forms of contractarianism, it remains deficient: it systematically denies that we have direct duties to those human beings who do not have a sense of justice—young children, for instance, and many mentally retarded humans. And yet it seems reasonably certain that, were we to torture a young child or a retarded elder, we would be doing something that wronged him or her, not something that would be wrong if (and only if) other humans with a sense of justice were upset. And since this is true in the case of these humans, we cannot rationally deny the same in the case of animals.

Indirect duty views, then, including the best among them, fail to command our rational assent. Whatever ethical theory we should accept rationally, therefore, it must at least recognize that we have some duties directly to animals, just as we have some duties directly to each other. . . .

Some people think that the theory we are looking for is utilitarianism. A utilitarian accepts two moral principles. The first is that of equality: everyone's interests count, and similar interests must be counted as having similar weight or importance. White or black, American or Iranian, human or animal—everyone's pain or frustration matters, and matters just as much as the equivalent pain or frustration of anyone else. The second principle a utilitarian accepts is that of utility: do the act that will bring about the best balance between satisfaction and frustration for everyone affected by the outcome.

As a utilitarian, then, here is how I am to approach the task of deciding what I morally ought to do: I must ask who will be affected if I choose to do one thing rather than another, how much each individual will be affected, and where the best results are most likely to lie—which option, in other words, is most likely to bring about the best results, the best balance between satisfaction and frustration. That option, whatever it may be, is the one I ought to choose. That is where my moral duty lies.

The great appeal of utilitarianism rests with its uncompromising egalitarianism: everyone's interests count and count as much as the like interests of everyone else. The kind of odious discrimination that some forms of contractarianism can justify—discrimination based on race or sex, for example—seems disallowed in principle by utilitarianism, as is speciesism, systematic discrimination based on species membership.

The equality we find in utilitarianism, however, is not the sort an advocate of animal or human rights should have in mind. Utilitarianism has no room for the equal moral rights of different individuals because it has no room for their equal inherent value or worth. What has value for the utilitarian is the satisfaction of an individual's interests, not the individual whose interests they are. A universe in which you satisfy your desire for water, food and warmth is, other things being equal, better than a universe in which these desires are frustrated. And the same is true in the case of an animal with similar desires. But neither you nor the animal have any value in your own right. Only your feelings do.

Here is an analogy to help make the philosophical point clearer: a cup contains different liquids, sometimes sweet, sometimes bitter, sometimes a mix of the two. What has value are the liquids: the sweeter the better, the bitterer the worse. The cup, the container, has no value. It is what goes into it, not what they go into, that has value. For the utilitarian you and I are like the cup; we have no value as individuals and thus no equal value. What has value is what goes into us, what we serve as receptacles for; our feelings of satisfaction have positive value, our feelings of frustration negative value.

Serious problems arise for utilitarianism when we remind ourselves that it enjoins us to bring about the best consequences. What does this mean? It doesn't mean the best consequences for me alone, or for my family or friends, or any other person taken individually. No, what we must do is, roughly, as follows: we must add up (somehow!) the separate satisfactions and frustrations of everyone likely to be affected by our choice, the satisfactions in one column, the frustrations in the other. We must total each column for each of the options before us. That is what it means to say the theory is aggregative. And then we must choose that option which is most likely to bring about the best balance of totaled satisfactions over totaled frustrations. Whatever act would lead to this outcome is the one we ought morally to perform—it is where our moral duty lies. And that act quite clearly might not be the same one that would bring about the best results for me personally, or for my family or friends, or for a lab animal. The best aggregated consequences for everyone concerned are not necessarily the best for each individual.

That utilitarianism is an aggregative theory—different individuals' satisfactions or frustrations are added, or summed, or totaled—is the key objection to this theory. My Aunt Bea is old, inactive, a cranky, sour person, though not physically ill. She prefers to go on living. She is also rather rich. I could make a fortune if I could get my hands on her money, money she intends to give me in any event, after she dies, but which she refuses to give me now. In order to avoid a huge tax bite, I plan to donate a handsome sum of my profits to a local children's hospital. Many, many children will benefit from my generosity, and much joy will be brought to their parents, relatives and friends. If I don't get the money rather soon, all these ambitions will come to naught. The once-in-a-lifetime opportunity to make a real killing will be gone. Why, then, not kill my Aunt Bea? Oh, of course I might get caught. But I'm no fool and, besides, her doctor can be counted on to cooperate (he has an eye for the same investment and I happen to know a good deal about his shady past). The deed can be done . . . professionally, shall we say. There is very little chance of getting caught. And as for my conscience being guilt-ridden, I am a resourceful sort of fellow and will take more than sufficient comfort—as I lie on the beach at Acapulco—in contemplating the joy and health I have brought to so many others.

Suppose Aunt Bea is killed and the rest of the story comes out as told. Would I have done anything wrong? Anything immoral? One would have thought that I had. Not according to utilitarianism. Since what I have done has brought about the best balance between totaled satisfaction and frustration for all those affected by the outcome, my action is not wrong. Indeed, in killing Aunt Bea the physician and I did what duty required.

This same kind of argument can be repeated in all sorts of cases, illustrating, time after time, how the utilitarian's position leads to results that impartial people find morally callous. It is wrong to kill my Aunt Bea in the name of bringing about the best results for others. A good end does not justify an evil means. Any adequate moral theory will have to explain why this is so. Utilitarianism fails in this respect and so cannot be the theory we seek.

What to do? Where to begin anew? The place to begin, I think, is with the utilitarian's view of the value of the individual—or, rather, lack of value. In its place, suppose we consider that you and I, for example, do have value as individuals—what we will call inherent value. To say we have such value is to say that we are something more than, something different from, mere receptacles. Moreover, to ensure that we do not pave the way for such injustices as slavery or sexual discrimination, we must believe that all who have inherent value have it equally, regardless of their sex, race, religion, birthplace and so on. Similarly to be discarded as irrelevant are one's talents or skills, intelligence and wealth, personality or pathology, whether one is loved and admired or despised and loathed. The genius and the retarded child, the prince and the pauper, the brain surgeon and the fruit vendor, Mother Teresa and the most unscrupulous used-car salesman—all have inherent value, all possess it equally, and all have an equal right to be treated with respect, to be treated in ways that do not reduce them to the status of things, as if they existed as resources for others. My value as an individual is independent of my usefulness to you. Yours is not dependent on your usefulness to me. For either of us to treat the other in ways that fail to show respect for the other's independent value is to act immorally, to violate the individual's rights.

Some of the rational virtues of this view—what I call the rights view—should be evident. Unlike (crude) contractarianism, for example, the rights view in principle denies the moral tolerability of any and all forms of racial, sexual or social discrimination; and unlike utilitarianism, this view in principle denies that we can justify good results by using evil means that violate an individual's rights—denies, for example, that it could be moral to kill my Aunt Bea to harvest beneficial consequences for others. That would be to sanction the disrespectful treatment of the individual in the name of the social good, something the rights view will not—categorically will not—ever allow.

The rights view, I believe, is rationally the most satisfactory moral theory. It surpasses all other theories in the degree to which it illuminates and explains the foundation of our duties to one another—the domain of human morality. On this score it has the best reasons, the best arguments, on its side. Of course, if it were possible to show that only human beings are included within its scope, then a person like myself, who believes in animal rights, would be obliged to look elsewhere.

But attempts to limit its scope to humans only can be shown to be rationally defective. Animals, it is true, lack many of the abilities humans possess. They can't read, do higher mathematics, build a bookcase or make baba ghanoush. Neither can many human beings, however, and yet we don't (and shouldn't) say that they (these humans) therefore have less inherent value, less of a right to be treated with respect, than do others. It is the similarities between those human beings who most clearly, most non-controversially have such value (the people reading this, for example), not our differences, that matter most. And the really crucial, the basic similarity is simply this: we are each of us the experiencing subject of a life, a conscious creature having an individual welfare that has importance to us whatever our usefulness to others. We want and prefer things, believe and feel things, recall and expect things. And all these dimensions of our life, including our pleasure and pain, our enjoyment and suffering, our satisfaction and frustration, our continued existence or our untimely death—all make a difference to the quality of our life as lived, as experienced, by us as individuals. As the same is true of those animals that concern us, . . . they too must be viewed as the experiencing subjects of a life, with inherent value of their own.

Some there are who resist the idea that animals have inherent value. "Only humans have such value," they profess. How might this narrow view be defended? Shall we say that only humans have the requisite intelligence, or autonomy, or reason? But there are many, many humans who fail to meet these standards and yet are reasonably viewed as having value above and beyond their usefulness to others. Shall we claim that only humans belong to the right species, the species Homo sapiens? But this is blatant speciesism. Will it be said, then, that all—and only—humans have immortal souls? Then our opponents have their work cut out for them. I am myself not ill-disposed to the proposition that there are immortal souls. Personally, I profoundly hope I have one. But I would not want to rest my position on a controversial ethical issue on the even more controversial question about who or what has an immortal soul. That is to dig one's hole deeper, not to climb out. Rationally, it is better to resolve moral issues without making more controversial assumptions than are needed. The question of who has inherent value is such a question, one that is resolved more rationally without the introduction of the idea of immortal souls than by its use.

Well, perhaps some will say that animals have some inherent value, only less than we have. Once again, however, attempts to defend this view can be shown to lack rational justification. What could be the basis of our having more inherent value than animals? Their lack of reason, or autonomy, or intellect? Only if we are willing to make the same judgment in the case of humans who are similarly deficient. But it is not true that such humans—the retarded child, for example, or the mentally deranged—have less inherent value than you or I. Neither, then, can we rationally sustain the view that animals, like them in being the experiencing subjects of a life, have less inherent value. All who have inherent value have it equally, whether they be human animals or not.

Inherent value, then, belongs equally to those who are the experiencing subjects of a life. Whether it belongs to others—to rocks and rivers, trees and glaciers, for example—we do not know and may never know. But neither do we need to know, if we are to make the case for animal rights. We do not need to know, for example, how many people are eligible to vote in the next presidential election before we can know whether I am. Similarly, we do not need to know how many individuals have inherent value before we can know that some do. When it comes to the case for animal rights, then, what we need to know is whether the animals that, in our culture, are routinely eaten, hunted and used in our laboratories, for example, are like us in being subjects of a life. And we do know this. We do know that many—literally, billions and billions—of these animals are the subjects of a life in the sense explained and so have inherent value if we do. And since, in order to arrive at the best theory of our duties to one another, we must recognize our equal inherent value as individuals, reason—not sentiment, not emotion—reason compels us to recognize the equal inherent value of these animals and, with this, their equal right to be treated with respect.

That, *very* roughly, is the shape and feel of the case for animal rights. Most of the details of the supporting argument are missing. They are to be found in the book to which I alluded earlier. Here, the details go begging, and I must, in closing, limit myself to four final points.

The first is how the theory that underlies the case for animal rights shows that the animal rights movement is a part of, not antagonistic to, the human rights movement. The theory that rationally grounds the rights of animals also grounds the rights of humans. Thus those involved in the animal rights movement are partners in the struggle to secure respect for human rights—the rights of women, for example, or minorities, or workers. The animal rights movement is cut from the same moral cloth as these.

Second, having set out the broad outlines of the rights view, I can now say why its implications for . . . science, among other fields, are both clear and uncompromising. In the case of the use of animals in science, the rights view is categorically abolitionist. Lab animals are not our tasters; we are not their kings. Because these animals are treated routinely, systematically as if their value were reducible to their usefulness to others, they are routinely, systematically treated with a lack of respect, and thus are their rights routinely, systematically violated. This is just as true when they are used in trivial, duplicative, unnecessary or unwise research as it is when they are used in studies that hold out real promise of human benefits. We can't justify harming or killing a human being (my Aunt Bea, for example) just for these sorts of reason. Neither can we do so even in the case of so lowly a creature as a laboratory rat. It is not just refinement or reduction that is called for, not just larger, cleaner cages, not just more generous use of anesthetic or the elimination of multiple surgery, not just tidying up the system. It is complete replacement. The best we can do when it comes to using animals in science is—not to use them. That is where our duty lies, according to the rights view. . . .

My last two points are about philosophy, my profession. It is, most obviously, no substitute for political action. The words I have written here and in other places by themselves don't change a thing. It is what we do with the thoughts that the words express—our acts, our deeds—that changes things. All that philosophy can do, and all I have attempted, is to offer a vision of what our deeds should aim at. And the why. But not the how.

Finally, I am reminded of my thoughtful critic, the one I mentioned earlier, who chastised me for being too cerebral. Well, cerebral I have been: indirect duty views, utilitarianism, contractarianism—hardly the stuff deep passions are made of. I am also reminded, however, of the image another friend once set before me—the image of the ballerina as expressive of disciplined passion. Long hours of sweat and toil, of loneliness and practice, of doubt and fatigue: those are the discipline of her craft. But the passion is there too, the fierce drive to excel, to speak through her body, to do it right, to pierce our minds. That is the image of philosophy I would leave with you, not "too cerebral" but disciplined passion. Of the discipline enough has been seen. As for the passion: there are times, and these not infrequent, when tears come to my eyes when I see, or read, or hear of the wretched plight of animals in the hands of humans. Their pain, their suffering, their loneliness, their innocence, their death. Anger. Rage. Pity. Sorrow. Disgust. The whole creation groans under the weight of the evil we humans visit upon these mute, powerless creatures. It is our hearts, not just our heads, that call for an end to it all, that demand of us that we overcome, for them, the habits and forces behind their systematic oppression. All great movements, it is written, go through three stages: ridicule, discussion, adoption. It is the realization of this third stage, adoption, that requires both our passion and our discipline, our hearts and our heads. The fate of animals is in our hands. God grant we are equal to the task.

Journal/Discussion Questions

✍ *In your own life, what moral standing or importance do animals have? What difference does animal suffering make to you? How were you* affected *by Regan's article?*

1. What does Regan mean by "indirect duty views"? What criticisms does he offer of them? In what ways do you agree/disagree with his criticisms?
2. According to Regan, what is "contractarianism"? What criticisms does he offer of the contractarian approach to morality?
3. Why, according to Regan, should we reject utilitarian approaches to the issue of our relationship to animals?
4. Why, according to Regan, is the rights view superior to all other approaches to the issue of our relationship to animals? Do you agree with Regan's assessment?

Bonnie Steinbock
"Speciesism and the Idea of Equality"*

Bonnie Steinbock is a professor of philosophy at the State University of New York at Albany. She specializes in biomedical ethics, philosophy of law, and public policy, and has published widely in these areas. Her works include Life Before Birth: The Moral and Legal Status of Embryos and Fetuses, Killing and Letting Die, *edited with Alastair Norcross; and* Ethical Issues in Modern Medicine, *edited with John D. Arras.*

Seeking a middle ground in the debate over the moral significance of animal suffering, Steinbock considers the thorny issue of what weight should be accorded to animal interests. She agrees with Singer's claim that animal pain has moral weight, but she points out important moral differences between animal pain and human suffering.

As You Read, Consider This:

1. What, according to Steinbock, are the differences between human beings and animals that justify treating them differently?
2. Singer has argued that we treat human beings who lack these distinctly human capabilities differently than we treat animals. How does Steinbock reply to Singer's claim?

Most of us believe that we are entitled to treat members of other species in ways which would be considered wrong if inflicted on members of our own species. We kill them for food, keep them confined, use them in painful experiments. The moral philosopher has to ask what relevant difference justifies this difference in treatment. A look at this question will lead us to re-examine the distinctions which we have assumed make a moral difference.

* *Philosophy,* Vol. 53, No. 204 (April 1978), pp. 247–256 of Cambridge University Press. Copyright 1978 Cambridge.

It has been suggested by Peter Singer that our current attitudes are "speciesist," a word intended to make one think of "racist" or "sexist." The idea is that membership in a species is in itself not relevant to moral treatment, and that much of our behavior and attitudes toward nonhuman animals is based simply on this irrelevant fact.

There is, however, an important difference between racism or sexism and "speciesism." We do not subject animals to different moral treatment simply because they have fur and feathers, but because they are in fact different from human beings in ways that could be morally relevant. It is false that women are incapable of being benefited by education, and therefore that claim cannot serve to justify preventing them from attending school. But this is not false of cows and dogs, even chimpanzees. Intelligence is thought to be a morally relevant capacity because of its relation to the capacity for moral responsibility.

What is Singer's response? He agrees that nonhuman animals lack certain capacities that human animals possess, and that this may justify different *treatment.* But it does not justify giving less consideration to their needs and interests. According to Singer, the moral mistake which the racist or sexist makes is not essentially the factual error of thinking that blacks or women are inferior to white men. For even if there were no factual error, even if it were true that blacks and women are less intelligent and responsible than whites and men, this would not justify giving less consideration to their needs and interests. It is important to note that the term "speciesism" is in one way like, and in another way unlike, the terms "racism" and "sexism." What the term "speciesism" has in common with these terms is the reference to focusing on a characteristic which is, in itself, irrelevant to moral treatment. And it is worth reminding us of this. But Singer's real aim is to bring us to a new understanding of the idea of equality. The question is, on what do claims to equality rest? The demand for *human* equality is a demand that the interests of all human beings be considered equally, unless there is a moral justification for not doing so. But why should the interests of all human beings be considered equally? In order to answer this question, we have to give some sense to the phrase, "All men (human beings) are created equal." Human beings are manifestly *not* equal, differing greatly in intelligence, virtue, and capacities. In virtue of what can the claim to equality be made?

It is Singer's contention that claims to equality do not rest on factual equality. Not only do human beings differ in their capacities, but it might even turn out that intelligence, the capacity for virtue, etc., are not distributed evenly among the races and sexes.

The appropriate response to those who claim to have found evidence of genetically based differences in ability between the races or sexes is not to stick to the belief that the genetic explanation must be wrong, whatever evidence to the contrary may turn up; instead we should make it quite clear that the claim to equality does not depend on intelligence, moral capacity, physical strength, or similar matters of fact. Equality is a moral ideal, not a simple assertion of fact. There is no logically compelling reason for assuming that a factual difference in ability between two people justifies any difference in the amount of consideration we give to satisfying their needs and interests. The principle of equality of human beings is not a description of an alleged actual equality among humans: it is a prescription of how we should treat humans.[2]

Insofar as the subject is human equality, Singer's view is supported by other philosophers. Bernard Williams, for example, is concerned to show that demands for equality cannot rest on factual equality among people, for no such equality exists.[3] The only respect in which all men are equal, according to Williams, is that they are all equally men. This seems to be a platitude, but Williams denies that it is trivial. Membership in the species *homo sapiens* in itself has no special moral significance, but rather the fact that all men are human serves as a *reminder* that being human involves the possession of characteristics that are morally relevant. But on what characteristics does Williams focus? Aside from the desire for self-respect (which I will discuss later), Williams is not concerned with uniquely human capacities. Rather, he focuses on the capacity to feel pain and the capacity to feel affection. It is in virtue of these capacities, it seems, that the idea of equality is to be justified.

Apparently Richard Wasserstrom has the same idea as he sets out the racist's "logical and moral mistakes" in "Rights, Human Rights and Racial Discrimination."[4] The racist fails to acknowledge that the black person is as capable of suffering as the white person. According to Wasserstrom, the reason why a person is said to have a right not to be made to suffer acute physical pain is that we all do in fact value freedom from such pain. Therefore, if anyone has a right to be free from suffering acute physical pain, *everyone* has this right, for there is no possible basis of discrimination. Wasserstrom says, "For, if all persons do have equal capacities of these sorts and if the existence of these capacities is the reason for ascribing these rights to anyone, then all persons ought to have the right to claim equality of treatment in respect to the possession and exercise of these rights."[5] The basis of equality, for Wasserstrom as for Williams, lies not in some uniquely human capacity, but rather in the fact that all human beings are alike in their capacity to suffer. Writers on equality have focused on this capacity, I think, because it functions as some sort of lowest common denominator, so that whatever the other capacities of a human being, he is entitled to equal consideration because, like everyone else, he is capable of suffering.

If the capacity to suffer is the reason for ascribing a right to freedom from acute pain, or a right to well-being, then it certainly looks as though these rights must be extended to animals as well. This is the conclusion Singer arrives at. The demand for human equality rests on the equal capacity of all human beings to suffer and to enjoy well being. But if this is the basis of the demand for equality, then this demand must include all beings which have an equal capacity to suffer and enjoy well being. That is why Singer places at the basis of the demand for equality, not intelligence or reason, but sentience. And equality will mean, not equality of treatment, but "equal consideration of interests." The equal consideration of interests will often mean quite different treatment, depending on the nature of the entity being considered. (It would be as absurd to talk of a dog's right to vote, Singer says, as to talk of a man's right to have an abortion.)

It might be thought that the issue of equality depends on a discussion of rights. According to this line of thought, animals do not merit equal consideration of interests because, unlike human beings, they do not, or cannot, have rights. But I am not going to discuss rights, important as the issue is. The fact that an entity does not have rights does not necessarily imply that its interests are going to count for less than the interests of entities which are right-bearers. According to the view of rights held by H.L.A. Hart and S.I. Benn, infants do not have rights, nor do the mentally defective, nor do the insane, in so far as they all lack certain minimal conceptual capabilities for having rights.[6] Yet it certainly does not seem that either Hart or Benn would agree that *therefore* their interests are to be counted for less, or that it is morally permissible to treat them in ways in which it would not be permissible to treat right-bearers. It seems to mean only that we must give different sorts of reasons for our obligations to take into consideration the interests of those who do not have rights.

We have reasons concerning the treatment of other people which are clearly independent of the notion of rights. We would say that it is wrong to punch someone because doing that infringes his rights. But we could also say that it is wrong because doing that hurts him, and that is, ordinarily, enough of a reason not to do it. Now this particular reason extends not only to human beings, but to all sentient creatures. One has a *prima facie* reason not to pull the cat's tail (whether or not the cat has rights) because it hurts the cat. And this is the only thing, normally, which is relevant in this case. The fact that the cat is not a "rational being," that it is not capable of moral responsibility, that it cannot make free choices or shape its life—all of these differences from us have nothing to do with the justifiability of pulling its tail. Does this show that rationality and the rest of it are irrelevant to moral treatment?

I hope to show that this is not the case. But first I want to point out that the issue is not one of cruelty to animals. We all agree that cruelty is wrong, whether perpetrated on a moral or nonmoral, rational or nonrational agent. Cruelty is defined as the infliction of unnecessary pain or suffering. What is to count as necessary or unnecessary is determined, in part, by the nature of the end pursued. Torturing an animal is cruel, because although the pain is logically necessary for the action to be torture, the end (deriving enjoyment from seeing the animal suffer) is monstrous. Allowing animals to suffer from neglect or for the sake of large profits may also be thought to be unnecessary and therefore cruel. But there may be some ends, which are very good (such as the advancement of medical knowledge), which can be accomplished by subjecting animals to pain in experiments. Although most people would agree that the pain inflicted on animals used in medical research ought to be kept to a minimum, they would consider pain that cannot be eliminated "necessary" and therefore not cruel. It would probably not be so regarded if the subjects were nonvoluntary human beings. Necessity, then, is defined in terms of human benefit, but this is just what is being called into question. The topic of cruelty to animals, while important from a practical viewpoint, because much of our present treatment of animals involves the infliction of suffering for no good reason, is not very interesting philosophically. What is philosophically interesting is whether we are justified in having different standards of necessity for human suffering and for animal suffering.

Singer says, quite rightly I think, "If a being suffers, there can be no moral justification for refusing to take that suffering into consideration."[7] But he thinks that the principle of equality requires that, no matter what the nature of the being, its suffering be counted equally with the like suffering of any other being. In other words sentience does not simply provide us with reasons for acting; it is the *only* relevant consideration for equal consideration of interests. It is this view that I wish to challenge.

I want to challenge it partly because it has such counterintuitive results. It means, for example, that feeding starving children before feeding starving dogs is just like a Catholic charity's feeding hungry Catholics before feeding hungry non-Catholics. It is simply a matter of taking care of one's own, something which is usually morally permissible. But whereas we would admire the Catholic agency which did not discriminate, but fed all children, first come, first served, we would feel quite differently about someone who had this policy for dogs and children. Nor is this, it seems to me, simply a matter of sentimental preference for our own species. I might feel much more love for my dog than for a strange child—and yet I might feel morally obliged to feed the child before I fed my dog. If I gave in to the feelings of love and fed my dog and let the child go hungry, I would probably feel guilty. This is not to say that we can simply rely on such feelings. Huck Finn felt guilty at helping Jim escape, which he viewed as stealing from a woman who had never done him any harm. But while the existence of such feelings does not settle the morality of an issue, it is not clear to me that they can be explained away. In any event, their existence can serve as a motivation for trying to find a rational justification for considering human interests above nonhuman ones.

However, it does seem to me that this *requires* a justification. Until now, common sense (and academic philosophy) have seen no such need. Benn says, "No one claims equal consideration for all mammals—human beings count, mice do not, though it would not be easy to say *why* not.

Although we hesitate to inflict unnecessary pain on sentient creatures, such as mice or dogs, we are quite sure that we do not need to show good reasons for putting human interests before theirs."[8]

I think we do have to justify counting our interests more heavily than those of animals. But how? Singer is right, I think, to point out that it will not do to refer vaguely to the greater value of human life, to human worth and dignity.

Faced with a situation in which they see a need for some basis for the moral gulf that is commonly thought to separate humans and animals, but can find no concrete difference that will do this without undermining the equality of humans, philosophers tend to waffle. They resort to high-sounding phrases like "the intrinsic dignity of the human individual." They talk of "the intrinsic worth of all men" as if men had some worth that other beings do not have or they say that human beings, and only human beings, are "ends in themselves," while "everything other than a person can only have value for a person." Why should we not attribute "intrinsic dignity" or "intrinsic worth" to ourselves? Why should we not say that we are the only things in the universe that have intrinsic value? Our fellow human beings are unlikely to reject the accolades we so generously bestow upon them, and those to whom we deny the honor are unable to object.[9]

Singer is right to be skeptical of terms like "intrinsic dignity" and "intrinsic worth." These phrases are no substitute for a moral argument. But they may point to one. In trying to understand what is meant by these phrases, we may find a difference or differences between human beings and nonhuman animals that will justify different treatment while not undermining claims for human equality. While we are not compelled to discriminate among people because of different capacities, if we can find a significant difference in capacities between human and nonhuman animals, this could serve to justify regarding human interests as primary. It is not arbitrary or smug, I think, to maintain that human beings have a different moral status from members of other species because of certain capacities which are characteristic of being human. We may not all be equal in these capacities, but all human beings possess them to some measure, and nonhuman animals do not. For example, human beings are normally held to be responsible for what they do. In recognizing that someone is responsible for his or her actions, you accord that person a respect which is reserved for those possessed of moral autonomy, or capable of achieving such autonomy. Secondly, human beings can be expected to reciprocate in a way that nonhuman animals cannot. Nonhuman animals cannot be motivated by altruistic or moral reasons; they cannot treat you fairly or unfairly. This does not rule out the possibility of an animal being motivated by sympathy or pity. It does rule out altruistic motivation in the sense of motivation due to the recognition that the needs and interests of others provide one with certain reasons for acting.[10] Human beings are capable of altruistic motivation in this sense. We are sometimes motivated simply by the recognition that someone else is in pain, and that pain is a bad thing, no matter who suffers it. It is this sort of reason that I claim cannot motivate an animal or any entity not possessed of fairly abstract concepts. (If some nonhuman animals do possess the requisite concepts—perhaps chimpanzees who have learned a language—they might well be capable of altruistic motivation.) This means that our moral dealings with animals are necessarily much more limited than our dealings with other human beings. If rats invade our houses, carrying disease and biting our children, we cannot reason with them, hoping to persuade them of the injustice they do us. We can only attempt to get rid of them. And it is this that makes it reasonable for us to accord them a separate and not equal moral status, even though their capacity to suffer provides us with some reason to kill them painlessly, if this can be done without too much sacrifice of human interests. Thirdly, as Williams points out, there is the "desire for self-respect": "a certain human desire to be identified with what one is doing, to be able to realize purposes of one's own, and not to be the instrument of another's will unless one has willingly accepted such a role."[11] Some animals may have some form of this desire, and to the extent that they do, we ought to consider their interest in freedom and self-determination. (Such considerations might affect our attitudes toward zoos and circuses.) But the desire for self-respect *per se* requires the intellectual capacities of human beings, and this desire provides us with special reasons not to treat human beings in certain ways. It is an affront to the dignity of a human being to be a slave (even if a well-treated one); this cannot be true for a horse or a cow. To point this out is of course only to say that the justification for the treatment of an entity will depend on the sort of entity in question. In our treatment of other entities, we must consider the desire for autonomy, dignity and respect, but only where such a desire exists. Recognition of different desires and interests will often require different treatment, a point Singer himself makes.

But is the issue simply one of different desires and interests justifying and requiring different treatment? I would like to make a stronger claim, namely, that certain capacities, which seem to be unique to human beings, entitle their possessors to a privileged position in the moral community. Both rats and human beings dislike pain, and so we have a *prima facie* reason not to inflict pain on either. But if we can free human beings from crippling diseases, pain and death through experimentation which involves making animals suffer, and if this is the only way to achieve such results, then I think that such experimentation is justified because human lives are more valuable than animal lives. And this is because of certain capacities and abilities that normal human beings have which animals apparently do not, and which human beings cannot exercise if they are devastated by pain or disease.

My point is not that the lack of the sorts of capacities I have been discussing gives us a justification for treating animals just as we like, but rather that it is these differences between human beings and nonhuman animals which provide a rational basis for different moral treatment and consideration. Singer focuses on sentience alone as the basis of equality, but we can justify the belief that human beings have a moral worth that nonhuman animals do not, in virtue of specific capacities, and without resorting to "high-sounding phrases."

Singer thinks that intelligence, the capacity for moral responsibility, for virtue, etc., are irrelevant to equality, because we would not accept a hierarchy based on intelligence any more than one based on race. We do not think that those with greater capacities ought to have their interests weighed more heavily than those with lesser capacities, and this, he thinks, shows that differences in such capacities are irrelevant to equality. But it does not show this at all. Kevin Donaghy argues (rightly, I think) that what entitles us human beings to a privileged position in the moral community is a certain minimal level of intelligence, which is a prerequisite for morally relevant capacities.[12] The fact that we would reject a hierarchical society based on degree of intelligence does not show that a minimal level of intelligence cannot be used as a cut-off point, justifying giving greater consideration to the interests of those entities which meet this standard.

Interestingly enough, Singer concedes the rationality of valuing the lives of normal human beings over the lives of nonhuman animals.[13] We are not required to value equally the life of a normal human being and the life of an animal, he thinks, but only their suffering. But I doubt that the value of an entity's life can be separated from the value of its suffering in this way. If we value the lives of human beings more than the lives of animals, this is because we value certain capacities that human beings have and animals do not. But freedom from suffering is, in general, a minimal condition for exercising these capacities, for living a fully human life. So, valuing human life more involves regarding human interests as counting for more. That is why we regard human suffering as more deplorable than comparable animal suffering.

But there is one point of Singer's which I have not yet met. Some human beings (if only a very few) are less intelligent than some nonhuman animals. Some have less capacity for moral choice and responsibility. What status in the moral community are these members of our species to occupy? Are their interests to be considered equally with ours? Is experimenting on them permissible where such experiments are painful or injurious, but somehow necessary for human well being? If it is certain of our capacities which entitle us to a privileged position, it looks as if those lacking those capacities are not entitled to a privileged position. To think it is justifiable to experiment on an adult chimpanzee but not on a severely mentally incapacitated human being seems to be focusing on membership in a species where that has no moral relevance. (It is being "speciesist" in a perfectly reasonable use of the word.) How are we to meet this challenge?

Donaghy is untroubled by this objection. He says that it is fully in accord with his intuitions, that he regards the killing of a normally intelligent human being as far more serious than the killing of a person so severely limited that he lacked the intellectual capacities of an adult pig. But this parry really misses the point. The question is whether Donaghy thinks that the killing of a human being so severely limited that he lacked the intellectual capacities of an adult pig would be less serious than the killing of that pig. If superior intelligence is what justifies privileged status in the moral community, then the pig who is smarter than a human being ought to have superior moral status. And I doubt that this is fully in accord with Donaghy's intuitions.

I doubt that anyone will be able to come up with a concrete and morally relevant difference that would justify, say, using a chimpanzee in an experiment rather than a human being with less capacity for reasoning, moral responsibility, etc. Should we then experiment on the severely retarded? Utilitarian considerations aside (the difficulty of comparing intelligence between species, for example), we feel a special obligation to care for the handicapped members of our own species, who cannot survive in this world without such care. Nonhuman animals manage very well, despite their "lower intelligence" and lesser capacities; most of them do not require special care from us. This does not, of course, justify experimenting on them. However, to subject to experimentation those people who depend on us seems even worse than subjecting members of other species to it. In addition, when we consider the severely retarded, we think, "That could be me." It makes sense to think that one might have been born retarded, but not to think that one might have been born a monkey. And so, although one can imagine oneself in the monkey's place, one feels a closer identification with the severely retarded human being. Here we are getting away from such things as "morally relevant differences" and are talking about something much more difficult to articulate, namely, the role of feeling and sentiment in moral thinking. We would be *horrified* by the use of the retarded in medical research. But what are we to make of this horror? Has it moral significance or is it "mere" sentiment, of no more import than the sentiment of whites against blacks? It is terribly difficult to know how to evaluate such feelings.[14] I am not going to say more about this, because I think that the treatment of severely incapacitated human beings does not pose an insurmountable objection to the privileged status principle. I am willing to admit that my horror at the thought of experiments being performed on severely mentally incapacitated human beings in cases in which I would find it justifiable and preferable to perform the same experiments on nonhuman animals (capable of similar suffering) may not be a moral emotion. But it is certainly not wrong of us to extend special care to members of our own species, motivated by feelings of sympathy, protectiveness, etc. If this is speciesism, it is stripped of its tone of moral condemnation. It is not racist to provide special care to members of your own race; it is racist to fall below your moral obligation to a person because of his or her race. I have been arguing that we are morally obliged to consider the interests of all sentient creatures, but not to consider those interests equally with human interests. Nevertheless, even this recognition will mean some radical changes in our attitude toward and treatment of other species.[15]

Endnotes

1. Peter Singer, *Animal Liberation* (A New York Review Book, 1975).
2. Singer, 5.
3. Bernard Williams, "The Idea of Equality," *Philosophy, Politics and Society* (Second Series), Laslett and Runciman (eds.) (Blackwell, 1962), 110–431, reprinted in *Moral Concepts,* Feinberg (ed.) (Oxford, 1970), 153–171.
4. Richard Wasserstrom, "Rights, Human Rights, and Racial Discrimination," *Journal of Philosophy* 61, No. 20 (1964), reprinted in *Human Rights,* A.I. Melden (ed.) (Wadsworth, 1970), 96–110.
5. Ibid., 106.
6. H.L.A. Hart, "Are There Any Natural Rights?" *Philosophical Review* 64 (1955), and S.I. Benn, "Abortion, Infanticide, and Respect for Persons," *The Problem of Abortion,* Feinberg (ed.) (Wadsworth, 1973), 92–104.
7. Singer, 9.
8. Benn, "Equality, Moral, and Social," *The Encyclopedia of Philosophy* 3, 40.
9. Singer, 266–267.
10. This conception of altruistic motivation comes from Thomas Nagel's *The Possibility of Altruism* (Oxford, 1970).
11. Williams, *op. cit.,* 157.
12. Kevin Donaghy, "Singer on Speciesism," *Philosophic Exchange* (Summer 1974).
13. Singer, 22.
14. We run into the same problem when discussing abortion. Of what significance are our feelings toward the unborn when discussing its status? Is it relevant or irrelevant that it looks like a human being?
15. I would like to acknowledge the help of, and offer thanks to, Professor Richard Arneson of the University of California, San Diego; Professor Sidney Gendin of Eastern Michigan University; and Professor Peter Singer of Monash University, all of whom read and commented on earlier drafts of this paper.

Journal/Discussion Questions

✍ *Steinbock notes that we are horrified at the thought of experimentation upon the mentally retarded, and she notes that this same problem occurs in our discussions of abortion. What status are we to accord to feelings in the moral life?*

1. What is Steinbock's position on the moral significance of animal pain versus human suffering? Do you agree with her? Discuss.
2. Why does the issue of our treatment of the retarded come up in this discussion? Do you agree or disagree with Steinbock's position on this issue?
3. What place, according to Steinbock, should sympathy have in life? Do you agree with her? Discuss.

Gary E. Varner
"The Prospects for Consensus and Convergence in the Animal Rights Debate"

Gary E. Varner is an assistant professor in the department of philosophy at Texas A&M University, College Station. He has published widely in the areas of environmental ethics and animal rights.

Despite political posturing, both sides in the animal rights debate—the "animal welfarists" and the "animal rightists"—in Varner's eyes have a surprising potential for agreeing at least at the level of policy (convergence), and sometimes even at the level of moral theory (consensus). Peter Singer's utilitiarianism is less absolutist than often realized, and allows that animal experimentation may in some (rare and largely hypothetical) cases be justified. Often disagreements turn on empirical rather than moral matters—how much pain animals actually suffer and what benefits actually flow from a particular research project. Even Tom Regan's defense of animal rights reocgnizes that in some cases human interests clearly take precedence over animal interests. Varner concludes with a cautionary note about extremist statements on both sides of this debate.

As You Read, Consider This:

1. How are animal welfarists distinguished—both philosophically and politically—from animal rightists?
2. Varner distinguishes between the approaches of Peter Singer and Tom Regan. What is the most important philosophical basis for distinguishing their positions?

Controversies over the use of nonhuman animals (henceforth animals) for science, nutrition, and recreation are often presented as clear-cut standoffs, with little or no common ground between opposing factions and, consequently, with little or no possibility for consensus-formation. As a philosopher studying these controversies, my sense is that the apparent intransigence of opposing parties is more a function of political posturing than theoretical necessity, and that continuing to paint the situation as a clear-cut standoff serves the interests of neither side. A critical look at the philosophical bases of the animal rights movement reveals surprising potential for convergence (agreement at the level of policy despite disagreement at the level of moral theory) and, in some cases, consensus (agreement at both levels).[1] Recognizing this should make defenders of animal research take animal rights views more seriously and could refocus the animal rights debate in a constructive way.

In response to the growth of the animal rights movement, animal researchers have begun to distinguish between animal rights views and animal welfare views, but they have not drawn the distinction the way a philosopher would. Researchers typically stress two differences between animal welfarists and animal rightists. First, welfarists argue for reforms in research involving animals, whereas rightists argue for the total abolition of such research. Second, welfarists work within the system, whereas rightists advocate using theft, sabotage, or even violence to achieve their ends. A more philosophical account of the animal rights/animal welfare distinction cuts the pie very differently, revealing that many researchers agree with some animal rights advocates at the level of moral theory, and that, even where they differ dramatically at the level of moral theory, there is some potential for convergence at the level of policy.

Animal Welfare: The Prospects for Consensus

Peter Singer's *Animal Liberation* is the acknowledged Bible of the animal rights movement. Literally millions of people have been moved to vegetarianism or animal activism as a result of reading this book. PETA (People for the Ethical Treatment of Animals) distributed the first edition of the book as a membership premium, and the number of copies in print has been cited as a measure of growth in the animal rights movement. However, Singer wrote *Animal Liberation* for popular consumption, and in it he intentionally avoided discussion of complex philosophical issues.[2] In particular, he avoided analyzing the concepts of "rights" and "harm," and these concepts are crucial to drawing the animal rights/animal welfare distinction in philosophical terms.

In *Animal Liberation,* Singer spoke loosely of animals having moral "rights," but all that he intended by this was that animals (at least some of them) have some basic moral standing and that there are right and wrong ways of treating them. In later, more philosophically rigorous work—summarized in his *Practical Ethics,* a second edition of which has just been issued[3]—he explicitly eschews the term rights, noting that, as a thoroughgoing utilitarian, he must deny not only that animals have moral rights, but also that human beings do.

When moral philosophers speak of an individual "having moral rights," they mean something much more specific than that the individual has some basic moral standing and that there are right and wrong ways of treating him or her. Although there is much controversy as to the specifics, there is general agreement on this: to attribute moral rights to an individual is to assert that the individual has some kind of special moral dignity, the cash value of which is that certain things cannot justifiably be done to him or her (or it) for the sake of benefit to others. For this reason, moral rights have been characterized as "trump cards" against utilitarian arguments. Utilitarian arguments are based on aggregate benefits and aggregate harms. Specifically, utilitarianism is the view that right actions maximize aggregate happiness. In principle, nothing is inherently or intrinsically wrong, according to a utilitarian; any action could be justified under some possible circumstances.

One way of characterizing rights views in ethics, by contrast, is that there are some things which, regardless of the consequences, it is simply wrong to do to individuals, and that moral rights single out these things.

Although a technical and stipulative definition of rights, this philosophical usage reflects a familiar concept. In day-to-day discussions, appeals to individuals' rights are used to assert, in effect, that there is a limit to what individuals can be forced to do, or to the harm that may be inflicted upon them, for the benefit of others. So the philosophical usage of rights talk reflects the commonsense view that there are limits to what we can justifiably do to an individual for the benefit of society.

To defend the moral rights of animals would be to claim that certain ways of treating animals cannot be justified on utilitarian grounds. But in *Practical Ethics* Peter Singer explicitly adopts a utilitarian stance for dealing with our treatment of nonhuman animals. So the author of "the Bible of the animal rights movement" is not an animal rights theorist at all, and the self-proclaimed advocates of animal welfare are appealing to precisely the same tradition in ethics as is Singer. Both believe that it is permissible to sacrifice (even involuntarily) the life of one individual for the benefit of others, where the aggregated benefits to others clearly outweigh the costs to that individual. (At least they agree on this as far as animals are concerned. Singer is a thoroughgoing utilitarian, whereas my sense is that most animal researchers are utilitarians when it comes to animals, but rights theorists when it comes to humans.)

Many researchers also conceive of harm to animals very similarly to Singer, at least where nonmammalian animals are concerned. In *Animal Liberation,* Singer employs a strongly hedonistic conception of harm. He admits that the morality of killing is more complicated than that of inflicting pain (p. 17) and that although pain is pain wherever it occurs, this "does not imply that all lives are of equal worth" (p. 20). This should be stressed, because researchers commonly say that according to animal rights philosophies, of which Singer's is their paradigm, all animals' lives are of equal value. No fair reading of Singer's *Animal Liberation* would yield this conclusion, let alone any fair reading of *Practical Ethics,* where he devotes four chapters to the question of killing.

The morality of killing is complicated by competing conceptions of harm. In *Animal Liberation,* Singer leaves the question of killing in the background and uses a strongly hedonistic conception of animal welfare. He argues that the conclusions reached in the book, including the duty to refrain from eating animals, "flow from the principle of minimizing suffering alone" (p. 21). To conceive of harm hedonistically is to say that harm consists in felt pain or lost opportunities for pleasure. For a utilitarian employing a hedonistic conception of harm, individuals are replaceable in the following sense. If an individual lives a pleasant life, dies a painless death, and is replaced by an individual leading a similarly pleasant life, there is no loss of value in the world. Agriculturalists appear to be thinking like hedonistic utilitarians when they defend humane slaughter in similar terms. Researchers employ a similarly hedonistic conception of harm when they argue that if all pain is eliminated from an experimental protocol then, ethically speaking, there is nothing left to be concerned about.

Singer conceives of harm to "lower" animals in hedonistic terms and thus agrees with these researchers and agriculturalists. He even acknowledges that the replaceability thesis could be used to defend some forms of animal agriculture, although not intensive poultry systems, where the birds hardly live happy lives or die painless deaths. However, Singer argues that it is implausible to conceive of harm in hedonistic terms when it comes to "self-conscious individuals, leading their own lives and wanting to go on living" (p. 125), and he argues that all mammals are self-conscious in this sense.

Singer equates being self-conscious with having forward-looking desires, especially the desire to go on living. He argues that such self-conscious individuals are not replaceable, because when an individual with forward-looking desires dies, those desires go unsatisfied even if another individual is born and has similar desires satisfied. With regard to self-conscious individuals, Singer is still a utilitarian, but he is a preference utilitarian rather than a hedonistic utilitarian. Singer cites evidence to demonstrate that the great apes are self-conscious in his sense (pp. 11–16) and states, without saying what specific research leads him to this conclusion, that neither fish nor chickens are (pp. 95, 133), but that "a case can be made, though with varying degrees of confidence," that all mammals are self-conscious (p. 132).

It is easy to disagree with Singer about the range of self-consciousness, as he conceives of it, in the animal kingdom.[4] Probably most mammals have forward-looking desires, but the future to which they look is doubtless a very near one. Cats probably think about what to do in the next moment to achieve a desired result, but I doubt that they have projects (long-term, complicated desires) of the kind suggested by saying that they are "leading their own lives and wanting to go on living."

However, even if we grant Singer the claim that all mammals have projects, so long as we remain utilitarians this just means that research on mammals carries a higher burden of justification than does research on "lower" animals like reptiles or insects, a point many researchers would readily grant. A preference utilitarian is still a utilitarian, and in at least some cases, a utilitarian must agree that experimentation is justified.

In the following passage from *Practical Ethics,* Singer stresses just this point:

> In the past, argument about animal experimentation has often . . . been put in absolutist terms: would the opponent of experimentation be prepared to let thousands die from a terrible disease that could be cured by experimenting on one animal? This is a purely hypothetical question, since experiments do not have such dramatic results, but as long as its hypothetical nature is clear, I think the question should be answered affirmatively—in other words, if one, or even a dozen animals had to suffer experiments in order to save thousands, I would think it right and in accordance with equal consideration of interests that they should do so. This, at any rate, is the answer a utilitarian must give. (p. 67)

Singer doubts that most experiments are justified, not because he believes experimentation is wrong simpliciter, but because he doubts that the benefits to humans significantly outweigh the costs to the animals. In the pages preceding the passage just quoted, Singer cites examples of experiments he thinks cannot plausibly be said "to serve vital medical purposes": testing of new shampoos and food colorings, armed forces experiments on the effects of radiation on combat performance, and H.E Harlow's maternal deprivation experiments. "In these cases, and many others like them," he says, "the benefits to humans are either nonexistent or uncertain, while the losses to members of other species are certain and real" (p. 66).

So the disagreement between Singer and the research establishment is largely empirical, about how likely various kinds of research are to lead to important human benefits. Researchers often argue that we cannot be expected to know ahead of time which lines of research will yield dramatic benefits. Critics respond that these same scientists serve on grant review boards, whose function is to permit funding agencies to make such decisions all the time. Here I want only to emphasize that this is an empirical dispute that cannot be settled a priori or as a matter of moral theory. One of the limitations of utilitarianism is that its application requires very detailed knowledge about the effects of various actions or policies. When it comes to utilitarian justifications for animal research, the probability—and Singer is correct that it is never a certainty—that various lines of research will save or significantly improve human lives must be known or estimated before anything meaningful can be said. Singer is convinced that most research will not meet this burden of proof; most researchers are convinced of just the opposite.

Animal Rights: The Prospects for Convergence

Most animal researchers agree to a surprising extent with the Moses of the animal rights movement. Their basic ethical principles are the same (at least where nonhuman animals are concerned), and they apply to all animals the same conception of harm which Singer applies to all animals except mammals. Where they disagree with Singer is at the level of policy; they see the same ethical theory implying different things in practice. Dramatic disagreement at the level of moral theory emerges only when we turn to the views of Tom Regan, whose ethical principles and conception of harm are dramatically different from Singer's and the researchers'.

Regan's *The Case for Animal Rights*[5] is a lengthy and rigorous defense of a true animal rights position. It is impossible to do justice to the argument of a 400-page book in a few paragraphs, so here I will simply state the basic destination Regan reaches, in order to examine its implications for animal research.

For Regan, there is basically one moral right: the right not to be harmed on the grounds that doing so benefits others, and all individuals who can be harmed in the relevant way have this basic right. Regan conceives of harm as a diminution in the capacity to form and satisfy desires, and he argues that all animals who are capable of having desires have this basic moral right not to be harmed. On Regan's construal, losing an arm is more of a harm than stubbing one's toe (because it frustrates more of one's desires), but death is always the worst harm an individual can suffer because it completely destroys one's capacity to form and satisfy desires. As to which animals have desires, Regan explicitly defends only the claim that all mentally normal mammals of a year or more have desires, but he says that he does this to avoid the controversy over "line drawing," that is, saying precisely how far down the phylogenetic scale one must go to find animals that are incapable of having desires. Regan is confident that at least all mammals and birds have desires, but acknowledges that the analogical evidence for possession of desires becomes progressively weaker as we turn to herpetofauna (reptiles and amphibians), fish, and then invertebrates.[6]

Regan defends two principles to use in deciding whom to harm where it is impossible not to harm someone who has moral rights: the miniride and worse-off principles. The worse-off principle applies where noncomparable harms are involved, and it requires us to avoid harming the worse-off individual. Regan's discussion of this principle makes it clear that for him, harm is measured in absolute, rather than relative terms. If harm were measured relative to the individual's original capacity to form and satisfy desires, rather than in absolute terms, then death would be uniformly catastrophic wherever it occurs. But Regan reasons that although death is always the greatest harm which any individual can suffer (because it forecloses all of that individual's opportunities for desire formation and satisfaction), death to a normal human being is noncomparably worse than death to any nonhuman animal, because a normal human being's capacity to form and satisfy desires is so much greater. To illustrate the use of the worse-off principle, Regan imagines that five individuals, four humans, and a dog are in a lifeboat that can support only four of them. Since death to any of the human beings would be noncomparably worse than death to the dog, the worse-off principle applies, and it requires us to avoid harming the human beings, who stand to lose the most.

The miniride principle applies to cases where comparable harms are involved, and it requires us to harm the few rather than the many. Regan admits that, where it applies, this principle yields the same conclusions as the principle of utility, but he emphasizes that the reasoning is nonutilitarian. The focus, he says, is on individuals rather than the aggregate. What the miniride principle instructs us to do is minimize the overriding of individuals' rights, rather than to maximize aggregate happiness. To illustrate the miniride principle's application, Regan imagines that a runaway mine train must be sent down one of two shafts, and that fifty miners would be killed by sending it down the first shaft but only one by sending it down the second. Since the harms that the various individuals in the example would suffer are comparable (only humans are involved, and all are faced with death), the miniride principle applies, and we are obligated to send the runaway train down the second shaft.

Regan argues that the rights view (as he labels his position) calls for the total abolition of animal research. In terms of the basic contrast drawn above between rights views and utilitarianism, it is easy to see why one would think this. The fundamental tenet of rights views is opposition to utilitarian justifications for harming individuals, and as we saw above, researchers' justification for animal research is utilitarian. They argue that by causing a relatively small number of individuals to suffer and die, a relatively large number of individuals can live or have their lives significantly improved.

However, Regan's worse-off principle, coupled with his conception of harm, would seem to imply that at least some research is not only permissible but required, even on a true animal rights view. For as we just saw, Regan believes that death for a normal human is noncomparably worse than death for any nonhuman animal. So if we knew that by performing fatal research on a given number of nonhuman animals we could save even one human life, the worse-off principle would apply, and it would require us to perform the research. In the lifeboat case referred to above, Regan emphasizes that where the worse-off principle applies, the numbers do not matter. He says:

> Let the number of dogs be as large as one likes; suppose they number a million; and suppose the lifeboat will support only four survivors. Then the rights view still implies that, special considerations apart, the million dogs should be thrown overboard and the four humans saved. To attempt to reach a contrary judgment will inevitably involve one in aggregative i.e., utilitarian considerations. (p. 325)

The same reasoning, in a hypothetical case like that described by Singer (where we know, with absolute certainty, that one experiment will save human lives) would imply that the experiment should be performed.

One complication is that the empirical dispute over the likelihood of significant human benefits emerging from various lines of research, which makes utilitarian justifications of experimentation so complex, will reappear here. Having admitted that some research is justified, animal rights advocates would doubtless continue to disagree with researchers over which research this is. Nevertheless, the foregoing discussion illustrates how the implications of a true animal rights view can converge with those of researchers' animal welfare philosophy. Even someone who attributes moral rights in the philosophical sense to animals, and whose ethical theory thus differs dramatically from most animal researchers', could think that some medical research is justified. This warrants stressing, because researchers commonly say things like, "According to animal rightists, a rat is a pig is a dog is a boy," and, "Animal rightists want to do away with all uses of animals, including life-saving medical research." However, no fair reading of either Singer or Regan would yield the conclusion that they believe that a rat's or a pig's life is equal to a normal human's. And, consequently, it is possible for someone thinking with Singer's or Regan's principles to accept research that actually saves human lives.

It is possible, but Regan himself continues to oppose all animal research to benefit humans. His basis is not the worse-off principle, but that the principle applies, "special considerations apart." One of those considerations is that "risks are not morally transferable to those who do not voluntarily choose to take them," and this, he claims, blocks application of the worse-off principle to the case of medical experimentation (p. 377). For example, subjects used to screen a new vaccine run higher risks of contracting the disease when researchers intentionally expose them to it. Humans can voluntarily accept these risks, but animals cannot. Consequently, the only kind of research on "higher" animals (roughly, vertebrates) that Regan will accept is that which tests a potential cure for a currently incurable disease on animals that have already acquired the disease of their own accord.

However, most people believe that in at least some cases, we can justifiably transfer risks without first securing the agreement of those to whom the risks are transferred. For instance, modifying price supports can redistribute the financial risks involved in farming, and changing draft board policies in time of war can redistribute the risk of being killed in defense of one's country. Yet most people believe such transfers are justifiable even if involuntary. In these cases, however, the individuals among whom risks are redistributed are all members of a polis through which, arguably, they give implicit consent to the policies in question. Still, in some cases there cannot plausibly be said to be even implicit consent. When we go to war, for instance, we impose dramatic risks on thousands or even millions of people who have no political influence in our country. But if the war is justified, so too, presumably, are the involuntarily imposed risks.

The Prospects for Conversation

It has not been my purpose in this paper to decide which particular forms of experimentation are morally justifiable, so I will not further pursue a response to Regan's abolitionist argument. My goal has been to refocus the animal rights debate by emphasizing its philosophical complexity. The question is far more complicated than is suggested by simplistic portrayals by many researchers and in the popular media.

According to the common stereotype, an animal rights advocate wants to eliminate all animal research and is a vegetarian who even avoids wearing leather. But the first "serious attempt . . . to assess the accuracy of" this stereotype, a survey of about 600 animal activists attending the June 1990 "March for Animal Rights" in Washington, DC, found that: nearly half of all activists believe the animal rights movement should not focus on animal research as its top priority; over a third eat red meat, poultry, or seafood; and 40 percent wear leather.[7] I have often heard agriculturalists and scientists say that it is hypocritical for an animal rights advocate to eat any kind of meat, wear leather, or use medicines that have been developed using animal models. But it would only be hypocritical if there were a single, monolithic animal rights philosophy that unambiguously ruled them all out.

In this essay, I have stressed the philosophical diversity underlying the animal rights movement. The "animal rights philosophies" of which many researchers are so contemptuous run the philosophical gamut from a utilitarianism very similar to their own to a true animal rights view that is quite different from their own. On some of these views, certain kinds of animal agriculture are permissible, but even on a true animal rights view like Regan's, it is possible to endorse some uses of animals, including experimentation that is meaningfully tied to saving human lives.

Continuing to paint all advocates of animal rights as unreasoning, antiscience lunatics will not make that movement go away, any more than painting all scientists who use animal models as Nazis bent on torturing the innocent will make animal research go away. Animal protection movements have surfaced and then disappeared in the past, but today's animal rights movement is squarely grounded in two major traditions in moral philosophy and, amid the stable affluence of a modern, industrialized nation like the United States, cannot be expected to go away. By the same token, twentieth-century medical research has dramatically proven its capacity to save lives and to improve the quality of human life, and it cannot be expected to go away either. So the reality is going to involve some level of some uses of animals, including some kinds of medical research.

A more philosophical understanding of the animal welfare/animal rights distinction can help replace the current politics of confrontation with a genuine conversation. Researchers who understand the philosophical bases of the animal rights movement will recognize similarities with their own views and can rest assured that genuinely important research will not be opposed by most advocates of animal rights. In the last analysis, what animal rights views do is increase the burden of proof the defenders of research must meet, and this is as it should be. Too often, pain and suffering have been understood to be "necessary" whenever a desired benefit could not be achieved without them, without regard to how important the benefit in question was.[8]

When it comes to research on animals, "academic freedom" cannot mean freedom to pursue any line of research one pleases, even in the arena of medical research. In most areas of research, someone who spends her career doing trivial work wastes only the taxpayers' money. But a scientist who spends his career doing trivial experiments on animals can waste the lives of hundreds or even thousands of sentient creatures. There will be increasing public oversight of laboratory research on animals, because major traditions in Western ethical theory support at least basic moral consideration for all sentient creatures. Researchers who react by adopting a siege mentality, refusing to disclose information on research and refusing to talk to advocates of animal rights, only reinforce the impression that they have something to hide.

Endnotes

1. I owe this account of the consensus/convergence distinction to Bryan G. Norton, *Toward Unity among Environmentalists* (New York: Oxford University Press, 1991), pp. 237–243.
2. Peter Singer, *Animal Liberation,* 2nd ed. (New York: Avon Books, 1990), pp. x–xi.
3. Peter Singer, *Practical Ethics,* 2nd ed. (New York: Cambridge University Press, 1993).
4. In any case, as Raymond Frey has pointed out, it is not clear that having forward-looking desires is a necessary condition for being self-conscious. R. G. Frey, *Rights, Killing, and Suffering: Moral Vegetarianism and Applied Ethics* (Oxford: Basil Blackwell, 1983), p. 163.

5. Tom Regan, *The Case for Animal Rights* (Berkeley and Los Angeles: University of California Press, 1983).
6. This evidence is reviewed in my *In Nature's Interests? Interests, Animal Rights, and Environmental Ethics,* in manuscript.
7. S. Plous, "An Attitude Survey of Animal Rights Activists," *Psychological Science* 2 (May 1991): 194–196.
8. Susan Finsen, "On Moderation," in *Interpretation and Explanation in the Study of Animal Behavior,* ed. Marc Bekoff and Dale Jamieson, vol. 2 (Boulder, CO: Westview Press, 1990), pp. 394–419.

Journal/Discussion Questions

✍ *In your own life, do you find yourself looking for some middle ground between the animal rights position and those that Varner describes as "animal welfarists"? Discuss.*

1. Animal rights activists are sometimes portrayed as fanatics, yet Varner suggests that they are a much more diverse group than many outsiders recognize. What basis does he offer for this assertion? Do you think that animal rights activists are inconsistent if they are not strict vegetarians?
2. According to Varner, is there a morally relevant difference between experimentation on mammals versus experimentation on nonmammals? Where do Singer and Regan stand on this issue? In what ways do you agree/disagree with them? Discuss your reasons.
3. Explain the miniride and the worse-off principles. Under what circumstances is each applicable? How do these affect Regan's views on animal experimentation?

Concluding Discussion Questions

Where Do You Stand Now?

Instructions

You have already answered the following questions in your moral problems self-quiz at the beginning of this book. Now that you have studied the material in this section, take a moment to answer the same questions again.

	Strongly Agree	*Agree*	*Undecided*	*Disagree*	*Strongly Disagree*	*Chapter 10: Living Together with Animals*
46.	❑	❑	❑	❑	❑	There's nothing morally wrong with eating veal.
47.	❑	❑	❑	❑	❑	It's morally permissible to cause animals pain in order to do medical research that benefits human beings.
48.	❑	❑	❑	❑	❑	All animals have the same moral standing.
49.	❑	❑	❑	❑	❑	Zoos are a morally good thing.
50.	❑	❑	❑	❑	❑	There is nothing morally wrong with hunting.

Compare your answers to the present self-quiz with the answers to the initial self-quiz. How, if at all, have your answers changed? How have the *reasons* for your answers changed?

Journal/Discussion Questions

✍ *In light of the material in this chapter, how have your views changed on the ethical treatment of animals in regard to issues such as keeping pets, eating meat, wearing fur and animal products (such as leather shoes), using animals for testing shampoos, and using animals for medical research?*

1. In light of all the readings in this chapter, what changes (if any) do you think we should make in the ways in which animals are treated in our society? Why should people be motivated to make these changes if they involve some degree of sacrifice on their part?
2. If we grant animals rights, then we are accepting the general principle that nonhumans can have rights. One of the issues in the abortion debate has been the claim that the fetus is not (yet) a human being and thus does not have rights. If animals have rights, does this have moral implications for the rights of fetuses?

3. Drawing on the readings in this and the previous chapter, discuss the relationship between animals rights, vegetarianism, and world hunger. To what extent could problems of world hunger be solved by vegetarianism, an option that would at the same time reduce animal suffering? How would a utilitarian answer this question? How do you answer it?

FOR FURTHER READING

Web Resources

For extensive resources on ethical issues in our relationships with animals, see the animal rights page of *Ethics Updates* (http://ethics.acusd.edu).

Bibliographies

See Charles Magel, *A Bibliography of Animal Rights and Related Matters* (Washington, DC: University Press of America, 1981); and his *Keyguide to Information Sources on Animal Rights* (Jefferson, NC: McFarland, 1989).

Journals

In addition to the standard journals in ethics discussed in the bibliographical essay at the end of Chapter 1, there are two journals devoted solely to issues related to animals: *Ethics and Animals* and *Between the Species.*

Survey Articles

Tom Regan's "Treatment of Animals," in *Encyclopedia of Ethics,* edited by Lawrence Becker (New York: Garland, 1992), Vol. I, pp. 42–46 provides an excellent, short survey of the principal ethical issues surrounding the treatment of animals; it includes a bibliography. Lori Gruen's "Animals," in *A Companion to Ethics,* edited by Peter Singer (Oxford: Blackwell, 1991), pp. 343–353 also provides an excellent summary of these issues along with a bibliography. For a broader social history of the animal rights movement, see "Man's Mirror; History of Animal Rights," *The Economist,* Vol. 321, No. 7733 (November 16, 1991) p. 21 ff.

Anthologies

There are a number of excellent anthologies dealing with issues of the moral status of animals, including the issue entitled "In the Company of Animals," *Social Research,* 62, 1 (Fall 1995), with articles by Vikki Hearne, Stephen Jay Gould, Daniel Dennett, Cora Diamond, Colin McGinn, Wendy Doniger, and others. *Animal Rights: Opposing Viewpoints,* edited by Andrew Harnack (San Diego: Greenhaven Press, 1996) contains an excellent collection of short articles; it also includes a list of organizations involved in the animal rights issue and how to contact them. *Animal Rights and Welfare,* edited by Jeanne Williams (New York: H.W. Wilson Company, 1991), in the series The Reference Shelf, Vol. 63, No. 4., is a well-edited, short (168 pages) collection of short and often popular articles on the issues of animal rights, animals in research, and changes in the animal rights movement. *Ethics and Animals,* edited by Harlan B. Miller and William H. Williams (Clifton, NJ: Humana Press, 1983) is an excellent anthology of philosophical articles by well-known philosophers (including Tom Regan, Jan Narveson, Annette Baier, Bernard Rollin, Dale Jamieson, Lawrence Becker, James Rachels, R.G. Frey, and many others) and includes a very good bibliography. *On the Fifth Day: Animal Rights and Human Ethics,* edited by Richard Knowles Morrow and Michael W. Fox (Washington, DC: Acropolis Books, 1978) is a volume sponsored by the Humane Society of the United States and contains twelve essays on the moral status of animals and a statement of the Principles of the Humane Society. *The Animal Rights/Environmental Ethics Debate,* edited by Eugene C. Hargrove (Albany: State University of New York Press, 1992) contains eleven very good articles dealing specifically with the question of the relationship between animals rights issues and issues about environmental ethics. On the issue of animal experimentation, see F. Barbara Orlans, Tom L. Beauchamp, Rebecca Dresser, David B. Morton, and John P. Gluck, *The Human use of Animals* (New York: Oxford, 1997) and *Animal Experimentation: The Moral Issues,* edited by Robert M. Baird and Stuart E. Rosenbaum (Buffalo, NY: Prometheus Books, 1991) contains fifteen articles on animal rights and experimentation and a short bibliography. Also see R.G. Frey, *Rights, Killing, and Suffering: Moral Vegetarianism and Applied Ethics* (Oxford: Basil Blackwell, 1983); *Animal Sacrifices: Religious Perspectives on the Use of Animals in Science,* edited by Tom Regan (Philadelphia: Temple University Press, 1986); *In Defense of Animals,* edited by Peter Singer (New York: Blackwell, 1985); and *Animals' Rights: A Symposium,* edited by David Paterson and Richard Ryder (Fontwell, Sussex: Centaur, 1979). Tom Regan and Peter Singer co-edited *Animal Rights and Human Obligations* (Englewood Cliffs: Prentice-Hall, 1976). Peter Singer's *Ethics* (New York: Oxford, 1994) is not an anthology about animal rights, but rather a very interesting anthology about ethics from the standpoint of a strong advocate of animal rights.

Single-Author Works

Although there are certainly some early works that defended the rights of animals, such as Lewis Gompertz's *Moral Inquiries on the Situation of Man and of Brutes* (1824) and Henry S. Salt, *Animals' Rights* (1892), it was not until the past three decades that strong defenses of animal rights gained significant ground. Peter Singer's *Animal Liberation,* now in its second edition (New York: Avon Books, 1990), first appeared in 1976. Also see his *Practical Ethics,* 2nd ed. (New York: Cambridge University Press, 1993). Equally influential has been the work of Tom Regan, whose *The Case for Animal Rights* (Berkeley, CA: University of California Press, 1983) and *The Three Generation: Reflections on the Coming Revolution* (Philadelphia: Temple University Press, 1991), a collection of his recent essays, including "Christians Are What Christians Eat," have both had a wide impact. Mary Midgley, *Animals and Why They Matter* (Athens, GA: University of Georgia Press, 1983) is admirably argued, as is James Rachels, *Created from Animals: The Moral Implications of Darwinism* (Oxford: Oxford University Press, 1991). Bernard E. Rollin, *The Unheeded Cry: Animal Consciousness, Animal Pain, and Science,* with a Foreword by Jane Goodall (Oxford: Oxford University Press, 1989) surveys changing attitudes toward animal consciousness and deals specifically with the issue of how we can know and measure animal pain, and his *Animal Rights and Human Morality,* revised edition (Buffalo, NY: Prometheus Books, 1992): well-written, articulate defense of animal rights. In *The Animals Issue* (Cambridge: Cambridge University Press, 1992), Peter Carruthers, defends a contractualist account of ethics and argues that animals do not have direct moral significance. Michael P.T. Leahy's *Against Liberation: Putting Animals in Perspective* (London and New York: Routledge, 1991) offers a Wittgensteinian critique of contemporary defenses of animal rights. In *Interests and Rights: The Case Against Animals* (Oxford: Clarendon Press, 1980), R.G. Frey argues that animals are part of the moral community, but that their lives are not of equal value to adult human lives. For a nuanced discussion of these issues by a philosopher whose primary concern is with the concept of rights rather than animals, see Chapter 6 of A.I. Melden, *Rights in Moral Lives* (Berkeley: University of California Press, 1988). Also see Steven F. Sapontzis, *Morals, Reason, and Animals* (Philadelphia: Temple University Press, 1987); Richard Ryder, *Victims of Science* (London: David-Poynter, 1975); Marian Stamp Dawkins, *Animal Suffering: The Science of Animal Welfare* (London and New York: Chapman and Hall, 1980). In *The Case for Animal Experimentation* (Berkeley: University of California Press, 1986), Michael A. Fox argues that animals lack the critical self-awareness necessary for membership in the moral community; however, he renounced this view almost immediately after publication of the book. See Michael A. Fox, "Animal Experimentation: A Philosopher's Changing Views," *Between the Species,* Vol. 3 (1987), pp. 55–60. On the historical origins of the Western dabate, see Richard Sorabji, *Animal Minds and Human Morals* (Ithaca: Cornell, 1993).

Andrew Linzey, in *Animal Rights: A Christian Assessment* (London: SCM Press, 1976) and *Christianity and the Rights of Animals* (New York: Crossroad, 1988) develops a critique of Christianity's neglect of animals and offers a theological foundation for a more positive Christian attitude toward the rights of animals.

Articles

In addition to the articles contained in the anthologies mentioned above, see Peter Singer's "Ten Years of Animal Liberation," *New York Review of Books* 31 (1985), pp. 46–52; Dale Jamieson, "Utilitarianism and the Morality of Killing," *Philosophical Studies* Vol. 45, (1984), pp. 209–221; R.G. Frey, "Moral Standing, the Value of Lives, and Speciesism," *Between the Species,* Vol. 4, No. 3 (Summer 1988), pp. 191–201; and M. Kheel, "The Liberation of Nature: A Circular Affair," *Environmental Ethics,* Vol. 7, No. 2 (Summer 1985), 135–149.

CHAPTER 11

Environmental Ethics

NARRATIVE ACCOUNT

N. Scott Momaday
"Native American Attitudes toward the Environment"

N. Scott Momaday is the author of numerous works, including House Made of Dawn *and* The Way to Rainy Mountain.

In an informal context, Mr. Momaday discusses the ways in which Native Americans understand their relationship to the natural environment. He focuses on several key ideas: the ways in which the relationship between human beings and the environment is one of mutual appropriation, the ways in which Native Americans understand what an "appropriate" relationship is between a person and the environment, and the important role played by imagination in understanding these issues.

As You Read, Consider This:

1. How does Mr. Momaday use stories to develop his ideas? Would you draw the same conclusions from his stories that Mr. Momaday does?
2. What does Mr. Momaday mean by "appropriateness"?

The first thing to say about the Native American perspective on environmental ethics is that there is a great deal to be said. I don't think that anyone has clearly understood yet how the Indian conceives of himself in relation to the landscape. We have formulated certain generalities about that relationship, and the generalities have served a purpose, but they have been rather too general. For example, take the idea that the Indian reveres the earth, thinks of it as the place of his origin and thinks of the sky also in a personal way. These statements are true. But they can also be misleading because they don't indicate anything about the nature of the relationship which is, I think, an intricate thing in itself.

I have done much thinking about the "Indian worldview," as it is sometimes called. And I have had some personal experience of Indian religion and Indian societies within the framework of a worldview. Sometime ago I wrote an essay entitled "An American Land Ethic" in which I tried to talk in certain ways about this idea of a Native American attitude toward the landscape. And in that essay I made certain observations. I tried to express the notion first that the Native American ethic with respect to the physical world is a matter of reciprocal appropriation: appropriations in which man invests himself in the landscape, and at the same time incorporates the landscape into his own most fundamental experience. That suggests a dichotomy, or a paradox, and I think it is a paradox. It is difficult to understand a relationship which is defined in these terms, and yet I don't know how better to define it.

Secondly, this appropriation is primarily a matter of the imagination. The appropriation is realized through an act of the imagination which is moral and kind. I mean to say that we are all, I suppose, at the most fundamental level what we imagine ourselves to be. And this is certainly true of the American Indian. If you want a definition, you would not go, I hope, to the stereotype which has burdened the American Indian for many years. He is not that befeathered spectacle who is always chasing John Wayne across the silver screen. Rather, he is someone who thinks of himself in a particular way and his idea comprehends his relationship to the physical world, among other things. He imagines himself in terms of that relationship and others. And it is that act of the imagination, that moral act of the imagination, which I think constitutes his understanding of the physical world.

Thirdly, this imagining, this understanding of the relationship between man and the landscape, or man and the physical world, man and nature, proceeds from a racial or cultural experience. I think his attitude toward the landscape has been formulated over a long period of time, and the length of time itself suggests an evolutionary process perhaps instead of a purely rational and decisive experience. Now I am not sure that you can understand me on this point; perhaps I should elaborate. I mean that the Indian has determined himself in his imagination over a period of untold generations. His racial memory is an essential part of his understanding. He understands himself more clearly than perhaps other people, given his situation in time and space. His heritage has always been rather closely focused, centered upon the landscape as a particular reality. Beyond this, the Native American has a particular investment in vision and in the idea of vision. You are familiar with the term "vision quest" for example. This is another essential idea to the Indian worldview, particularly that view as it is expressed among the cultures of the Plains Indians. This is significant. I think we should not lose the force of the idea of seeing something or envisioning something in a particular way. I happen to think that there are two visions in particular with reference to man and his relationship to the natural world. One is physical and the other is imaginative. And we all deal in one way or another with these visions simultaneously. If I can try to find an analogy, it's rather like looking through the viewfinder of a camera, the viewfinder which is based upon the principle of the split image. And it is a matter of trying to align the two planes of that particular view. This can be used as an example of how we look at the world around us. We see it with the physical eye. We see it as it appears to us, in one dimension of reality. But we also see it with the eye of the mind. It seems to me that the Indian has achieved a particularly effective alignment of those two planes of vision. He perceives the landscape in both ways. He realizes a whole image from the possibilities within his reach. The moral implications of this are very far-reaching. Here is where we get into the consideration of religion and religious ideas and ideals.

There is another way in which I think one can very profitably and accurately think of the Indian in relation to the landscape and in terms of his idea of that relationship. This is to center on such a word as *appropriate*. The idea of "appropriateness" is central to the Indian experience of the natural world. It is a fundamental idea within his philosophy. I recall the story told to me some years ago by a friend, who is not himself a Navajo, but was married for a time to a Navajo girl and lived with her family in Southern Utah. And he said that he had been told this story and was passing it on to me. There was a man living in a remote place on the Navajo reservation who had lost his job and was having a difficult time making ends meet. He had a wife and several children. As a matter of fact, his wife was expecting another child. One day a friend came to visit him and perceived that his situation was bad. The friend said to him "Look, I see that you're in tight straits, I see you have many mouths to feed, that you have no wood and that there is very little food in your larder. But one thing puzzles me. I know you're a hunter, and I know, too, there are deer in the mountains very close at hand. Tell me, why don't you kill a deer so that you and your family might have fresh meat to eat?" And after a time the man replied, "No, it is inappropriate that I should take life just now when I am expecting the gift of life."

The implications of that idea, and the way in which the concept of appropriateness lies at the center of that little parable is a central consideration within the Indian world. You cannot understand how the Indian thinks of himself in relation to the world around him unless you understand his conception of what is appropriate; particularly what is morally appropriate within the context of that relationship.

QUESTION: Could you probe a little deeper into what lies behind the idea of appropriate or inappropriate behavior regarding the natural world. Is it a religious element? Is it biological or a matter of survival? How would you characterize what makes an action appropriate or inappropriate?

MOMADAY: It is certainly a fair question but I'm not sure that I have the answer to it. I suspect that whatever it is that makes for the idea of appropriateness is a very complex thing in itself. Many things constitute the idea of appropriateness. Basically, I think it is a moral idea as opposed to a religious one. It is a basic understanding of right within the framework of relationships, and, within the framework of that relationship I was talking about a moment ago, between man and the physical world. That which is appropriate within this context is that which is *natural.* This is another key word. My father used to tell me of an old man who has lived a whole life. I have often thought of this image. The old man used to come to my grandfather's house periodically to pay visits, and my father has very vivid recollections of this man whom I never knew. But his name was Chaney. Father says that Chaney would come to the house and he would make himself perfectly at home. He would be passing by going from one place to another, exercising his ethnic prerogative for nomadism. But he would make my grandfather's house a kind of resting place. He stayed there on many occasions. My father says that every morning when Chaney was there as a guest he would get up in the first light, paint his face, go outside, face the east, and bring the sun out of the horizon. Then he would pray. He would pray aloud to the rising sun. He did that because it was appropriate that he should do that. He understood. Or perhaps I should say that in terms of his own understanding, the sun was the origin of his strength. He understood the sun, within a more formal religious context, similar to the way someone else understands the presence of a deity. And in the face of that recognition, he acted naturally or appropriately. Through the medium of prayer, he returned some of his strength to the sun. He did this everyday. It was a part of his daily life. It was as natural and appropriate to him as anything could be. There is in the Indian worldview this kind of understanding of what is and what is not appropriate. It isn't a matter of intellection. It is respect for the understanding of one's heritage. It is a kind of racial memory and it has its origin beyond any sort of historical experience. It reaches back to the dawn of time.

QUESTION: When talking about vision, you said that the Indians saw things physically and also with the eye of the mind, I think this is the way you put it. You also said that this was a whole image, and that it had certain moral implications. Would you elaborate further?

MOMADAY: I think there are different ways of seeing things. I myself am particularly interested in literature, and in the traditions of various peoples, the Indians in particular. I understand something of how this works within the context of literature. For example, in the nineteenth century in America, there were poets who were trying very hard to see nature and to write about it. This is one kind of vision. They succeeded in different ways, some succeeding more than others. They succeeded in seeing what was really there on the vision plain of the natural world and they translated that vision, or that perception of the natural world, into poetry. Many of them had a kind of scientific training. Their observations were trained through the study of botany, astronomy, or zoology, etc. This refers, of course, to one kind of vision.

But, obviously, this is not the sort of view of the landscape which characterizes the Indian world. His view rather is of a different and more imaginative kind. It is a more comprehensive view. When the Native American looks at nature, it isn't with the idea of training a glass upon it, or pushing it away so that he can focus upon it from a distance. In his mind, nature is not something apart from him. He conceives of it, rather, as an element in which he exists. He has existence within that element, much in the same way we think of having existence within the element of air. It would be unimaginable for him to think of it in the way the nineteenth century "nature poets" thought of looking at nature and writing about it. They employed a kind of "esthetic distance," as it is sometimes called. This idea would be alien to the Indian. This is what I meant by trying to make the distinction between two sides of a split image.

QUESTION: So then, presumably in moral terms, the Indian would say that a person should not harm nature because it's something in which one participates oneself.

MOMADAY: This is one aspect of it. There is this moral aspect, and it refers to perfect alignment. The appropriation of both images into the one reality is what the Indian is concerned to do: to see what is really there, but also to see what is *really* there. This reminds me of another story. It is very brief. It was told to me by the same fellow who told me about the man who did not kill the deer. (To take a certain liberty with the title of a novel that I know well.) He told me that while he himself was living in southern Utah with his wife's family, he became very ill. He contracted pneumonia. There was no doctor, no physician nearby. But there was a medicine man close at hand. The family called in a diagnostician (the traditional thing to do), who came and said that my friend was suffering from a particular malady whose cure would be the red-ant ceremony. So a man who is very well versed in that ceremony, a seer, a kind of specialist in the red-ant ceremony, came in and administered it to my friend. Soon after that my friend recovered completely. Not long after this he was talking to his father-in-law, and he was very curious about what had taken place. He said, "I wonder about the red-ant ceremony. Why is it that the diagnostician prescribed that particular ceremony for me?" His father-in-law looked at him and said, "Well, it was obvious to him that there were red ants in your system, and so we had to call in a seer to take the red ants out of your system." At this point, my friend became very incredulous, and said, "Yes, but surely you don't mean that there were red ants inside of me." His father-in-law looked at him for a moment, then said, "Not ants, but ants." Unless you understand this distinction, you might have difficulty understanding something about the Indian view of the natural world.

Endnote

This paper was adapted from transcriptions of oral remarks Professor Momaday made on this subject, informally, during a discussion with faculty and students.

Journal/Discussion Questions

✍ *Mr. Momaday suggests that "appropriateness" is a central concept in terms of which Native Americans understand their relationship to the natural world. In your own life, what role—if any—does this notion play in your understanding of your own relationship to the natural world. Does this concept shed light on any parts of your experience that you hadn't reflected on before?*

1. Explain what Mr. Momaday means by appropriateness. How could this idea be used to develop environmental policies?
2. Think about the way in which Mr. Momaday responds to questions. He usually tells a story. What does this suggest about the way in which Native Americans maintain and transmit moral wisdom? How does this relate to the role of imagination?

AN INTRODUCTION TO THE ETHICAL ISSUES IN OUR RELATIONSHIPS WITH THE ENVIRONMENT

Should we view the world in scientific or natural terms?

Perhaps more than any of the other issues that we have considered in this book, questions about our relationships with animals and the environment take us to the heart of a fundamental clash of worldviews. It is, moreover, not like the familiar clashes between liberal and conservative, theist and atheist, or the like; it is, rather, a clash between a *scientific* and *technological worldview*—which encompasses liberal and conservative, theist and atheist, and other divisions familiar to us—and a diverse set of *natural worldviews*—many of them echoing the cultures of indigenous peoples—which emphasize the continuity and interdependence of human beings and the natural world.

One of the by-products of this clash of worldviews is that much of environmental ethics calls into question the foundations of traditional (i.e., Western European) ethics. This has been both an asset and a liability for the development of environmental ethics. On the plus side, it has resulted in a number of interesting discussions that illuminate aspects of the foundations of Western ethics that might not otherwise be brought as sharply into focus. In particular, it has called attention to the ways in which Western ethics conceptualizes the natural world and understands the place of human beings in it. On the negative side, however, the concern with such foundational questions has detracted, at least in the eyes of some, from environmental ethic's principal task as *applied* ethics. Rather than concentrating on specific moral issues facing those concerned with the environment (as well as those who are not concerned with it!), environmental ethics has concentrated on issues that exist on such a high level of abstraction that they are not immediately fruitful for making decisions about the specific environmental issues.

The Central Questions

As we turn toward a consideration of environmental ethics, three questions present themselves:

1. *Who,* or what, *has moral weight* (i.e., is deserving of direct moral consideration)?
2. *How much* moral weight does each (type of) entity have?
3. How do we make *decisions* when there are *conflicts* among different types of beings, each of which have moral weight?

An adequate environmental ethic must eventually provide answers to all three of these questions. In recent work by environmentalists, considerable attention has been paid to the first of these questions. Here the debate has centered around the question of whether individual animals, species, plants, rivers, etc. have moral weight (i.e., whether we should give moral consideration to the question of their well-being or continued flourishing). Sometimes this question is posed in relation to individuals (e.g., this specific plant) and sometimes it is posed in relation to species (e.g., the spotted owl). In the next section of this introduction, we shall examine a number of specific answers to these questions.

The second question—how much moral standing something has—is both crucial and usually neglected. It is crucial because ethics must eventually provide guidance for our actions, and if we have no way of ranking how much moral consideration a given entity merits, we are left without assistance in resolving conflicts among morally considerable beings. The answer to the third question obviously presupposes an answer to the first two questions. We shall consider each of these three questions here, but first sketch out an overview of the main schools of thought in environmental ethics.

An Overview

Since this is relatively uncharted territory for many of us, it may be helpful to see an overview of the conceptual terrain and the various positions that have been marked out on it by the current participants in the discussion of environmental ethics. We may initially divide these approaches into two categories. *Human-centered approaches* to the environment take human beings as their moral point of reference and consider questions of the environment solely from that perspective. They ask, in other words, environmental questions from the standpoint of the effects of the answers to such questions on human beings in one way or another. In contrast to these approaches, we find in recent years that a number of *expanded-circle approaches* (to borrow a term from the title of Peter Singer's *The Expanding Circle*) that draw the circle of morally considerable beings—that is, entities deserving of moral respect in some way—with an increasingly wide radius. Let's examine each of these in somewhat more detail.[1]

Human-Centered Approaches

Human-centered approaches to the environment do not necessarily neglect the environment, but typically they recognize as valid moral reasons only those reasons acceptable to traditional moral theories. These theories are of the various types we discussed in the Introduction to this book.

Ethical egoists recognize only reasons of self-interest as an adequate moral justification for treating the environment in a particular way. For example, ethical egoists could well imagine people wanting a particular landscape preserved because it provided them personally with an aesthetically pleasing view, but it would also see those who wanted to strip mine that particular landscape as morally justified if it maximized their own self-interest.

Group egoists are also concerned with self-interest, but the net of self-interest is more broadly cast to include not only one's personal interests, but the interests of the group with which one most strongly affiliates. The boundaries of the group may be comparatively narrow (one's family), intermediate (one's neighborhood, one's corporation, one's church group), or quite broad (one's nation, all those who share one's religious beliefs). What is characteristic of these approaches is that only the interests of one's group are to be given moral weight in making decisions. Similarly, there are approaches in *virtue ethics* which concentrate on developing those character traits that contribute to the welfare of the group: loyalty, a spirit of self-sacrifice, obedience to authority, and so on. Aristotle, for example, sought to determine those character traits that would make a person a good member of the *polis,* the Greek city-state. Much more recently, William Bennett and others have sought to determine the virtues we should foster in order to have a better civic and communal life in the United States. One of the principal differences between group egoist and virtue ethics is that egoism focuses on the question of what actions we should perform, while virtue ethics looks at the kind of person we should be.

Utilitarians, like egoists, are consequentialists, that is, they determine whether particular actions are right or wrong by looking at their consequences. However, whereas the ethical egoist looks at consequences only insofar as they affect the egoist personally, the utilitarian looks at consequences insofar as they affect all human beings. Often courses of action that would be justified from the standpoint of ethical egoism are not morally justified from a utilitarian standpoint, since they may benefit the egoist but not provide sufficient benefit to humanity as a whole (when judged in relation to competing courses of action).

Preserving the natural environment may be an important value to utilitarians if doing so provides the maximal benefit to humanity. There are a variety of ways in which this could be so. For example, preservation—or at least careful management—of the natural environment may provide long-term resources for all of humanity. Thus, we may want to preserve the rain forests because, even though destroying them might bring short-term profit to a small group of people, preserving them provides irreplaceable benefits to humanity in terms of air quality, natural resources, etc. Notice that there is no claim here that the rain forest is valuable in itself; its value derives from the ways in which it contributes to human well-being. If in the long-run human well-being would best be served by destroying the rain forests, then utilitarianism would not only permit this, it would require it.

Expanded-Circle Approaches

Expanded utilitarianism. Traditionally, utilitarianism has been concerned with the effects of various actions on the well-being of human beings. The underlying rationale has been that the whole point of ethics is to increase pleasure or happiness and to decrease pain, suffering or unhappiness. As we saw in the previous chapter, a number of philosophers, most notably Peter Singer, have taken the next step and asked why only *human* suffering counts in the utilitarian calculus. If we are concerned with reducing suffering, should we be concerned with reducing the suffering of *all* sentient beings. Thus this version of utilitarianism has expanded the circle of morally considerable beings to include nonhuman animals. Although this is far from a full-fledged environmental ethic, it is an important step beyond a purely anthropocentric ethic.

Biocentrism represents the first step toward a genuinely environmental ethic, for it maintains that all living beings—this includes plants, fauna, and so on as well as human and nonhuman animals—are deserving of moral consideration in their own right. Biocentric approaches focus on individual entities, and the premise here seems to be primarily a teleological one. All living beings have some *telos* or final goal, and this is usually understood in terms of flourishing or growing in some sense. They are thus entitled to moral consideration from us—that is, we should not act in ways which thwart their movement toward their natural goal.

Ecocentrism, which is often called deep ecology by its supporters, expands the circle to its maximal terrestrial limits by taking the entirety of what exists on the earth as morally considerable, inanimate as well as animate. It comes in two versions, the latter of which is much more plausible than the former. *Individualistic ecocentrism* gives moral weight to each and every entity within the ecosystem. The difficulty with this approach flows from the fact that individualistic ecocentrism has been unable to provide a criterion for assigning different weights to different individuals—and if everything has an equal moral weight, then it is virtually impossible to arrive at a decision procedure in particular cases in which precedence must be given to one individual over another.

The more plausible variant of ecocentrism is to be found in *holistic ecocentrism,* which gives moral weight to each species, type, etc. in the ecosystem. Thus holistic ecocentrism is concerned with the preservation of species, and concern about individuals is only a means to the end of species-preservation. Similarly, ecocentric environmentalists may be concerned about the preservation of particular types of environments—wetlands, sand dunes, rain forest—both in their own right and insofar as they are parts of larger ecosystems. The ultimate ecosystem is the earth as a whole.

As we have already seen in Chapter 9, many philosophers argued that the moral circle ought to be expanded to include nonhuman animals. As we shall see in this chapter, some philosophers want to expand this circle even further to include all of the natural environment.

Criteria of Moral Considerability

Clearly, those who want to "expand the circle" are claiming that entities which previously had not been recognized as having moral weight should now be given moral consideration. On what basis should they be accorded this moral respect? In nonanthropocentric approaches, it must be on the basis of some property that they possess, rather than on the basis of their impact on human beings. In the previous chapter, we examined several proposed criteria for expanding the circle of moral considerability to include nonhuman animals, but most of those criteria were limited to the world of humans and animals. When the circle is extended even further, criteria such as the ability to use language or manipulate tools are of little help. Several proposal have been advanced for criteria of moral considerability which extend the moral domain beyond humans and animals.

Intrinsic Value

To say that something has intrinsic value is to say that it can't be used merely as a means. Most people admit that human beings have intrinsic value (i.e., that we can't morally use people merely as a means to our own ends). On the other hand, we would all agree that something like a hammer has no intrinsic value—we can use it for whatever purposes we want, whether to pound nails or as a doorstop, without worrying about being disrespectful to the hammer. Indeed, we can even destroy it without feeling like we are violating the hammer in some morally significant way. It has no intrinsic value, and thus in itself merits no moral respect.

Yet what quality or characteristic accords intrinsic value to human beings and not to hammers—and what other types of beings share this characteristic? Claims about intrinsic value turn out to be mere resting places along the path of a longer argument, for advocates of intrinsic value must then specify the characteristics that form the basis of intrinsic value. Some philosophers, like Immanuel Kant, have maintained that *rationality* is the foundation of intrinsic value; thus any being possessing rationality would merit moral respect. More recently, Kenneth Goodpaster and others have argued that being alive should be our criterion of moral considerability and that all *living* beings have intrinsic value.[2] At least one philosopher has maintained that the only nonarbitrary criterion of moral considerability and intrinsic value is *"being in existence."*[3] On this view, everything that exists would have intrinsic value.

It is clear that the appeal to intrinsic value in itself sheds little light on the issue of moral considerability, since such an appeal must quickly be filled in with a specification of the basis for attributing intrinsic value—and at this point we are back to the broader issue of criteria of moral considerability. However, this discussion indirectly illuminates an interesting and sometimes neglected background issue. In modern industrialized countries like the United States, the assumption is often that things have *only* instrumental value unless there is evidence to the contrary. This is in sharp contrast to other cultures that make the opposite assumption: they assume that everything is deserving of respect, and that we ought not to use things as mere means unless there is a good justification for doing so. The burden of proof is then on the other side.

Teleology

A second way of approaching this problem has been to argue that, at least in the living world, there is a natural teleology: plants move toward flowering, animals toward reproduction, and so on. Certainly this is true, and one simply has to walk through a lush forest to understand what natural flourishing is like. Similarly, one only has to walk through a forest that has been clear-cut to understand what devastation induced by human beings is like. So there is something intuitively plausible about appeals to teleology.

Yet the teleological argument does not take us far enough, or at least does not yield the conclusions that some environmentalists would like to see. First, we get different and conflicting views of flourishing, depending on whether we consider the flourishing of the individual, the species, or the ecosystem. What promotes the flourishing of one might not promote the flourishing of the others. The flourishing of individual animals often depends on killing other animals. The flourishing of a species may well depend on preventing overpopulation of the species, and that may in turn depend on the early deaths of a certain percentage of the species. Similarly, the flourishing of the ecosystem may depend on diminishing or destroying certain species. Flourishing in an ecosystem is a complex phenomenon, and it includes things such as animals killing one another and forest fires and floods and droughts.

Second, the flourishing of one individual or species is often bought at the price of the flourishing of another. Yet environmentalists often seem to advocate some form of noninterference with the environment, which seems at odds with the way in which species often seem to conflict with, and prey upon, one another. Teleology doesn't seem to provide much support for an ethic of noninterference with the environment.

Third, how do we think about the natural teleology of human beings? It seems reasonable to maintain that human beings need many things to flourish that may be harmful to the environment. Again, it would seem that teleology might well justify much that many environmentalists oppose.

Aesthetic Value

Certainly one of the most powerful motivating forces in the work of many environmentalists has been their appreciation of the beauty of nature. If you have experienced the beauty of nature, then you understand how compelling this motivation can be. If you have not experienced it, it is unlikely that any description will convince you of the power of the experience.

To what extent should we respect nature because of its beauty?

Yet there are difficulties associated with allowing the moral weight of nature to depend on its aesthetic value. We have already alluded to one of those difficulties in the previous paragraph: beauty, while not perhaps solely in the eye of the beholder, is not universally and objectively accessible. The Florida everglades are a good example—beautiful to some, a bug-infested swamp to others. Moreover, even if there were relatively widespread agreement about beauty, is *all* of nature beautiful? It seems improbable that some of it wouldn't be ugly—and if so, does it deserve less moral consideration than the beautiful parts? Finally, even granting the beauty of the natural world, are we willing to commit ourselves to a principle that aesthetic value outweighs other types of value? It seems unlikely that we would be willing to do so outside of environmental ethics, so allowing the moral value of nature to rest on its aesthetic value seems to be a risky proposition.

Sacredness

Religious traditions have played a major role in shaping people's attitudes toward the environment, although we often find within a single religious tradition different and at times conflicting ways of understanding and appreciating the environment. Consider the Christian, the Native American, and the Taoist traditions.

The Christian traditions: Dominion and stewardship. Throughout its history, there have been two distinct traditions in Christianity about the relationship between human beings and the environment. The dominant tradition has been one of *dominion,* and its origins are found in the first chapter of Genesis, where human beings are given control over the world to use it to their own ends. The other tradition, perhaps never dominant but often more powerful than it has been in the twentieth century, is one of *stewardship,* in which human beings are seen as being charged by God with the task of preserving the natural environment. Environmentalists typically criticize the former tradition in Christianity, while they tend—if they acknowledge its existence—to laud the latter.

Native American traditions: Reciprocity and respect. Although there is a considerable degree of diversity within Native American religious traditions, in general Native American traditions emphasize the sacredness of nature—the natural world is much more imbued with spirits than it is for, say, the traditional Christian—and the ways in which it therefore merits respect. However, in contrast to many contemporary environmentalists who espouse noninterference by humans in the natural world, Native Americans see the relationship between human beings and the natural world as one of reciprocal interaction. Hunting, for example, is an important activity in many Native American traditions; although unnecessary killing of animals is prohibited, hunting in order to meet one's own basic needs (and the needs of one's family) is not only permitted, but on occasion even celebrated. Interestingly, killing an animal is not seen as necessarily incompatible with respecting it.

Future Generations, Predictibility, and the Environment

Concern for the environment is all the more complex because often the principal issue is not the immediate effects of one particular action, but rather the long-range effects of a policy carried out for decades, perhaps even centuries. Two aspects of this issue are especially troublesome: the moral status of future generations, and the limits of our predictive powers.

Future Generations: Their Rights, Our Responsibilities

Part of this complexity centers around the issue of future generations. Often we are concerned, not just about the short-term effects on the environment at present, but even more about the long-term effects of policies on the environment and the impact of the resulting changes on the lives of our descendants. Nuclear waste, for example, might be a significant problem now, but it could well be a mammoth, unmanageable problem in another century if present trends continue.

What do we owe future generations in terms of the environment we leave them?

A number of philosophical perplexities surround the issue of future generations. Perhaps the most pressing of these concerns the issue of the kind of rights that future generations can have. Since future generations do not exist yet (by definition), then how is it possible for non-existent beings to have rights? Indeed, if we pursue certain environmentally destructive courses of action, they may well never exist. In what sense, if any, can counter-factual individuals—persons who would have existed if we had acted differently—exert a moral claim on us? This is slippery conceptual terrain, and it is not clear that we can traverse it without stumbling.

The more promising way of dealing with this issue is to leave aside the issue of the rights of future generations and concentrate on the maxims that guide our own situation. Some moral guideline—for example, that we should leave the earth in no worse a condition than we received it—might provide a basis for considering the interests of future generations. Or we might make metaphorical use of the concept of parenthood as a foundation for our concern for the well-being of future generations. We are all children of parents; some of us may also be (or become) parents ourselves; all of us can pass on parental concern, whether biologically grounded or not, by acting in ways which promote the welfare of future generations. These lines of argumentation seem more plausible than a concern with the narrowly defined issue of the rights of future generations.

Predictability

To what extent can we predict the long-term environmental consequences of our actions?

The other way in which this whole issue is complex centers around the issue of predictability. As we deal with increasingly complex systems, it becomes more and more difficult to know reliably in advance precisely what will occur. Our predictions are often accompanied by a restriction: "all other things being equal." Yet in complex systems, other things are rarely if ever equal.

In recent years, an entire branch of mathematics—called "chaos theory"—has been devoted solely to this issue. Chaos theory grew in part out of the difficulties in forecasting the weather, and chaos theorists now maintain that it is impossible *in principle,* not just in practice, to predict the weather with absolute accuracy, even with an infinite number of weather sensors covering the entire globe. Infinitesimal variations—a butterfly fluttering its wings in South America—produce unanticipated results—a thunderstorm in New York two months later.

Coupled with this is the fact that we cannot easily foretell what additional developments, particularly technological ones, will have an impact on our predictions. A century ago, for example, dire predictions warned that New York City would eventually be overcome by horse manure, given the steadily increasing amount of horse traffic on the city streets. The advent of the automobile eliminated this problem while substituting other types of problems in its place. So, too, we are unsure of the ways in which future inventions may reshape our environmental problems.

What are we to conclude from this? Clearly, we cannot simply give up on prediction. In fact, our predictions are often accurate. However, we must be especially aware of our own fallibility, our own ability to make mistakes, as we make predictions on a global scale about long-term future events and trends. However, such an awareness should not be seen as a justification of complacency based in a feeling of futility about prediction.

Endnotes

1. This typology draws on several sources, most notably Carolyn Merchant's "Environmental Ethics and Political Conflict," and J. Baird Callicott's "Environmental Ethics," *Encyclopedia of Ethics,* edited by Lawrence and Charlotte Becker (New York: Garland, 1992), Vol. I, pp. 311–315.
2. Kenneth E. Goodpaster, "On Being Morally Considerable," *Journal of Philosophy,* LXXV, 6 (June 1978), 308–324.
3. W. Murray Hunt, "Are Mere Things Morally Considerable?" *Environmental Ethics,* 2 (Spring 1980), 59–65.

THE ARGUMENTS

Robert Elliott
"Environmental Ethics"

Robert Elliot is senior lecturer in the Department of Philosophy at the University of New England, Armidale, New South Wales. He is published widely in environmental ethics, including Environmental Ethics *and* Faking Nature: The Ethics of Environmental Restoration.

In this article, Elliott provides us with an overview of major options in environmental ethics. He looks at individualistic approaches that are human-centered, animal-centered, life-centered, and holistic. He then turns to a consideration of the justification of environmental ethics and what deserves moral consideration.

As You Read, Consider This:

1. What are the factors that move us from a human-centered ethic to an animal-centered ethic? From an animal-centered ethic to a life-centered ethic?
2. On what basis are we justified in attributing intrinsic value to something?

What Is an Environmental Ethic?

Kakadu National Park in Australia's Northern Territory, contains rugged woodlands, swamps and waterways supporting a rich variety of life; it contains species found nowhere else, including some, such as the Hooded Parrot and the Pig-nosed Turtle, which are endangered. Kakadu affords aesthetic enjoyment and recreational and research opportunities. Many think it is a place of immense beauty and ecological significance. It is of spiritual significance to the Jawoyn aboriginals. Kakadu is also rich in gold, platinum, palladium and uranium, which some think should be mined. If this happens then, environmentalists claim, aesthetic, recreational and research opportunities will be reduced, the beauty of Kakadu will be lessened, species will disappear, ecological richness will decrease, the naturalness of the place will be compromised and the spiritual values of the Jawoyn discounted. Mining already goes on in the Kakadu area and there is pressure to allow more. Should more mining be allowed? Should any mining at all be allowed? How exactly might we reach answers to these ethical questions?

Empirical or factual evidence certainly plays a role. For example, opponents of mining claim that it is likely to pollute rivers, poison wildlife, endanger species and disrupt ecosystems. This opposition to mining relies on empirical claims; that is, claims about what does and will in fact happen. Many supporters dispute these empirical claims and there are some who think that even if the claims are true it is better to go ahead with mining. Settling the facts does not ensure that the issue is settled. Arguments about such facts only have a point, only make sense, against a certain kind of background, and differences in this background give rise to different assessments of what should be done. What constitutes this background are such things as desires, preferences, aims, goals and principles, including moral principles. An environmentalist might want to know whether mining is a threat to wildlife because he or she desires that wildlife be protected or, more seriously, because he or she thinks it is morally wrong to cause the death of wildlife. The evaluative background need not include moral principles; some people might be amoral. However, many people do want their own actions and the actions of others, including corporations and governments, to conform to moral principles. For such people the resolution of the Kakadu controversy requires an appeal to principles which offer moral guidance in our treatment of wild nature and which enable us to answer questions like: would it matter if our actions caused a species to become extinct? Would it matter if our actions caused the death of individual animals? Would it matter if we caused widespread erosion in Kakadu? Would it matter if we turned the South Alligator River into a watercourse devoid of life? Is it better to protect Kakadu or to generate increased material wealth which might improve the lives of a number of people? Is the extinction of a species an acceptable price to pay for increased employment opportunities? Such sets of principles, which would guide our treatment of wild nature, constitute an environmental ethic in the most general sense. There is a variety of competing, including partly overlapping, environmental ethics.

People who have views of a moral kind about environmental issues are committed to an environmental ethic consisting of at least one, but usually a number of principles. Consider environmentalists who say that the extinction of species as a result of human actions is a bad thing, maybe even a bad thing no matter what the cause. This might be a basic principle in an environmental ethic. Without having explicitly represented it as such, an environmentalist might nevertheless be committed to the view that the extinction of species etc. is bad considered in itself, quite apart from any consequences it might have. Another possibility is that the principle is not itself basic but rests on a principle enjoining concern for human welfare, combined with the belief that humans are harmed by the extinction of species. Making the ethical commitment explicit is a first step in subjecting it to critical appraisal or justification. Justification is necessary if we are to adjudicate between the various competing environmental ethics we encounter. It is not enough that an environmental policy conform to the principles of some or other environmental ethic, it should conform to the correct, or best justified, one. We have two questions: how might an environmental ethic be fleshed out? How might putative environmental ethics be justified?

1. Human-Centered Ethics

Some think that environmental policies should be evaluated solely on the basis of how they affect humans (see Baxter, 1974, and Norton, 1988). This entails a human-centered environmental ethic. Although the classical utilitarians include animal suffering in their ethical calculation, a variant of utilitarianism, which enjoins us to maximize the surplus of human happiness over human unhappiness, is one example of a human-centered ethic. Taking this ethic seriously obliges us to calculate the varying effects of the Kakadu options on human happiness and unhappiness. We might discover that mining would reduce the ecological richness of the wetlands and that if this happened then some people would be made unhappy; for instance, some might be moved by the plight of individual animals, some might be saddened by the loss of species, some, including members of future generations, might miss out on the chance of particular recreational or aesthetic enjoyments, some might be adversely affected by resultant climatic changes, changes in flood patterns and so on, some might be psychologically harmed by the despoliation of areas to which they have a spiritual attachment. These negative effects would have to be subtracted from any increases in happiness which resulted from mining in Kakadu. A human-centered ethic could lead to substantial agreement with environmentalists about policy. This would depend on the facts about the effects on humans of changes to the natural environment. However, this decision would have been reached by considering the interests of humans alone. A helpful way of putting this is to say that this ethic treats only humans as morally considerable. Something is morally considerable if it enters into ethical evaluation in its own right, independently of its usefulness as a means to other ends. Consider the Pig-nosed Turtle. On the human-centered ethic just now described neither the species as a whole nor the individual members of it are morally considerable: it is only the happiness and unhappiness of humans which is morally considerable and this might or might not be affected by what happens to the turtles.

2. Animal-Centered Ethics

There is a view of ethics which counts not only humans as morally considerable but non-human animals as well; it includes all animals in its scope. Many of the things which we do to the natural environment do affect non-humans adversely and this, it is suggested, must be taken into account. For example, if we thought that cyanide pollution in the South Alligator River would cause non-humans to suffer then this is a moral minus which must be taken into account independently of how things will be for humans. The example is not fanciful: consider the effect on non-humans caused by clear-cutting forests, damming river valleys, quarrying mountains, constructing pipelines and so on. An animal-centered ethic enjoins the moral consideration of individual animals not of species: what happens to species is only of indirect concern insofar as it affects individual animals.

While an animal-centered ethic counts all animals as morally considerable it does not necessarily rank them equally. A useful way of putting this is to say that some animal-centered ethics will accord different moral significance to animals of different kinds. One form this differentiation might take involves the arbitrary, and many would say unjustified, discounting of the interests of non-humans simply because they are the interests of non-humans. Just how this will affect judgments about policy will depend on the degree of the discounting. It could be such as to make human interests always count for more than non-human interests no matter what the intensity or strength of the interests and no matter what the numbers involved. It could be such as to allow stronger or more numerous non-human interests to prevail over weaker or fewer human interests. Avoiding arbitrariness seems to require that equal interests be treated equally. This would leave scope for differentiation, which might still be made on the basis of interests which not all animals have. For example, humans have a capacity for developing theoretical knowledge or for rational autonomous action, which are arguably not capacities of kangaroos. These capacities might underpin certain interests which, because they lack them, kangaroos could not have. Such additional interests might swing a decision in favor of humans and against kangaroos. This is particularly likely in, although not restricted to, cases in which their common interests are equally threatened or equally protected: the appeal to the additional, unshared interest acts as a tie-breaker. Imagine that some important medical breakthrough depended on confining either humans or kangaroos. Keeping kangaroos in a very large enclosure in order to study them may be morally preferable if it threatens no interests of theirs; if they are not treated cruelly, if they are fed, if they are able to behave according to their nature. Confining humans in the same way is not morally acceptable because of the additional interests of humans. This mode of differentiation treats equal interests equally regardless of species and it also allows that unshared interests leave room for degrees of moral significance.

3. Life-Centered Ethics

The class of living things includes more than humans and non-human animals; it includes plants, algae, single-celled organisms, perhaps viruses and, it is sometimes suggested, ecosystems and even the whole biosphere itself (see Attfleld, 1983, Goodpaster, 1978, & Taylor, 1986). The complexity of a life-centered ethic will depend on how the question "What is living?" is answered. However this question is settled it will make much of the idea of a self-regulating system which strives, not necessarily consciously, toward certain goals. Moreover, it is this feature which is typically supposed to confer moral considerability on living things. A life-centered ethic counts all living things as morally considerable, although not necessarily of equal moral significance. So, it might be better to save a Pig-nosed Turtle than a waratah shrub, even though both are morally considerable. The former, however, might be more morally significant because it is a more complex living thing. Here complexity acts as an intensifier: if living, then the more complex, the more morally significant. To take a different kind of case, it morally might be preferable to save some plant rather than to save the Pig-nosed Turtle, because only that plant can fill its particular ecological niche, whereas the Pig-nosed Turtle fills a niche that perhaps could be filled by similar turtles of a different species. Here the differentiation is based on a moral assessment of the respective consequences of the plant ceasing to exist and the Pig-nosed Turtle ceasing to exist, and not on internal characteristics of the living things themselves.

A life-centered ethic requires that in deciding how we should act we need to take account of the impact of our actions on every living thing affected by them. For example, if mining goes on in Kakadu, it will involve cutting down trees and destroying other plants; it will cause the death of some animals and impair, if not destroy, wetland ecosystems. These facts and others count against mining and collectively must be weighed against the good things that might result if mining does go ahead. Since the good things would seem to include only material benefits for some humans, it would be difficult to do the evaluation sum in such a way that it sanctioned mining. This is not to say that it is never morally permissible to fell trees, to flatten dunes, to kill animals, to modify ecosystems and so on. Whether it is permissible depends on what the outcomes are and on differences in moral significance within the class of the morally considerable. A life-centered ethic, incidentally, might take a radical form: it might claim that not only are all living things morally considerable but also that they are of equal moral significance. (See Naess, 1979.) This biotic egalitarianism, if it could be justified, would make it very difficult indeed to defend morally human interventions in the natural environment. It would allow only quantitative judgments; for example, that two living things count for more than one. Most proposed life-centered ethics allow for differential significance within the class of living things, although humans might not be counted the most significant. The preservation of the biosphere and of large ecosystems might be thought more significant than the preservation of large numbers of humans.

4. Rights for Rocks?

The ethics so far considered each evaluate actions by considering consequences for individuals and adding them. What distinguishes these ethics are the kinds of individuals within their scope; moreover, the later ones include all individuals included by earlier ones in the list. It could be argued that we are drawn inexorably to a life-centered ethic; that there is no non-arbitrary way of stopping the drift from the ethic of narrowest scope to the ethic of widest scope. Why not take the argument another step and count non-living things too as morally considerable? There is no attempt here to attribute a mental life or a point of view to non-living things; that would be to enter into an entirely different dispute. The claim is that non-living things, which, like many living things, lack consciousness and which also lack even rudimentary biological organization, are morally considerable. Call this ethic the everything ethic.

Take rocks for example. Mining will involve smashing up rocks, disturbing geological structures, spoiling fossils and the like. Is there anything wrong in doing these things? Here we must take care to forget for a moment the consequential damage which would be done to plants, animals and ecosystems; we must ask whether these things would be wrong considered in themselves. Another example might highlight the issue. Imagine a plan to test a missile by firing it at some distant and completely lifeless celestial body which will be thereby destroyed. Would this be wrong considered in itself? On the ethic which attributes "rights" to rocks, so to speak, it would be. All things considered it might not be wrong, but according to this ethic that is a case which must be made. Like the life-centered ethic, this one can be fleshed out in a variety of ways. It may allow degrees of moral significance and attribute comparatively minimal moral significance to non-living things. It may mirror biological egalitarianism and deny that there are gradations of moral significance, or it may fall somewhere in between.

5. Ecological Holism

It was earlier said that any ethic which would guide us in our treatment of the natural environment is, in the most general sense, an environmental ethic. The term "environmental ethic" sometimes has narrower uses. It is sometimes used to indicate an ethic which counts as morally considerable individuals other than humans and which provides some solid purchase for the moral demands of environmentalists. A life-centered ethic is an environmental ethic in this sense, an animal-centered ethic less clearly so. However, some reserve the term for a specific ethic, ecological holism, presumably because they think that only such an ethic provides morally satisfactory protection for the natural environment. (See Callicott, 1979.) Ecological holism counts two kinds of things as morally considerable; the biosphere as a whole and the large ecosystems which constitute it. Individual animals, including humans, as well as the plants, rocks, molecules etc. which constitute these large systems are not morally considerable; they matter only insofar as they contribute to the maintenance of the significant whole to which they belong. Why should we worry if some species is caused to become extinct? We should worry not because of what this implies for its individual members or even for the species itself but because the extinction runs counter to the goal of maintaining the biosphere or ecosystems. It is a moot point whether ecological holism should be thought to differ structurally from the other ethics. They had as their focus individuals, and "holism" might be thought to signal a different focus. However, it is possible to view the biosphere and ecosystems as individuals, albeit extremely complex ones. If so, the holism amounts to the view that individuals many have hitherto regarded as morally considerable are not. Note that, although the principles of ecological holism differ from those of the other ethics, this does not entail that it differs from all of them in its policy implications. The life-centered ethic and the everything ethic are likely to sanction similar environmental policies as a result of the nature of the mechanisms which maintain ecosystems and the biosphere. Also, it is possible to combine ecological holism with any of the other ethics described. If, for instance, it was combined with the animal-centered ethic we would be enjoined to consider the interests of animals and the goal of biospheric maintenance. Where these conflict, for example, in some odd case where animals can only be saved by simplifying an ecosystem, then some kind of trade-off or balancing would be required.

Justifying an Environmental Ethic

It is not too difficult to appreciate what is compelling about the claim that humans are morally considerable. Most obviously they are considerable because they have interests which can be harmed or advanced. These interests are based on capacities which humans have; for example, the capacity to experience pain and pleasure, the capacity for rational choice, the capacity for free action. Less obviously, they are considerable because of properties or characteristics which they possess which do not give rise to interests, to things in which they themselves have a stake. For example, it might be argued that anything which has the property of being a complex living thing is, to that extent, intrinsically valuable, which is to say that there is a moral reason for preserving it for its own sake independently of whatever uses it serves.

What is compelling about a human-centered ethic pushes us toward an animal-centered ethic, possibly further. (This argument is developed by Lori Gruen in Article 30, "Animals," in *A Companion to Ethics.*) Consistency and the avoidance of arbitrary moral distinctions fuel the shift from a human-centered ethic to an animal-centered ethic. Also, in thinking about non-humans we might notice new reasons for moral considerability; for example, non-humans might have aesthetic properties such as beauty, which we might think make them morally considerable. This, too, is a case where they are morally considerable not because they have interests but because they possess some property which gives them intrinsic value.

Do the reasons advanced in support of animal-centered ethics also support life-centered ethics? If plants (and ecosystems or the biosphere) can be said to have interests, such as an interest in continued existence, then perhaps they do. The concept of *interest* is often explained in terms of a thing having a good of its own which can be harmed or promoted. Some claim that plants have a good of their own; for example, that the good of a tree is promoted by sufficient nutrients for its continued flourishing and harmed when it is deprived of nutrients. A plant's good is determined by the kind of thing it is, by the type of biological organization it exemplifies, by what it is for it to be a flourishing member of its kind. Plants have a good in this sense but this is obviously not enough to ground the claim that they have interests in any morally relevant sense. Plants do not have a point of view from which they experience the world. It doesn't matter to the tree that it withers and dies from want of water; it would matter to a kangaroo. While plants have natural goals, they have no attitude to those goals and progress toward them is not something which they experience. Similar points can be made about the biosphere and about ecosystems. It is this difference which is thought by some to stop the drift, by providing a non-arbitrary cut-off, from an animal-centered to a life-centered ethic.

Even if it is denied that plants have interests, however, it does not follow that they are not morally considerable. Recall that there were reasons suggested, which did not have to do with interests, in virtue of which humans and non-humans are morally considerable. These concerned the property of being a complex living thing and the property of being beautiful. Plants can possess these properties and if animals are morally considerable in virtue of possessing them, then so too are plants. The key to defending thus a life-centered ethic is to establish that the properties appealed to are intrinsically valuable.

Is there anything that might be said in defense of a life-centered ethic which pushes us toward an everything ethic? The property of being a complex living thing cannot be exemplified by rocks etc. but a related property, namely that of being a complex system, can be exemplified by collections of non-living things exhibiting certain relationships with one another. If it is organizational complexity *per se* that makes something morally considerable, then some non-living things will be morally considerable; for example, the bodies which make up the solar system, patterns of weathering on a cliff and a snowflake. The relevance of this suggestion to the Kakadu case depends, among other things, on whether ecosystems count as living things. If they do not then they are non-living things which exhibit complexity and which, given the suggestion, are morally considerable. The fact that they are morally considerable would provide an ethical reason for opposing mining. Or again, we might judge that one reason we think that living things are morally considerable is because they exemplify beauty. In some cases beauty might be exemplified by a thing's more general, external features, as in the case of tigers, whales, orchids and proteas. In addition, beauty might be exemplified in the more specific detail of a thing's biological functioning. Now some non-living things such as boulders, dunes, lifeless moons and icebergs can be beautiful, so, if exemplification of beauty is a basis for attributing moral considerability to living things, then at least some non-living things are morally considerable. The claim that exemplifying beauty is a basis for moral considerability is contentious; however, it is strongly supported by some, for example, Rolston, 1988. Those who oppose it typically urge that it is the appreciation of beauty rather than beauty itself which is morally significant.

So, one way in which the move from one ethic to the next is accomplished is by finding a determinant of moral considerability in that ethic and showing that a rigorous application of it leads us to the next kind of ethic. Another way is by showing that there are new morally relevant features which the more restrictive ethics unjustifiably ignore. One such feature might be the property of being a natural object; that is, an object which is not the product of human technology and culture. Rocks are natural objects and so on this view it would be wrong, although perhaps not all things considered wrong, to destroy them. There are other candidate properties: for example, the property of exhibiting diversity of parts, the property of functional integration of parts, the property of exhibiting harmony and the property of being a self-regulating system. This last group of properties, if deemed determinants of moral considerability, move us in the direction of ecological holism or in the direction of a mixed ethic. This is because they are properties quintessentially exemplified by ecosystems and the biosphere. If we accept that they are determinants of moral considerability, then we are provided with a reason, in addition to any we might derive from the other ethics we have considered, for resisting policies which would lead to disruption of ecosystems.

How do we decide whether candidate determinants of moral considerability are in fact such? Consider naturalness and exhibiting diversity of parts. Imagine that a certain mine requires the destruction of a group of trees on a rocky outcrop and of the outcrop itself. Environmentalists protest that this involves an uncompensated loss of value. The mining company promises to reconstruct the outcrop from synthetic parts and to replace the trees with plastic models. This bit of artificial environment will be indistinguishable, except by laboratory analysis, from what was originally there. It will be exactly as appealing to look at, no animals will be harmed as a consequence and no ecosystem will be disrupted. Neither the human-centered ethic nor the animal-centered ethic provides space for an environmentalist rejoinder. The life-centered ethic does to the extent that it permits a complaint about the killing of living trees. However, this does not seem to some to be the only thing morally amiss with the mining company's proposal. Isn't it also morally suspect because it replaces the natural with the artificial? Imagine a modified case in which only a rock outcrop, devoid of life, is removed and later replaced with synthetic rock. Not even the life-centered ethic allows for a complaint about the morality of this. Some people think that even in the modified case the mining company does something to which a moral minus attaches. If this thought is persistent it provides support for a variant of an everything ethic which includes within its scope all natural items. (See Elliot, in VanDeVeer & Pierce, 1986, 142–150.) It is difficult to be entirely sure about the source of the belief, if we have it, that naturalness is a determinant of moral considerability. It is possible that we think that there is something dubious about the artificial outcrop because we cannot distance ourselves from the thought that it will be detectably different or from the belief that it will harm animal interests or that it will result in ecosystemic disruption. If these are the sources of our belief, then we have no basis for the view that naturalness is a determinant of moral considerability. There is another possibility to which we should be alert. Naturalness might be a conditional determinant; that is, it might require the presence of some other property, for instance complexity. So, it isn't natural items which are morally considerable but things which are both natural and complex.

Consider the property of having a diversity of parts. Is this a determinant of moral considerability? Here we might compare an area which is covered with rainforest with an area which has been cleared of rainforest and is under cultivation. Which is more valuable in itself? Again we must distance ourselves from certain thoughts; for example, the thought that clearing rainforests is contrary to long-term human interests, the thought that wild animals would have suffered during the clearing or the thought that aboriginal peoples were displaced. Having attempted this, many would say that the rainforest is of more value. Imagine, then, that only one of these areas could be saved from massive devastation. Many would say that, considering them just in themselves, the rainforest should be saved. Moreover, one reason that will be given is that the rainforest exhibits more diversity; it is constituted in a more complex, richer fashion. There are other reasons that might also be given; for example, that there are aesthetic properties possessed by the rainforest but not possessed by the cultivated area. Our preparedness, by the way, to attribute aesthetic properties, such as beauty, to the rainforest, may well depend on whether we have an understanding of it as an ecological system: knowing how the parts work in concert to maintain the whole might assist us in seeing it as a thing of beauty. Counting these kinds of reasons as reasons for avoiding environmental despoliation provides the basis for an environmental ethic which reaches beyond either a human or animal-centered one and possibly beyond a life-centered one as well.

Even if we accept, for example, that the ecosystems of Kakadu are morally considerable, how do we weigh this against human (or other) interests? A first step is to ask whether there are alternative ways of satisfying human interests. Often there are. Moreover, the modification of ecosystems is often contrary to long-term human interests. Sometimes there will be cases of genuine conflict where the different moral considerations pull in different directions. Here we must carefully enumerate the relevant moral considerations, ask ourselves how important they are and then make an all-things-considered judgment. There is no decisive calculus available to assist us in these judgments. It is not correct to say that humans should always come first nor is it correct to say that preserving an ecosystem is always more important than protecting any set of human interests. Nevertheless there will be cases, such as Kakadu, where the morally appropriate policy is clear enough.

References

Attfleld, K. *The Ethics of Environmental Concern* (Oxford: Blackwell, 1983).

Baxter, W.F. *People or Penguins: The Case for Optimal Pollution* (New York: Columbia University Press, 1974).

Callicott, I.B. Elements of an Environmental Ethic: Moral Considerability and the Biotic Community, *Environmental Ethics* (1979), 71–81.

Goodpaster, K. On Being Morally Considerable, *Journal of Philosophy,* 75 (1978), 308–325.

Naess, A. Self-Realisation in Mixed Communities of Humans, Bears, Sheep, and Wolves, *Inquiry,* 22 (1979), 231–242.

Norton, B. *Why Preserve Natural Variety?* (Princeton: Princeton University Press, 1988).

Rolston III, H. *Environmental Ethics: Duties to and Values in the Natural World* (Philadelphia: Temple University Press, 1988).

Taylor, P. *Respect for Nature* (Princeton: Princeton University Press, 1986).

VanDeVeer, D. and Pierce, C., eds. *People, Penguins and Plastic Trees: Basic Issues in Environmental Ethics* (Belmont, CA: Wadsworth, 1986).

Further Reading

Elliot, R. and Arran, G., eds. *Environmental Philosophy: A Collection of Readings* (St. Lucia: University of Queensland Press, 1983).

Mannison, D., McRobbie, M., and Routley, R., eds. *Environmental Philosophy* (Canberra: Research School of Social Sciences, Australian National University, 1980).

Partridge, E., ed. *Obligations to Future Generations* (Buffalo: Prometheus, 1981).

Regan, T., ed. *Earthbound: New Introductory Essays in Environmental Ethics* (New York: Random House, 1984).

Sylvan, R. *A Critique of Deep Ecology* (Canberra: Research School of Social Sciences, Australian National University, 1985).

Journal/Discussion Questions

✍ *Which of the approaches that Elliott describes—human-centered, animal-centered, or life-centered—most closely reflects your own initial views?*

1. What are the principal limitations of a human-centered ethic? Discuss.
2. What are the principal limitations of an animal-centered ethic? Discuss.
3. What are the principal limitations of a life-centered ethic? Discuss.
4. What, according to Elliott, are the characteristics of moral considerability? Do you agree with Elliott's analysis? Discuss.

Janna Thompson
"A Refutation of Environmental Ethics"

Janna Thompson is a senior lecturer in the School of Philosophy at the University of LaTrobe. Thompson's research interests include environmental ethics and political philosophy, especialy issues of global justice. Her works include Justice and World Order *and* Discourse and Knowledge: Defense of a Collectivist Ethics.

Environmental ethics, Thompson maintains, holds that some entities in nature are intrinsically valuable. She argues that either environmental ethics fails to satisfy the requirements for any ethic theory in general or else that it fails to provide a sufficient account of its intrinsic values. Environmental ethics, she concludes, is not properly ethics at all.

As You Read, Consider This:

1. Where is the difference between "shallow" and "deep" ecological theories?
2. What, according to Thompson, are the formal requirements that any ethics has to fulfill?

An environmental ethic holds that some entities in nature or in natural states of affairs are intrinsically valuable. I argue that proposals for an environmental ethic either fails to satisfy requirements which any ethical system must satisfy to be an ethic or they fail to give us reason to suppose that the values they promote are intrinsic values. If my arguments are correct, then environmental ethics is not properly ethics at all.

In "The Shallow and the Deep, Long Range Ecology Movement" Arne Naess distinguishes between two responses to ecological degradation. The shallow response recommends that we be nice to nature so that nature will be nice for us. The deep ecological response, on the other hand, insists that a proper appreciation of nature leads to a recognition that "the equal right to live and blossom is an intuitively clear and obvious value axiom."[1]

Following Naess, a considerable number of philosophers and others have chosen the deep ecology path, and they have understood this to require the development of an ethic which values things in nature for their own sake. John Rodman expresses a common motivation for having such an ethic:

> I need only to stand in the midst of a clearcut forest, a stripmined hillside, a defoliated jungle, or a dammed canyon to feel uneasy with assumptions that could yield the conclusion that no human action can make any difference to the welfare of anything but sentient animals.[2]

Val and Richard Routley in "Human Chauvinism and Environmental Ethics" argue that only a truly environmental ethic which regards natural systems or their properties as valuable in themselves can adequately express the standpoint of those who want to preserve wilderness and who abhor strip-mined hillsides and defoliated jungles.[3] More recently Holmes Rolston, III in *Environmental Ethics*[4] and Paul W. Taylor in *Respect for Nature*[5] have both argued for an ethic which recognizes value in nature.

An environmental ethic, as I understand it, is an ethic which holds that natural entities and/or states of affairs are intrinsically valuable, and thus deserve to be the object of our moral concern. What exactly it means to say that something is intrinsically valuable depends on the account given of what values are and where they come from.[6] At a minimum, however, those who find intrinsic value in nature are claiming two things: first, that things and states which are of value are valuable for what they are in themselves and not because of their relations to us (and in particular, not because they provide us with pleasure and satisfaction). Second, the intrinsic value which these states of nature have is objective in the sense that its existence is not a matter of individual taste or personal preference. Any rational, morally sensitive person ought to be able to recognize that it is there. This means, of course, that those who claim that intrinsic value exists in nature must provide some criteria for identifying what is of value and some reasons for believing that the things and states in question are valuable.

In general, an ethic is supposed to tell us two things: (1) what states of affairs, things, and properties are intrinsically desirable or valuable (as opposed to what is valuable as a means to an end); and (2) what we should do or not do in order to promote, protect, or bring into existence that which is of intrinsic value. Given that an ethic is supposed to tell us these things, it must satisfy the following formal requirements in order to count as an ethic at all:

(1) The requirement of consistency. If a thing or state of affairs is thought to be intrinsically valuable, then all things that are like it in relevant respects must also be judged to have intrinsic value. On the other hand, if something is thought not to have intrinsic value, then all things that are like that thing in relevant respects must be regarded as not having intrinsic value. Supporters of animal liberation and environmental ethics have made heavy use of the consistency requirement in their condemnations of "human chauvinism." They argue, for example, that if human beings are regarded as being intrinsically valuable, and if some animals are like human beings in all respects that seem relevant, then a consistent ethic must regard these animals as valuable. If animals are not regarded as being valuable, then those human beings that are like animals in relevant respects (babies, children, the mentally retarded) must be judged by a consistent ethic not to have intrinsic value.[7]

The requirement of consistency presupposes that the ethic in question has provided us with an account of what differences and similarities are relevant and why. If that ethic is to have any claim to being objective, then that account must not seem arbitrary. In other words, if something is thought to be of value and another thing is not, then there must be reason for believing that the differences between them justify making that judgment, and if two things are regarded to be of equal value then the similarities they have must be such so that this judgment can reasonably be made.

(2) The requirement of non-vacuity. The criteria for determining what things or states of affairs are intrinsically valuable must not be such so that it turns out that every thing and every state of affairs counts as equally valuable. The reason why this requirement must be satisfied should be clear.

An ethic is supposed to tell us what we ought or ought not to do; however, it cannot do so if it turns out that all things and states of affairs are equally valuable, for if they are, then there is no reason to do one thing rather than another, to bring about one state of affairs rather than another.

(3) The decidability requirement. The criteria of value which an ethic offers must be such that in most cases it is possible to determine what counts as valuable and what does not. Probably all ethical systems will have problems with borderline cases. For example, an ethic which regards sentient creatures as objects of moral concern and their well-being as something that we should promote may have difficulties determining what counts as a sentient creature and what the well-being of a particular creature consists of. Nevertheless, in general it is usually clear what satisfies the criteria and what does not. A more serious difficulty arises if the criteria leave us in doubt in most cases. If this happens, then we do not simply have a problem within an ethic, but a problem regarding something as an ethic in the first place.[8] The reason for having a decidability requirement is much the same as the reason for requiring non-vacuity. If an ethic is to make prescriptions, then we have to have a good idea of what we are supposed to be promoting and avoiding. If an ethic can't tell us this, if it leaves us uncertain in too many cases about what things or states of affairs are valuable and which are more valuable than others, then its claim to be an ethic is brought into question.

My claim is that proposals for an environmental ethic either fail to satisfy one or more of these formal criteria or fail to give us reason to suppose that the values they promote are intrinsic values. It should be noted that my objection to environmental ethics is not that its ideas about what is valuable are implausible, or that rational, morally sensitive people should not value what environmental ethicists tell them to value. Rather, if my arguments are correct, what is called environmental ethics is not properly ethics at all.

What can go wrong with environmental ethics is illustrated by an argument presented by Paul Taylor in *Respect for Nature.* The argument is meant to establish that there is no good reason for thinking that sentient creatures alone have intrinsic value (*inherent worth*), indeed, that there is no reason to deny that nonsentient creatures—plants, lower animals—have less intrinsic value than sentient creatures. Human beings, Taylor admits, have properties that many living things do not have—e.g., intelligence—and some philosophers, most notoriously Descartes, have believed that human beings are distinguished from all other creatures by the possession of mind. Apart from the question of whether other creatures do not have minds, however, there is no reason in nature why we should regard the qualities that human beings happen to have as making them more valuable than living creatures that do not have these qualities—no reason why creatures who can think or feel should be regarded as more valuable than plants and other nonsentient creatures.[9]

A natural response to this argument is to ask, "Why stop here?" Why should we regard rocks, rivers, volcanoes, molecules as being of less value simply because they happen to lack the properties associated with life? Why indeed should we say that anything is more valuable than any other thing? The argument Taylor uses to overthrow human chauvinism seems to undermine the very possibility of an ethic. We might conclude that if we leave it up to nature to tell us what we should or should not value, that we get no answer—that we can only find nature to be valuable insofar as natural states of affairs are related to us: to our interests and concerns, or more generally the interests and concerns of sentient creatures. This is in fact the position I hold, but to establish it requires much more argument, for environmental ethicists do think that they can give us criteria for discovering objective value in nature, criteria which do not set us on the slippery slope into inconsistency, vacuity, or undecidability.

There are two ways in which environmental ethicists have tried to establish their thesis that there are intrinsic values in nature. The first is to argue by analogy. Taylor (and sometimes Rolston) does this. Let us assume that human individuals are intrinsically valuable and that it is desirable that their well-being be promoted. The reason we think that this is so (the argument goes) is that human individuals have interests, preferences, purposes—a good that can be frustrated or furthered. But if this is our criterion for having value, then in all consistency we must recognize that since some animals also have interests, preferences, and purposes, they too should count as having intrinsic value. Plants, nonsentient creatures, may not have interests in a true sense, but they do have a good (unlike a rock). "Once we come to understand the life cycle of a butterfly," Taylor says, "and know the environmental conditions it needs to survive in a healthy state, we have no difficulty speaking about what is beneficial to it and what might be harmful to it."[10] The same can be said about bacteria or plants. Furthermore, the good that a butterfly and a blue gum have is a good of their own. Unlike machines, the good of which is determined by human purposes, we can say what is good for a natural organism without reference to any other entity. Thus, we can understand how nonsentient organisms can be candidates for having intrinsic value, and once we come to appreciate their nature and the role that they play in environmental systems, we will be inclined to say that they do have "intrinsic value."[11]

The second approach to environmental ethics is not to argue by analogy but simply to try to persuade us as valuers that there are certain things or states of affairs in nature that we as rational, morally sensitive people ought to regard as having a value independent of our needs and interests and that there are other states of affairs (like defoliated jungles or exotic pine plantations) that we ought to regard as having a disvalue. We simply have to come to recognize that these values or disvalues are there, and the job of the proponent of environmental ethics is to encourage us to do this by persuading us to appreciate certain aspects of nature and by trying to show us that an ethic which does not acknowledge these values cannot satisfy our intuitive understanding of what is bad or good, right or wrong. The Routleys take this approach, and so do Rodman and sometimes Rolston.

The Routleys argue in "Human Chauvinism and Environmental Ethics" that environmental systems are to be valued according to their possession of a mix of factors: diversity, naturalness, integrity, stability, and harmony,[12] and that people who appreciate wilderness, who are reluctant to destroy natural systems even if the destruction does not harm sentient creatures, should accept this criterion of value. Rolston maintains that not only organisms as self-maintaining systems deserve to be valued, but also species as entities with a history and an essence and ecosystems as "integrated cybernetic systems." He argues that only if we are prepared to value these things for themselves do we have an ethical basis for preserving and protecting what many sensitive people want to preserve and protect.

Because both approaches claim to be laying the foundations of an environmental ethic, it is presupposed that they can satisfy the formal requirements of an ethic. Indeed, it seems that they do satisfy these requirements. Each claims to have the virtue of consistency—unlike ethics which are described as being "human chauvinist." Each tells us that some things or states of affairs are valuable and some are not; and each presents criteria that we are supposed to be able to use to decide what is valuable and to what extent.

But what exactly is valuable? On this matter environmental ethicists do not speak with one voice. Taylor insists that it is individual organisms that have intrinsic value and not environmental systems or species. The Routleys regard environmental systems as holders of value. Rolston thinks that individual organisms, species, and ecosystems all have value, though perhaps to different degrees. Is this disagreement about what in nature has value a little problem that environmental ethicists should be able to solve among themselves, or is it a symptom of a larger difficulty? To answer this question let us look more closely at each of the two approaches.

Once again I take Taylor's argument as illustrating what goes wrong with the analogical approach. Taylor argues that if a thing has a good of its own, then it is a candidate for having intrinsic value. He assumes that it is individual living organisms and only individual living organisms that can have this value. But there is nothing in the criterion, or the mode of argument used to support it, that requires this limitation. It is not difficult to use Taylor's way of determining what is of value to insist that other kinds of things must also have the same intrinsic value if we are to be true to the consistency requirement.

Why can't we say, for example, that hearts, lungs, livers, and kidneys have intrinsic value and thus deserve in themselves to be objects of our moral concern? Once we come to appreciate how a kidney or some other internal organ develops within the embryo, how it functions and maintains itself, what makes it flourish and what harms it, then surely as in the case of the butterfly or the bacteria we have to recognize that it has a good of its own.

But isn't the good of a kidney defined in terms of the good of the organism that has the kidney? It is true that my own good and the good of my kidneys are intimately related. We depend upon each other (though modern technology has made it possible for me to get on without my kidneys and my kidneys to continue to exist without me). But my purposes and goals do not define what is good for a kidney. This can be determined independently to the same extent that the good of a wood-boring insect can be determined independently of the good of the tree it feeds on or that the good of intestinal bacteria can be defined independently of the good of the intestine or the good of the creature who has the intestine. Kidneys, like insects and bacteria, need certain kinds of nourishment; they are healthy under some conditions and are caused harm by others. These conditions can be specified without mentioning the organism in which the organs reside.

So using the same kind of argument which Taylor uses to persuade us that organisms have a good of their own, we have to conclude that internal organs have such a good too. For the same reason, it seems that we also ought to say that individual leaves, buds, and bits of bark have a good of their own and are equally candidates for having intrinsic value. And what will stop us from saying that a piece of skin, a bodily cell, or a DNA molecule has a good of its own?

Why discriminate against rocks? Once we appreciate how crystals form according to a pattern determined by molecular structure, what conditions make it possible for this pattern to form in a characteristic way, what maintains its structural integrity, and what conditions cause it to be deformed or to break up, then surely we will want to say that in an extended sense of the phrase a crystal has a "good of its own." It is true that it sounds odd to say this. But why should we be any more impressed by the fact that crystals, strictly speaking, do not have a good of their own than Taylor is impressed by the fact that nonsentient creatures, strictly speaking, do not have interests? Surely it is the relevant similarities between bacteria, cells, and crystals that should be crucial for our ethical reasoning, just as it is the relevant similarities between sentient creatures and nonsentient creatures that are crucial for Taylor. The same thing that is said about crystals can be said about any natural entity, whether a rock, a molecule, an atom, or a solar system. Each has an integrity of its own which it can maintain under certain conditions, but which will be destroyed under others.

It is time to reassess the status of machines. Although it is true that we think that the purpose of a machine is to serve a human need, the matter is really not so simple, for machines, because of their structure, have a potential, a way of doing things, of their own, and in order to accomplish their purposes people often have to conform to the ways of the machine. In fact, it is frequently the case that people have to redefine their goals or are caused to discover new ones as a consequence of realizing the potential of a machine or in the course of adapting themselves to it. It seems as if the good of a machine is best defined in terms of the structures and capacities it has and what operations will realize its potential and which ones will tend to destroy it or not allow it to fulfill its potential. Moreover, if a machine has a good of its own, then so do the parts of a machine for the same reason that a liver or a heart have a good of its own.

What can be said about a machine might also be said about other constructed entities like social institutions and societies, for these also have a structure, a potential, a way of operating which the individuals in them don't necessarily appreciate. The same can be said of ecological systems. Taylor objects to regarding systems as being objects of respect, probably because he assumes that the good of a system is reducible to the goods of the individual animal and plant populations that make it up; however, ecological systems, like social systems, have a potential for change and development and a dynamic which may be compatible with the destruction of particular populations—as when a forest develops toward a climax state. So why not admit that ecological systems have a good of their own and are thus in themselves candidates for our moral concern? If ecological systems are entities with a good of their own, then why not parts of ecological systems—e.g., the relation between a predator population and a prey population? Why not a whole wilderness? Why not the relations between plants and animals on a continent? Why not nature as a whole?

One of the problems which this vigorous use of analogy brings out in the open is the problem of determining what should count as an individual for the purposes of environmental ethics. It is perhaps natural to think that particular plants and animals are the individuals that we need to be concerned with. But why shouldn't we count the parts of an animal or plant as individuals, their cells, organs, or molecules? Why not the complex consisting of an animal or a plant and its various parasites and bacteria? Why not the plant and the soil that nourishes it? Why not an interrelated system of animals and plants? There doesn't seem to be any good reason why one thing should be counted as an individual and others not. How we divide up the world depends upon context and convenience. But surely an environmental ethic which claims to discover intrinsic value in nature shouldn't depend upon the way we happen to look at things.

Once we do (somehow) pick out the individuals we are concerned with it is still a problem to decide what is good for them. So far, like Taylor, I have assumed that this is generally obvious. However, there is another way of viewing the matter. An individual plant or animal has a genetic potential to manifest a range of properties, but what properties it realizes depends on its environment. Why should we regard it to be for the good of a plant if it realizes one aspect of its potential rather than another? Once again it is natural to think that it is for the good of a plant to be raised in conditions which encourage it to be vigorous and healthy and that disease and poor nutrition are bad for a plant. Nevertheless, a diseased plant displays properties, realizes a potential, which it would not have manifested if it had been healthy. Why should we regard it as a worse thing for it if it has these properties? The answer might be that if the ability of a plant to survive and reproduce is threatened, then this is not to its good. However, if this is our criterion of what is bad for natural things, why should we say that it is bad for the plant's sake that it dies of disease rather than that this is bad for its genes or bad for the species? Moreover, why should it be bad for the plant's sake to live a short time rather than a longer time? One reason why we find it so natural to suppose that it is better for an organism's sake that it be healthy and have a long, productive life is because this is what we want for ourselves and what we want for the plants we grow. Nevertheless, plants don't want anything. Thus, as this discussion shows, determining what a nonsentient organism's own good is is not as straightforward as it sometimes appears and this difficulty throws into question the analogy between sentient creatures and nonsentient organisms upon which Taylor's approach to environmental ethics depends.

Other attempts to argue by analogy have not been any more successful. Rolston suggests that what living creatures from the most complex to the simplest have in common is that they are self-contained systems and that it is this which makes them deserving of respect. Nevertheless, virtually anything can be regarded as a self-contained system in the same sense, be it a liver, a molecule, or a solar system. Moreover, Rolston, like Taylor, faces the problem of determining in a nonarbitrary way what states of a system count as good.

Because of these problems, I conclude that neither Taylor nor Rolston succeed in providing the foundations for an environmental ethic. The criteria they use to determine what is of value not only fail to rule out many things that they would probably wish to exclude (e.g., lungs and livers), but also fail to satisfy the formal requirements of an ethic. First, their proposals probably fail to satisfy the requirement of non-vacuity, for if we push the analogies that they depend upon to their logical conclusion, then we end up regarding virtually everything as valuable. Second, even if we can somehow resist this result, it is clear that the proposals won't satisfy the decidability requirement, for the criteria leave us radically uncertain about what counts as an object of moral concern and what states of affairs should be regarded as good.

Of course, the fact that a few proponents of environmental ethics have failed to establish that there can be such an ethic is not conclusive. Is there a way of improving the argument from analogy and/or sharpening up the criteria of value so that they satisfy the requirements? It might be suggested that environmental ethicists should simply declare that what is of intrinsic value are living creatures, or wilderness, or ecological systems. The obvious problem with this idea, however, is that in making this declaration they would be committing the same sin of arbitrariness which they accuse human chauvinists of committing. If they claim to be uncovering intrinsic values in nature, then we are entitled to get an answer to the question, "What is it about living creatures or wilderness that is valuable?" and when the answer is given, in attempting to satisfy the consistency requirement for the ethic, they are likely once again to encounter the problems I have already discussed above.

Maybe the environmental ethicist can give a better answer than the ones so far considered. What distinguishes living things from nonliving things is their complexity. They are not only self-contained systems, but also systems with parts that are related in a complex way, systems which carry out complex processes. Perhaps we should say that something is intrinsically valuable if it has a certain degree of complexity, or that things are valuable according to their degree of complexity. The latter is sometimes suggested by Rolston.

If we adopt the complexity criterion, we might be able to satisfy the requirement of non-vacuity. However, accusations of arbitrariness can still be made. Why should the cutoff point that determines what is of value or what degree of value something has be in one place rather than another? Why should a slightly lesser degree of complexity be regarded as a relevant difference? In addition, it is doubtful whether the criterion can satisfy the decidability requirement. How is complexity to be defined in general and how are we to compare the complexity of different kinds of things? Is an individual less complex than the ecological system or social institution to which he/she/it belongs? Is a heart or liver or brain less complex than the creature it belongs to? Moreover, it is not clear what systems we are talking about. Virtually anything, as I have pointed out, can be regarded as a system: an individual animal or plant, the relationship between several animals and plants, an ecological system, the planet Earth, a heart or kidney, a molecule, an interacting system of molecules, etc. Until we know what we are comparing and how, it is not going to be possible to answer the question, "What should be the object of our moral concern?" Finally, even if we can determine what systems we ought to be concerned with, there remains the difficulty of how we should determine, in a nonarbitrary way, what states of these systems count as good.

Given that there are so many problems with the analogical approach to environmental ethics, one might suppose that the second approach is bound to be preferable. I argue, however, that it encounters the same difficulties. Let us begin with the Routleys' multifactored criterion for evaluating natural systems: diversity, naturalness, integrity, stability, and harmony. The Routleys allow that there can be difficulties in determining how these different factors should be weighed, for example, whether and in what cases a greater diversity can make up for a lack of naturalness. They would also undoubtedly admit that there may be difficulties in determining what "stability" or "harmony" amount to in a dynamic system. But they do claim that this criterion gives us clear reasons for preferring a wilderness over a monoculture pine plantation and for condemning the defoliation of a jungle or the clear-cutting of a forest, and they argue that the judgments that we make using it correspond to our intuitions about what is of value in nature.

That the Routleys don't escape the problems we have already encountered becomes evident as soon as we ask the question: "What is it exactly that we are supposed to be evaluating?" Although they assume that their criterion applies primarily to large environmental systems, such as wilderness, why should we assume this? What prevents us from applying the criterion more widely?[13] For example, compost and dung heaps are little environmental systems that can be evaluated according to the diversity of creatures or processes which they contain, their naturalness, integrity, stability, and harmony. Likewise, individual animals and plants can be regarded as environmental systems containing a greater or lesser diversity of parts and functions, parts that tend to maintain harmony and stability. And, of course, parts of these systems, e.g., livers and lungs, are also systems with a complexity of parts, with an integrity, harmony, etc. of their own. Finally, why should we suppose that the criterion must apply only to systems of living things? How about a solar system, a molecule, or an atom? Why can't a society be regarded as a diverse, stable, harmonious cybernetic system?

Once again we have a problem of determining and limiting the scope of the application of the value criterion. It won't do any good to insist that it is only to be applied to ecological systems. This is a mere piece of legislation. If other systems are like ecological systems in relevant respects, then they too should be judged as valuable. If we don't want to say that they are valuable, then we have to find a relevant respect in which they are different.

The difficulty involved in determining what should be the objects of our moral concern translates into a difficulty about what states of affairs we should be promoting. Is the diversity, integrity, naturalness, etc. contained in a compost heap or a tree less worthy of our concern than the diversity, integrity, naturalness, etc. of a forest? Is a monoculture pine plantation full of creatures, which in themselves have diversity, integrity, etc., necessarily of less worth than the wilderness that it replaced?

Even if we focus on ecological systems, it is difficult to determine what ought to be preserved and protected and why. If we degrade an environmental system, make it less diverse, natural, stable, etc., then we have rendered it less valuable according to our criterion. But in the future this system may recover, becoming as diverse and integrated as before (though perhaps with different species), or another system just as diverse, etc. may eventually replace it (perhaps in a thousand or a million years). If we have good reason to think that this will happen, then why should we be terribly concerned about what we now do to our environment? What counts as harm?

One answer might be that a state of affairs is worse if it is brought about by our tampering. What environmental ethics above all wants to condemn is unnecessary human interventions in nature. Its message is "Leave it alone." The Routleys, for example, place a lot of weight on "naturalness." Even if our interventions increase the diversity of a system and do not damage its stability and harmony, they can still be condemned because they make it less natural.

It is puzzling that an ethic which purports to find objective value in nature should be so concerned about what states of affairs human beings bring about. Although it is true that human actions do have a detrimental effect on environmental systems, so do storms, floods, volcanoes, and glaciers. Exotic species can be introduced into a system by winds or the migration of birds. Given these natural disturbances, how can environmental ethicists justify condemning a human action when it does not (in the long term, at least) make a system any less stable, diverse, harmonious, etc.? Moreover, why aren't they concerned to prevent (if possible) natural occurrences that threaten the stability, integrity, and diversity of an environmental system? The emphasis environmental ethicists place on limiting human interventions, on preserving and protecting the natural communities which we are in contact with, suggests that their real concern is to encourage a better relationship between humans and their environment. Their ideas about what we should value and why—that, for example, we should value the creatures and systems that now happen to exist—depend on a covert reference to the human point of view, to our interests and concerns.

Other recent attempts to develop a criterion for making value judgments have been no more successful than the Routleys' criterion. Rolston, for example, argues that species deserve to be respected because they are discrete entities with a history of their own. A species, he says, is a kind of an essence.[14] But what history a species has, what turns out to be its essence, depends upon the environmental forces which act upon it. Why should one outcome be regarded as better than another? Why should existing species be regarded as better than others that could take their place (whether now or in several thousand or million years)? If a species is an essence, then why not say that any population with a distinct genetic character is an essence? Why not an individual, etc.?

Although I cannot rule out the possibility that someone might someday state a criterion of value which would include in its scope all and only those things and states that environmental ethicists want included and which would satisfy the formal requirements of ethics, it seems to me to be unlikely. The problem, as I have suggested, is that how we view the world, how we divide it up into individuals and systems, what we regard as good or bad for an individual or a system is too arbitrary—i.e., too dependent on point of view, interest, and convenience—to support an ethic that purports to be based on value in nature independent of our interests and concerns. Every criterion of environmental value seems to depend for its application on our taking a particular point of view, or on using a particular set of concepts, and there does not seem to be any nonarbitrary reason (as far as ethics is concerned) for taking up one point of view or using one set of concepts rather than another. As a result, the attempt to be objective and to avoid assuming an interest or a point of view risks vacuity or at the very least producing something too indeterminate in scope to be useful as an ethic.

If there is something so fundamentally wrong with environmental ethics, then two questions are critical. First, is any ethic possible at all? If environmental ethics is flawed, then what reason do we have for supposing that a nonenvironmental ethic is any less arbitrary or any more likely to satisfy formal requirements? Second, if environmental ethics is impossible, what we are going to say about those practices—our destruction of wilderness, species, environmental systems, creatures—which environmental ethicists believe that they need an environmental ethics to condemn?

To establish the possibility of ethics it is enough to give an example of a system of ethics which satisfies the formal criteria for an ethic and includes reference to intrinsic values. I believe that an ethic which takes individuals who have a point of view (i.e., that are centers of consciousness) as having intrinsic value—an ethic which supports the satisfaction of the interests, needs, and preferences of those individuals—is such an ethic. The fact that individuals have a point of view, and can therefore be caused anguish, frustration, pleasure, or joy as the result of what we do, is one good reason for valuing such individuals and requiring that their interests and preferences be a matter of moral concern to all rational, morally sensitive agents. Equally important, in satisfying the formal requirements of an ethic, is the fact that individuals with a point of view—with consciousness, desires, feelings, goals, etc.—are self-defining. What in the framework of the ethic counts as an individual is not an arbitrary matter, not a question of the valuer's point of view. That they have a point of view decides the matter. It is also not an arbitrary matter, not a question of the valuer's point of view, that counts as the good of such individuals. They themselves define their good by how they feel, what they say, by how they behave. Because we are able to use the value criteria of this ethic consistently, nonvacuously, and without any overwhelming problems of undecidability, it is clear that a nonarbitrary ethic is possible, though, of course, much more discussion is needed to determine what an ethic which values sentient beings requires of us.[15]

If environmental ethics is nonviable, if we are stuck with a sentient-being-centered ethic, then what about the needs of the environment? What do we say about the intuitions and attitudes of those people who think that we ought to preserve wilderness, species, and nonsentient organisms even when these things have no instrumental value for human beings or other sentient creatures? Do we really need an environmental ethic in order to do justice to the standpoint of the environmentalist who abhors a defoliated jungle or a strip-mined hillside?

Perhaps the reason why so many people think we do is because they are operating within an unnecessarily narrow conception of what is instrumentally valuable. They think that within the framework of a human-centered or sentient-being-centered ethic we can only value natural things if they satisfy a well-defined need which we (or some other sentient creatures) have. Dissatisfied with this ethic, they mistakenly want to argue for the preservation of something that is not valuable in this sense and thus feel obliged to embark on the project of constructing an environmental ethic. Fortunately, there is another possibility. We might be able to argue that something is valuable and therefore ought to be preserved because our lives and our conception of ourselves will be enhanced—in a spiritual sense—if we learn to appreciate it for what it is and we learn how to live with it in harmony.[16] Although such an approach does not pretend to go beyond the human point of view, beyond our concerns and interests, it is not confined to a concern with obvious and traditional material and psychological needs, for it permits us to define a new conception of what we are as individuals and what a good life is. My view is that those who want to develop a deep approach to environmental concerns have everything to gain and nothing to lose by following this approach. Environmental ethics is not only a dead end, but also an unnecessary diversion.

Endnotes

1. Arne Naess, "The Shallow and the Deep, Long Range Ecology Movement: A Summary," *Inquiry* 16 (1973): 96.
2. John Rodman, "Liberation of Nature," *Inquiry* 20 (1977): 89.
3. Val and Richard Routley, "Human Chauvinism and Environmental Ethics," in *Environmental Philosophy,* edited by Don Mannison, Michael McRobbie, and Richard Routley, Monograph Series 2, Department of Philosophy, Research School of Social Sciences (Canberra: Australian National University, 1980). See also Val and Richard Routley, "Against the Inevitability of Human Chauvinism," in Kenneth Goodpaster and Kenneth Sayre, eds., *Ethics and the Problems of the 21st Century* (Notre Dame: University of Notre Dame Press, 1987).
4. Holmes Rolston III, *Environmental Ethics* (Philadelphia: Temple University Press, 1988). See also *Philosophy Gone Wild: Essays in Environmental Ethics* (Buffalo: Prometheus Books, 1986).
5. Paul W. Taylor, *Respect for Nature: A Theory of Environmental Ethics* (Princeton: Princeton University Press, 1986).
6. The Routleys ("Human Chauvinism and Environmental Ethics") hold that there are no values without valuers, but that valuers can and should value things which are not instrumental to their needs and purposes (p. 152). Rolston (*Environmental Ethics*) argues that values are as much in the world as objects like trees (see chap. 3); see also Holmes Rolston, III, "Are Values in Nature Subjective or Objective?" in Robert Elliot and Arran Gare, eds., *Environmental Philosophy* (University Park: Pennsylvania University Press, 1983). Although these accounts of values are metaphysically diverse, they nevertheless satisfy what I call the minimum conditions for being intrinsic values.
7. See for example the Routleys' arguments against human chauvinism in "Against the Inevitability of Human Chauvinism."
8. One might distinguish between being decidable in principle and being decidable in practice. For example, hedonistic utilitarianism might satisfy "in principle" decidability because it gives us a formula for determining what we should do (in terms of the net balance of pleasure and pain). However, in practice it may be impossible to apply this formula, and if this is so, then hedonistic utilitarianism gives us no way in practice of determining what we ought to do. It is undecidability in practice with which I am concerned here.
9. Taylor, *Respect for Nature,* p. 129.
10. Ibid., p. 66.
11. Taylor's strategy is, first, to persuade us that nonsentient organisms have a good of their own, and thus are plausible candidates for having what he calls an *inherent worth,* and, second, to argue that if we adopt a biocentric outlook (which includes accepting the argument against the superiority of human beings and sentient creatures criticized above), we will then believe that they do indeed have inherent worth.

12. Routley and Routley, "Human Chauvinism and Environmental Ethics," p. 170.
13. In Richard Sylvan, "Critique of Deep Ecology," *Radical Philosophy* no. 40 (1984): 2–12, and no. 41 (1985): 1–22, Richard Sylvan (Routley) does suggest that natural systems are not the only things which satisfy his criterion of value. However, he does not attempt to say exactly what satisfies.
14. Rolston's *Environmental Ethics,* chap. 7.
15. Peter Singer in *Expanding Circle* (Oxford: Clarendon Press, 1981) also insists that distinction between sentient and nonsentient creatures is not an arbitrary one from a moral point of view. He stresses the importance of creatures being capable of feeling pleasure or pain, whereas I emphasize the importance of their having a point of view. Whether this difference makes a difference to the content of an ethic is not something I can explore here.
16. I argue in more detail for this position in "Preservation of Wilderness and the Good Life," in Elliot and Gare, *Environmental Philosophy.*

Journal/Discussion Questions

1. Thompson discusses what she calls the analogical approach in environmental ethics. What does she mean by this? What does she see as its shortcomings? Do you agree? Discuss.
2. Thompson suggests that, "It is puzzling that an ethic which purports to find objective value in nature should be so concerned about what states of affairs human beings bring about." What does she mean by this? Do you agree?
3. Environmental ethics, Thompson maintains, wants to condemn unnecessary human interventions in nature. Is this description of environmental ethics accurate? Why, in Thompson's eyes, is this a shortcoming? Do you agree?

Holmes Rolston, III
"Challenges in Environmental Ethics"*

Holmes Rolston III is University Distinguished Professor at Colorado State University. Rolston's research covers a variety of areas but he is especially known for his work in environmental ethics, including Philosophy Gone Wild, Environmental Ethics, *and* Conserving Natural Value. *He is also a cofounder and associate editor of the* Journal of Environmental Ethics *and founding past-president of the International Society of Environmental Ethics. Rolston is also a backpacker, a field naturalist, and a bryologist.*

Rolston presents a biocentric view of environmental ethics, arguing that all living things are intrinsically valuable. He argues, however, that this is a matter of degree, with sentient beings having more intrinsic value

*This essay was originally prepared for an American Philosophical Association symposium on Rolston's *Environmental Ethics.* A revised version appears in *Ecology, Economics, Ethics: The Broken Circle* (New Haven: Yale University Press, 1991).

than plants and nonsentient animals, and with self-conscious rational animals (human beings) having more intrinsic value than those which are not self-conscious. He also accords a special value to species and to ecosystems.

As You Read, Consider This:

1. What, according to Rolston, does environmental ethics teach us about ethics in general?
2. What, according to Rolston, is radically wrong with anthropencentric value?

Ethicists had settled on at least one conclusion as ethics became modern in Darwin's century: that the moral has nothing to do with the natural. To argue otherwise commits the naturalistic fallacy, moving without justification from what *is* in nature *ought to be* in culture. Science describes natural history, natural law; ethics prescribes human conduct, moral law; and to confuse the two makes a category mistake. Nature simply *is,* without objective value; the preferences of human subjects establish value; and these human values, appropriately considered, generate human duties. Only humans are ethical subjects and only humans are ethical objects. Nature is amoral; the moral community is interhuman.

In the last third of this century, unsettled as we enter the next millennium, there is foreboding revolution. Only the human species contains moral agents, but perhaps conscience on such an earth ought not be used to exempt every other form of life from consideration, with the resulting paradox that the sole moral species acts only in its collective self-interest toward all the rest. There is something overspecialized about an ethic, held by the dominant class of *Homo sapiens,* that regards the welfare of only one of several million species as an object and beneficiary of duty. We need an interspecific ethics. Whatever ought to be in culture, this biological world that *is* also *ought to be;* we must argue from the natural to the moral.

If this requires a paradigm change about the sorts of things to which duty can attach, so much the worse for those humanistic ethics no longer functioning in, nor suited to, their changing environment. The anthropocentrism associated with them was fiction anyway. There is something Newtonian, not yet Einsteinian, besides something morally naive, about living in a reference frame where one species takes itself as absolute and values everything else relative to its utility. If trite to their specific epithet, ought not *Homo sapiens* value this host of life as something with a claim to care in its own right? Man may be the only measurer of things, but is man the only measure of things? The challenge of environmental ethics is a principled attempt to redefine the boundaries of ethical obligation.

Still there is the sense of anomaly that forebodes paradigm overthrow. An ecological conscience? Sometimes this seems to be a category mistake, joining a scientific adjective with an ethical noun, rather like Christian biochemistry mismatches a religious adjective and a scientific noun. With analysis, we suspect that the relation is three-place. Person A has a duty to person B concerning the environment C, and no one has ever denied that natural things have instrumental value to humans. Humans are helped or hurt by the condition of their environment, and we have duties to humans that concern their valuable environment, an environment they are able to value. So conservatives may shrink back into the persistent refusal of philosophers to think biologically, to naturalize ethics in the deep sense. They will fear that it is logically incoherent to suppose there is a nonanthropogenic value, or that this is too metaphysically speculative ever to be operational and that it does not make any pragmatic difference anyway, claiming that an adequate environmental ethic can be anthropogenic, even anthropocentric.

When we face up to the crisis, however, we undergo a more direct moral encounter. Environmental ethics is not a muddle; it is an invitation to moral development. All ethics seeks an appropriate respect for life, but respect for human life is only a subset of respect for all life. What ethics is about, in the end, is seeing outside your own sector of self-interest, of class interest. A comprehensive ethic will find values in and duties to the natural world. The vitality of ethics depends on our knowing what is really vital, and there will be found the intersection of value and duty. An ecological conscience requires an unprecedented mix of science and conscience, of biology and ethics.

1. Higher Animals

We have direct encounters with life that has eyes, at least where our gaze is returned by something that itself has a concerned outlook. The relation is two-place: I-thou, subject to subject. Compared with concern about soil and water, which are instrumentally vital but blind, when we meet the higher animals there is somebody there behind the fur and feathers. "The environment" is external to us all, but where there is inwardness in this environment, perhaps we ought to be conscious of other consciousness. Whatever matters to animals, matters morally.

Wild animals defend their own lives, because they have a good of their own. Animals hunt and howl, seek shelter, build nests and sing, care for their young, flee from threats, grow hungry, thirsty, hot, tired, excited, sleepy, seek out their habitats and mates. They suffer injury and lick their wounds. They can know security and fear, endurance and fatigue, comfort and pain. When they figure out their helps and hurts in the environment, they do not make man the measure of things at all; more, man is not the only measurer of things.

Still, man is the only moral measurer of things, and how should he count these wild, nonmoral things? One might expect classical ethics to have sifted well an ethics for animals. Our ancestors did not think about endangered species, ecosystems, acid rain, or the ozone layer, but they lived in closer association with wild and domestic animals than do we. Nevertheless, until recently, the scientific, humanistic centuries since the so-called Enlightenment have not been sensitive ones for animals. Animals were mindless, living matter; biology was mechanistic. Even psychology, rather than defending animal experience, was behaviorist. Philosophy, as we have already said, thought man the measure of things. Across several centuries of hard science and humanist ethics there has been little compassion for animals. We eat millions of them every year and we use many millions more in industry and research, as though little matters unless it matters to humans.

So far as we got ethically, we rather oddly said that we should be humane toward nonhuman animals. "The question is not," said Bentham, "Can they reason, nor Can they talk? but, Can they suffer?" These nonhumans do not share with humans the capacity to reason or talk, but they do share the capacity to suffer, and human ethics can be extended so far forth to our animal cousins. We may be unsure about insects and fish, but at least we will need an avian and a mammal ethics.

The progress of recent science itself has increasingly smeared the human-nonhuman boundary line. Animal anatomy, biochemistry, perception, cognition, experience, behavior, and evolutionary history are kin to our own. Animals have no immortal souls, but then persons may not either, or beings with souls may not be the only kind that count morally. Ethical progress further smeared the boundary. Sensual pleasures are a good thing, ethics should be egalitarian nonarbitrary, nondiscriminatory. There are ample scientific grounds that animals enjoy pleasures and suffer pains; and ethically no grounds to value these in humans and not in animals. The *is* in nature and the *ought* in ethics are not so far apart after all. We should treat animals humanely, that is, treat animals equally with ourselves where they have equal interests.

Recently, then, there has been a vigorous reassessment of human duties to sentient life. More has been written on this subject in the past fifteen years than in the previous fifteen centuries. The world cheered in the fall of 1988 when humans rescued two whales from the winter ice. A sign in Rocky Mountain National Park enjoins humans not to harass bighorn sheep: "Respect their right to life." We have passed animal welfare legislation and set up animal care committees in our universities. We have made a vital breakthrough past humans, and the first lesson in environmental ethics has been learned.

But the risk of ethical inadequacy here lies in a moral extension that expands rights as far as mammals and not much further, a psychologically based ethic that counts only felt experience. We respect life in our nonhuman but near-human animal cousins, a semi-anthropic and still quite subjective ethics. Justice remains a concern for just-us subjects. Extending our human ethics, we say that the sheep, too, have rights and that we should be humane to the whales. There has, in fact, not been much theoretical breakthrough, no paradigm shift. We do not yet have a biologically based ethics.

We certainly need an ethic for animals, but that is only one level of concern in a comprehensive environmental ethics. When we try to use culturally extended rights and psychologically based utilities to protect the flora or even the insentient fauna, to protect endangered species or ecosystems, we can only stammer. Indeed, we get lost trying to protect bighorns, because in the wild the cougar is not respecting the rights or utilities of the sheep she slays. There are no rights in the wild, and nature is indifferent to the welfare of particular animals. Further, in culture, humans slay sheep and eat them regularly, while humans have every right not to be eaten by either humans or cougars.

A bison fell through the ice into a river in Yellowstone Park; the environmental ethic there, letting nature take its course, forbade would-be rescuers from either saving or mercy killing the suffering animal. A drowning human would have been saved at once. It was as vital to the struggling bison as to any human to get out; the poor thing froze to death that night. Was the Yellowstone ethic callous to life, inhumane? Or had it other vitalities to consider? This ethic seems rather to have concluded that a moral extension is too nondiscriminating; we are unable to separate an ethics for humans from an ethics for wildlife. To treat wild animals with compassion learned in culture does not appreciate their wildness.

Man, said Socrates, is the political animal; humans maximally are what they are in culture, where the natural selection pressures (impressively productive in ecosystems) are relaxed without detriment to the species *Homo sapiens,* and indeed with great benefit to its member persons. Wild and even domestic animals cannot enter culture; they do not have that capacity. They cannot acquire language at sufficient levels to take part in culture; they cannot make their clothing, or build fires, much less read books or receive an education.

Worse, cultural protection can work to their detriment; with too much human or humane care their wildness is made over into a human artifact. A cow does not have the integrity of a deer, a poodle that of a wolf. Culture is a good thing for humans, often a bad thing for animals. Culture does make a relevant ethical difference, and environmental ethics has different criteria from inter-human ethics.

Can they talk? and, Can they reason? indicating cultural capacities, are relevant questions, not just, Can they suffer? Compassionate respect for life in its suffering is only part of the analysis. Sometimes in an environmental ethic we do need to follow nature, and not so much to treat animals humanely, like we do humans, as to treat animals naturally, for what they are by themselves. Even when we treat them humanely within culture, part of the ethic may also involve treating them naturally.

"Equality" is a positive word in ethics, "discriminatory" a pejorative one. On the other hand, simplistic reduction is a failing in the philosophy of science and epistemology; to be "discriminating" is desirable in logic and value theory. Something about treating humans as equals with bighorns and cougars seems to "reduce" humans to merely animal levels of value, a "no more" counterpart in ethics of the "nothing but" fallacy often met in science. Humans are "nothing but" naked apes. Something about treating sheep and cougars as the equals of humans seems to elevate them unnaturally, unable to value them for what they are. There is something insufficiently discriminating in such judgments—species blind in a bad sense, blind to the real differences between species, valuational differences that do count morally. To the contrary, a discriminating ethicist will insist on preserving the differing richness of valuational complexity, wherever found.

Two tests of discrimination are pain and diet. It might be thought that pain is a bad thing, whether in nature or culture. Perhaps when dealing with humans in culture, additional levels of value and utility must be protected by conferring rights that do not exist in the wild, but meanwhile at least we should minimize animal suffering. That is indeed a worthy imperative in culture where animals are removed from nature and bred, but it may be misguided where animals remain in ecosystems. When the bighorn sheep of Yellowstone caught pinkeye—blinded, injured, and starving in result—300 bighorns, over half the herd, perished. Wildlife veterinarians wanted to treat the disease, as they would have in any domestic herd, and as they did with Colorado bighorns infected with an introduced lungworm, but the Yellowstone ethicists left them to suffer, seemingly not respecting their life. Had they no mercy? Was this again inhumane?

They knew rather that, while intrinsic pain is a bad thing whether in humans or in sheep, pain in ecosystems is instrumental pain, through which the sheep are naturally selected for a more satisfactory adaptive fit. Pain in a medically skilled culture is pointless, once the alarm to health is sounded, but pain operates functionally in bighorns in their niche, even after it becomes no longer in the interests of the pained individuals. To have interfered in the interests of the blinded sheep would have weakened the species. The question, Can they suffer? is not as simple as Bentham thought. What we *ought* to do depends on what *is*. The *is* of nature differs significantly from the *is* of culture, even when similar suffering is present in both.

Some ethicists will insist that at least in culture we can minimize animal pain, and that will constrain our diet. There is predation in nature; humans evolved as omnivores. But humans, the only moral animals, should refuse to participate in the meat-eating phase of their ecology, just as they refuse to live merely by the rules of natural selection. Humans do not look to the behavior of wild animals as an ethical guide in other matters (marriage, truth telling, promise keeping, justice, charity). There they do not follow nature. Why should they justify their dietary habits by watching what animals do?

But the difference is that these other matters are affairs of culture; these are person-to-person events, not events at all in spontaneous nature. By contrast, eating is omnipresent in wild nature; humans eat because they are in nature, not because they are in culture. Eating animals is not an event between persons, but is a human-to-animal event; and the rules for this come from the ecosystems in which humans evolved and which they have no duty to remake. We must eat to live; nature absolutely requires that. We evolved to eat as omnivores; that animal nature underruns over human nature. Even in culture meat eating is still relatively natural; there is nothing immoral about fitting into one's ecology. We follow nature, treat animals naturally, capture nutritional values, and learn our place in the scheme of life and death. This respects life, profoundly so. Humans, then, can model their dietary habits from their ecosystems, though they cannot and should not so model their interpersonal justice or charity. When eating they ought to minimize animal suffering, and they also may gladly affirm their ecology. The boundary between animals and humans has not been rubbed out after all; only what was a boundary line has been smeared into a boundary zone. We have discovered that animals count morally, though we are only beginning to solve the challenge of how to count them.

2. Organisms

In college zoology I did an experiment on nutrition in rats, to see how they grew with and without vitamins. When the experiment was completed, I was told to take the rats out and drown them. I felt squeamish but did it. In college botany I did an experiment on seedlings to test how they grew with this or that fertilizer. The experiment over, I threw out the seedlings without a second thought. While there can be ethics about sentient animals, after that perhaps ethics is over. Respect for life ends somewhere in zoology; it is not part of botany. No consciousness, no conscience. Without sentience, ethics is nonsense.

Or do we want an ethic that is more objective about life? In Yosemite National Park for almost a century humans entertained themselves by driving through a tunnel cut in a giant sequoia. Two decades ago the Wawona tree, weakened by the cut, blew down in a storm. People said: Cut us another drive—through sequoia. The Yosemite environmental ethic, deepening over the years, said no! You ought not to mutilate majestic sequoias for amusement. Respect their life! Indeed, some ethicists count the value of redwoods so highly that they will spike redwoods, lest they be cut. In the Rawah Wilderness in alpine Colorado, old signs read, "Please leave the flowers for others to enjoy" When they rotted out, the new signs urged a less humanist ethic: "Let the flowers live!"

But trees and flowers cannot care, so why should we? We are not considering animals that are close kin, nor can they suffer or experience anything. There are no humane societies for plants. Plants are not valuers with preferences that can be satisfied or frustrated. It seems odd to claim that plants need our sympathy, odd to ask that we should consider their point of view. They have no subjective life, only objective life.

Fishermen in Atlantic coastal estuaries and hays toss beer bottles overboard, a convenient way to dispose of trash. On the bottom, small crabs, attracted by the residual beer, make their way inside the bottles and become trapped, unable to get enough foothold on the slick glass neck to work their way out. They starve slowly. Then one dead crab becomes bait for the next victim, an indefinitely resetting trap! Are those bottle traps of ethical concern, after fishermen have been warned about this effect? Or is the whole thing out of sight, out of mind, with crabs too mindless to care about? Should sensitive fishermen pack their bottle trash back to shore—whether or not crabs have much, or any, felt experience?

Flowers and sequoias live; they ought to live. Crabs have value out of sight, out of mind. Afraid of the naturalistic fallacy, conservative ethicists will say that people should enjoy letting flowers live or that it is silly to cut drive-through sequoias, aesthetically more excellent for humans to appreciate both for what they are. The crabs are out of sight, but not really out of mind; humans value them at a distance. But these ethically conservative reasons really do not understand what biological conservation is in the deepest sense. Nothing matters to a tree, but much is *vital.*

An organism is a spontaneous, self-maintaining system, sustaining and reproducing itself, executing its program, making a way through the world, checking against performance by means of responsive capacities with which to measure success. It can reckon with vicissitudes, opportunities, and adversities that the world presents. Something more than physical causes, even when less than sentience, is operating within every organism. There is *information* super-intending the causes; without it the organism would collapse into a sand heap. This information is a modern equivalent of what Aristotle called formal and final causes; it gives the organism a *telos,* "end," a kind of (non-felt) goal. Organisms have ends, although not always ends-in-view.

All this cargo is carried by the DNA, essentially a *linguistic* molecule. By a serial "reading" of the DNA, a polypeptide chain is synthesized, such that its sequential structure determines the bioform into which it will fold. Ever-lengthening chains (like ever-longer sentences), are organized into genes (like paragraphs and chapters). Diverse proteins, lipids, carbohydrates, enzymes—all the life structures are "written into" the genetic library. The DNA is thus a *logical set,* not less than a biological set, informed as well as formed. Organisms use a sort of symbolic logic, use these molecular shapes as symbols of life. The novel resourcefulness lies in the epistemic content conserved, developed, and thrown forward to make biological resources out of the physicochemical cause and effect system, and partly something more: partly a historical information system discovering and evaluating ends so as to map and make a way through the world, partly a system of significances attached to operations, pursuits, resources. In this sense, the genome is a set of *conservation* molecules.

The genetic set is really a *propositional set*—to choose a provocative term—recalling how the Latin *proposition* is an assertion, a set task, a theme, a plan, a proposal, a project, as well as a cognitive statement. From this it is also a motivational set, unlike human books, since these life motifs are set to drive the movement from genotypic potential to phenotypic expression. Given a chance, these molecules seek organic self-expression. They thus proclaim a life way, and with this an organism, unlike an inert rock, claims the environment as source and sink, from which to abstract energy and materials and into which to excrete them. It "takes advantage" of its environment, life thus arises out of earthen sources (as do rocks), but life turns back on its sources to make resources out of them (unlike rocks). An acorn becomes an oak; the oak stands on its own.

So far we have only description. We begin to pass to value when we recognize that the genetic set is a *normative set;* it distinguishes between what *is* and what *ought to be.* This does not mean that the organism is a moral system, for there are no moral agents in nature; but the organism is an axiological, evaluative system. So the oak grows, reproduces, repairs its wounds, and resists death. The physical state that the organism seeks, idealized in its programmatic form, is a valued state. *Value* is present in this achievement. *Vital* seems a better word for it than *biological.* We are not dealing simply with an individual defending its solitary life but with an individual having situated fitness in an ecosystem. Still, we want to affirm that the living individual, taken as a "point experience" in the web of interconnected life, is *per se* an intrinsic value.

A life is defended for what it is in itself, without necessary further contributory reference, although, given the structure of all ecosystems, such lives necessarily do have further reference. The organism has something it is conserving, something for which it is standing: its life. Organisms have their own standards, fit into their niche though they must. They promote their own realization, at the same time that they track an environment. They have a technique, a know-how. Every organism has a *good-of-its-kind;* it defends its own kind as a *good kind.* In that sense, as soon as one knows what a giant sequoia tree is, one knows the biological identity that is sought and conserved. Man is neither the measurer nor the measure of things; value is not anthropogenic, it is biogenic.

There seems no reason why such own-standing normative organisms are not morally significant. A moral agent deciding his or her behavior, ought to take account of the consequences for other evaluative systems. This does not follow nature, if we mean by that to imitate ethical agents there, for nature is amoral. But it does follow nature, if we mean by that we respect these amoral organic norms as we shape our conduct. Such an ethic will be teleological, I suppose, since it values the *telos* in organisms, but it seems equally deontological, since it owes (Gk: *deont-*) respect for life in itself, intrinsically, and not just instrumentally, consequentially. (Frankly, the classical teleological/deontological distinction seems as troublesome as helpful in moral analysis here.)

Within the community of moral agents one has not merely to ask whether X is a normative system, but, since the norms are a personal option, to judge the norm and the consequences. But within the biotic community organisms are amoral normative systems, and there are no cases where an organism seeks a good of its own that is morally reprehensible. The distinction between having a good of its kind and being a good kind vanishes, so far as any faulting of the organism is concerned. To this extent, everything with a good of its kind is a good kind and thereby has intrinsic value.

One might say that an organism is a bad organism if, during the course of pressing its normative expression, it upsets the ecosystem or causes widespread disease, bad consequences. Remember though, that an organism cannot be a good kind without situated environmental fitness. By natural selection the kind of goods to which it is genetically programmed must mesh with its ecosystemic role. Despite the ecosystem as a perpetual contest of goods in dialectic and exchange, it is difficult to say that any organism is a bad kind in this instrumental sense either. The misfits are extinct, or soon will be. In spontaneous nature any species that preys upon, parasitizes, competes with, or crowds another will be a bad kind from the narrow perspective of its victim or competitor.

But if we enlarge that perspective it typically becomes difficult to say that any species is a bad kind overall in the ecosystem. An "enemy" may even be good for the "victimized" species, though harmful to individual members of it, as when predation keeps the deer herd healthy. Beyond this, the "bad kinds" typically play useful roles in population control, in symbiotic relationships, or in providing opportunities for other species. The *Chlamydia* microbe is a bad kind from the perspective of the bighorns, but when one thing dies, something else lives. After the pinkeye outbreak, the golden eagle population in Yellowstone flourished, preying on the bighorn carcasses. For them *Chlamydia* is a good kind instrumentally.

Some biologist-philosophers will say that, even though an organism evolves to have a situated environmental fitness, not all such situations are good arrangements; some can be clumsy or bad. True, the vicissitudes of historical evolution do sometimes result in ecological webs that are sub-optimal solutions, within the biologically limited possibilities and powers of interacting organisms. Still, such systems have been selected over millennia for functional stability; and at least the burden of proof is on a human evaluator to say why any natural kind is a bad kind and ought not to call forth admiring respect. Something may be a good kind intrinsically but a bad kind instrumentally in the system; these will be anomalous cases, however, with selection pressures against them. These claims about good kinds do not say that things are perfect kinds, or that there can be no better ones, only that natural kinds are good kinds until proven otherwise.

What is almost invariably meant by a "bad" kind is that an organism is instrumentally bad when judged from the viewpoint of human interests, of humane interests. "Bad" so used is an anthropocentric word; there is nothing at all biological or ecological about it, and so it has no force evaluating objective nature, however much humanist force it may sometimes have.

A really *vital* ethic respects all life, not just animal pains and pleasures, much less just human preferences. In the Rawah, the old signs, "Leave the flowers for others to enjoy," were application signs using an old, ethically conservative, humanistic ethic. The new ones invite a change of reference frame—a wilder, more logical because more biological ethic, a radical ethic that goes down to the roots of life, that really is conservative because it understands biological conservation at depths. What the injunction, "Let the flowers live!" means is: "Daisies, marsh-marigolds, geraniums, larkspurs are evaluative systems that conserve goods of their kind, and, in the absence of evidence to the contrary, are good kinds. There are trails here by which you may enjoy these flowers. Is there any reason why your human interests should not also conserve these good kinds?" A drive-through sequoia causes no suffering; it is not cruel, but it is callous and insensitive to the wonder of life. The ethically conservative will complain that we have committed the naturalistic fallacy; rather, we invite a radical commitment to respect all life.

3. Species

Certain rare species of butterflies occur in hummocks (slightly elevated forested ground) on the African grasslands. It was formerly the practice of unscrupulous collectors to go in, collect a few hundred specimens, and then burn out the hummock with the intention of destroying the species, thereby driving up the price of their collections. I find myself persuaded that they morally ought not do this. Nor will the reason resolve into the evil of greed, but it remains the needless destruction of a butterfly species.

This conviction remains even when the human goods are more worthy. Coloradans are considering whether to build the Two Forks Dam to supply urban Denver with water. This would require destroying a canyon and altering the Platte River flow, with many negative environmental consequences, including endangering a butterfly, the Pawnee montane skipper, *Hesperia leonardus montana,* as well as endangering the whooping crane downstream. I doubt whether the good of humans who wish more water for development, both for industry and for bluegrass lawns, warrants endangering species of butterflies and cranes.

Sometimes the stakes are alleged to rise even higher. The Bay checkerspot, *Euphydryas editha bayensis,* proposed to be listed as an endangered species, inhabits peripheral tracts of a large facility on which United Technologies Corporation, a missile contractor, builds and tests Minuteman and Tomahawk propulsion systems. The giant defense contractor has challenged the proposed listing and thinks it airy and frivolous that a butterfly should slow the delivery of warhead missile propulsion systems, and so went ahead and dug a water pipeline through a butterfly patch. They operated out of the classical ethics that says that butterflies do not count but that the defense of humans does.

But a more radical, environmental ethics demurs. The good of humans might override the good of butterfly species but the case must be argued. Lest this seem the foolishness of a maverick philosopher, I point out that such conviction has been written into national law. The Endangered Species Act requires that the case must be argued before a high level "God" committee.

A species exists; a species ought to exist. Environmental ethics must make both claims and move from biology to ethics with care. Species exist only instantiated in individuals, yet are as real as individual plants or animals. The claim that there are specific forms of life historically maintained in their environments over time seems as certain as anything else we believe about the empirical world. At times biologists revise the theories and taxa with which they map these forms, but species are not so much like lines of latitude and longitude as like mountains and rivers, phenomena objectively there to be mapped. The edges of these natural kinds will sometimes be fuzzy, to some extent discretionary. One species will slide into another over evolutionary time. But it does not follow from the fact that speciation is sometimes in progress that species are merely made up, not found as evolutionary lines with identity in time as well as space.

A consideration of species is revealing and challenging because it offers a biologically based counterexample to the focus on individuals—typically sentient and usually persons—so characteristic in classical ethics. In an evolutionary ecosystem, it is not mere individuality that counts, but the species is also significant because it is a dynamic life form maintained over time. The individual represents (re-presents) a species in each new generation. It is a token of a type, and the type is more important than the token.

A species lacks moral agency, reflective self-awareness, sentience, or organic individuality. The older, conservative ethic will be tempted to say that specific-level processes cannot count morally. Duties must attach to singular lives, most evidently those with a psychological self, or some analogue to this. In an individual organism, the organs report to a center; the good of a whole is defended. The members of a species report to no center. A species has no self. It is not a bounded singular. There is no analogue to the nervous hookups or circulatory flows that characterize the organism.

But singularity, centeredness, selfhood, individuality, are not the only processes to which duty attaches. A more radically conservative ethic knows that having a biological identity reasserted genetically over time is as true of the species as of the individual. Identity need not attach solely to the centered organism; it can persist as a discrete pattern over time. Thinking this way, the life that the individual has is something passing through the individual as much as something it intrinsically possesses. The individual is subordinate to the species, not the other way around. The genetic set, in which is coded the *telos,* is as evidently the property of the species as of the individual through which it passes. A consideration of species strains any ethic fixed on individual organisms, much less on sentience or persons. But the result can be biologically sound even though it revises what was formerly thought logically permissible or ethically binding. This is a higher teleological ethic, finding now the specific *telos,* and concerned about consequences at that level; again, it is deontological, duty bound to the dynamic form of life for what it is in itself.

The species line is the *vital* living system, the whole, of which individual organisms are the essential parts. The species too has its integrity, its individuality, its "right to life" (if we must use the rhetoric of rights); and it is more important to protect this vitality than to protect individual integrity. The right to life, biologically speaking, is an adaptive fit that is right for life, that survives over millennia, and this generates at least a presumption that species in niche are good right where they are, and therefore that it is right for humans to let them be, to let them evolve.

Processes of value that we earlier found in an organic individual reappear at the specific level: defending a particular form of life, pursuing a pathway through the world, resisting death (extinction), regeneration maintaining a normative identity over time, creative resilience discovering survival skills. It is as logical to say that the individual is the species' way of propagating itself as to say that the embryo or egg is the individual's way of propagating itself. The dignity resides in the dynamic form; the individual inherits this, exemplifies it, and passes it on. If, at the specific level, these processes are just as evident, or even more so, what prevents duties arising at that level? The appropriate survival unit is the appropriate level of moral concern. This would be following nature specifically.

Sensitivity to this level, however, can sometimes make an environmental ethicist seem callous. On San Clemente Island, the U.S. Fish and Wildlife Service and the California Department of Fish and Game planned to shoot 2,000 feral goats to save three endangered plant species, *Malacothamnus clementinus, Castilleja grisea, Delphinium kinkiense,* of which the surviving individuals numbered only a few dozens. After a protest, some goats were trapped and relocated. But trapping all was impossible and many hundreds were killed. Is it inhumane to count plant species more than mammal lives, a few plants more than a thousand goats?

Those who wish to restore rare species of big cats to the wilds have asked about killing genetically inbred, inferior cats, presently held in zoos, in order to make space available for the cats needed to reconstruct and maintain a population genetically more likely to survive upon release. All the Siberian tigers in zoos in North America are descendants of seven animals; if these were replaced by others nearer to the wild type and with more genetic variability, the species could be saved in the wild. When we move to the level of species, we may kill individuals for the good of their kind.

Or we may now refuse to let nature take its course. The Yellowstone ethicists let the bison drown, callous to its suffering; they let the blinded bighorns die. But in the spring of 1984 a sow grizzly and her three cubs walked across the ice of Yellowstone Lake to Frank Island, two miles from shore. They stayed several days to feast on two elk carcasses, when the ice bridge melted. Soon afterward, they were starving on an island too small to support them. This time the Yellowstone ethicists promptly rescued the grizzlies and released them on the mainland, in order to protect an endangered species. They were not rescuing individual bears so much as saving the species. They thought that humans had already and elsewhere imperiled the grizzly, and that they ought to save this form of life.

Humans have more understanding than ever of the natural world they inhabit, of the speciating processes, more predictive power to foresee the intended and unintended results of their actions, and more power to reverse the undesirable consequences. The duties that such power and vision generate no longer attach simply to individuals or persons but are emerging duties to specific forms of life. The wrong that humans are doing, or allowing to happen through carelessness, is stopping the historical vitality of life, the flow of natural kinds.

Every extinction is an incremental decay in this stopping life, no small thing. Every extinction is a kind of superkilling. It kills forms (*species*), beyond individuals. It kills "essences" beyond "existences," the "soul" as well as the "body." It kills collectively, not just distributively. It kills birth as well as death. Afterward nothing of that kind either lives or dies. A shutdown of the life stream is the most destructive event possible. Never before has this level of question—superkilling by a superkiller—been deliberately faced. What is ethically callous is the malestrom of killing and insensitivity to forms of life and the sources producing them. What is required is principled responsibility to the biospheric earth.

Several billion years' worth of creative toil, several million species of teeming life, have been handed over to the care of this late-coming species in which mind has flowered and morals have emerged. Life on earth is a many splendored thing; extinction dims its luster. If, in this world of uncertain moral convictions, it makes any sense to claim that one ought not to kill individuals, without justification, it makes more sense to claim that one ought not to superkill the species, without superjustification. That moves from what *is* to what *ought to be;* and the fallacy is not committed by naturalists who so argue but by humanists who cannot draw these conclusions.

4. Ecosystems

"A thing is right," urged Aldo Leopold, concluding his land ethic, "when it tends to preserve the integrity, stability, and beauty of the biotic community; it is wrong when it tends otherwise." Again, we have two parts to the ethic: first that ecosystems exist, both in the wild and in support of culture; secondly that ecosystems ought to exist, both for what they are in themselves and as modified by culture. Again, we must move with care from the biological claims to the ethical claims.

Classical, humanistic ethics finds ecosystems unfamiliar territory. It is difficult to get the biology right, and, superimposed on the biology, to get the ethics right. Fortunately, it is often evident that human welfare depends on ecosystemic support, and in this sense all our legislation about clean air, clean water, soil conservation, national and state forest policy, pollution controls, oil spills, renewable resources, and so forth is concerned about ecosystem level processes. Further, humans find much of value for themselves in preserving wild ecosystems and our wilderness and park system is accordingly ecosystem oriented.

Still, a comprehensive environmental ethics needs the best, naturalistic reasons, as well as the good, humanistic ones, for respecting ecosystems. The ecosystem is the community of life; in it the fauna and flora, the species have entwined destinies. Ecosystems generate and support life, keep selection pressures high, enrich situated fitness, evolve congruent kinds in their places with sufficient containment. The ecologist finds that ecosystems are objectively satisfactory communities in the sense that organismic needs are sufficiently met for species long to survive, and the critical ethicist finds (in a subjective judgment matching the objective process) that such ecosystems are satisfactory communities to which to attach duty. Our concern must be for the fundamental unit of survival.

Giant forest fires raged over Yellowstone National Park in the summer of 1988, consuming nearly a million acres, despite the efforts of a thousand firefighters. By far the largest fires ever known in the park, the fires seemed a disaster. But the Yellowstone land ethic enjoins: Let nature take its course. Let it burn! So the fires were not fought at first, but in midsummer national authorities overrode that policy and ordered the fires put out. Even then, weeks later, fires continued to burn, partly because they were too big to control, but partly, too, because Yellowstone personnel did not altogether want the fires put out. Despite the evident destruction of trees, shrubs, and wildlife, they believe that fires are a good thing. Fires reset succession, release nutrients, recycle materials, renew the biotic community. (Nearby, in the Teton wilderness, a storm blew down 15,000 acres of trees, and some proposed that the area be declassified as wilderness for commercial salvage of the timber. But a similar environmental ethics said: No, let it rot.)

Aspen are important in the Yellowstone ecosystem. While some aspen stands are climax and self-renewing, many are seral and give way to conifers. Aspen groves support many birds and much wildlife, especially the beavers, whose activities maintain the riparian zones. Aspen are rejuvenated after fires, and the Yellowstone land ethic wants the aspen for its critical role in the biotic community. Elk browse the young aspen stems. To a degree this is a good thing, since it gives elk critical nitrogen, but in excess it is a bad thing. The elk have no predators, since the wolves are gone, and as a result they overpopulate. Excess elk also destroy the willows and this in turn destroys the beavers. Rejuvenating the aspen might require managers to cull hundreds of elk—all for the sake of a healthy ecosystem.

The Yellowstone ethic wishes to restore wolves to the greater Yellowstone ecosystem. At the level of species, this is partly for what the wolf is in itself, but it is partly because the greater Yellowstone ecosystem does not have its full integrity, stability, and beauty without this majestic animal at the top of the trophic pyramid. Restoring the wolf as a top predator would mean suffering and death for many elk, but that would be a good thing for the aspen and willows, for the beavers and riparian habitat, with mixed benefits for the bighorns and mule deer, whose food the over-populating elk consume, but who would also be consumed by the wolves. The Yellowstone ethic demands wolves, as it does fires, in appropriate respect for life in its ecosystem.

Letting nature take its ecosystemic course is why the Yellowstone ethic forbade rescuing the drowning bison, but rescued the sow grizzly with her cubs, the latter to insure that the big predators remain. After the bison drowned, coyotes and magpies, foxes and ravens fed on the carcass. Later, even a grizzly bear fed on it. All this is a good thing because the system cycles on. On that account rescuing the whales trapped in the winter ice seems less of a good thing, when we note that rescuers had to drive away polar bears that attempted to eat the dying whales.

An ecosystem, the conservative ethicist will say, is too low a level of organization to be respected intrinsically. Ecosystems can seem little more than random, statistical processes. A forest can seem a loose collection of externally related parts, the collection of fauna and flora a jumble, hardly a community. The plants and animals within an ecosystem have needs, but their interplay can seem simply a matter of distribution and abundance, birth rates and death rates, population densities, parasitism and predation, dispersion, cheeks and balances, stochastic process. Much is not organic at all (rain, groundwater, rocks, soil particles, air), while some organic material is dead and decaying debris (fallen trees, scat, humus). These things have no organized needs. There is only catch-as-catch-can scrimmage for nutrients and energy—a game played with loaded dice, not really enough integrated process to call the whole a community.

Unlike higher animals, ecosystems have no experiences; they do not and cannot care. Unlike plants, an ecosystem has no organized center; no genome. It does not defend itself against injury or death. Unlike a species, there is no ongoing *telos,* no biological identity reinstantiated over time. The organismic parts are more complex than the community whole. More troublesome still, an ecosystem can seem a jungle where the fittest survive, a place of contest and conflict, beside which the organism is a model of cooperation. In animals, the heart, liver, muscles and brain are tightly integrated, as are the leaves, cambium, and roots in plants. But the ecosystem community is pushing and shoving between rivals, each aggrandizing itself or else indifference and haphazard juxtaposition, nothing to call forth our admiration.

Environmental ethics must break through the boundary posted by disoriented ontological conservatives, who hold that only organisms are "real," actually existing as entities, whereas ecosystems are nominal—just interacting individuals. Oak trees are real but forests are nothing but collections of trees. But any level is real if it shapes behavior on the level below it. Thus the cell is real because that pattern shapes the behavior of amino acids; the organism because that pattern coordinates the behavior of hearts and lungs. The biotic community is real because the niche shapes the morphology of the oak trees within it. Being real at the level of community only requires an organization that shapes the behavior of its members.

The challenge is to find a clear model of community and to discover an ethics for it—better biology for better ethics. Even before the rise of ecology, biologists began to conclude that the combative survival of the fittest distorts the truth. The more perceptive model is coaction in adapted fit. Predator and prey, parasite and host, grazer and grazed are contending forces in dynamic process where the well-being of each is bound up with the other—coordinated (orders that couple together) as much as heart and liver are coordinated organically. The ecosystem supplies the coordinates through which each organism moves, outside which the species cannot really be located. A species is what it is where it is.

The community connections are looser than the organism's internal interconnections—but not less significant. Admiring organic unity in organisms and stumbling over environmental looseness is like valuing mountains and despising valleys. The matrix the organism requires in order to survive is the open, pluralistic ecology. Internal complexity—heart, liver, muscles, brain—arises as a way of dealing with a complex, tricky environment. The skin-out processes are not just the support, they are the subtle source of the skin-in processes. In the complete picture, the outside is as *vital* as the inside. Had there been either simplicity or lock-step concentrated unity in the environment, no organismic unity could have evolved. Nor would it remain. There would be less elegance in life.

To look at one level for what is appropriate at another makes a categorical mistake. One should not look for a single center or program in ecosystems, much less for subjective experiences. Instead, one should look for a matrix, for interconnections between centers (individual plants and animals, dynamic lines of speciation), for creative stimulus and open-ended potential. Everything will be connected to many other things, sometimes by obligate associations, more often by partial and pliable dependencies and, among other things, there will be no significant interactions. There will be functions in a communal sense: shunts and criss-crossing pathways, cybernetic subsystems, and feedback loops. An order arises spontaneously and systematically when many self-concerned units jostle and seek their own programs, each doing their own thing and forced into informed interaction.

An ecosystem is a productive, projective system. Organisms defend only their selves, with individuals defending their continuing survival and species increasing the numbers of kinds. But the evolutionary ecosystem spins a bigger story, limiting each kind, locking it into the welfare of others, promoting new arrivals, bringing forth kinds and the integration of kinds. Species *increase their kind;* but ecosystems *increase kinds,* superimposing the latter increase onto the former. *Ecosystems are selective systems, as surely as organisms are selective systems.* The natural selection comes out of the system and is imposed on the individual. The individual is programmed to make more of its kind, but more is going on systemically than that; the system is making more kinds.

This extends natural selection theory beyond the merely tautological formulation that the system selects the best adapted to survive. Ecosystems select for those features that appear over the long ranges, for individuality, for diversification, for sufficient containment, for quality supervening on quantity of life. They do this, appropriately to the community level, by employing conflict, decenteredness, probability, succession, spontaneous generation of order, and historicity. Communal processes—the competition between organisms, more or less probable events, plant and animal successions, speciation over historical time—generate an ever-richer community.

Hence the evolutionary toil, elaborating and diversifying the biota, that once began with no species and results today in five million species, increasing over time the quality of lives in the upper rungs of the tropic pyramids. One-celled organisms evolved into many-celled, highly integrated organisms. Photosynthesis evolved and came to support locomotion—swimming, walking, running, flight. Stimulus-response mechanisms became complex instinctive acts. Warm-blooded animals followed cold-blooded ones. Complex nervous systems, conditioned behavior and learning emerged. Sentience appeared—sight, hearing, smell, tastes, pleasure, pain. Brains coupled with hands. Consciousness and self-consciousness arose. Culture was superimposed on nature.

These developments do not take place in all ecosystems or at every level. Microbes, plants, and lower animals remain, good of their kinds, and serving continuing roles, good for other kinds. The understories remain occupied. As a result, the quantity of life and its diverse qualities continue—from protozoans to primates to people. There is a push-up, lock-up, ratchet effect that conserves the upstrokes and the outreaches. The later we go in time the more accelerated are the forms at the top of the tropic pyramids, the more elaborated are the multiple tropic pyramids of earth. There are upward arrows over evolutionary time.

The system is a game with loaded dice, but the loading is a prolife tendency, not mere stochastic process. Though there is no *nature* in the singular, the system has a nature, a loading that pluralizes, putting *natures* into diverse kinds, $nature_1$, $nature_2$, natures . . . $nature_n$. It does so using random elements (in both organisms and communities), but this is a secret of its fertility, producing steadily intensified interdependencies and options. An ecosystem has no head, but it has a "heading" for species diversification, support, and richness. Though not a superorganism, it is a kind of vital field.

Instrumental value uses something as a means to an end; *intrinsic value* is worthwhile in itself. No warbler eats insects to become food for a falcon; the warbler defends its own life as an end in itself and makes more warblers as it can. A life is defended intrinsically without further contributory reference. But neither of these traditional terms is satisfactory at the level of the ecosystem. Though it has value *in* itself, the system does not have any value *for* itself. Though a value producer, it is not a value owner. We are no longer confronting instrumental value, as though the system were of value instrumentally as a fountain of life. Nor is the question one of intrinsic value, as though the system defended some unified form of life for itself. We have reached something for which we need a third term: *systemic value*. Duties arise in an encounter with the system that projects and protects these member components in biotic community. If you like, that is an ethic that is teleological again, but since we are respecting both processes and products, perhaps a better word for it now is communitarian. We follow nature, this time ecologically.

Ethical conservatives, in the humanist sense, will say that ecosystems are of value only because they contribute to human experiences. But that mistakes the last chapter for the whole story, one fruit for the whole plant. Humans count enough to have the right to flourish there, but not so much that they have the right to degrade or shut down ecosystems, not at least without a burden of proof that there is an overriding cultural gain. Earlier, environmental ethics will say that ecosystems are of value because they contribute to animal experiences or to organismic life. Later, the deeper, more conservative and more radical view sees that the stability, integrity, and beauty of biotic communities are what are most fundamentally to be conserved.

5. Value Theory

In practice the ultimate challenge of environmental ethics is the conservation of life on earth. In principle the ultimate challenge is a value theory profound enough to support that ethic. We need an account of how nature carries value, and an ethics that appropriately respects those values. For subjectivists both the theory and the ethics will be nothing but human constructs; but objectivists in environmental ethics will use such theory to discover facts, how nature carries values, and from this sometimes there will follow what humans ought to do. The values that nature carries belong as much to the biology of natural history as to the psychology of human experience. Some of the values that nature carries are up to us, our assignment. But fundamentally there are powers in nature that move to us and through us. The splendors of earth do not simply lie in their roles as human resources, supports of culture, or stimulators of experience.

There is no value without an evaluator. So runs a well-entrenched dogma. Humans clearly evaluate their world; sentient animals may also. But plants cannot evaluate their environment; they have no options and make no choices. *A fortiori,* species and ecosystems, earth and nature cannot be bona fide evaluators. Value, like a tickle or remorse, must be felt to be there. Its *esse* is *percipi.* Nonsensed value is nonsense. There are no thoughts without a thinker, no percepts without a perceiver, no deeds without a doer, no targets without an aimer. Valuing is felt preferring; value is the product of this process.

If value arrives only with consciousness, experiences where humans find value then have to be dealt with as appearances of various sorts. The value has to be relocated in the valuing subject's creativity as a person meets a valueless world, or even a valuable one—one *able to be valued*—but which before the human bringing of value ability contains only possibility and not any actual value. Value can only be extrinsic to nature, never intrinsic to it. Nature offers but the standing possibility of valuation; value is not generated until humans appear with their valuing ability.

But the valuing subject in an otherwise valueless world is an insufficient premise for the experienced conclusions of those who respect all life. Conversion to a biological view seems truer to world experience and more logically compelling. Here the order of knowing reverses—and also enhances—the order of being. This, too, is a perspective, but ecologically better informed. Science has been steadily showing how the consequents (life, mind) are built on their precedents (energy, matter), however much they overleap them. Life and mind appear where they did not before exist, and with this levels of value emerge that did not before exist. But that gives no reason to say that all value is an irreducible emergent at the human (or upper animal) level. Nature does, of course, offer possibilities for human valuation, but the vitality of the system is not something that goes on in the human mind, nor is its value. The possibility of valuation is carried to us by evolutionary and ecological natural history, and such nature is already valuable before humans arrive to evaluate what is taking place.

How do we humans come to be charged up with values, if there was and is nothing in nature charging us up so? Some value is anthropogenic, generated by humans, but some is biogenic, in the natural genesis. A comprehensive environmental ethics reallocates value across the whole continuum. Value increases in the emergent climax, but is continuously present in the composing precedents. The system is *value-able, able* to produce *value*. Human evaluators are among its products. But when we value we must not forget our communal bonds. Sometimes we need to evaluate (appraise the worth of) what we ourselves may not value (personally prefer). Against the standard view that all value requires a beholder, some value requires only a holder, and some value is held within the historic system that carries value to and through individuals.

Here we do not want a subjective morality but an objective one, even though we find that subjectivity is the most valuable output of the objective system. Is there any reason for ethical subjects to discount the vital systemic processes unless and until accompanied by sentience? Perhaps to evaluate the entire biological world on the basis of sentience is as much a categorical mistake as to judge it according to whether justice and charity are found there. The one mistake judges biological places by extension from psychology, the other from culture. What is "right" about the biological world is not just the production of pleasures and positive experiences. What is "right" includes ecosystemic patterns, organisms in their generating, sustaining environments.

Some value depends on subjectivity, yet all value is generated within the geosystemic and ecosystemic community. Systemically, value fades from subjective to objective value, but also fans out from the individual to its role and matrix. Things do not have their separate natures merely in and for themselves, but they face outward and co-fit into broader natures. Value-in-itself is smeared out to become value-in-togetherness. Value seeps out into the system, and we lose our capacity to identify the individual as the sole locus of value.

Intrinsic value, that of an individual "for what it is in itself," becomes problematic in a holistic web. True, the system produces such values more and more with its evolution of individuality and freedom. Yet to decouple this from the biotic, communal system is to make value too internal and elementary; this forgets relatedness and externality. Every intrinsic value has leading and trailing *ands* pointing to value from which it comes and toward which it moves. Adapted fitness makes individualistic value too system independent. Intrinsic value is a part in a whole, not to be fragmented by valuing it in isolation. An isolated *telos* is biologically impossible; the ethic cannot be teleological in that sense, nor can we term it deontological either, if this requires respect for an intrinsic value regardless of ecosystemic consequences. (The classical distinction fails again.)

Everything is good in a role, in a whole, although we can speak of objective intrinsic goodness wherever a good kind defends itself. We can speak of subjective intrinsic goodness when such an event registers as a point experience, at which point humans pronounce both their experience and what it is of good without need to enlarge their focus. The system is a value transformer where form and being, process and reality, fact and value are inseparably joined. Intrinsic and instrumental values shuttle back and forth, parts-in-wholes and wholes-in-parts, local details of value embedded in global structures, gems in their settings, and their setting-situation a corporation where value cannot stand alone. Every good is in community.

This is what is radically wrong with anthropocentric or merely anthropogenic value. It arrogates to humans what permeates the community. Subjective self-satisfactions are, and ought to be, sufficiently contained within the objectively satisfactory system. The system creates life, selects for adaptive fit, constructs increasingly richer life in quantity and quality, supports myriads of species, escalates individually, autonomy, and even subjectivity, within the limits of decentralized community. When persons appraise this natural history if such land is not a valuable, satisfactory biotic community; why not? Does earth and its community of life not claim their concern and care?

In environmental ethics one's beliefs about nature, which are based upon but exceed science, have everything to do with beliefs about duty. The way the world *is* informs the way it *ought* to be. We always shape our values in significant measure in accord with our notion of the kind of universe that we live in, and this drives our sense of duty. Our model of reality implies a model of conduct. Perhaps we can leave open what metaphysics ultimately underlies our cosmos, but for an environmental ethics at least we will need an earthbound metaphysics, a metaecology. Differing models sometimes imply similar conduct, but often they do not. A model in which nature has no value apart from human preferences will imply different conduct from one where natures projects fundamental values, some objective and others that further require human subjectivity superposed on objective nature.

This evaluation is not scientific description; hence not ecology per se, but we do move to metaecology. No amount of research can verify that, environmentally, the right is the optimum biotic community. Yet ecological description generates this valuing of nature, endorsing the systemic rightness. The transition from *is* to *good* and thence to *ought* occurs here; we leave science to enter the domain of evaluation, from which an ethic follows.

What is ethically puzzling and exciting is that an *ought* is not so much *derived* from an *is* as discovered simultaneously with it. As we progress from descriptions of fauna and flora, of cycles and pyramids, of autotrophs coordinated with heterotrophs, of stability and dynamism, on to intricacy, planetary opulence and interdependence, to unity and harmony with oppositions in counterpoint and synthesis, organisms evolved within and satisfactorily fitting their communities, arriving at length of beauty and goodness, it is difficult to say where the natural facts leave off and where the natural values appear. For some at least, the sharp *is/ought* dichotomy is gone; the values seem to be there as soon as the facts are fully in, and both alike properties of the system. This conviction, and the conscience that follows from it, can yield our best adaptive fit on earth.

Journal/Discussion Questions

✍ *Rolston provides a number of examples of environmental incidents. Were any of these of particular interest to you? Discuss.*

1. Rolston writes, "I doubt whether the good of humans who wish more water for development, both for industry and for bluegrass lawns, warrants endangering species of butterflies and cranes." Do you agree with this statement? Discuss.
2. How does Rolston deal with the question of whether human beings should have greater moral weight than other living beings? Critically assess Rolston's position.
3. At several points in his essay, Rolston refers to *ought* and *is*. Traditionally, most moral philosophers have maintained that it is impossible to derive an "ought" from an "is," that is, to derive a statement about moral obligation from a set of merely factual statements. What is Rolston's position on this issue? Do you agree?

Ramachandra Guha
"Radical American Environmentalism and Wilderness Preservation: A Third World Critique"

Ramachandra Guha is a member of the Centre for Ecological Sciences, Indian Institute of Science, Bangalore, India.

In this essay, Professor Guha presents a Third World critique of the trend in American environmentalism known as deep ecology, analyzing each of deep ecology's central tenets: the distinction between anthropocentrism and biocentrism, the focus on wilderness preservation, the invocation of Eastern traditions, and the belief that it represents the most radical trend within environmentalism. He argues that the anthropocentrism-biocentrism distinction is of little use in understanding the dynamics of environmental degradation, that the implementation of the wilderness agenda is causing serious deprivation in the Third World, that the deep ecologist's interpretation of Eastern traditions is highly selective, and that in other cultural contexts (e.g., West Germany and India) radical environmentalism manifests itself quite differently, with a far greater emphasis on equity and the integration of ecological concerns with livelihood and work. He concludes that despite its claims to universality, deep ecology is firmly rooted in American environmental and cultural history and is inappropriate when applied to the Third World.

As You Read, Consider This:

1. Often, those outside our own culture can help us see things about ourselves that would not otherwise have been visible to us. In what ways does Guda help you to see things about the American environment movement more clearly?
2. According to Guha, many of us in the West have misperceptions of Eastern spirituality. What are some of these misperceptions?

Even God dare not appear to the poor man except in the form of bread

—Mahatma Gandhi

I. Introduction

The respected radical journalist Kirkpatrick Sale recently celebrated "the passion of a new and growing movement that has become disenchanted with the environmental establishment and has in recent years mounted a serious and sweeping attack on it—style, substance, systems, sensibilities and all."[1] The vision of those whom Sale calls the "New Ecologists"—and what I refer to in this article as deep ecology—is a compelling one. Decrying the narrowly economic goals of mainstream environmentalism, this new movement aims at nothing less than a philosophical and cultural revolution in human attitudes toward nature. In contrast to the conventional lobbying efforts of environmental professionals based in Washington, it proposes a militant defense of "Mother Earth," an unflinching opposition to human attacks on undisturbed wilderness. With their goals ranging from the spiritual to the political, the adherents of deep ecology span a wide spectrum of the American environmental movement. As Sale correctly notes, this emerging strand has in a matter of a few years made its presence felt in a number of fields: from academic philosophy (as in the journal *Environmental Ethics*) to popular environmentalism (for example, the group Earth First!).

In this article I develop a critique of deep ecology from the perspective of a sympathetic outsider. I critique deep ecology not as a general (or even a foot soldier) in the continuing struggle between the ghosts of Gifford Pinchot and John Muir over control of the U.S. environmental movement, but as an outsider to these battles. I speak admittedly as a partisan, but of the environmental movement in India, a country with an ecological diversity comparable to the U.S., but with a radically dissimilar cultural and social history.

My treatment of deep ecology is primarily historical and sociological, rather than philosophical, in nature. Specifically, I examine the cultural rootedness of a philosophy that likes to present itself in universalistic terms. I make two main arguments: first, that deep ecology is uniquely American, and despite superficial similarities in rhetorical style, the social and political goals of radical environmentalism in other cultural contexts (e.g., West Germany and India) are quite different; second, that the social consequences of putting deep ecology into practice on a worldwide basis (what its practitioners are aiming for) are very grave indeed.

II. The Tenets of Deep Ecology

While I am aware that the term deep ecology was coined by the Norwegian philosopher Arne Naess, this article refers specifically to the American variant.[2] Adherents of the deep ecological perspective in this country, while arguing intensely among themselves over its political and philosophical implications, share some fundamental premises about human-nature interactions. As I see it, the defining characteristics of deep ecology are fourfold:

First, deep ecology argues, that the environmental movement must shift from an "anthropocentric" to a "biocentric" perspective. In many respects, an acceptance of the primacy of this distinction constitutes the litmus test of deep ecology. A considerable effort is expended by deep ecologists in showing that the dominant motif in Western philosophy has been anthropocentric—i.e., the belief that man and his works are the center of the universe—and conversely, in identifying those lonely thinkers (Leopold, Thoreau, Muir, Aldous Huxley, Santayana, etc.) who, in assigning man a more humble place in the natural order, anticipated deep ecological thinking. In the political realm, meanwhile, establishment environmentalism (shallow ecology) is chided for casting its arguments in human-centered terms. Preserving nature, the deep ecologists say, has an intrinsic worth quite apart from any benefits preservation may convey to future human generations. The anthropocentric-biocentric distinction is accepted as axiomatic by deep ecologists, it structures their discourse, and much of the present discussion remains mired within it.

The second characteristic of deep ecology is its focus on the preservation of unspoilt wilderness—and the restoration of degraded areas to a more pristine condition—to the relative (and sometimes absolute) neglect of other issues on the environmental agenda. I later identify the cultural roots and portentous consequences of this obsession with wilderness. For the moment, let me indicate three distinct sources from which it springs. Historically, it represents a playing out of the preservationist (read radical) and utilitarian (read reformist) dichotomy that has plagued American environmentalism since the turn of the century. Morally, it is an imperative that follows from the biocentric perspective; other species of plants and animals, and nature itself, have an intrinsic right to exist. And finally, the preservation of wilderness also turns on a scientific argument—viz., the value of biological diversity in stabilizing ecological regimes and in retaining a gene pool for future generations. Truly radical policy proposals have been put forward by deep ecologists on the basis of these arguments. The influential poet Gary Snyder, for example, would like to see a 90 percent reduction in human populations to allow a restoration of pristine environments, while others have argued forcefully that a large portion of the globe must be immediately cordoned off from human beings.[3]

Third, there is a widespread invocation of Eastern spiritual traditions as forerunners of deep ecology. Deep ecology, it is suggested, was practiced both by major religious traditions and at a more popular level by "primal" peoples in non-Western settings. This complements the search for an authentic lineage in Western thought. At one level, the task is to recover those dissenting voices within the Judeo-Christian tradition; at another, to suggest that religious traditions in other cultures are, in contrast, dominantly if not exclusively "biocentric" in their orientation. This coupling of (ancient) Eastern and (modern) ecological wisdom seemingly helps consolidate the claim that deep ecology is a philosophy of universal significance.

Fourth, deep ecologists, whatever their internal differences, share the belief that they are the "leading edge" of the environmental movement. As the polarity of the shallow/deep and anthropocentric/biocentric distinctions makes clear, they see themselves as the spiritual, philosophical, and political vanguard of American and world environmentalism.

III. Toward a Critique

Although I analyze each of these tenets independently, it is important to recognize, as deep ecologists are fond of remarking in reference to nature, the interconnectedness and unity of these individual themes.

(1) Insofar as it has begun to act as a check on man's arrogance and ecological hubris, the transition from an anthropocentric (human-centered) to a biocentric (humans as only one element in the ecosystem) view in both religious and scientific traditions is only to be welcomed.[4] What is unacceptable are the radical conclusions drawn by deep ecology, in particular, that intervention in nature should be guided primarily by the need to preserve biotic integrity rather than by the needs of humans. The latter for deep ecologists is anthropocentric, the former biocentric. This dichotomy is, however, of very little use in understanding the dynamics of environmental degradation. The two fundamental ecological problems facing the globe are (i) overconsumption by the industrialized world and by urban elites in the Third World and (ii) growing militarization, both in a short-term sense (i.e., on-going regional wars) and in a long-term sense (i.e., the arms race and the prospect of nuclear annihilation). Neither of these problems has any tangible connection to the anthropocentric-biocentric distinction. Indeed, the agents of these processes would barely comprehend this philosophical dichotomy. The proximate causes of the ecologically wasteful characteristics of industrial society and of militarization are far more mundane: at an aggregate level, the dialectic of economic and political structures, and at a micro-level, the life style choices of individuals. These causes cannot be reduced, whatever the level of analysis, to a deeper anthropocentric attitude toward nature;

on the contrary, by constituting a grave threat to human survival, the ecological degradation they cause does not even serve the best interests of human beings! If my identification of the major dangers to the integrity of the natural world is correct, invoking the bogy of anthropocentricism is at best irrelevant and at worst a dangerous obfuscation.

(2) If the above dichotomy is irrelevant, the emphasis on wilderness is positively harmful when applied to the Third World. If in the U.S. the preservationist/utilitarian division is seen as mirroring the conflict between "people" and "interests," in countries such as India the situation is very nearly the reverse. Because India is a long settled and densely populated country in which agrarian populations have a finely balanced relationship with nature, the setting aside of wilderness areas has resulted in a direct transfer of resources from the poor to the rich. Thus, Project Tiger, a network of parks hailed by the international conservation community as an outstanding success, sharply posits the interests of the tiger against those of poor peasants living in and around the reserve. The designation of tiger reserves was made possible only by the physical displacement of existing villages and their inhabitants; their management requires the continuing exclusion of peasants and livestock. The initial impetus for setting up parks for the tiger and other large mammals such as the rhinoceros and elephant came from two social groups, first, a class of ex-hunters turned conservationists belonging mostly to the declining Indian feudal elite and second, representatives of international agencies, such as the World Wildlife Fund (WWF) and the International Union for the Conservation of Nature and Natural Resources (IUCN), seeking to transplant the American system of national parks onto Indian soil. In no case have the needs of the local population been taken into account, and as in many parts of Africa, the designated wildlands are managed primarily for the benefit of rich tourists. Until very recently, wildlands preservation has been identified with environmentalism by the state and the conservation elite; in consequence, environmental problems that impinge far more directly on the lives of the poor—e.g., fuel, fodder, water shortages, soil erosion, and air and water pollution—have not been adequately addressed.[5]

Deep ecology provides, perhaps unwittingly, a justification for the continuation of such narrow and inequitable conservation practices under a newly acquired radical guise. Increasingly, the international conservation elite is using the philosophical, moral, and scientific arguments used by deep ecologists in advancing their wilderness crusade. A striking but by no means atypical example is the recent plea by a prominent American biologist for the takeover of large portions of the globe by the author and his scientific colleagues. Writing in a prestigious scientific forum, the *Annual Review of Ecology and Systematics,* Daniel Janzen argues that only biologists have the competence to decide how the tropical landscape should be used. As "the representatives of the natural world," biologists are "in charge of the future of tropical ecology," and only they have the expertise and mandate to "determine whether the tropical agroscape is to be populated only by humans, their mutualists, commensals, and parasites, or whether it will also contain some islands of the greater nature—the nature that spawned humans, yet has been vanquished by them." Janzen exhorts his colleagues to advance their territorial claims on the tropical world more forcefully, warning that the very existence of these areas is at stake: "if biologists want a tropics in which to biologize, they are going to have to buy it with care, energy, effort, strategy, tactics, time, and cash."[6]

This frankly imperialist manifesto highlights the multiple dangers of the preoccupation with wilderness preservation that is characteristic of deep ecology. As I have suggested, it seriously compounds the neglect by the American movement of far more pressing environmental problems within the Third World. But perhaps more importantly, and in a more insidious fashion, it also provides an impetus to the imperialist yearning of Western biologists and their financial sponsors, organizations such as the WWF and IUCN. The wholesale transfer of a movement culturally rooted in American conservation history can only result in the social uprooting of human populations in other parts of the globe.

(3) I come now to the persistent invocation of Eastern philosophies as antecedent in point of time but convergent in their structure with deep ecology. Complex and internally differentiated religious traditions—Hinduism, Buddhism, and Taoism—are lumped together as holding a view of nature believed to be quintessentially biocentric. Individual philosophers such as the Taoist Lao Tzu are identified as being forerunners of deep ecology. Even an intensely political, pragmatic, and Christian influenced thinker such as Gandhi has been accorded a wholly undeserved place in the deep ecological pantheon. Thus the Zen teacher Robert Aitken Roshi makes the strange claim that Gandhi's thought was not human-centered and that he practiced an embryonic form of deep ecology which is "traditionally Eastern and is found with differing emphasis in Hinduism, Taoism and in Theravada and Mahayana Buddhism."[7] Moving away from the realm of high philosophy and scriptural religion, deep ecologists make the further claim that at the level of material and spiritual practice "primal" peoples subordinated themselves to the integrity of the biotic universe they inhabited.

I have indicated that this appropriation of Eastern traditions is in part dictated by the need to construct an authentic lineage and in part a desire to present deep ecology as a universalistic philosophy. Indeed, in his substantial and quixotic biography of John Muir, Michael Cohen goes so far as to suggest that Muir was the "Taoist of the [American] West."[8] This reading of Eastern traditions is selective and does not bother to differentiate between alternate (and changing) religious and cultural traditions; as it stands, it does considerable violence to the historical record. Throughout most recorded history the characteristic form of human activity in the "East" has been a finely tuned but nonetheless conscious and dynamic manipulation of nature. Although mystics such as Lao Tzu did reflect on the spiritual essence of human relations with nature, it must be recognized that such ascetics and their reflections were supported by a society of cultivators whose relationship with nature was a far more *active* one. Many agricultural communities do have a sophisticated knowledge of the natural environment that may equal (and sometimes surpass) codified "scientific" knowledge; yet, the elaboration of such traditional ecological knowledge (in both material and spiritual contexts) can hardly be said to rest on a mystical affinity with nature of a deep ecological kind. Nor is such knowledge infallible; as the archaeological record powerfully suggests, modern Western man has no monopoly on ecological disasters.

In a brilliant article, the Chicago historian Ronald Inden points out that this romantic and essentially positive view of the East is a mirror image of the scientific and essentially pejorative view normally upheld by Western scholars of the Orient. In either case, the East constitutes the Other, a body wholly separate and alien from the West; it is defined by a uniquely spiritual and nonrational "essence," even if this essence is valorized quite differently by the two schools. Eastern man exhibits a spiritual dependence with respect to nature—on the one hand, this is symptomatic of his prescientific and backward self, on the other, of his ecological wisdom and deep ecological consciousness. Both views are monolithic, simplistic, and have the characteristic effect—intended in one case, perhaps unintended in the other of denying agency and reason to the East and making it the privileged orbit of Western thinkers.

The two apparently opposed perspectives have then a common underlying structure of discourse in which the East merely serves as a vehicle for Western projections. Varying images of the

East are raw material for political and cultural battles being played out in the West; they tell us far more about the Western commentator and his desires than about the "East." Inden's remarks apply not merely to Western scholarship on India, but to Orientalist constructions of China and Japan as well:

> Although these two views appear to be strongly opposed, they often combine together. Both have a similar interest in sustaining the Otherness of India. The holders of the dominant view, best exemplified in the past in imperial administrative discourse (and today probably by that of "development economics"), would place a traditional, superstition-ridden India in a position of perpetual tutelage to a modern, rational West. The adherents of the romantic view, best exemplified academically in the discourses of Christian liberalism and analytic psychology, concede the realm of the public and impersonal to the positivist. Taking their succor not from governments and big business, but from a plethora of religious foundations and self-help institutes, and from allies in the "consciousness industry," not to mention the important industry of tourism, the romantics insist that India embodies a private realm of the imagination and the religious which modern, western man lacks but needs. They, therefore, like the positivists, but for just the opposite reason, have a vested interest in seeing that the Orientalist view of India as "spiritual," "mysterious," and "exotic" is perpetuated.[9]

(4) How radical, finally, are the deep ecologists? Notwithstanding their self-image and strident rhetoric (in which the label "shallow ecology" has an opprobrium similar to that reserved for "social democratic" by Marxist-Leninists), even within the American context their radicalism is limited and it manifests itself quite differently elsewhere.

To my mind, deep ecology is best viewed as a radical trend within the wilderness preservation movement. Although advancing philosophical rather than aesthetic arguments and encouraging political militancy rather than negotiation, its practical emphasis—viz., preservation of unspoilt nature—is virtually identical. For the mainstream movement, the function of wilderness is to provide a temporary antidote to modern civilization. As a special institution within an industrialized society, the national park "provides an opportunity for respite, contrast, contemplation, and affirmation of values for those who live most of their lives in the workaday world."[10] Indeed, the rapid increase in visitations to the national parks in postwar America is a direct consequence of economic expansion. The emergence of a popular interest in wilderness sites, the historian Samuel Hays points out, was "not a throwback to the primitive, but an integral part of the modern standard of living as people sought to add new 'amenity' and 'aesthetic' goals and desires to their earlier preoccupation with necessities and conveniences."[11]

Here, the enjoyment of nature is an integral part of the consumer society. The private automobile (and the life style it has spawned) is in many respects the ultimate ecological villain, and an untouched wilderness the prototype of ecological harmony; yet, for most Americans it is perfectly consistent to drive a thousand miles to spend a holiday in a national park. They possess a vast, beautiful, and sparsely populated continent and are also able to draw upon the natural resources of large portions of the globe by virtue of their economic and political dominance. In consequence, America can simultaneously enjoy the material benefits of an expanding economy and the aesthetic benefits of unspoilt nature. The two poles of "wilderness" and "civilization" mutually coexist in an internally coherent whole, and philosophers of both poles are assigned a prominent place in this culture. Paradoxically as it may seem, it is no accident that Star Wars technology and deep ecology both find their fullest expression in that leading sector of Western civilization, California.

Deep ecology runs parallel to the consumer society without seriously questioning its ecological and socio-political basis. In its celebration of American wilderness, it also displays an uncomfortable convergence with the prevailing climate of nationalism in the American wilderness movement. For spokesmen such as the historian Roderick Nash, the national park system is America's distinctive cultural contribution to the world, reflective not merely of its economic but of its philosophical and ecological maturity as well. In what Walter Lippman called the American century, the "American invention of national parks" must be exported worldwide. Betraying an economic determinism that would make even a Marxist shudder, Nash believes that environmental preservation is a "full stomach" phenomenon that is confined to the rich, urban, and sophisticated. Nonetheless, he hopes that "the less developed nations may eventually evolve economically and intellectually to the point where nature preservation is more than a business.[12]

The error which Nash makes (and which deep ecology in some respects encourages) is to equate environmental protection with the protection of wilderness. This is a distinctively American notion, borne out of a unique social and environmental history. The archetypal concerns of radical environmentalists in other cultural contexts are in fact quite different. The German Greens, for example, have elaborated a devastating critique of industrial society which turns on the acceptance of environmental limits to growth. Pointing to the intimate links between industrialization, militarization, and conquest, the Greens argue that economic growth in the West has historically rested on the economic and ecological exploitation of the Third World. Rudolf Bahro is characteristically blunt:

> The working class here [in the West] is the richest lower class in the world. And if I look at the problem from the point of view of the whole of humanity, not just from that of Europe, then I must say that the metropolitan working class is the worst exploiting class in history. . . . What made poverty bearable in eighteenth or nineteenth-century Europe was the prospect of escaping it through exploitation of the periphery. But this is no longer a possibility, and continued industrialism in the Third World will mean poverty for whole generations and hunger for millions.[13]

Here the roots of global ecological problems lie in the disproportionate share of resources consumed by the industrialized countries as a whole *and* the urban elite within the Third World. Since it is impossible to reproduce an industrial monoculture worldwide, the ecological movement in the West must begin by cleaning up its own act. The Greens advocate the creation of a "no growth" economy, to be achieved by scaling down current (and clearly unsustainable) consumption levels.[14] This radical shift in consumption and production patterns requires the creation of alternate economic and political structures—smaller in scale and more amenable to social participation—but it rests equally on a shift in cultural values. The expansionist character of modern Western man will have to give way to an ethic of renunciation and self-limitation, in which spiritual and communal values play an increasing role in sustaining social life. This revolution in cultural values, however, has as its point of departure an understanding of environmental processes quite different from deep ecology.

Many elements of the Green program find a strong resonance in countries such as India, where a history of Western colonialism and industrial development has benefited only a tiny elite while exacting tremendous social and environmental costs. The ecological battles presently being fought in India have as their epicenter the conflict over nature between the subsistence and largely rural sector and the vastly more powerful commercial-industrial sector. Perhaps the most celebrated of these battles concerns the Chipko (Hug the Tree) movement, a peasant movement against deforestation in the Himalayan foothills. Chipko is only one of several movements that have sharply questioned the nonsustainable demand being placed on the land and vegetative base by urban centers and industry. These include opposition to large dams by displaced peasants, the conflict between small artisan fishing and large-scale trawler fishing for export, the countrywide movements against commercial forest operations, and opposition to industrial pollution among downstream agricultural and fishing communities.[15]

Two features distinguish these environmental movements from their Western counterparts. First, for the sections of society most critically affected by environmental degradation—poor and landless peasants, women, and tribals—it is a question of sheer survival, not of enhancing the quality of life. Second, and as a consequence, the environmental solutions they articulate deeply involve questions of equity as well as economic and political redistribution. Highlighting these differences, a leading Indian environmentalist stresses that "environmental protection per se is of least concern to most of these groups. Their main concern is about the use of the environment and who should benefit from it."[16] They seek to wrest control of nature away from the state and the industrial sector and place it in the hands of rural communities who live within that environment but are increasingly denied access to it. These communities have far more basic needs, their demands on the environment are far less intense, and they can draw upon a reservoir of cooperative social institutions and local ecological knowledge in managing the "commons"—forests, grasslands, and the waters—on a sustainable basis. If colonial and capitalist expansion has both accentuated social inequalities and signaled a precipitous fall in ecological wisdom, an alternate ecology must rest on an alternate society and polity as well.

This brief overview of German and Indian environmentalism has some major implications for deep ecology. Both German and Indian environmental traditions allow for a greater integration of ecological concerns with livelihood and work. They also place a greater emphasis on equity and social justice (both within individual countries and on a global scale) on the grounds that in the absence of social regeneration environmental regeneration has very little chance of succeeding. Finally, and perhaps most significantly, they have escaped the preoccupation with wilderness preservation so characteristic of American cultural and environmental history.[17]

IV. A Homily

In 1958, the economist J.K. Galbraith referred to overconsumption as the unasked question of the American conservation movement. There is a marked selectivity, he wrote, "in the conservationist's approach to materials consumption. If we are concerned about our great appetite for materials, it is plausible to seek to increase the supply, to decrease waste, to make better use of the stocks available, and to develop substitutes. But what of the appetite itself? Surely this is the ultimate source of the problem. If it continues its geometric course, will it not one day have to be restrained? Yet in the literature of the resource problem this is the forbidden question. Over it hangs a nearly total silence."[18]

The consumer economy and society have expanded tremendously in the three decades since Galbraith penned these words; yet his criticisms are nearly as valid today. I have said "nearly," for there are some hopeful signs. Within the environmental movement several dispersed groups are working to develop ecologically benign technologies and to encourage less wasteful life styles. Moreover, outside the self-defined boundaries of American environmentalism, opposition to the permanent war economy is being carried on by a peace movement that has a distinguished history and impeccable moral and political credentials.

It is precisely these (to my mind, most hopeful) components of the American social scene that are missing from deep ecology. In their widely noticed book, Bill Devall and George Sessions make no mention of militarization or the movements for peace, while activists whose practical focus is on developing ecologically responsible life styles (e.g., Wendell Berry) are derided as "falling short of deep ecological awareness."[19] A truly radical ecology in the American context ought to work toward a synthesis of the appropriate technology, alternate life style, and peace movements.[20] By making the (largely spurious) anthropocentric-biocentric distinction central to the debate, deep ecologists may have appropriated the moral high ground, but they are at the same time doing a serious disservice to American and global environmentalism.[21]

Acknowledgments

This essay was written while the author was a visiting lecturer at the Yale School of Forestry and Environmental Studies. He is grateful to Mike Bell, Tom Birch, Bill Burch, Bill Cronon, Diane Mayerfeld, David Rothenberg, Kirkpatrick Sale, Joel Seton, Tim Weiskel, and Don Worster for helpful comments.

Endnotes

1. Kirkpatrick Sale, "The Forest for the Trees: Can Today's Environmentalists Tell the Difference," *Mother Jones* 11, no. 8 (November 1986): 26.
2. One of the major criticisms I make in this essay concerns deep ecology's lack of concern with inequalities *within* human society. In the article in which he coined the term *deep ecology,* Naess himself expresses concerns about inequalities between and within nations. However, his concern with social cleavages and their impact on resource utilization patterns and ecological destruction is not very visible in the later writings of deep ecologists. See Arne Naess, "The Shallow and the Deep, Long-Range Ecology Movement: A Summary," *Inquiry* 16 (1973): 96 (I am grateful to Tom Birch for this reference).
3. Gary Snyder, quoted in Sale, "The Forest for the Trees," p. 32. See also Dave Foreman, "A Modest Proposal for a Wilderness System," *Whole Earth Review,* no. 53 (Winter 1986–1987): 42–45.
4. See, for example, Donald Worster, *Nature's Economy: The Roots of Ecology* (San Francisco, Sierra Club Books, 1977).
5. See Centre for Science and Environment, *India: The State of the Environment 1982: A Citizens Report* (New Delhi: Centre for Science and Environment, 1982); R. Sukumar, "Elephant-Man Conflict in Karnataka," in Cecil Saldanha, ed., *The State of Karnataka's Environment* (Bangalore: Centre for Taxonomic Studies, 1985). For Africa, see the brilliant analysis by Helge Kjekshus, *Ecology Control and Economic Development in East African History* (Berkeley: University of California Press, 1977).

6. Daniel Janzen, "The Future of Tropical Ecology," *Annual Review of Ecology and Systematics* 17 (1986): 305–306; emphasis added.
7. Robert Aitken Roshi, "Gandhi, Dogen, and Deep Ecology," reprinted as appendix C in Bill Devall and George Sessions, *Deep Ecology: Living as if Nature Mattered* (Salt Lake City: Peregrine Smith Books, 1985). For Gandhi's own views on social reconstruction, see the excellent three volume collection edited by Raghavan Iyer, *The Moral and Political Writings of Mahatma Gandhi* (Oxford: Clarendon Press, 1986–1987).
8. Michael Cohen. *The Pathless Way* (Madison: University of Wisconsin Press, 1984), p. 120.
9. Ronald Inden, "Orientalist Constructions of India," *Modern Asian Studies* 20 (1986): 442. Inden draws inspiration from Edward Said's forceful polemic, *Orientalism* (New York: Basic Books, 1980). It must be noted, however, that there is a salient difference between Western perceptions of Middle Eastern and Far Eastern cultures respectively. Due perhaps to the long history of Christian conflict with Islam, Middle Eastern cultures (as Said documents) are consistently presented in pejorative terms. The juxtaposition of hostile and worshipping attitudes that Inden talks of applies only to Western attitudes toward Buddhist and Hindu societies.
10. Joseph Sax, *Mountains Without Handrails: Reflections on the National Parks* (Ann Arbor: University of Michigan Press, 1980), p. 42. Cf. also Peter Schmitt, *Back to Nature: The Arcadian Myth in Urban America* (New York: Oxford University Press, 1969), and Alfred Runte, *National Parks: The American Experience* (Lincoln: University of Nebraska Press, 1979).
11. Samuel Hays, "From Conservation to Environment: Environmental Politics in the United States since World War Two," *Environmental Review 6* (1982): 21. See also the same author's book entitled *Beauty, Health and Permanence: Environmental Politics in the United States, 1955–1985* (New York: Cambridge University Press, 1987).
12. Roderick Nash, *Wilderness and the American Mind,* 3rd ed. (New Haven: Yale University Press, 1982).
13. Rudolf Bahro, *From Red to Green* (London: Verso Books, 1984).
14. From time to time, American scholars have themselves criticized these imbalances in consumption patterns. In the 1950s, William Vogt made the charge that the United states, with one-sixteenth of the world's population, was utilizing one-third of the globe's resources. (Vogt, cited in E.F. Murphy, *Nature, Bureaucracy and the Rule of Property* [Amsterdam: North Holland, 1977, p. 29].) More recently, zero Population Growth has estimated that each American consumes thirty-nine times as many resources as an Indian. See *Christian Science Monitor,* 2 March 1987.
15. For an excellent review, see Anil Agarwal and Sunita Narain, eds., *India: The Slate of the Environment 1984–1985: A Citizens Report* (New Delhi: Centre for Science and Environment, 1985). Cf. Also Ramachandra Guha, *The Unquiet Woods: Ecological Change and Peasant Resistance in the Indian Himalaya* (Berkeley: University of California Press, forthcoming).
16. Anil Agarwal, "Human-Nature Interactions in a Third World Country," *The Environmentalist* 6. no. 3 (1986): 167.
17. One strand in radical American environmentalism, the bioregional movement, by emphasizing a greater involvement with the bioregion people inhabit, does indirectly challenge consumerism.

However, as yet bioregionalism has hardly raised the questions of equity and social justice (international, intranational, and intergenerational) which I argue must be a central plank of radical environmentalism. Moreover, its stress on (individual) experience as the key to involvement with nature is also somewhat at odds with the integration of nature with livelihood and work that I talk of in this paper. Cf. Kirkpatrick Sale, *Dwellers in the Land: The Bioregional Vision* (San Francisco: Sierra Club Books, 1985).

18. John Kenneth Galbraith, "How Much Should a Country Consume?" in Henry Jarrett, ed., *Perspectives on Conservation* (Baltimore: Johns Hopkins Press, 1958), pp. 91–92.
19. Devall and Sessions, *Deep Ecology,* p. 122. For Wendell Berry's own assessment of deep ecology, see his "Amplications: Preserving Wildness," *Wilderness* 50 (Spring 1987): 39–40, 50–54.
20. See the interesting recent contribution by one of the most influential spokesmen of appropriate technology—Barry Commoner, "A Reporter at Large: The Environment," *New Yorker,* 15 June 1987. While Commoner makes a forceful plea for the convergence of the environmental movement (viewed by him primarily as the opposition to air and water pollution and to the institutions that generate such pollution) and the peace movement, he significantly does not mention consumption patterns, implying that "limits to growth" do not exist.
21. In this sense, my critique of deep ecology, although that of an outsider, may facilitate the reassertion of those elements in the American environmental tradition for which there is a profound sympathy in other parts of the globe. A global perspective may also lead to a critical reassessment of figures such as Aldo Leopold and John Muir, the two patron saints of deep ecology. As Donald Worster has pointed out, the message of Muir (and, I would argue, of Leopold as well) makes sense only in an American context; he has very little to say to other cultures. See Worster's review of Sterchen Fox's *John Muir and His Legacy,* in *Environmental Ethics* 5 (1983): 277–281.

Journal/Discussion Questions

✍ *What experience have you had in third world countries? How does your experience shed light on what Guha says in this article?*

1. Explain the difference between an anthropocentric and a biocentric perspective.
2. What are Guha's principal objections to deep ecology? Critically assess his objections.
3. How do you think environmental issues should best be handled in developing countries? What are the principal factors to consider? How does your answer to this relate to Guha's?

Concluding Discussion Questions

Where Do You Stand Now?

Instructions

You have already answered the following questions in your moral problems self-quiz at the beginning of this book. Now that you have studied the material in this section, take a moment to answer the same questions again.

	Strongly Agree	*Agree*	*Undecided*	*Disagree*	*Strongly Disagree*	*Chapter 11: Environmental Ethics*
51.	❑	❑	❑	❑	❑	Nature is just a source of resources for us.
52.	❑	❑	❑	❑	❑	The government should strictly regulate toxic waste.
53.	❑	❑	❑	❑	❑	We should make every effort possible to avoid infringing on the natural environment any more than we already have.
54.	❑	❑	❑	❑	❑	We owe future generations a clean and safe environment.
55.	❑	❑	❑	❑	❑	We should not impose our environmental concerns on developing nations.

Compare your answers to the present self-quiz with the answers to the initial self-quiz. How, if at all, have your answers changed? How have the *reasons* for your answers changed?

For Further Reading

Journal

In addition to the standard journals in ethics discussed in the bibliographical essay at the end of Chapter 1, see especially *Environmental Ethics,* which has been a rich source of scholarship and theory on issues of environmental ethics; also see the journal *Environmental Values,* edited by Alan Holland at Lancaster University, UK.

Review Articles

See the review articles by J. Baird Callicott, "Environmental Ethics," *Encyclopedia of Ethics,* edited by Lawrence C. Becker and Charlotte B. Becker (New York: Garland Publishing, Inc., 1992), Vol. I, pp. 311–314, and Robert Elliot, "Environmental Ethics," *A Companion to Ethics,* edited by Peter Singer (Oxford: Blackwell, 1991), pp. 284–293. Also see the articles in *Environmental Philosophy: From Animal Rights to Radical Ecology,* discussed below, and John Passmore, "Environmentalism," *A Companion to Contemporary Political Philosophy,* edited by Robert E. Goodin and Philip Pettit (Oxford: Blackwell, 1993), pp. 471–488.

Anthologies

The Environmental Crisis: Opposing Viewpoints, edited by Neal Bernards (San Diego: Greenhaven Press, 1991) contains chapters on pesticides, garbage, toxic waste, air and water pollution, and environmental protection. *Taking Sides: Clashing Views on Controversial Environmental Issues,* edited, selected, and with introductions by Theodore D. Goldfarb, 5th ed. (Guilford, CT: Dushkin Group, 1993) also covers a wide range of issues with a balanced selection of readings as does Donald VanDerVeer and Christine Pierce, eds., *People, Penguins, and Plastic Trees* (Belmont: Wadsworth, 1986). *The Environment in Question: Ethics and Global Issues,* edited by David E. Cooper and Joy A. Palmer (London: Routledge, 1992) contains a good balance of theoretical and applied issues. *Earthbound: New Introductory Essays in Environmental Ethics,* edited by Tom Regan (New York: Random House, 1984) in a very interesting collection of original essays on such topics as pollution, energy, economics, ocean resources, agriculture, rare species, future generations, and moral theory. Also see Donald Scherer and Thomas Attig, eds., *Ethics and the Environment* (Englewood Cliffs, NJ: Prentice-Hall, 1983). *Environmental Philosophy: From Animal Rights to Radical Ecology,* edited by Michael E. Zimmerman et al., 2nd ed. (Englewood Cliffs, NJ: Prentice-Hall, 1998) is a superb collection of essays, with introductions for individual sections done by representatives of each tradition, including ecofeminism, deep ecology, and social ecology. *Environmental Pragmatism,* edited by Andrew Light and Eric Katz (London: Routledge, 1998) stresses the importance of ethical pluralism and enviornmental pragmatism in understanding and resolving environmental issues.

Future generations. *Responsibilities to Future Generations,* edited by Ernest Partridge (Buffalo: Prometheus Press, 1980), *Obligations to Future Generations,* edited by R. I Sikora and Brian Barry (Philadelphia: Temple University Press, 1978), and *Obligations to Future Generations,* edited by E. Partridge (Buffalo: Prometheus, 1981) all contain articles about the issue of our responsibility to future generations for not destroying the natural environment. *Why Posterity Matters: Environmental Policies and Future Generations*, edited by Avner De-Shalit (London: Routledge, 1991) focuses specifically on the environmental dimensions of our obligations to future generations, and *Caring for Future Generations: Jewish, Christian and Islamic Perspectives* (Praeger Studies on the 21st Century), edited by Emmanuel Agius and Lionel Chircop (New York: Praeger, 1998) focuses on this issue in three major religious traditions.

Articles

Richard Routley's "Is There a Need for a New, an Environmental Ethic?" in *Proceedings of the 15th World Congress of Philosophy,* edited by Bulgarian Organizing Committee (Sophia, Bulgaria: Sophia-Press, 1973), Vol. 1, pp. 205–210, was one of the first statements of a need for a new environmental ethic.

Kenneth E. Goodpaster, "On Being Morally Considerable." *Journal of Philosophy* Vol. 22 (1978), pp. 308–325, argues that it is the capacity to live (not mere sentience) that gives an entity moral considerability; also see his "From Egoism to Environmentalism," in *Ethics and Problems of the 21st Century,* edited by K.E. Goodpaster and K.M. Sayre (Notre Dame: University of Notre Dame Press, 1979).

On the issue of the relationship between human beings and nature, see Bryan G. Norton, "Environmental Ethics and Weak Anthropocentrism." *Environmental Ethics* Vol. 6 (1984), pp. 131–148; Tom Regan, "The Nature and Possibility of an Environmental Ethic." *Environmental Ethics,* Vol. 3 (1981), pp. 19–34; Peter Singer, "Not for Humans Only: The Place of Non-humans in Environmental Issues," in *Ethics and Problems of the 21st Century,* edited by Kenneth E. Goodpaster (Notre Dame, IN: University of Notre Dame Press, 1979); and Donald VanDeVeer, "Interspecies Justice." *Inquiry,* Vol. 22 (1979), pp. 55–70.

J. Ronald Engel, "Ecology and Social Justice: The Search for a Public Environmental Ethic," in *Issues of Justice: Social Sources and Religious Meanings,* edited by Warren Copeland and Roger Hatch (Macon, GA: Mercer Press, 1988), pp. 243–266. On the relationship between feminism and environmental issues, see Karen Warren, "Feminism and Ecology: Making Connections," *Environmental Ethics* Vol. 9 (1987), pp. 3–20.

Books

Aldo Leopold's *A Sand County Almanac: With Essays on Conservation from Round River* (New York: Ballantine Books, 1970) is a classic of the environmental movement; J. Baird Callicott's *In Defense of the Land Ethic: Essays in Environmental Philosophy* (Albany: State University of New York Press, 1988) is a development of, and defense of, Leopold's land ethic. In this same tradition is Rolston, III, Holmes, *Environmental Ethics: Duties to and Values in the Natural World* (Philadelphia: Temple University Press, 1988) and *Philosophy Gone Wild: Essays in Environmental Ethics* (New York: Prometheus Books, 1986).

Among the more important works in this area, see Robin Attfield, *The Ethics of Environmental Concern* (New York: Columbia University Press, 1983); Hargrove, Eugene C. *Foundations of Environmental Ethics* (Englewood Cliffs, NJ: Prentice-Hall, 1989); Passmore, John, *Man's Responsibility for Nature: Ecological Problems and Western Traditions* (New York: Scribner's, 1974); W.F. Baxter, *People or Penguins: The Case for Optimal Pollution* (New York: Columbia University Press, 1974) and Christopher Manes, *Radical Environmentalism and the Unmaking of Civilization* (Boston: Little, Brown, 1990); Mark Sagoff, *The Economy of the Earth: Philosophy, Law, and the Environment* (Cambridge: Cambridge University Press, 1988); Paul W. Taylor, *Respect for Nature: A Theory of Environmental Ethics* (Princeton: Princeton University Press, 1986) defends a biocentric account of ethics; Lawrence E. Johnson, *A Morally Deep World: An Essay on Moral Significance and Environmental Ethics* (Cambridge: Cambridge University Press, 1991); and Richard Sylvan, *A Critique of Deep Ecology* (Canberra: Research School of Social Sciences, Australian National University, 1985).